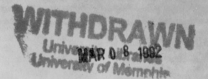

GHOST STORIES AND PHANTOM FANCIES

SHORT STORIES FOR ORAL FRENCH

THE WALTER–BALLARD FRENCH SERIES
PUBLISHED BY CHARLES SCRIBNER'S SONS

BEGINNER'S FRENCH. Ballard	$1.60
A FRENCH READER. Ballard	1.12
FRENCH SONGS. Ballard	.60

ANNOTATED TEXTS

SAND'S LA MARE AU DIABLE. Brooks	.68
CONTES DIVERS. Harvitt	.80
THEURIET'S L'ABBÉ DANIEL. Geddes	.76

Other volumes to follow

SHORT STORIES FOR ORAL FRENCH. Ballard	.88
PHONETIC FRENCH READER. Ballard and Tilly	.64

SHORT STORIES FOR ORAL FRENCH

BY

ANNA WOODS BALLARD, M.A.

Diplômée de l'Association phonétique internationale

ASSISTANT PROFESSOR OF FRENCH IN COLUMBIA UNIVERSITY,
IN CHARGE OF FRENCH IN THE SCHOOL OF PRACTICAL ARTS,
TEACHERS COLLEGE, COLUMBIA UNIVERSITY

CHARLES SCRIBNER'S SONS

NEW YORK   CHICAGO   BOSTON
          ATLANTA   SAN FRANCISCO

TO MY BEGINNERS
1910–1911
IN HORACE MANN HIGH SCHOOL, NEW YORK,
THEIR STORIES ARE INSCRIBED

PREFACE

THIS collection of simple stories is offered to teachers and pupils for oral work. It is difficult to find material easy enough and interesting enough for successful conversation; yet in oral work that he can thoroughly master, the pupil finds the most stimulating exercise in his modern-language work. Once the story is his own to tell freely, it is a short step for him to write it correctly.

It is a principle of the Reform Method never to require work to be written that cannot be spoken fluently; always to require a correct written reproduction of what is known orally. The willing spirit in which pupils meet these demands is the surest guarantee of their soundness.

Many of the easiest stories in this collection were used during the school year 1910–1911 with two classes of beginners in Horace Mann High School who had French every day. The method described on page xiii was followed closely. In many cases the pupils wrote out the stories without a mistake, and their interest in this type of work never flagged.

The very complete, some will say too complete, questions have been added to encourage the pupil who finds oral work difficult. Many find it very hard who would like to do it well.

The teacher will find his material ready, I hope, without the necessity for alteration or correction on his part. The pupil, even the slowest of mind, can prepare himself perfectly for any question on the text by mastering the questions set for him and will gain almost unconsciously the power to tell the story.

No attempt has been made to grade the stories as to difficulty except that the easiest come first. Practically all have been simplified and shortened. They can be used for oral work no matter what other textbooks are appointed, and suitable stories for all grades are included. They are arranged in the hope of helping and stimulating those who have hitherto done little oral work or who foresee difficulties in attempting it.

If the written work is required constantly as the sequence of the oral, the effort put forth by the pupils and the successful results will astonish teachers. What they love to do, they do well.

A. W. B.

TEACHERS COLLEGE
and
HORACE MANN HIGH SCHOOL
April, 1912

PREFACE TO REVISED EDITION

To this edition is added the work in pronunciation, beginning on page 81. These are the exercises done by my pupils while reading these stories in the "Phonetic French Reader."

The French-French vocabulary of earlier editions has been replaced by a French-English one which includes the irregular past definites, etc., translated.

This removes a difficulty where pupils have not yet studied the irregular verbs in detail, and will help the many teachers who are using successfully as a first reader this little book originally planned for oral work only.

A. W. B.

TEACHERS COLLEGE
COLUMBIA UNIVERSITY, N. Y.
September, 1918

ix

TABLE DES MATIÈRES

HOW TO USE THIS BOOK

1. Tell the story slowly with pupils' books closed, being sure all understand. Explain in French the meaning of any word new to the class; make constant use of action, often the easiest way to explain words.

2. Have the class open their books at the story; let the teacher pronounce it sentence by sentence, the class repeating after him; drill on words hard to pronounce; then have the class read the story through to be sure they pronounce correctly.

3. On the following day the pupils should be ready to answer orally any question on the story; they are to prepare to do this by trying to answer readily the questions that follow the story. The class should be able to tell the story at this lesson. Let them do so sentence by sentence in order as they sit.

4. The next day they should be able to write the story in class.

5. All stories learned should be frequently reviewed throughout the year. When they are well known, many stories can be told in fifteen minutes.

6. The method of treating the stories must vary according to the class. In the case of adults who

have done no oral work, the books should be open from the beginning; the story should be read sentence by sentence after the teacher until the class can read it fluently together. Then the questions should be read and answered in class before the lesson is assigned for home work. This method may be followed in the beginning with any class who have studied French without oral work and who do not understand the spoken language. The pupils will gradually gain this power, and then the stories can be treated as already outlined.

7. The French verb is so difficult for the ordinary pupil that verb drill should form a part of every kind of instruction, especially if power of sight-reading is aimed at. If the stories are used consecutively, the exercises following the stories will be found useful. For pupils who know little French, the easiest way is to teach first the endings of the Infinitives, the Present and Past Participles of the three conjugations, then the Present Indicative of a number of verbs used in the stories they have learned, and after that the Past Indefinite, Imperfect, Past Definite, Future and Conditional of the same verbs.

No effort has been made to "teach the French verb," but the idea has been to give here all the material the teacher needs while using this book for teaching the formation of the verb.

The Present has been given in full and a list of the irregular Past Definites and Futures has been added because they are so very easy for beginners to learn in this way. My own pupils in their first year learned their irregular verbs from typewritten sheets in just the form presented here.

For more advanced pupils, the principal parts of the verb can be used.

SHORT STORIES FOR ORAL FRENCH[1]

1. L'OISEAU QUI A FROID

C'est l'hiver. Il fait froid. Un petit oiseau a faim et froid. Il frappe à une fenêtre. Une petite fille ouvre la fenêtre et l'oiseau entre. Elle lui donne à manger et le soigne tout l'hiver. Au printemps l'oiseau est triste. Il ne chante plus. L'enfant ouvre la cage et l'oiseau s'envole.

1. Répondez à ces questions:

   1. Quelle est la saison?
   2. Quel temps fait-il?
   3. Qui a faim?
   4. Qui a froid?
   5. Comment est l'oiseau?
   6. Que fait-il?
   7. Où frappe-t-il?
   8. Qui ouvre la fenêtre?
   9. Que fait-elle?
  10. Que fait l'oiseau?
  11. Qu'est-ce que la jeune fille lui donne?
  12. Que fait-elle tout l'hiver?
  13. Comment est l'oiseau au printemps?
  14. Quand l'oiseau est-il triste?
  15. Est-ce qu'il chante?

[1] For phonetic transcription of these stories see " Phonetic French Reader " by Ballard and Tilly.

16. Que fait la petite fille?
17. Que fait l'oiseau?

   A. Comment se trouve l'oiseau?
   B. Pourquoi l'oiseau frappe-t-il à la fenêtre?
   C. Où entre-t-il?
   D. L'oiseau est triste: comment la petite fille le sait-elle?

2. Racontez l'histoire.
3. Vous êtes l'oiseau.   Racontez l'histoire.
4. Vous êtes la petite fille.   Racontez l'histoire.
5. Dites tout ce que fait l'oiseau.
6. Dites tout ce que fait l'enfant.

2. LE GANT

Une dame achète une paire de gants. Le marchand vend les gants. La dame paye les gants et sort du magasin. Elle perd un gant dans la rue. Une petite fille le trouve et le ramasse. La dame revient sur ses pas et cherche le gant. L'enfant le lui rend. La dame remercie la petite fille; elle est très contente.

1. Répondez à ces questions:

   1. Qui achète des gants?
   2. Que fait la dame?
   3. Qu'est-ce qu'elle achète?
   4. Qui vend les gants?
   5. Que fait le marchand?
   6. Que vend-il?
   7. Qui paye les gants?
   8. Qu'est-ce qu'elle paye?
   9. Que fait-elle ensuite?

10. Que perd-elle?
11. Où perd-elle le gant?
12. Qui le trouve?
13. Que fait la petite fille?
14. Que fait la dame?
15. Que cherche-t-elle?
16. Qui lui rend le gant?
17. Que fait la dame?
18. La dame est-elle contente?

A. D'où sort la dame?
B. Que fait la petite fille après avoir trouvé le gant?
C. Pourquoi la dame revient-elle sur ses pas?
D. Pourquoi remercie-t-elle la petite fille?
E. Que lui dit-elle?
F. Pourquoi est-elle contente?

2. Racontez l'histoire.
3. Racontez l'histoire au passé indéfini.
4. Vous êtes la dame. Racontez l'histoire au présent et au passé indéfini.

3. L'ENFANT QUI PLEURE

Un petit enfant pleure dans la rue. Un monsieur vient et lui dit: "Mon enfant, pourquoi pleures-tu?" "Ma mère m'a donné deux sous et je les ai perdus."

"Ne pleure plus," dit le monsieur, "Voici deux sous," et il donne deux sous à l'enfant. Le monsieur part. Il entend l'enfant qui pleure de plus belle. Il revient. "Pourquoi pleures-tu à présent?"

"Si je n'avais pas perdu mes deux sous, j'en aurais quatre à présent."

1. Répondez à ces questions:

   1. Qui pleure?
   2. Comment est l'enfant?
   3. Où pleure t-il?
   4. Que fait l'enfant?
   5. Qui vient?
   6. Qu'est-ce qu'il dit à l'enfant?
   7. Qu'est-ce que la mère a donné à l'enfant?
   8. Est-ce qu'il a les deux sous à présent?
   9. Pourquoi pas?
   10. Que dit le monsieur?
   11. Que donne t-il a l'enfant?
   12. Qu'est-ce qu'il fait ensuite?
   13. Qu'est-ce qu'il entend?
   14. Alors que fait le monsieur?
   15. Qu'est-ce qu'il dit?
   16. Que répond l'enfant?

A. Combien de sous la mère a-t-elle donnés à l'enfant?
B. Pourquoi le monsieur est-il revenu?

2. Racontez l'histoire.
3. Racontez l'histoire au passé indéfini.

4. LE CANIF

Un petit garçon trouve un canif sur la route. Il le ramasse. Il examine le canif. Le canif a plusieurs lames et un tire-bouchon. Il voit venir à lui un monsieur qui cherche quelque chose sur la route. Le petit garçon s'approche du monsieur en le saluant poliment. Celui-ci lui demande: "As-tu trouvé un canif neuf à plusieurs lames?" Le petit garçon tire le canif de sa poche et le rend au monsieur. "Merci, mille fois," dit l'homme, et il s'en va.

1. Répondez à ces questions:

    1. Qui trouve un canif?
    2. Comment est le garçon?
    3. Que fait-il?
    4. Qu'est-ce qu'il trouve?
    5. Où le trouve-t-il?
    6. Que fait-il?
    7. Que fait-il ensuite?
    8. Qu'est-ce qu'il examine?
    9. Combien de lames voit-il?
    10. Qu'est-ce qu'il voit encore?
    11. Qui vient à lui?
    12. Que fait le monsieur?
    13. Où cherche-t-il quelque chose?

14. Qui s'approche du monsieur?
15. Que fait le petit garçon?
16. Comment s'approche-t-il du monsieur?
17. Que lui dit le monsieur?
18. Où est le canif?
19. Que fait le petit garçon?
20. Que dit l'homme?
21. Que fait-il?

A. Faites une description du canif.
B. Que fait le petit garçon en s'approchant du monsieur?
C. D'où tire-t-il le canif?
D. Dites tout ce que fait le petit garçon.

2. Racontez l'histoire.
3. Racontez l'histoire au passé indéfini.

5. L'OISEAU QUI A SOIF

Un étourneau a soif. Il veut boire dans une carafe: mais son bec est trop court. Il frappe la bouteille pour la briser; mais le verre est trop dur. Il essaye de renverser la carafe; mais elle est trop lourde. Alors il apporte des petits cailloux et les jette dans l'eau. L'eau monte: l'oiseau apporte toujours des cailloux. Enfin il peut boire à son aise.

1. Répondez à ces questions:
    1. Qui a soif?
    2. Où veut-il boire?
    3. Peut-il boire dans la carafe?
    4. Pourquoi?
    5. Que fait-il?

6. Pourquoi?
7. Peut-il briser la bouteille?
8. Comment est le verre?
9. Qu'est-ce qu'il essaye de faire?
10. Renverse-t-il la carafe?
11. Et pourquoi pas?
12. Qu'est-ce qu'il apporte?
13. Que fait-il avec les cailloux?
14. Qu'est-ce qui arrive?
15. Qu'est-ce que l'oiseau continue à faire?
16. Enfin que peut-il faire?

   A. Pourquoi veut-il boire?
   B. Est-ce que la carafe est pleine d'eau?

2. Racontez l'histoire.
3. Racontez l'histoire au passé indéfini.
4. Employez dans de courtes phrases: soif, court, essaye, cailloux, toujours.

6. J'ÉCRIS UNE LETTRE

J'ai une lettre à écrire.   Je prends une feuille de
papier à lettre et je la pose devant moi sur la table.
Je prends un porte-plume, je trempe ma plume dans
l'encre et j'écris.   Je sèche l'écriture avec du papier
buvard.   Je prends une enveloppe, je l'ouvre, je plie
ma lettre en deux, je la glisse dans l'enveloppe, je ferme
l'enveloppe et j'écris l'adresse.   Je colle un timbre
dans le coin droit supérieur de l'enveloppe et je jette
la lettre dans la boîte aux lettres.

D'APRÈS GOUIN.

Exercices

1. Le professeur fait chaque action très lentement en
   parlant.   Il répète si les élèves ne comprennent pas.
   Il explique les mots nouveaux, en montrant la chose
   ou en faisant l'action.   Les élèves prononcent les
   mots.

2. Le professeur dit "*J'ai* une lettre à écrire"; les élèves
   disent "*Vous avez* une lettre à écrire"; et ainsi de
   suite.

3. Un élève fait le professeur et dit "J'ai une lettre à
   écrire, etc."   Un autre dit "Vous avez une lettre
   à écrire"; et le troisième dit, "Il a une lettre à
   écrire."

4. Tous les élèves parlent ensemble ou l'un après l'autre
   pendant que le professeur ou un des élèves fait les
   actions sans parler.

5. Le professeur fait les actions et les élèves écrivent ce
   qu'il fait.

7. UN ET DEUX FONT TROIS

Lorsque Frédéric revint du collège aux vacances de Pâques, il voulut montrer à tous sa science et son esprit. Au dîner la domestique servit deux poulets.

"Papa," dit Frédéric, "vous croyez qu'il y a deux poulets rôtis sur ce plat? Eh bien, je veux vous prouver qu'il y en a trois!"

"Voyons," dit le père.

"D'abord, celui-ci fait un et celui-là fait deux. Or, un et deux font trois. Nous avons donc trois poulets à manger ce soir."

"C'est parfaitement exact," répondit le père; "Maman va en prendre un, moi, j'en prends un aussi et le troisième sera pour toi!"

1. Répondez à ces questions:

    1. Qui revint du collège?
    2. Quand revint-il?
    3. Que voulut-il montrer?
    4. A qui voulut-il montrer son esprit?
    5. Que servit la domestique?
    6. Quand servit-elle les poulets?
    7. Combien de poulets servit-elle?
    8. Comment étaient les poulets?
    9. Que croit le père?
    10. Qu'est-ce que Frédéric va prouver?
    11. Que dit le père?
    12. Comment Frédéric prouve-t-il que un et deux font trois?
    13. Qui va manger un poulet?

14. Qui va manger un autre poulet?
15. Qui aura le troisième?

A. Est-ce que Frédéric a eu faim ce soir-là?
B. Et pourquoi?

2. Racontez l'histoire.
3. Racontez l'histoire au passé indéfini.
4. Employez dans des phrases: vacances, dîner, rôtis, d'abord, exact, aussi.

8. LA MÈRE AUX ÂNES

Des enfants sortent de l'école; ils sont bien contents car la classe est finie. Ils voient sur la route qui passe devant l'école une vieille femme montée sur un âne; elle a un long fouet à la main et elle chasse devant elle quatre autres ânes.

A ce spectacle, un des enfants, un de ces petits garçons mal élevés qui ne respectent personne, crie: "Bonjour, bonjour, la mère aux ânes!" Les autres petits garçons se mettent à rire et tous ensemble crient: "Bonjour, bonjour, la mère aux ânes."

La vieille femme les regarde en souriant et leur répond bien haut: "Bonjour, bonjour, mes enfants."

1. Répondez à ces questions:

1. Qui sort de l'école?
2. Comment sont-ils?
3. Pourquoi sont-ils contents?
4. Qui voient-ils sur la route?
5. Où passe la route?

6. Sur quoi la femme est-elle montée?
7. Qu'a-t-elle à la main?
8. Que chasse-t-elle devant elle?
9. Qui parle à la femme?
10. Est-ce un bon garçon?
11. Comment est-il?
12. Que crie-t-il?
13. Qu'est-ce que les autres garçons se mettent à faire?
14. Qu'est-ce que chacun crie à son tour?
15. Que fait la femme?
16. Comment les regarde-t-elle?
17. Que leur répond-elle?
18. Comment le dit-elle?

2. Racontez l'histoire:
3. Vous êtes un des petits garçons. Racontez l'histoire à votre façon.
4. Racontez l'histoire au passé indéfini.

9. LE POISSON

Un pêcheur jette sa ligne dans l'eau. Un petit poisson avale l'appât et l'hameçon. Le petit poisson est attrapé. Il dit: "Rendez-moi la liberté. Je suis si petit. Laissez-moi grandir."

Le pêcheur répond: "Non, ce soir même je te mangerai, car, dit-on

"Un Tiens vaut mieux que deux Tu l'auras:
L'un est sûr; l'autre ne l'est pas."

1. Répondez à ces questions :

1. Qui jette sa ligne dans l'eau?
2. Où jette-t-il sa ligne?
3. Que jette-t-il dans l'eau?
4. Que voit-on dans l'eau?
5. Que fait le poisson?
6. Comment est-il?
7. Que désire-t-il?
8. Pourquoi?
9. Que veut-il faire?
10. Quand le pêcheur mangera-t-il le poisson?
11. Qu'est-ce qui vaut mieux que deux "Tu l'auras?"
12. Pourquoi? Comment est un "Tiens?"
13. Est-ce que deux "Tu l'auras" sont sûrs?

2. Racontez l'histoire.
3. Racontez l'histoire au passé indéfini.

10. LUI, IL FUME

Un fumeur présente son porte-cigares ouvert à son voisin de droite. "Merci, je ne fume pas."

Il se retourne vers son voisin de gauche. "Je ne fume pas, merci."

Sa femme lui dit tout bas: "Tu n'en offres pas au capitaine?"

"Ah! non; lui, il fume!"

1. Répondez à ces questions:

1. A qui le fumeur présente-t-il son porte-cigares?
2. Comment est le porte-cigares?
3. Que répond le voisin de droite?
4. Vers qui se retourne-t-il?
5. Que répond ce voisin?
6. Que lui dit sa femme?
7. Comment le dit-elle?
8. Que répond le fumeur?

2. Racontez l'histoire.

11. LUNETTES POUR LIRE

Un paysan va en ville. Il remarque tout ce qu'il voit. Par exemple il remarque que beaucoup de personnes lisent un journal et presque toutes portent un lorgnon ou des lunettes. Le paysan entre chez un opticien et demande des lunettes pour lire. L'opticien lui en essaye plusieurs paires pendant que le paysan regarde dans un livre: mais à chaque essai il répond: "Non, je ne puis lire." L'opticien fatigué de lui essayer ses verres, finit par dire au client: "Mais savez-vous lire?"—"Quelle question! Si je savais lire je ne vous aurais pas demandé des lunettes pour lire."

1. Répondez à ces questions:

1. Où va le paysan?
2. Que remarque-t-il?
3. Qu'est-ce que beaucoup de personnes lisent?
4. Que portent-elles?
5. Chez qui entre le paysan?
6. Que demande-t-il?
7. Que lui essaye l'opticien?
8. Que fait le paysan?
9. Que répond-il à chaque essai?
10. Comment est l'opticien?
11. Que finit-il par dire?
12. Que répond le paysan?

2. Racontez l'histoire.
3. Racontez l'histoire au passé indéfini.
4. Employez dans de courtes phrases: beaucoup, chez, plusieurs, chaque, par, mais.

12. BON POIDS

Jacques Dupont, un boulanger, achetait son beurre chez Jean Rigot, un paysan qui habitait le même village.

Au bout de quelque temps il s'aperçut qu'il ne recevait pas assez de beurre pour son argent, et rencontrant Rigot, il l'accusa de malhonnêteté.

Le paysan nia vivement l'accusation, et Dupont porta sa plainte devant le juge de paix.

"Apportez-moi," dit le juge à Rigot, "votre balance et vos poids."

"Voilà ma balance," répondit Rigot; "quant à mes poids, je n'en ai pas."

"Alors comment faites-vous pour peser le beurre?"

"Oh! c'est bien simple. J'achète à mon voisin Dupont un pain de quatre livres, et ce pain me sert de poids pour peser le beurre que je lui envoie tous les samedis. Je le place dans l'un des plateaux de la balance et je mets le beurre dans l'autre."

"Eh bien!" dit le juge à Dupont, "vous devez être satisfait."

1. Répondez à ces questions:

1. Comment s'appelait le boulanger?
2. Où achetait-il son beurre?
3. Est-ce que le boulanger demeurait près du paysan?
4. De quoi s'aperçut-il?
5. Qui rencontra-t-il?
6. De quoi l'accusa-t-il?

7. Que fit le paysan?
8. Comment nia-t-il l'accusation?
9. Devant qui le paysan porta-t-il sa plainte?
10. Que dit le juge à Rigot?
11. Que répondit Rigot?
12. Que lui dit le juge alors?
13. Est-ce que Rigot trouve cela difficile?
14. Qu'est-ce qu'il achète à son voisin?
15. A quoi sert ce pain?
16. Combien de fois par semaine envoie-t-il du beurre à Dupont?
17. Où place-t-il le pain?
18. Où met-il le beurre?
19. Que dit le juge à Dupont?

2. Racontez l'histoire.
3. Racontez l'histoire à l'indicatif présent.
*4. Le professeur peut demander à trois élèves de jouer la dernière partie de cette histoire.

* For a complete treatment of this story, with pupils who have studied French for a year and a half, see "Max Walter's French Lessons," pp. 161–168.

13. LE CORBEAU ET LE RENARD

Un corbeau est perché sur la branche d'un arbre. Dans son bec il tient un fromage. Au pied de l'arbre est le renard. Il dit: "Bonjour, monsieur le Corbeau." Le corbeau regarde le renard, mais il ne répond pas, car il a un fromage dans le bec.

Le renard dit: "Que vous êtes beau, monsieur le Corbeau! Quelles belles plumes noires! Quel joli bec!" Le corbeau a l'air content, mais il ne dit rien.

Le renard devient impatient; il agite la queue: "Oui, vous êtes beau," dit-il, "et si votre voix est aussi belle que votre plumage, vous êtes le prince des oiseaux."

Le corbeau a l'air très content. Il ouvre le bec pour montrer sa belle voix. Le fromage tombe, le renard le ramasse et s'en va vite.

D'APRÈS LA FONTAINE.

1. Répondez à ces questions :

    1. Qui est perché sur un arbre?
    2. Où est-il perché?
    3. Que tient-il dans son bec?
    4. Où est le fromage?
    5. Qui est au pied de l'arbre?
    6. Où est le renard?
    7. Que dit le renard?
    8. Que fait le corbeau?
    9. Parle-t-il?
    10. Pourquoi?
    11. Que dit le renard alors?

12. Comment sont ses plumes?
13. Comment est son bec?
14. Quel air a le corbeau?
15. Est-ce qu'il parle au renard?
16. Comment devient le renard?
17. Que fait-il?
18. Que veut-il entendre?
19. Que dit-il au corbeau?
20. Comment se trouve le corbeau?
21. Que fait-il?
22. Pourquoi?
23. Qu'est-ce qui arrive?
24. Que fait le renard?
25. Comment s'en va-t-il?

A. Pourquoi le renard flatte-t-il le corbeau?

2. Racontez l'histoire.
3. Racontez l'histoire au passé indéfini.

14. MOI, J'ATTENDS

Lili va à l'école mais elle ne s'y amuse pas beaucoup. Son oncle l'interroge: "Lili, que fais-tu à l'école? Sais-tu lire un peu?" Lili secoue la tête. "Sais-tu écrire?" Lili recommence à secouer la tête. "Alors qu'est-ce que tu y fais?"—"Moi, j'attends qu'on sorte."

1. Répondez à ces questions:

    1. Où va Lili?
    2. Est-ce qu'elle s'y amuse?
    3. Qui lui parle?
    4. Que lui demande-t-il?
    5. Est-ce qu'elle sait lire ou écrire?
    6. Comment répond-elle à son oncle?
    7. Que dit-elle qu'elle fait à l'école?

2. Racontez l'histoire.
3. Employez dans des phrases: beaucoup, que, secoue, y, attends.

15. LE SAVETIER ET LE FINANCIER. I

Le savetier Grégoire demeurait près de la maison d'un riche financier.

Dès la pointe du jour, le joyeux savetier chantait en travaillant. Le financier, fatigué par ses affaires, se plaignait de ne pouvoir dormir ou s'il dormait, d'être réveillé par les chants de son voisin.

Un jour, il fit venir Grégoire dans son cabinet.

"Je veux," dit-il, "que vous soyez aussi riche qu'un roi. Prenez ces cent écus et gardez-les avec soin pour vous en servir à l'occasion."

Le savetier, qui n'avait jamais vu tant d'argent, ouvrit les yeux avec surprise. Après avoir remercié le financier, il rentra chez lui au plus vite, et cacha son trésor au fond de sa cave.

1. Répondez à ces questions:

    1. Où demeurait le savetier?
    2. Comment s'appelait-il?
    3. Comment était le financier?
    4. Quand chantait le joyeux savetier?
    5. Que faisait-il en chantant?
    6. Pourquoi le financier était-il fatigué?
    7. Dormait-il bien?
    8. Qu'est-ce qui le réveillait?
    9. Où fit-il venir Grégoire?
    10. Que veut le financier?
    11. Que donne-t-il au savetier?
    12. Comment faut-il garder l'argent?
    13. Comment était le savetier?

14. Qui remercia-t-il?
15. Où rentra-t-il.
16. Comment rentra-t-il chez lui?
17. Où cacha-t-il son trésor?

A. De quoi le financier se plaignait-il?

2. Racontez l'histoire.
3. Racontez l'histoire au présent.

16. LE SAVETIER ET LE FINANCIER. II

A partir de ce moment, le savetier n'eut plus repos.
Dans la crainte d'être volé, il délaissait tout le jour son
travail pour faire le guet. La nuit, si quelque chat
faisait du bruit, le chat prenait l'argent et vite Grégoire
courait voir son trésor.

Il ne pouvait travailler, ne dormait pas, et ne chantait plus. Quant au financier, il pouvait maintenant
dormir toute la matinée.

Au bout de quelque semaines, le savetier comprit
que sa richesse le rendait fort malheureux. Prenant
alors son argent, il retourna chez son voisin. "Rendez-
moi," lui dit-il, "mes chansons et mon somme et reprenez vos cent écus."

Rentré chez lui, Grégoire retrouva son entrain au
travail, sa gaieté et ses chansons.

D'APRÈS LA FONTAINE.

1. Répondez à ces questions:

1. A partir de ce moment, dans quel état fut le savetier?
2. Que craignait-il?

3. La nuit si quelque chat faisait du bruit, que pensait Grégoire?
4. Où se rendait-il vite?
5. Pourquoi le financier pouvait-il dormir maintenant?
6. Que comprit le savetier au bout de quelques semaines?
7. Que prit-il?
8. Où se rendit-il?
9. Que dit-il au financier?
10. Que retrouva-t-il?

2. Racontez l'histoire.
3. Racontez l'histoire à l'indicatif présent.
4. Employez dans de courtes phrases: repos, crainte, guet, plus, matinée, somme, entrain, chansons.

17. LE CHAT ET LA SOURIS

Une souris sort de son trou; elle trotte dans la chambre. Le chat est couché dans un coin; il aperçoit la souris. Il se relève sans bruit; il bondit sur elle. La souris crie; le chat la laisse s'échapper. Elle court bien vite vers son trou, mais le chat la rattrape, et la mange. Pauvre petite souris!

1. Répondez à ces questions:

1. Qui sort de son trou?
2. Où trotte-t-elle?
3. Qui est dans un coin?
4. Comment est le chat?
5. Où est le chat?
6. Que voit-il?
7. Où est la souris?

8. Que fait le chat?
9. Comment se relève-t-il?
10. Que fait-il ensuite?
11. Que fait la souris?
12. Est-ce que le chat mange la souris tout de suite?
13. Où court la souris?
14. Comment court-elle vers son trou?
15. Entre-t-elle dans son trou?
16. Pourquoi?
17. Que fait le chat?

18. ALEXANDRE ET DIOGÈNE

Un jour Alexandre, passant par Corinthe, eut la curiosité de voir Diogène:

"Je suis le grand roi Alexandre," lui dit-il.

"Et moi, je suis Diogène," répondit le philosophe.

"Ne me crains-tu point?" continua Alexandre.

"Es-tu bon ou mauvais?" reprit Diogène.

"Je suis bon," repartit Alexandre.

"Hé! qui craint ce qui est bon?" reprit Diogène.

Alexandre admira l'esprit et la franchise de Diogène, et il lui dit: "Tu es pauvre, Diogène; je serais bien aise de te secourir; demande-moi tout ce que tu voudras."

"Mets-toi un peu de côté," répondit Diogène; "tu m'empêches de jouir du soleil."

FÉNELON.

1. Répondez à ces questions:

1. Qui passait par Corinthe?
2. Qui eut-il la curiosité de voir?

3. Racontez leur conversation?
4. Qu'est-ce que le roi admira?
5. Comment était Diogène?
6. Que lui dit le roi?
7. Que demanda Diogène au roi?

2. Racontez l'histoire au passé indéfini et au présent.
3. Le professeur peut faire jouer le rôle d'Alexandre par un élève et celui de Diogène par un autre.

19. ET VOUS?

On dit qu'Alexandre Dumas n'est pas l'auteur de plusieurs romans qui portent sa signature. Un jour il rencontra son fils et lui dit: "Eh bien, que penses-tu de mon dernier roman? l'as-tu lu?"—"Non, je ne l'ai pas lu, mon père, et vous?" répondit Alexandre Dumas fils dont la réputation pour l'esprit est bien connue et bien méritée.

1. Répondez à ces questions:

1. Que dit-on d'Alexandre Dumas?
2. Qui rencontra-t-il un jour?
3. Que lui dit-il?
4. Que répondit le fils?
5. Quelle était sa réputation?

2. Racontez l'histoire.
3. Racontez l'histoire au passé indéfini.

20. L'AMÉRICAIN EN ANGLETERRE

"Comment trouvez-vous l'Angleterre?" demanda-t-on à un Américain qui revenait d'un voyage en Europe. "C'est un pays bien agréable, très riche, et bien cultivé," répond l'Américain; "mais je n'y étais pas à mon aise."—"Et pourquoi cela?"—"J'aime à faire une promenade après le déjeuner; or, l'Angleterre— c'est une île si petite que je n'osais faire ma promenade habituelle; j'avais peur d'aller trop près du bord et de tomber."

1. Répondez à ces questions:

   1. D'où revenait l'Américain?
   2. Que lui demanda-t-on?
   3. Comment est l'Angleterre?
   4. Y était-il content?
   5. Qu'aime-t-il à faire?
   6. Est-ce que l'Angleterre est grande?
   7. Pourquoi n'osait-il pas faire sa promenade habituelle?

2. Racontez l'histoire.
3. Racontez l'histoire au passé indéfini.

21. IL VOYAIT LOIN

Un berger breton, debout sur la crête d'une haute falaise, contemplait l'océan.　Un touriste survint qui l'aborde et lui dit: "Il y a une belle vue d'ici! Vous voyez loin, n'est-ce pas?"—"Très loin."—"Vous voyez l'Amérique?"—"Je vois plus loin!"—"Oh! oh! et comment cela?"—"Attendez que ce nuage soit passé, et je verrai la lune."

1. Répondez à ces questions:

    1. Où le berger était-il debout?
    2. Que contemplait-il?
    3. Qui survint?
    4. Que dit le touriste au berger?
    5. Que répond le berger?
    6. Comment peut-il voir plus loin que l'Amérique?

2. Le professeur peut faire jouer le rôle du berger par un élève et celui du touriste par un autre.

3. Employez dans de courtes phrases: debout, vue, loin, nuage.

22. JE VOUDRAIS L'ÊTRE

Un Français et un Anglais se disputaient au sujet de la gloire militaire, littéraire et scientifique de leur patrie. Chacun restait persuadé que sa patrie était la première de toutes. Cependant le Français voulant terminer poliment la dispute, dit: "Du reste, Monsieur, si je n'étais pas Français je voudrais être Anglais." "Et moi," répondit fièrement l'Anglais. "Si je n'étais pas Anglais, je voudrais l'être."

1. Répondez à ces questions:
    1. Qui se disputait?
    2. À propos de quoi se disputaient-ils?
    3. De quoi chacun était-il persuadé?
    4. Qui voulait terminer la dispute?
    5. Comment voulait-il la terminer?
    6. Que dit-il?
    7. Que lui répondit l'Anglais?

2. Racontez l'histoire à l'indicatif présent.
3. Employez dans de courtes phrases: sujet, chacun, dispute, fièrement.

23. L'ANGLAIS EN AMÉRIQUE

Un Anglais avait passé un an aux États-Unis. Au moment où il allait se rembarquer pour l'Europe, un de ses amis lui demanda: "Eh bien, que pensez-vous de notre climat?"—"Votre climat! Mais vous n'avez pas de climat; vous n'en avez que des échantillons!"

1. Répondez à ces questions:
    1. Où un Anglais avait-t-il passé un an?
    2. Pour quel pays allait-il se rembarquer?
    3. Qui lui a parlé?
    4. Que lui a-t-il dit?
    5. Qu'est-ce que l'Anglais a répondu?

24. L'ACTEUR ET L'AUTEUR

A la répétition générale, un acteur, disait trop vite quelques mots qu'il avait à prononcer. "Allez plus lentement," lui cria l'auteur; "prenez votre temps, il y a un point et virgule." "Non, monsieur," répond le débutant, "il n'y a qu'une virgule." "Eh bien!" reprit l'auteur en riant, "mettez un point et virgule." "Ma foi, monsieur," s'écria ce pauvre jeune homme, "si vous faites toujours des changements, je ne serai jamais prêt pour demain."

1. Répondez à ces questions:
    1. Que faisait un acteur à la répétition générale?
    2. Que lui cria l'auteur?
    3. Quelle était la ponctuation, selon l'auteur?
    4. Que trouve l'acteur?

5. Que reprit l'auteur?
6. Que crie le pauvre acteur?

2. Racontez l'histoire au passé indéfini.
3. Racontez l'histoire à l'indicatif présent.

25. JOSEPH II ET LA MARCHANDE

Joseph II, empereur d'Allemagne, parcourait souvent les rues de Vienne dans un cabriolet qu'il conduisait lui-même. Un jour, en traversant une place, il renversa la charrette d'une marchande de fruits et de légumes, qui, ne le reconnaissant pas, lui débita mille injures, en ramassant ses choux et ses carottes.

A peine l'empereur fut-il de retour au palais, qu'il envoya une douzaine de ducats à cette bonne femme, en disant: "Je crois qu'elle aura lieu d'être contente; je répare le tort que je peux lui avoir fait, et je lui ai donné tout le temps de pester à son aise contre moi."

1. Répondez à ces questions:
    1. Que faisait souvent Joseph II?
    2. Qui conduisait son cabriolet?
    3. Que traversait-il un jour?
    4. Que renversa-t-il?
    5. Que fit la femme?
    6. Tout en lui disant des injures, que faisait-elle?
    7. Reconnut-elle l'empereur?
    8. Que lui envoya l'empereur?
    9. Pourquoi aura-t-elle lieu d'être contente?

2. Racontez l'histoire au passé indéfini.
3. Racontez l'histoire au présent de l'indicatif.

26. L'ARAIGNÉE ET LE VER A SOIE

L'araignée en ces mots raillait le ver à soie:
"Mon Dieu! que de lenteur dans tout ce que tu fais!
    Vois combien peu de temps j'emploie
A tapisser un mur d'innombrables filets."
—"Soit!" répondit le ver; "mais ta toile est fragile,
    Et puis à quoi sert-elle? à rien.
    Pour moi, mon travail est utile:
    Si je fais peu, je le fais bien." LE BAILLY.

1. Répondez à ces questions:

    1. Qui raillait le ver à soie?
    2. Pourquoi? Comment travaille le ver à soie?
    3. Qu'est-ce que l'araignée peut faire en peu de temps?
    4. Que répond le ver?
    5. Comment est la toile de l'araignée?
    6. A quoi sert-elle?
    7. Comment est le travail du ver à soie?
    8. Comment le fait-il?

2. A apprendre par coeur.
3. Employez dans de courtes phrases: que de, peu, toile.

27. BRAVOURE DES GAULOIS

1. Les Gaulois aimaient la guerre et la faisaient souvent.

2. Ils étaient braves. Les jours de bataille, ils sortaient des rangs; ils s'avançaient à quelques pas de l'ennemi: "Qui veut combattre avec moi?" criaient-ils.

3. C'était une joie pour eux que d'être blessés, et ils montraient avec orgueil le sang qui décorait leur poitrine.

4. Ils étaient fiers quand ils avaient vaincu un ennemi. Ils lui coupaient la tête pour la mettre à la pointe de leur lance, ou la pendre à la selle de leurs chevaux, comme font encore aujourd'hui les peuples barbares.

5. Malheureusement, ils n'étaient point fermes et patients, comme il faut l'être dans les batailles. Ils attaquaient l'ennemi avec une bravoure éclatante; mais, si l'ennemi leur résistait, ils se fatiguaient et se décourageaient. A cause de cela, tout en étant braves, ils n'étaient pas de bons soldats; car le bon soldat reste calme et brave jusque dans la défaite.

LAVISSE.

1. Répondez à ces questions:

   1. Qu'est-ce que les Gaulois aimaient?
   2. Comment étaient-ils?
   3. D'où sortaient-ils le jour de bataille?
   4. Où s'avançaient-ils?

5. Que criaient-ils?
6. Qu'est-ce qui les rendait joyeux?
7. Que montraient-ils avec orgueil?
8. De quoi étaient-ils fiers?
9. Que faisaient-ils?
10. Où mettaient-ils la tête de leurs ennemis?
11. Qui fait encore cela aujourd 'hui?
12. Comment faut-il être dans les batailles?
13. Est-ce que les Gaulois l'étaient?
14. Comment attaquaient-ils l'ennemi?
15. Que faisaient-ils quand l'ennemi leur résistait?
16. Pourquoi n'étaient-ils pas de bons soldats?
17. Quelle est la conduite du bon soldat?

2. Racontez l'histoire à l'indicatif présent.
3. Racontez l'histoire à la troisième personne du singulier

28. VENGEANCE D'UN ÉLÉPHANT

Un jour un cornac conduisait un éléphant à l'abreuvoir. Ils passèrent, tous les deux, devant l'atelier
d'un tailleur qui travaillait, assis près de sa fenêtre
grande ouverte. L'éléphant, voyant quelques fruits
sur la table, allongea sa trompe et en saisit un. Le
tailleur, pour le punir lui piqua la trompe avec son
aiguille. L'éléphant continua son chemin et semblait avoir oublié l'incident, mais après avoir fini de
boire, il remplit sa trompe d'eau. Le cornac le ra-
mena, et, lorsqu'ils arrivèrent devant l'atelier du
tailleur, l'éléphant s'arrêta et lança toute l'eau au
visage de son ennemi; c'est ainsi qu' il prit sa revanche.

1. Répondez à ces questions :

1. Qui conduisait l'éléphant ?
2. Où conduisait-il l'éléphant ?
3. Devant quel atelier passèrent-ils ?
4. Que faisait le tailleur ?
5. Où était-il assis ?
6. Comment était la fenêtre ?
7. Qu'y avait-il sur la table ?
8. Qui vit les fruits ?
9. Qu'est-ce qu'il allongea ?
10. Que fit-il ?
11. Que fit le tailleur avec son aiguille ?
12. Pourquoi piqua-t-il l'éléphant ?
13. Où alla l'éléphant ?
14. Après avoir fini de boire, que fit-il ?
15. Où arrivèrent-ils ?
16. Que fit-il ?
17. Où lança-t-il l'eau ?
18. Pourquoi le fit-il ?

2. Racontez l'histoire au présent et au passé indéfini.

3. Prenez le rôle de l'éléphant et racontez l'histoire à votre façon.

29. POUVOIR DE LA CONCORDE

Un homme qui avait douze fils, les fit appeler autour
de son lit de mort. Il leur montra un faisceau de
flèches et ordonna à chacun d'eux de rompre les flèches
toutes à la fois ainsi attachées. Personne ne put le faire.

Il leur dit ensuite de les rompre l'une après l'autre.
Ils les rompirent avec facilité.

"Voilà un emblême du pouvoir de la concorde," leur
dit le père; "aussi longtemps que vous resterez unis,
personne ne pourra vous vaincre."

D'APRÈS OTTO.

1. Répondez à ces questions:

   1. Combien de fils avait l'homme?
   2. Où les fit-il appeler?
   3. Que leur montra-t-il?
   4. Que leur ordonna-t-il?
   5. Est-ce que les fils y réussirent?
   6. Comment leur dit-il ensuite de rompre les flèches?
   7. Qu'est-ce qui arriva?
   8. Que leur dit-il?
   9. Comment faut-il rester?

2. Prenez le rôle d'un des fils et racontez l'histoire.

30. UN ÉGOISTE

Chérubini, le célèbre compositeur, se rendait un jour à pied, par une pluie battante, au Conservatoire. Un de ses admirateurs, homme fort riche, le voit de sa voiture. Il fait arrêter, et descendant, appelle le musicien: "Il pleut trop fort, cher maître," dit-il, "prenez ma voiture. Moi, je ne vais pas du même côté; seulement, prêtez-moi votre parapluie." "Mon parapluie," s'écrie Chérubini, "je ne le prête jamais. Allons un peu vite," continue-t-il en s'adressant au cocher, "je suis en retard."

1. Répondez à ces questions:
   1. Quel temps faisait-il?
   2. Qui était Chérubini?
   3. Où allait-il?
   4. Comment y allait-il?
   5. Qui le voit?
   6. Où est l'admirateur?
   7. Que fait-il?
   8. Que dit-il au musicien?
   9. Où monte Chérubini?
   10. Pourquoi l'admirateur ne monte-t-il pas dans la voiture?
   11. Que demande-t-il à Chérubini?
   12. Pourquoi Chérubini ne veut-il pas prêter son parapluie?
   13. Que dit-il au cocher?

   A. Pourquoi l'histoire a-t-elle pour titre "Un Égoiste"?

2. Racontez l'histoire.
3. Racontez l'histoire au passé indéfini.

31. LE VALET FAIT UNE BÊTISE

Un valet reçoit de son maître l'ordre de prendre les lettres qu'il trouvera sur son bureau, et de les porter à la poste. Il y en avait trois dont une n'avait pas d'adresse. Le valet les porte toutes trois à la poste. Le maître s'apercevant de l'erreur et lui demandant pourquoi il avait porté à la poste une lettre qui n'avait pas d'adresse: "Je croyais," répond le valet, "que vous ne vouliez pas qu'on sût à qui vous l'adressiez."

1. Répondez à ces questions:

    1. Qui parle à un valet?
    2. Où sont les lettres?
    3. Où faut-il les porter?
    4. Combien de lettres y a-t-il?
    5. Combien de lettres n'ont pas d'adresse?
    6. Est-ce que le valet porte cette lettre à la poste?
    7. De quoi s'aperçoit le maître?
    8. Que dit-il au valet?
    9. Que répond le valet?

    A. Que dit le maître au valet en l'envoyant à la poste?
    B. Qu'est-ce qui manque à une lettre?
    C. Au retour du valet, que lui demande son maitre?

2. Racontez l'histoire.
3. Employez dans de courtes phrases: en, dont, poste, bureau, pas de.

32. LES DOMESTIQUES

Quand Louis XIV allait à la chasse, on portait à sa suite quarante bouteilles de vin. C'était moins pour le roi que pour les piqueurs, les palefreniers et ceux-là même qui portaient ce vin, et qui se faisaient payer pour le distribuer. Un jour le roi avait soif et il demanda un verre de vin. "Sire," lui répondit-on, "il n'y en a plus." "N'en prend-on pas toujours quarante bouteilles?" dit le roi. "Oui, Sire," mais on a tout bu." "Prenez-en à l'avenir quarante-et-une, pour qu'il en reste une pour moi."

1. Répondez à ces questions:
    1. Où Louis quatorze allait-il quelquefois?
    2. Que portait-on à sa suite?
    3. Le roi buvait-il beaucoup de vin?
    4. Qui le buvait?
    5. Est-ce que ceux qui portaient le vin le donnaient aux autres?
    6. Qu'est-ce qui arriva un jour?
    7. Que demanda le roi?
    8. Que lui répondit-on?
    9. Que dit le roi?
    10. Pourquoi n'y en a-t-il plus?
    11. Que répondit le roi?

2. Racontez l'histoire à l'indicatif présent.
3. Le professeur peut demander à un élève de prendre le rôle de Louis XIV et à un autre celui du domestique.

33. LE PANIER DE PAIN

Ésope fut vendu à un marchand d'esclaves, qui,
peu de temps après, entreprit le voyage d'Éphèse pour
revendre ceux qu'il avait. Chacun était obligé de
porter un fardeau. Ésope prit le plus pesant, c'était
le panier au pain. Ses camarades crurent qu'il
l'avait fait par bêtise, mais au premier repas le pain
fut entamé, et le fardeau devint moins pesant; il en
fut de même le soir, et de même le lendemain, de sorte
qu'à la fin il n'avait plus rien à porter.

1. Répondez à ces questions:

   1. A qui Ésope fut-il vendu?
   2. Quel voyage le marchand entreprit-il?
   3. Quand entreprit-il ce voyage?
   4. Pourquoi y alla-t-il?
   5. Qu'est-ce que chacun était obligé de **faire?**
   6. Quel fardeau choisit Ésope?
   7. Que crurent ses camarades?
   8. Quand le pain fut-il entamé?
   9. Comment était le fardeau?
  10. Qu'est-ce qui arriva le soir et le lendemain?
  11. A la fin avait-il beaucoup à porter?

2. Vous êtes Ésope. Racontez l'histoire à votre façon.

3. Employez dans de courtes phrases: esclaves, chacun,
pesant, bêtise, entamé, de même.

34. L'EMPEREUR AURÉLIEN

L'empereur Aurélien, étant arrivé devant la ville
de Tyane, et en ayant trouvé les portes fermées, jura
dans sa colère qu'il ne laisserait seulement pas un
chien en vie dans cette ville rebelle. Les soldats se
réjouissaient d'avance dans l'espoir de faire un grand
butin. La ville ayant été prise, Aurélien dit à ses
troupes, qui le conjuraient de tenir son serment:
"J'ai juré de ne pas laisser un chien dans cette ville;
tuez donc, si vous voulez, tous les chiens mais ne
faites aucun mal aux habitants."

1. Répondez à ces questions:

1. Où l'empereur Aurélien était-il arrivé?
2. Comment étaient les portes de la ville?
3. Qu'est-ce qu'il a juré dans sa colère?
4. Comment étaient les soldats?
5. Qu'espéraient-ils faire?
6. La ville fut prise. Qu'est-ce que les troupes conjurè-
   rent l'empereur de faire?
7. Quel était son serment?
8. Que dit-il aux soldats pour le tenir?

2. Racontez l'histoire.

35. LE CHEVAL VOLÉ

On avait volé le cheval d'un paysan. Celui-ci se rendit à une foire aux chevaux pour en acheter un autre. Il reconnut son propre cheval parmi ceux qui étaient en vente.

"Ce cheval est à moi," dit-il à l'homme qui le gardait, "on me l'a volé il y a trois jours."

"Ce n'est pas possible," dit l'autre, "il y a trois ans que je l'ai."

"Trois ans?" dit le paysan; "j'en doute." Puis, mettant subitement les mains sur les deux yeux du cheval: "De quel œil est-il borgne?"

"De l'œil gauche," dit l'autre.

Le paysan ôte sa main et l'œil gauche paraît clair et brillant.

"Oh! je me suis trompé," dit l'autre; "je veux dire de l'œil droit."

"Il n'est borgne ni de l'œil droit, ni de l'œil gauche," dit le paysan, en ôtant l'autre main. "Il est évident que vous êtes un voleur; vous le voyez, vous autres!" continua-t-il en s'adressant à la foule autour de lui.

Le voleur essaya de se sauver, en entendant ces mots. Mais il fut saisi et conduit devant le magistrat, et le paysan reprit possession de son cheval.

1. Répondez à ces questions:

   1. Qu'avait-on volé?
   2. A qui l'avait-on volé?
   3. Où celui-ci se rendit-il?

4. Pourquoi s'y rendit-il?
5. Que vit-il?
6. Que dit-il à l'homme?
7. Que répondit-il?
8. Le paysan crut-il cela?
9. Où posa-t-il les mains?
10. Que dit-il à l'homme?
11. Que répondit l'homme?
12. Que fait le paysan alors?
13. Comment est l'œil gauche?
14. Qu'est-ce que le voleur se hâte **de dire?**
15. Que dit le paysan?
16. Que fait-il en disant cela?
17. A qui s'adresse-t-il?
18. Qu'est-ce que le voleur essaya de **faire?**
19. Qu'est-ce qu'il est devenu?
20. Qui reprit possession du cheval?

2. Le professeur peut faire jouer les rôles du paysan, du voleur, et du cheval par trois élèves.

36. LE CARDINAL ET SON SOUPER

On raconte cette histoire du cardinal Dubois, ministre de Louis XV. Le souper du cardinal consistait en un poulet qu'il mangeait toujours seul. Un soir, le poulet fut oublié par ses domestiques. Au moment d'aller se coucher il sonna et réclama son souper, leur demandant pourquoi on le servait si tard. Les domestiques l'écoutent froidement et lui répondent qu'il a mangé son poulet il y a une heure. "Comment!" s'écria-t-il, "j'ai mangé mon poulet?" Les domestiques dirent que oui. "C'est bien! allez," leur dit-il, et il se coucha sans souper.

1. Répondez à ces questions:

   1. De qui le cardinal Dubois était-il ministre?
   2. En quoi consistait son souper?
   3. Qu'arriva-t-il un soir?
   4. Que fit-il?
   5. Que leur demanda-t-il?
   6. Comment les domestiques l'écoutent-ils?
   7. Que lui répondent-ils?
   8. Quand l'a-t-il mangé?
   9. Quelle fut sa réponse?
   10. Que dirent les domestiques?
   11. Que leur dit-il?
   12. Comment se coucha-t-il?

2. Racontez l'histoire.

37. A QUOI SERT LA VACCINE

Un homme très crédule disait qu'il n'avait pas confiance dans la vaccine.

"A quoi sert-elle?" ajouta-t-il; "je connaissais un enfant beau comme le jour, que sa famille avait fait vacciner; eh bien! il est mort deux jours après."

"Comment! deux jours après?"

"Oui, il est tombé du haut d'un arbre et s'est tué. Faites donc vacciner vos enfants après cela!"

1. Répondez à ces questions :

   1. Que disait un homme un jour?
   2. Comment était l'homme?
   3. Qui connaissait-il?
   4. Qu'est-ce que la famille a fait?
   5. Quand l'enfant est-il mort?
   6. Quelle fut l'exclamation?
   7. Comment l'enfant est-il mort?
   8. A la fin que dit l'homme crédule?

2. Racontez l'histoire.

38. LA CHENILLE

Un jour, causant entre eux, différents animaux
  Louaient beaucoup le ver à soie:
"Quel talent," disaient-ils, "cet insecte déploie
En composant ces fils si doux, si fins, si beaux
  Qui de l'homme font la richesse!"
Tous vantaient son travail, exaltaient son adresse;
Une chenille seule y trouvait des défauts,
Aux animaux surpris en faisait la critique,
  Disait des *mais* et puis des *si*.
Un renard s'écria: "Messieurs, cela s'explique;
  C'est que madame file aussi."

FLORIAN.

1. Répondez à ces questions:

 1. Qui causait un jour?
 2. Qui louaient-ils?
 3. Que fait le ver à soie?
 4. Comment sont les fils du ver à soie?
 5. Qu'est-ce que tous vantaient?
 6. Qu'est-ce que tous exaltaient?
 7. Qui trouvait des défauts?
 8. Quelle fut la réflexion du renard?

2. A apprendre par cœur.

39. LE FLEUVE TARI

Au bord d'un lac il y avait un berger qui gardait les chameaux d'un village. Un jour, il s'aperçut que l'eau du lac fuyait. Il ferma l'issue souterraine avec une grosse pierre, mais il y laissa tomber son bâton de berger. Quelque temps après, un fleuve tarit dans une des provinces de la Perse. Le sultan envoya des émissaires dans tous les royaumes environnants pour découvrir comment la source de son fleuve avait été tarie. Ces ambassadeurs portaient le bâton du berger que le fleuve avait apporté. Le berger se souvint de son bâton; il comprit que son lac était la source du fleuve.

"Que fera le sultan pour celui qui lui rendra son fleuve?" demanda-t-il aux envoyés.

"Il lui donnera," répondirent-ils, "sa fille et la moitié de son royaume."

"Allez donc," répliqua-t-il, "et le fleuve perdu arrosera la Perse et réjouira le cœur du sultan."

Le berger ôta la grosse pierre, et les eaux allèrent remplir de nouveau le lit du fleuve. Le sultan envoya de nouveaux ambassadeurs avec sa fille à l'heureux berger, et lui donna la moitié de ses provinces.

D'APRÈS LAMARTINE.

1. Répondez à ces questions:

    1. De qui parle l'histoire? Quel était son occupation?
    2. Où gardait-il ses chameaux?
    3. De quoi s'aperçut-il un jour?

4. Comment ferma-t-il l'issue?

5. Qu'est-ce qu'il laissa tomber dans l'eau?

6. Qu'est-ce qui arriva quelque temps après?

7. Que fit le sultan?

8. Pourquoi envoya-t-il les émissaires?

9. Que portaient les ambassadeurs?

10. Où l'avaient-ils trouvé?

11. De quoi le berger se souvint-il?

12. Que comprit-il?

13. Que demanda-t-il aux envoyés?

14. Qu'est-ce que le sultan lui donnera?

15. Que promit-il aux envoyés?

16. Que fit alors le berger?

17. Où coulèrent les eaux?

18. Qui est venu avec les nouveaux ambassadeurs?

19. Qu'est-ce que le sultan donna aussi au berger?

2. Vous êtes le berger. Racontez à votre façon l'histoire au passé indéfini.

40. LE PINSON ET LA PIE

"Apprends-moi donc une chanson!"
Demandait la bavarde Pie
A l'agréable et gai Pinson,
Qui chantait au printemps sur l'épine fleurie.
    "Allez, vous vous moquez, ma mie;
A gens de votre espèce, ah! je gagerais bien
    Que jamais on n'apprendra rien."
    "Eh quoi! la raison, je te prie!"
"Mais c'est que pour s'instruire et savoir bien
    chanter,
    Il faudrait savoir écouter;
    Et jamais babillard n'écouta de sa vie!"
                    MME DE LA FÉRANDIÈRE.

1. Répondez à ces questions:

    1. Comment est la Pie?
    2. Comment est le Pinson?
    3. Que demande celle-là à celui-ci?
    4. Que faisait le Pinson?
    5. Que répond-il à la Pie?
    6. Que gagerait-il?
    7. Pour savoir bien chanter, que faudrait-il apprendre?
    8. Est-ce que la Pie bavarde écoute bien?

2. A apprendre par cœur.

41. ALEXANDRE ET SES SOLDATS

Pendant une marche longue et pénible dans un pays aride, l'armée d'Alexandre souffrait extrêmement de la soif. Quelques soldats, envoyés par le roi à la découverte, trouvèrent un peu d'eau dans le creux d'un rocher, et l'apportèrent au roi dans un casque. Alexandre montra cette eau à ses soldats, pour les encourager à supporter la soif avec patience, puisqu'elle leur annonçait une source voisine. Alors, au lieu de boire, il jeta l'eau par terre aux yeux de toute l'armée. Quel est le soldat qui, sous un tel chef, se serait plaint des privations et des fatigues?

1. Répondez à ces questions:

    1. Comment était la marche?
    2. Comment était le pays?
    3. De quoi souffrait l'armée d'Alexandre?
    4. Que trouvèrent quelques soldats?
    5. Où la trouvèrent-ils?
    6. Comment l'apportèrent-ils au roi?
    7. A qui l'empereur montra-t-il l'eau?
    8. Pourquoi?
    9. Qu'est-ce que l'eau annonçait?
    10. Est-ce que l'empereur but l'eau?
    11. Que fit-il alors?
    12. De quoi ne peut-on se plaindre sous un tel chef?

2. Racontez l'histoire.

42. L'AIGLE ET LE CHAT

Un jour un aigle, tournant autour d'une ferme, crut voir un lièvre; il tomba sur sa proie, la saisit dans ses serres et l'emporta dans les airs. L'aigle s'aperçut bientôt que malgré la finesse de sa vue il s'était trompé: c'était un chat qu'il avait pris. Le chat en se débattant s'était dégagé peu à peu des serres de l'aigle, puis l'avait saisi au corps avec ses quatre griffes et maintenant lui enfonçait ses dents dans le cou. "Lâche-moi," s'écria l'aigle, "et je te lâcherai." "Je n'ai nulle envie," dit le chat, "de m'écraser en tombant d'une telle hauteur. Tu m'as enlevé, descends-moi à présent et remets-moi où tu m'as pris." L'aigle, déchiré par les dents et les griffes du chat, comprit qu'il devait faire ce que l'autre lui disait, aussi descendit-il au plus vite.

D'APRÈS FRANKLIN.

1. Répondez à ces questions:

   1. Où tournait un aigle un jour?
   2. Que crut-il voir?
   3. Que fit-il?
   4. Comment la saisit-il?
   5. Où emporta-t-il sa proie?
   6. De quoi s'aperçut-il bientôt?
   7. Qu'est-ce qu'il avait pris?
   8. Que faisait le chat dans les serres de l'aigle?
   9. Comment s'était-il dégagé?
   10. Comment avait-il saisi l'aigle?
   11. Où lui enfonçait-il les dents?
   12. Qu'est-ce que l'aigle cria?

13. De quoi le chat n'a-t-il pas envie?
14. Où faut-il que l'aigle le remette?
15. Que comprit l'aigle?
16. Que fit-il?

2. Racontez au passé indéfini.
3. Racontez à l'indicatif présent.

43. LE MÉDECIN ET LE PETIT CADEAU

Un célèbre médecin avait soigné un petit enfant pendant une maladie dangereuse. La mère reconnaissante arrive chez le sauveur de son fils. "Docteur," dit-elle, "il y a des services qui ne se payent pas. Je ne savais comment reconnaître vos soins. J'ai pensé que vous voudriez bien accepter ce porte-monnaie que j'ai brodé de ma main." "Madame," répliqua un peu rudement le docteur, "la médecine n'est pas une affaire de sentiment et nos soins veulent être rémunérés en argent. Les petits cadeaux entretiennent l'amitié mais ils n'entretiennent pas nos maisons." "Mais docteur," dit la dame surprise et blessée, "parlez, fixez un chiffre."—"Madame, c'est deux mille francs." La dame ouvre le porte-monnaie, en tire cinq billets de banque de mille francs, en donne deux au médecin, remet les trois autres dans le porte-monnaie, salue froidement et se retire.

1. Répondez à ces questions:

   1. Qui un médecin avait-il soigné?
   2. Ce médecin était-il connu?

3. Comment était la maladie?
4. Comment est la mère?
5. Où arrive-t-elle?
6. De quels services parle-t-elle?
7. Qu'est-ce qu'elle ne savait pas?
8. Que veut-elle lui donner?
9. De quelle manière répliqua le docteur?
10. Que dit-il?
11. Que font les petits cadeaux?
12. Qu'est-ce qu'ils ne font pas?
13. Comment était la dame?
14. Que dit-elle?
15. Que répond le médecin?
16. Qu'est-ce que la dame ouvre?
17. Qu'est-ce qu'elle en tire?
18. Combien en donne-t-elle au médecin?
19. Où met-elle les autres?
20. Que fait-elle ensuite?

2. Racontez l'histoire.

44. IL FAUT PAYER D'AVANCE

Un curé italien, célèbre par ses bons mots s'embarqua
pour un voyage, et fut prié par plusieurs de ses amis
de leur faire des emplettes au pays où il allait. Ils lui
en donnèrent tous des mémoires; un seul lui donna
l'argent nécessaire. Le curé employa l'argent pour
acheter les marchandises demandées et ne songea pas
aux commissions des autres. Quand il fut de retour
chez lui, chacun vint s'informer s'il avait fait les emplettes. "Messieurs," leur dit le curé, "lorsque je fus
embarqué, je mis tous vos mémoires sur le pont du
navire, pour les ranger par ordre; mais il s'éleva un
vent qui les emporta tous dans la mer. Il m'a donc été
impossible de faire vos commissions." "Cependant,"
dit l'un d'eux, "vous avez fait telle emplette pour un
tel." "C'est vrai," répliqua le curé; "mais c'est qu'il
avait enveloppé dans son mémoire l'argent qu'il fallait
pour en payer le montant, et le poids a empêché que
le vent l'emportât."

1. Répondez à ces questions:
    1. Par quoi le curé italien était-il célèbre?
    2. Que fit-il?
    3. Que lui demandèrent plusieurs de ses amis?
    4. Qui lui donna de l'argent?
    5. Quel argent lui donna-t-il?
    6. Que fit le curé?
    7. A quoi ne songea-t-il pas?
    8. Quand il fut de retour qui vint chez lui?
    9. Pourquoi les amis vinrent-ils?

10. Où le curé avait-il mis leurs mémoires?
11. Pourquoi?
12. Qu'arriva-t-il?
13. Que lui dit l'un d'eux?
14. Comment avait-il enveloppé son argent?
15. Qu'est-ce que le poids de l'argent empêcha?

2. Racontez l'histoire au passé indéfini.

45. COMMENT ON DEVIENT MARÉCHAL DE FRANCE

Le maréchal Lefebvre avait un camarade de régiment qui vint le voir un jour et qui admira, non sans un sentiment d'envie, son bel hôtel, ses belles voitures, ses nombreux serviteurs, tout le train enfin d'un grand dignitaire de l'empire.

"Parbleu," lui dit-il, "il faut avouer que tu es bien heureux, et que le ciel t'a bien traité!"

"Veux-tu," lui répondit le maréchal, "avoir tout cela?"

"Oui, certainement."

"La chose est très simple: tu vas descendre dans la cour de mon hôtel; je mettrai à chaque fenêtre deux soldats qui tireront sur toi. Si tu échappes aux balles, je te donnerai tout ce que tu m'envies. C'est comme cela que je l'ai obtenu."

SAINT-MARC GIRARDIN.

1. Répondez à ces questions:

1. De quel maréchal parle-t-on?
2. Qui vint le voir un jour?
3. Qu' admira-t-il?

4. Que pense-t-il?
5. Que lui demande le maréchal?
6. Que répond le camarade?
7. Où faut-il descendre?
8. Qui sera à chaque fenêtre?
9. Que feront les soldats?
10. S'il échappe aux balles, que lui donnera le maréchal?
11. Qui l'a obtenu ainsi?

46. UN MARCHÉ

Un vieil avare fait venir un médecin pour voir sa femme très malade. Le médecin qui connaissait son homme, demande à s'arranger d'abord pour ses honoraires. "Soit," dit l'avare, "je vous donnerai deux cents francs, que vous tuiez ma femme ou que vous la guérissiez." Le médecin accepte, mais malgré ses soins, la femme meurt. Quelque temps après, il vient réclamer son argent. "Quel argent?" dit l'avare. "Avez-vous guéri ma femme?"—"Non, je ne l'ai pas guérie."—"Alors vous l'avez tuée?"—"Tuée! quelle horreur! Vous savez bien que non."—"Eh bien, puisque vous ne l'avez ni guérie ni tuée, que demandez-vous?"

1. Répondez à ces questions:
    1. Qui fait venir un médecin?
    2. Qui est malade?
    3. Que demande le médecin?
    4. Pourquoi demande-t-il cela?
    5. Que dit l'avare?
    6. Qu'est-ce qui arrive, malgré les soins du médecin?

7. Pourquoi le médecin vient-il quelque temps après?
8. Que dit l'avare?
9. Que lui répond le médecin?
10. Que reprit l'avare?
11. Quelle fut l'exclamation du médecin?
12. Qu'est-ce que l'avare finit par dire?

47. LA SOURCE

Tout près du lac filtre une source,
Entre deux pierres, dans un coin;
Allègrement l'eau prend sa course
Comme pour s'en aller bien loin.

Elle murmure: "Oh! quelle joie!
Sous la terre il faisait si noir!
Maintenant ma rive verdoie,
Le ciel se mire à mon miroir.

"A ma coupe l'oiseau s'abreuve . . .
Qui sait? après quelques détours
Peut-être deviendrai-je un fleuve
Baignant vallons, rochers et tours.

"Je broderai de mon écume
Ponts de pierre, quais de granit,
Emportant le steamer qui fume
A l'Océan où tout finit."

Ainsi la jeune source jase,
Formant cent projets d'avenir;
Comme l'eau qui bout dans un vase,
Son flot ne peut se contenir;

Mais le berceau touche à la tombe,
Le géant futur meurt petit:
Née à peine la source tombe
Dans le grand lac qui l'engloutit.

THÉOPHILE GAUTIER.

1. Répondez à ces questions :

   1. Près de quoi filtre la source?
   2. Entre quoi filtre-t-elle?
   3. Dans quoi filtre-t-elle?
   4. Comment coule l'eau?
   5. Que murmure-t-elle?
   6. Maintenant que fait la rive?
   7. Où le ciel se mire-t-il?
   8. Que fait l'oiseau?
   9. Que deviendra peut-être la source?
10. Que baignera-t-elle?
11. Que brodera-t-elle de son écume?
12. Qu'emportera t-elle?
13. Où tout finit-il?
14. Que forme la jeune source en jasant ainsi?
15. À quoi ressemble-t-elle?
16. Où touche le berceau?
17. Comment meurt le géant?
18. Où tombe la source?
19. Qu'engloutit le grand lac?

48. DEUX VOLUMES

Frédéric Guillaume III, roi de Prusse, avait un aide de camp, peu fortuné; il lui envoie un petit porte-feuille, en forme de livre, où il avait placé cinq cents thalers. Quelque temps après il rencontre l'officier. "Eh bien!" lui dit-il, "comment avez-vous trouvé l'ouvrage que je vous ai adressé?"

"Parfait, sire," répond le colonel, "et même tellement intéressant que j'en attends le second volume avec impatience."

Le roi sourit; et, quand vint la fête de l'officier, il lui envoya un nouveau portefeuille absolument semblable au premier, avec ces mots en tête du livre: "Cette œuvre n'a que deux volumes."

1. Répondez à ces questions:

   1. De quel pays Frédéric Guillaume III était-il roi?
   2. Quel était l'état de fortune de son aide-de-camp?
   3. Que lui envoie-t-il?
   4. Comment est le portefeuille?
   5. Qu'avait-il placé dans le portefeuille?
   6. Qui rencontre-t-il quelque temps après?
   7. Que lui dit le roi?
   8. Le livre était-il intéressant?
   9. Qu'est-ce qui le prouve?
  10. Que fit-le roi?
  11. Quand lui envoya-t-il un nouveau **portefeuille?**
  12. Comment était-il?
  13. Quels mots étaient en tête du livre?

2. Racontez l'histoire au passé indéfini.

49. ALPHONSE V ET LE PAYSAN

Alphonse V, roi d'Aragon, rencontra un jour un paysan qui était fort embarrassé, parce que son âne chargé de farine venait de s'enfoncer dans la boue. Le roi descendit aussitôt de cheval et se dirigea vers le pauvre homme pour l'aider. Arrivé à l'endroit où était l'âne, le roi et le paysan se mirent à le tirer par la tête, afin de le faire sortir du bourbier. A peine eurent-ils réussi à retirer la bête, que les gens de la suite d'Alphonse arrivèrent, et voyant le roi tout couvert de boue, ils s'empressèrent de l'essuyer et de lui procurer d'autres vêtements. Le paysan, fort étonné de voir que c'était le roi qui lui était venu en aide, commença à lui faire des excuses et à lui demander pardon. Mais le roi le rassura avec bonté, et lui dit que les hommes étaient faits pour s'aider.

1. Répondez à ces questions:

1. Qui Alphonse V rencontra-t-il un jour?
2. Comment était le paysan?
3. De quoi son âne était-il chargé?
4. Où venait-il de s'enfoncer?
5. Que fit le roi?
6. Où se dirigea-t-il?
7. Où arriva-t-il?
8. Que se mit-il à faire?
9. A ce moment qui arriva?
10. Comment était le roi?
11. Qu'est-ce que les gens du roi s'empressèrent de faire?
12. Que lui procurèrent-ils?

13. Pourquoi le paysan était-il étonné?
14. Que commença-t-il à faire?
15. Que fit le roi?
16. Que dit-il au paysan?

2. Racontez l'histoire au passé indéfini.
3. Racontez l'histoire au présent de l'indicatif.

50. LA VEUVE

Un jour, Azora revenant tout en colère d'une promenade, faisait de grandes exclamations, "Qu'avez-vous," lui dit Zadig son époux, "qui vous peut mettre ainsi hors de vous-même?"—"Hélas," dit-elle, "vous seriez comme moi, si vous aviez vu ce que j'ai vu. J'ai été consoler la jeune veuve Cosrou, qui vient d'élever un tombeau à son jeune époux auprès du ruisseau qui borde cette prairie. Dans sa douleur, elle a promis aux dieux, de demeurer auprès de ce tombeau aussi longtemps que ce ruisseau y coulerait."

"Eh bien!" dit Zadig, "voilà une femme estimable qui aimait véritablement son mari."

"Ah!" reprit Azora, "si vous saviez à quoi elle s'occupait quand je lui ai rendu visite!"

"A quoi donc, belle Azora?"

"Elle faisait détourner le ruisseau."

D'APRÈS VOLTAIRE.

1. Répondez à ces questions:

1. Que fit Azora un jour?
2. Comment était-elle?

3. Que faisait-elle?
4. Que lui dit son époux?
5. Qui voulut-elle consoler?
6. Qu'est-ce que Cosrou vient d'élever?
7. Où est le tombeau?
8. Où a-t-elle promis aux dieux de demeurer?
9. Combien de temps a-t-elle promis d'y demeurer?
10. Que dit Zadig à Azora?
11. A quoi la veuve s'occupait-elle quand Azora lui a rendu visite?

51. LE SOI-DISANT M. CHOSE

Monsieur Chose, musicien francais, avait ses entrées libres au Théâtre-Français, mais il n'y allait jamais. Un soir cependant, passant par là, il entre. Il donne son nom, mais le contrôleur le regarde sévèrement et lui dit: "Monsieur, nous connaissons très bien Monsieur Chose; il vient tous les soirs, il est déjà dans la salle." "Eh bien," dit le vrai M. Chose, "veuillez me donner une place à côté de lui—je serais heureux de faire sa connaissance."

Monsieur Chose paya donc et entra. Pendant l'entr'acte il parla au soi-disant Chose.

"Vous êtes vraiment M. Chose," lui dit-il, "vous en êtes sûr?"

"Mais, Monsieur," balbutia l'autre, un peu inquiet.

"Vous m'étonnez," dit doucement le musicien. "Depuis cinquante ans je croyais que c'était moi."

1. Répondez à ces questions :

  1. Où Monsieur Chose avait-il ses entrées libres?
  2. Y allait-il souvent?
  3. Que fait-il un soir?
  4. Que fait le contrôleur lorsqu'il donne son nom?
  5. Que lui dit le contrôleur?
  6. Ce soi-disant Monsieur Chose vient-il souvent?
  7. Où est-il déjà?
  8. Que demande le vrai M. Chose au contrôleur?
  9. Que fit-il pendant l'entr'acte?
  10. Que dit-il à son voisin?
  11. Qu'éprouve-t-il?
  12. Pourquoi le musicien est-il étonné?

52. LES SOULIERS DE VOLTAIRE

Voltaire avait à son service un brave garçon, fidèle, mais paresseux, qui recevait, comme gages, vingt-cinq francs par mois. "Joseph," lui dit un jour son maître, "apporte-moi mes souliers." Joseph arrive, et Voltaire s'apercevant que ses souliers étaient encore couverts de boue, s'écria avec colère: "Je ne conçois pas que tu oses m'apporter des souliers aussi sales." Le domestique répondit: "Mais, monsieur, je ne vois pas quelle importance cela peut avoir, puisque les rues sont pleines de boue. Dans deux heures vos souliers seront aussi sales que maintenant." Voltaire se chaussa et sortit. Mais Joseph courut après lui et dit: "Monsieur! la clef?" "La clef! Quelle clef?" "Oui, la clef du buffet, pour déjeuner." "Mon ami," répondit Voltaire, "à quoi bon? Deux

heures après tu auras aussi faim que maintenant."
A partir de ce jour-là, Joseph cira toujours les souliers
de son maître.

1. Répondez à ces questions:

    1. Qui Voltaire avait-il à son service?

    2. Quelles gages recevait-il?

    3. Que lui dit son maître?

    4. De quoi les souliers étaient-ils couverts?

    5. Quelle fut l'exclamation de Voltaire?

    6. Le domestique trouve-t-il cela important?

    7. Quel est l'état des rues?

    8. Comment seront les souliers?

    9. Que fit Voltaire?

    10. Que fit Joseph?

    11. Que demanda-t-il?

    12. Pourquoi?

    13. Que répondit Voltaire?

    14. Que fit Joseph à partir de ce jour-là?

2. Le professeur peut faire jouer le rôle de Voltaire par un
élève et celui de Joseph par un autre.

3. Employez dans des phrases: gages, couvert, puisque,
plein, faim.

53. LE LOUP REMERCIE

Un loup très goulu, et très affamé, avait avalé gloutonnement un quartier d'agneau, et un os pointu lui était demeuré dans le gosier. Il s'agite, ouvre la gueule, baisse la tête, essaie de retirer l'os avec sa patte; peine inutile! il ne peut le retirer. Une cigogne au long cou passa par hasard près de l'endroit où maître Loup s'agitait et se tourmentait. "Qu'avez-vous?" lui demanda-t-elle. "Puis-je vous être utile?" Le loup lui fit signe qu'il avait dans la gorge quelque chose qui le gênait. Dame Cigogne retire l'os avec son bec. L'opération étant terminée, la cigogne dit au loup: "Ma récompense, monsieur, s'il vous plaît." "Votre récompense!" répliqua le loup. "Vous plaisantez, madame. N'est-ce pas assez que de vous avoir laissé retirer votre tête de mon gosier? Vous êtes une ingrate."

D'APRÈS LA FONTAINE.

1. Répondez à ces questions:

1. Comment était le loup?
2. Qu'avait-il avalé?
3. Qu'est-ce qui le gênait?
4. Où l'os était-il demeuré?
5. Qu'est-ce qu'il ne pouvait pas faire?
6. Qui passa près de lui?
7. Que lui demanda-t-elle?
8. Le loup ne pouvant parler, quel signe fit-il?
9. Que fait la cigogne?

10. Que dit-elle ensuite au loup?
11. Quelle est sa récompense?

2. Prenez le rôle du loup. Racontez l'histoire.
3. Prenez le rôle du cigogne. Racontez l'histoire.

54. LE RICHE ET LE PAYSAN

A sa mort un pauvre bon paysan vint à la porte du paradis. Un riche seigneur monta au ciel en même temps que lui. Saint Pierre arriva avec ses clefs, ouvrit la porte, et fit entrer le seigneur; mais sans doute il n'avait pas vu le paysan, car il le laissa dehors et ferma la porte. Le paysan entendit la joyeuse réception que le ciel faisait au riche, avec chant et musique. Quand le concert fut terminé, Saint Pierre revint et fit entrer le pauvre homme. Celui-ci s'attendait qu'à son entrée le chant et la musique allaient recommencer. Mais tout resta tranquille. On le reçut de bon cœur; mais personne ne chanta. Il demanda à Saint Pierre pourquoi on ne faisait pas de musique pour lui comme pour le riche, et si la partialité régnait au ciel comme sur la terre. "Tu nous es aussi cher qu'aucun autre," lui répondit le saint; "mais, vois-tu, des pauvres paysans comme toi, il en entre tous les jours ici, tandis que des riches il n'en vient pas ur tous les cent ans."

1. Répondez à ces questions:

1. Qui mourut?
2. Où alla-t-il?

3. Qui y monta en même temps que lui?
4. Qui arriva?
5. Que portait-il?
6. Qu'ouvrit-il?
7. Qui fit-il entrer?
8. Où laissa-t-il le paysan?
9. Qu'est-ce que le paysan entendit?
10. Que fit Saint Pierre ensuite?
11. A quoi s'attendait le paysan?
12. Fit-on de la musique?
13. Comment le reçut-on?
14. Que demanda-t-il à Saint Pierre?
15. Que lui répond Saint Pierre?

2. Racontez l'histoire au passé indéfini.

55. UNE LEÇON DE GÉNÉROSITÉ

Un ami du doyen Swift lui envoya un jour un turbot par un jeune domestique qui n'avait jamais reçu de la part du doyen la moindre marque de générosité. Entré dans la maison, le jeune homme ouvrit la porte du cabinet du doyen, et, déposant brusquement le poisson, dit à voix haute: "Mon maître vous envoie un turbot." "Jeune homme," dit Swift, "est-ce ainsi que vous faites votre commission? Je vais vous donner une leçon de politesse: asseyez-vous dans mon fauteuil; nous allons changer de rôle et je vais vous montrer comment à l'avenir vous devrez vous comporter." Notre garçon s'assit, et le doyen se dirigea de la porte vers la table d'un pas respectueux, fit une profonde révérence et dit: "Monsieur, mon maître vous fait ses amitiés, il aime à penser que vous vous portez bien, et vous prie d'accepter ce petit présent." "Vraiment?" répliqua le garçon, "faites-lui tous mes remerciements, et prenez pour vous-même cette demi-couronne." Le doyen, ainsi contraint à un acte de générosité, rit de bon cœur et lui donna une couronne.

1. Répondez à ces questions:

    1. De qui parle-t-on dans l'histoire?
    2. Qu'apporta le domestique?
    3. Où entra-t-il?
    4. Qu'ouvrit-il?
    5. Que fit-il?
    6. Que dit-il?
    7. Que lui dit le doyen?
    8. Que veut-il donner au domestique?
    9. Que va-t-il lui montrer.
    10. Où le domestique s'assit-il?
    11. Comment marcha le doyen?
    12. Que fit-il?
    13. Que dit-il?
    14. Que répondit le garçon?
    15. Que fit le doyen?

2. Racontez l'histoire au passé indéfini.

56. BONAPARTE ET LA SENTINELLE

Après avoir gagné la bataille d'Arcole qui avait duré trois jours, Bonaparte sous un vêtement fort simple, parcourait son camp, afin d'examiner par lui-même si les fatigues de trois journées aussi pénibles n'avaient rien fait perdre à ses soldats de leur discipline et de leur surveillance habituelles. Le général trouve une sentinelle endormie, lui enlève doucement son fusil sans l'éveiller, et monte la faction à sa place. Quelques moments après, le soldat se réveille; se voyant ainsi désarmé et reconnaissant son général, il s'écrie: "Je suis perdu!" "Rassure-toi," lui dit Bonaparte avec douceur, "après tant de fatigues, il peut être permis à un brave tel que toi de succomber au sommeil; mais une autre fois choisis mieux ton temps."

1. Répondez à ces questions:

1. Combien de jours dura la bataille d'Arcole?
2. Qui la gagna?
3. Que fit-il ensuite?
4. Comment était son vêtement?
5. Que voulait-il examiner?
6. Qu'est-ce qui arrive?
7. Que fait Bonaparte?
8. Quand le soldat se réveille-t-il?
9. Comment se voit-il?
10. Qui reconnaît-il?
11. Que cria-t-il?
12. Comment lui parle son général?
13. Qu'est-ce qui peut être permis à un brave?
14. Que faut-il faire une autre fois?

57. LE VILLAGEOIS CHANGE D'AVIS

Un villageois se promenait à la campagne, par une chaude journée d'été. En regardant les chênes, il vit que ces arbres portaient un petit fruit pas plus gros que le pouce. Il remarqua, en même temps, une petite plante, qui, rampant à terre, portait des citrouilles quatre fois plus grosses que sa tête. Cet homme se dit en lui-même: "Il me semble que si j'avais été à la place du Créateur, j'aurais mieux arrangé les choses: la citrouille aurait dû pousser sur ce grand arbre, et le gland sur cette petite plante rampante." Le sommeil le gagnant il alla se coucher sous un grand chêne. Pendant qu'il dormait, un gland lui tomba sur le nez, et le réveilla. Portant aussitôt la main au visage, il trouva le gland pris dans sa barbe. Alors notre sage s'écria: "J'avoue que Dieu a raison d'avoir arrangé les choses telles qu'elles sont. Que serais-je devenu si la citrouille avait été sur le chêne? En tombant elle m'aurait écrasé la tête!"

D'APRÈS LA FONTAINE.

1. Répondez à ces questions:
   1. Que faisait un villageois?
   2. Quel temps faisait-il?
   3. Quels arbres regardait-il?
   4. Que vit-il?
   5. Quelle petite plante remarqua-t-il?
   6. Que portait-elle?
   7. Qu'aurait-il fait s'il avait été à la place du Créateur?
   8. Qu'aurait-il changé de place?
   9. Où alla-t-il se coucher?

10. Pourquoi?
11. Qu'arriva-t-il?
12. Où trouva-t-il le gland?
13. Quelle fut son exclamation?

2. Racontez l'histoire au passé indéfini.

58. LE PORTE-DRAPEAU

Un régiment français était en bataille contre toute l'armée prussienne. Les officiers criaient: "Couchez-vous!" Mais personne ne voulait obéir, et le fier régiment restait debout, groupé autour de son drapeau.

De temps en temps le drapeau qui flottait agité au vent de la mitraille, sombrait dans la fumée: alors une voix s'élevait grave et fière: "Au drapeau, mes enfants, au drapeau!" Aussitôt un officier s'élançait, et l'héroïque enseigne, planait encore au-dessus de la bataille.

Vingt-deux fois elle tomba! Vingt-deux fois sa hampe, échappée d'une main mourante, fut saisie, redressée; et, lorsqu'au soleil couchant ce qui restait du régiment—à peine une poignée d'hommes—battit lentement en retraite, le drapeau n'était plus qu'une guenille aux mains du sergent Hornus, le vingt-troisième porte-drapeau de la journée.

D'APRÈS ALPHONSE DAUDET (CONTES DU LUNDI).

1. Répondez à ces questions:

1. Que faisait le régiment français?
2. Contre qui était-il en bataille?
3. Que criaient les officiers?

4. Qui voulait obéir?
5. Comment était le régiment?
6. Comment restait-il?
7. Autour de quoi était-il groupé?
8. Qu'entendait-on?
9. Qu'est-ce qui l'agitait?
10. De temps en temps que faisait le drapeau?
11. Qu'est-ce qui s'élevait?
12. Comment était la voix?
13. Que disait la voix?
14. Qui s'élançait aussitôt?
15. Où planait encore le drapeau?
16. Combien de fois tomba l'héroïque enseigne?
17. D'où s'échappait la hampe?
18. Que restait-il du régiment au soleil couchant?
19. Que fit le régiment?
20. Comment était le drapeau?
21. Qui le tenait?
22. Combien y avait-il eu de porte-drapeaux dans la journée?

59. JOSEPH II CHEZ LE FORGERON

L'empereur Joseph II voyageant seul en Italie s'arrêta dans un village pour faire réparer le fer d'une des roues de sa voiture. Il entra dans l'atelier du serrurier et lui demanda de réparer la roue sur-le-champ. "Il faudra attendre un peu, monsieur," dit l'ouvrier: "c'est fête aujourd'hui, et tout le monde est à l'église. Je n'ai personne pour faire jouer le soufflet."—"Qu'à cela ne tienne!" répondit l'empereur; "je ferai bien jouer le soufflet moi-même; et puis, cela me rechauffera."

Tous deux se mirent donc au travail, le monarque soufflant, l'ouvrier forgeant, et en une demi-heure la voiture était prête. "Combien est-ce?" demanda Joseph. "Six sous," répondit l'autre. "Tiens, voilà," et l'empereur lui mit six ducats dans la main. Le serrurier ouvrit de grands yeux. "Vous vous trompez, monsieur; vous me donnez six pièces d'or et, de plus, je n'ai point de monnaie." "Garde tout, mon brave," dit Joseph en souriant; "le surplus de tes six sous est pour le plaisir que j'ai eu à souffler."

1. Répondez à ces questions:

1. Où voyageait l'empereur Joseph II?
2. Où s'arrêta-t-il?
3. Que fallait-il faire réparer?
4. Où entra-t-il?
5. Que lui demanda-t-il?
6. Pourquoi faudra-t-il attendre?
7. Où est tout le monde?
8. Pourquoi le serrurier ne peut-il pas réparer la roue tout seul?
9. Qui fera jouer le soufflet?
10. Que faisait le monarque?
11. Que faisait l'ouvrier?
12. Quand la voiture fut-elle prête?
13. Que demanda Joseph?
14. Que répondit l'autre?
15. Combien lui donna l'empereur?
16. Que fit le serrurier?
17. Que dit-il?
18. Que répond Joseph?
19. Pourquoi lui donne-t-il le surplus?

60. LES SACS DE POUDRE

Dix-huit contrebandiers, chargés chacun d'un sac de poudre, passaient sur une route coupée dans des rochers. Le dernier s'apercevant que son sac s'allégeait, se douta que l'allègement était aux dépens de la charge. On voyait une longue traînée de poudre sur le chemin qu'ils avaient parcouru. C'était un indice qui pouvait trahir la marche de la troupe et compromettre l'entreprise. Il cria halte, et, à ce cri, les autres s'assirent sur les sacs, pour boire un coup et s'essuyer le front. Pendant ce temps, l'autre revint sur ses pas jusqu'au commencement de la traînée de poudre. Il y arriva au bout de deux heures de marche, et avec sa pipe y mit le feu pour en détruire les traces. Deux minutes après, il entendit une détonation formidable, qui se répercutait dans les vallées et dans les gorges: c'étaient les dix-sept sacs, qui, rejoints par la traînée sautaient en l'air avec les dix-sept pères de famille assis dessus.

D'APRÈS TÖPFFER.

1. Répondez à ces questions :

    1. Où passaient les contrebandiers ?
    2. Combien y avait-il de contrebandiers ?
    3. Par où passaient-ils ?
    4. De quoi étaient-ils chargés ?
    5. De quoi s'aperçut le dernier ?
    6. De quoi se doutait-il ?
    7. Qu'est-ce qui se voyait sur sa trace ?
    8. Que cet indice pouvait-il trahir ?

9. Que pouvait-il compromettre?
10. Que cria-t-il?
11. Où s'assirent les autres?
12. Que firent-ils?
13. Que faisait l'autre pendant ce temps?
14. Quand y arriva-t-il?
15. Que fit-il?
16. Comment?
17. Pourquoi y mit-il le feu?
18. Qu'entendit-il deux minutes après?
19. Où entendit-on la détonation?
20. Qu'est-ce qui faisait ce bruit?
21. Comment furent-ils rejoints?
22. Qu'arriva-t-il?
23. Qui était assis dessus?

2. Prenez le rôle du dernier. Racontez l'histoire.
3. Racontez l'histoire au présent.

61. LOUIS XVI EN PRISON

Le 10 août 1792, Louis XVI fut enfermé dans la
prison du Temple avec sa sœur, la reine et ses deux
enfants. Au Temple, la famille royale se réunissait
dans la journée; lorsque le temps le permettait, on
descendait au jardin. Le soir, le roi quittait sa famille
pour monter au premier étage qu'il occupait seul;
chaque soir il se demandait s'il reverrait sa famille le
lendemain. Louis XVI était en prison depuis cinq
mois, lorsque la Convention décréta qu'il serait jugé
par elle. Robespierre voulait sa mort sans jugement.
"Vous n'avez point," dit-il aux représentants, "de

sentence à rendre, mais une mesure de salut public à prendre." Le 11 décembre, le roi parut devant l'assemblée. Toute défense était inutile. La Convention déclara que Louis XVI avait conspiré contre la liberté publique, et le condamna à mort.

1. Répondez à ces questions:

1. Quand Louis XVI fut-il enfermé dans la prison du Temple?
2. Qui était avec lui?
3. Que faisait la famille royale dans la journée?
4. Où descendait-on?
5. Le soir que faisait le roi?
6. Que se demandait-il chaque soir?
7. Que décréta la Convention?
8. Depuis quand Louis XVI était-il en prison?
9. Que voulait Robespierre?
10. Que dit-il aux représentants?
11. Quand le roi parut-il devant l'assemblée?
12. Pouvait-il se défendre?
13. Que déclara la Convention?
14. A quoi le condamna-t-elle?

62. NAPOLÉON ET JUNOT

Le 27 août 1793, les royalistes du midi de la France livrèrent le port de Toulon aux Anglais. Pour le reprendre, le jeune Napoléon y fut envoyé en qualité de commandant d'artillerie, et la ville se rendit après un siège resté célèbre. Ce fut pendant le siège que Napoléon rencontra Junot, qui devait plus tard rendre

de grands services à l'empire. Un jour, pendant que
le jeune commandant d'artillerie faisait construire une
batterie, il eut besoin d'écrire, et demanda un sergent
ou un caporal pour lui servir de secrétaire. Il s'en
présenta un aussitôt, et Napoléon, le faisant asseoir
sur le terrain même, lui dicta sa correspondance. La
lettre était à peine terminée qu'un boulet, tombant
tout près, la couvrit de terre. "Bon," dit le soldat
écrivain, "je n'aurai pas besoin de sable." C'était
Junot, et cette preuve de courage et de sang-froid
suffit pour le recommander à son commandant, qui le
poussa ensuite aux premiers grades de l'armée.

1. Répondez à ces questions:

1. Qui livra Toulon aux Anglais?
2. Qui y fut envoyé?
3. Qu'arriva-t-il?
4. Qui Napoléon rencontra-t-il?
5. Que devait-il faire plus tard?
6. Que faisait construire Napoléon?
7. De quoi avait-il besoin?
8. Qui demanda-t-il?
9. Où le secrétaire s'assit-il?
10. Qu'arriva-t-il?
11. Que dit le secrétaire?
12. Qu'est-ce qui le recommanda à Napoléon?
13. Jusqu' où Napoléon poussa-t-il Junot?

63. EPITAPHE DE FRANKLIN

A Philadelphie pas loin de la maison où mourut Franklin, on voit sur une modeste tombe couverte de mousse sauvage, cette épitaphe, composée par lui-même plusieurs années avant sa mort:

CI-GÎT LE CORPS DE BENJAMIN FRANKLIN, IMPRIMEUR,
SEMBLABLE À LA COUVERTURE D'UN VIEUX LIVRE
DONT LA TABLE DES MATIÈRES A ÉTÉ ARRACHÉE,
DONT LES CARACTÈRES ONT ÉTÉ EFFACÉS ET LA DORURE TERNIE
LA PÂTURE DES VERS.
CEPENDANT L'OUVRAGE LUI-MÊME NE SERA PAS PERDU,
CAR IL PARAÎTRA SOUS UN AUTRE FORMAT
DANS UNE NOUVELLE ÉDITION
CORRIGÉE ET PURIFIÉE PAR L'AUTEUR.

I. Répondez à ces questions :

1. Où est la tombe de Franklin?
2. Comment est-elle?
3. De quoi est-elle couverte?
4. Près de quelle maison est-elle?
5. Que voit-on sur la tombe?
6. Qui l'a composée?
7. Quand l'a-t-il composée?
8. A quoi le corps est-il semblable?
9. Qu'est-ce qui a été arraché?
10. Comment sont les caractères?
11. Comment est la dorure?
12. Comment paraîtra l'ouvrage?
13. Comment sera la nouvelle édition?
14. De quel auteur parle-t-on ici?

EXERCICES SUR LES VERBES

I. (HISTORIETTES 1-10)

1. Quel est l'infinitif de:
2. A quel temps est:

1. Il fait. 2. Il a. 3. Il frappe. 4. Il ouvre. 5. Il entre. 6. Il donne. 7. Il chante. 8. Il s'envole. 9. Vous êtes. 10. Dites. 11. Elle achète. 12. Il vend. 13. Elle paye. 14. Elle sort. 15. Elle perd. 16. Elle revient. 17. Elle rend. 18. Elle remercie. 19. Il est. 20. Il veut. 21. Il essaye. 22. Il jette. 23. Il peut. 24. J'écris. 25. Je prends. 26. Je sèche. 27. Il répète. 28. Ils écrivent. 29. Il revint. 30. Il voulut. 31. Vous croyez. 32. Je veux. 33. Ils font. 34. Ils étaient. 35. Ils sont. 36. Ils voient. 37. Il crie. 38. Ils mettent. 39. Rendez. 40. Laissez. 41. Il vaut. 42. Tu auras. 43. Ouvert.

II. (HISTORIETTES 11-14)

1. Quel est l'infinitif de:
2. A quel temps est:

1. Il va. 2. Il remarque. 3. Il voit. 4. Ils lisent. 5. Ils portent. 6. Il entre. 7. Il demande. 8. Il essaye. 9. Il regarde. 10. Il répond. 11. Je puis. 12. Il finit. 13. Je savais. 14. J'aurais demandé. 15. Il achetait. 16. Il habitait. 17. Il s'aperçut. 18. Il recevait. 19. Il accusa. 20. Il nia. 21. Il porta. 22. Vous faites. 23. Apportez. 24. Il répondit. 25. J'ai. 26. J'achète. 27. Il sert. 28. J'envoie. 29. Je mets. 30. Vous devez. 31. Il dit. 32. Il tient. 33. Vous êtes. 34. Il devient. 35. Il s'en va. 36. Tu sais. 37. Tu fais. 38. J'attends.

III. (Historiettes 15–20)

1. Quel est l'infinitif de:

2. A quel temps est:

1. Ils fatiguaient. 2. Il se plaignait. 3. Il fit. 4. Je veux. 5. Il dit. 6. Vous soyez. 7. Prenez. 8. Gardez. 9. Il avait vu. 10. Il ouvrit. 11. Il avait. 12. Il faisait. 13. Il prenait. 14. Il allait. 15. Il ¦pouvait. 16. Il comprit. 17. Rentré. 18. Il sort. 19. Il aperçoit. 20. Il se relève. 21. Il court. 22. Il mange. 23. Il eut. 24. Je suis. 25. Il répondit. 26. Tu crains. 27. Il continua. 28. Il reprit. 29. Je serais. 30. Tu es. 31. Tu as. 32. J'ai lu. 33. Connu. 34. J'étais. 35. J'osais. 36. J'avais.

IV. (Historiettes 21–26)

1. Quel est l'infinitif de:

2. A quel temps est:

1. Il voyait. 2. Il survient. 3. Il dit. 4. Il y a. 5. Vous voyez. 6. Qu'il soit. 7. Je verrai. 8. Il peut. 9. Il était. 10. Voulant. 11. Il va. 12. Il disait. 13. Il avait. 14. Allez. 15. Il reprit. 16. Mettez. 17. Vous faites. 18. Je serai. 19. Il faisait. 20. Il conduisait. 21. Reconnaissant. 22. Il fut. 23. Je crois. 24. Elle aura. 25. Fait. 26. J'ai donné. 27. Elle fit. 28. Disant. 29. Elle reconnut. 30. Elle aura. 31. Elle sert.

V. (Historiettes 27–33)

1. Quel l'infinitif de:

2. A quel temps est:

1. Il veut. 2. Vaincu. 3. Ils font. 4. Il faut. 5. Ils attaquaient. 6. Etant. 7. Conduisait. 8. Assis. 9. Voyant. 10. Il allongea. 11. Il saisit. 12. Il prit. 13. Il put. 14. Ils rompirent. 15. Il pourra. 16. Ils réussirent. 17. Il se rendait. 18. Il voit. 19. Il pleut. 20. Je vais. 21. J'appelle. 22. Allons. 23. Je suis. 24. S'apercevant. 25. Je croyais. 26. Il sut. 27. Revenu. 28. Ils faisaient. 29. Bu. 30. Il buvait. 31. Vendu. 32. Il entreprit. 33. Ils crurent. 34. Il choisit.

VI. (HISTORIETTES 34–42)

1. Quel est l'infinitif de:

2. A quel temps est:

1. Etant. 2. Ayant. 3. Eté. 4. Tuez. 5. Faites. 6. Ils espéraient. 7. Il fut. 8. Il dit. 9. Il se rendit. 10. Il reconnut. 11. Il paraît. 12. Je veux. 13. Vous voyez. 14. Il crut. 15. Il mangeait. 16. Ils dirent. 17. Il disait. 18. Je connais. 19. Il est mort. 20. Faites. 21. Ils font. 22. Il faisait. 23. Il s'aperçut. 24. Il fuyait. 25. Eté. 26. Il se souvint. 27. Il comprit. 28. Il faudrait. 29. Plaint. 30. Il crut. 31. Pris. 32. Qu'il remette.

VII. (HISTORIETTES 43–50)

1. Quel est l'infinitif de:

2. A quel temps est:

1. Il répliqua. 2. Ils entretiennent. 3. Il savait. 4. Ils font. 5. Il met. 6. Il songea. 7. Il vint. 8. Je mis. 9. Il fallait. 10. Venu. 11. Obtenu. 12. Il sera. 13. Il meurt. 14. Je deviendrai. 15. Il bout. 16. Il peut. 17. Il envoie. 18. J'attends. 19. Il sourit.

20. Il fit. 21. Il venait. 22. Il se dirigea. 23. Il se mit.
24. Ils eurent. 25. Couvert. 26. Il revint. 27. Faisant.
28. Vous seriez. 29. Promis. 30. Voulu.

VIII. (Historiettes 51–59)

1. Quel est l'infinitif de:
2. A quel temps est:

1. Veuillez. 2. Nous connaissons. 3. Je serai. 4.
Vous êtes. 5. Je croyais. 6. Il plaît. 7. Il pouvait.
8. Il mourut. 9. Vu. 10. Il reçut. 11. Tu es. 12. Tu
vois. 13. Reçu. 14. Asseyez-vous. 15. Vous devrez.
16. Faites. 17. Il rit. 18. Il parcourait. 19. Il enlève.
20. Voyant. 21. Permis. 22. J'aurais. 23. Dû. 24.
Voyageant. 25. Il faudra. 26. Je ferai. 27. Ils se
mirent. 28. Tiens. 29. Il mit.

IX. (Historiettes 59–63)

1. Quel est l'infinitif de:
2. A quel temps est:

1. Parcouru. 2. Il voyait. 3. Suivi. 4. Il pouvait.
5. Ils s'assirent. 6. Rejoint. 7. Assis. 8. Il reverrait.
9. Il parut. 10. Qu'il pût. 11. Il voit.

EXERCICES DE PRONONCIATION

[The black face numerals in these exercises refer to the stories. See note p. xv.]

ÉCRIVEZ LES SONS ET PRONONCEZ LES MOTS:

1. Premier son dans: 1. envole.

Deuxième son dans: 1. manger.

Avant-dernier son dans: 1. hiver. 2. oiseau. 3. soigne.

Dernier son dans: 1. hiver. 2. froid. 3. faim. 4. soigne. 5. printemps. 6. plus. 7. sage.

2. Deuxième son dans: 1. dame. 2. paire. 3. marchand. 4. paye. 5. sort. 6. perd. 7. revient. 8. contente.

Dernier son dans: 1. gants. 2. vend. 3. paye. 4. magasin. 5. rue. 6. pas. 7. contente.

3. Premier son dans: 1. aurais. 2. quatre.

Deuxième son dans: 1. petite. 2. part. 3. deux.

Avant-dernier son dans: 1. pleure.

Dernier son dans: 1. pourquoi. 2. plus. 3. entend. 4. aurais.

4. Premier son dans: 1. examine. 2. homme.

Deuxième son dans: 1. examine. 2. lame. 3. poliment. 4. celui. 5. neuf. 6. poche.

Avant-dernier son dans: 1. approche.

Dernier son dans: 1. rend. 2. fois.

5. Premier son dans: 1. essaie. 2. eau. 3. enfin. 4. aise.

Deuxième son dans: 1. court. 2. dur.

Avant-dernier son dans: 1. soif. 2. boire. 3. bouteille. 4. essaie. 5. alors. 6. cailloux.

Dernier son dans: 1. veut. 2. trop. 3. court. 4. bouteille. 5. essaie. 6. enfin. 7. aise.

6. Premier son dans: 1. encre.

Deuxième son dans: 1. feuille. 2. sèche. 3. buvard. 4. colle. 5. timbre. 6. supérieur.

Avant-dernier son dans: 1. trempe. 2. écriture. 3. enveloppe. 4. supérieur. 5. boîte.

Dernier son dans: 1. moi. 2. avec. 3. buvard. 4. coin.

7. Premier son dans: 1. exact. 2. aussi.

Deuxième son dans: 1. science. 2. domestique. 3. rôti. 4. père. 5. donc. 6. sera.

Avant-dernier son dans: 1. collège. 2. vacances. 3. Pâques. 4. abord. 5. soir.

Dernier son dans: 1. revint. 2. tous. 3. esprit. 4. donc. 5. soir. 6. toi.

8. Premier son dans: 1. âne. 2. chasse. 3. autres. 4. ensemble. 5. haut.

Deuxième son dans: 1. contents. 2. car. 3. vieille, 4. femme. 5. long. 6. fouet. 7. chasse. 8. devant. 9. leur.

Troisième son dans: 1. ensemble.

Avant-dernier son dans: 1. école. 2. personne.

Dernier son dans: 1. contents. 2. voient. 3. vieille. 4. fouet.

9. Premier son dans: 1. hameçon.

Deuxième son dans: 1. poisson. 2. pêcheur. 3. rendez. 4. laissez.

Avant-dernier son dans: 1. pêcheur. 2. mieux.

Dernier son dans: 1. ligne. 2. appât. 3. mangerai. 4. vaut. 5. mieux.

10. Premier son dans: 1. offre.

Deuxième son dans: 1. retourne. 2. femme.

Avant-dernier son dans: 1. fumeur. 2. cigare. 3. droite. 4. capitaine.

Dernier son dans: 1. pas. 2. bas.

11. Premier son dans: 1. opticien. 2. essaye. 3. question. 4. aurais.

Deuxième son dans: 1. lunettes. 2. paysan. 3. beaucoup. 4. lorgnon. 5. paire.

Avant-dernier son dans: 1. lorgnon. 2. personne. 3. essaye. 4. question.

Dernier son dans: 1. opticien. 2. client. 3. aurais.

12. Premier son dans: 1. envoie. 2. autre.

Deuxième son dans: 1. Jacques. 2. Dupont. 3. Jean. 4. beurre. 5. juge. 6. simple.

Avant-dernier son dans: 1. plainte.

Dernier son dans: 1. Dupont. 2. temps. 3. balance. 4. poids.

Sons nasaux dans: 1. rencontrant. 2. envoie. 3. balance. 4. un. 5. bien. 6. boulanger. 7. Jean. 8. Dupont. 9. temps. 10. en. 11. pain. 12. comment. 13. dans. 14. plainte. 15. paysan.

13. Premier son dans: 1. impatient. 2. aussi. 3. air.

Deuxième son dans: 1. corbeau. 2. monsieur. 3. car. 4. joli. 5. content. 6. devient. 7. agite.

Troisième son dans: 1. fromage.

Avant-dernier son dans: 1. branche. 2. plume. 3. noir. 4. prince.

Dernier son dans: 1. pied. 2. content. 3. devient. 4. queue. 5. voix.

14. Premier son dans: 1. interroge.

Deuxième son dans: 1. sais. 2. secoue.

Avant-dernier son dans: 1. secouer.

Dernier son dans: 1. attends. 2. sorte.

15. Premier son dans: 1. joyeux. 2. occasion. 3. yeux.

Deuxième son dans: 1. dormir. 2. voisin. 3. soyez. 4. cacha. 5. cave.

Troisième son dans: 1. pointe. 2. joyeux.

Avant-dernier son dans: 1. affaires. 2. plaignait. 3. réveillé.

Dernier son dans: 1. joyeux. 2. voisin. 3. cabinet. 4. soin. 5. tant. 6. yeux. 7. fond.

16. Premier son dans: 1. entrain. 2. guet.

Deuxième son dans: 1. moment. 2. vole. 3. comprit. 4. fort. 5. somme. 6. chanson. 7. reprenez.

Avant-dernier son dans: 1. crainte.

Dernier son dans: 1. travail. 2. guet. 3. chat. 4. malheureux. 5. entrain. 6. moment.

17. Deuxième son dans: 1. chambre. 2. laisse. 3. pauvre. 4. sort.

Dernier son dans: 1. coin. 2. aperçoit.

18. Premier son dans: 1. philosophe. 2. aise. 3. empêcher.

Deuxième son dans: 1. curiosité. 2. mauvais. 3. jouir.

Troisième son dans: 1. Diogène.

Avant-dernier son dans: 1. Corinthe. 2. Diogène.

Dernier son dans: 1. point. 2. serai.

20. Premier son dans: 1. Europe. 2. aise. 3. or. 4. Angleterre. 5. osais.

Deuxième son dans: 1. revenait. 2. pays. 3. cultivé. 4. faire. 5. peur. 6. bord. 7. tomber.

Troisième son dans: 1. voyage. 2. promenade.

Quatrième son dans: 1. déjeuner.

Avant-dernier son dans: 1. Europe. 2. Angleterre.

Dernier son dans: 1. pays. 2. riche. 3. répond. 4. pourquoi. 5. cela.

21. Premier son dans: 1. haute. 2. océan.

Deuxième son dans: 1. lune. 2. verrai. 3. loin.

Troisième son dans: 1. breton. 2. crête. 3. loin.

Dernier son dans: 1. Amérique. 2. océan.

Sons nasaux dans: 1. contempler. 2. breton. 3. océan. 4. loin.

22. Deuxième son dans: 1. sujet. 2. scientifique. 3. leur. 4. toutes. 5. poliment. 6. fièrement.

Troisième son dans: 1. gloire. 2. première.

Dernier son dans: 1. chacun. 2. monsieur. 3. anglais.

23. Premier son dans: 1. état. 2. unis.

Deuxième son dans: 1. vingt. 2. passe. 3. moment. 4. rembarquer. 5. pensez. 6. notre. 7. votre.

Troisième son dans: 1. échantillons.

Avant-dernier son dans: 1. échantillons.

Dernier son dans: 1. climat.

Sons nasaux dans: 1. vingt. 2. moment. 3. rembarquer. 4. pensez. 5. échantillons.

24. Premier son dans: 1. auteur. 2. homme.

Deuxième son dans: 1. lentement. 2. jeune. 3. faites. 4. changement.

Troisième son dans: 1. prononcer. 2. prenez.

Avant-dernier son dans: 1. virgule.

Dernier son dans: 1. mot. 2. plus. 3. temps. 4. point. 5. non. 6. répond. 7. riant. 8. foi. 9. serai. 10. prêt. 11. demain.

Sons nasaux dans: 1. temps. 2. point. 3. répond. 4. riant. 5. demain.

25. Premier son dans: 1. Joseph. 2. empereur. 3. aura.

Deuxième son dans: 1. Vienne. 2. peine. 3. ducat. 4. femme. 5. tort.

Avant-dernier son dans: 1. carottes. 2. douzaine.

Dernier son dans: 1. Joseph. 2. Allemagne. 3. cabriolet. 4. chou. 5. palais. 6. crois. 7. lieu. 8. tort. 9. peux. 10. temps. 11. moi.

26. Premier son dans: 1. emploie. 2. utile.

Avant-dernier son dans: 1. toile. 2. travail.

Dernier son dans: 1. soie. 2. dieu. 3. vois. 4. peu. 5. emploie. 6. soit.

27. Premier son dans: 1. aimaient. 2. ennemi. 3. orgueil. 4. encore. 5. aujourd'hui. 6. heureuse.

Deuxième son dans: 1. guerre. 2. faisaient. 3. leurs. 4. lances. 5. comme. 6. peuples. 7. patient. 8. cause. 9. soldat. 10. car. 11. calme. 12. jusque.

Avant-dernier son dans: 1. bataille. 2. encore. 3. barbare. 4. éclatante. 5. défaite.

Dernier son dans: 1. rang. 2. criaient. 3. joie. 4. orgueil. 5. sang. 6. heureuse. 7. point. 8. patient. 9. faut. 10. défaite.

Sons nasaux dans: 1. encore. 2. lances. 3. patient. 4. éclatante. 5. rang. 6. point.

28. Premier son dans: 1. éléphant. 2. aiguille. 3. incident.

Deuxième son dans: 1. vengeance. 2. tailleur. 3. saisit. 4. semblait. 5. boire. 6. remplit. 7. lorsque.

Troisième son dans: 1. atelier. 2. allongea. 3. tailleur.

Avant-dernier son dans: 1. atelier. 2. travaillait. 3. trompe. 4. piqua. 5. revanche.

Dernier son dans: 1. aiguille. 2. chemin. 3. incident.

Sons nasaux dans: 1. éléphant. 2. incident. 3. vengeance. 4. semblait. 5. remplit. 6. allongea. 7. trompe. 8. revanche. 9. chemin. 10. incident.

29. Premier son dans: 1. homme. 2. ainsi. 3. ensuite. 4. autre. 5. emblème. 6. aussi. 7. uni.

Deuxième son dans: 1. montra. 2. personne. 3. longtemps. 4. vaincre.

Troisième son dans: 1. appeler. 2. flèche.

Dernier son dans: 1. fils. 2. longtemps.

30. Premier son dans: 1. Chérubini.

Deuxième son dans: 1. pied. 2. fort. 3. descendant. 4. maître. 5. vais. 6. même. 7. côté. 8. seulement. 9. votre. 10. cocher.

Troisième son dans: 1. voiture. 2. appelle. 3. prenez.

Quatrième son dans: 1. compositeur.

Avant-dernier son dans: 1. battante. 2. conservatoire. 3. retard.

Dernier son dans: 1. trop. 2. moi. 3. jamais.

31. Deuxième son dans: 1. poste. 2. bureau.

Avant-dernier son dans: 1. erreur.

Dernier son dans: 1. trois. 2. pas. 3. pourquoi. 4. répond.

32. Premier son dans: 1. oui.

Deuxième son dans: 1. Louis. 2. faisaient. 3. paye. 4. mais.

Avant-dernier son dans: 1. bouteille. 2. soif.

Dernier son dans: 1. bouteille. 2. moins. 3. roi. 4. ceux.

33. Premier son dans: 1. Éphèse. 2. oblige.

Deuxième son dans: 1. porter. 2. fardeau. 3. pesant. 4. lendemain. 5. sorte.

Troisième son dans: 1. premier. 2. soir.

Avant-dernier son dans: 1. Ésope. 2. esclave.

Dernier son dans: 1. marchand. 2. après. 3. pain.

34. Premier son dans: 1. Aurélien. 2. empereur. 3. espoir. 4. ayant.

Deuxième son dans: 1. colère. 2. seulement. 3. cette. 4. rebelle. 5. tenir. 6. donc. 7. serment.

Avant-dernier son dans: 1. empereur. 2. colère. 3. espoir.

35. Premier son dans: 1. œil. 2. essaya.

Deuxième son dans: 1. voler. 2. paysan. 3. foire. 4. ceux. 5. possession.

Troisième son dans: 1. trompe.

Dernier son dans: 1. trois. 2. œil. 3. borgne. 4. droit. 5. mots.

36. Premier son dans: 1. quinze. 2. histoire. 3. heure.

Deuxième son dans: 1. seul. 2. soir. 3. domestique. 4. moment. 5. tard.

Avant-dernier son dans: 1. soir.

Dernier son dans: 1. Dubois. 2. quinze. 3. poulet. 4. sans.

Sons nasaux dans: 1. quinze. 2. moment. 3. sans.

39. Premier son dans: 1. heureux.

Deuxième son dans: 1. pierre. 2. mais. 3. bâton.
4. lac. 5. temps. 6. sultan. 7. donna.

Troisième son dans: 1. fleuve. 2. provinces. 3.
royaume. 4. moitié. 5. arrosera.

Quatrième son dans: 1. souterraine.

Avant-dernier son dans: 1. émissaire.

Dernier son dans: 1. heureux.

41. Deuxième son dans: 1. pays. 2. peu. 3. creux.
4. casque. 5. patience. 6. leur.

Troisième son dans: 1. soif. 2. lieu.

42. Deuxième son dans: 1. lâche. 2. descends.

43. Deuxième son dans: 1. cadeau. 2. service. 3.
payent. 4. veulent. 5. maison.

Dernier son dans: 1. médecin. 2. médecine. 3. billet.

44. Premier son dans: 1. emplettes. 2. ordre.

Deuxième son dans: 1. curé. 2. voyage. 3. leur.
4. marchandises. 5. commissions. 6. lorsque. 7. payer.

Troisième son dans: 1. informer. 2. impossible.

Avant-dernier son dans: 1. plusieurs. 2. mémoires.
3. donnèrent. 4. nécessaire. 5. employa. 6. emplettes.

Dernier son dans: 1. italien. 2. célèbre. 3. mots.
4. voyage. 5. chez. 6. vrai. 7. poids.

Sons nasaux dans: 1. emplettes. 2. marchandises.
3. informer. 4. impossible. 5. italien.

45. Sons nasaux dans: 1. devient. 2. France. 3.
vint. 4. sans. 5. sentiment. 6. envie. 7. nombreux.
8. train. 9. enfin. 10. grand. 11. empire. 12. bien.
13. répondit. 14. simple.

46. Premier son dans: 1. horreur.

Deuxième son dans: 1. femme. 2. connaissait.

Avant-dernier son dans: 1. avare. 2. guérissiez. 3. soin. 4. horreur.

Dernier son dans: 1. soit. 2. très. 3. connaissait.

48. Premier son dans: 1. aide. 2. Guillaume. 3. officier. 4. œuvre.

Deuxième son dans: 1. Guillaume. 2. cent. 3. cinq. 4. quelque. 5. colonel. 6. second. 7. absolument.

Avant-dernier son dans: 1. ouvrage.

Dernier son dans: 1. parfait. 2. roi.

50. Deuxième son dans: 1. veuve. 2. faisait.

Avant-dernier son dans: 1. hélas.

51. Deuxième son dans: 1. passant. 2. veuillez. 3. paya.

Troisième son dans: 1. théâtre. 2. soir. 3. vraiment. 4. inquiet.

Dernier son dans: 1. soi.

52. Premier son dans: 1. heures. 2. auras.

Deuxième son dans: 1. gages. 2. deux. 3. chassa. 4. maître.

Troisième son dans: 1. brave. 2. maintenant. 3. quoi.

53. Premier son dans: 1. essaie. 2. opération.

Deuxième son dans: 1. agneau. 2. pointu. 3. gosier. 4. gueule. 5. patte. 6. passa.

Troisième son dans: 1. pointu. 2. hasard. 3. plaisantez.

Dernier son dans: 1. os. 2. essaie. 3. cigogne. 4. long. 5. ingrate.

54. Premier son dans: 1. homme.

Deuxième son dans: 1. mort. 2. paysan. 3. seigneur. 4. ciel. 5. saint. 6. faisait. 7. comme. 8. cher.

Troisième son dans: 1. seigneur. 2. dehors. 3. joyeuse. 4. régnait. 5. soi.

55. Premier son dans: 1. haute. 2. ainsi. 3. aime.

Deuxième son dans: 1. turbot. 2. domestique. 3. part. 4. maison. 5. poisson. 6. politesse. 7. maître. 8. demi.

Troisième son dans: 1. doyen. 2. brusquement. 3. profonde. 4. vraiment. 5. faites. 6. prenez.

Avant-dernier son dans: 1. doyen. 2. couronne. 3. voix. 4. monsieur. 5. amitiés.

Dernier son dans: 1. doyen. 2. pas.

56. Premier son dans: 1. examiner.

Deuxième son dans: 1. gagne. 2. bataille. 3. Bonaparte. 4. moment.

Troisième son dans: 1. endormi. 2. enlève. 3. voyant.

Avant-dernier son dans: 1. bataille. 2. Arcole. 3. place. 4. faction. 5. douceur.

Dernier son dans: 1. bataille. 2. trois. 3. camp. 4. fusil. 5. temps.

57. Premier son dans: 1. aurais.

Deuxième son dans: 1. rampant. 2. sommeil. 3. barbe. 4. raison.

Avant-dernier son dans: 1. citrouille. 2. écraser.

Dernier son dans: 1. villageois. 2. citrouille. 3. fois. 4. gland. 5. sommeil. 6. dieu.

58. Premier son dans: 1. officier. 2. obéir. 3. aussitôt. 4. enseigne. 5. hampe.

Deuxième son dans: 1. fière. 2. sombrait. 3. saisit. 4. guenille. 5. Daudet. 6. lundi.

Troisième son dans: 1. flottait. 2. héroïque.

Avant-dernier son dans: 1. mitraille. 2. grave. 3. Alphonse.

Dernier son dans: 1. au-dessus. 2. bataille. 3. Daudet.

59. Premier son dans: 1. aujourd'hui. 2. or.

Deuxième son dans: 1. jouer. 2. pièces. 3. monnaie.

Troisième son dans: 1. plaisir.

Avant-dernier son dans: 1. surplus.

Dernier son dans: 1. ferai. 2. plus. 3. monnaie. 4. surplus.

60. Premier son dans: 1. halte. 2. air.

Deuxième son dans: 1. passaient. 2. rocher. 3. dernier. 4. longue. 5. formidable. 6. gorge. 7. sac.

Troisième son dans: traînée.

Dernier son dans: dépens.

Quel son a "a" dans détonation? dans formidable?

61. Deuxième son dans: 1. Louis. 2. temple. 3. reine. 4. mois. 5. Robespierre.

Dernier son dans: 1. roi. 2. salut.

62. Premier son dans: 1. août.

Deuxième son dans: 1. port. 2. siège. 3. commandant. 4. sergent.

Troisième son dans: 1. royaliste. 2. preuve. 3. grade.

Cinquième son dans: 1. artillerie.

Dernier son dans: 1. Anglais. 2. Napoléon. 3. **froid.**

LES VERBES

En français il y a trois conjugaisons:
I. L'Infinitif se termine en -er, donner.
II. L'Infinitif se termine en -ir, finir.
III. L'Infinitif se termine en -re, rompre.

I	II	III
donner	finir	rompre
to give	to end	to break

Participe Présent

donnant	finissant	rompant
giving	ending	breaking

Participe Passé

donné	fini	rompu
given	ended	broken

Temps Simples

Indicatif

Présent

je donne	je finis	je romps
tu donnes	tu finis	tu romps
il donne	il finit	il rompt
nous donnons	nous finissons	nous rompons
vous donnez	vous finissez	vous rompez
ils donnent	ils finissent	ils rompent
I give, am giving, do give	*I finish, am finishing, do finish*	*I break, am breaking, do break*

IMPARFAIT

je donnais	je finissais	je rompais
tu donnais	tu finissais	tu rompais
il donnait	il finissait	il rompait
nous donnions	nous finissions	nous rompions
vous donniez	vous finissiez	vous rompiez
ils donnaient	ils finissaient	ils rompaient
I was giving, used to give	*I was finishing, used to finish*	*I was breaking, used to break*

PASSÉ DÉFINI

je donnai	je finis	je rompis
tu donnas	tu finis	tu rompis
il donna	il finit	il rompit
nous donnâmes	nous finîmes	nous rompîmes
vous donnâtes	vous finîtes	vous rompîtes
ils donnèrent	ils finirent	ils rompirent
I gave	*I finished*	*I broke*

FUTUR

je donnerai	je finirai	je romprai
tu donneras	tu finiras	tu rompras
il donnera	il finira	il rompra
nous donnerons	nous finirons	nous romprons
vous donnerez	vous finirez	vous romprez
ils donneront	ils finiront	ils rompront
I shall give	*I shall finish*	*I shall break*

CONDITIONNEL

je donnerais	je finirais	je romprais
tu donnerais	tu finirais	tu romprais
il donnerait	il finirait	il romprait

nous donnerions	nous finirions	nous romprions
vous donneriez	vous finiriez	vous rompriez
ils donneraient	ils finiraient	ils rompraient
I should give	*I should finish*	*I should break*

Subjonctif

PRÉSENT

que je donne	que je finisse	que je rompe
que tu donnes	que tu finisses	que tu rompes
qu'il donne	qu'il finisse	qu'il rompe
que nous donnions	que nous finissions	que nous rompions
que vous donniez	que vous finissiez	que vous rompiez
qu'ils donnent	qu'ils finissent	qu'ils rompent
That I may give	*That I may finish*	*That I may break*

IMPARFAIT

que je donnasse	que je finisse	que je rompisse
que tu donnasses	que tu finisses	que tu rompisses
qu'il donnât	qu'il finît	qu'il rompît
que nous donnassions	que nous finissions	que nous rompissions
que vous donnassiez	que vous finissiez	que vous rompissiez
qu'ils donnassent	qu'ils finissent	qu'ils rompissent
That I might give	*That I might finish*	*That I might break*

Impératif

PRÉSENT

donne	finis	romps
donnons	finissons	rompons
donnez	finissez	rompez
Give, let us give	*Finish, let us finish*	*Break, let us break*

Terminaisons

1. Présent			2. Imparfait	3. Passé Défini	
I	II	III		I	II III
-e	-is	-s	-ais	-ai	-is
-es	-is	-s	-ais	-as	-is
-e	-it	-t[1]	-ait	-a	-it
	-ons		-ions	-âmes	-îmes
	-ez		-iez	-âtes	-îtes
	-ent		-aient	-èrent	-irent

4. Futur	5. Conditionnel	6. Participe Présent
-ai	-ais	-ant
-as	-ais	
-a	-ait	
-ons	-ions	
-ez	-iez	
-ont	-aient	

7. Participe Passé			8. Présent du Subjonctif	9. Imparfait du Subjonctif
I	II	III		
-é	-i	-u	-e	-sse
			-es	-sses
			-e	-̂t
			-ions	-ssions
			-iez	-ssiez
			-ent	-ssent

[1] Les verbes en " dre " ne prennent pas le *t*, ex. *rendre, il rend.*

Temps Primitifs

Les temps primitifs d'un verbe sont. 1. L'Infinitif. 2. Le Participe Présent. 3. Le Participe Passé. 4. Le Présent de l'Indicatif. 5. Le Passé Défini.

(1) donner; (2) donnant; (3) donné; (4) je donne; (5) je donnai.

(1) finir; (2) finissant; (3) fini; (4) je finis; (5) je finis.

(1) rompre; (2) rompant; (3) rompu; (4) je romps; (5) je rompis.

1. De *l'Infinitif* on forme le Futur et le Conditionnel, en y ajoutant les terminaisons. A la troisième conjugaison, on supprime -e avant d'ajouter les terminaisons.

2. Du *Participe présent,* on forme.

(1) le pluriel de l'Indicatif présent.

(2) l'Imparfait de l'Indicatif.

(3) le Subjonctif présent.

On supprime -**ant** et ajoute les terminaisons.

3. Du *Participe passé*, on forme tous les temps composés (voir p. 97).

4. De *l'Indicatif présent*, on forme l'Impératif, en supprimant les pronoms *tu*, *nous*, et *vous*. A la deuxième personne du singulier, les verbes de la première conjugaison on supprime -**s** . . . ~~tu~~ donnes ~~nous~~ donnons ~~vous~~ donnez

5. Du *Passé défini* on forme l'Imparfait du Subjonctif, en remplaçant *la dernière lettre* de la première personne, par les terminaisons.

VERBES IRRÉGULIERS

INFINITIF	INDICATIF PRÉSENT	
acheter.—	J'achète	nous achetons
	tu achètes	vous achetez
	il achète	ils achètent
aller.—	Je vais	nous allons
	tu vas	vous allez
	il va	ils vont
allonger.—	J'allonge	nous allongeons
	tu allonges	vous allongez
	il allonge	ils allongent
annoncer.—	J'annonce	nous annonçons
	tu annonces	vous annoncez
	il annonce	ils annoncent
apercevoir.—	J'aperçois	nous apercevons
	tu aperçois	vous apercevez
	il aperçoit	ils aperçoivent
s'appeler.—	Je m'appelle	nous nous appelons
	tu t'appelles	vous vous appelez
	il s'appelle	ils s'appellent
s'asseoir.—	Je m'assieds	nous nous asseyons
	tu t'assieds	vous vous asseyez
	il s'assied	ils s'asseyent
battre.—	Je bats	nous battons
	tu bats	vous battez
	il bat	ils battent

INFINITIF	INDICATIF PRÉSENT	
boire.—	Je bois	nous buvons
	tu bois	vous buvez
	il boit	ils boivent
connaître.—	Je connais	nous connaissons
	tu connais	vous connaissez
	il connaît	ils connaissent
courir.—	Je cours	nous courons
	tu cours	vous courez
	il court	ils courent
craindre.—	Je crains	nous craignons
	tu crains	vous craignez
	il craint	ils craignent
croire.—	Je crois	nous croyons
	tu crois	vous croyez
	il croit	ils croient
déployer.—	Je déploie	nous déployons
	tu déploies	vous déployez
	il déploie	ils déploient
devoir.—	Je dois	nous devons
	tu dois	vous devez
	il doit	ils doivent
dire.—	Je dis	nous disons
	tu dis	vous dites
	il dit	ils disent
dormir.—	Je dors	nous dormons
	tu dors	vous dormez
	il dort	ils dorment

Infinitif	Indicatif Présent	
écrire.—	J'écris	nous écrivons
	tu écris	vous écrivez
	il écrit	ils écrivent
enlever.—	J'enlève	nous enlevons
	tu enlèves	vous enlevez
	il enlève	ils enlèvent
espérer.—	J'espère	nous espérons
	tu espères	vous espérez
	il espère	ils espèrent
faire.—	Je fais	nous faisons
	tu fais	vous faites
	il fait	ils font.
fuir.—	Je fuis	nous fuyons
	tu fuis	vous fuyez
	il fuit	ils fuient
jeter.—	Je jette	nous jetons
	tu jettes	vous jetez
	il jette	ils jettent
mettre.—	Je mets	nous mettons
	tu mets	vous mettez
	il met	ils mettent
ouvrir.—	J'ouvre	nous ouvrons
	tu ouvres	vous ouvrez
	il ouvre	ils ouvrent
partir.—	Je pars	nous partons
	tu pars	vous partez
	il part	ils partent

INFINITIF	INDICATIF PRÉSENT	
plaindre.—	Je plains	nous plaignons
	tu plains	vous plaignez
	il plaint	ils plaignent
plaire.—	Je plais	nous plaisons
	tu plais	vous plaisez
	il plaît	ils plaisent
pouvoir.—	Je peux, *or* Je puis	nous pouvons
	tu peux	vous pouvez
	il peut	ils peuvent
prendre.—	Je prends	nous prenons
	tu prends	vous prenez
	il prend	ils prennent
recevoir.—	Je reçois	nous recevons
	tu reçois	vous recevez
	il reçoit	ils reçoivent
rejoindre.—	Je rejoins	nous rejoignons
	tu rejoins	vous rejoignez
	il rejoint	ils rejoignent
répéter.—	Je répète	nous répétons
	tu répètes	vous répétez
	il répète	ils répètent
rire.—	Je ris	nous rions
	tu ris	vous riez
	il rit	ils rient
savoir.—	Je sais	nous savons
	tu sais	vous savez
	il sait	ils savent

INFINITIF	INDICATIF PRÉSENT	
servir.—	Je sers	nous servons
	tu sers	vous servez
	il sert	ils servent
sortir.—	Je sors	nous sortons
	tu sors	vous sortez
	il sort	ils sortent
tenir.—	Je tiens	nous tenons
	tu tiens	vous tenez
	il tient	ils tiennent
vaincre.—	Je vaincs	nous vainquons
	tu vaincs	vous vainquez
	il vainc	ils vainquent
valoir.—	Je vaux	nous valons
	tu vaux	vous valez
	il vaut	ils valent
venir.—	Je viens	nous venons
	tu viens	vous venez
	il vient	ils viennent
voir.—	Je vois	nous voyons
	tu vois	vous voyez
	il voit	ils voient
vouloir.—	Je veux	nous voulons
	tu veux	vous voulez
	il veut	ils veulent

INFINITIF	PASSÉ DÉFINI
[1]allonger	j'allongeai
[2]annoncer	j'annonçai
apercevoir	j'aperçus
[1]arranger	j'arrangeai
s'asseoir	je m'assis
avoir	j'eus
boire	je bus
[2]commencer	je commençai
comprendre	je compris
conduire	je conduisis
[3]connaître	je connus
[1]corriger	je corrigeai
courir	je courus
craindre	je craignis
croire	je crus
devoir	je dus
dire	je dis
[1]diriger	je dirigeai
[2]élancer	j'élançai
[1]encourager	j'encourageai

NOTE 1. *All* verbs in -ger insert *e* after *g* before *a* or *o*. Like allonger, conjugate arranger, corriger, diriger, encourager, interroger, manger, voyager.

NOTE 2. *All* verbs in -cer have a cedilla under the *c* before *a* or *o*. Like annoncer, conjugate commencer, élancer, lancer.

NOTE 3. In stem, connaître and paraître have *î* everywhere before *t* = connaît, paraît, etc.

INFINITIF	PASSÉ DÉFINI
être	je fus
faire	je fis
falloir	il fallut
instruire	j'instruisis
[1]interroger	j'interrogeai
[2]lancer	je lançai
lire	je lus
[1]manger	je mangeai
mettre	je mis
mourir	je mourus
plaindre	je plaignis
plaire	je plus
pleuvoir	il plut
pouvoir	je pus
prendre	je pris
recevoir	je reçus
rejoindre	je rejoignis
savoir	je sus
tenir	je tins
vaincre	je vainquis
valoir	je valus
venir	je vins
vouloir	je voulus
[1]voyager	je voyageai

1, 2.—See notes on p. 103.

INFINITIF	FUTUR
acheter	j'achèterai
aller	j'irai
⁵apercevoir	j'apercevrai
⁴appeler	j'appellerai
asseoir	j'assiérai
avoir	j'aurai
courir	je courrai
⁶déployer	je déploierai
devenir	je deviendrai
⁵devoir	je devrai
⁶employer	j'emploierai
⁷enlever	j'enlèverai
entretenir	j'entretiendrai
⁵envoyer	j'enverrai
être	je serai
faire	je ferai
falloir	il faudra

NOTE 4. Many verbs in -eler double the *l* before the endings *e, es, ent,* and in Future and Conditional.

NOTE 5. *All* verbs in -oir drop -oi of infinitive to form future stem.

NOTE 6. Verbs ending in -oyer change *y* to *i* before endings *e, es, ent,* and in Future and Conditional.

NOTE 7. Verbs ending in -er preceded by a consonant that is not *l* or *t* and having an *e* mute in the stem (enl*e*ver, s*e*mer, m*e*ner) take a grave accent on the *e* mute of the stem before the endings *e, es, ent,* and in the Future and Conditional.

INFINITIF	FUTUR
[8]jeter	je jetterai
mourir	je mourrai
obtenir	j'obtiendrai
pouvoir	je pourrai
[7]se promener	je me promènerai
[5]recevoir	je recevrai
savoir	je saurai
tenir	je tiendrai
valoir	je vaudrai
venir	je viendrai
voir	je verrai
vouloir	je voudrai

5, 7.—See notes on p. 105.

NOTE 8. Many verbs ending in -eter double *t* before the endings *e*, *es*, *ent*, and in the Future and Conditional.

VERBES AUXILIAIRES

AVOIR

PARTICIPE PRÉSENT	PARTICIPE PASSÉ
ayant	eu

INDICATIF

PRÉSENT		IMPARFAIT	
j'ai	nous avons	j'avais	nous avions
tu as	vous avez	tu avais	vous aviez
il a	ils ont	il avait	ils avaient
(*I have*)		(*I used to have*)	

PASSÉ DÉFINI		FUTUR	
j'eus	nous eûmes	j'aurai	nous aurons
tu eus	vous eûtes	tu auras	vous aurez
il eut	ils eurent	il aura	ils auront
(*I had*)		(*I shall have*)	

CONDITIONNEL

j'aurais	nous aurions
tu aurais	vous auriez
il aurait	ils auraient
(*I would have*)	

SUBJONCTIF

PRÉSENT		IMPARFAIT	
que j'aie	que nous ayons	que j'eusse	que nous eussions
que tu aies	que vous ayez	que tu eusses	que vous eussiez
qu'il ait	qu'ils aient	qu'il eût	qu'ils eussent
(*That I may have*)		(*That I might have*)	

IMPÉRATIF

aie, *have*   ayons, *let us have*
ayez, *have*

ÊTRE

PARTICIPE PRÉSENT   [**PARTICIPE PASSÉ**
étant   été

INDICATIF

PRÉSENT

je suis	nous sommes
tu es	vous êtes
il est	ils sont
(I am)	

IMPARFAIT	PASSÉ DÉFINI
j'étais nous étions	je fus nous fûmes
tu étais vous étiez	tu fus vous fûtes
il était ils étaient	il fut ils furent
(I was, used to be)	*(I was)*

FUTUR	CONDITIONNEL
je serai nous serons	je serais nous serions
tu seras vous serez	tu serais vous seriez
il sera ils seront	il serait ils seraient
(I shall be)	*(I would be)*

SUBJONCTIF

PRÉSENT

que je sois	que nous soyons
que tu sois	que vous soyez
qu'il soit	qu'ils soient
(That I may be)	

IMPARFAIT

que je fusse	que nous fussions
que tu fusses	que vous fussiez
qu'il fût	qu'ils fussent
(That I might be)	

IMPÉRATIF

sois, *be*   soyons, *let us be*
soyez, *be*

TEMPS COMPOSÉS

TEMPS SIMPLES	TEMPS COMPOSÉS
PRÉSENT	PASSÉ INDÉFINI
Je donne	J'ai donné
IMPARFAIT	PLUS QUE PARFAIT
Je donnais	J'avais donné
PASSÉ DÉFINI	PASSÉ ANTÉRIEUR
Je donnai	J'eus donné
FUTUR	FUTUR ANTÉRIEUR
Je donnerai	J'aurai donné
CONDITIONNEL	CONDITIONNEL PASSÉ
Je donnerais	J'aurais donné
PRÉSENT DU SUBJONCTIF	PASSÉ DU SUBJONCTIF
Que je donne	Que j'aie donné
IMPARFAIT DU SUBJONCTIF	PLUS QUE PARFAIT DU SUBJONCTIF
Que je donnasse	Que j'eusse donné

VERBES IRRÉGULIERS

F. = Futur. S. = Subjonctif.

INFINITIF	PART. PRÉS.	PART. PASSÉ	PRÉS. DE L'INDICATIF	PASSÉ DÉFINI
acheter	achetant	acheté	j'achète	j'achetai
[1]F. achèter-	[2]S. achèt-			
aller	allant	allé	je vais	j'allai
F. ir-	S. aille			
[1]allonger	allongeant	allongé	j'allonge	j'allongeai
[2]annoncer	annonçant	annoncé	j'annonce	j'annonçai
[4]appeler	appelant	appelé	j'appelle	j'appelai
apercevoir	apercevant	aperçu	j'aperçois	j'aperçus
[5]F. apercevr-	S. aperçoiv-			
[1]arranger	arrangeant	arrangé	j'arrange	j'arrangeai
s'asseoir	s'asseyant	s'assis	je m'assieds	je m'assis
F. assiér-				
avoir	ayant	eu	j'ai	j'eus
F. aur-	S. aie			
	Impf. avais			

1, 2, 4, 5.—See notes on pp. 103 and 105.

battre	battant	battu	je bats	je battis
boire	buvant	bu	je bois	je bus
	S. boive			
bouillir	bouillant	bouilli	je bous	je bouillis
²commencer	commençant	commencé	je commence	je commençai
comprendre	(like prendre)			
conduire	conduisant	conduit	je conduis	je conduisis
²connaître	connaissant	connu	je connais	je connus
¹corriger	corrigeant	corrigé	je corrige	je corrigeai
courir	courant	couru	je cours	je courus
F. courr-				
couvrir	couvrant	couvert	je couvre	je couvris
			(Regular or 1st)	
craindre	craignant	craint	je crains	je craignis
croire	croyant	cru	je crois	je crus
	S. croie			
⁵déployer	déployant	déployé	je déploie	je déployai
F. déploier-	S. déploie			

1, 2, 3, 6.—See notes on pp. 103 and 105.

INFINITIF	PART. PRÉS.	PART. PASSÉ	PRÉS. DE L'INDICATIF	PASSÉ DÉFINI
devenir	(like venir)			
devoir F. devr–	devant S. doive	dû	je dois	je dus
dire	disant	dit	je dis	je dis
¹diriger	dirigeant	dirigé	je dirige	je dirigeai
dormir	dormant	dormi	je dors	je dormis
écrire	écrivant	écrit	j'écris	j'écrivis
²élancer	élançant	élancé	j'élance	j'élançai
¹encourager	encourageant	encouragé	j'encourage	j'encourageai
entretenir	(like tenir)			
envoyer F. enverr–	envoyant S. envoie	envoyé	j'envoie	j'envoyai
⁶employer F. emploier–	employant S. emploie	employé	j'emploie	j'employai
⁷enlever F. enlèver–	enlevant	enlevé	j'enlève	j'enlevai

1, 2, 6, 7.—See notes on pp. 103 and 105.

	espérant	espéré	j'espère	j'espérai
'espérer	espérant S. espère	espéré	j'espère	j'espérai
être F. ser-	étant S. sois (see p. 96)	été	je suis	je fus
faire F. fer-	faisant S. fasse	fait	je fais	je fis
falloir F. faudr-	(not used) S. faille	fallu	il faut	il fallut
fuir	fuyant	fui	je fuis	je fuis
s'instruire	s'instruisant	s'instruit	je m'instruis	je m'instruisis
¹interroger	interrogeant	interrogé	j'interroge	j'interrogeai
⁸jeter F. jetter-	jetant S. jette	jeté	je jette	je jetai
⁷lancer	lançant	lancé	je lance	je lançai
lire	lisant	lu	je lis	je lus

1, 2, 8.—See notes on pp. 103 and 106.

NOTE 9. Verbs ending in -er that have *é* in the stem change the acute accent to a grave accent before the endings *e*, *es*, *ent*. The accent *does not change* in the Future or Conditional.

INFINITIF	PART. PRÉS.	PART. PASSÉ	PRÉS. DE L'INDICATIF	PASSÉ DÉFINI
[1]manger	mangeant	mangé	je mange	je mangeai
mettre	mettant	mis	je mets	je mis
mourir F. mour-	mourant S. meure	mort	je meurs	je mourus
offrir	offrant	offert	j'offre (Regular of 1st)	j'offris
obtenir	(like tenir)			
ouvrir	(like couvrir)			
[3]paraître	(like connaître)			
partir	partant	parti	je pars	je partis
permettre	(like mettre)			
plaindre	plaignant	plaint	je plains	je plaignis
plaire	plaisant	plu	je plais	je plus
[5]pleuvoir F. pleuv-	pleuvant	plu	il pleut	il plut
pouvoir F. pourr-	pouvant S. puisse	pu	je peux	je pus

1, 3, 5.—See notes on pp. 103 and 105.

prendre	prenant	pris	je prends	je pris
'se promener	se promenant	se promené	je me promène	je me promenai
F. promèner-				
promettre	(like mettre)			
'recevoir	recevant / S. reçoive	reçu	je reçois	je reçus
F. recevr-				
reconnaître	(like connaître)			
'régner	régnant / S. règne	régné	je règne	je régnai
rejoindre	rejoignant	rejoint	je rejoins	je rejoignis
'répéter	répétant	répété	je répète	je répétai
revenir	(like venir)			
rire	riant	ri	je ris	je ris
savoir	sachant / Impf. savais	su	je sais	je sus
F. saur-				
'sécher	séchant	séché	je sèche	je séchai
servir	servant	servi	je sers	je servis

5, 7, 9.—See notes on pp. 105 and 113.

INFINITIF	PART. PRÉS.	PART. PASSÉ	PRÉS. DE L'INDICATIF	PASSÉ DÉFINI
sortir	sortant	sorti	je sors	je sortis
se souvenir de	(like venir)			
tenir	tenant	tenu	je tiens	je tins
F. tiendr–	S. tienne			
vaincre	vainquant	vaincu	je vaincs	je vainquis
	S. vainque			
valoir	valant	valu	je vaux	je valus
F. vaudr–	S. vaille			
venir	venant	venu	je viens	je vins
F. viendr–	S. vienne			
voir	voyant	vu	je vois	je vis
F. verr–	S. voie			
vouloir	voulant	voulu	je veux	je voulus
F. voudr–	S. veuille			
¹voyager	voyageant	voyagé	je voyage	je voyageai

1.—See note on p. 103.

VOCABULARY

A

aborder, to approach.

abreuver, to quench one's thirst.

abreuvoir, *m.*, drinking-trough.

à cause de, on account of.

accepter, to accept.

accuser, to accuse; il accusa, he accused, *past def. of* accuser.

acheter, to buy.

acteur, *m.*, actor.

action, *f.*, action.

admirateur, *m.*, admirer.

adresse, *f.*, address (*as on letter*); skill.

s'adresser (à), to speak to, to apply to.

affaire, *f.*, business.

affamé, famished.

afin, in order.

agiter, to shake, to wave.

agneau, *m.*, lamb.

aide, *f.*, aid, help.

aide de camp, *m.*, aide-de-camp.

aider, to help.

aigle, *m.*, eagle.

aiguille, *f.*, needle.

aimer, to love, to like.

ainsi, thus; — de suite, and so on.

air, *m.*, appearance.

aise, *f.*, ease; à mon aise, as I please.

aise, glad, pleased.

ajouter, to add.

s'alléger, to grow lighter.

Allemagne, *f.*, Germany.

aller, to go; s'en —, to go away; Allez! Come!

allonger, to lengthen, to extend.

alors, then.

Américain, *m.*, an American.

Amérique, *f.*, America.

à merveille, wonderfully, perfectly.

ami, *m.*, friend.

amitié, *f.*, ses —s, his kind regards.

s'amuser, to enjoy oneself.

an, *m.*, year.

âne, *m.*, donkey.

Anglais, -e, Englishman.

Angleterre, *f.*, England.

à partir de, from.

apercevoir, to see, notice.

il aperçoit, he sees, *pres. of* apercevoir.

il aperçut, he saw, *past def. of* apercevoir.

appât, *m.*, bait.

s'appeler, to be called, named.

apporter, bring.

approcher, approach, bring near; s'—, to go near.

après, after.

à présent, now.

araignée, *f.*, spider.

arbre, *m.*, tree.

argent, *m.*, silver, money.

aride, dry, barren.

armée, *f.*, army.
arracher, to snatch.
s'arrêter, to stop.
arriver, to happen; **Qu'est-ce qui arrive?** What happens?
arroser, to water.
s'asseoir, to sit down.
assis, seated.
attaquer, to attack.
attendre, to wait for.
attraper, to catch.
au bout de, at the end of.
aucun, any.
auprès de, near.
tu auras, you shall have, *fut. of* avoir.
aussi, also, as, accordingly.
aussitôt, immediately.
auteur, *m.*, author.
autour, around.
autre, other; **vous —s**, you (*emphatic*).
avaler, to swallow.
d'avance, beforehand.
s'avancer, to advance.
avare, *m.*, miser.
avec, with.
avenir, *m.*, future.
avis, *m.*, opinion.
avoir, to have.
avouer, to confess.

B

babillard, *m.*, chatterer.
baigner, bathe.
baisser, lower.
balance, *f.*, scales.
balbutier, stammer.
balle, *f.*, ball, bullet.
banque, *f.*, bank.
barbare, barbarous, uncivilized.

barbe, *f.*, beard.
bas, -se, low.
bataille, *f.*, battle.
bâton, *m.*, stick.
bavard, talkative.
beau, belle, fine, handsome.
beaucoup, much, many.
bec, *m.*, beak.
belle, de plus —, harder than ever.
berceau, *m.*, cradle.
berger, *m.*, shepherd.
besoin, *m.*, need.
bêtise, *f.*, stupid action, folly, blunder.
beurre, *m.*, butter.
bien, very; **Eh —!** Well!
bientôt, soon.
billet, *m.*, ticket.
blé, *m.*, corn.
blesser, to wound, offend.
boire, to drink; **— dans,** to drink out of; **— un coup,** to take a drink.
boîte, *f.*, box; **— aux lettres,** post-box, letter-box.
Bonaparte, family name of Napoleon.
bondir, to bound.
bonjour, good morning.
bonté, *f.*, kindness.
bord, *m.*, edge, bank, border.
border, to border on.
borgne, blind in one eye.
boue, *f.*, mud.
bouillir, to boil.
boulanger, *m.*, baker.
boulet, *m.*, bullet.
bourbier, *m.*, mire.
bout, *m.*, end.
il bout, it boils, *pres. ind. of* bouillir.
bouteille, *f.*, bottle.

branche, *f.*, branch.
brave, courageous.
bravoure, *f.*, courage.
Breton, -ne, a native of Brittany.
brillant, bright.
briser, to break.
broder, to embroider.
bruit, *m.*, noise.
brusquement, rudely, abruptly.
bu, drunk, *past part. of* boire.
buffet, *m.*, sideboard.
bureau, *m.*, desk, office, shop.
il but, he drank, *past def. of* boire.
butin, *m.*, booty.
il buvait, he was drinking, *imperf. of* boire.
buvard, *m.*, blotting-paper.

C

cabinet, *m.*, office.
cabriolet, *m.*, cab.
cacher, to hide.
cadeau, *m.*, present.
cage, *f.*, cage.
caillou, -x, *m.*, pebble.
camarade, *m.*, companion.
camp, *m.*, camp.
campagne, *f.*, country.
canif, *m.*, penknife.
capitaine, *m.*, captain.
caporal, *m.*, corporal.
car, for, because.
carafe, *f.*, decanter, crock, bottle.
cardinal, *m.*, cardinal.
carotte, *f.*, carrot.
casque, *m.*, helmet.
causer, to talk, chat.
cave, *f.*, cellar.
ce (cet), cette, ces, this, that.

célèbre, celebrated.
celui, celle, this one, that one; — -ci, the latter; — -là, the former.
cent, a hundred.
cependant, nevertheless, however.
certainement, assuredly.
chacun, each one, every one.
chambre, *f.*, room.
chameau, *m.*, camel.
changement, *m.*, change.
chanson, *f.*, song.
chant, *m.*, singing.
chanter, to sing.
chaque, each, every.
charge, *f.*, load, burden.
chargé, laden.
charrette, *f.*, cart.
chasse, *f.*, chase.
chasser, to hunt.
chat, -te, cat.
chaud, *m.*, heat.
chaud, warm.
se chausser, to put on one's shoes.
chef, *m.*, leader.
chemin, *m.*, road, way.
chêne, *m.*, oak.
chenille, *f.*, caterpillar.
cher, chère, dear.
chercher, to look for, seek.
cheval, -aux, *m.*, horse.
chez, at the house of, at the store of.
chien, *m.*, dog.
chiffre, *m.*, figure, cipher.
choisir, to choose.
chose, *f.*, thing.
Chose, Monsieur —, Mr. So-and-so, Mr. What's-his-name.
chou, -x, *m.*, cabbage.
ciel, cieux, *m.*, sky.

ci-gît, here lies.

cigogne, *f.*, swan.

cinquante, fifty.

cirer, to polish.

citrouille, *f.*, pumpkin.

clair, clear.

classe, *f.*, class.

clef, *f.*, key.

client, *m.*, customer.

climat, *m.*, climate.

cocher, *m.*, coachman.

cœur, *m.*, heart; de bon —, heartily.

coin, *m.*, corner.

colère, *f.*, anger.

colle, *f.*, paste.

collège, *m.*, high school, college.

coller, to stick, paste.

combattre, to fight.

combien, how much, how many.

commandant, *m.*, commanding officer.

comme, like.

commencer (à), to begin.

comment, how (*often begins a question to which the answer is an adjective*).

commission, *f.*, errand, message.

comporter, to permit, admit; se —, to behave.

composer, compose.

compositeur, *m.*, one who composes music: composer.

comprendre, to understand.

il comprit, he understood, *past def. of* comprendre.

compromettre, imperil.

concevoir, to conceive, understand.

concorde, *f.*, union, harmony.

condamner, to condemn.

conduire, to lead, to drive (*a cab, etc.*).

il conduisait, he was driving, *imperf. of* conduire.

confiance, *f.*, confidence, trust.

confus, confused.

conjurer, to implore.

je connaissais, I used to know, *imperf. of* connaître.

connaissance, *f.*, acquaintance.

connaître, to know, be acquainted with.

connu, known, *past part. of* connaître.

conservatoire, *m.*, conservatory.

consister, to consist of.

consoler, to comfort.

conspirer, to conspire.

construire, to build, construct.

conte, *m.*, story, tale.

contempler, to contemplate.

contenir, to contain.

content, happy, satisfied.

continuer, to continue.

contraint, compelled, restrained.

contre, against.

contrebandier, *m.*, smuggler.

contrôleur, *m.*, ticket-collector.

Convention, *f.*, provisional government under the Revolution.

corbeau, *m.*, crow.

cornac, *m.*, elephant-driver.

corps, *m.*, body, corps.

correspondance, *f.*, correspondence, letters.

corriger, to correct.

côté, *m.*, side; à — de, beside; de —, aside; du même —, in the same direction.

cou, *m.*, neck.

couchant, *m.*, west, sunset.

se coucher, to go to bed.

couler, to flow.

couloir, *m.*, corridor, passage.

coup, *m.*, blow, stroke; boire un —, to take a drink.

coupe, *f.*, cup.

couper, to cut.

courage, *m.*, courage, spirit, pluck.

courir, to run.

couronne, *f.*, crown.

course, *f.*, path.

court, short.

couvert, covered.

couvrir, to cover.

il craignait, he feared, *imperf. of* craindre.

craindre, to fear.

il craint, he fears.

crainte, *f.*, fear.

Créateur, *m.*, Creator.

crédule, credulous.

crête, *f.*, top.

creux, *m.*, hollow.

creux, -se, hollow.

crier, to shout, to proclaim.

critique, *f.*, criticism.

croire, to believe; vous croyez, you believe, *pres. of* croire.

il crut, he believed, *past def. of* croire.

cultivé, cultivated, tilled.

cure, *f.*, living, charge.

curiosité, *f.*, curiosity.

D

d'abord, at first, at once.

dame, *f.*, lady.

dangereux, -se, dangerous.

dans, in.

d'après, from, according to.

se débattre, to struggle.

débiter, to retail, recite; to sell.

debout, standing.

débutant, *m.*, beginner.

décembre, *m.*, December.

déchiré, torn.

décoré, decorated, adorned.

décourager, to discourage.

découverte, *f.*, discovery.

découvrir, to discover.

défaite, *f.*, defeat.

défaut, *m.*, defect, fault, want.

défence, *f.*, defence; prohibition.

dégager, to release, to clear.

dehors, outside.

déjà, already.

déjeuner, *m.*, breakfast, luncheon.

demain, to-morrow.

demander, to ask.

demeure, *f.*, residence, dwelling.

demeurer, to live, dwell.

demi-couronne, *f.*, half a crown.

demi-heure, *f.*, half an hour.

dent, *f.*, tooth.

dépens, *m.*, expense.

déployer, display, unfold, unfurl.

de plus belle, harder than ever.

déposer, to deposit.

depuis, since; — deux ans, for two years.

dernier, -ère, last.

des, of the, some.

dès, as soon as.

désarmé, disarmed.

descendre, to go down.

de sorte que, so as to.

dessus, upon.

destinée, f., destiny, fate.

de temps en temps, from time to time.

détonation, f., explosion.

détour, m., winding.

détourner, to turn aside.

détruire, to destroy.

deux, two; —ième, second.

devant, before.

devenir, to become.

je deviendrai, I shall become, fut. of devenir.

il devint, he became, past def. of devenir.

devoir, to owe.

devoir, m., duty, task.

Dieu, m., God.

dieux, gods.

difficile, difficult, hard.

dîner, m., dinner.

Diogène, Diogenes, Greek philosopher.

dire, to say, tell.

ils dirent, they said, told, past def. of dire.

diriger, to guide, direct; se —, to go.

il disait, he was saying, said, used to say, imperf. of dire.

discipline, f., discipline.

dispute, f., quarrel, discussion.

distribuer, to give out, share, divide.

domestique, m. et f., servant.

dont, of whom, whose.

dormir, to sleep.

dorure, f., gilding.

d'où, whence, from where.

doucement, gently, sweetly.

douceur, f., sweetness, gentleness.

doute, m., suspicion.

se douter (de), to suspect.

doux, douce, sweet, gentle, soft.

douzaine, f., dozen.

doyen, m., dean.

drapeau, m., flag.

dresser, to raise, erect.

droit, right; voisin de droite, right-hand neighbor or neighbor on right.

dû, past part. of devoir, to owe; aurait —, ought to have.

ducat, m., ducat.

Dumas, French author.

dur, hard.

durée, f., duration.

du reste, moreover.

E

eau, f., water.

échantillon, m., sample.

échapper or s'—, to escape.

échauffer, to warm.

éclatant, brilliant.

école, f., school.

écouter, to listen to.

écraser, to crush.

s'écrier, to cry out.

écrire, to write.

écriture, f., writing.

écrivain, m., writer.

écu, m., crown.

écume, f., foam.

édition, f., edition, publication.

effacé, worn out.

église, f., church.

égoiste, m., a selfish person.

éléphant, m., elephant.

élève, m. et f., pupil.

élever, to place higher, to bring up; s'—, rise.

s'embarquer, to embark.

embarrassé, ill at ease, perplexed.

emblème, *m.*, symbol.

émissaire, *m.*, envoy.

empêcher, to hinder.

empereur, *m.*, emperor.

empire, *m.*, empire.

emplette, *f.*, purchase.

employer, to use.

emporter, to carry away, to take with one.

empressement, *m.*, eagerness, special attention.

s'empresser, to hasten.

en, of it, of them, some, any.

encore, again.

encourager, to encourage.

encre, *f.*, ink.

endormi, asleep.

endroit, *m.*, place.

enfant, *m. et f.*, child.

enfermer, to shut up.

enfin, at last.

engloutir, to engulf, swallow up.

ennemi, *m.*, enemy.

ensuite, then, afterwards.

entamer, to begin.

entendre, to hear, understand.

entr'acte, *m.*, intermission.

entrain, *m.*, spirit, gaiety.

entre, between, among.

il entreprit, he undertook, *past def. of* entreprendre.

entrer, to enter.

entretenir, to keep, keep up, converse.

enveloppe, *f.*, envelope.

envelopper, to wrap up.

envie, *f.*, desire, wish.

environnant, surrounding.

il envoie, he sends, *pres. ind. of* envoyer.

s'envoler, to fly away.

envoyer, to send.

épi, *m.*, ear (*of grain*).

épine, *f.*, thorn.

épitaphe, *f.*, epitaph.

époux, -se, husband.

éprouver, to try, experience.

esclave, *m.*, slave.

Ésope, Æsop, Greek philosopher.

esprit, *m.*, spirit, wit.

essayer, to try.

essuyer, to wipe.

étage, *m.*, floor.

ils étaient, they were, used to be, *imperf. of* être.

état, *m.*, state.

États-Unis, United States.

été, been, *past part. of* être.

étonné, astonished.

étourneau, *m.*, starling.

être, to be.

ils eurent, they had, *past def. of* avoir.

il eut, he had, *past def. of* avoir.

éveiller, to awaken, arouse.

évident, clear.

exact, correct, right.

exalter, to praise.

examiner, to examine, look at carefully.

exclamation, *f.*, exclamation.

excuse, *f.*, excuse.

exemple, *m.*, model; **par —,** for instance.

expliquer, to explain.

extrêmement, extremely.

F

facilité, *f.*, ease.

façon, *f.*, way, fashion.

faction, *f.,* guard.

faim, *f.,* hunger.

faire, to do, make; — **venir,** to send for; — **le professeur,** act as teacher.

il faisait, he made or did, used to make or do, *imperf. of* **faire.**

faisceau, *m.,* bundle.

falaise, *f.,* cliff.

il fallait, it was necessary, *imperf. of* **falloir.**

famille, *f.,* family.

fardeau, *m.,* burden.

farine, *f.,* flour.

fatigué, tired.

se fatiguer, to get tired.

il faudra, it will be necessary, *fut. of* **falloir.**

il faudrait, it would be necessary, *cond. of* **falloir.**

il faut, it is necessary, *pres. of* **falloir.**

fauteuil, *m.,* armchair.

fenêtre, *f.,* window.

fer, *m.,* iron.

je ferai, I shall make or do, *fut. of* **faire.**

ferme, firm, fixed.

fermer, to shut.

fête, *f.,* birthday, celebration.

feu, *m.,* fire.

feuille, *f.,* leaf.

fidèle, faithful.

fier, fière, proud.

fièrement, proudly.

fil, *m.,* thread.

file, *f.,* file, line.

filer, to spin.

filet, *m.,* net.

fille, *f.,* daughter, girl.

fils, *m.,* son.

filtrer, to filter, ooze.

fin, *f.,* end.

financier, *m.,* financier.

finesse, *f.,* keenness.

finir, to end.

il fit, he did, he made, *past def. of* **faire.**

fixe, fixed, steady, regular.

flatter, to flatter.

fleuri, in bloom.

fleuve, *m.,* river.

flot, *m.,* wave, flood.

flotter, to float.

foi, *f.,* faith; **Ma —!** Upon my word! Well!

foire, *f.,* fair.

fois, *f.,* time; **deux —,** twice.

fond, *m.,* bottom.

ils font, they make, do, *pres. of* **faire.**

forger, to forge.

forgeron, *m.,* blacksmith.

format, *m.,* size.

forme, *f.,* form, pattern, manner.

former, to form, shape, mould.

formidable, terrible.

fort, very; strong.

fortune, *f.,* fortune, riches.

fouet, *m.,* whip.

foule, *f.,* crowd.

fragile, frail, brittle.

franc, *m.,* franc (*about* 20 *cents*).

franchise, *f.,* openness, freedom.

frapper, to strike.

froid, *m.,* cold.

froidement, calmly, coldly.

fromage, *m.,* cheese, piece of cheese.

front, *m.,* forehead.

fruit, *m.,* fruit.

fuir, to flee.

fumée, *f.*, smoke.
fumer, to smoke.
fumeur, *m.*, one who smokes, a smoker.
fusil, *m.*, gun.
fusillade, *f.*, volley.
il fut, he was, *past def. of* être.
futur, *m.*, future.
il fuyait, he was fleeing, *imperf. of* fuir.

G

gager, to wager.
gages, *m.*, wages.
gagner, to obtain; to overcome.
gai, joyous.
gaieté, *f.*, good humor.
gant, *m.*, glove.
garder, to keep.
gauche, left.
Gaulois, *m.*, a Gaul.
géant, *m.*, giant.
gêner, to embarrass.
général, *m.*, general.
générosité, *f.*, generosity.
gens, people.
gland, *m.*, acorn.
glisser, to slip, slide.
gloutonnement, greedily.
gorge, *f.*, throat; gorge.
gosier, *m.*, throat.
goulu, greedy, ravenous.
goûter, to taste, appreciate, enjoy.
grade, *f.*, rank.
grand, tall, great.
grandir, to grow, increase.
granit, *m.*, granite.
gras, -se, fat.
grave, grave, serious.
gros, -se, large.
groupe, *m.*, group.

guenille, *f.*, rag.
guérir, to cure.
guerre, *f.*, war.
gueule, *f.*, jaws.

H

habitant, *m.*, an inhabitant.
habiter, to live in.
habituel, -le, customary, habitual.
halte, *f.*, halt.
hameçon, *m.*, hook.
hampe, *f.*, handle, staff.
Harpagon, proper noun personifying a miser.
hasard, *m.*, chance.
haut, high, loud.
haut, *m.*, top.
hauteur, *f.*, height.
hé! Halloo!
hélas, alas.
héroïque, brave, heroic.
heure, *f.*, hour.
heureux, -se, happy, fortunate.
histoire, *f.*, story.
hiver, *m.*, winter.
homme, *m.*, man.
honoraires, *m.*, fee.
horizon, *m.*, horizon.
hors, outside.
hôtel, *m.*, hotel, mansion.

I

ici, here.
île, *f.*, island.
il y a, there is, there are.
impatience, *f.*, impatience.
imprimeur, *m.*, printer.
indice, *m.*, sign.
ingrat, *m.*, ungrateful person.
injures, *f.*, insult; **dire des —,** to abuse.

innombrable, countless.
inquiet, -ète, uneasy.
insecte, *m.*, insect.
s'instruire, to learn.
intéressant, interesting.
interroger, to question.
inutile, useless.
issue, *f.*, outlet.
Italien, -ne, an Italian.

J

jamais, ne —, never.
jardin, *m.*, garden.
jaser, to chatter.
je, I.
jeter, to throw; il jette, he throws, *pres. ind. of* jeter.
jeune, young.
joie, *f.*, joy.
joli, pretty.
Joseph II, emperor of Austria.
jouer, to play.
jouir, to enjoy.
jour, *m.*, day.
journal, *m.*, newspaper.
journée, *f.*, day.
joyeux, -se, joyous.
juge, *m.*, judge.
jugement, *m.*, judgment.
juger, to judge.
Junot, name of a French general.
jurer, to swear.
jusque, until.

L

lac, *m.*, lake.
lâche, cowardly.
lâcher, to let go.
laisser, to leave, to allow, let.
lame, *f.*, blade.

lancer, to throw.
leçon, *f.*, lesson.
Léfèbvre, French general.
légume, *m.*, vegetable.
lendemain, *m.*, next day.
lenteur, *f.*, slowness.
lettre, *f.*, letter.
leur, their, to them.
liberté, *f.*, liberty.
libre, free.
lier, to bind, fasten together.
lieu, *m.*, place; au — de, instead of.
lièvre, *m.*, hare
ligne, *f.*, line.
lire, to read.
lit, *m.*, bed.
littéraire, literary.
littérature, *f.*, literature.
livre, *m.*, book.
livre, *f.*, pound (500 *grammes*).
livrer, to give up.
loin, far.
long, -ue, long.
longtemps, for a long time.
lorgnon, *m.*, eye-glass.
lorsque, when.
loup, *m.*, wolf.
lourd, heavy.
lui, to him, to her, him.
lui-même, himself.
lune, *f.*, moon.
lunettes, *f.*, spectacles.

M

madame, madam, Mrs.
ma foi! Upon my word! Well!
magasin, *m.*, store.
magistrat, *m.*, magistrate.
main, *f.*, hand.
maintenant, now.
mais, but.

maison, *f.*, house.
maître, *m.*, master.
mal, badly.
malade, ill.
malade, *m. et f.*, a sick person.
maladie, *f.*, illness.
malgré, in spite of.
malheureusement, unfortunately.
malheureux, -se, unhappy.
malhonnêteté, *f.*, dishonesty.
manger, to eat.
manière, *f.*, manner, way.
manquer, to be lacking, to want, to miss.
marchand, *m.*, merchant.
marchandise, *f.*, goods.
marche, *f.*, march, course.
marché, *m.*, market, bargain.
maréchal, *m.*, marshal.
mari, *m.*, husband.
marque, *f.*, token, sign.
masse, *f.*, mass.
matière, *f.*, material; table des —s, contents.
matinée, *f.*, morning.
mauvais, bad.
médecin, *m.*, doctor.
médecine, *f.*, medicine.
même, same, very; ce soir —, this very evening.
mémoire, *m.*, memorandum.
merci, thanks.
mère, *f.*, mother.
mériter, to deserve.
merveille, à—, wonderfully.
mettre, to put; se — à, to begin.
il meurt, he dies, *pres. ind. of* mourir.
midi, *m.*, noon, south.
mie=amie.
mieux, better.
militaire, military.

mille, thousand.
ministre, *m.*, minister.
ils mirent, they put, *past. def. of* mettre.
se mirer, to look at one's self.
miroir, *m.*, mirror.
mis, put, placed, *past part. of* mettre.
il mit, he put, *past.def. of* mettre.
mitraille, *f.*, grape-shot.
modeste, modest, simple.
moindre, less.
mois, *m.*, month.
moitié, *f.*, half.
moment, *m.*, moment.
monarque, *m.*, monarch.
monde, *m.*, world; tout le —, everybody.
monnaie, *f.*, money, change.
monsieur, sir, Mr., gentleman.
montant, *m.*, amount.
monter, to rise, to go up.
montrer, to show, to point out.
se moquer de, to ridicule.
mort, *f.*, death.
mort, dead; died, *past part. of* mourir.
mot, *m.*, word.
mourir, to die.
il mourut, he died, *past def. of* mourir.
mousse, *f.*, moss.
murmure, *m.*, murmur.
musicien, *m.*, musician.
musique, *f.*, music.

N

naître, to be born.
naïveté, *f.*, simplicity, innocence.
Napoléon, emperor of the French.

né, born, *past part. of* naître.
nécessaire, necessary.
neuf, nine.
neuf, neuve, new.
nez, *m.*, nose.
il nia, he denied, *past def. of* nier.
nier, to deny.
noir, black.
nom, *m.*, name.
nombreux, -se, numerous.
non, no.
nous, we, us, to us.
nouveau, nouvelle, new.
nouvelles, *f.*, news.
nuage, *m.*, cloud.
nuit, *f.*, night.
nul, -le, not one, no.

O

obéir, to obey.
obligé, obliged, forced.
obtenir, to obtain.
occasion, *f.*, opportunity; à l'—, as opportunity offers.
occuper, to occupy; s'—, to give one's time to.
œil, *m.*, eye.
œuvre, *m.*, work.
officier, *m.*, officer.
offre, *f.*, offer.
oiseau, *m.*, bird.
on, one, they, people, we, you (*all used indefinitely*).
oncle, *m.*, uncle.
opération, *f.*, operation.
opticien, *m.*, optician.
or, now.
or, *m.*, gold.
orage, *m.*, storm.
ordre, *m.*, order.
orgueil, *m.*, pride.

os, *m.*, bone.
oser, to dare.
ôter, to take away.
ou, or.
où, where; d'où, whence, from where.
oublier, to forget.
oui, yes.
ouvert, open.
ouvrage, *m.*, work.
ouvrier, *m.*, workman.
ouvrir, to open.
il ouvrit, he opened, *past def. of* ouvrir.

P

pain, *m.*, bread, loaf.
paire, *m.*, pair.
paix, *f.*, peace.
palais, *m.*, palace.
palefrenier, *m.*, groom.
panier, *m.*, basket.
papier, *m.*, paper; — buvard, blotting-paper; — à lettre, writing-paper.
Pâques, *f.*, Easter.
par, by; — exemple, for instance.
paradis, Paradise.
paraître, to appear.
parapluie, *m.*, umbrella.
parbleu! Upon my word! Of course!
parcourir, to go through.
paresseux, -se, idle.
parfait, perfect.
parler, to speak.
partialité, *f.*, partiality.
partie, *f.*, part.
partir, to set out; à — de, from.
il parut, he appeared, *past def. of* paraître.

pas, *m.*, step.

passé, past.

patrie, *f.*, country, native land.

patte, *f.*, paw.

pâturage, *m.*, pasture.

pâture, *f.*, food.

pauvre, poor.

payer, to pay.

pays, *m.*, country.

paysan, *m.*, peasant, rustic.

pêcheur, *m.*, fisherman.

à peine, hardly.

pendant que, while.

pénible, difficult, painful.

penser, to think.

perché, perched.

perdre, to lose.

Perse, *f.*, Persia.

personne, ne —, nobody.

personne, *f.*, a person.

persuader, to persuade.

pesant, heavy.

peser, to weigh.

pester, contre, to storm, at.

petit, small, little.

peu, little.

peur, *f.*, fear.

il peut, he can, *pres. ind. of* pouvoir.

peut-être, perhaps.

phrase, *f.*, sentence.

philosophe, *m.*, philosopher.

pie, *f.*, magpie.

pied, *m.*, foot.

pierre, *f.*, stone.

pinson, *m.*, chaffinch.

piquer, to prick.

piqueur, *m.*, huntsman.

place, *f.*, place, square.

se plaindre de, to complain of.

plaint, complained, *past part. of* se plaindre.

plainte, *f.*, complaint.

plaisanter, to joke.

plaisir, *m.*, pleasure.

planer, to hover.

plante, *f.*, plant.

plat, *m.*, dish.

plateau, *m.*, plate *or* side of scales.

plein, full.

pleurer, to weep.

pleuvoir, to rain.

plier, to fold.

pluie, *f.*, rain.

plumage, *m.*, feathers.

plume, *f.*, pen, feather.

plus, more; ne —, no longer.

plusieurs, several.

poche, *f.*, pocket.

poids, *m.*, weight.

poignée, *f.*, handful.

point, ne . . . —, not at all (*emphatic for* ne . . . pas).

pointe, *f.*, la — du jour, dawn, daybreak.

pointu, pointed.

poisson, *m.*, fish.

poitrine, *f.*, breast.

poliment, politely.

politesse, *f.*, politeness.

pont, *m.*, bridge; deck.

il porta, he carried, brought, wore, *past def. of* porter.

porte, *f.*, door.

porte-cigares, *m.*, cigar-case.

porte-drapeau, *m.*, color-bearer, ensign.

portefeuille, *m.*, pocket-book.

porte-monnaie, *m.*, pocket-book.

porte-plume, *m.*, penholder.

porter, to carry, wear.

poser, to put, place.

possible, possible.

poste, *f.*, post.

pouce, *m.*, thumb.

poudre, *f.*, powder.

poulet, *m.*, chicken.
pourquoi, why.
il pourra, he will be able, *fut. of* pouvoir.
pousser, to grow, to advance.
pouvoir, to be able.
prairie, *f.*, meadow.
premier, -ère, first.
prendre, to take.
près de, near.
à présent, now.
presque, almost.
prêt, ready.
prêter, to lend.
preuve, *f.*, proof.
prier, to beg.
printemps, *m.*, spring.
prison, *f.*, prison.
il prit, he took, *past def. of* prendre.
privation, *f.*, privation.
procurer, to procure.
profond, deep.
proie, *f.*, prey.
projet, *m.*, plan.
promenade, *f.*, walk.
se promener, to take a walk.
promettre, to promise.
promis, promised.
prononcer, to pronounce.
à propos de, with reference to.
prouver, to prove.
province, *f.*, province.
Prusse, *f.*, Prussia.
public, publique, public.
puis, then.
je puis, I can, *pres. ind. of* pouvoir.
puisque, since.
punir, to punish.
purifier, to purify.
il put, he could, *past. def. of* pouvoir.

Q

quai, *m.*, wharf, platform.
qualité, *f.*, en — de, as.
quand, when.
quant à, as to.
quarante, forty.
quartier, *m.*, quarter.
quatre, four.
quel, -le, what, what a.
quelque chose, *m.*, something.
quelqu'un, some one.
qu'est-ce qui, what.
queue, *f.*, tail.
qui, who.
quitter, to leave, abandon.
quoi, what.

R

raconter, to relate.
railler, to joke, ridicule.
raison, *f.*, reason; avoir —, to be right.
ramasser, to pick up.
ramener, to bring back.
ramper, to climb.
rang, *m.*, rank.
ranger, to put in order.
raser, to raze.
rassurer, to calm, give confidence to.
rattraper, to catch again, to take back.
réception, *f.*, reception.
recevoir, to receive.
réchauffer, to warm.
il reçoit, he receives, *pres. ind. of* recevoir.
recommander, to recommend.
récompense, *f.*, reward.
reconnaissance, *f.*, gratitude.

reconnaissant, grateful; re-cognizing, *pres. part. of* re-connaître.

reconnaître, to recognize.

il reconnut, he recognized, *past def. of* reconnaître.

il reçut, he received, *past def. of* recevoir.

redresser, to set up again.

regarder, to look at, look.

régiment, *m.*, regiment.

régner, to reign.

reine, *f.*, queen.

rejoindre, to join again, to unite.

réjouir, to rejoice.

se relever, to get up.

remarquer, to observe.

rembarquer, to re-embark.

remercier, to thank.

remettre, to put back, to hand to.

remplir, to fill.

rémunérer, to reward.

renard, *m.*, fox.

rencontrer, to meet.

rendre, to return; — visite à, to pay a visit to; se — à, to go to.

renverser, to upset.

reparer, to repair.

repartir, to reply.

repas, *m.*, meal.

se répercuter, to resound.

répéter, to repeat.

répétition, *f.*, rehearsal.

répliquer, to reply.

il répondit, he answered, *past def. of* répondre.

répondre, to answer.

réponse, *f.*, answer.

repos, *m.*, rest.

reprendre, to answer, reply.

représentant, *m.*, representa-tive.

il reprit, he answered, *past def. of* reprendre.

résister, to resist.

respecter, to respect.

reste, du —, moreover.

rester, to remain.

retard, en —, late.

retirer, to withdraw.

retourner, to return, to turn round.

réussir, to succeed.

revanche, *f.*, revenge.

réveiller, to awake.

revenir, to come back, return.

révérence, *f.*, bow.

il reverrait, he would see again, *cond. of* revoir.

il revint, he came back, *past def. of* revenir.

revoir, to see again.

riche, rich.

richesse, *f.*, riches.

rien, ne . . . rien, nothing.

rire, to laugh.

rocher, *m.*, rock.

roi, *m.*, king.

rôle, *m.*, part.

roman, *m.*, novel.

ils rompirent, they broke, *past def. of* rompre.

rompre, to break.

rôtir, to roast.

roue, *f.*, wheel.

route, *f.*, road.

royal, royal.

royaliste, *m.*, royalist, sup-porter of the king.

royaume, *m.*, kingdom.

rudement, roughly.

rue, *f.*, street.

ruisseau, *m.*, spring.

S

sable, *m.*, sand.

sac, *m.*, sack.

s'adresser à, to turn to.

sage, wise; (of a child) good, well-behaved.

Saint Pierre, Saint Peter.

tu sais, you know, *pres. ind. of* savoir.

saisir, to seize.

il saisit, he seized, *past def. of* saisir.

saison, *f.*, season.

sale, dirty.

salle, *f.*, room.

s'alléger, to grow lighter.

saluer, to bow.

salut, *m.*, bow; safety.

samedi, *m.*, Saturday; tous les —s, every Saturday.

sang-froid, *m.*, coolness, assurance.

sans, without.

s'apercevoir, to notice.

s'appeler, to be called, named.

s'arrêter, to stop.

s'asseoir, to take a seat, to sit down.

satisfait, satisfied.

s'attendre (à), to expect.

sauter, to jump.

sauvage, wild, savage.

se sauver, to run away.

sauveur, saviour.

s'avancer, to advance.

savetier, *m.*, cobbler.

savoir, to know.

science, *f.*, science, knowledge.

scientifique, scientific.

sec, sèche, dry.

s'échapper, to escape.

sécher, to dry.

second, second.

secouer, to shake.

secourir, to help.

secours, *m.*, help, assistance.

secrétaire, *m.*, secretary.

seigneur, *m.*, lord.

s'élancer, to dash forward.

s'élever, to rise.

selle, *f.*, saddle.

selon, according (to).

semaine, *f.*, week.

s'embarquer, to embark.

semblable, like.

sembler, to seem.

s'empresser, to be eager, to hasten.

sentinelle, *f.*, guard.

je serai, I shall be, *fut. of* être.

je serais, I should be, *cond. of* être.

serment, *m.*, oath.

serre, *m.*, talon.

serrurier, *m.*, locksmith.

il sert, he (it) serves; — à, is used for, *pres. ind. of* servir.

servir, to serve; — à, to be used for.

sévèrement, severely.

si, if, so.

siège, *m.*, seat.

signature, *f.*, signature.

signe, *m.*, sign.

s'il vous plaît, if you please.

simple, simple.

s'instruire, to learn.

sire, *m.*, Sir, Sire.

six, six.

sœur, *f.*, sister.

soi-disant, self-styled, so-called.

soif, *f.*, thirst.

soigner, to take care of.

soin, *m.*, care; —s, attentions.

soir, *m.*, evening.
Soit! Be it so!
soldat, *m.*, soldier.
soleil, *m.*, sun.
sombrer, to disappear.
somme, *m.*, sleep, nap.
somme, *f.*, sum, amount; en
— , upon the whole.
songer, to think.
sonner, to ring.
sorte, *f.*, kind, manner; de —
que, so as to.
sortir, to go out.
sou, cent.
souffler, to blow.
soufflet, *m.*, bellows.
souffrir, to suffer.
soulier, *m.*, shoe.
souper, *m.*, supper.
source, *f.*, spring.
sourire, *m.*, smile.
souris, *f.*, mouse.
souterrain, underground.
se souvenir (de), to remember.
souvent, often.
soyez, be, *imp. of* être.
spectacle, *m.*, sight.
subitement, suddenly.
succomber, to yield, give way.
suite, *f.*, ainsi de —, and so on;
tout de —, immediately, at
once.
sujet, *m.*, subject.
sultan, *m.*, sultan.
supérieur, superior, upper.
supporter, to endure.
supposer, to suppose.
sûr, sure, certain.
sur, on, upon; — -le-champ,
immediately.
surplus, *m.*, remainder, what
is left over.
surpris, surprised.

surprise, *f.*, astonishment, surprise.
surveillance, *f.*, watch, supervision.
survenir, to happen, arrive
unexpectedly.
il sut, he knew, *past def. of*
savoir.
sût, vous ne vouliez pas qu'on
— , you didn't want any one
to know.

T

table, *f.*, table.
tailleur, *m.*, tailor.
talent, *m.*, talent.
tandis que, while.
tant, so much, so many.
tapisser, to paper.
tari, dried up.
tellement, so.
temple, *m.*, temple.
temps, *m.*, time; de — en —,
from time to time.
tenir, to hold.
terminer, to end.
terne, dull.
ternir, to tarnish.
terrain, *m.*, ground.
terre, *f.*, earth.
thaler, *m.*, dollar.
tienne, qu'à cela ne —, never
mind.
tiens, indeed.
il tient, he holds, *pres. ind. of* tenir.
timbre, *m.*, stamp.
tire-bouchon, *m.*, corkscrew.
tirer, to pull, draw, take out.
toit, *m.*, roof.
tombeau, *m.*, tomb.
tomber, to fall.
tort, *m.*, wrong; avoir —, to be
wrong.

toucher, to touch.
toujours, always, still.
tour, *f.*, tower.
tour, *m.*, trick, turn.
tourbillon, *m.*, whirlwind.
touriste, *m.*, tourist.
tourmenter, to torture.
tous deux, both.
tout, all.
trace, *f.*, mark, track.
trahir, to betray.
train, *m.*, pomp.
traînée, *f.*, train.
traité, *m.*, treaty.
tranquille, quiet.
travail, *m.*, work.
travailler, to work.
traverser, to cross.
tremper, to dip, soak.
trésor, *m.*, treasure.
triste, sad.
trompe, *f.*, trunk (*of an ele-phant*).
tromper, to deceive; se —, to be mistaken.
trop, too, too much.
trotter, to trot, to run.
troupe, *f.*, troop.
troupeau, *m.*, herd.
trouver, to find; se —, to be.
tuer, to kill.
turbot, *m.*, a turbot.

U

unir, to unite.
unisson, *m.*, unison.
utile, useful.

V

va, go, *imp. of* aller.
vacances, *f.*, holidays.
vaccine, *f.* vaccination.

vaincre, to overcome.
vaincu, conquered.
valet, *m.*, valet.
vallée, *f.*, valley.
vallon, *m.*, valley.
valoir mieux, to be better.
vanter, to boast of; to praise heartily.
vase, *m.*, vase.
il vaut, he (it) is worth, *pres. ind. of* valoir.
vendre, to sell.
vengeance, *f.*, revenge
venir, to come; — de, to have just.
vent, *m.*, wind.
vente, *f.*, sale.
ver, *m.*, worm; — à soie, silkworm.
verdoyer, to be or become green.
véritablement, truly.
je verrai, I shall see, *fut. of* voir.
verre, *m.*, glass, eye-glass.
vers, toward.
vêtement, *m.*, garment.
veuillez, be so good as to.
il veut, he wishes, *pres. ind. of* vouloir.
veuve, *f.*, widow.
vie, *f.*, life.
Vienne, *f.*, Vienna.
il vient, he comes, *pres. ind. of* venir.
vieux, vieil, vieille, old.
villageois, *m.*, villager.
ville, *f.*, town, city.
vin, *m.*, wine.
vint, he came, *past def. of* venir.
virgule, *m.*, comma; **point** et —, semicolon.
visage, *m.*, face.

visite, *f.*, visit.
il vit, he saw, *past def. of* voir.
vite, quickly.
vivement, vigorously.
voici, here is (vois + ici).
ils voient, they see, *pres. ind. of* voir.
voilà, there is (vois + là).
voir, to see.
voisin, *m.*, neighbor.
voisin, neighboring.
voiture, *f.*, carriage.
voix, *f.*, voice.
voler, to steal.
voleur, *m.*, thief.
tu voudras, you will wish, *fut. of* vouloir.

il voulait, he wished, *imperf. of* vouloir.
vouloir, to wish.
il voulut, he wished, *past def. of* vouloir.
voyager, to travel.
voyant, seeing, *pres. part. of* voir.
Voyons! Come!
vue, *f.*, view, sight.

Y

y, there, to it, in it.
y compris, with, included.
yeux, eyes.

FIFTY LETTERS
OF PLINY

FIFTY LETTERS
OF PLINY

Selected and edited
with introduction and notes

BY

A. N. SHERWIN-WHITE, M.A.

FELLOW AND TUTOR
ST. JOHN'S COLLEGE, OXFORD

OXFORD UNIVERSITY PRESS

1967

Oxford University Press, Ely House, London W. 1

GLASGOW NEW YORK TORONTO MELBOURNE WELLINGTON
CAPE TOWN SALISBURY IBADAN NAIROBI LUSAKA ADDIS ABABA
BOMBAY CALCUTTA MADRAS KARACHI LAHORE DACCA
KUALA LUMPUR HONG KONG TOKYO

PRINTED IN GREAT BRITAIN

PREFACE

THIS selection of Pliny's Letters, replacing the 1914 edition of G. B. Allen, is intended for use in sixth forms and certain university courses. The commentary is designed to help students who have no special knowledge of the social and political history of the Roman empire. It is based on my large-scale commentary published by the Clarendon Press, and deliberately confines citations of similarities and parallels to a minimum, while references to external sources are given only when the material is of special interest. Generally Pliny is illustrated from his own letters. The more learned may consult my long commentary. Linguistically, the use of a short Latin dictionary is assumed, but the meaning of rare or technical words is given in the notes. The selection of letters in intended to cover the whole range of Pliny's activities and interests, and so to provide a wide illustration of the private, public, and literary life of the capital of the Roman Empire in the early second century A.D. A representative group of the official correspondence of Pliny as governor of Bithynia with the Emperor Trajan is included, showing the variety of problems that confronted a provincial governor and the nature of his relations with the central government. These may be of use for detailed study by those reading special periods of imperial history at school or university level.

A. N. S.-W.

St. John's College, Oxford
January 1966

CONTENTS

The cover illustration shows *The Education of an Infant* from a Roman Sarcophagus now in the Louvre. *Mansell Collection.*

INTRODUCTION

THE AUTHOR

GAIUS Plinius Caecilius Secundus, commonly called Pliny the Younger, was a wealthy landowner who hailed from the prosperous borough of Comum (Como), in the Cisalpine region of North Italy. He was the first member of his family to become a senator of Rome, and owed his advancement to the influence of friends of his uncle, Gaius Plinius Secundus, who had held high offices in the second or 'equestrian' grade of the imperial service. The Letters contain accounts of the lives and characters of these friends, such as Corellius Rufus and Verginius Rufus (Letters 5, 8, 13, 37). Pliny, who was born in the year A.D. 61–62, lived in the fourth generation of the period of Roman history known as the Principate or Empire. This began with the foundation of a 'new order' in 27 B.C. by Augustus Caesar, after the end of the civil wars which destroyed the old Republic.

The 'new order' was a thinly disguised monarchy in which the 'First Man' (*princeps*) or emperor (*imperator*) had the supreme effective power. But a great deal of political influence and administrative work was left in the hands of the Senate, which still controlled certain provinces of the empire through annual proconsuls, though the great armies were all under the command of the Princeps and his *legati*. The emperors after Augustus were increasingly autocratic, and claimed ever more power at the expense of the Senate. Hence there were feuds between the emperors and leading senators, and periods of political oppression of varying severity under the Julio-Claudian emperors Claudius and Nero (A.D. 41–54, 54–68), who were descended from Augustus. Nero was succeeded, after a year of military revolutions in which three army commanders briefly held the Principate, by the Flavian dynasty of Vespasian and his sons Titus and Domitian (A.D. 70–96). Under Domitian (A.D. 81–96) relations between Senate and Princeps were severely strained. Pliny tells many stories in the Letters of these difficult times (Letters 5, 8, 15, 31, 37). But after the assassination of the hated Domitian and the brief reign of Cocceius Nerva (A.D. 96–98), who was chosen by the conspirators as a successor likely to placate all interests, M. Ulpius Traianus, an efficient army commander of consular rank, became Princeps as the adopted son of Nerva. His reign (A.D. 98–117) was a time of political reconciliation between senators and emperor, and of successful foreign wars which extended the frontiers of the empire beyond the Danube and the Euphrates.

Pliny's public career spanned the principates of Domitian, Nerva, and Trajan. He refers to most of his posts in various letters, and a long inscription survives giving his whole career (p. xviii). After military service as a legionary officer in the frontier army of Syria (A.D. 81, Letter 4. 2), he held the usual annual magistracies at Rome from quaestorship to praetorship (cf. Letter 35. 8 n.). These relics of the old Republican constitution were now unimportant but necessary preliminaries to gaining the major appointments in the service of the Princeps. Between A.D. 94 and 100 Pliny was head of the Military

Treasury and of the State Treasury (*Praefectus aerari Saturni*, Letter 4. 9). In A.D. 100 he held the consulship, which was the senior annual magistracy, and was chairman of the drainage-board of the city of Rome (*curator aluei Tiberis*) for some three years (A.D. 104–7). Then in about A.D. 110 he was sent on a special mission by Trajan to reorganize the province of Bithynia-with-Pontus (in modern Turkey) as *legatus Augusti*.

Pliny's appointments, though substantial, did not carry the highest distinction in the public service because they were non-military. The army commanders of the great frontier provinces such as Syria, the Danube provinces, and Britain had greater prestige. But Pliny's credit as an administrator is shown by the fact that he served several times as an adviser on the emperor's supreme judicial and administrative tribunal (Letter 20). Pliny was a civilian, and he made his name not in the army but as a barrister or advocate in the courts, which were always an alternative means of promotion in Roman society. Advocacy and soldiering were the only two professions open to the Roman upper classes. Pliny began his career as an advocate in the Centumviral court of civil law at the age of eighteen, and by A.D. 100 he was a notable legal figure, who could and did claim to be second only to the outstanding orator Cornelius Tacitus, the historian (Letters 10, 23, 38). Pliny writes a great deal about the theory and practice of oratory, describing his own court work and the final publication of his big speeches (Letters 22, 23, 26, 27). The most important of these were concerned with the accusation or defence of provincial governors tried on charges of extortion before the Senate (Letters 10, 31).

Late in life Pliny turned to other forms of literature, producing two books of light verse and dallying with the idea of writing history (Letters 22, 34). He encouraged others to write, assisted young advocates in their careers, and was patron of the needy satirist Martial (Letters 17, 26, 29, 39). Twice he provided material for the histories of Tacitus in the form of memoirs of famous events (Letters 25, 31). Literature was his personal enthusiasm, and many letters are devoted to its characteristic manifestation in Roman society, the formal recitation of new work (Letters 6, 27, 34). He admired the contemporary teachers of philosophy, but rather as preachers than as thinkers; like most Romans, his interest was in rules of conduct rather than in logical analysis. His intellect was more genuinely stirred by *quaestiones naturales*, or scientific problems. In letters on these themes he shows a capacity unusual in antiquity, after the age of the Greek scientists, for exact observation and inference from physical data (Letters 21, 25, 30).

Pliny's letters deal with a wide variety of topics. They hold a mirror up to the high society of the capital of the Roman empire at the time of its greatest prosperity. Pliny observes this society with a friendly and complacent eye, but he observes with precision, and provides a counter-check on the exaggerations of the contemporary satirists Martial and Juvenal, for whom all is vice and blackness. At times he reveals glimpses of a grimmer side of Roman life—the murder of a cruel slave-owner, the dodges of legacy hunters, the corruptions of provincial government (Letters 10, 11, 14). He writes much about his private life —his daily routine, his sensible marriage to a provincial girl from his home town, the treatment of slaves and servants, the management of estates and tenants (Letters 3, 16, 19, 24). Often Pliny's letters provide the only solid evidence for these aspects of Roman life.

Pliny's social background was that of the country gentry, brought up for generations in the atmosphere of a respectable *bourgeoisie*, which was easily shocked by the excessive self-indulgence and sophisticated vices that were characteristic of the older Roman nobility, and of the society of the capital in the days of the Julio-Claudian emperors. Tacitus says of Pliny's generation that 'the old aristocracy was replaced by new families from the remoter parts of Italy and from the provinces, which acquired wealth and political power but retained their native sobriety of behaviour'. This attitude of mind pervades the Letters. It appears in a rather priggish rectitude towards the failings of others (Letters 11, 29, 36), but also in Pliny's humane attitude towards his staff and servants (Letters 9, 24, 33), and in the practical shrewdness of the financial letters (Letters 16, 28). This trait of caution enabled Pliny to make his career as a young senator under the protection of the unpopular Emperor Domitian without compromising himself, either by too close an association with critics of the emperor such as Junius Mauricus, or by involving himself in Domitian's iniquities (Letters 20. 3–6, 31. 4–9). Most of Pliny's close friends had the same social background, and the same cautious attitude (Letters 5, 12).

PLINY IN BITHYNIA

In A.D. 109 or 110 Pliny was given an unusual appointment. The province of Bithynia-with-Pontus is a sector of

North-western Turkey, stretching from the eastern end
of the Propontis channel as far eastwards as Sinope and
Amisus on the Black Sea coast (p. 164). This province had
been under the control of the Senate and its annual proconsuls since the foundation of the Principate in 27 B.C. It
was a land in which the civilization and language were
Greek, and the local administration was based on a number of large self-governing Greek cities. These were rich
and prosperous, but their government was corrupt and
inefficient. The wealthy upper classes controlled the city
councils and monopolized the civic offices and magistracies, while the mass of the working population had
few rights beyond the power to elect these officers. Public money was being wasted on extravagant building
schemes, the rules of local government were often flouted,
faction and intrigue between local politicians were rife,
and the mass of the people were discontented. Pliny, who
had had considerable experience of financial management
in his career, but no practice in provincial administration,
was commissioned as the special envoy of the Princeps,
with the title *legatus Augusti consulari potestate*, to take over
the government of the province and to set matters right.
Pliny describes the similar mission of his friend Maximus
in the province of Achaea two years earlier in Letter 35.

Trajan gave Pliny a number of directives (Letters 47. 7,
49. 1 nn.), and encouraged the legate to consult him when
special difficulties arose. Pliny apparently died in office
some eighteen months later, and his official correspondence with Trajan was published together with the emperor's replies or 'rescripts'. He consulted Trajan some
thirty-seven times, mostly on issues where there was a

conflict between Trajan's directives and the needs of the local situation as Pliny saw it, or when he lacked experience in some problem. Five characteristic consultations, with Trajan's replies, are included in this collection (Letters 41–50). Pliny has often been criticized as timid and ineffectual by those who have not considered the terms of his appointment and the reasons underlying his consultations. But his own proposals show good sense, a quick eye for abuses, and a readiness to consider the best interests of the province.

On Pliny's life and times see Sir R. Syme, *Tacitus* (Oxford, 1958), chs. iii, vii, viii, and G. E. F. Chilver, *Cisalpine Gaul* (Oxford, 1941), ch. vi. 2.

THE FORM OF THE LETTERS

Only two Roman writers before Pliny are known to have had their letters formally published, Cicero and Seneca. Cicero's letters are genuine correspondence concerning matters of the day, written for the moment and in a moment, to a wide variety of recipients, without special regard for technical literary rules. Seneca's letters to Lucilius are epistles in moral philosophy, with a certain amount of anecdote and information, which hardly pretend to be letters at all. Pliny's letters are not quite like either of these two types. Though closer in intent and content to the letters of Cicero, whom he claims as his model (Ep. ix. 2. 2), they are closer to Seneca in their regard for literary form. They are *epistulae curatius* (or *diligentius*) *scriptae*, a term which recurs in the Letters (Letters 1. 1, 26. 8). In their contents they are letters of

831770 b

news, concerned with events and occasions, or letters
of advice, or letters of personal recommendation. But the
news-letter often develops into a character-sketch or a
miniature history, and the letter of particular advice into
an essay. Every letter is written with great attention to
style, and nearly all observe a strict rule that limits each
to a single subject, treated at moderate length. Pliny regularly apologizes for exceeding the appropriate length: 'ne
modum . . . in epistula excedam' (Ep. ii. 5. 13, cf. Letter
10. 25), and he once ingeniously invokes a rule of the
schools of oratory to justify the inclusion in one letter of
three different anecdotes illustrating a single theme (Letter
11. 9). Several other letters, such as 15 and 30, are constructed on this principle.

Pliny and his friends regularly exchanged letters of this
literary genre (Ep. ix. 28. 1, 5). But to form his collection
Pliny has often taken letters that were originally genuine
correspondence of the moment, and rewritten or edited
them according to the rules of the literary letter. This is
most apparent in the letters dealing with practical affairs,
such as Letters 16, 18, 28, and letters of commendation,
like Letter 12, which may be close to their original form.

Pliny developed the literary letter to something that is
without parallel in surviving Latin literature up to that
time. The closest resemblance is not to any other surviving Latin letters, but to the 'occasional' verses of
Statius, known as the *Silvae*, and to those of Martial,
dealing with such topics as a dinner party, the sketch of
a character or a man's career, or a building. Several of
Pliny's themes come straight from Martial, even when
they seem genuine items of correspondence (e.g. Letters

7, 9), and he sometimes exploits a topic from Cicero's letters (Letters 22. 2, 36. 1 nn.).

In style the literary intention is clear. Pliny regularly uses the devices and forms of Latin rhetoric for his purpose. Because he does not write 'periodic' sentences like Cicero, with an accumulation of subordinate clauses preceding the main statement, the sentence construction appears more 'natural' to an English ear. But the arrangement of words and clauses in sentences and paragraphs is regularly balanced with great care, and the vocabulary, especially in scenic descriptions, is very poetical (cf. Letters 25 pref., 26. 8 n., 32. 2 n.). Yet despite these devices the construction of sentences is plain and logical. Verbs are frequently placed at the beginning or in the middle of clauses, adjectives often precede their nouns, and genitives may follow instead of preceding the nouns on which they depend. A short example from Letter 10. 13 illustrates much of this: 'erat ergo perquam onerosum accusare damnatum, quem ut premebat (A) atrocitas (B) criminis (C) ita quasi peractae damnationis (C) miseratio (B) tuebatur (A).' The main sentence has the non-periodic word order with the verb and predicate thrust prominently forward, and the relative clause contains a sustained rhetorical 'chiasmus' of which the corresponding words are indicated by ABCCBA. The order of verbs and genitive dependent nouns is adjusted to secure this favourite effect. See also Letters 16. 4, 32. 3, 5, 39. 2 nn.

Unlike the private letters of Books I–IX the letters to Trajan from Book Ten, though carefully written, are not *curatius scriptae*, and seem to have been published in their original form.

Surprisingly Pliny, who writes so much about his oratory and his verses, never discusses the composition or the publication of his letters in the Letters themselves, except for the brief introduction formed by Letter 1. 1. A brief phrase from Letter 37. 1, where a friend quotes from a letter in Book VI, implies that the earlier volumes had been published before the compilation of Book IX. There is no evidence for the favourite theory that the letters were published in three groups of three books each. To judge by their contents, many of which refer to clearly dated or datable events, the letters were published in the years between Pliny's consulship in A.D. 100 and his departure to Bithynia in about A.D. 110. These questions of date, which can be discussed only in relation to the whole collection, do not affect the understanding of the letters themselves (see my *Historical Commentary*, 20 ff.). The dates of particular letters are either given precisely or relatively by their contents, or are inferred from the general date of the contents of each book.

INSCRIPTIONS OF PLINY AND HIS FAMILY

The following is the principal inscription recording Pliny's career, set up after his death at Comum, and published in *CIL* v. 5262 (*ILS* 2927). Others less complete may be found in *CIL* v. 5263 and 5667. The epigraphical abbreviations have been expanded, and missing words included in brackets.

C. Plinius, Luci filius Oufentina tribu, Caecilius [Secundus, consul] augur, legatus pro praetore prouinciae Pon[ti et Bithyniae] consulari potestate in eam prouinciam e[x senatus consulto missus ab] imperatore Caesare Nerua Traiano Augusto German[ico Dacico patre patriae], curator aluei Tiberis et riparum e[t cloacarum urbis], praefectus aerari Saturni, praefectus aerari mil[itaris, praetor, tribunus plebis], quaestor imperatoris, seuir equitum [Romanorum,] tribunus militum legionis [tertiae] Gallicae, [xuir stli]tibus iudicandis.

The posts held by Pliny are here given in reverse chronological order, i.e. starting from the end, and the consulship and augurate are placed, as was usual, out of order at the beginning. The inscription continues with an account of Pliny's bequests and donations to his city including the words 'item uiuus dedit in alimenta puerorum et puellarum plebis urbanae HS D'.

Another inscription about the building of a temple at Comum mentions persons who may be Pliny's dead father and sister, and himself as the dedicant (*CIL* v *Suppl. Italica I*, 745).

[Caeci]liae filiae suae nomine L. Cae[ciliu]s Gai filius Oufentina tribu Secundus, praefectus [fabrorum] a consule, IIIIuir iuri dicundo, pontifex, tem[plum] aeternitati Romae et Augu[sti c]um porticibus et ornamentis incohauit, [Caeci]lius Secundus filius dedicauit.

Forebears of Pliny may also be found at Comum in *CIL* v. 5279 (*ILS* 6728).

TRANSLATION

Pliny's Latin presents fewer difficulties than many Latin authors because he usually follows grammatical rules closely, and uses a syntactical system that seems more normal to the English reader than that of Cicero or Livy (above, p. xvii). But he uses some devices that may baffle the unaccustomed student. The omission of the verb *est*, *esse* in its various parts is extremely frequent. 'When in doubt supply the verb to be' is often helpful. Pliny also frequently omits conjunctions, especially *ut*, linking main and subordinate verbs, e.g. Letter 11. 10: 'rogo ... has mihi leges', Letter 10. 15: 'admoneret uoci laterique consulerem'. He normally omits *ut* after *licet*. He also omits verbs of saying and doing when they can be supplied from the context, e.g. Letter 26. 3: 'sedulo pensitare quid tu quid ille commodius (i.e. scripserit)'.

He often uses a *quod* clause as the subject or object of a main verb, e.g. Letter 27. 13: 'hoc ipsum quod nos recitaturos (i.e. esse) cogitamus emendat'. Letter 10. 6: 'adnotatumque (i.e. est) experimentis quod fauor et misericordia acres ... impetus habent'. Letter 37. 1: 'reprehendis quod iusserit'.

He inverts the order of nouns and relative clauses describing them, e.g. Letter 29. 8: 'iucundum est mihi quod ceperam gaudium scribendo retractare'. He is a great user of parentheses, usually placed in construction by the particle *enim* or *nam*, though sometimes a verb is merely inserted, as it were, in brackets, e.g. Letter 31. 1: 'illis— ingenue fatebor—inseri cupio'. Letter 27. 9: 'tunc commutata non dico plurima sed omnia cupis'.

He omits the correlate of *qui, quae* even when it is not clear, e.g. Letter 38. 3: 'notus (i.e. eis) quibus aliter ignotus est'. Letter 31. 4: 'ne bona dissipari sinant (i.e. ei) quorum esse in custodia debent'.

He occasionally uses a dative of the person concerned

instead of an ablative of the agent after passive verbs, e.g.
Letter 30. 6: 'inhabitantibus . . . tristes . . noctes uigilabantur'.

He often uses a subjunctive, mostly in the perfect tense,
to assert a fact or an opinion modestly, e.g. Letter 26. 3:
'nihil offuerit . . . scribere'.

Certain particles are used in an unfamiliar sense, e.g.
quamquam meaning 'yet' rather than 'although', as in
Letter 26. 15: 'quamquam dixi cum dicerem quae scribenda (i.e. sint)'. He normally uses *quamquam* as a conjunction with the subjunctive like *quamuis*. He often uses
uel in the sense of 'even', instead of *et* or *etiam*, and he
uses *quasi* very frequently in the positive sense of 'as'
rather than meaning 'as if' with the implication of a supposition. He sometimes leaves out *in* when he uses the
ablative in the sense of 'in', e.g. 30. 12.

THE TEXT

The text of this collection usually follows the edition of
Professor Sir R. A. B. Mynors in the Oxford Classical
Texts series, which is derived from three groups of manuscripts, known from their contents as the Eight-Book, the
Nine-Book, and the Ten-Book groups. The oldest of the
manuscripts go back to the ninth century A.D., but many
are very much later in date. The modern text has been
constructed by the comparison of the manuscript readings in the three groups, which often differ amongst
themselves. It is now generally thought that the three
groups are of equal value with one another as a whole,
though individual manuscripts of each group of different

dates may be of very unequal value. Differences of reading
are resolved by accepting the reading common to two
groups against the different reading of a third group, unless there are strong reasons in Pliny's use of language to
reject the majority reading. Thus in Letter 1. 1 two of the
groups read *epistulas si quas . . . curatius* (or *accuratius*)
scripsissem while the third group reads *cura maiore scripsissem*. It is clear that *curatius* is likely to be the original
reading, and *cura maiore* an explanation substituted for the
original, especially as Pliny elsewhere uses the similar
phrase *diligentius scripsissem* about writing letters. When
the three groups offer three different readings, Pliny's
usage elsewhere is the best guide.

The letters to Trajan (Book Ten) are known only from
the printed editions of Aldus and other early editors,
which were made from the same manuscript of the Ten-
Book group which is now lost. None of the surviving
Ten-Book manuscripts now contains more than Books
I–V. 6.

THE COMMENTARY

The notes are given in the order of sections in each
Letter, but within each section there are some divergences
from serial treatment in order to keep the continuity
of closely related comments. Hence notes on verbal and
grammatical points are sometimes put at the end of
sections. References to Pliny's letters not in this collection
are given in the form 'Ep. vi. 20. 5', etc.

LETTER 1

Editing the letters

C. PLINIVS SEPTICIO ⟨CLARO⟩ SVO S.

FREQVENTER hortatus es ut epistulas, si quas paulo cura- 1
tius scripsissem, colligerem publicaremque. Collegi non
seruato temporis ordine (neque enim historiam compone-
bam), sed ut quaeque in manus uenerat. Superest ut nec te 2
consilii nec me paeniteat obsequii. Ita enim fiet, ut eas
quae adhuc neglectae iacent requiram et si quas addidero
non supprimam. Vale.

LETTER 2

Pliny goes a-hunting

C. PLINIVS CORNELIO TACITO SVO S.

RIDEBIS, et licet rideas. Ego, ille quem nosti, apros tres et 1
quidem pulcherrimos cepi. 'Ipse?' inquis. Ipse; non tamen
ut omnino ab inertia mea et quiete discederem. Ad retia
sedebam; erat in proximo non uenabulum aut lancea, sed
stilus et pugillares; meditabar aliquid enotabamque, ut si
manus uacuas, plenas tamen ceras reportarem. Non est 2
quod contemnas hoc studendi genus; mirum est ut animus
agitatione motuque corporis excitetur; iam undique siluae
et solitudo ipsumque illud silentium quod uenationi datur,
magna cogitationis incitamenta sunt. Proinde cum uena- 3
bere, licebit auctore me ut panarium et lagunculam sic

831770   B

etiam pugillares feras: experieris non Dianam magis
montibus quam Mineruam inerrare. Vale.

LETTER 3

The daily round at Rome

C. PLINIVS MINICIO FVNDANO SVO S.

1 MIRVM est quam singulis diebus in urbe ratio aut constet aut constare uideatur, pluribus iunctisque non constet.
2 Nam si quem interroges 'Hodie quid egisti?', respondeat:
'Officio togae uirilis interfui, sponsalia aut nuptias frequen-
taui, ille me ad signandum testamentum, ille in aduoca-
3 tionem, ille in consilium rogauit.' Haec quo die feceris,
necessaria, eadem, si cotidie fecisse te reputes, inania
uidentur, multo magis cum secesseris. Tunc enim subit
recordatio: 'Quot dies quam frigidis rebus absumpsi!'
4 Quod euenit mihi, postquam in Laurentino meo aut lego
aliquid aut scribo aut etiam corpori uaco, cuius fulturis
5 animus sustinetur. Nihil audio quod audisse, nihil dico
quod dixisse paeniteat; nemo apud me quemquam sinistris
sermonibus carpit, neminem ipse reprehendo, nisi tamen
me cum parum commode scribo; nulla spe nullo timore
sollicitor, nullis rumoribus inquietor: mecum tantum et
6 cum libellis loquor. O rectam sinceramque uitam! O
dulce otium honestumque ac paene omni negotio pul-
chrius! O mare, o litus, uerum secretumque μουσεῖον,
7 quam multa inuenitis, quam multa dictatis! Proinde tu
quoque strepitum istum inanemque discursum et multum
ineptos labores, ut primum fuerit occasio, relinque teque

studiis uel otio trade. Satius est enim, ut Atilius noster 8
eruditissime simul et facetissime dixit, otiosum esse quam
nihil agere. Vale.

LETTER 4

A philosopher

C. PLINIVS ATTIO CLEMENTI SVO S.

SI quando urbs nostra liberalibus studiis floruit, nunc 1
maxime floret. Multa claraque exempla sunt; sufficeret 2
unum, Euphrates philosophus. Hunc ego in Syria, cum
adulescentulus militarem, penitus et domi inspexi, amari-
que ab eo laboraui, etsi non erat laborandum. Est enim
obuius et expositus, plenusque humanitate quam prae-
cipit. Atque utinam sic ipse quam spem tunc ille de me 3
concepit impleuerim, ut ille multum uirtutibus suis addi-
dit! aut ego nunc illas magis miror quia magis intellego.
Quamquam ne nunc quidem satis intellego; ut enim de 4
pictore scalptore fictore nisi artifex iudicare, ita nisi
sapiens non potest perspicere sapientem. Quantum tamen 5
mihi cernere datur, multa in Euphrate sic eminent et
elucent, ut mediocriter quoque doctos aduertant et ad-
ficiant. Disputat subtiliter grauiter ornate, frequenter
etiam Platonicam illam sublimitatem et latitudinem effin-
git. Sermo est copiosus et uarius, dulcis in primis, et qui
repugnantes quoque ducat impellat. Ad hoc proceritas 6
corporis, decora facies, demissus capillus, ingens et cana
barba; quae licet fortuita et inania putentur, illi tamen
plurimum uenerationis adquirunt. Nullus horror in cultu, 7

nulla tristitia, multum seueritatis; reuerearis occursum,
non reformides. Vitae sanctitas summa; comitas par: in-
sectatur uitia non homines, nec castigat errantes sed emendat. Sequaris monentem attentus et pendens, et persuaderi
8 tibi etiam cum persuaserit cupias. Iam uero liberi tres,
duo mares, quos diligentissime instituit. Socer Pompeius
Iulianus, cum cetera uita tum uel hoc uno magnus et
clarus, quod ipse prouinciae princeps inter altissimas condiciones generum non honoribus principem, sed sapientia
elegit.

9 Quamquam quid ego plura de uiro quo mihi frui non
licet? an ut magis angar quod non licet? Nam distringor
officio, ut maximo sic molestissimo: sedeo pro tribunali,
subnoto libellos, conficio tabulas, scribo plurimas sed
10 inlitteratissimas litteras. Soleo non numquam (nam id
ipsum quando contingit!) de his occupationibus apud
Euphraten queri. Ille me consolatur, adfirmat etiam esse
hanc philosophiae et quidem pulcherrimam partem, agere
negotium publicum, cognoscere iudicare, promere et
exercere iustitiam, quaeque ipsi doceant in usu habere.
11 Mihi tamen hoc unum non persuadet, satius esse ista
facere quam cum illo dies totos audiendo discendoque
consumere. Quo magis te cui uacat hortor, cum in urbem
proxime ueneris (uenias autem ob hoc maturius), illi te
12 expoliendum limandumque permittas. Neque enim ego
ut multi inuideo aliis bono quo ipse careo, sed contra:
sensum quendam uoluptatemque percipio, si ea quae mihi
denegantur amicis uideo superesse. Vale.

LETTER 5

A Roman suicide

C. PLINIVS CALESTRIO TIRONI SVO S.

IACTVRAM grauissimam feci, si iactura dicenda est tanti 1
uiri amissio. Decessit Corellius Rufus et quidem sponte,
quod dolorem meum exulcerat. Est enim luctuosissimum
genus mortis, quae non ex natura nec fatalis uidetur.
Nam utcumque in illis qui morbo finiuntur, magnum ex 2
ipsa necessitate solacium est; in iis uero quos accersita
mors aufert, hic insanabilis dolor est, quod creduntur
potuisse diu uiuere. Corellium quidem summa ratio, quae 3
sapientibus pro necessitate est, ad hoc consilium compulit,
quamquam plurimas uiuendi causas habentem, optimam
conscientiam optimam famam, maximam auctoritatem,
praeterea filiam uxorem nepotem sorores, interque tot
pignora ueros amicos. Sed tam longa, tam iniqua ualetu- 4
dine conflictabatur, ut haec tanta pretia uiuendi mortis
rationibus uincerentur. Tertio et tricensimo anno, ut
ipsum audiebam, pedum dolore correptus est. Patrius hic
illi; nam plerumque morbi quoque per successiones quasdam ut alia traduntur. Hunc abstinentia sanctitate, quoad 5
uiridis aetas, uicit et fregit; nouissime cum senectute in-
grauescentem uiribus animi sustinebat, cum quidem in-
credibiles cruciatus et indignissima tormenta pateretur.
Iam enim dolor non pedibus solis ut prius insidebat, sed 6
omnia membra peruagabatur. Veni ad eum Domitiani
temporibus in suburbano iacentem. Serui e cubiculo re- 7
cesserunt (habebat hoc moris, quotiens intrasset fidelior

amicus); quin etiam uxor quamquam omnis secreti capa-
8 cissima digrediebatur'. Circumtulit oculos et 'Cur' inquit
'me putas hos tantos dolores tam diu sustinere? ut scilicet
isti latroni uel uno die supersim.' Dedisses huic animo par
corpus, fecisset quod optabat. Adfuit tamen deus uoto,
cuius ille compos ut iam securus liberque moriturus,
9 multa illa uitae sed minora retinacula abrupit. Increuerat
ualetudo, quam temperantia mitigare temptauit; perseuerantem constantia fugit. Iam dies alter tertius quartus:
abstinebat cibo. Misit ad me uxor eius Hispulla com-
munem amicum C. Geminium cum tristissimo nuntio,
destinasse Corellium mori nec aut suis aut filiae precibus
inflecti; solum superesse me, a quo reuocari posset ad
10 uitam. Cucurri. Perueneram in proximum, cum mihi ab
eadem Hispulla Iulius Atticus nuntiat nihil iam ne me
quidem impetraturum: tam obstinate magis ac magis
induruisse. Dixerat sane medico admouenti cibum:
Κέκρικα, quae uox quantum admirationis in animo
11 meo tantum desiderii reliquit. Cogito quo amico, quo uiro
caream. Impleuit quidem annum septimum et sexagensi-
mum, quae aetas etiam robustissimis satis longa est; scio.
Euasit perpetuam ualetudinem; scio. Decessit superstitibus
suis, florente re publica, quae illi omnibus carior erat; et
12 hoc scio. Ego tamen tamquam et iuuenis et firmissimi
mortem doleo, doleo autem (licet me imbecillum putes)
meo nomine. Amisi enim, amisi uitae meae testem recto-
rem magistrum. In summa dicam, quod recenti dolore
contubernali meo Caluisio dixi: 'Vereor ne neglegentius
13 uiuam.' Proinde adhibe solacia mihi, non haec: 'Senex
erat, infirmus erat' (haec enim noui), sed noua aliqua, sed
magna, quae audierim numquam, legerim numquam.

Nam quae audiui quae legi sponte succurrunt, sed tanto dolore superantur. Vale.

LETTER 6

The state of literature

C. PLINIVS SOSIO SENECIONI SVO S.

MAGNVM prouentum poetarum annus hic attulit: toto 1 mense Aprili nullus fere dies, quo non recitaret aliquis. Iuuat me quod uigent studia, proferunt se ingenia hominum et ostentant, tametsi ad audiendum pigre coitur. Plerique in stationibus sedent tempusque audiendi fabulis 2 conterunt, ac subinde sibi nuntiari iubent, an iam recitator intrauerit, an dixerit praefationem, an ex magna parte euoluerit librum; tum demum ac tunc quoque lente cunctanterque ueniunt, nec tamen permanent, sed ante finem recedunt, alii dissimulanter et furtim, alii simpliciter et libere. At hercule memoria parentum Claudium Caesarem 3 ferunt, cum in Palatio spatiaretur audissetque clamorem, causam requisisse, cumque dictum esset recitare Nonianum, subitum recitanti inopinatumque uenisse. Nunc 4 otiosissimus quisque multo ante rogatus et identidem admonitus aut non uenit aut, si uenit, queritur se diem (quia non perdidit) perdidisse. Sed tanto magis laudandi pro- 5 bandique sunt, quos a scribendi recitandique studio haec auditorum uel desidia uel superbia non retardat. Equidem prope nemini defui. Erant sane plerique amici; neque 6 enim est fere quisquam, qui studia, ut non simul et nos amet. His ex causis longius quam destinaueram tempus in urbe consumpsi. Possum iam repetere secessum et scribere aliquid, quod non recitem, ne uidear, quorum recitationibus adfui, non auditor fuisse sed creditor. Nam ut in ceteris rebus ita in audiendi officio perit gratia si reposcatur. Vale.

LETTER 7

A polite party

C. PLINIVS SEPTICIO CLARO SVO S.

1 Hevs tu! promittis ad cenam, nec uenis? Dicitur ius: ad
2 assem impendium reddes, nec id modicum. Paratae erant lactucae singulae, cochleae ternae, oua bina, halica cum mulso et niue (nam hanc quoque computabis, immo hanc in primis quae perit in ferculo), oliuae betacei cucurbitae bulbi, alia mille non minus lauta. Audisses comoedos uel
3 lectorem uel lyristen uel (quae mea liberalitas) omnes. At tu apud nescio quem ostrea uuluas echinos Gaditanas maluisti. Dabis poenas, non dico quas. Dure fecisti: inuidisti, nescio an tibi, certe mihi, sed tamen et tibi.
4 Quantum nos lusissemus risissemus studuissemus! Potes adparatius cenare apud multos, nusquam hilarius simplicius incautius. In summa experire, et nisi postea te aliis potius excusaueris, mihi semper excusa. Vale.

LETTER 8

Death of a former hero

C. PLINIVS ROMANO SVO S.

POST aliquot annos insigne atque etiam memorabile 1
populi Romani oculis spectaculum exhibuit publicum
funus Vergini Rufi, maximi et clarissimi ciuis, perinde
felicis. Triginta annis gloriae suae superuixit; legit scripta 2
de se carmina, legit historias et posteritati suae interfuit.
Perfunctus est tertio consulatu, ut summum fastigium
priuati hominis impleret, cum principis noluisset. Caesares 3
quibus suspectus atque etiam inuisus uirtutibus fuerat
euasit, reliquit incolumem optimum atque amicissimum,
tamquam ad hunc ipsum honorem publici funeris re-
seruatus. Annum tertium et octogensimum excessit in 4
altissima tranquillitate, pari ueneratione. Vsus est firma
ualetudine, nisi quod solebant ei manus tremere, citra
dolorem tamen. Aditus tantum mortis durior longiorque,
sed hic ipse laudabilis. Nam cum uocem praepararet 5
acturus in consulatu principi gratias, liber quem forte ac-
ceperat grandiorem, et seni et stanti ipso pondere elapsus
est. Hunc dum sequitur colligitque, per leue et lubricum
pauimentum fallente uestigio cecidit coxamque fregit,
quae parum apte collocata reluctante aetate male coiit.

Huius uiri exsequiae magnum ornamentum principi 6
magnum saeculo magnum etiam foro et rostris attulerunt.
Laudatus est a consule Cornelio Tacito; nam hic supremus
felicitati eius cumulus accessit, laudator eloquentissimus.
Et ille quidem plenus annis abît, plenus honoribus, illis 7

etiam quos recusauit: nobis tamen quaerendus ac desi-
derandus est ut exemplar aeui prioris, mihi uero praecipue,
qui illum non solum publice quantum admirabar tantum
8 diligebam; primum quod utrique eadem regio, municipia
finitima, agri etiam possessionesque coniunctae, praeterea
quod ille mihi tutor relictus adfectum parentis exhibuit.
Sic candidatum me suffragio ornauit; sic ad omnes honores
meos ex secessibus accucurrit, cum iam pridem eiusmodi
officiis renuntiasset; sic illo die quo sacerdotes solent
nominare quos dignissimos sacerdotio iudicant, me sem-
9 per nominabat. Quin etiam in hac nouissima ualetudine,
ueritus ne forte inter quinqueuiros crearetur, qui minuendis publicis sumptibus iudicio senatus constituebantur,
cum illi tot amici senes consularesque superessent, me
huius aetatis per quem excusaretur elegit, his quidem
uerbis: 'Etiam si filium haberem, tibi mandarem.'
10   Quibus ex causis necesse est tamquam immaturam mortem eius in sinu tuo defleam, si tamen fas est aut flere aut
omnino mortem uocare, qua tanti uiri mortalitas magis
11 finita quam uita est. Viuit enim uiuetque semper, atque
etiam latius in memoria hominum et sermone uersabitur,
12 postquam ab oculis recessit. Volo tibi multa alia scribere,
sed totus animus in hac una contemplatione defixus est.
Verginium cogito, Verginium uideo, Verginium iam
uanis imaginibus, recentibus tamen, audio adloquor teneo;
cui fortasse ciues aliquos uirtutibus pares et habemus et
habebimus, gloria neminem. Vale.

A vulgar dinner-party

C. PLINIVS AVITO SVO S.

LONGVM est altius repetere nec refert, quemadmodum 1
acciderit, ut homo minime familiaris cenarem apud quendam, ut sibi uidebatur, lautum et diligentem, ut mihi,
sordidum simul et sumptuosum. Nam sibi et paucis 2
opima quaedam, ceteris uilia et minuta ponebat. Vinum
etiam paruolis lagunculis in tria genera discripserat, non
ut potestas eligendi, sed ne ius esset recusandi, aliud sibi
et nobis, aliud minoribus amicis (nam gradatim amicos
habet), aliud suis nostrisque libertis. Animaduertit qui 3
mihi proximus recumbebat, et an probarem interrogauit.
Negaui. 'Tu ergo' inquit 'quam consuetudinem sequeris?'
'Eadem omnibus pono; ad cenam enim, non ad notam
inuito cunctisque rebus exaequo, quos mensa et toro
aequaui.' 'Etiamne libertos?' 'Etiam; conuictores enim 4
tunc, non libertos puto.' Et ille: 'Magno tibi constat.'
'Minime.' 'Qui fieri potest?' 'Quia scilicet liberti mei non
idem quod ego bibunt, sed idem ego quod liberti.' Et 5
hercule si gulae temperes, non est onerosum quo utaris
ipse communicare cum pluribus. Illa ergo reprimenda,
illa quasi in ordinem redigenda est, si sumptibus parcas,
quibus aliquanto rectius tua continentia quam aliena con-
tumelia consulas.

Quorsus haec? ne tibi, optimae indolis iuueni, quorun- 6
dam in mensa luxuria specie frugalitatis imponat. Conuenit
autem amori in te meo, quotiens tale aliquid inciderit, sub

7 exemplo praemonere, quid debeas fugere. Igitur memento
nihil magis esse uitandum quam istam luxuriae et sor-
dium nouam societatem; quae cum sint turpissima discreta
ac separata, turpius iunguntur. Vale.

LETTER 10

Trial of a corrupt governor

C. PLINIVS ARRIANO SVO S.

1 SOLET esse gaudio tibi, si quid acti est in senatu dignum
ordine illo. Quamuis enim quietis amore secesseris, insidet
tamen animo tuo maiestatis publicae cura. Accipe ergo
quod per hos dies actum est, personae claritate famosum,
seueritate exempli salubre, rei magnitudine aeternum.
2 Marius Priscus accusantibus Afris quibus pro consule prae-
fuit, omissa defensione iudices petiit. Ego et Cornelius
Tacitus, adesse prouincialibus iussi, existimauimus fidei
nostrae conuenire notum senatui facere excessisse Priscum
immanitate et saeuitia crimina quibus dari iudices possent,
cum ob innocentes condemnandos, interficiendos etiam,
3 pecunias accepisset. Respondit Fronto Catius depreca-
tusque est, ne quid ultra repetundarum legem quaereretur,
omniaque actionis suae uela uir mouendarum lacrimarum
peritissimus quodam uelut uento miserationis impleuit.
4 Magna contentio, magni utrimque clamores aliis cognitionem senatus lege conclusam, aliis liberam solutamque
dicentibus, quantumque admisisset reus, tantum uindi-
5 candum. Nouissime consul designatus Iulius Ferox, uir
rectus et sanctus, Mario quidem iudices interim censuit

dandos, euocandos autem quibus diceretur innocentium poenas uendidisse. Quae sententia non praeualuit modo, 6 sed omnino post tantas dissensiones fuit sola frequens, adnotatumque experimentis, quod fauor et misericordia acres et uehementes primos impetus habent, paulatim consilio et ratione quasi restincta considunt. Vnde euenit ut, 7 quod multi clamore permixto tuentur, nemo tacentibus ceteris dicere uelit; patescit enim, cum separaris a turba, contemplatio rerum quae turba teguntur. Venerunt qui 8 adesse erant iussi, Vitellius Honoratus et Flauius Marcianus; ex quibus Honoratus trecentis milibus exsilium equitis Romani septemque amicorum eius ultimam poenam, Marcianus unius equitis Romani septingentis milibus plura supplicia arguebatur emisse; erat enim fustibus caesus, damnatus in metallum, strangulatus in carcere. Sed 9 Honoratum cognitioni senatus mors opportuna subtraxit, Marcianus inductus est absente Prisco. Itaque Tuccius Cerialis consularis iure senatorio postulauit, ut Priscus certior fieret, siue quia miserabiliorem siue quia inuidiosiorem fore arbitrabatur, si praesens fuisset, siue (quod maxime credo) quia aequissimum erat commune crimen ab utroque defendi, et si dilui non potuisset in utroque puniri.

Dilata res est in proximum senatum, cuius ipse con- 10 spectus augustissimus fuit. Princeps praesidebat (erat enim consul), ad hoc Ianuarius mensis cum cetera tum praecipue senatorum frequentia celeberrimus; praeterea causae amplitudo auctaque dilatione exspectatio et fama, insitumque mortalibus studium magna et inusitata noscendi, omnes undique exciuerat. Imaginare quae sollicitudo 11 nobis, qui metus, quibus super tanta re in illo coetu praesente Caesare dicendum erat. Equidem in senatu non

semel egi, quin immo nusquam audiri benignius soleo:
tunc me tamen ut noua omnia nouo metu permouebant.
12 Obuersabatur praeter illa quae supra dixi causae difficul-
tas: stabat modo consularis, modo septemuir epulonum,
13 iam neutrum. Erat ergo perquam onerosum accusare
damnatum, quem ut premebat atrocitas criminis, ita
14 quasi peractae damnationis miseratio tuebatur. Vtcumque
tamen animum cogitationemque collegi, coepi dicere non
minore audientium adsensu quam sollicitudine mea. Dixi
horis paene quinque; nam duodecim clepsydris, quas
spatiosissimas acceperam, sunt additae quattuor. Adeo illa
ipsa, quae dura et aduersa dicturo uidebantur, secunda
15 dicenti fuerunt. Caesar quidem tantum mihi studium,
tantam etiam curam (nimium est enim dicere sollici-
tudinem) praestitit, ut libertum meum post me stantem
saepius admoneret uoci laterique consulerem, cum me
uehementius putaret intendi, quam gracilitas mea perpeti
posset. Respondit mihi pro Marciano Claudius Marcel-
16 linus. Missus deinde senatus et reuocatus in posterum;
neque enim iam incohari poterat actio, nisi ut noctis
interuentu scinderetur.

17 Postero die dixit pro Mario Saluius Liberalis, uir sub-
tilis dispositus acer disertus; in illa uero causa omnes artes
suas protulit. Respondit Cornelius Tacitus eloquentissime
18 et, quod eximium orationi eius inest, σεμνῶς. Dixit pro
Mario rursus Fronto Catius insigniter, utque iam locus
ille poscebat, plus in precibus temporis quam in defensione consumpsit. Huius actionem uespera inclusit, non
tamen sic ut abrumperet. Itaque in tertium diem probationes exierunt. Iam hoc ipsum pulchrum et antiquum,
senatum nocte dirimi, triduo uocari, triduo contineri.

Cornutus Tertullus consul designatus, uir egregius et pro 19
ueritate firmissimus, censuit septingenta milia quae ac-
ceperat Marius aerario inferenda, Mario urbe Italiaque
interdicendum, Marciano hoc amplius Africa. In fine
sententiae adiecit, quod ego et Tacitus iniuncta aduoca-
tione diligenter et fortiter functi essemus, arbitrari senatum ita nos fecisse ut dignum mandatis partibus fuerit.
Adsenserunt consules designati, omnes etiam consulares 20
usque ad Pompeium Collegam: ille et septingenta milia
aerario inferenda et Marcianum in quinquennium rele-
gandum, Marium repetundarum poenae quam iam passus
esset censuit relinquendum. Erant in utraque sententia 21
multi, fortasse etiam plures in hac uel solutiore uel molliore. Nam quidam ex illis quoque, qui Cornuto uidebantur adsensi, hunc qui post ipsos censuerat sequebantur.
Sed cum fieret discessio, qui sellis consulum adstiterant, in 22
Cornuti sententiam ire coeperunt. Tum illi qui se Collegae
adnumerari patiebantur in diuersum transierunt; Collega
cum paucis relictus. Multum postea de impulsoribus suis,
praecipue de Regulo questus est, qui se in sententia quam
ipse dictauerat deseruisset. Est alioqui Regulo tam mobile
ingenium, ut plurimum audeat plurimum timeat.

Hic finis cognitionis amplissimae. Superest tamen 23
λειτούργιον non leue, Hostilius Firminus legatus Mari
Prisci, qui permixtus causae grauiter uehementerque uexa-
tus est. Nam et rationibus Marciani, et sermone quem ille
habuerat in ordine Lepcitanorum, operam suam Prisco ad
turpissimum ministerium commodasse, stipulatusque de
Marciano quinquaginta milia denariorum probabatur,
ipse praeterea accepisse sestertia decem milia foedissimo
quidem titulo, nomine unguentarii, qui titulus a uita

hominis compti semper et pumicati non abhorrebat.
24 Placuit censente Cornuto referri de eo proximo senatu;
tunc enim, casu an conscientia, afuerat.

25   Habes res urbanas; inuicem rusticas scribe. Quid arbu-
sculae tuae, quid uineae, quid segetes agunt, quid oues
delicatissimae? In summa, nisi aeque longam epistulam
reddis, non est quod postea nisi breuissimam exspectes.
Vale.

LETTER 11

The legacy hunter

C. PLINIVS CALVISIO SVO S.

1 ASSEM para et accipe auream fabulam, fabulas immo;
nam me priorum noua admonuit, nec refert a qua potissi-
2 mum incipiam. Verania Pisonis grauiter iacebat, huius
dico Pisonis, quem Galba adoptauit. Ad hanc Regulus
uenit. Primum impudentiam hominis, qui uenerit ad
aegram, cuius marito inimicissimus, ipsi inuisissimus
3 fuerat! Esto, si uenit tantum; at ille etiam proximus toro
sedit, quo die qua hora nata esset interrogauit. Vbi audiit,
componit uultum intendit oculos movet labra, agitat digitos computat. Nihil. Vt diu miseram exspectatione sus-
pendit, 'Habes' inquit 'climactericum tempus sed euades.
4 Quod ut tibi magis liqueat, haruspicem consulam, quem
5 sum frequenter expertus.' Nec mora, sacrificium facit,
adfirmat exta cum siderum significatione congruere. Illa
ut in periculo credula poscit codicillos, legatum Regulo
scribit. Mox ingrauescit, clamat moriens hominem nequam
perfidum ac plus etiam quam periurum, qui sibi per

salutem filii peierasset. Facit hoc Regulus non minus 6
scelerate quam frequenter, quod iram deorum, quos ipse
cotidie fallit, in caput infelicis pueri detestatur.

Velleius Blaesus ille locuples consularis nouissima ualetu- 7
dine conflictabatur: cupiebat mutare testamentum. Regulus qui speraret aliquid ex nouis tabulis, quia nuper captare
eum coeperat, medicos hortari rogare, quoquo modo
spiritum homini prorogarent. Postquam signatum est testa- 8
mentum, mutat personam, uertit adlocutionem isdemque
medicis: 'Quousque miserum cruciatis? quid inuidetis bona
morte, cui dare uitam non potestis?' Moritur Blaesus et,
tamquam omnia audisset, Regulo ne tantulum quidem.

Sufficiunt duae fabulae, an scholastica lege tertiam po- 9
scis? est unde fiat. Aurelia ornata femina signatura testa- 10
mentum sumpserat pulcherrimas tunicas. Regulus cum
uenisset ad signandum, 'Rogo' inquit 'has mihi leges.' 11
Aurelia ludere hominem putabat, ille serio instabat; ne
multa, coegit mulierem aperire tabulas ac sibi tunicas quas
erat induta legare; obseruauit scribentem, inspexit an
scripsisset. Et Aurelia quidem uiuit, ille tamen istud tamquam morituram coegit. Et hic hereditates, hic legata
quasi mereatur accipit.

Ἀλλὰ τί διατείνομαι in ea ciuitate, in qua iam pridem 12
non minora praemia, immo maiora nequitia et improbitas
quam pudor et uirtus habent? Adspice Regulum, qui ex 13
paupere et tenui ad tantas opes per flagitia processit, ut
ipse mihi dixerit, cum consuleret quam cito sestertium
sescentiens impleturus esset, inuenisse se exta duplicia,
quibus portendi miliens et ducentiens habiturum. Et habe- 14
bit, si modo ut coepit, aliena testamenta, quod est impro-
bissimum genus falsi, ipsis quorum sunt illa dictauerit. Vale.

LETTER 12

Promotion of a friend

C. PLINIVS VIBIO MAXIMO SVO S.

1 QVOD ipse amicis tuis obtulissem, si mihi eadem materia
2 suppeteret, id nunc iure uideor a te meis petiturus. Arrianus Maturus Altinatium est princeps; cum dico princeps, non de facultatibus loquor, quae illi large supersunt,
3 sed de castitate iustitia, grauitate prudentia. Huius ego
consilio in negotiis, iudicio in studiis utor; nam plurimum fide, plurimum ueritate, plurimum intellegentia
4 praestat. Amat me (nihil possum ardentius dicere) ut tu.
Caret ambitu; ideo se in equestri gradu tenuit, cum facile
possit ascendere altissimum. Mihi tamen ornandus excolen-
5 dusque est. Itaque magni aestimo dignitati eius aliquid
adstruere inopinantis nescientis, immo etiam fortasse
nolentis; adstruere autem quod sit splendidum nec mole-
6 stum. Cuius generis quae prima occasio tibi, conferas in
eum rogo; habebis me, habebis ipsum gratissimum debito-
rem. Quamuis enim ista non adpetat, tam grate tamen
excipit, quam si concupiscat. Vale.

LETTER 13

The life of a public official

C. PLINIVS BAEBIO MACRO SVO S.

1 PERGRATVM est mihi quod tam diligenter libros auunculi
mei lectitas, ut habere omnes uelis quaerasque qui sint
2 omnes. Fungar indicis partibus, atque etiam quo sint

ordine scripti notum tibi faciam; est enim haec quoque
studiosis non iniucunda cognitio. 'De iaculatione equestri 3
unus'; hunc cum praefectus alae militaret, pari ingenio
curaque composuit. 'De uita Pomponi Secundi duo'; a
quo singulariter amatus hoc memoriae amici quasi debi-
tum munus exsoluit. 'Bellorum Germaniae uiginti'; qui- 4
bus omnia quae cum Germanis gessimus bella collegit.
Incohauit cum in Germania militaret, somnio monitus:
adstitit ei quiescenti Drusi Neronis effigies, qui Germaniae
latissime uictor ibi periit, commendabat memoriam suam
orabatque ut se ab iniuria obliuionis adsereret. 'Studiosi 5
tres', in sex uolumina propter amplitudinem diuisi, quibus oratorem ab incunabulis instituit et perficit. 'Dubii
sermonis octo': scripsit sub Nerone nouissimis annis, cum
omne studiorum genus paulo liberius et erectius periculosum seruitus fecisset. 'A fine Aufidi Bassi triginta unus.' 6
'Naturae historiarum triginta septem', opus diffusum eruditum, nec minus uarium quam ipsa natura.

Miraris quod tot uolumina multaque in his tam scrupu- 7
losa homo occupatus absoluerit? Magis miraberis si scieris
illum aliquamdiu causas actitasse, decessisse anno sexto et
quinquagensimo, medium tempus distentum impedi-
tumque qua officiis maximis qua amicitia principum
egisse. Sed erat acre ingenium, incredibile studium, 8
summa uigilantia. Lucubrare Vulcanalibus incipiebat non
auspicandi causa sed studendi statim a nocte multa, hieme
uero ab hora septima uel cum tardissime octaua, saepe
sexta. Erat sane somni paratissimi, non numquam etiam
inter ipsa studia instantis et deserentis. Ante lucem ibat ad 9
Vespasianum imperatorem (nam ille quoque noctibus
utebatur), inde ad delegatum sibi officium. Reuersus

10 domum quod reliquum temporis studiis reddebat. Post
cibum saepe (quem interdiu leuem et facilem ueterum
more sumebat) aestate si quid otii iacebat in sole, liber
legebatur, adnotabat excerpebatque. Nihil enim legit
quod non excerperet; dicere etiam solebat nullum esse
11 librum tam malum ut non aliqua parte prodesset. Post
solem plerumque frigida lauabatur, deinde gustabat dor-
miebatque minimum; mox quasi alio die studebat in
cenae tempus. Super hanc liber legebatur adnotabatur, et
12 quidem cursim. Memini quendam ex amicis, cum lector
quaedam perperam pronuntiasset, reuocasse et repeti
coegisse; huic auunculum meum dixisse: 'Intellexeras
nempe?' Cum ille adnuisset, 'Cur ergo reuocabas? decem
13 amplius uersus hac tua interpellatione perdidimus.' Tanta
erat parsimonia temporis. Surgebat aestate a cena luce,
hieme intra primam noctis et tamquam aliqua lege
cogente.

14   Haec inter medios labores urbisque fremitum. In secessu
solum balinei tempus studiis eximebatur (cum dico balinei,
de interioribus loquor; nam dum destringitur tergitur-
15 que, audiebat aliquid aut dictabat). In itinere quasi
solutus ceteris curis, huic uni uacabat: ad latus notarius
cum libro et pugillaribus, cuius manus hieme manicis
muniebantur, ut ne caeli quidem asperitas ullum studii
tempus eriperet; qua ex causa Romae quoque sella uehe-
16 batur. Repeto me correptum ab eo, cur ambularem:
'poteras' inquit 'has horas non perdere'; nam perire omne
17 tempus arbitrabatur, quod studiis non impenderetur. Hac
intentione tot ista uolumina peregit electorumque commentarios centum sexaginta mihi reliquit, opisthographos
quidem et minutissimis scriptos; qua ratione multiplicatur

hic numerus.) Referebat ipse potuisse se, cum procuraret in Hispania, uendere hos commentarios Larcio
Licino quadringentis milibus nummum; et tunc aliquanto
pauciores erant. Nonne uidetur tibi recordanti, quantum 18
legerit quantum scripserit, nec in officiis ullis nec in amicitia principis fuisse; rursus cum audis quid studiis laboris
impenderit, nec scripsisse satis nec legisse? Quid est enim
quod non aut illae occupationes impedire aut haec instantia non possit efficere? Itaque soleo ridere cum me 19
quidam studiosum uocant, qui si comparer illi sum desi-
diosissimus. Ego autem tantum, quem partim publica
partim amicorum officia distringunt? quis ex istis, qui tota
uita litteris adsident, collatus illi non quasi somno et
inertiae deditus erubescat?

Extendi epistulam cum hoc solum quod requirebas 20
scribere destinassem, quos libros reliquisset; confido tamen
haec quoque tibi non minus grata quam ipsos libros
futura, quae te non tantum ad legendos eos uerum etiam
ad simile aliquid elaborandum possunt aemulationis stimu-
lis excitare. Vale.

LETTER 14

Murder of a master

C. PLINIVS ACILIO SVO S.

REM atrocem nec tantum epistula dignam Larcius Macedo 1
uir praetorius a seruis suis passus est, superbus alioqui
dominus et saeuus, et qui seruisse patrem suum parum,
immo nimium meminisset. Lauabatur in uilla Formiana. 2

Repente eum serui circumsistunt. Alius fauces inuadit,
alius os uerberat, alius pectus et uentrem, atque etiam
(foedum dictu) uerenda contundit; et cum exanimem
putarent, abiciunt in feruens pauimentum, ut experirentur
an uiueret. Ille siue quia non sentiebat, siue quia se non
sentire simulabat, immobilis et extentus fidem peractae
3 mortis impleuit. Tum demum quasi aestu solutus effer-
tur; excipiunt serui fideliores, concubinae cum ululatu et
clamore concurrunt. Ita et uocibus excitatus et recreatus
loci frigore sublatis oculis agitatoque corpore uiuere se (et
4 iam tutum erat) confitetur. Diffugiunt serui; quorum
magna pars comprehensa est, ceteri requiruntur. Ipse
paucis diebus aegre focilatus non sine ultionis solacio de-
5 cessit ita uiuus uindicatus, ut occisi solent. Vides quot
periculis quot contumeliis quot ludibriis simus obnoxii;
nec est quod quisquam possit esse securus, quia sit remissus
et mitis; non enim iudicio domini sed scelere perimuntur.
6   Verum haec hactenus. Quid praeterea noui? Quid?
Nihil, alioqui subiungerem; nam et charta adhuc superest,
et dies feriatus patitur plura contexi. Addam quod opportune de eodem Macedone succurrit. Cum in publico
Romae lauaretur, notabilis atque etiam, ut exitus docuit,
7 ominosa res accidit. Eques Romanus a seruo eius, ut
transitum daret, manu leuiter admonitus conuertit se nec
seruum, a quo erat tactus, sed ipsum Macedonem tam
8 grauiter palma percussit ut paene concideret. Ita balineum
illi quasi per gradus quosdam primum contumeliae locus,
deinde exitii fuit. Vale.

LETTER 15

Portrait of a heroine

C. PLINIVS NEPOTI SVO S.

ADNOTASSE uideor facta dictaque uirorum feminarum- 1
que alia clariora esse alia maiora. Confirmata est opinio 2
mea hesterno Fanniae sermone. Neptis haec Arriae illius,
quae marito et solacium mortis et exemplum fuit. Multa
referebat auiae suae non minora hoc sed obscuriora; quae
tibi existimo tam mirabilia legenti fore, quam mihi
audienti fuerunt. Aegrotabat Caecina Paetus maritus eius, 3
aegrotabat et filius, uterque mortifere, ut uidebatur. Filius
decessit eximia pulchritudine pari uerecundia, et parentibus non minus ob alia carus quam quod filius erat. Huic 4
illa ita funus parauit, ita duxit exsequias, ut ignoraret
maritus; quin immo quotiens cubiculum eius intraret,
uiuere filium atque etiam commodiorem esse simulabat,
ac persaepe interroganti, quid ageret puer, respondebat:
'Bene quieuit, libenter cibum sumpsit.' Deinde, cum diu 5
cohibitae lacrimae uincerent prorumperentque, egrediebatur; tunc se dolori dabat; satiata siccis oculis composito
uultu redibat, tamquam orbitatem foris reliquisset. Prae- 6
clarum quidem illud eiusdem, ferrum stringere, perfodere
pectus, extrahere pugionem, porrigere marito, addere
uocem immortalem ac paene diuinam: 'Paete, non dolet.'
Sed tamen ista facienti, ista dicenti, gloria et aeternitas
ante oculos erant; quo maius est sine praemio aeternitatis,
sine praemio gloriae, abdere lacrimas operire luctum,
amissoque filio matrem adhuc agere!

7 Scribonianus arma in Illyrico contra Claudium mouerat;
fuerat Paetus in partibus, et occiso Scriboniano Romam
8 trahebatur. Erat ascensurus nauem; Arria milites orabat,
ut simul imponeretur. 'Nempe enim' inquit 'daturi estis
consulari uiro seruolos aliquos, quorum e manu cibum
capiat, a quibus uestiatur, a quibus calcietur; omnia sola
9 praestabo.' Non impetrauit: conduxit piscatoriam naucu-
lam, ingensque nauigium minimo secuta est) Eadem apud
Claudium uxori Scriboniani, cum illa profiteretur indicium, 'Ego' inquit 'te audiam, cuius in gremio Scribonianus occisus est, et uiuis?' Ex quo manifestum est ei
10 consilium pulcherrimae mortis non subitum fuisse. Quin
etiam, cum Thrasea gener eius deprecaretur, ne mori pergeret, interque alia dixisset: 'Vis ergo filiam tuam, si mihi
pereundum fuerit, mori mecum?', respondit: 'Si tam diu
tantaque concordia uixerit tecum quam ego cum Paeto,
11 uolo.' Auxerat hoc responso curam suorum; attentius
custodiebatur; sensit et 'Nihil agitis' inquit; 'potestis enim
12 efficere ut male moriar, ut non moriar non potestis.' Dum
haec dicit, exsiluit cathedra aduersoque parieti caput in-
genti impetu impegit et corruit. Focilata 'Dixeram' inquit
'uobis inuenturam me quamlibet duram ad mortem
13 uiam, si uos facilem negassetis.') Videnturne haec tibi
maiora illo 'Paete, non dolet', ad quod per haec peruen-
tum est? cum interim illud quidem ingens fama, haec
nulla circumfert. Vnde colligitur, quod initio dixi, alia
esse clariora alia maiora. Vale.

LETTER 16

On buying an estate

C. PLINIVS CALVISIO RVFO SVO S.

ADSVMO te in consilium rei familiaris, ut soleo. Praedia 1
agris meis uicina atque etiam inserta uenalia sunt. In his me
multa sollicitant, aliqua nec minora deterrent. Sollicitat 2
primum ipsa pulchritudo iungendi; deinde, quod non
minus utile quam uoluptuosum, posse utraque eadem
opera eodem uiatico inuisere, sub eodem procuratore ac
paene isdem actoribus habere, unam uillam colere et
ornare, alteram tantum tueri. Inest huic computationi 3
sumptus supellectilis, sumptus atriensium topiariorum
fabrorum atque etiam uenatorii instrumenti; quae plurimum refert unum in locum conferas an in diuersa di-
spergas. Contra uereor ne sit incautum, rem tam magnam 4
isdem tempestatibus isdem casibus subdere; tutius uidetur
incerta fortunae possessionum uarietatibus experiri. Habet
etiam multum iucunditatis soli caelique mutatio, ipsaque
illa peregrinatio inter sua. Iam, quod deliberationis no- 5
strae caput est, agri sunt fertiles pingues aquosi; constant
campis uineis siluis, quae materiam et ex ea reditum sicut
modicum ita statum praestant. Sed haec felicitas terrae 6
imbecillis cultoribus fatigatur. Nam possessor prior saepius uendidit pignora, et dum reliqua colonorum minuit
ad tempus, uires in posterum exhausit, quarum defectione
rursus reliqua creuerunt. Sunt ergo instruendi eo pluris 7
quod frugi mancipiis; nam nec ipse usquam uinctos
habeo nec ibi quisquam. Superest ut scias quanti uideantur

posse emi. Sestertio triciens, non quia non aliquando
quinquagiens fuerint, uerum et hac penuria colonorum et
communi temporis iniquitate ut reditus agrorum sic
8 etiam pretium retro abiit. Quaeris an hoc ipsum triciens
facile colligere possimus. Sum quidem prope totus in
praediis, aliquid tamen fenero, nec molestum erit mutuari;
accipiam a socru, cuius arca non secus ac mea utor.
9 Proinde hoc te non moueat, si cetera non refragantur,
quae uelim quam diligentissime examines. Nam cum in
omnibus rebus tum in disponendis facultatibus plurimum
tibi et usus et prouidentiae superest. Vale.

LETTER 17

A poet retires

C. PLINIVS CORNELIO PRISCO SVO S.

1 AVDIO Valerium Martialem decessisse et moleste fero.
Erat homo ingeniosus acutus acer, et qui plurimum in
scribendo et salis haberet et fellis, nec candoris minus.
2 Prosecutus eram uiatico secedentem; dederam hoc amicitiae, dederam etiam uersiculis quos de me composuit.
3 Fuit moris antiqui, eos qui uel singulorum laudes uel
urbium scripserant, aut honoribus aut pecunia ornare;
nostris uero temporibus ut alia speciosa et egregia, ita hoc
in primis exoleuit. Nam postquam desîmus facere lau-
4 danda, laudari quoque ineptum putamus. Quaeris, qui
sint uersiculi quibus gratiam rettuli? Remitterem te ad
ipsum uolumen, nisi quosdam tenerem; tu, si placuerint
5 hi, ceteros in libro requires. Adloquitur Musam, mandat
ut domum meam Esquilîs quaerat, adeat reuerenter:

Sed ne tempore non tuo disertam
pulses ebria ianuam, uideto.
Totos dat tetricae dies Mineruae,
dum centum studet auribus uirorum
hoc, quod saecula posterique possint
Arpinis quoque comparare chartis.
Seras tutior ibis ad lucernas:
haec hora est tua, cum furit Lyaeus,
cum regnat rosa, cum madent capilli.
Tunc me uel rigidi legant Catones.

Meritone eum qui haec de me scripsit et tunc dimisi 6
amicissime et nunc ut amicissimum defunctum esse doleo?
Dedit enim mihi quantum maximum potuit, daturus
amplius si potuisset. Tametsi quid homini potest dari
maius, quam gloria et laus et aeternitas? At non erunt
aeterna quae scripsit: non erunt fortasse, ille tamen scripsit tamquam essent futura. Vale.

LETTER 18

Hiring a schoolmaster

C. PLINIVS CORNELIO TACITO SVO S.

SALVVM in urbem uenisse gaudeo; uenisti autem, si 1
quando alias, nunc maxime mihi desideratus. Ipse pauculis
adhuc diebus in Tusculano commorabor, ut opusculum
quod est in manibus absoluam. Vereor enim ne, si hanc 2
intensionem iam in fine laxauero, aegre resumam. Interim ne quid festinationi meae pereat, quod sum praesens
petiturus, hac quasi praecursoria epistula rogo. Sed prius

3 accipe causas rogandi, deinde ipsum quod peto. Proxime
cum in patria mea fui, uenit ad me salutandum municipis
mei filius praetextatus. Huic ego 'Studes?' inquam. Respondit: 'Etiam.' 'Vbi?' 'Mediolani.' 'Cur non hic?' Et
pater eius (erat enim una atque etiam ipse adduxerat
puerum): 'Quia nullos hic praeceptores habemus.' 'Quare
4 nullos? Nam uehementer intererat uestra, qui patres estis'
(et opportune complures patres audiebant) 'liberos uestros
hic potissimum discere. Vbi enim aut iucundius moraren-
tur quam in patria aut pudicius continerentur quam sub
5 oculis parentum aut minore sumptu quam domi? Quantu-
lum est ergo collata pecunia conducere praeceptores,
quodque nunc in habitationes, in uiatica, in ea quae
peregre emuntur (omnia autem peregre emuntur) im-
penditis, adicere mercedibus? Atque adeo ego, qui nondum liberos habeo, paratus sum pro re publica nostra,
quasi pro filia uel parente, tertiam partem eius quod con-
6 ferre uobis placebit dare. Totum etiam pollicerer, nisi
timerem ne hoc munus meum quandoque ambitu corrumperetur, ut accidere multis in locis uideo, in quibus
7 praeceptores publice conducuntur. Huic uitio occurri uno
remedio potest, si parentibus solis ius conducendi re-
linquatur, isdemque religio recte iudicandi necessitate col-
8 lationis addatur. Nam qui fortasse de alieno neglegentes,
certe de suo diligentes erunt dabuntque operam, ne a me
pecuniam non nisi dignus accipiat, si accepturus et ab ipsis
9 erit. Proinde consentite conspirate maioremque animum
ex meo sumite, qui cupio esse quam plurimum, quod de-
beam conferre. Nihil honestius praestare liberis uestris,
nihil gratius patriae potestis. Educentur hic qui hic nascun-
tur, statimque ab infantia natale solum amare frequentare

consuescant. Atque utinam tam claros praeceptores indu-
catis, ut in finitimis oppidis studia hinc petantur, utque
nunc liberi uestri aliena in loca ita mox alieni in hunc
locum confluant.'

Haec putaui altius et quasi a fonte repetenda, quo magis 10
scires, quam gratum mihi foret si susciperes quod iniungo.
Iniungo autem et pro rei magnitudine rogo, ut ex copia
studiosorum, quae ad te ex admiratione ingenii tui
conuenit, circumspicias praeceptores, quos sollicitare possimus, sub ea tamen condicione ne cui fidem meam
obstringam. Omnia enim libera parentibus seruo: illi
iudicent illi eligant, ego mihi curam tantum et impendium
uindico. Proinde si quis fuerit repertus, qui ingenio suo 11
fidat, eat illuc ea lege ut hinc nihil aliud certum quam
fiduciam suam ferat. Vale.

LETTER 19

Snapshot of a wife

C. PLINIVS CALPVRNIAE HISPVLLAE SVAE S.

Cvm sis pietatis exemplum, fratremque optimum et 1
amantissimum tui pari caritate dilexeris, filiamque eius ut
tuam diligas, nec tantum amitae ei adfectum uerum etiam
patris amissi repraesentes, non dubito maximo tibi gaudio
fore cum cognoueris dignam patre dignam te dignam auo
euadere. Summum est acumen summa frugalitas; amat 2
me, quod castitatis indicium est. Accedit his studium litterarum, quod ex mei caritate concepit. Meos libellos habet
lectitat ediscit etiam. Qua illa sollicitudine cum uideor 3

acturus, quanto cum egi gaudio adficitur! Disponit qui
nuntient sibi quem adsensum quos clamores excitarim,
quem euentum iudicî tulerim. Eadem, si quando recito,
in proximo discreta uelo sedet, laudesque nostras auidis-
4 simis auribus excipit. Versus quidem meos cantat etiam
formatque cithara non artifice aliquo docente, sed amore
5 qui magister est optimus. His ex causis in spem certissi-
mam adducor, perpetuam nobis maioremque in dies
futuram esse concordiam. Non enim aetatem meam aut
corpus, quae paulatim occidunt ac senescunt, sed gloriam
6 diligit. Nec aliud decet tuis manibus educatam, tuis prae-
ceptis institutam, quae nihil in contubernio tuo uiderit,
nisi sanctum honestumque, quae denique amare me ex
7 tua praedicatione consueuerit. Nam cum matrem meam
parentis loco uererere, me a pueritia statim formare
laudare, talemque qualis nunc uxori meae uideor, ominari
8 solebas. Certatim ergo tibi gratias agimus, ego quod illam
mihi, illa quod me sibi dederis, quasi inuicem elegeris. Vale.

LETTER 20

The Emperor's 'Cabinet'

C. PLINIVS SEMPRONIO RVFO SVO S.

1 INTERFVI principis optimi cognitioni in consilium adsumptus. Gymnicus agon apud Viennenses ex cuiusdam
testamento celebrabatur. Hunc Trebonius Rufinus, uir
egregius nobisque amicus, in duumuiratu tollendum
abolendumque curauit. Negabatur ex auctoritate publica
2 fecisse. Egit ipse causam non minus feliciter quam diserte.
Commendabat actionem, quod tamquam homo Romanus

et bonus ciuis in negotio suo mature et grauiter loquebatur. Cum sententiae perrogarentur, dixit Iunius Mauricus, 3 quo uiro nihil firmius nihil uerius, non esse restituendum Viennensibus agona; adiecit 'Vellem etiam Romae tolli posset.' Constanter, inquis, et fortiter; quidni? sed hoc a 4 Maurico nouum non est. Idem apud imperatorem Neruam non minus fortiter. Cenabat Nerua cum paucis; Veiento proximus atque etiam in sinu recumbebat: dixi omnia cum hominem nominaui. Incidit sermo de Catullo Mes- 5 salino, qui luminibus orbatus ingenio saeuo mala caecitatis addiderat: non uerebatur, non erubescebat, non miserebatur; quo saepius a Domitiano non secus ac tela, quae et ipsa caeca et improuida feruntur, in optimum quemque contorquebatur. De huius nequitia sanguinariisque senten- 6 tiis in commune omnes super cenam loquebantur, cum ipse imperator: 'Quid putamus passurum fuisse si uiueret?' Et Mauricus: 'Nobiscum cenaret.' Longius abii, libens 7 tamen. Placuit agona tolli, qui mores Viennensium infecerat, ut noster hic omnium. Nam Viennensium uitia intra ipsos residunt, nostra late uagantur, utque in corporibus sic in imperio grauissimus est morbus, qui a capite diffunditur. Vale.

LETTER 21

On the force of water

C. PLINIVS LICINIO SVRAE SVO S.

ATTVLI tibi ex patria mea pro munusculo quaestionem 1 altissima ista eruditione dignissimam. Fons oritur in 2 monte, per saxa decurrit, excipitur cenatiuncula manu

facta; ibi paulum retentus in Larium lacum decidit.
3 Huius mira natura: ter in die statis auctibus ac diminu-
tionibus crescit decrescitque. Cernitur id palam et cum
summa uoluptate deprenditur. Iuxta recumbis et uesceris,
atque etiam ex ipso fonte (nam est frigidissimus) potas;
4 interim ille certis dimensisque momentis uel subtrahitur
uel adsurgit. Anulum seu quid aliud ponis in sicco, ad-
luitur sensim ac nouissime operitur, detegitur rursus
paulatimque deseritur. Si diutius obserues, utrumque
5 iterum ac tertio uideas. Spiritusne aliquis occultior os fontis et fauces modo laxat modo includit, prout inlatus
6 occurrit aut decessit expulsus? quod in ampullis ceterisque
generis eiusdem uidemus accidere, quibus non hians nec
statim patens exitus. Nam illa quoque, quamquam prona
atque uergentia, per quasdam obluctantis animae moras
7 crebris quasi singultibus sistunt quod effundunt. An, quae
oceano natura, fonti quoque, quaque ille ratione aut impellitur aut resorbetur, hac modicus hic umor uicibus
8 alternis supprimitur egeritur? An ut flumina, quae in mare
deferuntur, aduersantibus uentis obuioque aestu retor-
quentur, ita est aliquid quod huius fontis excursum reper-
9 cutiat? An latentibus uenis certa mensura, quae dum
colligit quod exhauserat, minor riuus et pigrior; cum col-
10 legit, agilior maiorque profertur? An nescio quod libramentum abditum et caecum, quod cum exinanitum est,
suscitat et elicit fontem; cum repletum, moratur et
11 strangulat? Scrutare tu causas (potes enim), quae tantum
miraculum efficiunt: mihi abunde est, si satis expressi
quod efficitur. Vale.

LETTER 22

Writing history

C. PLINIVS TITINIO CAPITONI SVO S.

SVADES ut historiam scribam, et suades non solus: multi 1
hoc me saepe monuerunt et ego uolo, non quia commode
facturum esse confidam (id enim temere credas nisi expertus), sed quia mihi pulchrum in primis uidetur non
pati occidere, quibus aeternitas debeatur, aliorumque
famam cum sua extendere. Me autem nihil aeque ac 2
diuturnitatis amor et cupido sollicitat, res homine dignis-
sima, eo praesertim qui nullius sibi conscius culpae
posteritatis memoriam non reformidet. Itaque diebus ac 3
noctibus cogito, si 'qua me quoque possim tollere humo';
id enim uoto meo sufficit, illud supra uotum 'uictorque
uirum uolitare per ora'; 'quamquam o—': sed hoc satis
est, quod prope sola historia polliceri uidetur. Orationi 4
enim et carmini parua gratia, nisi eloquentia est summa:
historia quoquo modo scripta delectat. Sunt enim homines
natura curiosi, et quamlibet nuda rerum cognitione
capiuntur, ut qui sermunculis etiam fabellisque ducantur.
Me uero ad hoc studium impellit domesticum quoque
exemplum. Auunculus meus idemque per adoptionem 5
pater historias et quidem religiosissime scripsit. Inuenio
autem apud sapientes honestissimum esse maiorum uesti-
gia sequi, si modo recto itinere praecesserint. Cur ergo
cunctor? Egi magnas et graues causas. Has, etiamsi mihi 6
tenuis ex iis spes, destino retractare, ne tantus ille labor
meus, nisi hoc quod reliquum est studii addidero, mecum

7 pariter intercidat. Nam si rationem posteritatis habeas, quidquid non est peractum, pro non incohato est. Dices: 'Potes simul et rescribere actiones et componere historiam.' Vtinam! sed utrumque tam magnum est, ut 8 abunde sit alterum efficere. Vnodeuicensimo aetatis anno dicere in foro coepi, et nunc demum quid praestare debeat orator, adhuc tamen per caliginem uideo. Quid si 9 huic oneri nouum accesserit? Habet quidem oratio et historia multa communia, sed plura diuersa in his ipsis, quae communia uidentur. Narrat illa narrat haec, sed aliter: huic pleraque humilia et sordida et ex medio petita, illi omnia recondita splendida excelsa conueniunt; 10 hanc saepius ossa musculi nerui, illam tori quidam et quasi iubae decent; haec uel maxime ui amaritudine instantia, illa tractu et suauitate atque etiam dulcedine placet; postremo alia uerba alius sonus alia constructio. 11 Nam plurimum refert, ut Thucydides ait, κτῆμα sit an ἀγώνισμα; quorum alterum oratio, alterum historia est. His ex causis non adducor ut duo dissimilia et hoc ipso diuersa, quo maxima, confundam misceamque, ne tanta quasi colluuione turbatus ibi faciam quod hic debeo; ideoque interim ueniam, ut ne a meis uerbis recedam, 12 aduocandi peto. Tu tamen iam nunc cogita quae potissimum tempora adgrediar. Vetera et scripta aliis? Parata inquisitio, sed onerosa collatio. Intacta et noua? Graues 13 offensae leuis gratia. Nam praeter id, quod in tantis uitiis hominum plura culpanda sunt quam laudanda, tum si laudaueris parcus, si culpaueris nimius fuisse dicaris, 14 quamuis illud plenissime, hoc restrictissime feceris. Sed haec me non retardant; est enim mihi pro fide satis animi: illud peto praesternas ad quod hortaris, eligasque materiam,

ne mihi iam scribere parato alia rursus cunctationis et morae iusta ratio nascatur. Vale.

LETTER 23

A strict judge

C. PLINIVS SEMPRONIO RVFO SVO S.

DESCENDERAM in basilicam Iuliam, auditurus quibus 1 proxima comperendinatione respondere debebam. Sede- 2 bant iudices, decemuiri uenerant, obuersabantur aduocati, silentium longum; tandem a praetore nuntius. Dimittun- tur centumuiri, eximitur dies me gaudente, qui numquam ita paratus sum ut non mora laeter. Causa dilationis Nepos 3 praetor, qui legibus quaerit. Proposuerat breue edictum, admonebat accusatores, admonebat reos exsecuturum se quae senatus consulto continerentur. Suberat edicto sena- 4 tus consultum: hoc omnes qui quid negotii haberent iurare prius quam agerent iubebantur, nihil se ob aduoca- tionem cuiquam dedisse promisisse cauisse. His enim uer- bis ac mille praeterea et uenire aduocationes et emi uetabantur; peractis tamen negotiis permittebatur pecu- niam dumtaxat decem milium dare. Hoc facto Nepotis 5 commotus praetor qui centumuiralibus praesidet, delibera- turus an sequeretur exemplum, inopinatum nobis otium dedit. Interim tota ciuitate Nepotis edictum carpitur 6 laudatur. Multi: 'Inuenimus, qui curua corrigeret! Quid? ante hunc praetores non fuerunt? quis autem hic est, qui emendet publicos mores?' Alii contra: 'Rectissime fecit; initurus magistratum iura cognouit, senatus consulta legit,

reprimit foedissimas pactiones, rem pulcherrimam turpis-
7 sime uenire non patitur.' Tales ubique sermones, qui
tamen alterutram in partem ex euentu praeualebunt. Est
omnino iniquum, sed usu receptum, quod honesta con-
silia uel turpia, prout male aut prospere cedunt, ita uel
probantur uel reprehenduntur. Inde plerumque eadem
facta modo diligentiae modo uanitatis, modo libertatis
modo furoris nomen accipiunt. Vale.

LETTER 24

Illness of a servant

C. PLINIVS VALERIO PAVLINO SVO S.

1 VIDEO quam molliter tuos habeas; quo simplicius tibi
2 confitebor, qua indulgentia meos tractem. Est mihi semper in animo et Homericum illud πατὴρ δ' ὣς ἤπιος ἦεν et
hoc nostrum 'pater familiae'. Quod si essem natura aspe-
rior et durior, frangeret me tamen infirmitas liberti mei
Zosimi, cui tanto maior humanitas exhibenda est, quanto
3 nunc illa magis eget. Homo probus officiosus litteratus; et
ars quidem eius et quasi inscriptio comoedus, in qua plurimum facit. Nam pronuntiat acriter sapienter apte decen-
ter etiam; utitur et cithara perite, ultra quam comoedo
necesse est. Idem tam commode orationes et historias et
4 carmina legit, ut hoc solum didicisse uideatur. Haec tibi
sedulo exposui, quo magis scires, quam multa unus mihi
et quam iucunda ministeria praestaret. Accedit longa iam
5 caritas hominis, quam ipsa pericula auxerunt. Est enim
ita natura comparatum, ut nihil aeque amorem incitet et

accendat quam carendi metus; quem ego pro hoc non
semel patior. Nam ante aliquot annos, dum intente in- 6
stanterque pronuntiat, sanguinem reiecit atque ob hoc in
Aegyptum missus a me post longam peregrinationem
confirmatus redît nuper; deinde dum per continuos dies
nimis imperat uoci, ueteris infirmitatis tussicula admonitus
rursus sanguinem reddidit. Qua ex causa destinaui eum 7
mittere in praedia tua, quae Foro Iulii possides. Audiui
enim te saepe referentem esse ibi et aera salubrem et lac
eiusmodi curationibus accommodatissimum. Rogo ergo 8
scribas tuis, ut illi uilla, ut domus pateat, offerant etiam
sumptibus eius, si quid opus erit. Erit autem opus modico; 9
est enim tam parcus et continens, ut non solum delicias
uerum etiam necessitates ualetudinis frugalitate restringat.
Ego proficiscenti tantum uiatici dabo, quantum sufficiat
eunti in tua. Vale.

LETTER 25

Vesuvius erupts

C. PLINIVS TACITO SVO S.

PETIS ut tibi auunculi mei exitum scribam, quo uerius 1
tradere posteris possis. Gratias ago; nam uideo morti eius
si celebretur a te immortalem gloriam esse propositam.
Quamuis enim pulcherrimarum clade terrarum, ut populi 2
ut urbes memorabili casu, quasi semper uicturus occiderit,
quamuis ipse plurima opera et mansura condiderit, multum tamen perpetuitati eius scriptorum tuorum aeternitas
addet. Equidem beatos puto, quibus deorum munere 3

datum est aut facere scribenda aut scribere legenda, beatissimos uero quibus utrumque.) Horum in numero auunculus meus et suis libris et tuis erit. Quo libentius suscipio, deposco etiam quod iniungis.

4 Erat Miseni classemque imperio praesens regebat. Nonum kal. Septembres hora fere septima mater mea indicat ei adparere nubem inusitata et magnitudine et 5 specie. Vsus ille sole, mox frigida, gustauerat iacens studebatque; poscit soleas, ascendit locum ex quo maxime miraculum illud conspici poterat. Nubes—incertum procul intuentibus ex quo monte (Vesuuium fuisse postea cognitum est)—oriebatur, cuius similitudinem et formam 6 non alia magis arbor quam pinus expresserit. Nam longissimo uelut trunco elata in altum quibusdam ramis diffundebatur, credo quia recenti spiritu euecta, dein senescente eo destituta aut etiam pondere suo uicta in latitudinem uanescebat, candida interdum, interdum sordida et maculosa prout terram cineremue sustulerat. Magnum pro-7 piusque noscendum ut eruditissimo uiro uisum. Iubet liburnicam aptari; mihi si uenire una uellem facit copiam; respondi studere me malle, et forte ipse quod scriberem 8 dederat. Egrediebatur domo; accipit codicillos Rectinae Tasci imminenti periculo exterritae (nam uilla eius subiacebat, nec ulla nisi nauibus fuga): ut se tanto discrimini e-9 riperet orabat. Vertit ille consilium et quod studioso animo incohauerat obit maximo. Deducit quadriremes, ascendit ipse non Rectinae modo sed multis (erat enim frequens 10 amoenitas orae) laturus auxilium. Properat illuc unde alii fugiunt, rectumque cursum recta gubernacula in periculum tenet adeo solutus metu, ut omnes illius mali motus omnes figuras ut deprenderat oculis dictaret enotaretque.

Iam nauibus cinis incidebat, quo propius accederent, 11
calidior et densior; iam pumices etiam nigrique et ambusti et fracti igne lapides; iam uadum subitum ruinaque montis litora obstantia. Cunctatus paulum an retro
flecteret, mox gubernatori ut ita faceret monenti 'Fortes'
inquit 'fortuna iuuat: Pomponianum pete.' Stabiis erat 12
diremptus sinu medio (nam sensim circumactis curua-
tisque litoribus mare infunditur); ibi quamquam nondum
periculo adpropinquante, conspicuo tamen et cum cresceret proximo, sarcinas contulerat in naues, certus fugae
si contrarius uentus resedisset. Quo tunc auunculus meus
secundissimo inuectus, complectitur trepidantem consolatur hortatur, utque timorem eius sua securitate leniret,
deferri in balineum iubet; lotus accubat cenat, aut hilaris
aut (quod aeque magnum) similis hilari. Interim e Vesuuio 13
monte pluribus locis latissimae flammae altaque incendia
relucebant, quorum fulgor et claritas tenebris noctis excitabatur. Ille agrestium trepidatione ignes relictos desertasque uillas per solitudinem ardere in remedium formidinis
dictitabat. Tum se quieti dedit et quieuit uerissimo quidem
somno; nam meatus animae, qui illi propter amplitudinem corporis grauior et sonantior erat, ab iis qui limini
obuersabantur audiebatur. Sed area ex qua diaeta adibatur 14
ita iam cinere mixtisque pumicibus oppleta surrexerat, ut
si longior in cubiculo mora, exitus negaretur. Excitatus
procedit, seque Pomponiano ceterisque qui peruigilauerant
reddit. In commune consultant, intra tecta subsistant an in 15
aperto uagentur. Nam crebris uastisque tremoribus tecta
nutabant, et quasi emota sedibus suis nunc huc nunc illuc
abire aut referri uidebantur. Sub dio rursus quamquam 16
leuium exesorumque pumicum casus metuebatur, quod

tamen periculorum collatio elegit; et apud illum quidem
ratio rationem, apud alios timorem timor uicit.|Ceruicalia
capitibus imposita linteis constringunt; id munimentum
17 aduersus incidentia fuit. Iam dies alibi, illic nox omnibus
noctibus nigrior densiorque; quam tamen faces multae
uariaque lumina soluebant. Placuit egredi in litus, et ex
proximo adspicere, ecquid iam mare admitteret; quod ad-
18 huc uastum et aduersum permanebat. Ibi super abiectum
linteum recubans semel atque iterum frigidam aquam
poposcit hausitque. Deinde flammae flammarumque prae-
nuntius odor sulpuris alios in fugam uertunt, excitant
19 illum. Innitens seruolis duobus adsurrexit et statim con-
cidit, ut ego colligo, crassiore caligine spiritu obstructo,
clausoque stomacho qui illi natura inualidus et angustus et
20 frequenter aestuans erat. Vbi dies redditus (is ab eo quem
nouissime uiderat tertius), corpus inuentum integrum
inlaesum opertumque ut fuerat indutus:\habitus corporis
quiescenti quam defuncto similior.

21 Interim Miseni ego et mater—sed nihil ad historiam,
nec tu aliud quam de exitu eius scire uoluisti. Finem ergo
22 faciam. Vnum adiciam, omnia me quibus interfueram
quaeque statim, cum maxime uera memorantur, audieram,
persecutum. Tu potissima excerpes; aliud est enim epistulam aliud historiam, aliud amico aliud omnibus scribere.
Vale.

LETTER 26

The technique of an orator

C. PLINIVS FVSCO SVO S.

QVAERIS quemadmodum in secessu, quo iam diu frueris, 1
putem te studere oportere. Vtile in primis, et multi prae- 2
cipiunt, uel ex Graeco in Latinum uel ex Latino uertere in
Graecum. Quo genere exercitationis proprietas splen-
dorque uerborum, copia figurarum, uis explicandi, praeterea imitatione optimorum similia inueniendi facultas
paratur; simul quae legentem fefellissent, transferentem
fugere non possunt. Intellegentia ex hoc et iudicium ad- 3
quiritur. Nihil offuerit quae legeris hactenus, ut rem
argumentumque teneas, quasi aemulum scribere lectisque
conferre, ac sedulo pensitare, quid tu quid ille commodius.
Magna gratulatio si non nulla tu, magnus pudor si cuncta
ille melius. Licebit interdum et notissima eligere et cer-
tare cum electis. Audax haec, non tamen improba, quia 4
secreta contentio: quamquam multos uidemus eius modi
certamina sibi cum multa laude sumpsisse, quosque subse-
qui satis habebant, dum non desperant, antecessisse. Poteris 5
et quae dixeris post obliuionem retractare, multa retinere
plura transire, alia interscribere alia rescribere. Laboriosum 6
istud et taedio plenum, sed difficultate ipsa fructuosum,
recalescere ex integro et resumere impetum fractum
omissumque, postremo noua uelut membra peracto corpori intexere nec tamen priora turbare. Scio nunc tibi 7
esse praecipuum studium orandi; sed non ideo semper
pugnacem hunc et quasi bellatorium stilum suaserim. Vt

enim terrae uariis mutatisque seminibus, ita ingenia nostra
8 nunc hac nunc illa meditatione recoluntur. Volo interdum
aliquem ex historia locum adprendas, uolo epistulam
diligentius scribas. Nam saepe in oratione quoque non
historica modo sed prope poetica descriptionum necessitas
9 incidit, et pressus sermo purusque ex epistulis petitur. Fas
est et carmine remitti, non dico continuo et longo (id
enim perfici nisi in otio non potest), sed hoc arguto et
breui, quod apte quantas libet occupationes curasque dis-
10 tinguit. Lusus uocantur; sed hi lusus non minorem interdum gloriam quam seria consequuntur. Atque adeo (cur
enim te ad uersus non uersibus adhorter?)

11   ut laus est cerae, mollis cedensque sequatur
         si doctos digitos iussaque fiat opus
     et nunc informet Martem castamue Mineruam,
         nunc Venerem effingat, nunc Veneris puerum;
     utque sacri fontes non sola incendia sistunt,
         saepe etiam flores uernaque prata iuuant,
     sic hominum ingenium flecti ducique per artes
         non rigidas docta mobilitate decet.

12 Itaque summi oratores, summi etiam uiri sic se aut exerce-
bant aut delectabant, immo delectabant exercebantque.
13 Nam mirum est ut his opusculis animus intendatur remit-
tatur. Recipiunt enim amores odia iras misericordiam
urbanitatem, omnia denique quae in uita atque etiam in
14 foro causisque uersantur. Inest his quoque eadem quae
aliis carminibus utilitas, quod metri necessitate deuincti
soluta oratione laetamur, et quod facilius esse comparatio
ostendit, libentius scribimus.
15 Habes plura etiam fortasse quam requirebas; unum

tamen omisi. Non enim dixi quae legenda arbitrarer:
quamquam dixi, cum dicerem quae scribenda. Tu memi-
neris sui cuiusque generis auctores diligenter eligere.
Aiunt enim multum legendum esse, non multa. Qui sint 16
hi adeo notum probatumque est, ut demonstratione non
egeat; et alioqui tam immodice epistulam extendi, ut
dum tibi quemadmodum studere debeas suadeo, studendi
tempus abstulerim. Quin ergo pugillares resumis, et aliquid ex his uel istud ipsum quod coeperas scribis? Vale.

LETTER 27

On literary recitation

C. PLINIVS CELERI SVO S.

SVA cuique ratio recitandi; mihi quod saepe iam dixi, ut 1
si quid me fugit (ut certe fugit) admonear. Quo magis 2
miror, quod scribis fuisse quosdam qui reprehenderent
quod orationes omnino recitarem; nisi uero has solas non
putant emendandas. A quibus libenter requisierim, cur 3
concedant (si concedunt tamen) historiam debere recitari,
quae non ostentationi sed fidei ueritatique componitur; cur
tragoediam, quae non auditorium sed scaenam et actores; cur lyrica, quae non lectorem sed chorum et lyram
poscunt. At horum recitatio usu iam recepta est. Num 4
ergo culpandus est ille qui coepit? Quamquam orationes
quoque et nostri quidam et Graeci lectitauerunt. Super- 5
uacuum tamen est recitare quae dixeris. Etiam, si eadem
omnia, si isdem omnibus, si statim recites; si uero multa
inseras multa commutes, si quosdam nouos quosdam eosdem sed post tempus adsumas, cur minus probabilis sit

6 causa recitandi quae dixeris quam edendi? Sed difficile est ut oratio dum recitatur satisfaciat. Iam hoc ad laborem 7 recitantis pertinet, non ad rationem non recitandi. Nec uero ego dum recito laudari, sed dum legor cupio. Itaque nullum emendandi genus omitto. Ac primum quae scripsi mecum ipse pertracto; deinde duobus aut tribus lego; mox aliis trado adnotanda, notasque eorum, si dubito, cum uno rursus aut altero pensito; nouissime pluribus 8 recito, ac si quid mihi credis tunc acerrime emendo; nam tanto diligentius quanto sollicitius intendo. Optime autem reuerentia pudor metus iudicant, idque adeo sic habe: Nonne si locuturus es cum aliquo quamlibet docto, uno tamen, minus commoueris quam si cum multis uel in-9 doctis? Nonne cum surgis ad agendum, tunc maxime tibi ipse diffidis, tunc commutata non dico plurima sed omnia cupis? utique si latior scaena et corona diffusior; nam illos 10 quoque sordidos pullatosque reueremur. Nonne si prima quaeque improbari putas, debilitaris et concidis? Opinor, quia in numero ipso est quoddam magnum collatumque consilium, quibusque singulis iudicii parum, omnibus 11 plurimum. Itaque Pomponius Secundus (hic scriptor tragoediarum), si quid forte familiarior amicus tollendum, ipse retinendum arbitraretur, dicere solebat: 'Ad populum prouoco', atque ita ex populi uel silentio uel adsensu aut 12 suam aut amici sententiam sequebatur. Tantum ille populo dabat; recte an secus, nihil ad me. Ego enim non populum aduocare sed certos electosque soleo, quos intuear quibus credam, quos denique et tamquam singulos obseruem et 13 tamquam non singulos timeam. Nam, quod M. Cicero de stilo, ego de metu sentio: timor est, timor emendator asperrimus. Hoc ipsum quod nos recituros cogitamus

emendat; quod auditorium ingredimur emendat; quod pallemus horrescimus circumspicimus emendat. Proinde 14 non paenitet me consuetudinis meae quam utilissimam experior, adeoque non deterreor sermunculis istorum, ut ultro te rogem monstres aliquid quod his addam. Nihil 15 enim curae meae satis est. Cogito quam sit magnum dare aliquid in manus hominum, nec persuadere mihi possum non et cum multis et saepe tractandum, quod placere et semper et omnibus cupias. Vale.

LETTER 28

A charitable gift

C. PLINIVS CANINIO SVO S.

DELIBERAS mecum quemadmodum pecunia, quam muni- 1 cipibus nostris in epulum obtulisti, post te quoque salua sit. Honesta consultatio, non expedita sententia. Numeres rei publicae summam: uerendum est ne dilabatur. Des agros: ut publici neglegentur. Equidem nihil commodius 2 inuenio, quam quod ipse feci. Nam pro quingentis mili- bus nummum, quae in alimenta ingenuorum ingenuarum- que promiseram, agrum ex meis longe pluris actori publico mancipaui; eundem uectigali imposito recepi, tricena milia annua daturus. Per hoc enim et rei publicae 3 sors in tuto nec reditus incertus, et ager ipse propter id quod uectigal large supercurrit, semper dominum a quo exerceatur inueniet. Nec ignoro me plus aliquanto quam 4 donasse uideor erogauisse, cum pulcherrimi agri pretium

5 necessitas uectigalis infregerit. Sed oportet priuatis utili-
tatibus publicas, mortalibus aeternas anteferre, multoque
diligentius muneri suo consulere quam facultatibus. Vale.

LETTER 29

A gay old lady

C. PLINIVS GEMINO SVO S.

1 VMMIDIA Quadratilla paulo minus octogensimo aetatis
anno decessit usque ad nouissimam ualetudinem uiridis,
atque etiam ultra matronalem modum compacto corpore
2 et robusto. Decessit honestissimo testamento: reliquit
heredes ex besse nepotem, ex tertia parte neptem. Neptem
parum noui, nepotem familiarissime diligo, adulescentem
singularem nec iis tantum, quos sanguine attingit, inter
3 propinquos amandum. Ac primum conspicuus forma
omnes sermones malignorum et puer et iuuenis euasit,
intra quartum et uicensimum annum maritus, et si deus
adnuisset pater. Vixit in contubernio auiae delicatae
4 seuerissime, et tamen obsequentissime. Habebat illa pantomimos fouebatque, effusius quam principi feminae conuenit. Hos Quadratus non in theatro, non domi spectabat,
5 nec illa exigebat. Audiui ipsam cum mihi commendaret
nepotis sui studia, solere se, ut feminam in illo otio sexus,
laxare animum lusu calculorum, solere spectare pantomimos suos, sed cum factura esset alterutrum, semper se
nepoti suo praecepisse abiret studeretque; quod mihi non
amore eius magis facere quam reuerentia uidebatur.
6   Miraberis, et ego miratus sum. Proximis sacerdotalibus

ludis, productis in commissione pantomimis, cum simul
theatro ego et Quadratus egrederemur, ait mihi: 'Scis me
hodie primum uidisse saltantem auiae meae libertum?'
Hoc nepos. At hercule alienissimi homines in honorem 7
Quadratillae (pudet me dixisse honorem) per adulationis
officium in theatrum cursitabant exsultabant plaudebant
mirabantur ac deinde singulos gestus dominae cum canticis reddebant; qui nunc exiguissima legata, theatralis
operae corollarium, accipient ab herede, qui non spectabat. Haec, quia soles si quid incidit noui non inuitus 8
audire, deinde quia iucundum est mihi quod ceperam
gaudium scribendo retractare. Gaudeo enim pietate de-
functae, honore optimi iuuenis; laetor etiam quod domus
aliquando C. Cassi, huius qui Cassianae scholae princeps
et parens fuit, seruiet domino non minori. Implebit enim 9
illam Quadratus meus et decebit, rursusque ei pristinam
dignitatem celebritatem gloriam reddet, cum tantus
orator inde procedet, quantus iuris ille consultus. Vale.

LETTER 30
Ghosts

C. PLINIVS SVRAE SVO S.

ET mihi discendi et tibi docendi facultatem otium prae- 1
bet. Igitur perquam uelim scire, esse phantasmata et
habere propriam figuram numenque aliquod putes an
inania et uana ex metu nostro imaginem accipere. Ego ut 2
esse credam in primis eo ducor, quod audio accidisse
Curtio Rufo. Tenuis adhuc et obscurus, obtinenti Africam comes haeserat. Inclinato die spatiabatur in porticu;

offertur ei mulieris figura humana grandior pulchriorque. Perterrito Africam se futurorum praenuntiam dixit: iturum enim Romam honoresque gesturum, atque etiam cum summo imperio in eandem prouinciam reuersurum,
3 ibique moriturum. Facta sunt omnia. Praeterea accedenti Carthaginem egredientique naue eadem figura in litore occurrisse narratur. Ipse certe implicitus morbo futura praeteritis, aduersa secundis auguratus, spem salutis nullo suorum desperante proiecit.

4 Iam illud nonne et magis terribile et non minus mirum
5 est quod exponam ut accepi? Erat Athenis spatiosa et capax domus sed infamis et pestilens. Per silentium noctis sonus ferri, et si attenderes acrius, strepitus uinculorum longius primo, deinde e proximo reddebatur: mox adparebat idolon, senex macie et squalore confectus, promissa barba horrenti capillo; cruribus compedes, manibus
6 catenas gerebat quatiebatque. Inde inhabitantibus tristes diraeque noctes per metum uigilabantur; uigiliam morbus et crescente formidine mors sequebatur. Nam interdiu quoque, quamquam abscesserat imago, memoria imaginis oculis inerrabat, longiorque causis timoris timor erat. Deserta inde et damnata solitudine domus totaque illi monstro relicta; proscribebatur tamen, seu quis emere seu
7 quis conducere ignarus tanti mali uellet. Venit Athenas philosophus Athenodorus, legit titulum auditoque pretio, quia suspecta uilitas, percunctatus omnia docetur ac nihilo minus, immo tanto magis conducit. Vbi coepit aduesperascere, iubet sterni sibi in prima domus parte, poscit pugillares stilum lumen, suos omnes in interiora dimittit; ipse ad scribendum animum oculos manum intendit, ne uacua mens audita simulacra et inanes sibi metus fingeret.

Initio, quale ubique, silentium noctis; dein concuti fer- 8
rum, uincula moueri. Ille non tollere oculos, non remit-
tere stilum, sed offirmare animum auribusque praetendere.
Tum crebrescere fragor, aduentare et iam ut in limine,
iam ut intra limen audiri. Respicit, uidet agnoscitque
narratam sibi effigiem. Stabat innuebatque digito similis 9
uocanti. Hic contra ut paulum exspectaret manu significat
rursusque ceris et stilo incumbit. Illa scribentis capiti
catenis insonabat. Respicit rursus idem quod prius in-
nuentem, nec moratus tollit lumen et sequitur. Ibat illa 10
lento gradu quasi grauis uinçulis. Postquam deflexit in
aream domus, repente dilapsa deserit comitem. Desertus
herbas et folia concerpta signum loco ponit. Postero die 11
adit magistratus, monet ut illum locum effodi iubeant.
Inueniuntur ossa inserta catenis et implicita, quae corpus
aeuo terraque putrefactum nuda et exesa reliquerat uinculis; collecta publice sepeliuntur. Domus postea rite conditis manibus caruit.

Et haec quidem adfirmantibus credo; illud adfirmare 12
aliis possum. Est libertus mihi non inlitteratus. Cum hoc
minor frater eodem lecto quiescebat. Is uisus est sibi cernere quendam in toro residentem, admouentemque capiti
suo cultros, atque etiam ex ipso uertice amputantem
capillos. Vbi inluxit, ipse circa uerticem tonsus, capilli
iacentes reperiuntur. Exiguum temporis medium, et rur- 13
sus simile aliud priori fidem fecit. Puer in paedagogio
mixtus pluribus dormiebat. Venerunt per fenestras (ita
narrat) in tunicis albis duo cubantemque detonderunt et
qua uenerant recesserunt. Hunc quoque tonsum spar-
sosque circa capillos dies ostendit. Nihil notabile secutum, 14
nisi forte quod non fui reus, futurus, si Domitianus sub

quo haec acciderunt diutius uixisset. Nam in scrinio eius
datus a Caro de me libellus inuentus est; ex quo con-
iectari potest, quia reis moris est summittere capillum,
recisos meorum capillos depulsi quod imminebat periculi
signum fuisse.

15 Proinde rogo, eruditionem tuam intendas. Digna res
est quam diu multumque consideres; ne ego quidem
16 indignus, cui copiam scientiae tuae facias. Licet etiam
utramque in partem (ut soles) disputes, ex altera tamen
fortius, ne me suspensum incertumque dimittas, cum mihi
consulendi causa fuerit, ut dubitare desinerem. Vale.

LETTER 31

A political adventure

C. PLINIVS TACITO SVO S.

1 AVGVROR nec me fallit augurium, historias tuas immor-
tales futuras; quo magis illis (ingenue fatebor) inseri cupio.
2 Nam si esse nobis curae solet ut facies nostra ab optimo
quoque artifice exprimatur, nonne debemus optare, ut
operibus nostris similis tui scriptor praedicatorque con-
3 tingat? Demonstro ergo quamquam diligentiam tuam
fugere non possit, cum sit in publicis actis, demonstro
tamen quo magis credas, iucundum mihi futurum si
factum meum, cuius gratia periculo creuit, tuo ingenio
tuo testimonio ornaueris.

4 Dederat me senatus cum Herennio Senecione aduocatum

prouinciae Baeticae contra Baebium Massam, damna-
toque Massa censuerat, ut bona eius publice custodirentur.
Senecio, cum explorasset consules postulationibus uaca-
turos, conuenit me et 'Qua concordia' inquit 'iniunctam
nobis accusationem exsecuti sumus, hac adeamus consules
petamusque, ne bona dissipari sinant, quorum esse in
custodia debent.' Respondi: 'Cum simus aduocati a senatu 5
dati, dispice num peractas putes partes nostras senatus
cognitione finita.' Et ille: 'Tu quem uoles tibi terminum
statues, cui nulla cum prouincia necessitudo nisi ex bene-
ficio tuo et hoc recenti; ipse et natus ibi et quaestor in ea
fui.' Tum ego: 'Si fixum tibi istud ac deliberatum, sequar 6
te ut, si qua ex hoc inuidia, non tantum tua.' Venimus ad 7
consules; dicit Senecio quae res ferebat, aliqua subiungo.
Vixdum conticueramus, et Massa questus Senecionem
non aduocati fidem sed inimici amaritudinem implesse,
impietatis reum postulat. Horror omnium; ego autem 8
'Vereor,' inquam, 'clarissimi consules, ne mihi Massa
silentio suo praeuaricationem obiecerit, quod non et me
reum postulauit.' Quae uox et statim excepta, et postea
multo sermone celebrata est. Diuus quidem Nerua (nam 9
priuatus quoque attendebat his quae recte in publico
fierent) missis ad me grauissimis litteris non mihi solum,
uerum etiam saeculo est gratulatus, cui exemplum (sic
enim scripsit) simile antiquis contigisset. Haec, utcumque 10
se habent, notiora clariora maiora tu facies; quamquam
non exigo ut excedas actae rei modum. Nam nec historia
debet egredi ueritatem, et honeste factis ueritas sufficit.
Vale.

LETTER 32

The fountain

C. PLINIVS ROMANO SVO S.

1 VIDISTINE aliquando Clitumnum fontem? Si nondum
(et puto nondum: alioqui narrasses mihi), uide; quem ego
2 (paenitet tarditatis) proxime uidi. Modicus collis adsurgit,
antiqua cupressu nemorosus et opacus. Hunc subter exit
fons et exprimitur pluribus uenis sed imparibus, eluctatusque quem facit gurgitem lato gremio patescit, purus et
uitreus, ut numerare iactas stipes et relucentes calculos pos-
3 sis. Inde non loci deuexitate, sed ipsa sui copia et quasi
pondere impellitur, fons adhuc et iam amplissimum
flumen, atque etiam nauium patiens; quas obuias quoque
et contrario nisu in diuersa tendentes transmittit et perfert,
adeo ualidus ut illa qua properat ipse, quamquam per
solum planum, remis non adiuuetur, idem aegerrime
4 remis contisque superetur aduersus. Iucundum utrumque
per iocum ludumque fluitantibus, ut flexerint cursum,
laborem otio otium labore uariare. Ripae fraxino multa,
multa populo uestiuntur, quas perspicuus amnis uelut
mersas uiridi imagine adnumerat. Rigor aquae certauerit
5 niuibus, nec color cedit. Adiacet templum priscum et
religiosum. Stat Clitumnus ipse amictus ornatusque praetexta; praesens numen atque etiam fatidicum indicant
sortes. Sparsa sunt circa sacella complura, totidemque di.
Sua cuique ueneratio suum nomen, quibusdam uero etiam
fontes. Nam praeter illum quasi parentem ceterorum
sunt minores capite discreti; sed flumini miscentur, quod

ponte transmittitur. Is terminus sacri profanique: in 6
superiore parte nauigare tantum, infra etiam natare con-
cessum. Balineum Hispellates, quibus illum locum diuus
Augustus dono dedit, publice praebent, praebent et hospitium. Nec desunt uillae quae secutae fluminis amoeni-
tatem margini insistunt. In summa nihil erit, ex quo non 7
capias uoluptatem. Nam studebis quoque: leges multa
multorum omnibus columnis omnibus parietibus inscripta, quibus fons ille deusque celebratur. Plura laudabis,
non nulla ridebis; quamquam tu uero, quae tua humanitas, nulla ridebis. Vale.

LETTER 33

Household slaves

C. PLINIVS PATERNO SVO S.

CONFECERVNT me infirmitates meorum, mortes etiam, 1
et quidem iuuenum. Solacia duo nequaquam paria tanto
dolori, solacia tamen: unum facilitas manumittendi (uideor
enim non omnino immaturos perdidisse, quos iam liberos
perdidi), alterum quod permitto seruis quoque quasi testamenta facere, eaque ut legitima custodio. Mandant rogant- 2
que quod uisum; pareo ut iussus. Diuidunt donant
relinquunt, dumtaxat intra domum; nam seruis res publica
quaedam et quasi ciuitas domus est. Sed quamquam his 3
solaciis adquiescam, debilitor et frangor eadem illa humanitate, quae me ut hoc ipsum permitterem induxit. Non
ideo tamen uelim durior fieri. Nec ignoro alios eius modi
casus nihil amplius uocare quam damnum, eoque sibi

magnos homines et sapientes uideri. Qui an magni sapien-
4 tesque sint, nescio; homines non sunt. Hominis est enim
adfici dolore sentire, resistere tamen et solacia admittere,
5 non solaciis non egere. Verum de his plura fortasse quam
debui; sed pauciora quam uolui. Est enim quaedam etiam
dolendi uoluptas, praesertim si in amici sinu defleas, apud
quem lacrimis tuis uel laus sit parata uel uenia. Vale.

LETTER 34

Pliny publishes his poems

C. PLINIVS ARRIANO SVO S.

1 Vᴛ in uita sic in studiis pulcherrimum et humanissimum
existimo seueritatem comitatemque miscere, ne illa in tri-
2 stitiam, haec in petulantiam excedat. Qua ratione ductus
grauiora opera lusibus iocisque distinguo. Ad hos pro-
ferendos et tempus et locum opportunissimum elegi,
utque iam nunc adsuescerent et ab otiosis et in triclinio
audiri, Iulio mense, quo maxime lites interquiescunt, posi-
3 tis ante lectos cathedris amicos collocaui. Forte accidit ut
eodem die mane in aduocationem subitam rogarer, quod
mihi causam praeloquendi dedit. Sum enim deprecatus,
ne quis ut inreuerentem operis argueret, quod recita-
turus, quamquam et amicis et paucis, id est iterum amicis,
foro et negotiis non abstinuissem. Addidi hunc ordinem
me et in scribendo sequi, ut necessitates uoluptatibus,
seria iucundis anteferrem, ac primum amicis tum mihi
4 scriberem. Liber fuit et opusculis uarius et metris. Ita
solemus, qui ingenio parum fidimus, satietatis periculum

fugere. Recitaui biduo. Hoc adsensus audientium exegit;
et tamen ut alii transeunt quaedam imputantque quod
transeant, sic ego nihil praetereo atque etiam non praeter-
ire me dico. Lego enim omnia ut omnia emendem,
quod contingere non potest electa recitantibus. At illud 5
modestius et fortasse reuerentius; sed hoc simplicius et
amantius. Amat enim qui se sic amari putat, ut taedium
non pertimescat; et alioqui quid praestant sodales, si
conueniunt uoluptatis suae causa? Delicatus ac similis
ignoto est, qui amici librum bonum mauult audire quam
facere. Non dubito cupere te pro cetera mei caritate quam 6
maturissime legere hunc adhuc musteum librum. Leges,
sed retractatum, quae causa recitandi fuit; et tamen non
nulla iam ex eo nosti. Haec emendata postea uel, quod
interdum longiore mora solet, deteriora facta quasi noua
rursus et rescripta cognosces. Nam plerisque mutatis ea
quoque mutata uidentur, quae manent. Vale.

LETTER 35

Advice to a provincial governor

C. PLINIVS MAXIMO SVO S.

AMOR in te meus cogit, non ut praecipiam (neque enim 1
praeceptore eges), admoneam tamen, ut quae scis teneas
et obserues, aut nescire melius. Cogita te missum in 2
prouinciam Achaiam, illam ueram et meram Graeciam,
in qua primum humanitas litterae, etiam fruges inuentae
esse creduntur; missum ad ordinandum statum liberarum
ciuitatum, id est ad homines maxime homines, ad liberos

maxime liberos, qui ius a natura datum uirtute meritis
3 amicitia, foedere denique et religione tenuerunt. Reuerere
conditores deos et nomina deorum, reuerere gloriam
ueterem et hanc ipsam senectutem, quae in homine
uenerabilis, in urbibus sacra. Sit apud te honor antiquitati,
sit ingentibus factis, sit fabulis quoque. Nihil ex cuiusquam
dignitate, nihil ex libertate, nihil etiam ex iactatione de-
4 cerpseris. Habe ante oculos hanc esse terram, quae nobis
miserit iura, quae leges non uictis sed petentibus dederit,
Athenas esse quas adeas, Lacedaemonem esse quam regas;
quibus reliquam umbram et residuum libertatis nomen
5 eripere durum ferum barbarum est. Vides a medicis,
quamquam in aduersa ualetudine nihil serui ac liberi differant, mollius tamen liberos clementiusque tractari. Re-
cordare quid quaeque ciuitas fuerit, non ut despicias quod
6 esse desierit; absit superbia asperitas. Nec timueris con-
temptum. An contemnitur qui imperium qui fasces habet,
nisi humilis et sordidus, et qui se primus ipse contemnit?
Male uim suam potestas aliorum contumeliis experitur,
male terrore ueneratio adquiritur, longeque ualentior
amor ad obtinendum quod uelis quam timor. Nam timor
abit si recedas, manet amor, ac sicut ille in odium hic in
7 reuerentiam uertitur. Te uero etiam atque etiam (repetam
enim) meminisse oportet officii tui titulum ac tibi ipsum
interpretari, quale quantumque sit ordinare statum liberarum ciuitatum. Nam quid ordinatione ciuilius, quid
8 libertate pretiosius? Porro quam turpe, si ordinatio euersione, libertas seruitute mutetur! Accedit quod tibi cer-
tamen est tecum: onerat te quaesturae tuae fama, quam
ex Bithynia optimam reuexisti; onerat testimonium principis; onerat tribunatus, praetura atque haec ipsa legatio

quasi praemium data. Quo magis nitendum est ne in 9
longinqua prouincia quam surburbana, ne inter seruientes
quam liberos, ne sorte quam iudicio missus, ne rudis et
incognitus quam exploratus probatusque humanior melior
peritior fuisse uidearis, cum sit alioqui, ut saepe audisti
saepe legisti, multo deformius amittere quam non adsequi
laudem.

Haec uelim credas, quod initio dixi, scripsisse me ad- 10
mouentem, non praecipientem; quamquam praecipientem quoque. Quippe non uereor, in amore ne modum
excesserim. Neque enim periculum est ne sit nimium
quod esse maximum debet. Vale.

LETTER 36

At the races

C. PLINIVS CALVISIO SVO S.

OMNE hoc tempus inter pugillares ac libellos iucundis- 1
sima quiete transmisi. 'Quemadmodum' inquis 'in urbe
potuisti?' Circenses erant, quo genere spectaculi ne leuis-
sime quidem teneor. Nihil nouum nihil uarium, nihil
quod non semel spectasse sufficiat. Quo magis miror tot 2
milia uirorum tam pueriliter identidem cupere currentes
equos, insistentes curribus homines uidere. Si tamen aut
uelocitate equorum aut hominum arte traherentur, esset
ratio non nulla; nunc fauent panno pannum amant, et si
in ipso cursu medioque certamine hic color illuc ille huc
transferatur, studium fauorque transibit, et repente agitatores illos equos illos, quos procul noscitant, quorum

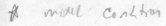

3 clamitant nomina relinquent. Tanta gratia tanta auctoritas
in una uilissima tunica, mitto apud uulgus, quod uilius
tunica, sed apud quosdam graues homines; quos ego cum
recordor, in re inani frigida adsidua, tam insatiabiliter
desidere, capio aliquam uoluptatem, quod hac uoluptate
4 non capior. Ac per hos dies libentissime otium meum in
litteris colloco, quos alii otiosissimis occupationibus per-
dunt. Vale.

LETTER 37

The consular orders his tomb

C. PLINIVS RVSONI SVO S.

1 SIGNIFICAS legisse te in quadam epistula mea iussisse
Verginium Rufum inscribi sepulcro suo:

Hic situs est Rufus, pulso qui Vindice quondam
imperium adseruit non sibi sed patriae.

Reprehendis quod iusserit, addis etiam melius rectiusque
Frontinum, quod uetuerit omnino monumentum sibi
fieri, meque ad extremum quid de utroque sentiam con-
2 sulis. Vtrumque dilexi, miratus sum magis quem tu
reprehendis, atque ita miratus ut non putarem satis um-
quam posse laudari, cuius nunc mihi subeunda defensio
3 est. Omnes ego qui magnum aliquid memorandumque
fecerunt, non modo uenia uerum etiam laude dignissimos
iudico, si immortalitatem quam meruere sectantur, uictu-
rique nominis famam supremis etiam titulis prorogare
4 nituntur. Nec facile quemquam nisi Verginium inuenio,
cuius tanta in praedicando uerecundia quanta gloria ex

facto. Ipse sum testis, familiariter ab eo dilectus pro- 5
batusque, semel omnino me audiente prouectum, ut de
rebus suis hoc unum referret, ita secum aliquando Cluuium
locutum: 'Scis, Vergini, quae historiae fides debeatur;
proinde si quid in historiis meis legis aliter ac uelis rogo
ignoscas.' Ad hoc ille: 'Tune ignoras, Cluui, ideo me
fecisse quod feci, ut esset liberum uobis scribere quae
libuisset?' Age dum, hunc ipsum Frontinum in hoc ipso, 6
in quo tibi parcior uidetur et pressior, comparemus.
Vetuit exstrui monumentum, sed quibus uerbis? 'Impensa monumenti superuacua est; memoria nostri durabit, si uita meruimus.' An restrictius arbitraris per orbem
terrarum legendum dare duraturam memoriam suam
quam uno in loco duobus uersiculis signare quod feceris?
Quamquam non habeo propositum illum reprehendendi, 7
sed hunc tuendi; cuius quae potest apud te iustior esse
defensio, quam ex collatione eius quem praetulisti? Meo 8
quidem iudicio neuter culpandus, quorum uterque ad
gloriam pari cupiditate, diuerso itinere contendit, alter
dum expetit debitos titulos, alter dum mauult uideri contempsisse. Vale.

LETTER 38

Pliny and Tacitus

C. PLINIVS MAXIMO SVO S.

FREQVENTER agenti mihi euenit, ut centumuiri cum 1
diu se intra iudicum auctoritatem grauitatemque tenuissent, omnes repente quasi uicti coactique consurgerent
laudarentque; frequenter e senatu famam qualem maxime 2

optaueram rettuli: numquam tamen maiorem cepi uoluptatem, quam nuper ex sermone Corneli Taciti. Narrabat sedisse secum circensibus proximis equitem Romanum. Hunc post uarios eruditosque sermones requisisse: 'Italicus 3 es an prouincialis?' Se respondisse: 'Nosti me, et quidem ex studiis.' Ad hoc illum: 'Tacitus es an Plinius?' Exprimere non possum, quam sit iucundum mihi quod nomina nostra quasi litterarum propria, non hominum, litteris redduntur, quod uterque nostrum his etiam ex studiis notus, quibus aliter ignotus est.

4   Accidit aliud ante pauculos dies simile. Recumbebat mecum uir egregius, Fadius Rufinus, super eum municeps ipsius, qui illo die primum uenerat in urbem; cui Rufinus demonstrans me: 'Vides hunc?' Multa deinde de studiis 5 nostris; et ille 'Plinius est' inquit. Verum fatebor, capio magnum laboris mei fructum. An si Demosthenes iure laetatus est, quod illum anus Attica ita noscitauit: Οὗτός ἐστι Δημοσθένης, ego celebritate nominis mei gaudere 6 non debeo? Ego uero et gaudeo et gaudere me dico. Neque enim uereor ne iactantior uidear, cum de me aliorum iudicium non meum profero, praesertim apud te qui nec ullius inuides laudibus et faues nostris. Vale.

LETTER 39

The African dolphin

C. PLINIVS CANINIO SVO S.

1 INCIDI in materiam ueram sed simillimam fictae, dignamque isto laetissimo altissimo planeque poetico ingenio; incidi autem, dum super cenam uaria miracula

hinc inde referuntur. Magna auctori fides: tametsi quid
poetae cum fide? Is tamen auctor, cui bene uel historiam
scripturus credidisses. Est in Africa Hipponensis colonia 2
mari proxima. Adiacet nauigabile stagnum; ex hoc in
modum fluminis aestuarium emergit, quod uice alterna,
prout aestus aut repressit aut impulit, nunc infertur mari,
nunc redditur stagno. Omnis hic aetas piscandi nauigandi 3
atque etiam natandi studio tenetur, maxime pueri, quos
otium lususque sollicitat. His gloria et uirtus altissime
prouehi: uictor ille, qui longissime ut litus ita simul
natantes reliquit. Hoc certamine puer quidam audentior 4
ceteris in ulteriora tendebat. Delphinus occurrit, et nunc
praecedere puerum nunc sequi nunc circumire, postremo
subire deponere iterum subire, trepidantemque perferre
primum in altum, mox flectit ad litus, redditque terrae et
aequalibus. Serpit per coloniam fama; concurrere omnes, 5
ipsum puerum tamquam miraculum adspicere, inter-
rogare audire narrare. Postero die obsident litus, pro-
spectant mare et si quid est mari simile. Natant pueri,
inter hos ille, sed cautius. Delphinus rursus ad tempus,
rursus ad puerum. Fugit ille cum ceteris. Delphinus, quasi
inuitet et reuocet, exsilit mergitur, uariosque orbes impli-
cat expeditque. Hoc altero die, hoc tertio, hoc pluribus, 6
donec homines innutritos mari subiret timendi pudor.
Accedunt et adludunt et adpellant, tangunt etiam per-
trectantque praebentem. Crescit audacia experimento.
Maxime puer, qui primus expertus est, adnatat nanti, in-
silit tergo, fertur referturque, agnosci se amari putat,
amat ipse; neuter timet, neuter timetur; huius fiducia,
mansuetudo illius augetur. Nec non alii pueri dextra 7
laeuaque simul eunt hortantes monentesque. Ibat una (id

quoque mirum) delphinus alius, tantum spectator et
comes. Nihil enim simile aut faciebat aut patiebatur, sed
alterum illum ducebat reducebat, ut puerum ceteri pueri.
8 Incredibile, tam uerum tamen quam priora, delphinum
gestatorem collusoremque puerorum in terram quoque
extrahi solitum, harenisque siccatum, ubi incaluisset in
9 mare reuolui. Constat Octauium Auitum, legatum pro-
consulis, in litus educto religione praua superfudisse un-
guentum, cuius illum nouitatem odoremque in altum
refugisse, nec nisi post multos dies uisum languidum et
maestum, mox redditis uiribus priorem lasciuiam et solita
10 ministeria repetisse. Confluebant omnes ad spectaculum
magistratus, quorum aduentu et mora modica res publica
nouis sumptibus atterebatur. Postremo locus ipse quietem
suam secretumque perdebat: placuit occulte interfici, ad
11 quod coibatur. Haec tu qua miseratione, qua copia deflebis
ornabis attolles! Quamquam non est opus adfingas aliquid
aut adstruas; sufficit ne ea quae sunt uera minuantur. Vale.

LETTER 40

Life in the country

C. PLINIVS FVSCO SVO S.

1 QVAERIS, quemadmodum in Tuscis diem aestate disponam. Euigilo cum libuit, plerumque circa horam primam, saepe ante, tardius raro. Clausae fenestrae manent;
mire enim silentio et tenebris ab iis quae auocant abductus
et liber et mihi relictus, non oculos animo sed animum
oculis sequor, qui eadem quae mens uident, quotiens non

uident alia. Cogito si quid in manibus, cogito ad uerbum 2
scribenti emendantique similis, nunc pauciora nunc plura,
ut uel difficile uel facile componi teneriue potuerunt.
Notarium uoco et die admisso quae formaueram dicto;
abit rursusque reuocatur rursusque dimittitur. Vbi hora 3
quarta uel quinta (neque enim certum dimensumque tempus), ut dies suasit, in xystum me uel cryptoporticum confero, reliqua meditor et dicto. Vehiculum ascendo. Ibi
quoque idem quod ambulans aut iacens; durat intentio
mutatione ipsa refecta. Paulum redormio, dein ambulo,
mox orationem Graecam Latinamue clare et intente non
tam uocis causa quam stomachi lego; pariter tamen et
illa firmatur. Iterum ambulo ungor exerceor lauor. Cenanti 4
mihi, si cum uxore uel paucis, liber legitur; post cenam
comoedia aut lyristes; mox cum meis ambulo, quorum in
numero sunt eruditi. Ita uariis sermonibus uespera ex-
tenditur, et quamquam longissimus dies bene conditur.
Non numquam ex hoc ordine aliqua mutantur; nam, si 5
diu iacui uel ambulaui, post somnum demum lectionem-
que non uehiculo sed, quod breuius quia uelocius, equo
gestor. Interueniunt amici ex proximis oppidis, partemque
diei ad se trahunt interdumque lasso mihi opportuna
interpellatione subueniunt. Venor aliquando, sed non sine 6
pugillaribus, ut quamuis nihil ceperim non nihil referam.
Datur et colonis, ut uidetur ipsis, non satis temporis,
quorum mihi agrestes querelae litteras nostras et haec
urbana opera commendant. Vale.

LETTER 41

On the treatment of convicts

C. PLINIVS TRAIANO IMPERATORI

1 SALVA magnitudine tua, domine, descendas oportet ad meas curas, cum ius mihi dederis referendi ad te, de quibus 2 dubito. In plerisque ciuitatibus, maxime Nicomediae et Nicaeae, quidam uel in opus damnati uel in ludum similiaque his genera poenarum publicorum seruorum officio ministerioque funguntur, atque etiam ut publici serui annua accipiunt. Quod ego cum audissem, diu mul- 3 tumque haesitaui, quid facere deberem. Nam et reddere poenae post longum tempus plerosque iam senes et, quantum adfirmatur, frugaliter modesteque uiuentes nimis seuerum arbitrabar, et in publicis officiis retinere damnatos non satis honestum putabam; eosdem rursus a re publica pasci otiosos inutile, non pasci etiam periculosum existi- 4 mabam. Necessario ergo rem totam, dum te consulerem, in suspenso reliqui. Quaeres fortasse, quem ad modum euenerit, ut poenis in quas damnati erant exsoluerentur: et ego quaesii, sed nihil comperi, quod adfirmare tibi possim. Vt decreta quibus damnati erant proferebantur, ita nulla monumenta quibus liberati probarentur. 5 Erant tamen, qui dicerent deprecantes iussu proconsulum legatorumue dimissos. Addebat fidem, quod credibile erat neminem hoc ausum sine auctore.

LETTER 42

On the treatment of convicts (2)

TRAIANVS PLINIO

MEMINERIMVS idcirco te in istam prouinciam missum, 1
quoniam multa in ea emendanda adparuerint. Erit autem
uel hoc maxime corrigendum, quod qui damnati ad
poenam erant, non modo ea sine auctore, ut scribis,
liberati sunt, sed etiam in condicionem proborum mini-
strorum retrahuntur. Qui igitur intra hos proximos decem 2
annos damnati nec ullo idoneo auctore liberati sunt, hos
oportebit poenae suae reddi; si qui uetustiores inuenientur
et senes ante annos decem damnati, distribuamus illos in
ea ministeria, quae non longe a poena sint. Solent et ad
balineum, ad purgationes cloacarum, item munitiones
uiarum et uicorum dari.

LETTER 43

On fire brigades

C. PLINIVS TRAIANO IMPERATORI

CVM diuersam partem prouinciae circumirem, Nicome- 1
diae uastissimum incendium multas priuatorum domos et
duo publica opera, quamquam uia interiacente, Gerusian
et Iseon absumpsit. Est autem latius sparsum, primum 2
uiolentia uenti, deinde inertia hominum quos satis constat
otiosos et immobiles tanti mali spectatores perstitisse; et

alioqui nullus usquam in publico sipo, nulla hama, nullum denique instrumentum ad incendia compescenda. Et
3 haec quidem, ut iam praecepi, parabuntur; tu, domine, dispice an instituendum putes collegium fabrorum dumtaxat hominum CL. Ego attendam, ne quis nisi faber recipiatur neue iure concesso in aliud utantur; nec erit difficile custodire tam paucos.

LETTER 44

On fire brigades (2)

TRAIANVS PLINIO

1 TIBI quidem secundum exempla complurium in mentem uenit posse collegium fabrorum apud Nicomedenses constitui. Sed meminerimus prouinciam istam et praecipue ipsas ciuitates eius modi factionibus esse uexatas. Quodcumque nomen ex quacumque causa dederimus iis, qui in
2 idem contracti fuerint, hetaeriae eaeque breui fient. Satius itaque est comparari ea, quae ad coercendos ignes auxilio esse possint, admonerique dominos praediorum, ut et ipsi inhibeant ac, si res poposcerit, adcursu populi ad hoc uti.

LETTER 45

Feuds among the gentry

C. PLINIVS TRAIANO IMPERATORI

1 CVM Prusae ad Olympum, domine, publicis negotiis intra hospitium eodem die exiturus uacarem, Asclepiades

magistratus indicauit adpellatum me a Claudio Eumolpo.
Cum Cocceianus Dion in bule adsignari ciuitati opus cuius
curam egerat uellet, tum Eumolpus adsistente Flauio
Archippo dixit exigendam esse a Dione rationem operis,
ante quam rei publicae traderetur, quod aliter fecisset ac
debuisset. Adiecit etiam esse in eodem positam tuam 2
statuam et corpora sepultorum, uxoris Dionis et filii,
postulauitque ut cognoscerem pro tribunali. Quod cum 3
ego me protinus facturum dilaturumque profectionem
dixissem, ut longiorem diem ad struendam causam darem
utque in alia ciuitate cognoscerem petiit. Ego me audi- 4
turum Nicaeae respondi. Vbi cum consedissem cogniturus,
idem Eumolpus tamquam si adhuc parum instructus dilationem petere coepit, contra Dion ut audiretur exigere.
Dicta sunt utrimque multa, etiam de causa. Ego cum 5
dandam dilationem et ⟨te⟩ consulendum existimarem in
re ad exemplum pertinenti, dixi utrique parti ut postu-
lationum suarum libellos darent. Volebam enim te
ipsorum potissimum uerbis ea quae erant proposita cognoscere. Et Dion quidem se daturum dixit. Eumolpus 6
respondit complexurum se libello quae rei publicae peteret,
ceterum quod ad sepultos pertineret non accusatorem se
sed aduocatum Flaui Archippi, cuius mandata pertulisset.
Archippus, cui Eumolpus sicut Prusae adsistebat, dixit
se libellum daturum. At nec Eumolpus nec Archippus
quam⟨quam⟩ plurimis diebus exspectati adhuc mihi libellos dederunt; Dion dedit, quem huic epistulae iunxi. Ipse 7
in re praesenti fui et uidi tuam quoque statuam in biblio-
theca positam, id autem in quo dicuntur sepulti filius et
uxor Dionis in area collocatum, quae porticibus includi-
tur. Te, domine, rogo ut me in hoc praecipue genere 8

cognitionis regere digneris, cum alioqui magna sit exspectatio, ut necesse est in ea re quae et in confessum uenit
et exemplis defenditur.

LETTER 46

Feuds among the gentry (2)

TRAIANVS PLINIO

1 POTVISTI non haerere, mi Secunde carissime, circa id de
quo me consulendum existimasti, cum propositum meum
optime nosses, non ex metu nec terrore hominum aut
criminibus maiestatis reuerentiam nomini meo adquiri.
2 Omissa ergo ea quaestione, quam non admitterem etiam
si exemplis adiuuaretur, ratio totius operis effecti sub cura
Cocceiani Dionis excutiatur, cum et utilitas ciuitatis exi-
gat nec aut recuset Dion aut debeat recusare.

LETTER 47

On the punishment of Christians

C. PLINIVS TRAIANO IMPERATORI

1 SOLLEMNE est mihi, domine, omnia de quibus dubito ad
te referre. Quis enim potest melius uel cunctationem
meam regere uel ignorantiam instruere? Cognitionibus de
Christianis interfui numquam: ideo nescio quid et qua-
2 tenus aut puniri soleat aut quaeri. Nec mediocriter haesi-

taui, sitne aliquod discrimen aetatum, an quamlibet teneri
nihil a robustioribus differant; detur paenitentiae uenia,
an ei, qui omnino Christianus fuit, desisse non prosit;
nomen ipsum, si flagitiis careat, an flagitia cohaerentia
nomini puniantur. Interim, ⟨in⟩ iis qui ad me tamquam
Christiani deferebantur, hunc sum secutus modum. Inter- 3
rogaui ipsos an essent Christiani. Confitentes iterum ac
tertio interrogaui supplicium minatus: perseuerantes duci
iussi. Neque enim dubitabam, qualecumque esset quod
faterentur, pertinaciam certe et inflexibilem obstinationem
debere puniri. Fuerunt alii similis amentiae, quos, quia 4
ciues Romani erant, adnotaui in urbem remittendos.

Mox ipso tractatu, ut fieri solet, diffundente se crimine
plures species inciderunt. Propositus est libellus sine 5
auctore multorum nomina continens. Qui negabant esse
se Christianos aut fuisse, cum praeunte me deos adpellarent et imagini tuae, quam propter hoc iusseram cum
simulacris numinum adferri, ture ac uino supplicarent,
praeterea male dicerent Christo, quorum nihil cogi posse
dicuntur qui sunt re uera Christiani, dimittendos putaui.
Alii ab indice nominati esse se Christianos dixerunt et 6
mox negauerunt; fuisse quidem sed desisse, quidam ante
triennium, quidam ante plures annos, non nemo etiam
ante uiginti. ⟨Hi⟩ quoque omnes et imaginem tuam
deorumque simulacra uenerati sunt et Christo male
dixerunt. Adfirmabant autem hanc fuisse summam uel 7
culpae suae uel erroris, quod essent soliti stato die ante
lucem conuenire, carmenque Christo quasi deo dicere
secum inuicem seque sacramento non in scelus aliquod
obstringere, sed ne furta ne latrocinia ne adulteria com-
mitterent, ne fidem fallerent, ne depositum adpellati

abnegarent. Quibus peractis morem sibi discedendi fuisse
rursusque coeundi ad capiendum cibum, promiscuum
tamen et innoxium; quod ipsum facere desisse post
edictum meum, quo secundum mandata tua hetaerias esse
8 uetueram. Quo magis necessarium credidi ex duabus
ancillis, quae ministrae dicebantur, quid esset ueri, et per
tormenta quaerere. Nihil aliud inueni quam superstitionem prauam et immodicam.

9 Ideo dilata cognitione ad consulendum te decucurri.
Visa est enim mihi res digna consultatione, maxime propter periclitantium numerum. Multi enim omnis aetatis,
omnis ordinis, utriusque sexus etiam uocantur in periculum et uocabuntur. Neque ciuitates tantum, sed uicos
etiam atque agros superstitionis istius contagio peruagata
10 est; quae uidetur sisti et corrigi posse. Certe satis constat
prope iam desolata templa coepisse celebrari, et sacra sol-
lemnia diu intermissa repeti passimque uenire ⟨carnem⟩
uictimarum, cuius adhuc rarissimus emptor inueniebatur.
Ex quo facile est opinari, quae turba hominum emendari
possit, si sit paenitentiae locus.

LETTER 48

On the punishment of Christians (2)

TRAIANVS PLINIO

1 ACTVM quem debuisti, mi Secunde, in excutiendis causis
eorum, qui Christiani ad te delati fuerant, secutus es.
Neque enim in uniuersum aliquid, quod quasi certam
2 formam habeat, constitui potest. Conquirendi non sunt;

si deferantur et arguantur, puniendi sunt, ita tamen ut,
qui negauerit se Christianum esse idque re ipsa manifestum fecerit, id est supplicando dis nostris, quamuis suspectus in praeteritum, ueniam ex paenitentia impetret.
Sine auctore uero propositi libelli ⟨in⟩ nullo crimine
locum habere debent. Nam et pessimi exempli nec nostri
saeculi est.

LETTER 49

A case of equity

C. PLINIVS TRAIANO IMPERATORI

ECDICVS, domine, Amisenorum ciuitatis petebat apud 1
me a Iulio Pisone denariorum circiter quadraginta milia
donata ei publice ante uiginti annos bule et ecclesia consentiente, utebaturque mandatis tuis, quibus eius modi
donationes uetantur. Piso contra plurima se in rem publi- 2
cam contulisse ac prope totas facultates erogasse dicebat.
Addebat etiam temporis spatium postulabatque, ne id,
quod pro multis et olim accepisset, cum euersione reliquae
dignitatis reddere cogeretur. Quibus ex causis integram
cognitionem differendam existimaui, ut te, domine, consulerem, quid sequendum putares.

LETTER 50

A case of equity (2)

TRAIANVS PLINIO

Sicvt largitiones ex publico fieri mandata prohibent, ita, ne multorum securitas subruatur, factas ante aliquantum temporis retractari atque in inritum uindicari non oportet. Quidquid ergo ex hac causa actum ante uiginti annos erit, omittamus. Non minus enim hominibus cuiusque loci quam pecuniae publicae consultum uolo.

NOTES

Editing the letters

Clarus is a Roman knight who later had a successful career in the imperial service, until the emperor Hadrian, in about A.D. 119, dismissed him from the command of the Praetorian Guard because of a mysterious intrigue which also involved another equestrian friend of Pliny, the biographer Suetonius Tranquillus.

This note acts as a preface to Pliny's first experimental publication of letters. Statius and Martial attached similar prefaces in letter-form to some of their books of verses (e.g. Martial I and II), but no other volume of Pliny's letters has a letter of introduction like this, and Pliny expresses a dislike of explanatory introductions elsewhere (Ep. iv. 14. 8). By dedicating the volume to the obscure Clarus Pliny avoided giving offence to any distinguished senator in his circle. Roman society was notoriously touchy about minor slights (Ep. ii. 18. 5, iv. 17. 11).

1. **epistulas si quas paulo curatius scripsissem.** Cf. Letter 26. 8 'uolo epistulam diligentius scribas'. Pliny's letters are of a literary type which at this period were regularly exchanged by way of polite correspondence between gentlemen of leisure. See Introduction p. xv, and Ep. ii. 13. 7, ix. 28. 5: 'adicis alias te litteras curiosius scriptas misisse; an acceperim quaeris'.

collegi non seruato temporis ordine. A fairly regular chronological order can be detected throughout the letters of Books II–IX, but those of Book I are spread through the years A.D. 96–99 with no particular attention to their sequence. Our Letter 4, for example, belongs to A.D. 98 or 99, while Letter 6 is datable to April 97. So this remark does not apply to the whole collection of nine books, which were probably not published all together. See p. xviii.

2. **obsequii,** 'deference', usually of juniors to seniors, or of citizens to rulers.

LETTER 2 (I. 6). TO CORNELIUS TACITUS

Pliny goes a-hunting

More letters in the collection are addressed to Cornelius Tacitus, the historian who wrote the *Annals* and *Histories*, than to any other person. Their tone is rather formal and suggests that the friendship was not very intimate, though Pliny claims in Ep. vii. 20. 2: 'qua concordia qua simplicitate uixerimus'. At this date, about A.D. 97–98, Tacitus, who as a suffect consul of 97 was senior to Pliny in senatorial rank, was known only as a leading advocate in the civil courts, who delivered the funeral oration over the famous statesman Verginius Rufus (Letter 8. 6), and had just published or was about to publish his biography of Julius Agricola, the conqueror of Scotland. Later Pliny wrote his account of Vesuvius to give Tacitus material for his Histories, and the letter about the trial of Baebius Massa (Letters 25, 31). In one of his last letters he is proud to be equated with Tacitus (Letter 38) as an orator.

1. **apros . . . cepi.** Pliny hunted on his Tuscan estate (Letter 40. 6). It was the one regular sport of the Roman gentry.

ad retia sedebam. The nets formed a curving trap into which the beasts were driven and then slain, with skill and danger, by the thrusting spear (*uenabulum*) or the throwing javelin (*lancea*). See the mosaics of ancient hunting reproduced in S. Aymard, *Essai sur les chasses romaines* (Paris, 1951), and G. Jennison, *Animals for Show and Pleasure etc.* (Manchester, 1937), p. 145.

stilus et pugillares. Cf. Letter 40. 6: 'uenor aliquando sed non sine pugillaribus'. These waxed wooden tablets, and the metal-tipped *stilus* for scratching them, were the notebooks and biros of antiquity.

2. **magna cogitationis incitamenta sunt.** He repeats this idea in Letter 3. 6, and in Ep. ix. 10. 2 quotes Tacitus as saying that writing poetry is easier *inter nemora et lucos*. This romantic notion occurs in Tacitus' *Dialogus* (9. 6, 12. 1) as a commonplace among poets, and in Quintilian also (*Inst.* 10. 3. 22 f.). The basic idea is as old as Horace, *Sermones* 2. 6. 60 ff.

By *cogitatio* he means any form of composition, as in Letter 40. 2: 'cogito ad uerbum scribenti . . . similis'.

3. panarium et lagunculam, 'satchel of bread, and wine-flask'.

feras. Subjunctive dependent on *licebit*.

non Dianam magis . . . quam Mineruam. The goddesses of the chase and of the arts respectively.

LETTER 3 (I. 9). TO MINICIUS FUNDANUS

The daily round at Rome

This letter is addressed to one of Pliny's more serious-minded friends, Minicius Fundanus, a student of philosophy, who at this time was a junior senator. Its theme, the vexatious daily round of city life, recurs in some verses of Martial (4. 78), which may be Pliny's model. Martial includes some things omitted by Pliny, such as the daily morning calls or *salutatio* at the houses of friends and patrons, and the perpetual recitation parties that Pliny loved (Letter 6).

1. ratio . . . constet. The 'accounts of life' should balance like a business ledger.

2. officio togae uirilis. Pliny mainly lists personal and family occasions. The Roman boy marked his 'coming of age' between the ages of fourteen and sixteen by a ceremony (*officium*) at which he put on the stripeless toga instead of the purple-edged one, was registered in his family 'tribe' in the civic lists, and thus acquired civil and political rights and duties.

Betrothal ceremonies (*sponsalia*) in the older Roman style involved the signing of a contract between the parents or guardians, and the settlement of dowries. At marriages (*nuptiae*) the completion of legal contracts of different sorts (*coemptio*) was followed by sacrifices and the taking of auspices, a feast in the bride's home, and the solemn transfer of the lady to the husband's home. For examples see Tacitus, *Annals* 11. 26, Juvenal 2. 119–21, 132–5.

ad signandum testamentum. See Letter 11. 10 for an instance. Seven witnesses were required to be present.

in aduocationem. In Pliny this word normally refers to the activities of professional lawyers in courts.

in consilium. Senators with experience in the law were frequently asked to act as assessors to the civic magistrates, who being elected annually often knew little about the law. Pliny in Letter 20 also helps the Emperor Trajan in this way.

3. **secesseris.** This verb is regularly used of withdrawal from Rome to one's country estate or township. Cf. Letters 6. 6, 8. 8, 10. 1.

4. **Laurentino meo.** Pliny describes this seaside villa near Ostia, eighteen miles from Rome, at great length in Ep. ii. 17. He often speaks of the opportunities for quiet study at his country villas, as in Letter 40. 2–3.

corpori uaco, 'I am free for physical exercise', as in Letter 13. 15: 'huic uni uacabat'. He describes the daily routine of walking, riding, sunning, and bathing in Letter 40. 3. See also Ep. iii. 1. 5–8.

6. **μουσεῖον.** The reading halls of the great library of Alexandria had this name, literally 'the place of the Muses', who were the 'spirits of learning'.

quam multa inuenitis. The thought is the same as in Letter 2. 2.

7. **multum.** Used as an adverb qualifying *ineptos*, because he does not wish to use the superlative adjective here, after the positive *inanem*.

8. **Atilius noster.** Atilius Crescens was a needy friend of Pliny, and a sharp wit.

LETTER 4 (I. 10). TO ATTIUS CLEMENS

A philosopher

Addressed to Attius Clemens, a man of letters, probably in A.D. 98 after Pliny had become prefect of the chief Roman treasury (s. 9). The subject, a portrait of a Greek literary figure visiting Rome, recurs in Ep. ii. 3, iii. 11, depicting Isaeus and Artemidorus.

1. **nunc maxime floret.** The professional philosophers, expelled from Rome by the Emperor Domitian in 93 because of their political

intrigues, returned when his successor Nerva restored a measure of liberty of thought in 96–97. Cf. Letter 5. 6–8 n.

2. **Euphrates philosophus.** This man was a characteristic figure of the age. Skilled in the Greek oratory and philosophy of the period, he came to make his fortune at Rome, like the hero of Lucian's essay *The Hirelings* (*De mercede conductis*), but had to return to his home in Syria at the time of the expulsions. Little is known of him, except that he was a pupil of the Stoic teacher Musonius Rufus, some of whose essays or sermons survive in an abbreviated form (s. 6 n.).

cum . . . militarem. Pliny served as a military tribune or staff officer of the *legio tertia Gallica* in Syria about A D. 81, where he also met the philosopher Artemidorus (Ep. iii. 11).

amari . . . laboraui, 'I worked to secure his friendship'. The infinitive, instead of a purpose clause, is not uncommon with *laboro*.

3. **aut ego . . . .** Pliny sometimes uses *aut* singly, in the sense 'or else'. Cf. Ep. viii. 15. 2.

4. **nisi artifex . . . non . . .,** 'only a craftsman can . . .'.

sapiens, i.e. a student of philosophy, as in Letter 5. 3.

5. **disputat subtiliter grauiter ornate,** 'with fineness of argument, seriousness of purpose, and literary skill'. Each adverb has a distinct meaning, and like the adjectives in this section belongs to the language of technical rhetoric, commending his style rather than his logic.

qui . . . ducat impellat, 'the sort to guide and drive you'.

6. **ingens . . . barba.** Epictetus (iv. 8) quotes a fragment of Euphrates against ostentation, and commends him for *not* flaunting the long beard that so impressed Pliny. The cult of the beard derived from Musonius, who insisted on the natural growth of beards as the mark of man, and spoke much about the details of behaviour and incidents of daily life, food and clothing, furniture and haircuts (*Reliquiae* xviii–xxi). Euphrates' remarks to Pliny are in his master's strain.

7. **in cultu.** In his dress and style of life, as in Ep. i. 22. 4: 'quam modicus in cultu'.

occursum, 'the meeting'. Cf. Tac. *Annals* 4. 60, 'uitare . . . occursum'.

persuaderi, 'to go on being persuaded'.

8. Pompeius Iulianus . . . prouinciae princeps. Cf. Letter 12. 2: 'Maturus . . Altinatium princeps'. Julianus, who was a Roman citizen, would be a wealthy man, chief magistrate of his city, and a deputy of the provincial council.

inter altissimas condiciones, 'amid distinguished offers', i.e. though more exalted alliances were available. So too Musonius, though a Roman knight, married his daughter to the philosopher Artemidorus.

9. quid ego plura? i.e. 'dicam'.

officio . . . molestissimo. Pliny became prefect of the Treasury of Saturn in January 98. The duties described in s. 10—*cognoscere, iudicare*—fit that post well. The prefects administered the complicated inheritance tax (*uicesima hereditatum*), and settled problems arising from the application of its rules, like a modern inspector of income-tax. They also handled suits brought under the marriage laws against childless citizens, whose legacies were forfeited to the treasury.

subnoto libellos. Written petitions were settled by a comment (*nota*) inscribed beneath the original document.

conficio tabulas. The prime duty of the prefects was to keep the accounts of the public monies which passed through the *aerarium*.

11. uacat. Impersonal.

LETTER 5 (I. 12). TO CALESTRIUS TIRO

A Roman suicide

The character-sketch of a leading man, often combined with an account of his illness or death, is a favourite type with Pliny. Compare the descriptions of Verginius Rufus, the Elder Pliny, and Ummidia Quadratilla (Letters 8, 13, 29).

Calestrius Tiro, the recipient, was a praetorian senator whose early career went step by step with Pliny's (Ep. vii. 16). The letter was written in 97.

1. Corellius Rufus. This senator, after a consulship in about A.D. 78, governed the province of Upper Germany at the beginning of Domitian's reign, but seems not to have held any other posts under Domitian. So his anger may be that of a discarded official. He helped Pliny's promotion in the public service, and guided him with advice, though when Pliny undertook the prosecution of Domitian's henchman Publicius Certus, a few months before this letter, he omitted to consult Corellius as being 'too slow and cautious' (Ep. iv. 17. 5–6, ix. 13. 6). Pliny has much to say about the family, which had some connexion with Comum (Ep. vii. 11).

si iactura dicenda est. The word, which has commercial undertones, recurs only in vi. 8. 6, with a financial sense. Corellius' death was no ordinary loss. But in the Verginius letter he takes a different line: great men do not die but live on in human memory (Letter 8. 10–11).

nec fatalis. He is thinking of the political misfortunes that overwhelmed many leading men in this period.

2. utcumque in illis, 'at any rate in those who die naturally'. He uses *utcumque* here as a particle, not a conjunction, much as in v. 5. 2: 'hoc utcumque tolerabile, grauius illud'.

accersita, 'summoned', i.e. 'deliberate'.

3. summa ratio quae sapientibus pro necessitate est. Corellius is a follower of philosophy (*sapiens*), and evidently of Stoicism, which encouraged suicide in such circumstances. He follows the advice of the Stoic Seneca (*Ep.* 58. 32–36), who recommended suicide to avoid incurable disease; 'because it interfered with everything that made life worth living'. So he coolly calculates the rival claims of his family and his sufferings, to find the 'total calculation' or 'final argument'. Pliny combines the two possible meanings of *summa ratio*.

quamquam ... habentem. Pliny often used *quamquam* with adjectives and participles as in s. 7 below, 'quamquam ... capacissima'.

optimam conscientiam. This word means a man's knowledge of his own deeds, as in Ep. ii. 22. 5: 'omnia ad conscientiam refert recteque facti mercedem ... ex facto petit'.

filiam uxorem nepotem. The daughter Corellia recurs in Ep. iii. 3, iv. 17, where Pliny finds a school for her son (*nepotem*) and defends her interests in a lawsuit. Hispulla, the rare name of Corellius' wife, may connect her with Calpurnia Hispulla of Comum, aunt of Pliny's wife (Letter 19).

6. Domitiani temporibus. The last three years of the tyrannical Domitian from August 93 onward formed the worst period of his political repression of the senatorial class. Cf. Tacitus, *Agricola* 45. 1.

suburbano. A country villa, some miles outside Rome (s. 10).

iacentem. In bed, with the implication of illness, as in Letter 11. 2: 'Verania . . . grauiter iacebat'.

7. hoc moris. A 'partitive' genitive common with *mos*, as in Letter 17. 3: 'fuit moris antiqui'.

quotiens intrasset. Pliny uses the subjunctive (as often in 'silver' Latin) in dependent clauses denoting frequent acts, as in Letters 9. 6, 15. 4. These are in past tenses. In 40. 1 he uses the indicative for the present tense.

uxor . . . secreti capacissima. Trusty ladies are a feature of North Italy in Pliny's letters. Cf. Ep. i. 14. 6. 'Nosti loci mores. Serrana tamen Patauinis quoque seueritatis exemplum est.' But even the naughty Quadratilla had a sense of social responsibility (Letter 29).

8. isti latroni. Domitian was called a brigand because he confiscated the estates of his political victims, and was apt to expect a share in the inheritances of wealthy men on slight grounds. Suetonius, *Domitian* 3. 2, 12. 1–2.

dedisses . . . fecisset. The English idiom explains this omission of *si*. 'Had you given him . . . he would have . . .'. Pliny implies that Corellius wanted to have a hand in the assassination of Domitian. No senator was concerned in the affair, which was managed by his household servants. Suetonius, *Domitian* 17. Cassius Dio 67. 15–16.

ut iam securus liberque. Pliny minimizes for effect the length of the interval between Domitian's assassination on 18 September A.D. 96, and Corellius' death some time in the middle of 97.

9. perseuerantem constantia fugit, 'he escaped the disease as it grew worse by his resolution'. The quality of *constantia* was one of the Stoic virtues.

9–10. C. Geminium . . . Iulius Atticus. Persons unknown.

9. destinasse Corellium. The accusative and infinitive are dependent on the sense of *nuntio*.

11. quae aetas etiam robustissimis satis longa est. The elder Pliny gave a statistical account of longevity in his Natural History (7. 153–64), noting that eighty-five centenarians were registered in Italy at the census of A.D. 74. The lawyer Ulpian remarked that the expectation of life between fifty-five and sixty was seven years, reaching the very age of Corellius. Our Pliny generally looked forward to old age, contrary to the general opinion of Latin writers, summed up by Seneca's phrase: 'senectus insanabilis morbus est' (*Ep.* 108. 28–29).

12. in summa, i.e. *re*. 'Altogether'. A favourite phrase with Pliny; cf. Letters 7. 4, 10. 25.

meo Caluisio. Pliny frequently writes to his friend Calvisius Rufus, a landowner of Comum, about politics and business affairs. See Letters 11, 16, 36.

13. quae audierim numquam, 'such as I have never heard'. The subjunctive is generic.

LETTER 6 (I. 13). TO SOSIUS SENECIO

The state of literature

The letter was written in April 97, a year when Pliny was free from public business, to Sosius Senecio, later a leading member of the Emperor Trajan's administration, but at this time a junior senator. He had literary tastes and was a patron of the Greek essayist Plutarch, who addressed his *de fraterno amore* to him.

1. magnum prouentum, 'a great crop of poets'.

quo non recitaret aliquis. The subjunctive is due to the negation contained in *nullus erat*, with *quo non* in place of *quin*, like *ut non* in s. 6.

The formal recitation, introduced in the time of Augustus, was a great literary and social feature of the imperial period. It filled the gap left by the disappearance of political assemblies as occasions for displays of oratory, and was soon adapted to other forms of literature. In the absence of printing it gave a quick and cheap means of publishing a new work to the educated audiences of Rome. Pliny frequently describes the recitations of poets and historians and of his own speeches (cf. s. 6 n.). This was an age of literary amateurs, all suffering from the 'bad habit of writing' disliked by Juvenal (*scribendi cacoethes, Sat.* 1. 1–21, 7. 52).

uigent studia. The liberal régime of Nerva was thought to have restored life to literature after the political censorship of Domitian. Tacitus speaks later of the 'happy novelty' which allowed men: 'sentire quae uelis et quae sentias dicere' (*Histories* 1. 1.).

2. in stationibus sedent. Men of leisure congregated in the porticoes of the imperial *Fora*, the great Baths, and the library of the temple of Apollo. When canvassing for a friend at elections Pliny says: 'stationes circumeo' (ii. 9. 5).

iam . . . intrauerit. Recitations were private parties, attended by invitation (s. 4).

praefationem. Works were introduced by preliminary remarks, like the prose prefaces of Martial and Statius.

euoluerit librum. The book is a papyrus roll. The audience wait until the author is well launched into the book.

ante finem. The usual length of recitations may be judged by the fact that Pliny took three sessions to recite his *Panegyricus*, which runs to some 2,700 lines in modern texts, and two sessions to read his volume of verses, probably as long as a book of Martial (Letter 34. 4).

3. hercule. A literary oath 'by Hercules', fairly common in Pliny, cf. Letter 29. 7.

ferunt, 'they say'.

in Palatio spatiaretur. Claudius was walking about in the grounds of the *Domus Tiberiana* on the Palatine hill.

clamorem, i.e. applause.

Nonianum. The works of the senator M. Servilius Nonianus, orator and historian, have not survived.

4. multo ante rogatus. Invitations were written and formal (*per libellos*), and large numbers might be asked: 'quasi populum in auditorium non in cubiculum amicos aduocarim' (Ep. iii. 18. 4, v. 3. 11). The seating was hired at great expense for the occasion (Letter 34. 3. Tacitus, *Dialogus* 9. 3).

6. qui studia, ut non simul et nos amet. Supply *amat* after *studia*. The *ut* clause is consecutive.

repetere secessum, i.e. at one of his country villas, as in Letter 3. 3.

quod non recitem, 'but not in order to recite it'. Pliny adopted the habit of recitation reluctantly at first (Ep. ii. 19). But after the success of his *Panegyricus* he became an ardent reciter (Ep. iii. 18. Letters 27, 34). — The subjunctive is either final or concessive.

creditor. A lender, i.e. of time.

LETTER 7 (I. 15). TO SEPTICIUS CLARUS

A polite party

Septicius is the Roman knight to whom the book is dedicated in Letter 1. The letter exploits a favourite theme, an invitation to a dinner-party contrasting inexpensive good taste with vulgar luxury. Martial's verses in v. 78 may be Pliny's model.

1. promittis ad cenam, i.e. 'te uenturum esse'.

dicitur ius, 'the magistrate is dealing with your case'. The metaphor of a breach of contract is kept up in s. 2 'computabis' and s. 3 'dabis poenas'.

2. paratae erant lactucae. Pliny does not attempt to give a complete menu for either side. His own list is limited to cheap land-produce, salads, eggs, and snails (*cochleae*), the other to expensive luxuries.

oliuae betacei cucurbitae bulbi. Olives, beetroot, cucumbers, onions.

halica cum mulso et niue. Pliny slips. *Halica*, a kind of barley-water, was a poor man's drink, but *mulsum*, a mixture of wine and honey, was a luxury, even unchilled. Martial has the right contrast in xiii. 6: 'nos halicam, poterit mulsum tibi mittere diues'. The use of snow, brought from the Appennines and kept in store to cool drinks, was a great extravagance (Pliny, *Nat. Hist.* 19. 54).

audisses comoedos uel lectorem uel lyristen. Pliny speaks of the custom of listening to recitations or music during or just after dinner, at his uncle's house and his own villa (Letters 13. 11–12, 40. 4). The entertainers were usually specialists. The *lector* read poetry, history, or oratory, the *comoedus* recited selections from Menander, Terence, or Plautus, and the *lyristes* was a soloist musician. Pliny's freedman Zosimus was exceptional in combining the three talents (Letter 24. 3). The old classical plays were now more often heard than seen, since spectacles, mimes, and pantomimes tended to monopolize the public theatres. See Letter 29. 4–5.

quae mea liberalitas. Parenthesis. 'For such is my generosity'. Cf. Letter 32. 7 n. *Quae* replaces *ea enim*.

3. ostrea uuluas echinos. Oysters, offal, sea-urchins.

Gaditanas maluisti. So too Martial (v. 78. 26) promises his friend a single flautist instead of the singers and dancers of Gades.

4. in summa. Cf. Letter 5. 12 n.

LETTER 8 (II. 1). TO VOCONIUS ROMANUS

Death of a former hero

This letter, like the account of Corellius (Letter 5) combines a character sketch with anecdotes about the life and death of a famous man. It is addressed to Voconius Romanus, a Roman knight from Spain, for whom Pliny secured promotion to the status of a senator (Ep. x. 4).

1. **publicum funus.** The state paid the expenses of a 'public funeral' out of the Treasury of Saturn. The consuls presided over the cere-monies, which were attended by the whole Senate and a formal parade of the Roman knights. Only the greatest men received this honour, on the proposal of the Princeps and the Senate.

2. **gloriae suae.** See Letter 37. 1 n. Verginius Rufus, as army com-mander of the Upper Rhine (*Germania superior*) in A.D. 68, played an ambiguous part in the fall of Nero, by first subduing a rebellion against Nero in Gaul and afterwards turning against him, though refusing to be made emperor himself.

de se . . . historias. Pliny has in mind Cluvius Rufus' history of the times of Claudius and Nero, which is now lost, though the story is known from Plutarch, *Galba* 10, and Cassius Dio, *Hist.* 63. 23–25.

posteritati suae interfuit, 'he lived to see the record of his fame'. Cf. Ep. ix. 3. 1: 'certus . . . posteritatis . . . cum futura gloria uiuit'.

summum fastigium priuati hominis. The consulship was a titular distinction in this period, held for a few months of the year, during which the consul presided over the fortnightly deliberations of the Senate; it opened the door to high promotion in the service of the Princeps, in army commands and provincial governorships. Dis-tinguished officers of this sort sometimes received a second consul-ship, but a third was a very rare honour. Only three were given in the twenty-seven years of the Flavian period.

3. **Caesares quibus suspectus . . . fuerat.** Galba, who succeeded Nero, dismissed Rufus from his army, and the Flavian emperors did not use him, but he returned to influence when Nerva succeeded Domitian in 96.

reliquit incolumem optimum. M. Cocceius Nerva became Prin-ceps after the murder of Domitian on 18 September A.D. 96, and died on 25 January, 98. Verginius was *consul ter* in January 97 and evidently died during the year. Nerva was popular with senators because he restored the political exiles after Domitian's repressive reign, and gave the Senate a freer hand in affairs (Letters 5. 7–8, 20. 4–6, 31. 9 nn.).

4. **citra,** 'this side of', hence 'without'.

sed hic ipse laudabilis, 'the man himself was splendid in this phase'. *Hic* is adverbial.

5. **uocem praepararet.** Orators were much given to rehearsals.

acturus in consulatu principi gratias. Consuls on entering office made a speech of thanks to the Princeps. Pliny's *Panegyricus Traiani* survives as an example, in which he praises the régime of the new ruler; he describes that speech in Ep. iii. 18.

hunc dum sequitur. The long papyrus roll unwinds, and he chases it.

6. **foro et rostris.** The funeral oration was delivered from the official pulpit of the Roman tribunes (*rostra*) in the Roman Forum.

a consule Cornelio Tacito. This is the historian Tacitus, who was consul in A.D. 97 and held several imperial posts, though little is known for certain about his career. Pliny reckoned him the foremost orator and advocate of his times in the Roman courts (Letter 2 pref.).

7. **publice,** 'in public life', as commonly in Pliny.

8. **municipia finitima, agri etiam.** Verginius came from Mediolanum (Milan), in Northern Italy, which was the administrative centre (*municipium*) of a large region next to Comum. An inscription thence names the manager of his estates: 'L. Verginius Rufi (libertus) Pylades saltuarius' (Dessau, *ILS* 982).

ille mihi tutor relictus. Orphaned minors remained under the control of a guardian (*tutor*) till the age of only fourteen in Roman law. When Pliny was seventeen he was living with his uncle at Misenum (Letter 25. 7; Ep. vi. 20. 5).

candidatum me suffragio ornauit. Young men aiming at a senatorial career had to secure a series of annual posts, including the quaestorship, tribunate, and praetorship, for which in the Empire the Senate was the electoral body. Influential senators promised their support (*suffragium*) beforehand.

ad omnes honores . . . accucurrit. Friends attended the formal entry into office of the new magistrates.

illo die quo sacerdotes solent nominare. The great priestly Brotherhoods or 'collegia', in which office was for life, were recruited by formal elections within the 'colleges', but the effective appointment was made by the Princeps from among the names put forward by the colleges. Pliny eventually secured the augurship thus, after his consulship (Ep. iv. 8, x. 13).

solent. The subject is *sacerdotes*—the members of the colleges—and the object is (εος) quos . . .'.

ex secessibus. Verginius lived in retirement at Alsium on the Etruscan coast, where he was buried (Letter 37. 1 n.).

9. **inter quinqueuiros crearetur,** 'given office on the Board of Five'. Pliny uses *creare*, a word connected with elections, because the Senate elects the board.

minuendis publicis sumptibus. The board was appointed to cut down the expenses of the Senate's administration of the public services of the city of Rome. These were paid directly out of the *aerarium populi Romani* (otherwise known as the *aerarium Saturni*, Letter 4. 9 n.). Hence the word *publicis* is used. The board cut down the cost of certain festivals, including the chariot races (Cassius Dio 68. 2. 3).

me huius aetatis, 'a man of my age'. The genitive is descriptive. Pliny was a senator of the second or praetorian grade at this time, and aged about thirty-five.

per quem excusaretur. Pliny is to present Verginius' refusal of the post to the Senate.

tibi mandarem, 'I would give you this task', i.e. of making the apology.

10. **mortalitas magis finita quam uita est,** 'his mortal condition rather than his life is ended'. The order is a little strained since *magis* does not qualify *finita*.

LETTER 9 (II. 6). TO JUNIUS AVITUS

A vulgar dinner-party

This is a letter of social advice to a young protégé, Junius Avitus, who was preparing to enter public life at this time, about A.D. 98. A year or two later he was serving as military tribune in the Danube army (Ep. viii. 23. 5).

1. familiaris. Pliny uses this word, or *sodalis* or *contubernalis*, for intimate friends, and *amicus* for cooler acquaintances. Cf. Letter 37. 5 n. and Ep. iv. 17. 2: 'est ... mihi cum isto ... non plane familiaris sed tamen amicitia'. *Homo ... familiaris* is in apposition to the subject (*ego*) of the verb.

2. sibi et paucis opima ... ceteris uilia ... ponebat. This un-pleasant custom is regularly criticized by the satirist Martial, Pliny's senior contemporary, who crisply asks in 3. 60. 9: 'cur sine te ceno cum tecum, Pontice, cenem?' Juvenal later scoffs at the vulgar Virro's banquet (*Sat.* 5. 146 f.): 'uilibus ancipites fungi ponentur amicis, boletus domino.'

gradatim amicos habet. Roman society was very finely graded, as Pliny admits in Ep. vii. 3. 2: 'amicitiae tam superiores quam minores', while Seneca earlier distinguished between 'first grade' and 'second grade' friends (*De beneficiis* 6. 33. 4–34. 5).

3. qui mihi proximus recumbebat. The party is arranged by *triclinia*, sets of three couches, each couch seating three persons in a re-clining position. Pliny and his friend are at the top set, and notice what is going on at the other sets.

ad notam. The metaphor is taken from the mark which the Roman censors placed against the names of ill-conditioned citizens in their lists.

etiamne libertos? The presence of freedmen at the dinner-party is remarkable, even though at lower tables. They would be favourite ex-slaves. Many hosts preferred to make a cash-present or *sportula* ('little basket') to their freedmen. That custom never appears in Pliny's letters, who was generous to his freedmen (Letter 24) and probably disliked it, like the Emperor Domitian, who at one time tried to suppress it (Suetonius, *Domitian* 7), but it is frequent in Martial.

4. magno tibi constat, 'it costs you a great deal'. The following *qui* is the interrogative adverb.

5. hercule. As in Letter 6. 3.

si gulae temperes. Here and below, *si parcas*, the present sub-junctive is used in the *si* clause in conjunction with compound phrases that are virtual imperatives ('non est onerosum . . . communicare', 'reprimenda . . . est'), to express a future conditional sense.

quo utaris. This is the object of *communicare*.

quibus . . . rectius tua continentia . . . consulas, 'you could deal with them better by personal restraint than by insulting others'.

6. quorundam in mensa luxuria. By using the preposition and noun instead of the genitive *mensarum* Pliny avoids a double genitive with *luxuria*. The development of a living language is apparent here.

specie frugalitatis, 'by its appearance of economy'.

sub exemplo praemonere. Pliny writes thus to juniors, to soften the edge of criticism. Cf. Ep. vii. 1. 7: 'quae tibi scripsi . . . ut te non sine exemplo monerem'.

7. nouam, i.e. 'strange', as often.

LETTER 10 (II. 11). TO ARRIANUS MATURUS

Trial of a corrupt governor

This letter describes the first of three great political cases in which Pliny prosecutes or defends a Roman provincial governor accused of extortion at the end of his tenure. The trials took place before the Senate sitting as a court with a consul acting as its president (s. 10). If the charge was limited to the taking of money and goods the Senate referred it to a committee of the House to investigate (s. 2: 'dari iudices'); the penalty was then restitution of the objects taken, and the loss of personal status and all public positions (s. 12). But if serious charges of cruelty and corrupt administration were involved (s. 2), the whole Senate tried the case and imposed severer penalties. The trial of Priscus is peculiar because he is tried by both methods, when the more serious charges should have excluded the lesser. This is an instance of the neglect of correct procedure by the Roman

Senate and magistrates which recurs several times in the Letters (cf. Letter 23), and which Pliny criticizes as *iuris senatorii obliuio* in Ep. viii. 14. 2–3. The treatment of the legate Firminus is another instance (s. 23 n.).

The recipient is Arrianus Maturus of Altinum, a Roman knight whom Pliny recommends for promotion in Letter 12.

1. secesseris. He retired temporarily to his country estate at Altinum.

2. Marius Priscus. A senator of Spanish origin, he was consul in about A.D. 81 and became proconsul of Africa for the year 97–98. He was accused in late 98, before the consulship of Julius Ferox (s. 5), and brought up for his final trial in December 99 and January 100 (s. 10).

accusantibus Afris. In Ep. iii. 9. 4 Pliny reveals that the charges were brought by several individuals and by a city, identified in s. 23 as Lepcis in African Tripolitania. The complaints were laid before the consuls at Rome, who brought them before the Senate.

pro consule. The Roman province of Africa covered Eastern Algeria, all modern Tunisia, and Tripolitania. It was governed by annual proconsuls under the direct authority not of the emperor but of the Senate, which selected the proconsuls by drawing lots among the senior ex-consuls, some sixteen years after their consulships.

omissa defensione iudices petiit. He pleads guilty to the lesser charges, heard by the judicial committee, in the hope of avoiding trial on the serious issues.

adesse prouincialibus iussi. At the first hearing of the charges the Senate assigned experienced senators to represent the plaintiffs at the trial.

excessisse . . . saeuitia crimina quibus dari iudices possent, 'by his cruelty he overstepped the charges for which a committee could be assigned'. See Introduction above. *Saeuitia* is the term normally used to indicate such actions of criminal extortion in Pliny and Tacitus.

ob innocentes condemnandos . . . pecunias accepisset. The offence lay technically in the taking of money. It was not practicable to prove that a Roman governor had given unjust sentences in his court. So the law punished the taking of bribes, which could be proved. Naturally the party which gave the bribes did not sue Priscus, but the facts leaked out when the evidence for the lesser charges was examined, as related in s. 23.

Cornelius Tacitus. For the advocate and historian Tacitus, who had been consul in 97, see Letter 2 pref.

3. Fronto Catius. The advocates named here and in ss. 16, 17 are senior senators defending Priscus.

ne quid ultra repetundarum legem quaereretur. Pliny is writing loosely here. The procedure for charges of criminal extortion was an extension of the earlier extortion law, and had been developed by rulings of the Senate in the preceding century based on the original *lex Iulia repetundarum.* Hence writers often speak as if there was a distinction between the law covering charges of cruelty involving extortion and that of simple extortion.

4. aliis cognitionem senatus lege conclusam aliis liberam solutamque dicentibus, 'some maintained that the Senate's jurisdiction was bound by the text of the law, others that it was unfettered'. The second claim was correct, because the extortion law referred to the old jury courts or *quaestiones* of the Republican period, the function of which had been taken over gradually and without legislation by the Senate since the Principate of Augustus. The Senate for practical purposes usually followed the guidance of the old law as a convenient rule-book, but it never regarded itself as bound by the old statute laws in the imposition of penalties.

5. consul designatus Iulius Ferox. He was consul in late 98 or early 99. There were several successive pairs of consuls each year at this period, normally holding office for three or four months in turn.

Mario quidem iudices interim censuit dandos. In all the numerous cases recorded in Tacitus and Pliny elsewhere the hearing of the lesser charges excludes a further trial, on the principle that a man can only be charged once for the same offence. The proper procedure was for the Senate to defer the lesser charges and hear all together.

euocandos autem quibus diceretur . . . poenas uendidisse. Usually the prosecution in a case of criminal extortion was given the right to summon witnesses compulsorily from the province (*inquisitio*) before the trial began (Ep. v. 20. 2). The difficulty in this case was that no charges of this sort had been formally brought.

censuit. The deliberation is conducted by the presiding consul, who reaches a decision by asking the opinions of the senior senators in turn, as in s. 20, beginning with the *consules designati*, i.e. those who were waiting after their election to take office as consuls in the current year. He then puts to the vote the opinions that command most support, as in s. 21.

6. fuit sola frequens, 'this alone had numerous support'. A well-attended Senate was called *frequens*. Cf. s. 10 *senatorum frequentia*.

adnotatumque experimentis quod . . ., 'it was discovered by trial that . . .'. The *quod* clause takes the place of an accusative and infinitive construction; see Introduction p. xx.

7. quod . . . tuentur, 'what many maintain'.

patescit . . ., cum separaris a turba, contemplatio rerum quae turba teguntur, 'the view of the things hidden by the crowd becomes clear only when you stand outside it'.

8. trecentis milibus, i.e. 'sestertiorum'.

exsilium . . . plura supplicia. A proconsul could not ordinarily sentence a Roman citizen to death or to the most severe form of exile, or even to a birching, if the accused exercised his right of appeal to the court of the Princeps at Rome, like St. Paul in the Acts of the Apostles (25. 10–11). Yet Pliny does not suggest that the sentences were illegal in themselves. Possibly certain crimes were exempted for practical reasons from the right of appeal.

9. Marcianus inductus est. This is the second session of the Senate recorded in the letter. It took place on the Ides of December, the regular business meeting before that mentioned in s. 10.

iure senatorio. A senator could make special requests at the beginning of public business.

10. erat enim consul. Trajan was consul in A.D. 100 for the third time, and presided over senatorial business during the month of January.

cetera, 'in general'. Accusative (plural) of extent.

frequentia. Ablative case.

noscendi. Construe with *studium*.

12. septemuir epulonum. The 'seven commissioners of sacred banquets' formed one of the four great priesthoods of the Roman state, which were much prized by leading senators and awarded by the favour of the Princeps. See Letter 8. 8.

iam neutrum. Marius has been found guilty on the lesser charges by the judicial committee (cf. Introduction), and hence has lost his personal standing or *dignitas*.

13. peractae damnationis miseratio, 'pity for his former condemnation'.

14. horis paene quinque. The normal time allowance was six hours or twenty-four turns of the 'water glass' (*clepsydra*—the ancient clock) for the prosecution. Pliny's share was twelve. He was then given four extra. This should make four hours in all. It amounted to nearly five because the glasses were *spatiosissimas*. Either the glasses were of unusual size or they were regulated to run slower than usual.

horis. Pliny often uses ablative instead of accusative for duration of time. Cf. s. 18 'triduo', and Letter 18. 1: 'pauculis . . . diebus . . . commorabor'.

illa ipsa. The points urged in ss. 11–13.

15. consulerem. Dependent on *admoneret*.

18. probationes. The examination of written evidence and witnesses, including the items in s. 23.

19. Cornutus Tertullus. His career was linked to Pliny's. They were colleagues as prefects of the Treasury of Saturn, and as consuls this year, and later Tertullus succeeded Pliny as governor of Bithynia (Ep. v. 14. 5).

censuit. The senators do not vote 'guilty' or 'not guilty', but propose a punishment, since the penalty was not automatic.

aerario inferenda. The money is confiscated to the State Treasury of Saturn (Letter 4. 9–10) because it was taken as a bribe, not by extortion.

Mario urbe Italiaque interdicendum. This is a sentence of *relegatio* or expulsion from the named areas for life, with no further penal consequences. It is distinct from *exilium*, which took the form of deportation to an island and by extinguishing all the civil rights (*caput*) of the exiled person was in law a kind of death sentence.

21. plures in hac . . . molliore. Senators judging fellow senators tended to let them off as lightly as possible. But there are no scandalous acquittals in the trials recorded by Pliny (Ep. iii. 9, iv. 9). Even the proposal of Collega would leave Priscus a politically ruined man.

22. cum fieret discessio. The House votes by 'dividing', like the House of Commons, to one side or the other. This was known as *pedibus ire in sententiam*.

qui sellis consulum adstiterant. The presence of Trajan influences those near him to support the better cause.

de Regulo. Aquilius Regulus, the advocate whose social tricks are described in Letter 11, here characteristically induces a more distinguished senator to sponsor his own proposal, and then abandons it when he sees that it may bring him no credit.

23. λειτούργιον. A civic duty.

legatus Mari. The proconsul of Africa had three junior senators called *legati propraetore* to assist him. They are distinct from the *legati Augusti propraetore* who govern the emperor's provinces.

rationibus Marciani et sermone . . . commodasse . . . probabatur. These are the main elements in this complicated sentence. The construction of *stipulatus* (*esse*) is a nominative and infinitive with the passive verb of statement (*probabatur*).

The parties involved were usually required to produce their account books (*rationes*) as evidence. These were likely to contain incriminating entries such as this item 'under the head of scent-material' (*nomine unguentarii*), because wealthy Romans kept their accounts with remarkable care. Evidently the item was 'Ten thousand sesterces to Firminus for scent-material'.

in ordine Lepcitanorum. *Ordo* is the usual word for town-council; it was later replaced by *curia*. The councils consisted of a large number of members holding office for life (*decuriones*).

The speech is made by Marcianus (*ille*), while the subject of the main sentence is Firminus (*ipse*).

pumicati, 'smoothed (with pumice-stone)'. Hence 'effeminate'.

24. **placuit . . . referri de eo.** This is a formal resolution, for which *placuit* (i.e. *patribus, senatui*) is the normal term.

Firminus had not been formally accused, but all provincial officials were liable under the extortion law. So the Senate instructs the consuls to arraign him. He was sentenced to the moderate penalty of exclusion from future provincial appointments (Ep. ii. 12. 1–2).

casu an conscientia. A compressed parenthesis with verb omitted, e.g. 'nescio casu an . . .'. Cf. Ep. i. 14. 5: 'ambitioni dicam an dignitati'.

LETTER 11 (II. 20). TO CALVISIUS RUFUS

The legacy hunter

The recipient was a landowner and alderman of Comum to whom Pliny writes about business affairs and political gossip (cf. Letters 16, 36). This letter describes *captatio*, a notable feature of Roman society, much discussed by the satirists, as in Horace, *Sermones* v. 5 and Juvenal, *Saturae* 3. The custom was connected with the Roman notion of *amicitia*. Assiduous attention was regarded as a proper means of securing personal support from seniors, and men were expected to reward their *amici* by leaving them legacies. Pliny approves of young Julius Naso (Ep. vi. 6. 5) because: 'parauit amicos, quos parauerat coluit'. The custom became an abuse when attention was directed to wealthy and elderly childless persons (*orbi*) for financial gain rather than advancement.

1. assem para. He speaks as a professional story-teller in the market-place.

noua, i.e. 'fabula'.

2. Verania Pisonis . . . quem Galba adoptauit. Her husband, L. Calpurnius Piso, was adopted as his heir by the short-lived Emperor Sulpicius Galba who displaced Nero in A.D. 68 and was murdered with Piso early in 69 by the supporters of Otho. Her father Q. Veranius had been the army commander in Britain in A.D. 58.

Regulus. This man, M. Aquilius Regulus, a leading advocate in the civil courts whom Pliny admired and detested, appears in several letters (Ep. iv. 2, 7, vi. 2). As a young man he prosecuted senators for treason in the interest of the Emperor Nero. One of his victims was Crassus, the brother of Piso, and he was rumoured to have savaged the head of Piso after his assassination. Hence the feud: *ipsi inuisissimus.* Under Vespasian he narrowly escaped punishment and abandoned the role of prosecutor. Tacitus tells the story in *Histories* iv. 42.

ipsi, i.e. to Verania. The relative *cui* is omitted.

3. digitos. Romans used the right hand for hundreds, and the left for units and tens.

climactericum tempus. An astrological term. The critical points in human life were determined by multiples of seven as the ages of 35, 49, and 63 (cf. Gellius, *Noctes Atticae* iii. 10. 9).

4. haruspicem consulam. Regulus was genuinely superstitious (Ep. vi. 2. 2), and frequently consulted *haruspices* on his own account, though here he intends a fraud. He was too cunning to consult astrologers, as their foreign practices were illegal at Rome. The *haruspices*, whose divination depended on the examination of entrails of sacrificial animals, were an Italian institution and officially recognized.

5. in periculo credula. Pliny did not expect his social equals to be so superstitious and disapproved of exotic cults (Letters 39. 9, 47. 8).

poscit codicillos. A Roman will (*testamentum*) could be extended by a separate and later document called *codicilli* or 'note-papers', adding fresh legacies, if this was properly attested by witnesses.

nequam. Indeclinable adjective, 'worthless'.

per salutem filii. The death of this boy is recorded some five years later in Ep. iv. 2, where Pliny does not recall this scandalous detail, which may be false.

7. **Velleius Blaesus.** Little is known of this man, whose death is mentioned by Martial (8. 38) about A.D. 93.

tabulis. The word is used of any formal document.

8. **bona morte.** Pliny uses the ablative for the object of *invideo*. Cf. Letter 4. 12 'inuideo aliis bono'.

Regulo ne tantulum quidem, i.e. 'legat'. Everyone was surprised because convention required Blaesus to leave Regulus something as an *amicus*.

9. **scholastica lege.** Quintilian (4. 5. 3) quotes the 'rule of rhetoricians' (*scholastici*) that three examples sufficed to establish a case. Letters 15 and 30, about Arria and about ghosts, follow the pattern of three anecdotes.

est unde fiat, 'there is a supply'.

10. **Aurelia.** She belonged to a well-known consular family.

signatura testamentum. These occasions are included in Pliny's account of the daily round at Rome in Letter 3. 2.

11. **ne multa,** i.e. *dicam*.

12. τί διατείνομαι, 'why do I continue?'

13. **cum consuleret,** i.e. 'haruspicem', as in s. 4–5.

sestertium sescentiens. This fortune of nearly sixty million sesterces compares with the immense sums of two and three hundred millions amassed by two great advocates in the time of Vespasian (Tacitus, *Dialogus* 8. 1). Pliny was much less wealthy (Letter 16. 7–8). But all senators owned far more than the nominal million sesterces which was the minimum legal qualification for senatorial status. Regulus and his like made most of their money by charging high fees for advocacy. Attempts were made to check this by enforcing a maximum charge of S. 10,000 a brief. See Letter 23. No modern equivalent can be given for these sums. Conversion tables for turning Greek or Roman money into £. s. d. are quite meaningless because of the change in values due to the industrial revolution. The comparative value of wages is some guide. A family could be kept on four sesterces (one silver denarius) a day, and a child maintained for a third of a sesterce a day (see Letter 28. 2 n.). A legionary soldier was paid at the rate of S. 1,200 a year, but high officials were paid salaries ranging from S. 60,000 to S. 1,000,000 a year. Larger sums may be evaluated as capital in terms of land value, reckoning S. 2,000–3,000 per Roman acre as an average price. See Letter 16. 7 n.

14. **illa.** The subject of *sunt*.

LETTER 12 (III. 2). TO VIBIUS MAXIMUS

Promotion of a friend

Pliny recommends his friend Arrianus Maturus for a provincial appointment to Vibius Maximus, who was the equestrian governor or prefect of Egypt from A.D. 103 onwards. The provincial governors could appoint men to military commissions in the army under their command as *tribuni militum* and *praefecti cohortis* if the candidates had the general approval of the Princeps. There are several similar testimonials in the collection, e.g. Ep. ii. 13, iii. 8, iv. 4.

1. **materia.** Cf. Ep. ii. 13. 2: 'regis exercitum amplissimum, hinc tibi beneficiorum larga materia'. Such promotions were known as *beneficia*, and promoted soldiers were called *beneficiarii*.

2. **Arrianus Maturus.** A wealthy man who had held the local magistracies of his city Altinum in North Italy, *Altinatium . . . princeps*. Many such men enter the equestrian service of the Princeps in their middle thirties after gaining experience in local government. After military service they pass on to civil service as *procuratores Augusti*, mostly on the financial side of the administration, and may eventually reach the governorship of certain provinces reserved for equestrians, as Vibius Maximus did. Cf. Letter 13, pref., and ss. 3, 17 n.

castitate . . . prudentia. These civilian virtues would be welcome in Egypt where the armed forces were more concerned with internal administration than with fighting.

3. huius . . . iudicio in studiis utor. Pliny consults Arrianus about the publication of speeches and verses, and reports the prosecution of Marius Priscus to him (Letters 10, 34. Ep. i. 2).

4. caret ambitu. Letter 10. 1: 'quietis amore secesseris' refers to the same dislike for politics.

ascendere altissimum. He means that Arrianus could have entered the Senate. Many rich men preferred unspectacular but profitable posts in the equestrian service to the political risks involved in the public life of a senator, who might arouse the jealousy of the Princeps if he was too successful as an army commander. Minicius Macrinus, another friend of Pliny, resigned the status of praetorian senator under Vespasian: 'honestam quietem huic nostrae ambitioni . . . praetulit' (Ep. i. 14. 5).

5. dignitati eius aliquid adstruere, 'to secure some addition to his rank'.

fortasse nolentis. An odd remark, in a recommendation, even if Pliny was planning a surprise. Possibly this is an addition to the original version of the letter. Arrianus accepted the appointment, for in Ep. iv. 12. 7 he writes to Pliny from overseas.

6. cuius generis quae prima occasio tibi, i.e 'whatever is the first opportunity of that sort (of appointment), give it him'.

LETTER 13 (III. 5). TO BAEBIUS MACER

The life of a public official

The senator Baebius Macer, consul in A.D. 103, governed several provinces. This letter tells most of what is known about Pliny's uncle, C. Plinius Secundus, the author of a remarkable encyclopedia of geographical, physical, and technical knowledge of the Roman world called the *Naturalis Historia*. After military commissions in the army of the Rhine from A.D. 47 to 51 he became an equestrian *procurator Augusti*, or financial administrator, in various provinces (s. 17 n.), and finally prefect of the fleet of Misenum (s. 9 n.) probably from about A.D. 74 until his death in the eruption of Vesuvius, as related in Letter 25. Other appointments have been conjectured from his references to his travels in the *Natural History*: possibly he was once procurator of Africa.

1. **libros auunculi mei.** Very little is known about these books of the Elder Pliny. Tacitus occasionally cites the 'Wars in Germany' and the 'History after Aufidius' in his *Annals*. The *Wars* covered events from Julius Caesar's wars in Gaul (58–50 B.C.) down to the reign of Tiberius (A.D. 14–37), and the *History* described the period from the accession (or a little later) of Claudius (A.D. 41) to that of Vespasian (A.D. 69–70). No more is certain, if so much.

3. **cum praefectus alae militaret.** The command of a cavalry regiment followed a military tribunate in a legion as the second step in the career of a Roman knight. Cf. Arrianus in Letter 12. Pliny probably served part of the time in the army of the Upper Rhine when his friend Pomponius Secundus was its commander (c. A.D. 50–51. Tacitus, *Annals* 12. 27). A piece of armour inscribed *Plinio praefec*, from Vetera on the Lower Rhine, may have been his (*CIL* xii. 10026, 22).

Pomponi Secundi. This consular senator, who was also an amateur dramatist (Letter 27. 11), was evidently the protector of the elder Pliny, who tried to rescue his son Pomponianus from the Vesuvius disaster (Letter 25. 11).

4. **Drusi Neronis.** Nero Claudius Drusus, brother of the future Emperor Tiberius, directed the Germanic wars of 12–9 B.C., but died after reaching the Elbe (*C.A.H.* x. 358).

5. **'Studiosi tres'.** This handbook of rhetoric is quoted by Quintilian, sometimes with disapproval (e.g. *Inst.* 3. 1. 21, 11. 3. 143).

sex uolumina, i.e. rolls of papyrus.

ab incunabulis, 'from the cradle', i.e. from the primary stage.

'Dubii sermonis'. He calls it *de grammatica* in *Nat. Hist.* Pref. 28, and it was much used by later grammarians. His own Latin in the *Nat. Hist.* is decidedly odd at times.

nouissimis annis. Nero became oppressive after the unexpected conspiracy of Piso in A.D. 65, and showed his jealousy of literary men by the execution of the poet Lucan and the exile of the philosopher Musonius.

periculosum. This is the predicate; the preceding words go directly with *genus*.

6. 'A fine Aufidi Bassi'. Pliny continued the history of Aufidius Bassus, who covered the period from the death of Julius Caesar (44 B.C.) to the accession of Gaius (A.D. 37). This is the usual form for the title of a Roman history. Cf. *ab urbe condita* for Livy, and *ab excessu diui Augusti* for the *Annals* of Tacitus.

diffusum eruditum . . . uarium. So it is. Pliny, whom Gellius called 'the most learned man of his age', claims to have included 20,000 items drawn from 2,000 book-rolls.

7. actitasse. The frequentative form of *agere*.

qua . . . qua. Like *partim . . . partim* in s. 19.

officiis maximis. His procuratorships.

amicitia principum. He was one of the so-called *amici principis* who sat, like the younger Pliny under Trajan (Letter 20), in the advisory cabinet of Vespasian (s. 9).

8. summa uigilantia. His motto was *uita uigilia est* (*Nat. Hist.* Pref. 18).

lucubrare. To work by lamplight.

Vulcanalibus. The feast of Vulcanus was on 28 August.

non auspicandi causa. The *auspicia* were taken after a night vigil. This was the only duty for which an official might be expected to 'keep watch'.

erat . . . somni paratissimi. Descriptive genitive, cf. 'erat moris' Letter 17. 3.

9. ille quoque noctibus utebatur. Suetonius also tells how Vespasian dealt with his business papers and consulted his cabinet in the dawn-hours (*Vesp.* 21).

delegatum . . . officium. His duties as a prefect of the fleet in the later years of Vespasian were partly performed at Rome, partly at Misenum, Letter 25. 4 n.

quod reliquum temporis, i.e. 'erat'. The routine of the elder Pliny, described here and in Letter 25. 4–5, differs from the country round of his nephew in Letter 40, but Martial's account of the Roman day (iv. 8. 5–8) makes it clear. His working day ends about the fifth hour after dawn with a light meal (*cibum . . . leuem*). Then comes rest, bath, and a second light meal (*gustabat*), which took him to the seventh hour (Letter 25. 4). Sleep and study continued until the main meal (*cena*), taken at the ninth or tenth hour in summer (s. 13). In winter his time-table was altered to make the most of the warmer hours.

10. si quid otii, i.e. 'erat'.

liber legebatur, i.e. by a trained reader, as at Pliny's dinner-party, Letter 7. 2 n.

excerpebatque. Doubtless making his collection of material for his *Natural History*.

11. frigida, i.e. 'aqua', ablative.

12. nempe. Cf. Letter 15. 8: 'nempe enim'. The particle may be equated with 'of course'.

14. in secessu, 'when away from Rome', i.e. at a country house, as in Letter 40.

eximebatur, 'was free of reading'.

de interioribus. The scraping took place in the outer room or *unctorium*, and the inner rooms held the actual baths, as in Pliny's villa (Ep. ii. 17. 11).

15. notarius cum . . . pugillaribus. A shorthand writer who takes down Pliny's comments in a leaved notebook (*codex*), cf. Letter 2. 1 n.

Seneca (*Ep.* 90. 25) mentions 'word-signs in which the fastest speech is taken down'.

manicis, 'sleeves'.

17. **electorumque commentarios,** 'record-books of selected passages'.

opisthographos. He displays eccentric meanness. It was rare for a roll to be written on both sides unless a book overran its estimated length.

cum procuraret in Hispania. He was then the financial agent of the Princeps (*procurator Augusti*) in charge of imperial revenue and expenditure in Northern Spain (Hispania Tarraconensis) at a time when Larcius Licinius was the imperial governor (*legatus Augusti propraetore*), probably about A.D. 72–74.

18. **nec scripsisse,** i.e. *uidetur*.

19. **amicorum officia,** 'services to friends', i.e. he defended their interests in courts of law as an advocate.

LETTER 14 (III. 14). TO ACILIUS

Murder of a master

Acilius is probably a wealthy friend of Pliny from Patavium in North Italy mentioned in Ep. i. 14. 6.

The murder of a master by a slave at Rome caused the sort of horror that is felt for a child-murder in modern times, for the reasons that Pliny's letter makes clear. Such crimes were not frequent, but a year or two later all Rome was appalled when a consul in office was found dead in suspicious circumstances (Ep. viii. 14. 12). Tacitus comments at length on the similar murder of Pedanius Fuscus, the head of the Roman police, in *Annals* 14. 42–45.

1. **Larcius Macedo . . . seruisse patrem.** It is difficult to explain how this man could be the son of a slave, because strict rules barred the descendants of slaves even from the functions of the equestrian order for three generations, except by the special favour of the

Princeps. Possibly the father was a household favourite who was first freed and then adopted by a member of the well-known senatorial family of Larcii. No other senator in this period can be proved to have been the son of a slave, though the great-grandfather of the Emperor Vitellius was believed to have been servile.

alioqui ... saeuus, 'altogether a brute'; *alioqui* ('otherwise') is a favourite particle of Pliny's. Cf. Letters 26. 16, 34. 5.

2. **in uilla Formiana.** At Formiae on the Campanian coast south of Rome.

fidem ... mortis, 'the conviction of death'.

4. **aegre focilatus,** 'barely brought to life'. The metaphor in *focilor* is from a household fire (*focus*).

uindicatus. The rule was that all slaves who were in the house at the time of the murder were put to death. The servile households in the palaces of the Roman aristocracy were very large. That of Pedanius Fuscus numbered 400. Hence the panic and the severity of the deterrent.

5. **non ... iudicio domini ... perimuntur,** 'masters are not murdered on grounds of reason'. Pliny betrays his panic, because he has admitted that the murder of the savage Larcius was rational.

6. **quid ... noui.** Partitive genitive.

dies feriatus. On such days of festival the courts did not sit, and Pliny was at leisure.

in publico ... lauaretur. The great Baths at Rome were patronized by rich and poor, for whom they filled the role of cafés, clubs, and swimming-pools in modern cities.

LETTER 15 (III. 16). TO MAECILIUS NEPOS

Portrait of a heroine

The recipient is an obscure senator to whom two or three other letters are addressed, unless the manuscript is emended to identify him with a well-known consular administrator called Metilius Nepos.

The letter, like Letter 11, tells three anecdotes to illustrate a theme according to the *lex scholastica* (ibid., s. 9).

2. neptis haec Arriae illius. The story of these ladies is mostly known from the letters of Pliny, who was a family friend. The heroine of this letter is the elder Arria, wife of Caecina Paetus and mother of the younger Arria. The latter married the heroic Thrasea Paetus, a consular senator who championed the rights of the Senate under Nero, and was condemned to death on a charge of disloyalty (s. 10 n.). Their daughter Fannia (*neptis haec*) married Thrasea's friend Helvidius Priscus, and was involved in the family opposition to the Principate under Vespasian and Domitian. Pliny tells the story of the political misfortunes of Fannia in Ep. vii. 19, and in Ep. ix. 13 recounts how he tried to secure her redress after the death of Domitian.

4. quin immo. Particles, not conjunctions: 'moreover'.

quotiens . . . intraret. Cf. Letter 5. 7 *quotiens intrasset* for the subjunctive in an indefinite clause after *quotiens*, contrary to the earlier usage of the indicative. But in Letter 40 he uses present indicative tense.

commodiorem, 'better'. This somewhat colloquial word is a favourite of Pliny in the chameleon senses of the English 'nice'. Cf. Ep. iii. 20. 11: 'ecquid commode uales?'; Letter 24. 3: 'commode orationes . . . legit', and Letter 28. 2.

5. orbitatem, 'her loss of a child'.

foris. Outside the room where her husband was.

6. illud eiusdem, 'that deed of hers'. Pliny anticipates the end of the story, the suicide of Arria and Paetus, which followed the events recounted in ss. 7–12. Cassius Dio 60. 16. 5–6 tells the same story.

quo maius. An exclamation, 'how much greater a thing it is . . .!'

7. Scribonianus arma in Illyrico . . . mouerat. This took place in A.D. 42 during Claudius' reign. Pliny's is the earliest account. The events are told in Dio (60. 15–16) and mentioned in Tacitus, *Annals* (12. 52. 1–2). See the *Cambridge Ancient History*, x. 671. L. Arruntius Camillus Scribonianus, commander of two legions in Dalmatia

(*Illyricum superius*, the southern part of modern Yugoslavia), was in touch with conspirators at Rome. But his army failed to support them, a soldier slew him (s. 9), and all was over in fifteen days.

fuerat . . . in partibus. The regular phrase for taking sides in a revolt. Paetus, a consular senator, was present as an advisory member (*comes*) of the staff of Camillus.

8. **nempe enim,** 'of course'. Cf. Letter 13. 12 n.

daturi . . . consulari . . . seruolos aliquos. Even a traitor was treated according to his station.

9. **minimo,** i.e. *nauigio*; instrumental ablative occurs with *sequor*.

apud Claudium. The trial took place in the Senate. Claudius was present, but the consuls presided (Dio).

cum illa profiteretur indicium. Vibia had been with Scribonianus. She was accused of complicity, and offered information against her friends, but was exiled. Tacitus (*Hist.* 2. 75) names Volaginius as her husband's assassin.

10. **ne mori pergeret.** Arria, who was protected by Messalina, wife of Claudius, was not accused, and her suicide was voluntary (Dio).

uis . . . filiam tuam . . . mori mecum? This very situation arose when Thrasea was sentenced in A.D. 66, and he duly persuaded his wife (*filiam tuam*) to go on living for the sake of Fannia (Tacitus, *Annals* 16. 34).

12. **exsiluit cathedra.** This incident precedes the final act described in s. 6.

cathedra. A seat.

focilata. Letter 14. 4 n.

13. **'Paete, non dolet'.** Paetus must have been allowed the free choice of death allowed to senators condemned to execution on political charges.

LETTER 16 (III. 19). TO CALVISIUS RUFUS

On buying an estate

Rufus is the alderman of Comum to whom Pliny wrote Letter 11.

Several of Pliny's letters deal with his estate business, and give information about the tenancy system which is not found in the contemporary Columella's book about agriculture. His lands were divided into separate farms which may have varied from fifteen to forty acres in size, and were let (*locare*) on short five-year leases to working farmers (*coloni*) for a cash rent. Every fifth year there was a general renewal of leases, and large numbers of tenants changed their farms, moving from estate to estate. Part of the land was kept in the owner's hands and farmed through a slave steward (*uilicus*) with servile labour. This 'home farm' was usually around the great country house (*uilla*) of the landowner. In Ep. v. 6 Pliny describes his *uilla* and estate at Tifernum Tiberinum on the upper Tiber, to which he hopes to add the lands described in this letter.

2. eodem procuratore. Pliny as a senator was obliged to live at Rome for at least ten months a year. So he manages his lands through an agent and staff (*actoribus*) whose duty it is to exact the obligations of the tenants and to perform those of the landlord, and to supervise the steward of the home farm.

unam uillam colere. Pliny's country house at Tifernum (Ep. v. 6. 14–40) was an elaborate building with many apartments, porticoes, and pleasure-grounds, which were maintained by the technicians listed in s. 3.

3. topiariorum. Topiary was a great feature of Roman gardens. At Tifernum there were box-trees in the shapes of wild animals, and forming the letters of Pliny's name (Ep. v. 6. 16, 35). The *atrienses* are the household-servants, the *fabri* are the carpenters and maintenance men.

uenatorii instrumenti. Hunting gear. For Pliny's hunting see Letter 2. 1.

plurimum refert . . . conferas, 'it makes a great difference whether you centralize . . .'.

4. incerta fortunae. Construe together. Note the contrast expressed in the rhetorical figure of a *chiasmus*: 'incerta (*a*) fortunae (*b*) possessionum (*b*) uarietatibus (*a*)'. Cf. p. xvii.

6. felicitas terrae . . . fatigatur, 'the fertile land is being exhausted'.

uendidit pignora . . . reliqua colonorum minuit . . . sunt . . . instruendi. The tenants pledged their working equipment and other property as security (*pignora*) for their rental payments. When these fell into arrears (*reliqua*), the owner distrained and sold the goods. Hence the farms now lack equipment, which Pliny must provide (*instruendi*) if the tenants are to continue. Normally working equipment was provided partly by the tenant and partly by the owner, who was responsible for the heavy tools, such as oil-presses and wine-vats.

7. instruendi eo pluris quod frugi mancipiis, 'the lands must be equipped with slaves, at all the greater cost because (it must be) with decent ones'. The Latin is compressed, but correct: *pluris* is a genitive of price. It was unusual for the landlord to provide the working slaves on leased farms. Pliny also has in mind the need for slaves on the 'home farm'.

nec . . . uinctos habeo. The chain-gang, housed in great prison-camps (*ergastula*), much used in the Late Republic, was now falling out of fashion, and the agricultural slave was an expensive trained worker.

sestertio triciens. Three million sesterces. For comparative values see Letter 11. 13 n. The price can be converted to an acreage by dividing the earlier valuation of 5,000,000 by the price of some 2,000 to 3,000 sesterces for a Roman acre of improved farm land, quoted by Columella about a generation earlier. This would give an estate of between 1,000 and 1,500 Roman acres, a unit which was about two-thirds of an English acre (Columella, *de re rustica* 3. 3. 8).

non quia non . . . fuerint. We can say 'not that they were not once'. The effect of this double negative with a causal conjunction and subjunctive verb is concessive—'although the price was once five millions'.

communi temporis iniquitate. Four times in ten years Pliny complains about the difficulties of landlords and tenants. Good tenants are scarce (*penuria colonorum*), and good and bad alike fail to pay their rents in full. Finally, Pliny tried the experiment of replacing cash rents by a fixed proportion of the crops, to reduce the burden in bad seasons (Ep. ix. 37). It is possible that Italian vineyards were suffering from the competition of the European provinces, where the vine was being widely planted in areas in which it had never been grown before. Hence the export of wine from Italy to North Europe may have declined and prices fallen. The Emperor Domitian had even ordered the destruction of provincial plantations and the limitation of vineyards in Italy. For a discussion see G. E. F. Chilver, *Cisalpine Gaul*, pp. 150 ff.; M. Rostovtzeff, *Social and Economic History of the Roman Empire*² (1957), 199 ff.

8. sum . . . prope totus in praediis. In English too one can say 'I am almost entirely in land'.

aliquid . . . fenero, 'I have some of my money out on loans'. In the absence of the capitalist system of stocks and shares, money-lending was the only form of short-term investment in the Roman world, for those who were not directly engaged in commerce or small-scale industry. Agriculture was the only great industry, and land the only permanent investment.

a socru. This lady, Pompeia Celerina, mother of Pliny's former wife, was still on very good terms with him (Ep. i. 4).

9. uelim . . . examines. Cf. Ep. v. 12. 4; vi. 8. 8. When the subject of the verb changes, Pliny uses the subjunctive instead of the infinitive after *uolo* as a polite imperative.

LETTER 17 (III. 21). TO CORNELIUS PRISCUS

A poet retires

Priscus is a consular senator who held office in about A.D. 102–3.

The letter is the only evidence about the death of the poet Martial, which should fall between 102 and 104, since Martial's last book refers to an event of 101 or 102, and no letter of Pliny's third book is as late as 105. The death of a man of letters is a recurrent theme in Pliny, who records the death of Silius Italicus in Ep. iii. 7 and that of the biographer Fannius in Ep. v. 5.

1. **salis . . . fellis . . . candoris.** Salt for wit, gall for satire, and light for charm, give the three chief moods of Martial's verses.

2. **prosecutus . . . uiatico.** He pays his travelling expenses, as for his freedman Zosimus in Letter 19.

secedentem. Martial, who had been publishing his light and satirical verses about social life at Rome since A.D. 84, returned to his native town of Bilbilis in Spain in 97 or 98, after the production of his eleventh volume at Rome when Nerva was Princeps. When he published the twelfth three years later at Bilbilis, he regretted his return, in the words of his preface: 'hac prouinciali solitudine . . . ubi sine solacio et sine excusatione secesserim'.

3. **fuit moris.** Cf. Letter 5. 7, n.: 'habebat hoc moris'.

desîmus for *desiimus*.

4. **qui sint uersiculi.** They appear in Martial 10. 20 (19), written about A.D. 96 when Pliny was only a praetorian senator. Pliny summarizes the first ten lines, and quotes the most flattering.

tenerem, i.e. 'in my memory'. Cf. Letter 40. 2: 'componi teneriue'.

5. **Esquilîs quaerat.** The Muse Thalia, who is to deliver a volume of verses to Pliny, has to climb up from Martial's humble lodging through the Suburra to Pliny's palace on the Esquiline hill.

disertam. Martial fêtes Pliny as an eloquent advocate, busy in the court of the Centumviri (Letter 23 nn.), like a second Cicero.

studet auribus, 'prepares for the ears of the Hundred'.

Arpinis . . . chartis. The pages of Cicero, who came from Arpinum.

tetricae. The goddess of the arts (cf. Letter 2. 3) is 'severe' in the demands that she makes.

Lyaeus, i.e. Bacchus.

rigidi Catones. The first Cato, a politician of the second century

B.C., was a Roman 'of the old school', and the 'younger Cato', an opponent of Julius Caesar, was a strict Stoic. But both were addicted to the bottle, as Martial hints.

6. **daturus amplius,** 'he would have given more'; the participle, with *erat* omitted, replaces the normal conditional tense (*dedisset*).

at non erunt aeterna. Despite Martial's survival the comment is perhaps just, like that on Silius Italicus in Ep. iii. 7. 5: 'scribebat carmina maiore cura quam ingenio'. Martial's pleasanter poems are written much in the tone of Pliny's letters, and may be their model (p. xvi). Both pass for minor classics, full of charm, but not 'eternal'.

LETTER 18 (IV. 13). TO CORNELIUS TACITUS

Hiring a schoolmaster

For Tacitus, the distinguished advocate, busy at this period preparing to write his *Histories*, see Letter 2.

1. **pauculis . . . diebus.** For ablative of duration see Letter 10. 14 n.

in Tusculano. A country house near Tusculum, in the hills outside Rome.

opusculum. His first volume of verses is described in Ep. iv. 14, the next letter to this in Book IV. He uses this word only for his verse. Cf. Letter 34. 4 'liber . . . opusculis uarius et metris'.

2. **ne quid . . . pereat,** 'that I may lose no time'. Literally 'that nothing may be lost to my haste'. He might equally have written *festinationis* as a partitive genitive.

quasi praecursoria. The letter is a scout, *praecursor*.

3. **in patria mea.** Comum, on Lake Como.

uenit ad me salutandum . . . filius praetextatus. The hour for formal calls was the levée at dawn, when dependants called on their patrons. Boys wore the purple-bordered *toga* until about fifteen, when they came of age; cf. Letter 3. 2 n.

'studes?' Pliny is inquiring about the second stage in Roman education, the course in rhetoric, given by a *rhetor Latinus*, which followed the primary course in Greek and Latin language and literature given by a *grammaticus*. The words *studia*, *studes* throughout the letters commonly refer to rhetorical study; cf. Ep. iii. 3. 4: 'iam studia . . . proferenda sunt, iam circumspiciendus rhetor Latinus'. The primary course was available at Comum, where Pliny himself learned his 'grammar' with his fellow citizens (Ep. i. 19. 1). The course in rhetoric dealt with forensic oratory, and aimed at producing trained advocates. Quintilian's *Institutio* contains an elaborate account of the methods of the *rhetor Latinus* at their highest level. At an advanced stage the pupils produced set speeches on special themes, of which samples are given in the elder Seneca's *Controuersiae*. See further E. P. Parks, *Roman Rhetorical Schools* (Baltimore, 1945), ch. 3; H. I. Marrou, *History of Education in Antiquity* (English Translation), ii ch. vi.

Mediolani. Milan was the chief city of the western area of Cisalpine Gaul in north Italy.

4. uestra. The adjectival form, in the ablative, is normal instead of a pronoun after *interest*, with *re* understood.

pudicius continerentur. In Ep. iii. 3. 3–5 Pliny is concerned with the morals of the public schools of rhetoric at Rome, and recommends the establishment of the severe Julius Genitor as a place where boys will learn 'nothing that they would be better without'.

5. conducere praeceptores. A 'school' was nothing but a booth or room, or an alcove in a public portico, where a teacher gave instruction at so much a head. Pliny calls the teachers of Rome simply 'omnes qui profitentur' (Ep. ii. 18. 3). Sometimes town councils hired teachers for a salary (s. 6), but private enterprise was common.

habitationes, 'lodgings'. Everything other than the teaching depended on personal arrangements.

peregre, 'abroad', i.e. outside the home-town, *republica nostra*.

adicere mercedibus. By increasing the fee they can attract a better man. A famous professor at Rome might charge as much as 2,000 sesterces a head and make 40,000 a year. The municipal teachers fared less well, though figures are not known in detail (Marrou, op. cit. ii, ch. 6).

pro republica nostra, i.e. 'for my municipality'. Cf. s. 3: *patria*. The Romans thought of their native city as a second native land after the Roman state.

6. **munus . . . ambitu . . . corrumperetur.** Pliny fears nepotism if the choice of professors is left to the municipal council, just as he feared the ruin of his local charity at Comum if he left its management entirely to the city (Letter 28. 1).

quandoque, 'at some time'.

publice conducuntur. Gellius (*Noctes Atticae,* 16. 6. 2) tells how a *grammaticus* was hired from Rome by the city of Brundisium, and Tacitus mentions a school for the sons of the Gallic aristocracy at Augustodunum (Autun) in *Annals* 3. 43. Vespasian encouraged such schools by granting teachers exemption from taxation. Later the number of privileged teachers had to be limited to three, four, or five for each subject ('grammar', rhetoric, and medicine also), according to the size of the cities, while to prevent corrupt practices, such as Pliny feared, the cities were required to apply proficiency tests (Marrou, op. cit. iii, ch. viii).

7. **religio recte iudicandi,** 'scrupulous care for fair judgement'. For *religio* implies both 'precision' and 'obligation'. Cf. Letter 22. 5, of a historian, 'religiosissime scripsit'.

10. **ex copia studiosorum quae ad te . . . conuenit.** The great advocates such as Tacitus did not give formal instruction for fees, but they had a circle of followers, including men of humble means who might welcome the present opportunity. These they trained by informal discussion and example, just as Pliny did for his aristocratic pupil Ummidius Quadratus (Letter 29. 2 n.). Society was shocked when the senator Licinianus in exile turned rhetorician: 'nunc eo decidit ut . . . rhetor de oratore fieret' (Ep. iv. 11. 1).

illi iudicent. They may ask the competitors to demonstrate their talents, like the *grammaticus* at Brundisium (s. 6 n.), who gave a trial lecture.

altius et . . . a fonte repetenda, 'this should be traced back to its origins'; cf. 9. 1: 'longum est altius repetere'.

11. **ea lege ut,** 'on condition that'.

LETTER 19 (IV. 19). TO CALPURNIA HISPULLA

Snapshot of a wife

Hispulla is the daughter of Calpurnius Fabatus, a local magnate and councillor of Comum. Pliny has recently married her niece, also called Calpurnia, whose father, the son of Fabatus, is dead (s. 1). This was apparently Pliny's third marriage (Ep. x. 2. 2), made after A.D. 100, though little is known of his second wife (Letter 16. 8 n.) and nothing of his first.

Pliny's description of his marriage has been criticized by modern readers as patronizing and cool. Roman marriages were based not on romance but on convenience and the propagation of the family. Wives were married very young. Calpurnia was probably not more than fifteen when she married Pliny, who was over forty. Yet Pliny expects more from his marriage than convenience. He looks forward to a genuine sharing of interests, however solemnly he may express it, and in an age when divorce was frequent he hopes for a lasting marriage. Elsewhere he speaks approvingly of devoted wives, united marriages, and couples who share their worst troubles (Letter 5. 7, Ep. vi. 24, viii. 5, 18. 8).

1. **euadere,** i.e. *illam.*

2. **amat me quod castitatis indicium est.** Pliny at least has no opinion of his own looks. Cf. Ep. i. 14. 8: 'facies liberalis . . . debet . . . castitati puellarum quasi praemium dari'.

meos libellos. His prose works, such as his *de ultione Heluidii* (Ep. ix. 13. 1).

3. **qua illa sollicitudine.** Construed with *adficitur.* The word-order of both clauses with the same verb corresponds exactly, just as in s. 8: 'ego quod, etc.'

acturus, 'when I am going to plead in court'.

si quando recito. Pliny was devoted to the practice of reciting his speeches and verses to select audiences (Letter 27, 34; cf. Letter 6, for recitations in general).

4. uersus quidem meos cantat. Pliny began to write and publish light verses in the style of Martial about the time of his marriage to Calpurnia. Ep. iv. 14 describes his first, and Letter 34 his second book of verse. The sample in Letter 26. 11 has little merit.

formatque cithara. Not 'set to music' so much as 'regulate by music'. Verse was chanted to the accompaniment of the stringed zither.

5. gloriam diligit. A way of saying that she shares his interests.

7. matrem meam . . . uererere. Pliny is marrying modestly within the circle of local family friends, instead of trying to make a match at Rome with a wealthy heiress of high rank.

ominari, 'forecast', i.e. by omens.

8. illam mihi . . . me sibi dederis. The thought is almost modern.

LETTER 20 (IV. 22). TO SEMPRONIUS RUFUS

The Emperor's 'Cabinet'

The letter describes an administrative inquiry before the Emperor Trajan in about A.D. 104. It is suitably addressed to a junior senator who was later consul.

1. principis optimi cognitioni. Trials before the emperor were called *cognitiones*. He sat as judge with a committee of advisers (*consilium*), whose opinion he took before giving his decision (s. 3, *sententiae perrogarentur*). They were not a jury, and the emperor was not bound to follow the majority opinion, though he usually did so, as on this occasion (s. 7, *placuit*). The advisers were senators or knights invited for particular sessions (*in consilium adsumptus*). Juvenal in his 'fish satire' (*Sat.* 4) parodies an investigation before Domitian at which the assessors numbered ten. Pliny describes two other sessions of the imperial court which he attended (Ep. vi. 22, 31). The procedure was quick and simple. Decisions on each case were reached in a single day, unlike the protracted trials before the Senate (Letter 10).

gymnicus agon. Pliny uses the Greek word for competition, because this was a festival in the Greek style with athletic and musical competitions instead of the usual Roman 'games' (*ludi*) involving beast-fights and gladiators.

apud Viennenses. Vienna on the Rhône, modern Vienne in Provence, once the capital of the Celtic tribe called Allobroges, was now a flourishing Romanized city with a Roman theatre that still survives, and a taste for Greek culture derived from the formerly Greek city of Massilia (Marseilles).

in duumuiratu tollendum ... curauit. Rufinus, as one of the two senior annual magistrates (*duouiri*) or mayors of Vienna, had the chief executive power in local government. But the magistrates were expected to act with the advice of the town council (*ex auctoritate publica*), which should have debated the abolition of the festival. Since Rufinus had not done so the council appealed to the emperor at Rome to reverse the action of the magistrate. Surprisingly they do not seem to have consulted the governor of the province about the matter.

2. egit ipse causam ... tamquam homo Romanus. All wealthy men attended the schools of forensic rhetoric, as in Letter 18. 4–5, and learned the rudiments of the art. Vienna was a borough of Roman citizens of Gallic origin.

commendabat. The subject is the *quod* clause.

actionem. A forensic speech.

3. perrogarentur, 'were asked in turn'.

Iunius Mauricus. This consular senator, who had been exiled on a political charge by Domitian, returned under Nerva in A.D. 97. See Letters 5. 6–8, 30. 14.

quo uiro. Supply *est*.

4. idem. Supply *egit* with *fortiter*.

Veiento proximus. Fabricius Veiento, the senior consular senator at this time, had been one of Domitian's counsellors, and retained his influence under Nerva.

recumbebat. For the arrangement of a Roman dinner-party see Letter 9. They lay on couches instead of sitting on chairs.

5. Catullus Messalinus. This man, Valerius Catullus Messalinus, had assisted Domitian's political purges, not as a prosecuting counsel (*delator*), but by proposing severe sentences of punishment when the Senate conducted treason trials. Each senator could give a formal *sententia*, and that of Catullus called for the death penalty (*sanguinariis sententiis*). Cf. Letter 10. 5, 22 n.

mala caecitatis. Pliny here uses *malum* as a noun. The 'evils' are indicated by the following verbs, *non uerebatur*, etc.

quo saepius, 'all the more often'.

6. passurum fuisse si uiueret. The mixture of tenses, with *uiueret* instead of *uixisset*, is idiomatic. 'If he were alive today' is more effective than 'if he had survived'. Cf. Letter 17. 6 n. for a similar mixture.

7. longius abii. Pliny apologizes because he has broken the rule that a literary letter was concerned with one subject only; cf. Letter 11. 9 n.

placuit. This is the verdict given to Trajan by his counsellors.

ut noster hic omnium. He means that the great Roman festival called Quinquatrua, instituted by Domitian on Greek lines, has corrupted the *mores omnium*. Roman writers are full of similar denunciations of pure athletics, which they suspected of encouraging homosexual tendencies. Cf. Tacitus, *Annals* 14. 20: 'degeneret iuuentus, gymnasia et otia et turpes amores exercendo'.

LETTER 21 (IV. 30). TO LICINIUS SURA

On the force of water

This is one of a group of letters, including Letters 25, 30, and Ep. viii. 20, in which Pliny first describes and then tries to give a rational explanation of physical phenomena. This letter contains a genuine effort to discover a theoretical or scientific explanation of observed facts, but reveals the weakness of ancient scientific thinking in the lack of a systematic experimental method.

Licinius Sura, trusted adviser of the Emperor Trajan in affairs of government, was an advocate by profession, like Pliny, and a savant by inclination. Pliny also addressed to him his inquiry into the nature of dreams and visions (Letter 30).

1. **ex patria mea,** i.e. from Comum.

2. **fons oritur.** The spring can still be seen in the grounds of the 'Villa Pliniana', which is a Renaissance palace. It behaves much the same as in antiquity. Pliny fails to give an impression of the considerable body of water, and the thunderous noise of the waterfall, though his uncle described it as *fons largus* (*Nat. Hist.* 2. 232).

cenatiuncula. Diminutive of *cenatio* (dining-room), i.e. a grotto for picnics. Pliny, like all Italians, delighted to have water in and around his houses. At his Tuscan villa he contrived a similar dining-arbour around a fountain (Ep. v. 6. 36–37).

3. **deprenditur,** 'is noted' or 'observed'.

4. **nouissime,** 'finally'.

5. **spiritusne aliquis occultior.** Pliny thinks of this hidden current of air as entering the vents of the spring (*os et fauces*) from inside the earth, like the air inside the bottles (s. 6). The analogy and argument are rational.

prout inlatus, 'according as it enters and meets (the water) or is pushed out and departs'.

6. **non hians nec statim patens,** i.e. bottles with narrow and long necks. The *ampulla* was a long jar, swelling in the middle, particularly suited to this experiment.

per . . . obluctantis animae moras, 'through checks due to the resistant air'. This is a 'subjective' genitive: the air causes the delay.

sistunt quod effundunt, 'check their flow'.

7. **an quae oceano natura fonti quoque?** 'Does the spring have the

same principle as the ocean?' The Romans had only come to know much about oceanic tides since the conquest of North Gaul and Britain. Pliny writes as if he was not aware of the lunar attraction, which was known to his uncle in the *Nat. Hist.* 2. 212.

8. **an ut flumina?** He now suggests external air pressure, instead of internal as in ss. 6–7.

aestu, i.e. the waters of the sea.

repercutiat, 'drives back'.

9. **certa mensura quae dum colligit?** 'Is there a water-gauge of fixed capacity, and is the stream diminished while this is storing up again the amount of water that it had drawn out?' Now, and in s. 10, Pliny applies his knowledge of the Roman aqueducts to the problem, and supposes that some natural feature is acting like the gauges of the aqueducts. *Mensura* can mean either a water-gauge or the act of measuring the water (Frontinus, *de aquis* 66, 69).

10. **nescio quod libramentum?** 'Is there a levelling device which, when emptied, draws out the water, etc.?' When used of water *libramentum* may mean the difference of height between the head and the foot of a supply, or the level itself. In other contexts it means a counterpoise. Pliny imagines either some reservoir through which the underground stream flows, and which controls the action of the water, or else a device like a ball-cock, rising and sinking to free or to block the passage of the water. Neither explanation is fully worked out, but both are logical and practical.

LETTER 22 (V. 8). TO TITINIUS CAPITO

Writing history

Written about A.D. 105–6. Titinius Capito was an imperial official of the equestrian grade. He had been the secretary of state called *ab epistulis*, in charge of the correspondence between the emperor and the provincial governors and army commanders, under Nerva and Trajan, and was now head of the fire-service at Rome (*praefectus uigilum*). He wrote historical biographies in prose and verse as a hobby (Ep. i. 17. 3; viii. 12. 1–4), and was a patron of young writers. He was probably much older than Pliny, whom he here encourages to write history.

1. **cum sua,** i.e. 'fama'.

2. **me . . . diuturnitatis . . . cupido sollicitat.** The letter echoes several passages in Cicero's famous letter to Lucceius urging him to write a history of Cicero's own consulship (*Ad fam*. v. 12). Compare ibid. i: 'me . . . commemoratio posteritatis . . . rapit'.

4. **nisi eloquentia est summa.** Pliny did not have exaggerated ideas about his own ability as an orator, though he took great pride in his successes (Letter 10. 19). He hopes for no more than *diuturnitas*, not for the *aeternitas* of great writers. His tone is modest throughout this letter, and if he takes up history he does not expect to do it very well (s. 11).

historia quoquo modo scripta delectat. This is a rare attitude in antiquity, when history was generally regarded as requiring a high degree of literary skill, with truth as a secondary object. But Pliny respects accuracy: 'nec historia debet egredi ueritatem' (Letter 31. 10), as in his scientific observations (Letters 21, 25).

sermunculis, 'gossip'. Diminutive of *sermo*.

5. **auunculus meus idemque per adoptionem pater.** For the elder Pliny's life see Letter 13. He seems to have adopted Pliny in the Roman fashion by will, after his death in the eruption of Vesuvius (Letter 25).

historias. The elder Pliny wrote a history of the German wars of Rome, and another of the reigns of Claudius and Nero (Letter 13. 4, 6 n.).

religiosissime, i.e. 'very scrupulously'.

6. **graues causas.** He means his prosecution of Baebius Massa in 93, of Marius Priscus in 99–100 (Letters 10, 31), and of the associates of Caecilius Classicus (Ep. iii. 9), all for extortion as governors of Roman provinces.

has . . . destino retractare. Pliny was a great believer in the careful revision and refinement of writing before publication, both of his oratory and his verses, as described in Letters 27. 5–8, 34. 4–5.

7. **abunde sit,** 'it is enough'. The adverb is used with the verb instead of an adjective, much like the phrase *pro non incohato est* above.

8. **unodeuicensimo aetatis anno dicere in foro coepi,** i.e. when aged eighteen. He was over seventeen in A.D. 79–80, the year after his uncle's death (Ep. vi. 20. 5), and mentions twice a case that he undertook when a very young man (Ep. i. 18. 3, iv. 24. 1). It was the fashion to begin in the courts thus, under the guidance of some leading advocate. Pliny himself introduced young Pedanius Fuscus and Quadratus to the Bar (Letters 26 pref., 29. 9).

in foro. The basilica Julia, court-house of the Centumviral bar (Letter 23. 1 n.), lay off the Forum Romanum.

9. **narrat illa narrat haec.** Throughout this section *illa* is history, and *haec* is oratory. Elsewhere Pliny reckons the style of history closer to poetry than to that of oratory, following his master Quintilian (*Inst. or.* 10. 1. 31). In Ep. i. 16. 1 he says that history requires *suauitas, splendor, sublimitas narrandi*.

10. **hanc . . . nerui, illam tori . . . decent.** The orator should be lean or sinewy and well muscled like a long-distance runner, the historian should have well-fleshed bulges (*tori*) and full mane (*iubae*) rather like an all-in wrestler. Quintilian assigns *athletarum tori* to history and *militum lacerti* to oratory.

alia uerba, 'their vocabularies differ'.

11. **ut Thucydides ait.** Pliny reverses the notion of Thucydides (i. 22. 4) that history as a 'possession for ever' should not be in a poetical style. For Pliny since history is a 'possession' (κτῆμα), not a 'competition' (ἀγώνισμα), it must be more, not less, ornate. But Thucydides wanted his history free from superfluous embellishments.

sit. The construction is an indirect question, with *utrum* to be supplied, after *refert*. 'It is important whether . . .'.

hoc ipso diuersa, quo maxima, i.e. *sunt*. 'differ in the very quality which gives them greatness'.

colluuione. Usually this has a bad sense; a *nasty* mixture of styles is here intended.

ueniam . . . aduocandi peto, 'I beg to be excused the brief for history'.

a meis uerbis recedam, 'not to abandon my vocabulary', i.e. of oratory.

12. **parata inquisitio sed onerosa collatio.** Pliny would find the research already assembled in existing histories, but it would be a labour to compare the different authors.

intacta et noua. He is thinking of a history of his own times, from A.D. 70 onwards, such as Tacitus was already writing in his *Historiae* at this moment, which Pliny first mentions in a letter of the next book (Letter 25. 1), and then in Letter 31.

graues offensae. Society was very touchy about political history. Tacitus in his preface (*Hist.* 1. 1) insisted: 'neque amore quisquam et sine odio dicendus est'. In Ep. ix. 27 Pliny tells how an unnamed author of a contemporary history shocked his audience, and abandoned its recitation at the request of interested parties.

14. **pro fide satis animi.** The varying meanings of *pro* (on behalf of, in the place of, in proportion to) and of *fides* (confidence, belief, trustworthiness, pledge), make this ambiguous. But the context requires the meaning 'I have enough spirit to give me confidence'.

illud . . . praesternas, 'prepare that road for me'. The metaphor is from road-building.

LETTER 23 (V. 9). TO SEMPRONIUS RUFUS

A strict judge

Sempronius Rufus is the junior senator to whom Letter 20 is addressed. The letter was written in early 105, when Licinius Nepos had just begun his year's work as praetor (s. 2).

1. **basilicam Iuliam.** This building, a colonnaded hall on the south

side of the Roman Forum, was the regular meeting-place of the Centumviral court, where Pliny had much legal practice.

proxima comperendinatione respondere, 'to which I had to reply at the next session'. Literally a *comperendinatio* was an adjournment till 'the day after tomorrow'. The court met on alternate days, and Pliny expects his opponents to take the whole of the first day over their case.

2. **sedebant iudices, decemuiri uenerant.** The court consisted of 180, not 100, jurors, and sat in four sections to hear different cases, under the presidency of the *decemuiri stlitibus iudicandis*, an annual magistracy held by future senators at the beginning of their careers. These young men were under the general administrative control of a praetor (s. 5). The court handled major cases of disputes about wills and inheritances, and as it was the only court of private or civil law with a jury, it attracted the outstanding advocates of the day, such as Pliny and Regulus, who liked the popular audience. See Letter 38. 1.

obuersabantur, 'walked about in front of' (*ob*) the tribunal on which the judges and jury sat.

eximitur dies, 'the day is taken out' (i.e. of the schedule of sessions).

3. **Nepos praetor, qui legibus quaerit.** Licinius Nepos in A.D. 105 was one of the annual praetors in charge of the various Roman law-courts. His own court was a criminal tribunal or *quaestio*, which was created to 'inquire under statute laws' (*legibus*). Each *quaestio* was concerned with a particular type of crime, but Pliny does not indicate which was Nepos' sphere. Nepos was an active senator who as praetor tried to check a number of judicial abuses, as here (Ep. v. 4, 13; vi. 5).

exsecuturum se quae senatus consulto continerentur. The praetors were free to regulate their courts by rules which they laid down in an 'edict', in general agreement with the provisions of laws and of decrees of the Senate. Their edict applied only to their own courts.

4. **iurare . . . iubebantur.** The rule was difficult to enforce because it was unpopular with advocates and clients alike. So the law had to

rely on oaths to secure obedience, with little success. The whole question had recently been stirred up by a case of flagrant violation to which Nepos had drawn attention (Ep. v. 4). Pliny uses the imperfect here and below because the rule was no longer in force.

nihil se ob aduocationem cuiquam dedisse. The rule was laid down by a decree of the Senate in A.D. 46, when an attempt was made to forbid payment of advocates altogether. Wealthy Roman gentry like Pliny gave their services free to their friends and dependants, but the mass of attorneys expected to make a living, or even a fortune, out of fees. Pliny's detested rival Regulus managed to amass some sixty million sesterces in thirty years, despite the law (Letter 11. 13).

cauisse, 'to have made a formal undertaking'.

5. **an sequeretur exemplum.** The praetors hoped by their official encouragement to induce persons to lay information about violations of the law. The emperor finally intervened with a statement supporting the action of Nepos (Ep. v. 13. 7–8).

6. **tota ciuitate,** 'throughout the city', or, as we say, 'in town'. This is a new meaning of *ciuitas*, which properly means the body of citizens, or the rights of citizenship. Cf. Letter 41. 2 n. The new usage is more frequent in the less literary letters to Trajan than in the private letters, in which Pliny normally uses *urbs* for Rome.

7. **ex euentu praeualebunt,** 'one side or other of the critical gossip will gain the day according to the result of Nepos' action'.

LETTER 24 (V. 19). TO VALERIUS PAULINUS

Illness of a servant

Valerius Paulinus at the time of this letter was a praetorian senator junior to Pliny, and held the consulship a few years later, in A.D. 107. He hailed from Gallia Narbonensis (Provence), where his estates were at Forum Iulii (Fréjus). Pliny wrote to him again about domestic affairs in Ep. ix. 37.

1. **quam molliter tuos habeas.** This letter, with Letters 9 and 33,

shows the civilized attitude of men like Pliny towards their dependants (*tuos*), both slaves and freedmen. Compare his disapproval of the brutal Larcius in Letter 14. Seneca writes in a similar strain (*Ep.* 47, *de clementia* i. 18). Pliny's comments suggest that his standard was above the normal. But generally household slaves were well treated, and the freeing of faithful and industrious slaves was extremely common, though slaves were usually expected to make some payment for their freedom, which came out of the servile earnings that their masters allowed them. Romans depended entirely upon slaves and freedmen for responsible staff in their households and estates, and even for personal assistants when they themselves were holding public appointments. See J. Carcopino, *Daily Life in Ancient Rome*, pp. 56 f.

2. **πατὴρ δ' ὣς ἤπιος ἦεν**, 'he was gentle as a father', a phrase applied to kings in Homer.

liberti mei Zosimi. His full name would be C. Plinius Zosimus. Freed slaves took the family name and *praenomen* of their master, and retained their own personal name as a third name or *cognomen*. They usually remained in the service of their former master, and lived in his household. In Letter 9. 4 they dine at his table. For the custom of manumission see Letter 33. 1 n.

illa. Ablative after *eget*.

3. **ars quidem eius . . . comoedus.** Servile labour was highly specialized. The *comoedus* did not usually do anything except recite from the repertoire of comedy. See Letter 7. 2 n.: 'audisses comoedos uel lectorem uel lyristen'.

inscriptio. The label of a slave at the slave-market, giving his particulars.

6. **in Aegyptum missus.** Pliny's friend Maturus Arrianus, who had recently been in the Egyptian administration, may have looked after Zosimus (Letter 12).

rursus sanguinem reddidit. The medical writers Celsus and Galen recommended the journey to Egypt, for the sea-voyage rather than the Egyptian climate, and also the milk and fresh-air method (s. 7), as treatment for tuberculosis. But they noted that relapses were frequent, as with Zosimus.

nimis imperat uoci, 'while making excessive demands on his voice'.

8. scribas tuis ut illi uilla . . . pateat. Wealthy Romans frequently used each others' country-houses when travelling, thus making good the lack of high-grade hotels in the Roman Empire. Cf. Ep. i. 4; vi. 10. 1.

offerant. The object of the verb is given by the clause 'si quid opus erit'.

9. opus modico. The verbal phrase *opus est* takes either the nominative or the ablative of the 'thing needed'. Pliny here uses both. Note the careful balance of the two phrases using the same or corresponding words in reverse order: 'si quid (*a*) opus (*b*) erit (*c*). erit (*c*) autem opus (*b*) modico (*a*)'.

ualetudinis. Dependent on *delicias* and *necessitates*, which are put before the genitive noun for emphasis.

tantum uiatici, 'so much (of) journey-money', a partitive genitive.

dabo quantum sufficiat. Pliny is not being mean. It was dangerous for private persons to travel with large quantities of silver or gold. Pliny tells in Ep. vi. 25 of the murder of a centurion travelling from Comum to Rome with 10,000 silver denarii in his baggage. So he arranges a draft on his friend's provincial household for Zosimus.

LETTER 25 (VI. 16). TO CORNELIUS TACITUS

Vesuvius erupts

Pliny sends the historian Tacitus this account of his uncle's death, in the first eruption of Vesuvius known in historical times, as a contribution for his Histories. He continues it in Ep. vi. 20 with an account of his own adventures at the same time, and sends Tacitus another contribution, about events of A.D. 93, in Letter 31. These three letters are the only evidence for dating the composition of the Histories.

Cornelius Tacitus was at this time a consular senator and a leading advocate. See Letter 2 pref. He was resident at Rome a year or two earlier (Letter 18. 1).

The style of the letter is colourful and poetical, especially in vocabulary (cf. ss. 5, 6, 11, 15, 19), true to Pliny's definition of historical style in Letter 22. 9–10 as *recondita splendida excelsa*. The writing is more compressed and rhetorical than Pliny there seems to recommend. Cf. phrases noted in ss. 2, 3, 8, 11, 12, 13, 17.

1. **auunculi mei.** For Pliny's uncle, and adoptive father, C. Plinius Secundus, and his career see Letter 13 nn. He was aged fifty-five at this moment (ib. s. 5).

2. **ut urbes memorabili casu,** 'like cities (*sc.* that perish) by a famous disaster'.

uicturus. From *uiuo*.

3. **quibus utrumque,** i.e. 'datum est'.

4. **erat Miseni.** A division of the imperial fleet was based on the harbour of Misenum, at the northern end of the bay of Naples. Plinius Secundus, an imperial procurator of long experience, was its admiral (*praefectus classis Misenensis*). His duties were mostly administrative, since the fleet had no warlike function when the whole Mediterranean was under Roman rule. It acted as a transport and water police force, and the admiral's duties were mostly done ashore (*praesens regebat*).

Nonum kal. Septembres hora fere septima, i.e. '*during* (accusative) the 24 August, *at* (ablative) about the seventh hour'. The twelve hours of daylight varied in length with the seasons, though not so much as in more northerly latitudes. The moment would be between 1 and 2 p.m. The year A.D. 79 is given by Cassius Dio.

adparere nubem. Pliny's observations begin after the first phase, described in Dio 66. 22. 4. After a great explosion, not noted by Pliny, the volcano cleared its vent by hurling out great rocks, torrents of flame, and smoke.

5. **usus ille sole . . . iacens studebat.** The routine of Secundus'

midday siesta and afternoon is as described in Letter 13. 10–11. His working day was over by the fourth or fifth hour.

frigida, i.e. *aqua.*

ex quo monte. Supply *oreretur* from *oriebatur.*

Vesuuium. When the geographer Strabo visited the sleeping volcano before A.D. 14 the top was fairly level, the prehistoric crater was filled in, and vineyards clothed the mountain side. Strabo noted slight signs of volcanic action, though the elder Pliny in his Natural History himself dismissed the mountain a few years before the disaster without any comment: 'haud procul spectato monte Vesuuiano'. Another great eruption took place in A.D. 203 during the lifetime of Cassius Dio, and it has been irregularly active ever since. See Strabo, v. 4. 8, p. 247; Pliny, *Nat. Hist.* 3. 62; Dio 66. 21–24, 76 (77). 2. 1.

pinus expresserit. The Mediterranean stone-pine has a flattened, spreading head that gives the very shape of a volcanic, or of an atomic explosion, cloud.

6. recenti spiritu euecta, dein senescente, etc. As in his other descriptions of natural phenomena (Letter 21 nn.) Pliny describes what he has seen for himself with an accuracy worthy of a 'scientist'. Cf. s. 11 n. He omits all the supernatural portents recorded by Dio.

credo. In parenthesis.

7. uisum. To be taken with *magnum* and *noscendum.*

liburnicam. The light vessel of the Roman fleet, invented by Liburnian pirates for fast work. The quadriremes of s. 9, with four banks of oars, were the battleships.

quod scriberem dederat. He was busy excerpting a book of Livy to improve his style (Ep. vi. 20. 5).

8. egrediebatur, i.e. just as he was setting out, he receives the message.

accipit codicillos Rectinae Tasci, 'he receives a message from Rectina, the wife of Tascius'. This is the normal form for indicating a married woman.

The word *codicilli*, used in the plural, means a wad of papyrus or parchment sheets used in book form instead of a roll. Cf. Letter 11. 5.

9. maximo, i.e. *animo.*

frequens amoenitas orae, 'the beautiful coast was dense with habitations'.

10. dictaret enotaretque. Secundus always kept a slave at hand to note down his observations (Letter 13. 15).

11. quo propius accederent. The subjunctive may be causal, as in a *cum* clause.

iam pumices . . . lapides. The stones predominate in this account (ss. 14–16). What geographers call a 'Vesuvian' eruption produces steam, dust, and stone, and sometimes streams of lava, absent on this occasion.

ambusti, 'burnt up'.

ruinaque montis litora obstantia, 'shores blocked with the debris of the mountain'. This is the report of others. Pliny himself more accurately observed that the shore line rose through an earthquake: 'mare . . . tremore terrae . . . repelli *uidebamus*' (Ep. vi. 20. 9).

12. Stabiis erat diremptus sinu medio. An inner bay, now filled in by the advance of the coast, separated Pomponianus at Stabiae from Secundus at or near Herculaneum. Pliny does not make it clear whether Secundus abandons the attempt to help Rectina at this point, or whether she has been already picked up by a detachment without further mention. For *multis . . . laturus auxilium*, etc. (ss. 9–10) may imply a general operation by the whole fleet.

mare infunditur. Literally 'the sea is poured into the curve of the coasts'.

cum cresceret proximo. Supply *futuro*. 'When it grew bigger it would be very close'.

contrarius uentus. A great wind rises as the cool air rushes in from the sea to the heat centre.

certus fugae. Following Virgil (*Aen.* iv. 554 'certus eundi') Pliny, like Tacitus, uses *certus* with the genitive, meaning 'determined on'.

secundissimo, i.e. *uento.*

deferri in balineum. Secundus coolly resumes his interrupted routine, s. 5 n.

13. **fulgor . . . excitabatur,** 'was intensified'. The verb is here metaphorical, as 'incitet et accendat' in Letter 24. 5.

desertasque uillas . . . ardere. The houses are on fire, not 'illuminated', because ancient lamps cast a very dim light.

meatus animae, 'the passage of his breath', i.e. his snores. Cf. s. 19.

limini obuersabantur. Cf. Letter 23. 2 n.

14. **area . . . cinere mixtisque pumicibus oppleta surrexerat.** This is exactly how Pompeii and Herculaneum were overwhelmed (Carrington, *Pompeii,* p. 7).

diaeta. An apartment in a villa, sometimes self-contained.

16. **collatio elegit,** 'the comparison of evils preferred this'.

incidentia. Neuter plural.

linteis, 'cloths', hardly 'napkins', cf. s. 18.

ceruicalia, 'cushions'.

17. **iam dies alibi.** The second day, 25 August, following the night described in ss. 13–16. His body was found on 26 August (s. 20).

quam . . . faces . . . soluebant. The fires noted in s. 13 above 'break up the blackness' due to the clouds of dust.

admitteret, 'allow'.

19. **frequenter aestuans,** 'his windpipe (*stomachus*) was often inflamed'. Secundus was perhaps asthmatical (s. 13, 'meatus animae . . . gravior'), and perished like a victim of smoky fog in modern times.

20. **dies redditus . . . tertius.** It is 26 August, the third day by Roman inclusive reckoning.

corpus inuentum integrum. A careful investigation would be made, after so important a personage's death, to make sure that he had not been murdered by his slaves when Pomponianus and the rest fled. See Letter 14 nn. Suetonius in his short 'Life' of Secundus reports a rumour that he asked his slave to kill him.

22. **quae . . . statim . . . audieram.** Pliny received the news at Misenum, apparently from Pomponianus and the slaves (Ep. vi. 20. 20). He must have questioned them carefully to secure the details which he reports: cf. s. 19: 'ut ego colligo'.

LETTER 26 (VII. 9). TO PEDANIUS FUSCUS SALINATOR

The technique of an orator

Pedanius Fuscus, son of an old consular family, was one of a group of young aristocrats, including Ummidius Quadratus (Letter 29. 9), who regarded Pliny as their mentor at the Roman bar. He celebrates their first appearances in court (Ep. vi. 11) and advises them on technical training, as here, and also on the routine of social life, as in Letter 40. Here Pliny, like his master Quintilian (*Inst. or.* x. 5. 2), recommends the practice of translation as an exercise in analysis and imagination.

1. **in secessu,** i.e. when living on his country estate, as in Letter 40.

2. **copia figurarum.** The patterns of sentences and of phrases, and artificial arrangements of words, were all catalogued in the handbooks of rhetoric as 'figures'.

imitatione optimorum. Take with *paratur*.

3. **notissima eligere,** 'to select famous passages in literature'.

offuerit. The subjunctive is used, as with *fefellissent* above, to express a mild assertion or supposition: 'It would be . . .'.

quid ille, i.e. *scripserit*.

6. **noua uelut membra . . . corpori intexere.** Pliny enlarged his speeches thus (cf. Letter 27. 5 'si multa inseras'), notably his Panegyric, which survives in a much expanded form.

7. **orandi,** 'of public advocacy'.

8. **non historica modo sed prope poetica descriptionum necessitas.** For Pliny historical style should be half poetical (cf. Letter 22.

9–10 n.), full of 'softness' and 'sweetness'. The epithets here are transferred. Properly they belong to *descriptionum*.

epistulam diligentius scribas, i.e. in the literary style of Pliny's own formal letters (Letter 1. 1 n.).

pressus sermo purusque. The usual terms for a plain and uninflated style, cf. Ep. i. 8. 5: 'stilus . . . pressus demissusque'. In Ep. i. 16 Pliny approved the simplicity of Terence for letter-writing. But his own descriptive letters such as Letter 25 are rich rather than simple in vocabulary.

9. fas est et carmine remitti, 'to relax in poetry'. Pliny deftly switches the subject to draw in his new interest in versification (Letter 34 nn.). He published two volumes of verses in these years.

arguto. Sharp and witty. He has in mind the style of his model Martial.

10. lusus uocantur. His usual word for his verses: 'triflings'. Cf. Ep. iv. 14. 3, cited below.

11. ut laus est cerae. There was a minor art of working figures in wax. These verses are evidently Pliny's own. He quotes others in Letter 34. 4. The opening *ut* is taken up by *sic* in l. 7 of the verses.

informet, 'give shape to'.

iussaque fiat opus, 'becomes a work of art when bidden'.

fontes non sola incendia sistunt, 'water is not only used to put out fires'. The conceit is very strained.

13. recipiunt . . . amores odia iras misericordiam urbanitatem. Pliny lists the contents of any book of Martial, who was his protégé (Letter 17). Cf. Ep. iv. 14. 3: 'his (uersibus) iocamur ludimus amamus dolemus'.

14. soluta oratione, i.e. 'prose', which is free from the rules of verse.

15. quamquam. Here a particle, not a subordinate conjunction: 'yet'.

sui cuiusque generis auctores, 'the leading exponents of each type'. He is to read only the great authors, e.g. Cicero for ornate oratory, Lysias for the plain style.

multum legendum esse, non multa, i.e. 'read the same selection again and again'.

16. **quin ergo?** Interrogative conjunction. 'Why not then?'

pugillares. See Ep. 2. 3 n.

istud ipsum quod coeperas. Pliny appears to be referring to something mentioned in Fuscus' letter.

LETTER 27 (VII. 17). TO CELER

On literary recitation

Celer is unknown; he may be a relative of Pliny's first mother-in-law, Pompeia Celerina.

In this letter Pliny defends his practice of giving formal recitations of his speeches. This was unusual (s. 2). The other recitations mentioned in the Letters are limited to poetry, history, or drama. Pliny had begun with the recitation of his speech against Marius Priscus (Ep. ii. 19), and continued with his Panegyric of Trajan (Ep. iii. 18). He is now devoted to recitation, because it gives him ample opportunity for revision, just as in his verse recitations (Letter 34), since he uses his audience as an editorial committee. The customs of the *auditorium* are described in Letter 6.

3. **quae . . . actores.** Supply *poscit* from *poscunt* below.

4. **nostri quidam . . . lectitauerunt.** Suetonius (*Augustus* 89. 3) notes it as unusual that speeches were recited a century earlier in the time of Augustus.

5. **quae dixeris,** 'what you have already delivered'.

etiam, 'yes'.

quosdam nouos, i.e. *auditores*.

7. **dum legor,** i.e. after publication of the book concerned.

8. tanto diligentius. Supply *emendo*. *Intendo* is intransitive, 'exert myself'.

idque adeo sic habe, 'so consider the matter as follows'.

uel indoctis, 'even though uneducated'.

9. cum surgis ad agendum. He now considers the effect on the speaker of appearances in court.

dico. This is in parenthesis.

corona. Usual word for the crowd round the tribunal.

sordidos pullatosque. The common people wearing dark clothing.

10. opinor, 'I think so'.

magnum collatumque consilium, 'a great body of advice'. Pliny runs together the meanings of 'advice' and 'body of advisers'. It was the Roman custom to take advice in every emergency, public or private, from a group of friends. In Ep. v. 3. 8 he claims to settle points of style 'quasi ex consilii sententia', just as if it was a court-case (Letter 20. 1 n.).

quibusque singulis . . . plurimum. There are two separate parallel clauses here, after *quia*, and requiring *est*.

11. Pomponius Secundus. A consular senator, friend of Pliny's uncle (Letter 13. 3).

12. quos . . . quibus . . . quos. Again, the clauses are parallel.

certos electosque. Cf. Ep. v. 3. 11, 'in cubiculum amicos aduocarim', of another recitation.

13. Cicero de stilo. Cf. Cicero, *De oratore* i. 150, 'stilus optimus . . . dicendi . . . magister'. A *stilus* literally is the pen itself.

hoc ipsum quod, 'the fact that'. The *quod* clauses are the subjects of the main verbs.

14. istorum, i.e. the critics mentioned in s. 2.

monstres aliquid, i.e. 'give me some new ideas about revision', not 'give me some fresh arguments'.

15. **dare aliquid in manus hominum,** i.e. to publish for sale: *edere* or *publicare* is more common. Cf. Ep. i. 2. 6: 'est aliquid edendum ... quod libelli quos emisimus dicuntur in manibus esse'.

LETTER 28 (VII. 18). TO CANINIUS RUFUS

A charitable gift

Pliny advises his friend Caninius Rufus, a landowner of Comum, about a charitable foundation.

1. **municipibus nostris.** The endowment would be placed under the control of the city council of Comum for the benefit of the local citizens (*municipes*).

in epulum. An annual banquet for all the citizens on the local register was a common form of benefaction.

non expedita . . ., 'my advice is not ready to hand'.

numeres, 'suppose you pay over'. The simplest use of the subjunctive. But he could have written 'si numeres . . . uerendum est'.

ne dilabatur. There was much waste and corruption in municipal finances. In Ep. x. 70 Pliny tells how a large house which was left as a legacy to the city of Prusa had crumbled into ruins sixty years later. See Letters 43–44, 49–50. It was to correct such waste that Pliny was sent to Bithynia (p. xiv).

2. **quingentibus milibus nummum.** Half a million sesterces, which was more than the minimum financial requirement for membership of the equestrian order, would purchase an estate of some 200–250 Roman acres.

in alimenta ingenuorum ingenuarumque promiseram. This was about ten years earlier, as recounted in Ep. i. 8. 10. He was following the example set by the Emperor Nerva (and later Trajan), who established municipal funds in many parts of Italy to support needy, free-born children with monthly allowances. Boys received S. 16 and girls S. 12 monthly in a scheme known from a long inscription found at Veleia in North Italy (Dessau, *ILS* 6675). Pliny's endowment at these rates could support about 120 boys and forty girls. The allowance would go a fair way towards providing basic necessities. A common soldier's total daily pay, including keep, at this time was rather less than four sesterces. The motive in the imperial schemes was partly political: 'hi subsidium bellorum . . . publicis sumptibus . . . aluntur' (Pliny, *Pan*. 28. 4–5). For money values see Letter 11. 13 n.

agrum . . . longe pluris, 'an estate of much greater value'.

actori publico mancipaui: eundem uectigali imposito recepi. Pliny made a nominal transfer of the land to the land-agent of the city by the legal process known as *mancipatio*, and then received it back by the same formality, subject to a permanent annual charge (*uectigal*) of S. 30,000 payable to the local authority. This represents 6 per cent. on the sum originally promised, a more generous rate than that given on the imperial benefactions of this sort.

3. sors, 'capital'.

propter id quod uectigal large supercurrit. The subject of the verb is *ager*, from the main sentence, and *uectigal* is the object. 'The value of the estate greatly exceeds the charge.'

4. erogauisse. This verb regularly means to pay a tax or public subscription.

agri pretium necessitas uectigalis infregerit. The existence of a fixed charge, which could not be reduced in a bad season, would depress the price by more than the S. 500,000 on which the dues were calculated.

LETTER 29 (VII. 24). TO ROSIANUS GEMINUS

A gay old lady

A character sketch in the form of an obituary notice is a favourite type of letter. Cf. Letters 8, 17. Pliny combines it here with a portrait of a distinguished pupil.

Rosianus Geminus was a praetorian senator who in A.D. 100 had been Pliny's assistant quaestor when Pliny was consul.

1. **Ummidia Quadratilla.** She was the daughter of C. Ummidius Quadratus, a great consular senator and administrator in the time of Claudius and Nero. The family came from Casinum in Italy, where there are inscriptions of herself and her dancer (s. 6) (*ILS* 5183, 5628).

2. **honestissimo testamento.** She left her estates within the family, and did not bequeath excessive sums to toadies and acquaintances pursuing the usual game of legacy hunting (s. 7), described in Letter 11. Society paid great attention to the details of wills. Pliny comments approvingly on the multimillionaire Domitius Tullus that 'cum se captandum praebuisset reliquit filiam heredem ... frustratus improbas spes hominum' (Ep. viii. 28. 2–3).

ex besse. The heirs receive the named proportions of the whole estate—two-thirds and one-third—after the legacies and the 5 per cent. inheritance tax have been paid.

nepotem familiarissime diligo. The young Ummidius Quadratus, who was just beginning a career as a senator and advocate under Pliny's guidance, reached the consulship in 118 and was a leading figure thereafter at the court of Hadrian. Though an Ummidius only by female descent he used the family name, as was not uncommon at this period in exalted families, in preference to his father's name, which is unknown.

inter propinquos. Since *propinquus* is a synonym of *cognatus*, this repeats the meaning of *quos sanguine attingit*.

3. **intra quartum et uicensimum annum maritus.** He married even earlier than the law required. The Lex Iulia *de maritandis ordinibus* imposed disadvantages on those who were unmarried and childless after the age of twenty-five, and rewarded the married by allowing them to hold public office a year earlier for each child, according to the number of their children. Ummidius would be just about to stand for the quaestorship, normally held at twenty-five.

et ... pater. Supply *futurus*.

auiae delicatae. Ummidia's tastes were those of the age of Nero, *luxuriem imperii ueterem* (Juvenal). So Pliny calls her *delicata* in the sense of idle and luxurious, rather than wanton. Cf. Ep. ix. 32:

'scribere nolim . . . tamquam delicatus . . . nihil est . . . pigrius delicatis'.

4. pantomimos fouebat . . . effusius quam principi feminae conuenit. Pliny's comments reflect the change of tone that spread through senatorial society at Rome in the generation after Nero (p. xiii). The new senators from North Italy and the provinces brought in a severer morality which affected the standards of taste at the capital. Tacitus writes with similar disapproval of Nero's passion for the stage and the races at the Circus, like Pliny in Letter 36. The Flavian emperors all showed some puritanism towards public entertainments. Domitian even forbade the public performances of *pantomimi*, and Titus would not watch his own dancers in public (Pliny, *Pan.* 46. 2–4. Suetonius, *Titus* 7. 2).

The 'pantomime' of the Empire was a combination of tragedy, opera, and ballet, in which the leading role was played by a 'star' *pantomimus*, supported by chorus and orchestra. See M. Bieber, *History of the Greek and Roman Theatre*[2], (1961), p. 235.

exigebat, 'nor did she demand that he should watch them'.

5. in illo otio sexus. Women of wealth had no serious occupation except to hold a general supervision over their households, which were kept by a large staff of slaves, and no arts or sports were open to them. So Quadratilla owned a troop of slaves trained as *pantomimi* to amuse herself.

lusu calculorum. An ancient form of draughts or backgammon. Pliny regards even this as improper, perhaps because of its connexion with gambling. Cf. Letter 36. 2 n.

6. proximis . . . ludis, 'at the recent priestly Games'. The officers of state, including the various 'colleges' of priests, gave public entertainments at Rome on some 150 days a year.

in commissione. A competition for drama at a festival like that mentioned in Letter 20.

libertum. Quadratilla has given freedom to her leading *pantomimus*.

7. alienissimi, 'mere acquaintances'.

gestus dominae cum canticis reddebant. Both the toadies in the audience and the chorus (*cantici*) copy the enthusiastic gestures of Quadratilla.

theatralis operae corollarium. Like hired applauders they have earned their 'wages for theatrical work'.

hercule. See Letter 6. 3 n.

8. quod ceperam gaudium. The clause is the object of *retractare*.

Cassianae scholae princeps et parens. C. Cassius Longinus, a leading civil lawyer in the time of Claudius and Nero, was the leader of the legal tradition known as 'Sabinian', after the name of an Augustan lawyer called Masurius Sabinus. Cassius and his successors gave informal instruction about cases and principles to young men like Quadratus, just as Pliny and Tacitus did for the practice of advocacy. Cf. Letter 18. 10: 'copia studiosorum quae ad te ex admiratione ingenii tui conuenit'. The 'school' consisted of a lecture and discussion in a public place, cf. Letter 18 nn.

9. tantus orator. Pliny describes briefly the first court appearance of Quadratus in a case against Pliny's other aristocratic pupil Pedanius Fuscus, in Ep. vi. 11. In Ep. vi. 29 he instructs Quadratus in the choice of briefs.

decebit. A personal verb, with Quadratus as subject.

LETTER 30 (VII. 27). TO LICINIUS SURA

Ghosts

This is the second letter about scientific problems addressed to the consular Licinius Sura, for whom see Letter 21 pref.

1. esse phantasmata. Pliny summarizes the two main theories of antiquity about ghosts and apparitions. Demetrius of Abdera explained them as physical emanations which penetrate the pores of the recipient, and Lucretius gave a similar account in terms of atomic structure (iv. 45 f., 84 f., 721 f.). The alternative, preferred by Pliny, was the Aristotelian theory attributing visions to the physical or mental state of the patient. See E. R. Dodds, *The Greeks and the Irrational*, pp. 117 ff.

Pliny's letter should be compared with the collection of exaggerated bogy stories in Lucian's *Philopseudes*. Pliny's account is clear and sober, as in his other descriptions of natural phenomena. The relative feebleness of the stories by modern standards is partly due to the lack of a romantic and isolated environment. The small size and compact arrangement of ancient houses, and the intense urban life, did not favour the development of a Gothic tradition of ghost stories in the nineteenth-century manner.

numen . . . aliquod. An element of spirit or divine force was thought to animate human beings, and to survive physical death.

2. accidisse Curtio Rufo. Tacitus tells much the same story in *Ann.* 11. 21. Rufus was a self-made man, promoted to high senatorial office by the Emperors Tiberius and Claudius, and finally became proconsul of Africa in an unknown year, as here related.

obtinenti Africam, 'the person holding Africa', i.e. the proconsul.

comes haeserat, 'had managed to attach himself'. Any member of a governor's staff was called *comes*. Tacitus makes him a junior assistant of the quaestor or provincial treasurer.

inclinato die. Midday with empty streets when every one is taking siesta is a good time for a Mediterranean ghost to appear.

Africam se . . . dixit, 'she said she was the divinity called Africa'. Cities and regions possessed a divine spirit or *genius*.

cum . . . imperio, i.e. with the authority of a proconsul.

5. erat Athenis . . . domus. Lucian, op. cit. 22, tells a similar story about a philosopher Arignotus and a house at Corinth, in a more extravagant vein.

6. inhabitantibus. A dative of the 'person interested', instead of *ab* with ablative, to be taken with the passive verb (*uigilabantur*). But as in gerundive constructions. Cf. s. 12. n.

damnata solitudine, 'sentenced to vacancy'.

proscribebatur, 'it was advertised', cf. *titulum* s. 7, the notice.

7. Athenodorus. A Stoic teacher of this name from Tarsus was a favourite of the Emperor Augustus.

sterni, 'a bed to be laid'.

in prima domus parte. A group of rooms around a passage precedes the inner court (*aream* s. 10), beyond which lie the main apartments.

8. concuti. This and the following verbs are infinitives of rapid narration.

animum auribus . . . praetendere, 'makes his thoughts a screen for his ears'.

stabat innuebatque digito. This is plain and factual. Lucian obscures the point with idiotic incidents; the ghost assumes the shapes of animals, and Arignotus masters it by spells. After the series of narrative infinitives in s. 8 Pliny dramatically reverts to the indicative mood, using present or imperfect as the action requires. Cf. Letter 39. 4 n.

9. ceris. Wax writing tablets.

11. adit magistratus. The city officials were concerned because the burial of a corpse inside the town was improper, and its removal was their business. Pliny's detail is again relevant.

exesa . . . uinculis. To be taken together.

publice, 'at the expense of the city'. Cf. Letter 8. 1 n.

rite conditis manibus caruit. As in the stories about the burial of the heroes Misenus and Palinurus in *Aeneid* vi, when the bodies of the dead are 'properly buried' their spirits (*manes*) are at rest. Pliny by compression transfers the burial from the body to the ghost.

12. illud adfirmare . . . possum. Pliny now adds a third story to illustrate his theme in accordance with the *lex scholastica* mentioned in Letter 11. 9.

sibi. For the dative common with *uideor* cf. s. 6 n.. 'He seemed to see'.

13. **exiguum temporis.** Partitive genitive. *medium* is the predicate after *erat* (understood).

priori . . ., 'gave credit to the earlier vision'.

14. **nihil notabile secutum.** Pliny expresses a belief in dreams in Ep. i. 18. 2; iv. 5. 5–6. He was involved because the slave-boy was his property.

in scrinio eius datus a Caro de me libellus. Mettius Carus was a notorious political prosecutor who helped the Emperor Domitian to secure the condemnation of suspected senators during the last three years of his reign (A.D. 93–96). But Pliny was in high favour in those years, holding his praetorship and the prefecture of the *aerarium militare* by imperial appointment. He claims several times with little justification to have done risky political things under Domitian. See Letter 31. 7–9. The imperial archives were called *scrinia*. *Libelli* were any petitions or addresses to the emperor not written in the form of a personal letter (*epistula*).

moris est. Cf. Letter 5. 7 n.

16. **tamen fortius,** 'but support one side more strongly'.

LETTER 31 (VII. 33). TO CORNELIUS TACITUS

A political adventure

Pliny having provided the material about his uncle's death for the new History that Tacitus was writing about the Flavian period, and having perhaps read the first books, as Ep. vii. 20; viii. 7 suggest, is now anxious to make sure of his own appearance in it. For Tacitus see Letter 2 pref.

1. **auguror.** A mild joke. Pliny was in fact a member of the priestly college of augurs.

2. **praedicator,** 'publisher'. *Praedicare* with its derivatives is a favourite word of Pliny for historical publicity, cf. Letter 37. 4.

3. **cum sit in publicis actis.** Pliny expects that Tacitus will consult

the public records, i.e. the *acta senatus*, or minute-book of the Senate's proceedings, and the *acta populi diurna*, a summary bulletin of events at Rome. These were available in the archives kept in the *aerarium Saturni*. But the imperial archives or *commentarii principum* would not be accessible.

gratia, 'value' or 'favour'.

4. dederat me senatus . . . aduocatum. The advocates were appointed to assist the plaintiffs, just as in the trial of Marius Priscus, cf. Letter 10. 2 n.

prouinciae Baeticae. The charge was brought by the whole province, probably acting through its provincial Council. This was the province of Southern Spain, named from its great river Baetis, and officially called *prouincia Hispania ulterior Baetica*.

contra Baebium Massam. This praetorian senator had been one of the tools used by Domitian, like Mettius Carus and Catullus Messalinus, to secure the judicial condemnation of suspected senators (Letters 20. 5 n., 30. 14 n.). But his corrupt behaviour as proconsul of Baetica in A.D. 92–93 offended Domitian, who expected a high standard of behaviour from his provincial governors. The trial took place in August 93 after the end of Massa's term of office. Massa was accused, like Marius Priscus, of the more serious form of extortion, for which the penalty included exile (*relegatio*, Letter 10. 19 n.) and loss of public position.

ut bona eius publice custodirentur. His estate and goods were placed under the control of the officials of the state treasury (*aerarium Saturni*), so as to ensure repayment of what he had extorted.

Senecio. Herennius Senecio was a junior senator in the circle of Junius Mauricus (Letter 20. 4 n.), which criticized and opposed Domitian. A few months later he was charged with treason, tried, and executed.

ne bona dissipari sinant. He fears that collusion between the officials, themselves senators, and Massa would enable him to conceal his assets or transfer them to a conniving third party, and thus defraud the plaintiffs.

sinant. The subject of this verb is (*ei*) *quorum*, and the subject of *debent* is *bona*, supplied from the previous clause.

5. **num peractas putes partes nostras.** Pliny was right. It was not the duty of the prosecutors to see that the penalty was exacted. He shows his own doubts by using the phrase *dispice num*.

nulla . . . necessitudo. Pliny had ties through his uncle with the northern province of Tarraconensis, but not with Baetica (Letter 13. 17 n.). His *beneficium* is his advocacy in this suit.

natus ibi. Many senators at this date were wealthy provincials from Southern Gaul and the Spanish provinces, including the Emperor Trajan himself and his right-hand man Licinius Sura (Letters 38. 2 n., and 32 pref.).

quaestor in ea. The annual quaestors served as treasury officials in the provinces governed by proconsuls.

6. **ut . . . non tantum tua.** Supply *sit*.

7. **uenimus ad consules.** Not in the Senate, but sitting in public on their tribunal. They were the chief administrative authority at Rome after the emperor.

impietatis reum postulat. Senecio had exceeded his duty as an advocate (*fidem*) by his officiousness, thus going beyond what *pietas* required. So Massa tried to turn the Roman law of *calumnia* against him. This laid down penalties for advocates who showed excessive zeal in prosecution (*inimici amaritudinem*), and especially aimed at the prevention of unwarranted prosecutions. If Massa's influential friends could induce the Senate to construe Senecio's action as *calumnia*, Massa's sentence would be quashed. But the consuls saw through Massa's dodge, and refused to accept the complaint.

8. **mihi . . . praeuaricationem obiecerit.** The offence of collusion, or helping the other side, was the opposite of *calumnia*. Hence Pliny's remark: 'by omitting me from his charge against my fellow advocate he must mean that I was in collusion with his own side'.

9. **diuus . . . Nerua . . . priuatus.** In A.D. 93 M. Cocceius Nerva was a senior senator closely associated with the régime of Domitian as an

administrative adviser, but he was not a political prosecutor like Massa. This is why he was chosen by the conspirators in September 96 to take Domitian's place after his assassination.

By *priuatus* Pliny means only that Nerva was not then emperor (cf. Letter 8. 2). He calls him *diuus* because by the date of the letter Nerva was dead and officially deified in the state cult.

saeculo est gratulatus. Nerva indicated that the government was pleased with Pliny's move. Some time later, in 94–95, Pliny was promoted by Domitian to be head of the *aerarium militare*. By *saeculum* he means 'the times', cf. Letter 48. 2.

10. utcumque se habent, 'whatever their status'. Pliny is hoping to secure merit in senatorial society for having helped one of Domitian's victims at a critical moment, though he lets the cat out of the bag by relating the intervention of Nerva.

quamquam non exigo. Pliny is trying to reconcile two contradictory attitudes held about the writing of history in antiquity—that it should 'glorify actions', and that it should tell the truth. He has in mind Cicero's letter inviting Lucceius to write up the events of his consulship (*Ad fam.* v. 12. 3). See Letter 22. 1–4 nn.

LETTER 32 (VIII. 8). TO VOCONIUS ROMANUS

The fountain

The recipient is an equestrian from Saguntum in Spain for whom Pliny secured senatorial status by the favour of Nerva and Trajan (Ep. x. 4). Letter 8 also is addressed to him.

Pliny, travelling to his Tuscan villa by a new route, visits the Clitumnus spring for the first time.

1. Clitumnum fontem. The stream is a branch of the Tinia, which joins the Tiber. Its springs lie above the bridge (s. 5) which carried the branch of the Via Flaminia linking Narnia, Spoletium, and Forum Flaminii, near the modern village of Le Vene. This is the only letter in which Pliny describes a picturesque scene for its own sake. His other natural descriptions are concerned with scientific problems, *quaestiones naturales*, as Seneca called them (Letters 21, 25, and Ep. vi. 20; viii. 20). The Romans, living in Italy, could take natural beauty for granted, but they were fully conscious of it. Pliny stresses the fine views of the countryside which his Tuscan villa possessed (Ep. v. 6. 14, 18, 28).

Pliny's description is original. The Clitumnus is frequently mentioned in Latin literature, but always for the fame of the local white oxen (e.g. Virgil, *Georgics* ii. 146). This is the one thing that Pliny does not include.

2. subter, 'at the foot of'.

exprimitur pluribus uenis, 'it issues in several runnels'. These coalesce to form the pool (*gurges*).

eluctatusque quem facit gurgitem. The main stream struggles out of the pool which it forms with its runnels. Pliny is straining after effect by compression, which causes obscurity. The *fons* is personified throughout.

gurgitem. Pliny, like Tacitus (*Hist.* 3. 59), uses *eluctor* as a transitive verb. Note the use of poetic and often Virgilian phraseology throughout, e.g. here *gurges* and *cupressu nemorosus*.

iactas stipes. They throw coins into the pool as an offering to the deity. Cf. Suetonius, *Aug.* 57.

3. amplissimum flumen. The quantity of water maintained in high summer when the rest of the Tiber tributaries were low and dry makes the charm of the Clitumnus.

nauium patiens. Latin is short of words for small boats. He uses *naucula* in a more prosaic context (Letter 15. 9), but *nauis* again in a picturesque passage in Ep. viii. 20. 5.

obuias . . . in diuersa tendentes. Either this refers to two sets of boats, going upstream and downstream, or else (less probably) he is elaborating the picture of those struggling against the current.

adeo ualidus. The subject is still *fons*. Pliny now expands what he summarized as *in diuersa tendentes*.

illa qua properat, i.e. *uia*. All are ablative.

contis superetur aduersus, 'it can be mastered with difficulty by poles when it is against you'. Note the cunning arrangement of words in the pattern ABBA, known as *chiasmus*: 'remis non . . . aegerrime remis', while *aduersus* at the end corresponds to *qua properat* at the beginning. This pattern recurs in s. 4, 'fraxino multa multa populo', and s. 6, 'balineum . . . praebent, praebent et hospitium'. See p. xvii.

4. per iocum . . . fluitantibus, 'on a pleasure cruise'.

ut flexerint, 'whenever they change course'. For the subjunctive cf. Letters 5. 7 n., 9. 6. They row themselves (*labore*), not using slaves.

rigor, 'sharpness'.

certauerit. Perfect subjunctive, as of a possibility, cf. Letter 26. 3: 'it could rival snow'.

5. religiosum, 'with an atmosphere of sanctity'.

stat Clitumnus ipse. The river-god was known locally as Juppiter Clitumnus, because he was a manifestation of the sky-god in the waters of the spring.

praetexta. A real, not a carved, toga with scarlet border.

praesens numen atque etiam fatidicum indicant sortes, 'tallies show that a spirit is present, and that it is prophetic'. The *sortes* were slips of wood or metal on which oracular statements were written. They were shaken together when required and one was drawn out.

totidemque di. In Roman primitive belief each natural object has its spirit.

minores capite discreti, 'lesser streams with separate springs'. These join the Clitumnus between the pool and the bridge.

6. profani. In its proper sense of 'outside the sanctuary'.

etiam natare. Human bodies would defile the sacred water. So too Pliny says of the Vadimon pool 'nulla in hoc nauis (sacer enim)' (Ep. viii. 20. 5). Observe the word order again in this sentence (s. 3 n.) 'in superiore parte (A) nauigare (B) tantum (C), infra (A) etiam (C) natare (B).

balineum Hispellates . . . publice praebent. The municipality of Hispellum though remote from the site instead of exploiting tourists provided free lodging and baths. Cf. Letter 39. 10.

7. **inscripta.** Informal scribblings rather than inscriptions carved on separate tablets.

multorum, 'of many hands', dependent on *multa*, not on *inscripta*.

quae tua humanitas, 'such is your human understanding'. The phrase could have been 'qua humanitate es'. In it *quae* replaces Pliny's favourite device of a parenthesis introduced by *enim* or *nam* (e.g. Letter 21. 3, 11). Cf. Letter 7. 2: 'quae mea liberalitas'.

LETTER 33 (VIII. 16). TO PLINIUS PATERNUS

Household slaves

The recipient was a literary friend of Pliny, but despite his name not closely related to him. The letter is a companion to Letter 24, on the illness of the freedman Zosimus.

1. **infirmitates meorum,** 'my people', as in Letter 24. 1: 'meos tractem'. He has Zosimus in mind, and his reader Encolpius, reported sick in Ep. viii. 1. For some of Pliny's domestic arrangements for his freedmen and slaves see Letter 30. 12–13.

facilitas manumittendi. The freeing of household slaves was common in Roman society, out of enlightened self-interest. The slave worked to earn his freedom, and the *libertus* made a trustworthy personal servant because he usually continued to live in his master's household, at a higher level than before (Letter 9. 3 n.), and looked to his master for advancement of himself and his children (Letter 24. nn.).

Full manumission gave the freedmen nearly all the rights in civil law of a Roman citizen, including the free disposal of most of their property, though they remained subject to limitations in public life, from which their children and descendants became free (Letter 14.

1 n.). A less favourable form of manumission (*Latinitas Iuniana*) gave them such rights only during their lifetime. But Pliny implies that he gave all his freedmen the better status, when he says he allowed his slaves *also* (*quoque*) to make wills, which 'Junian Latins' could not do.

permitto seruis quoque quasi testamenta facere. Though slaves by custom were paid pocket money and even wages, and held possessions, in law all these belonged to their masters, and they had no right of testamentary disposition. Pliny's generosity was most unusual. His remarks in s. 3 sum up the usual Roman attitude of 'rem quocumque modo rem'. Cf. Ep. v. 7. 1: 'hoc si ius adspicias inritum, si defuncti uoluntatem ratum . . . est. mihi autem defuncti uoluntas . . . antiquior iure est'.

2. **mandant rogantque.** Their instructions in wills concerning, for example, the building of a tomb, or the establishment of a charitable trust, or a religious endowment in memory of the testator, at the expense of the heirs. Such requests might take the legal form of a *fidei commissum* or 'request on trust'.

quod uisum, 'as they think fit'.

diuidunt. This and *relinquunt* refer to the division of the property among the heirs and legatees.

donant. Gifts could only be made by the living and were subject to legal rules. Not all gifts were valid in law.

seruis res publica . . . domus est. The idea recurs in Seneca (*Ep.* 47. 14); Tacitus (*Annals* 14. 27. 4) says similarly of a colony of veteran soldiers 'ut consensu et caritate rempublicam efficerent'.

3. **sapientes.** This word is frequently used by Pliny in the sense of 'philosophers'. Cf. Letter 5. 3: 'ratio . . . quae sapientibus . . . pro necessitate est'. For Pliny's general attitude compare his dislike of the mean treatment of freedmen in Letter 9.

5. **plura.** Supply, for example, *scripsi*.

LETTER 34 (VIII. 21). TO ARRIANUS MATURUS

Pliny publishes his poems

Pliny here describes the recitation of his second book of verses, following up the first which he discussed in Ep. iv. 14 and Letter 26. 9–14.

Arrianus is the equestrian from Altinum for whom he secured an administrative post in Letter 12, and who receives several letters about politics, oratory, and style, including Letter 10.

1. **petulantiam,** 'indecency'. In Ep. iv. 14. 4 he defended his writing of *petulantiora* on the ground that it was the fashion for the most respectable people, but claims that he avoided *nuda uerba* and *lasciuia rerum*. He follows Martial in including a percentage of mildly indecent verses with a majority of pleasant subjects.

2. **grauiora opera,** i.e. his forensic speeches.

lusibus. See Letter 26. 9–14 for a fuller account of his 'trifles'.

in triclinio audiri, i.e. at a formal recitation. See Letters 6 and 27.

quo maxime lites interquiescunt, 'when law-cases are mostly having a holiday'. There was no fixed calendar or recess for the courts of civil law, which sat throughout the year with numerous but irregular breaks for public holidays. Cf. Ep. iii. 18. 4: 'numquam . . . aut ualde uacat Romae aut commodum est audire recitantem'. Even the hour was difficult to fix, because of the informality of sudden business, as on this occasion, and because of the daily round of other social occasions (Letter 3. 2), while the long afternoon was taken up by siesta, bath, and exercise (Letter 13. 10–11, 40. 3).

ante. Adverbial, with *positis*.

amicos. Pliny's recitations were always by invitation, cf. Letter 27. 12.

3. **in aduocationem subitam.** As in Letter 3. 2: 'ille in aduocationem, ille in consilium rogauit'.

causam praeloquendi. Pliny rather disliked the use of *praefationes*: 'liber . . . sine praefatione intellegatur' (Ep. iv. 14. 8; v. 12. 3. Cf. Letter 6. 2).

ut inreuerentem, i.e. *me.*

et in scribendo. Here *et* has the force of *etiam*.

primum amicis. Dative, 'for the benefit of my friends'.

4. opusculis uarius et metris, i.e. varied in the subject and metres of its contents, like a book of Martial. Pliny's first book contained only verses in the hendecasyllabic metre (Ep. iv. 14. 8). Pliny quotes only elegiac couplets (Letter 26. 11) and hexameters (Ep. vii. 4. 6) of his own writing.

recitaui biduo, 'on two days'. Since his Panegyric of Trajan took three sessions to recite, it may be calculated roughly that a session lasted from one and a half to two hours (Ep. iii. 18. 4).

imputant ... quod transeant, 'take credit for their omissions'.

ut omnia emendem. See Letter 27. 7–10 for his similar method of revising his speeches with the help of his friends.

electa. The object of *recitantibus*.

5. delicatus. Cf. Letter 29. 3 n. for the sense of an idle fop, or 'social butterfly'.

ignoto, i.e. a total stranger.

6. adhuc museum librum, 'unmatured', like newly made wine.

LETTER 35 (VIII. 24). TO MAXIMUS

Advice to a provincial governor

Pliny had several correspondents with the final name (cognomen) Maximus. This man is a senator who has recently held the praetorship, possibly a certain Sextus Quintilius Valerius Varus Maximus from Alexandria Troas in the province of Asia (s. 8 n.).

1. non ut praecipiam ... admoneam tamen. Pliny regularly instructed his younger friends in the rules of behaviour, according to the Roman social convention which gave great weight to the *auctoritas* of seniors, but he preferred to veil his advice under polite forms, as in Letter 9. 6: 'conuenit . . . amori . . . meo . . . sub exemplo praemonere quid debeas fugere'.

ut quae scis teneas . . . aut nescire melius. Both *teneas* and *nescire* are after *admoneam*, corresponding to its double meaning as a verb of advice and of statement: 'I must urge you to remember . . . and warn you that otherwise it is better to know nothing'. For *teneas* see Letter 17. 4, and for *aut* used singly Letter 4. 3.

2. in prouinciam Achaiam. The land of classical Hellas, excluding the part of Northern Greece known in antiquity as Macedonia, had been a Roman province since 146 B.C.

in qua primum humanitas litterae . . . inuentae esse creduntur. Pliny speaks as a 'philhellenic' Roman who acknowledges the debt which his civilization owed to classical Greece, and who also admired the contemporary Greek writers and thinkers, such as the philosopher Euphrates and the orator Isaeus (Letter 4, Ep. ii. 3). He echoes passages of a letter that Cicero wrote to his brother when governor of Asia in the same strain. But many Roman writers of the Empire were irritated by the pretensions of contemporary Greeks (s. 3 'iactatione'), and derided them as *Graeculi*, 'silly little Greeks'. So Juvenal in a famous passage (*Sat.* 3. 77–78): 'Omnia nouit Graeculus esuriens: in caelum iusseris, ibit'. But Cicero (*ad Quint. fratrem* I. i. 27) spoke of 'ei generi . . . a quo ad alios peruenisse putetur etiam humanitas', and wrote similarly in his *pro Flacco* 61–62.

humanitas, litterae. The literature and philosophy of the period down to the fourth century B.C., beginning with Homer and ending with Plato and Aristotle.

meram. Old Greece is contrasted with the lands of Asia Minor, such as Bithynia (s. 8), to which Greek civilization spread after Alexander had conquered the Asiatic empire of the Persians.

missum ad ordinandum statum liberarum ciuitatum. Maximus has been sent on a special mission like that of Pliny to Bithynia later (p. xiii). Many of the cities of Greece were 'free states' enjoying a great measure of independence from the Roman governors, whose writ ran inside their territories only in matters of defence. But their

internal affairs had now fallen into disorder, and Maximus is to set them to rights. Compare the instructions given by Trajan to Pliny in Ep. x. 115: 'ut formandis istius prouinciae moribus ipse moderareris et ea constitueres quae ad perpetuam eius . . . quietem essent profutura'.

homines maxime homines. Pliny again echoes Cicero's letter (op. cit. 6), 'genere . . . quod est ex hominum omni genere humanissimum'.

ius . . . uirtute meritis amicitia foedere . . . religione tenuerunt. The Greeks had defended their liberty first by their own efforts (as in the wars against the Persians), and later by loyalty to and association with Rome (*amicitia*, etc.) against the kings of Macedon and Asia. By *foedere . . . et religione* he means scrupulous observance of their treaties with Rome. The word *religio* is a rare word in Pliny, and takes its meaning from the context. In Ep. vi. 2. 8 he speaks of the *religio* of a *iudex*, meaning faithfulness, much as here.

3. reuerere conditores deos. The Greeks thought of each city as founded and protected by a great deity, as Athens by Athena.

nomina deorum, 'titles'. He is playing on the double meaning of *nomen*, 'name' and 'fame'.

ex cuiusquam dignitate. Pliny advises a proconsul 'ut discrimina ordinum dignitatumque custodias' in Ep. ix. 5. 3. *Dignitas* means personal rank.

4. nobis miserit iura. There was a tradition that the early Romans sent to Athens for advice about the drafting of the Twelve Tables of the civil law in 450 B.C. (Livy 3. 31. 8).

5. quod esse desierit, 'because it has ceased to be such'.

6. fasces. The bundles of rods were the formal symbol of the official power (*imperium*) of a Roman governor.

male uim suam . . . experitur, 'it is bad that authority should try out its power by insults to others'.

aliorum contumeliis. An 'objective' genitive.

8. mutetur, 'is exchanged for'.

quaesturae tuae fama. Maximus had been the treasury official (*quaestor*) of Bithynia. This helps to identify him with Quintilius Valerius Varus Maximus, who also had been quaestor of Bithynia, as is known from an inscription of Alexandria Troas which gives his early career only (*ILS* 1018). Another inscription of about A.D. 115 mentions a Quintilius Maximus interfering in the affairs of Sparta. But it is not certain that either inscription refers to Pliny's friend, whose mission to Achaea was in about A.D. 107–9.

testimonium principis. Trajan, the ruling *princeps*, publicly commended him for his action.

tribunatus, praetura. These with the quaestorship are the regular annual offices of state at Rome which all senators normally held before proceeding to longer appointments in the imperial service (p. x).

legatio. Governors appointed by the emperor were called *legati Augusti propraetore*.

9. in longinqua . . . quam suburbana. In this list the first term in each pair refers to Bithynia and the second to Achaea.

suburbana. Metaphorical. Achaea was nearer to Rome than was Bithynia in north-west Turkey.

seruientes. The inhabitants of an ordinary province were subject to the absolute power of the governor (*fasces*, above).

sorte. The quaestors were assigned to their special posts by drawing lots.

iudicio, i.e. *principis*.

LETTER 36 (IX. 6). TO CALVISIUS RUFUS

At the races

Rufus is the wealthy friend from Comum who receives Letters 11, 16, 39.

1. inter pugillares ac libellos, 'in my study'; cf. Letter 2. 1 n. for *pugillares*.

quemadmodum . . . in urbe. See Letter 3. 2 for the daily round at Rome.

circenses erant. Understand *ludi*. There were races on many days throughout the year in the Circus Maximus at Rome, of which the ruins can be seen between the Palatine and Aventine hills.

nihil nouum. Pliny follows Cicero's lead in his intellectual snobbery, whose letter *Ad fam.* 7. 1 may be his model here. Seneca takes the same line in his *Ep.* 7. 4.

2. nunc fauent panno, 'actually they support the silks'. Four companies of trainers organized the races by hiring out teams to promoters who paid the expenses. These were senatorial magistrates and priests (Letter 29. 6 n.), and often the emperor himself. The teams were distinguished by their coloured shirts: *tunica russata* (red), *prasina* (pale green), *ueneta* (sea blue), *albata* (white). Pliny implies that gambling was the great motive, though this was nominally forbidden by law.

agitatores . . . equos. There are many inscriptions in honour of great jockeys and horses, such as 'Aquilo, by Aquilo', which won 130 races, and was 'placed' 125 times (*ILS* 5295). These were chariot or car races. There was no racing of ridden horses in the modern style.

3. mitto apud uulgus. This is a parenthesis: 'setting aside the common folk'.

apud . . . graues homines. Compare Pliny's strictures of Quadratilla for keeping pantomime actors (Letter 29. 4). Tacitus, who was shocked by the stories of Nero taking part as a charioteer in the public races (*Annals* 14. 14), is found attending the Circus in Letter 38. 2.

in re . . . adsidua, 'common', 'well worn'.

desidere, 'to idle'.

The consular orders his tomb

Cremutius Ruso was one of Pliny's young aristocratic friends. The story of Verginius Rufus' death and of his tomb is picked up from Letter 8 and Ep. vi. 10.

1. **in quadam epistula mea,** i.e. in Ep. vi. 10, where Pliny feared that through the neglected state of his tomb Verginius would be forgotten. This remark suggests that Ruso has read Book VI in a published edition before Book IX was published.

iussisse, i.e. in his will. It was customary to prescribe such arrangements by will.

Verginium Rufum. The elderly consular whose death in A.D. 97 is reported in Letter 8.

pulso . . . Vindice. As governor of Upper Germany in A.D. 68 Rufus suppressed the revolt of C. Julius Vindex, governor of Central Gaul (Gallia Lugdunensis), who had raised provincial forces to support Galba, the governor of Northern Spain, against the reigning Princeps Nero. After the battle Rufus' troops wanted to proclaim him emperor, but he refused, saying that the choice of emperor belonged to the Senate. Later Galba succeeded in displacing Nero, who committed suicide. Rufus then faced an awkward situation, and Galba recalled him from his post. This letter shows how Rufus tried to explain away his actions.

imperium adseruit non sibi sed patriae. This is deliberately ambiguous. *Imperium* can mean either 'the power of the Princeps' or 'the power of Rome over the world'. Since some accounts regard Vindex, who was a Gaul by birth, as a rebel against Rome, the sentence can mean either that Rufus saved the 'empire' for Rome from the hands of the Gallic rebel Vindex, or that he reserved the choice of emperor for the nation.

rectiusque Frontinum, i.e. *fecisse*. C. Julius Frontinus was another senior consular like Rufus. As governor of Britain in A.D. 74–78 he conquered the Silures of Southern Wales, and in 97–98 he had a hand in the choice of Trajan to succeed Nerva as Princeps.

3. prorogare. Metaphorical. This word properly means 'to propose the extension' of something in an assembly of the Roman people.

4. in praedicando uerecundia, 'modesty in publicity'. Cf. Letter 31. 2, 'praedicator' n.

5. familiariter . . . dilectus, 'a genuine friend'. Contrast Letter 9. 1, 'homo minime familiaris'. The word *amicus* means only an associate.

prouectum. Supply *esse Verginium.*

hoc unum referret ita . . . locutum, 'reported this one thing about his actions, that once Cluvius conversed with him as follows'.

Cluvius Rufus wrote a history of the period of Nero, now lost. He was a private friend of Nero, and supported Galba after Nero's death.

aliter ac uelis. Evidently Cluvius criticized Verginius Rufus, either for failing to support Nero properly, or for supporting him too well against Galba. Verginius tried to place the blame for the destruction of Vindex upon his troops, alleging that they took the initiative in attacking Vindex when Verginius was negotiating with him. See Cassius Dio 63. 24. 2–3.

quae historiae fides debeatur. See Letters 22. 4, 31. 10 nn. for Pliny's views of history.

ut esset liberum uobis scribere quae libuisset. Verginius claims to have championed freedom by reserving the choice of emperor for the Senate, which as a survival of the old Republican constitution was regarded as the symbol of political liberty.

scribere. Cf. Tacitus' definition of liberty at this time: 'sentire quae uelis et quae sentias dicere' (*Hist.* 1. 1. 5).

6. parcior . . . et pressior, 'rather spare and bare', cf. Letter 26. 8, 'pressus sermo' n.

uetuit exstrui monumentum. Frontinus was exceptional. Romans great and small, from serving soldiers to consular senators, went in for elaborate tombs and lengthy inscriptions recording every detail of their public life. The *monumentum* was the whole structure. In Ep. vi. 10 Pliny notes that Verginius' tomb though small was unfinished, and the famous inscription ironically had not been set up.

legendum dare . . . , 'to provide for publication of the fact that . . .'.

orbem terrarum, 'the world'. But the phrase often refers to the Roman Empire. In fact the will would be read only by the interested parties.

7. quamquam, 'yet'. Particle, not subordinate conjunction.

LETTER 38 (IX. 23). TO MAXIMUS

Pliny and Tacitus

This letter is one of a series in which Pliny compares the joint standing and relationship of Tacitus and himself as men of letters.

Maximus is an elder man, addressed with marked respect in **s. 6**, distinct from the legate of Achaea to whom Letter 35 is addressed, and from Vibius Maximus of Letter 12.

1. centumuiri. For this court see Letter 23. 1–2 nn. Its prestige is shown by the fact that Pliny equates it with the Senate.

se intra iudicum auctoritatem . . . tenuissent, 'confined themselves to the impressive demeanour of judges'.

2. Corneli Taciti. See Letters 2, 25, preff.

circensibus proximis. See Letter 36 nn.

Italicus es an prouincialis? Large numbers of wealthy provincials by this time were not only Roman citizens in status, but had become Roman 'knights' and senators holding responsible positions in the administration or becoming distinguished advocates, such as Licinius Sura (Letter 21 pref.), Herennius Senecio (Letter 31. 5 n.), and Marius Priscus (Letter 10. 2 n.). Tacitus himself may have been a provincial from Narbonensis, but this anecdote does not prove it (R. Syme, *Tacitus*, ch. xlv).

3. **ex studiis.** His oratory, as nearly always in Pliny. Tacitus had so far published only his short *Agricola* and *Dialogus*, but was a distinguished advocate.

quasi litterarum propria, 'as belonging to literature'. Pliny often uses *quasi* without the sense of supposition.

notus, quibus. Supply *eis* after *notus*.

4. **recumbebat,** 'sat at dinner'. For the Roman dinner-party arrangements see Letter 9. 3 n.

Fadius Rufinus. A junior senator, later consul in A.D. 113.

municeps ipsius. A fellow townsman, whom he would entertain. Tacitus tells in *Dialogus* 7. 4 how visiting strangers from distant parts of Italy and from the provinces would hunt out the great orators of the day at Rome.

uides hunc? They are lying on the same couch with Fadius between them, yet they have not been introduced.

Plinius est. He is known by his family name, which was rare, but Tacitus, whose family name Cornelius was very common, is indicated above by his very unusual cognomen.

5. **uerum.** Adjective, not conjunction.

anus Attica. This story is often told, for example by Cicero, *Tusculan. Disput.* 5. 103.

6. **aliorum . . . non meum.** Both go with *iudicium*.

apud te, 'in your presence'.

LETTER 39 (IX. 33). TO CANINIUS RUFUS

The African dolphin

Pliny offers a poetical subject to his literary friend Caninius of Comum, whom he had long been urging to write some composition, including a poetical version of Trajan's Dacian wars (Ep. iii. 7. 14–15; viii. 4).

1. **super cenam,** 'over dinner', as we say. Cf. Letter 13. 11.

magna auctori fides. Pliny probably means his uncle, who inserted a collection of dolphin stories in his *Natural History* (ix. 24–32), including a shorter version of this one (ibid. 26–27). Pliny combines separate anecdotes from his uncle's account, and differs on several details of substance (below ss. 3, 8, 9). Either Pliny had a separate source or he used the material freely.

uel, 'even'.

2. **Hipponensis colonia.** Pliny's description still fits the site of Hippo Diarrhytus, modern Bizerta in Tunisia, which lies on a great lagoon connected to the sea by a narrow tidal channel.

aestus. The slight Mediterranean tide is noticeable because of the narrow channel.

colonia. Hippo was by origin a city settled by Roman legionary veterans.

aut . . . aut . . . nunc . . . nunc. The order of related words is A–B–B–A, a rhetorical chiasmus, cf. p. xvii. For *repressit* corresponds to *redditur*, and *impulit* to *infertur*, since the river flows out when the tide gives it way.

3. **hic.** Adverbial, i.e. at the estuary.

maxime pueri. The boys, the calling by name, and the stranding (ss. 6, 8) come from different stories in the elder Pliny, who does not mention the water sports, while our Pliny omits the feeding of the dolphin by hand, which his uncle gives.

gloria et uirtus altissime prouehi, 'it is their heroic boast to swim far out to sea'.

4. **delphinus occurrit.** Most of the details of this and other dolphin stories have been vindicated by modern study of the dolphin, which is a remarkably tame and docile creature. A photograph of a boy mounted on a dolphin is published in *Greece & Rome*, 1960, pp. 82 f.

praecedere . . . sequi . . . mox flectit. He changes from narrative infinitives to the present indicative and back to infinitives in s. 5, *concurrere . . . adspicere.* Cf. Letter 30. 8 n.

5. **mari simile.** He means the lagoon.

ad tempus. Evidently at a particular hour.

6. **praebentem,** i.e. *se tangi*.

8. **gestatorem collusoremque puerorum.** There is a touch of mock epic in this title. Strictly, only one boy mounted the dolphin, though all played with it.

extrahi solitum. Pliny goes astray. In his uncle's version the dolphin comes to land for love of man and perishes, as it would once its skin became dry. These stories may derive from the accidental stranding of dolphins.

9. **Octauium Auitum.** The elder Pliny has a similar version of the dolphin's death, but names a different official, the proconsul Flavianus who governed Africa in a year between A.D. 70 and 77.

educto, i.e. the dolphin.

religione praua. This is Pliny's own comment, not taken from his uncle. Compare his disapproval of the Christians as a *superstitio praua immodica* (Letter 47. 8) and of the *nimia superstitio* of Regulus (Ep. vi. 2. 2).

odorem . . . in altum refugisse, 'fled from the smell into the sea'.

10. **magistratus quorum aduentu . . . modica res publica . . . atterebatur.** The Roman governors and their staff expect to be billeted and entertained by the municipality (*res publica*) of Hippo. Cf. Letter 32. 6: 'Hispellates . . . praebent . . . hospitium', and 45. 1.

placuit . . . interfici ad quod coibatur, 'it was decided that the object of these throngs should be slain'. By *placuit* he refers to a resolution of the town council.

LETTER 40 (IX. 36). TO PEDANIUS FUSCUS SALINATOR

Life in the country

The recipient is his young friend and pupil, the well-born Pedanius (Letter 26, pref.). This account of the daily life of a country gentleman is the counterpart of Letter 13. 8–11, on the daily life of his uncle in town, and it completes his advice to Pedanius on how to live in the country (Letter 26. 1).

1. **quaeris quemadmodum.** This is a formal letter of instruction, and it begins with the same phrase as Letter 26 to Fuscus.

in Tuscis. The villa on his estates at Tifernum Tiberinum, to which he proposed to add the lands described in Letter 16, is the subject of a long letter, Ep. v. 6.

diem aestate disponam. The day falls into two parts: the morning activities, ss. 1–3, followed by the siesta, exercise, and dinner, ss. 3–4.

circa horam primam. The hour after daybreak. Like his uncle he begins the day early (Letter 13. 8 n.).

clausae fenestrae. Shutters or curtains keep out the light.

animum oculis sequor, i.e. 'he visualizes his thoughts'.

quotiens . . . uident. Elsewhere he uses subjunctive after *quotiens*, when the verb is in past tense (Letter 5. 7 n.).

2. **ad uerbum scribenti emendantique similis.** He is 'like one who is writing and rewriting word by word', because he is working by thought and memory alone. There is no writing until the copying-clerk (*notarius*) comes in. He composes in short sections (*partes, membra*), as he advised Fuscus in Letter 26. 5–6. For the clerk and his tablets see Letter 13. 15.

teneriue, 'held in memory'. See Letters 17. 4 n., 26. 3.

3. **in xystum me uel cryptoporticum confero.** The terrace and the colonnade were great features of the country house, designed to provide a varied choice of places of exercise in a small area (cf. Ep. v. 6. 16, 27–29, 32) according to the weather (*ut dies suasit*).

uehiculum ascendo. He rides in a carriage or on horseback (s. 5) round the *hippodromos*, and walks (s. 4) round the *gestatio*. These were short oval or rectangular tracks laid out round gardens or shrubberies within his gardens, which he never leaves. The Romans took their exercise like passengers pacing the deck of an ocean liner.

ibi . . . idem, e.g. *ago.*

refecta. This agrees with *intentio*.

redormio. The hour of siesta.

non tam uocis causa quam stomachi. Pliny mentions this weakness in the account of his prosecution of Marius Priscus (Letter 10. 15). The ancient doctors prescribed reading aloud and other exercises as remedies. His uncle also suffered from a weak wind-pipe (Letter 25. 19).

4. iterum ambulo ungor exerceor lauor. The afternoon ritual is like his uncle's (Letter 13. 11), but closer still to that of Spurinna, a country gentleman, described in Ep. iii. 1. 5–8.

cenanti . . . liber legitur. As at his uncle's house (Letter 13. 11), where serious study always came first.

post cenam comoedia aut lyristes. At a formal dinner-party these accompanied the meal. See Letter 7. 2 n.

cenam. The only meal mentioned, and probably the only meal of the day, as in the house of Spurinna (Ep. iii. 1. 9), whereas the elder Pliny took three meals a day (Letter 13. 10–11).

cum meis. His slaves and freedmen, as in Letter 33. 1, such as the *libertus non inlitteratus* mentioned in Letter 30. 12.

quamquam longissimus dies bene conditur, 'the day is well concluded however long'. For *quamquam* cf. Letter 5. 7.

5. si diu iacui, i.e. in the phase described in ss. 1–2.

6. uenor . . . non sine pugillaribus. Just as in Letter 2. 1.

LETTER 41 (X. 31). TO TRAJAN

On the treatment of convicts

This letter shows some of the problems that lurked below the surface of city government in the Roman Empire. For Pliny's mission in Bithynia–Pontus, see pp. xiii–xv.

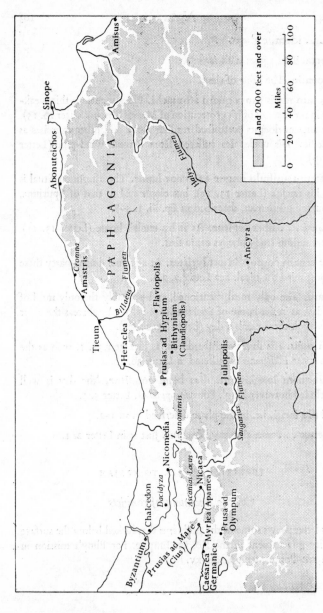

The cities of Bithynia and proconsular Pontus, and adjacent areas

1. **salua magnitudine tua.** We too can say 'saving your majesty'. Compare Ep. x. 41. 1 for the meaning: 'fortunae tuae et animi magnitudinem'.

ius mihi dederis referendi ad te. Pliny is quoting his original instructions. As his was a special mission of reconstruction (p. xiv) he was encouraged to consult the central government where a routine governor would have been left more to his own devices. Pliny consults Trajan about this problem because he wants to change the previous usage.

2. **ciuitatibus.** The word means 'towns' instead of 'communities' in the less literary and more colloquial language of Book Ten, and is contrasted with *uici* and *agri*. Cf. Letter 44: 'ipsas ciuitates' and Letter 47. 9: 'neque ciuitates tantum sed uicos etiam atque agros . . . contagio peruagata est'.

Nicomediae et Nicaeae. Modern Ismit and Isnik. These were the two greatest cities of Bithynia. Nicomedia was the provincial capital, and Nicaea was its great rival. They managed their own affairs as self-governing municipalities under the general control of the Roman governor.

in opus damnati uel in ludum. Condemned criminals were sentenced to long periods of hard labour in mines and quarries (*opus*) owned by the Roman state or by the cities, or to the service of the amphitheatres (*ludum*), either as attendants or as fighters in the beast-shows and gladiatorial contests.

publicorum seruorum officio. The executive and clerical work of the boroughs was done under the control of the annually elected magistrates by slaves that the city owned. These received a maintenance allowance (*annua*), and were responsible among other things for guarding prisoners (Ep. x. 19). Evidently there was a convenient impropriety: either the cities were saving themselves the expense of buying slaves by using the convict labour, or else the slaves themselves were using the convicts as substitutes to do their own work.

3. **nimis seuerum arbitrabar.** For Pliny's kindliness towards the underprivileged see Letters 24, 33.

non satis honestum, i.e. not befitting the public service (*honos*).

a re publica pasci. Usually the cities fed the prisoners, and repaid themselves by their work in the mines.

periculosum. Some of the prisoners might be trained gladiators and capable of causing serious trouble.

4. decreta. The formal sentences of the proconsuls were recorded in writing.

monumenta. Documents or records.

liberati probarentur, 'proved to have been set free'.

5. erant . . . qui dicerent. For the subjunctive compare Ep. x. 58. 2: 'fuerunt qui dicerent'. These are factual, not generic, unlike Ep. vi. 21. 1: 'sum ex eis qui mirer antiquos'. But possibly there is a touch of purpose: 'there were people to say'.

deprecantes . . . dimissos, 'that they begged for remission and were released'. But though freed from a particular sentence they were still condemned criminals. Hence their employment as a kind of slave.

iussu, i.e. on oral instructions only. The *legati* here mentioned were the assistants of the proconsuls.

LETTER 42 (X. 32). TO PLINY

On the treatment of convicts (2)

1. quoniam multa in ea emendanda adparuerint. In Ep. x. 117 Trajan writes: 'prudentiam tuam elegi ut formandis istius prouinciae moribus ipse moderareris'.

2. uetustiores, i.e. persons whose sentences date further back than ten years, though they are not themselves old men.

ad balineum. To service as cleaners and stokers at the public baths.

munitiones. Building and paving roads. The *uiae* are the main thoroughfares, and the *uici* are the side-streets that divide up the blocks of houses. The latter is a secondary meaning, since the wards of the cities are also called *uici*.

On fire-brigades

1. **Nicomediae uastissimum incendium.** For Nicomedia see Letter 41. 2 n. Though stone and brick rather than wood were the principal building materials, fire was a persistent menace to the cities of the Roman empire. Rome itself was frequently devastated by great fires despite the service of a large professional fire-brigade. For the worst of these see Tacitus, *Annals* 15. 38–41.

Gerusian. This building housed the association of civic elders which was also called the *Gerusia*.

Iseon. The temple of Isis, an Egyptian deity whose cult was a popular form of personal religion throughout the Roman empire. Both these words are Greek accusatives.

2 **inertia hominum.** There was much social unrest between the rich and the poor, who would not stir themselves to save the mansions of the wealthy. Hence Trajan's suspicions in Letter 44.

sipo . . . hama. These are hand-worked pumps, like stirrup-pumps, and buckets.

instrumentum. Ladders, poles, and large blankets (*centones*), soaked in water, were part of the fire-fighting equipment in common use. In Italy the professional craftsmen who owned or made these (*fabri*, *centonarii*) were organized into amateur fire-brigades by the cities. Hence Pliny's proposal below.

3. **an instituendum putes collegium fabrorum.** This was how the amateur fire-brigades were organized in Italy, and in the western provinces, as Pliny would know. The trade guilds undertook the job of fire-fighting. But such guilds did not exist in the eastern Greek-speaking provinces. Besides, Trajan had instructed Pliny to abolish

all social clubs throughout the province (Letter 47. 7), because they became organized centres of civic disturbances.

ne quis nisi faber recipiatur. This is to stop one of the dodges by which subversive agents infiltrated into the guilds.

LETTER 44 (X. 34). TO PLINY

On fire-brigades (2)

1. secundum exempla complurium. Pliny had not mentioned any precedents, but Trajan's secretaries have been at work looking up the files, and given the Princeps the information on which he bases his reply to Pliny.

ipsas ciuitates. The towns as distinct from villages, cf. Letter 41. 2 n.

factionibus . . . uexatas. A *factio* is much the same as an *hetaeria* (below). The contemporary Bithynian politician Cocceianus Dio in his municipal speeches tells how the richer folk at Prusa organized themselves in groups to control elections and public business and political trials in the town council and assembly, and at the court of the proconsul. The disorder was sometimes so great that the proconsul suspended the meetings of the assembly (Dio, *Or.* 43. 2–11, 45. 7–9, 50. 3–4).

hetaeriae eaeque breui fient, 'they will become political clubs, and that quickly'. The word *hetaeria* is Greek. The organization of political 'bands of companions' has a long history in Greek lands in antiquity, stretching back to the 'clubs' which carried out the anti-democratic revolution at Athens in 411 B.C.

2. dominos praediorum. The owners of tenement blocks. *Praedia* means 'real estate', whether in town or country.

ipsi inhibeant. They are to establish local centres of fire-control. The scheme seems inefficient, but no other form of fire-brigade was allowed in the great cities of the eastern provinces henceforth. Even at Rome, where a professional brigade existed, Nero after the great fire ordered that fire-fighting equipment was to be kept in the court-yards of the city tenements (Tacitus *Annals* 15. 43. 4). Perhaps in the narrow and crowded streets of the ancient cities such methods were more effective than an amateur brigade which lacked transport, large hoses, and water under pressure. But Trajan seems more afraid of riots than of fires.

adcursu populi ad hoc uti. Isidore (*Orig.* 20. 6. 9) records (s.v. *sifon*) that 'in the eastern empire when they see a house on fire people rush with pumps full of water and put out the fires'.

LETTER 45 (X. 81). TO TRAJAN

Feuds among the gentry

1. Prusae. A city of Western Bithynia at the foot of the Olympus range.

intra hospitium. A civic guest-house, cf. Letter 32. 6 n.

uacarem, 'when I was attending to', literally 'was free for'. Cf. Letter 3. 4 n.

magistratus. One of the annual magistrates of the city.

appellatum me. The provincial governor intervenes in ordinary civic affairs only when invited thus.

a Claudio Eumolpo. All the persons named seem to be civic council-lors. Their double names indicate that they also hold the Roman citizenship, except Asclepiades.

Cocceianus Dion. Author of many surviving essays and speeches about the civic politics of Bithynia, and about philosophical and literary subjects. He was a leading citizen of Prusa, and a few years earlier had initiated a programme of public building.

bule. A Greek word for town council. These councils had up to 300 or 400 members, elected for life by the popular assembly. With the city magistrates they controlled the city's affairs. Cf. Letter 20. 1 n.

adsignari ciuitati opus, 'that the city should take over the building'.

ciuitati. See Letter 41. 2 n.

curam egerat. Local citizens were made responsible for organizing such jobs. The city paid the bill, but the *curator* had to produce his accounts (*rationem operis*) for audit.

adsistente. Eumolpus is the primary figure, speaking with the support of Archippus on the main issue about the money. See s. 6 n.

2. ut cognoscerem pro tribunali, 'that I should conduct an official investigation'. This is an example of *cognitio extra ordinem*. No named charge is brought against Dio, but there is an allegation of improper conduct which the governor will adjudicate in accordance with his own opinion, and not according to any statute law.

pro, 'on (not 'in front of') my judicial bench'. Flavius Archippus was a professional teacher of philosophy who was involved in feuds with sundry persons at Prusa including Dio, who had earlier tried to secure his disgrace by alleging that he was an escaped convict (Ep. **x.** 58). He is now seeking his revenge.

4. Nicaeae. See Letter 41. 2 n.

parum instructus, 'inadequately briefed'.

5. etiam de causa. About the main charge as well as the procedure.

ad exemplum pertinenti. Pliny and Trajan were frequently anxious to avoid setting undesirable precedents, cf. Letter 48. 2: 'pessimi exempli est'.

6. non accusatorem se sed aduocatum. Eumolpus still takes the lead on the issue of the accounts, but claims only to be acting as the representative of Archippus on the treason charge. He wants to avoid responsibility for this, because he fears a counter-charge of malicious prosecution (*calumnia*). Cf. Letter 31. 7 n.

iunxi. The dossier was attached to the bottom of the covering letter with glue.

7. in re praesenti, 'on the spot'. The idiom is usual in official texts.

tuam quoque statuam. The burial of bodies near the statue of the emperor could be construed as a disrespectful act of the sort which emperors, jealous of their personal dignity, used to accept as the ground of a charge of treason under the *lex maiestatis minutae*.

sepulti. Burial inside the city precinct was contrary to civic regulations in many provinces. Evidently the rule was not strictly observed in Bithynia.

8. **exemplis defenditur,** 'the precedents are on the side of the defence'.

LETTER 46 (X. 82). TO PLINY

Feuds among the gentry (2)

1. **propositum meum.** The neuter passive participle is here used as a noun, like *decretum* or *praeceptum*.

optime nosses. Trajan had made it clear from his accession onwards that he would not allow frivolous charges of treason such as Domitian had encouraged for the suppression of political opposition (Letters 20. 5-6, 30. 14, 31. 7-8 nn.). Pliny had enlarged upon Trajan's attitude in his Panegyricus speech, delivered in A.D. 100.

2. **etiam si exemplis adiuuaretur,** 'even if the precedents were on the side of the prosecution'. Cf. Letter 45. 8.

excutiatur, 'let it be shaken out', like a bag.

LETTER 47 (X. 96). TO TRAJAN

On the punishment of Christians

This letter, with Trajan's reply, contains the earliest pagan evidence about the attitude of the Roman government to Christians and about the life and liturgy of the Christian communities. It was written about ten years earlier than Tacitus' account in his *Annals* (15. 44) of the execution of Christians at Rome after the great fire of A.D. 65. The letters also form part of a series of documents illustrating the treatment of foreign sects of all sorts by the Roman state. As it is the longest single text dealing with all these themes it has given rise to much comment, and some disagreement, among historians. Pliny's letter was known to the Christian apologist Tertullian, who summarizes it accurately in his *Apology* (ch. 2), written in A.D. 197.

Greeks and Romans alike believed that the safety of their states depended upon the proper observance of cults of local gods by each community (Letter 35. 3). The civic gods would be angry if any alien deity received offerings and worship from the inhabitants of their own territory, or if their own cult was neglected. But the management of the civic cults was left to civic magistrates and priests, drawn from the upper classes, while private individuals were left to their own devices, and tended, in the complex civilization of the Roman empire, to turn for personal religion to foreign cults and sects. These provided a deeper psychical satisfaction than did the old Graeco-Roman cults of personalized deities who were treated in literature and mythology as merely super-men and super-women. Thus the Egyptian cult of Isis flourished at Nicomedia (Letter 43. 1). The Roman government had always disapproved of its own citizens doing this, and from time to time banned particular cults at Rome and expelled the clergy of foreign sects, such as the priests of Isis and the Magian practitioners of the occult. But no statute laws were made to deal with the whole question. Each case was handled as it arose by magistrates at Rome and by governors in the provinces. They acted by the general power of control which they exercised over the behaviour of ordinary citizens, and which they enforced by the jurisdiction known as *cognitio extra ordinem* (cf. Letter 45. 2 n.). Usually they were immediately concerned not with the religious aspect of the cults, which seldom threatened the worship of the civic gods, but with the personal behaviour of the devotees. If cults gave rise to criminal or scandalous behaviour (*scelera, flagitia*), a magistrate would place a ban on the sect. But such bans were easy to elude, because the Roman police organization was very rudimentary, and forbidden cults easily re-established themselves after an interval. Besides, the Romans realized that foreigners ought to propitiate and worship their own native gods even when resident outside their homeland. Hence the

Romans tended to tolerate foreign cults provided that the adherents respected the official religion and cults of the country in which they were living, whether in Roman Italy or provincial territory.

But the Christians were in a worse position than the devotees of other private cults. First, because the church was not a civic or national cult, once it had broken free from Judaism, in Roman eyes it had no claim to recognition. Second, and worse, the Christians as monotheists totally refused to recognize the validity of any other form of religion. They were actively hostile to other peoples' gods, and hence were a positive danger to the safety of the civic community in which they lived. Even if free from other vices the sect offended against the basic principle on which the Romans were prepared to tolerate alien sects. But the Christians were also suspected of indulging in social misconduct of a kind that the Romans had found associated with other personal cults (*flagitia* s. 2 n.). So, in circumstances that are not clear, the Christians from A.D. 65 onwards came to be regarded as practitioners of an undesirable cult and could be prosecuted as such, following a precedent established by Nero (*nomen* s. 2 n.). The enforcement of such bans depended in Roman legal usage upon the activity of unofficial accusers or *delatores* (*deferebantur* s. 2 n.). There was no public prosecutor for this or any crime in the Roman world. Hence the 'persecution' of Christians was very limited and occasional during the first two centuries A.D., even when governors accepted the evidence of mere informers (s. 6 n.). The operation of Christian prosecutions is made known in any accurate technical detail only by Pliny's letter. Later accounts, such as the various *Acta martyrorum*, and the *Apology* of Tertullian tend to represent the Christian viewpoint and to slur over the technical aspects.

See further the Appendix in my *Historical Commentary*, and G. E. F. de Ste Croix, *Past and Present* (xxvi), 1963, 'Why were the Christians persecuted?'.

The letter was written from a city of Pontus, not Bithynia, which may be either Amisus or Amastris, about whose affairs Pliny wrote to Trajan in adjacent letters (Ep. x. 92, 98). The date lies between 18 September and 3 January of Pliny's second year in his province, i.e. not later than A.D. 112.

1. sollemne, 'usual'.

cognitionibus. For the term see Letters 20. 1 n., 45. 2 n. Any trial before a magistrate sitting without a regular jury was a *cognitio*. Barely two trials of Christians are known at Rome in Pliny's age.

nescio. Pliny does not hesitate to undertake the trial. As in other affairs he takes local advice (s. 10 'constat' n.), and follows the *exempla proconsulum*. Cf. Ep. x. 72 'postulantibus quibusdam ut . . . secundum exempla proconsulum ipse cognoscerem', and Letter 44. 1: 'secundum exempla complurium'.

quid et quatenus. The order of words is a *chiasmus* (p. xvii), i.e. *quid* goes with *quaeri*—'What is the object of investigation'—and *quatenus* with *puniri*.

2. nec mediocriter haesitaui. Pliny asks Trajan three questions in the following sentence, but lays most stress on that concerning *paenitentiae uenia* in the rest of the letter, and Trajan devotes most of his reply to this. Pliny is not pleading for an abandonment of the punishment of Christians.

sitne aliquod discrimen aetatum. A subsidiary question not affecting the main principle. Roman lawyers sometimes allowed for this in fixing the penalties for ordinary crimes.

nomen ipsum. The nature of this charge is indicated by the words 'an essent Christiani', i.e. simple adherence to the cult, without any assessment of their actions and behaviour. This is the regular procedure in all the accounts of Christian persecutions. Tertullian in his *Apology* (ch. 2) objects at length that by *accusatio nominis* the Christians were given no opportunity of proving the innocence of their lives. He attributes the invention of the procedure to the Emperor Nero, evidently at the time of the great fire of A.D. 65. But similar forms of prosecution had been used in the past against other sects from 186 B.C. onwards, when large numbers of persons were punished for being worshippers of Bacchus, and the Senate ordained that all shrines of Bacchus should be destroyed throughout Italy (Livy 39. 18).

an flagitia cohaerentia nomini. Alien sects had frequently been banned, like the Bacchanals, because they were associated with criminal and anti-social acts. The Druids were officially abolished by the Emperors Tiberius and Claudius because of their practice of human sacrifice. Tacitus in his account of the trial of Christians in A.D. 65 mentions *flagitia*, and calls them *sontes et nouissima exempla meritos*. They were popularly believed to indulge in incest and cannibalism. But later in the second century the well-informed Lucian knew nothing of such charges, and considered that 'atheism', i.e. hostility to the established religion, was their crime (*Alexander* 25, *De morte peregrini* 11–14). Pliny in ss. 7–8 raises a doubt about the existence of *flagitia*, but does not positively argue that Christians were inoffensive, and in s. 10 he refers to the effect of their 'atheism' on the civic cults of Pontus.

deferebantur. This technical term refers to formal accusation by a third party, a private accuser, who conducts the accusation before the governor, as in the accusation of Dio at Prusa (Letter 45. 2).

confitentes iterum ac tertio interrogaui. This procedure occurs in all well-attested trials of Christians, but not elsewhere. Since the Christians did not defend themselves, the accusers did not need to develop their case. The Roman judges could have sentenced them forthwith. But the Romans were reluctant to sentence an undefended prisoner, especially since there was a possibility of malicious prosecution (*calumnia*, Letter 31. 7 n.). Compare the questioning of the silent Christ by Pontius Pilatus (Mark xv. 2–4; Matt. xxvii. 11–15).

supplicium minatus. Punishment, not torture (cf. Letter 10. 8). The purpose is to induce the Christian to abandon his cult. He is punished only when he refuses to obey the implied order.

duci, 'to be led off to execution'.

pertinaciam . . . et inflexibilem obstinationem. Roman officials objected strongly to the behaviour of the kind commonly called *contumacia*—wanton and prolonged disobedience of a magistrate, whether in a court of law or in the course of administration. Cf. Ep. 57. 2: 'neque . . . sufficit eum poenae suae restitui quam contumacia elusit'. Marcus Aurelius in his Meditations (11. 3) remarks that Christians chose death out of 'sheer disobedience'.

4. quia ciues Romani erant. Roman governors were restricted in the power to execute Roman citizens by the latter's right to appeal to a court at Rome. Hence such prisoners usually were sent to Rome for trial. But cf. Letter 10. 8 n. for an exception.

5. praeeunte me. Pliny 'leads' the prayer and the others repeat it after him. Cf. x. 52: 'praeiuimus . . . commilitonibus iusiurandum'.

deos adpellarent et imagini tuae . . . supplicarent. In all provinces there was an official cult of the emperor, organized by civic magistrates, which acted as a focus of political loyalty to Rome. But it was not compulsory for the mass of the population. Hence neither Pliny nor Trajan regarded the refusal to participate as itself a crime. The test was simply a practical expedient to make certain of the guilt of the prisoners. Trajan particularly objected to supposed slights to his dignity being made the basis of charges of treason (Letter 46. 1 n.). But in the late second century it became a regular count against the Christians that they refused to respect the imperial cult, and they were then regarded as *maiestatis rei*.

The verbs *adpellarent*, *supplicarent*, refer to different acts of worship, 'calling by name upon', and 'making prayers accompanied by offerings'.

male dicerent Christo. Tablets containing curses of all sorts (*tabellae defixionum*), directed against private persons, survive from antiquity. Cf. Dessau, *ILS* 8172–8208.

6. indice. A spy or informer, who does not make a formal accusation.

quidam ante triennium. The dates may refer to earlier persecutions of Christians in Pontus.

7. stato die ante lucem conuenire. Pliny describes the regular services, already established, of the 'day of the Lord'. The dawn ceremony is the 'service of the word', a combination of prayers, psalms, or hymns, and a reading from 'holy writ'. There is doubt whether the second service, the taking of food, is the *agapé*, the customary communal meal of the early Christians, or the Eucharist. Pliny's description could cover either, though it is unlikely that the

Christians would abandon the Eucharist, their basic sacrament, rather than the *agapê*, in response to Pliny's edict about clubs.

ante lucem. The working day began at dawn for everyone. Cf. Letters 13. 9, 40. 1.

carmen . . . dicere . . . seque sacramento . . . obstringere. These phrases have been taken to refer to the repetition of a baptismal vow, or to the formula of renunciation of 'the world' in the baptismal service itself. But since *carmen dicere* is the ordinary Latin for singing a poem or song, hymns with responses (*inuicem*) are probably meant by the first phrase. By *sacramentum* Pliny can only mean an oath, as in Ep. x. 29. 2 ('iam dixerant sacramentum, *sc.* tirones').

quasi deo, 'as to god'. In Pliny *quasi* is used commonly without the idea of supposal. Cf. Letters 32. 3, 38. 3 n.

non in scelus aliquod. The following list resembles catalogues of prohibited sins in the Epistles, e.g. 1 Thess. iv. 3–6, 1 Pet. 15, rather than the Ten Commandments (as later recited at the Eucharist), which lack the last two items.

secundum mandata tua. Trajan gave Pliny specific instructions about various parts of his administrative duties. Where these required publicity Pliny published them in the form of an official proclamation.

hetaerias esse uetueram. For this veto on trade-guilds and social or political clubs see Letters 43–44 nn. It is clear that the Christians are not charged with violating this edict, though some historians have supposed this. Pliny examined the deacons to make certain about this, since the holding of communal banquets was a common form of club life.

8. **ministrae dicebantur.** Pliny seems to have learned of this term for 'deacon' (διάκονος) from the Christians, and misinterpreted it to mean servants or slaves, since only slaves were usually submitted as witnesses to judicial torture.

superstitionem prauam. Pliny's verdict is like that of Tacitus (loc. cit.) 'exitiabilis superstitio', and Suetonius (*Nero* 16. 2). The noun has a bad sense in Pliny, cf. Ep. vi. 2. 2: 'haruspices consulebat . . . a nimia superstitione'. Cf. also Letter 39. 9 n.

9. **ciuitates,** 'cities', cf. Letter 41. 2 n.

10. **satis constat,** 'it is quite agreed'. He is quoting the evidence of others, probably the civic priests and their underlings who expected to make profits out of the sale of sacrificial meat, and hence had an interest in stirring up these prosecutions, like the silversmiths of Ephesus who accused St. Paul when their trade in silver images was threatened (Acts xix. 24–40).

uenire carnem uictimarum, 'the flesh of sacrificial victims is on sale again'. Vast quantities of beasts were slaughtered at the regular festivals of the civic deities, which were maintained extravagantly by the local magnates. The carcasses were sold on the meat market after the ceremonies, but Christians refused to touch such meat. St. Paul discusses the question in 1 Cor. x. 18–21.

si sit paenitentiae locus. As in Ep. x. 39. 6 and Letter 45. 8, two other letters to Trajan of unusual length, Pliny rams home the point of the letter in the final paragraph.

LETTER 48 (x. 97). TO PLINY

On the punishment of Christians (2)

1. **actum quem debuisti.** Trajan confirms the general correctness of Pliny's judicial procedure (*actus*). This is Trajan's reply to Pliny's main question. Since he approves of the accusation based on the *nomen ipsum*, he does not need to reply to the question about *flagitia cohaerentia*, or to define degrees of punishment (*quatenus*).

neque ... in uniuersum aliquid ... constitui potest. The formula recurs in Ep. x. 113, where Trajan recommends Pliny to allow local variations in administration. He means that he will not lay down a uniform rule about punishment for all cases irrespective of age and sex, but makes it clear that he favours the punishment of adult male Christians after proper trial.

2. **conquirendi non sunt.** Governors were encouraged in their *mandata* to hunt down notorious criminals such as brigands. By refusing to

apply such methods to the treatment of Christians, and by leaving them to the processes of the common law, Trajan did a great deal to diminish the scale of the persecution of Christians in the following century, when there in fact were only limited and local outbreaks of trouble stimulated by private prosecutors.

puniendi sunt. Trajan does not specify execution, but leaves the degree of punishment to the discretion of the governor, as was normal in *cognitio extra ordinem* (Letters 41. 2, 45. 2 n).

ueniam ex paenitentia impetret. This might suggest that Trajan did not believe in the criminal *scelera* alleged against Christians, since common crimes could not be lightly set aside. But when other sects were banned because of associated *scelera*, this did not mean that all their practitioners were believed always to have committed crimes, but that such things were thought to happen from time to time. The Jews and the worshippers of Isis were expelled from Rome in A.D. 19 each because of the crime of a single person (Tacitus, *Annals* 2. 85. 5, with Josephus, *Antiquities*, 18. 3. 4–5).

pessimi exempli nec nostri saeculi. Cf. Ep. x. 55: 'non est ex iustitia nostrorum temporum', and Letter 45. 5 n.

LETTER 49 (X. 110). TO TRAJAN

A case of equity

1. ecdicus . . . Amisenorum . . . petebat apud me. The city of Amisus in the eastern part of Pliny's province was technically a free state which was not under the jurisdiction of the governor's court (cf. Letter 35. 2 n.). So it seems likely that enemies of Piso took the case to Pliny out of malice, because the business was not actionable in their own local court. Here, as in Letter 45, Pliny deals with cases arising from the personal feuds that racked the province (cf. Letter 44. 1: 'factionibus . . . uexatas').

The *ecdicus* was the official city attorney for financial affairs. Pliny normally uses the Greek civic terms (*bule, ecclesia*), as in Letter 43. 1: 'Gerusian'.

Iulio Pisone. He possesses the Roman citizenship, and is a 'bigwig' of Amisus.

denariorum . . . quadraginta milia. A large sum by local standards, equivalent to the ownership of a substantial farm. Cf. Letter 16. 7 n.

bule et ecclesia consentiente. The grant from public funds had been proposed in the city council (*bule*) and ratified by the city assembly (*ecclesia*). The councils had the main power in managing the city's affairs, but exceptional expenditure required the assembly's approval.

mandatis tuis. These were official instructions issued by Trajan to Pliny for his general guidance, including items like the veto on political clubs (Letters 43. 3, 47. 7 nn.). But these only became binding for Amisus as a free state when the city referred its case to Pliny.

2. plurima se in rem publicam contulisse. The wealthy men in the cities spent very large sums on benefactions for their boroughs, just as Pliny did at Comum: Letters 18. 5, 28. 2.

totas facultates erogasse, 'contributed all his resources'. For the connexion of *erogare* with civic payments see Letter 28. 4 n.

euersione reliquae dignitatis, 'with the loss of his remaining personal standing'. If he lost his fortune he would lose any official status that depended upon a financial qualification, such as his seat as a town councillor, if, as is probable, he was one.

LETTER 50 (X. III). TO PLINY

A case of equity (2)

ne multorum securitas subruatur. Trajan, though anxious to prevent abuses, is anxious also to protect the interests of the propertied classes, on whose political support the Romans depended to keep the masses everywhere under control. Cf. Letter 43. 2–3 nn. In Ep. x. 109 he refuses to sanction another financial ruling *in iniuriam priuatorum*.

INDEX

This contains words, topics, and persons discussed in the notes at length.

PRINTED IN GREAT BRITAIN
AT THE UNIVERSITY PRESS, OXFORD
BY VIVIAN RIDLER
PRINTER TO THE UNIVERSITY

PENGUIN BOOKS

THE BOOK OF CATS

George MacBeth was born in Scotland in 1932 and was educated at New College, Oxford. He joined the BBC in 1955, and was until 1976 a producer of radio talks and documentaries. He has published twelve books of poems, among them *Collected Poems 1958–1970* and, most recently, *Buying A Heart*. He has also published four novels, including *The Transformation* and *The Seven Witches*, and five anthologies of verse, including *Poetry 1900–1965*. George MacBeth has a cat called Orlando, successor to Peter who is immortalized in two poems in *The Book of Cats*.

Martin Booth was born in 1944 and educated in Hong Kong. He has published four collections of poems in Great Britain, the most recent obtaining the Poets' Yearbook Award, with another book, *The Knotting Sequence*, appearing in the USA. He is poetry critic for *Tribune* and has broadcast widely on BBC radio as poet, critic and features programme writer; four of his children's stories and a commissioned play have been televised by the BBC. He has travelled widely as a writer to Romania and to the USA, where he has lectured in universities and presented his own television programmes on poetry. He has written a novel, *The Carrier*, published in 1978. Martin Booth lives in a Bedfordshire hamlet with his wife and son, a dog and a ferret.

THE
BOOK OF CATS

EDITED BY

George MacBeth

AND

Martin Booth

PENGUIN BOOKS

Penguin Books Ltd, Harmondsworth, Middlesex, England
Penguin Books, 625 Madison Avenue, New York, New York 10022, U.S.A.
Penguin Books Australia Ltd, Ringwood, Victoria, Australia
Penguin Books Canada Ltd, 2801 John Street, Markham, Ontario, Canada L3R 1B4
Penguin Books (N.Z.) Ltd, 182–190 Wairau Road, Auckland 10, New Zealand

—

First published by Martin Secker & Warburg 1976
Published in Penguin Books 1979
Reprinted 1979, 1980

—

The Acknowledgements on pages 351–3 constitute an extension of this copyright page

—

Made and printed in Great Britain by
Butler & Tanner Ltd, Frome and London
Set in Monophoto Ehrhardt

CONTENTS

[5]

VII. CAT'S AGE

VIII. CAT'S DEATH

IX. CAT'S RESURRECTION

Cat, *n*. A soft, indestructible automaton provided by nature to be kicked when things go wrong in the domestic circle.

    This is a dog,
        This is a cat,
    This is a frog,
        This is a rat.
    Run, dog, mew, cat,
    Jump, frog, gnaw, rat.
    Elevenson (*Ambrose Bierce*)

PART I

Cat's Youth

How the Cat Became

TED HUGHES

THINGS were running very smoothly and most of the creatures were highly pleased with themselves. Lion was already famous. Even the little shrews and moles and spiders were pretty well known.

But among all these busy creatures there was one who seemed to be getting nowhere. It was Cat.

Cat was a real oddity. The others didn't know what to make of him at all.

He lived in a hollow tree in the wood. Every night, when the rest of the creatures were sound asleep, he retired to the depths of his tree – then such sounds, such screechings, yowlings, wailings! The bats that slept upside-down all day long in the hollows of the tree branches awoke with a start and fled with their wing-tips stuffed into their ears. It seemed to them that Cat was having the worst nightmares ever – ten at a time.

But no. Cat was tuning his violin.

If only you could have seen him! Curled in the warm smooth hollow of his tree, gazing up through the hole at the top of the trunk, smiling at the stars, winking at the moon – his violin tucked under his chin. Ah, Cat was a happy one.

And all night long he sat there composing his tunes.

Now the creatures didn't like this at all. They saw no use in his music, it made no food, it built no nest, it didn't even keep him warm. And the way Cat lounged around all day, sleeping in the sun, was just more than they could stand.

'He's a bad example,' said Beaver, 'he never does a stroke of work! What if our children think they can live as idly as he does?'

'It's time,' said Weasel, 'that Cat had a job like everybody else in the world.'

So the creatures of the wood formed a Committee to persuade Cat to take a job.

Jay, Magpie, and Parrot went along at dawn and sat in the topmost twigs of Cat's old tree. As soon as Cat poked his head out, they all began together, 'You've to get a job. Get a job! Get a job!'

That was only the beginning of it. All day long, everywhere he went, those birds were at him, 'Get a job! Get a job!'

[13]

And try as he would, Cat could not get a wink of sleep.

That night he went back to his tree early. He was far too tired to practise on his violin and fell fast asleep in a few minutes. Next morning, when he poked his head out of the tree at first light, the three birds of the Committee were there again, loud as ever, 'Get a job!'

Cat ducked back down into his tree and began to think. He wasn't going to start grubbing around in the wet woods all day, as they wanted him to. Oh no. He wouldn't have any time to play his violin if he did that. There was only one thing to do and he did it.

He tucked his violin under his arm and suddenly jumped out at the top of the tree and set off through the woods at a run. Behind him, shouting and calling, came Jay, Magpie, and Parrot.

Other creatures that were about their daily work in the undergrowth looked up when Cat ran past. No one had ever seen Cat run before.

'Cat's up to something,' they called to each other. 'Maybe he's going to get a job at last.'

Deer, Wild Boar, Bear, Ferret, Mongoose, Porcupine, and a cloud of birds set off after Cat to see where he was going.

Harleian manuscript (British Library, London)

After a great deal of running they came to the edge of the forest. There they stopped. As they peered through the leaves they looked sideways at each other and trembled. Ahead of them, across an open field covered with haycocks, was Man's farm.

But Cat wasn't afraid. He went straight on, over the field, and up to Man's door. He raised his paw and banged as hard as he could in the middle of the door.

Man was so surprised to see Cat that at first he just stood, eyes wide, mouth open. No creature ever dared to come on to his fields, let alone knock at his door. Cat spoke first.

'I've come for a job,' he said.

'A job?' asked Man, hardly able to believe his ears.

'Work,' said Cat. 'I want to earn my living.'

Man looked him up and down, then saw his long claws.

'You look as if you'd make a fine rat-catcher,' said Man.

Cat was surprised to hear that. He wondered what it was about him that made him look like a rat-catcher. Still, he wasn't going to miss the chance of a job. So he stuck out his chest and said, 'Been doing it for years.'

'Well then, I've a job for you,' said Man. 'My farm's swarming with rats and mice. They're in my haystacks, they're in my corn sacks, and they're all over the pantry.'

So before Cat knew where he was, he had been signed on as a Rat-and-Mouse-Catcher. His pay was milk, and meat, and a place at the fireside. He slept all day and worked all night.

At first he had a terrible time. The rats pulled his tail, the mice nipped his ears. They climbed on to rafters above him and dropped down – thump! on to him in the dark. They teased the life out of him.

But Cat was a quick learner. At the end of the week he could lay out a dozen rats and twice as many mice within half an hour. If he'd gone on laying them out all night there would pretty soon have been none left, and Cat would have been out of a job. So he just caught a few each night – in the first ten minutes or so. Then he retired into the barn and played his violin till morning. This was just the job he had been looking for.

Man was delighted with him. And Mrs Man thought he was beautiful. She took him on to her lap and stroked him for hours on end. What a life! thought Cat. If only those silly creatures in the dripping wet woods could see him now!

Well, when the other farmers saw what a fine rat-and-mouse-catcher

Cat was, they all wanted cats too. Soon there were so many cats that our Cat decided to form a string band. Oh yes, they were all great violinists. Every night, after making one pile of rats and another of mice, each cat left his farm and was away over the fields to a little dark spinney.

Then what tunes! All night long ...

Pretty soon lady cats began to arrive. Now, every night, instead of just music, there was dancing too. And what dances! If only you could have crept up there and peeped into the glade from behind a tree and seen the cats dancing – the glossy furred ladies and the tomcats, some pearly grey, some ginger red, and all with wonderful green flashing eyes. Up and down the glade, with the music flying out all over the night.

At dawn they hung their violins in the larch trees, dashed back to the farms, and pretended they had been working all night among the rats and mice. They lapped their milk hungrily, stretched out at the fireside, and fell asleep with smiles on their faces.

The Kitten's Eclogue

RUTH PITTER

Auctor
Tell now, good kit, of three months' age, or less,
Whence dost thou bring thy perfect blessedness?
Beast which must perish, and all black to view,
What makes the happiness of such as you?

Bogy Baby
My sable hue, like Ethiopian queen,
My raven tincture and my jetty dye,
Not as defect or blemish can be seen
By anybody that hath half an eye.
What sight more welcome than the night above?
What hue more honoured in the courts of love?

Unseen at night I ramble, being black,
And against black you will not hear me rail.
They kept the sooty whelp for fortune's sake
When all my stripy brethren plumbed the pail.
Their mice I kill, I stuff me with their tuck,
And no man kicks me lest he spoil his luck.

[16]

Black Cat, photo John Elliot (*Tourist Photo Library*)

The sex, which some a sorry burthen deem,
I glory in, and mightily rejoice;
Though but a babe, before the fire I dream
Already that I hear my lover's voice;
What music shall I have – what dying wails –
The seldom female in a world of males!

And when love's star above the chimneys shines,
And in my heart I feel the sacred fire,
Upon the ridge-tile will I hymn these lines
With which great Venus doth my soul inspire;
Then see the toms, in gallant cavalcade,
Come flying to the lovesick fair one's aid!

What mortal dame, what merely human she,
What strong enchantress, could thus honoured sit;
What maid could draw her suitors on like me,
Sing such a tune and get away with it?
What charmer could men's souls so nearly touch?
What nymph, I ask, could do one half as much?

[17]

Hold me not foul for that I wanton be.
These amorous frolics are but innocence;
I court no fickle immortality,
And fear no judgement when I go from hence:
No hope, no dread my little grave contains,
Nor anything beside my scant remains!

BOGY BABY'S EMBLEM. O felis semper felix!
EVERYBODY ELSE'S EMBLEM. MUD.

The Cat that Walked by Himself

RUDYARD KIPLING

HEAR and attend and listen; for this befell and behappened and became and was, O my Best Beloved, when the Tame animals were wild. The Dog was wild, and the Horse was wild, and the Cow was wild, and the Sheep was wild, and the Pig was wild – as wild as wild could be – and they walked in the Wet Wild Woods by their wild lones. But the wildest of all the wild animals was the Cat. He walked by himself, and all places were alike to him.

Of course the Man was wild too. He was dreadfully wild. He didn't even begin to be tame till he met the Woman, and she told him that she did not like living in his wild ways. She picked out a nice dry Cave, instead of a heap of wet leaves, to lie down in; and she strewed clean sand on the floor; and she lit a nice fire of wood at the back of the Cave; and she hung a dried wild-horse skin, tail-down, across the opening of the Cave; and she said, 'Wipe your feet, dear, when you come in, and now we'll keep house.'

That night, Best Beloved, they ate wild sheep roasted on the hot stones, and flavoured with wild garlic and wild pepper; and wild duck stuffed with wild rice and wild fenugreek and wild coriander; and marrow-bones of wild oxen; and wild cherries, and wild grenadillas. Then the Man went to sleep in front of the fire ever so happy; but the Woman sat up, combing her hair. She took the bone of the shoulder of mutton – the big flat blade-bone – and she looked at the wonderful marks on it, and she threw more wood on the fire, and she made a Magic. She made the First Singing Magic in the world.

The Cat that Walked by Himself, Rudyard Kipling

Out of the Wet Wild Woods all the wild animals gathered together where they could see the light of the fire a long way off, and they wondered what it meant.

Then Wild Horse stamped with his wild foot and said, 'O my Friends and O my Enemies, why have the Man and the Woman made that great light in that great Cave, and what harm will it do us?'

Wild Dog lifted up his wild nose and smelled the smell of the roast mutton, and said, 'I will go up and see and look, and say; for I think it is good. Cat, come with me.'

'Nenni!' said the Cat. 'I am the Cat who walks by himself, and all places are alike to me. I will not come.'

'Then we can never be friends again,' said Wild Dog, and he trotted off to the Cave. But when he had gone a little way the Cat said to himself, 'All places are alike to me. Why should I not go too and see and look and come away at my own liking?' So he slipped after Wild Dog softly, very softly, and hid himself where he could hear everything.

When Wild Dog reached the mouth of the Cave he lifted up the dried horse-skin with his nose and sniffed the beautiful smell of the roast mutton, and the Woman, looking at the blade-bone, heard him, and laughed, and said, 'Here comes the first. Wild Thing out of the Wild Woods, what do you want?'

Wild Dog said, 'O my Enemy and Wife of my Enemy, what is this that smells so good in the Wild Woods?'

Then the Woman picked up a roasted mutton-bone and threw it to Wild Dog and said, 'Wild Thing out of the Wild Woods, taste and try.' Wild Dog gnawed the bone, and it was more delicious than anything he had ever tasted, and he said, 'O my Enemy and Wife of my Enemy, give me another.'

The Woman said, 'Wild Thing out of the Wild Woods, help my Man to hunt through the day and guard this Cave at night, and I will give you as many roast bones as you need.'

'Ah!' said the Cat, listening. 'This is a very wise Woman, but she is not so wise as I am.'

Wild Dog crawled into the Cave and laid his head on the Woman's lap, and said, 'O my Friend and Wife of my Friend, I will help your Man to hunt through the day, and at night I will guard your Cave.'

'Ah!' said the Cat, listening. 'That is a very foolish Dog.' And he went back through the Wet Wild Woods waving his wild tail, and walking by his wild lone. But he never told anybody.

When the Man waked up he said, 'What is Wild Dog doing here?'

[20]

And the Woman said, 'His name is not Wild Dog any more, but the First Friend, because he will be our friend for always and always and always. Take him with you when you go hunting.'

Next night the Woman cut great green armfuls of fresh grass from the water-meadows, and dried it before the fire, so that it smelt like new-mown hay, and she sat at the mouth of the Cave and plaited a halter out of horse-hide, and she looked at the shoulder-of-mutton bone – at the big broad blade-bone – and she made a Magic. She made the Second Singing Magic in the world.

Out of the Wild Woods all the wild animals wondered what had happened to Wild Dog, and at last Wild Horse stamped with his foot and said, 'I will go and see and say why Wild Dog has not returned. Cat, come with me.'

'Nenni!' said the Cat. 'I am the Cat who walks by himself, and all places are alike to me. I will not come.' But all the same he followed Wild Horse softly, very softly, and hid himself where he could hear everything.

When the Woman heard Wild Horse tripping and stumbling on his long mane, she laughed and said, 'Here comes the second. Wild Thing out of the Wild Woods, what do you want?'

Wild Horse said, 'O my Enemy and Wife of my Enemy, where is Wild Dog?'

The Woman laughed, and picked up the blade-bone and looked at it, and said, 'Wild Thing out of the Wild Woods, you did not come here for Wild Dog, but for the sake of this good grass.'

And Wild Horse, tripping and stumbling on his long mane, said, 'That is true; give it me to eat.'

The Woman said, 'Wild Thing out of the Wild Woods, bend your wild head and wear what I give you, and you shall eat the wonderful grass three times a day.'

'Ah!' said the Cat, listening. 'This is a clever Woman, but she is not so clever as I am.'

Wild Horse bent his wild head, and the Woman slipped the plaited-hide halter over it, and Wild Horse breathed on the Woman's feet and said, 'O my Mistress, and Wife of my Master, I will be your servant for the sake of the wonderful grass.'

'Ah!' said the Cat, listening. 'That is a very foolish Horse.' And he went back through the Wet Wild Woods, waving his wild tail and walking by his wild lone. But he never told anybody.

When the Man and the Dog came back from hunting, the Man said,

Man and Dog Hunting, 1822

'What is Wild Horse doing here?' And the Woman said, 'His name is not Wild Horse any more, but the First Servant, because he will carry us from place to place for always and always and always. Ride on his back when you go hunting.'

Next day, holding her wild head high that her wild horns should not catch in the wild trees, Wild Cow came up to the Cave, and the Cat followed, and hid himself just the same as before; and everything happened just the same as before; and the Cat said the same things as before; and when Wild Cow had promised to give her milk to the Woman every day in exchange for the wonderful grass, the Cat went back through the Wet Wild Woods waving his wild tail and walking by his wild lone, just the same as before. But he never told anybody. And when the Man and the Horse and the Dog came home from hunting and asked the same questions same as before, the Woman said, 'Her name is not Wild Cow any more, but the Giver of Good Food. She will give us the warm white milk for always and always and always, and I will take care of her while you and the First Friend and the First Servant go hunting.'

Next day the Cat waited to see if any other Wild Thing would go up to the Cave, but no one moved in the Wet Wild Woods, so the Cat walked there by himself; and he saw the Woman milking the Cow, and he saw the light of the fire in the Cave, and he smelt the smell of the warm white milk.

[22]

Cat said, 'O my Enemy and Wife of my Enemy, where did Wild Cov go?'

The Woman laughed and said, 'Wild Thing out of the Wild Woods, go back to the Woods again, for I have braided up my hair, and I have put away the magic blade-bone and we have no more need of either friends or servants in our Cave.'

Cat said, 'I am not a friend, and I am not a servant. I am the Cat who walks by himself, and I wish to come into your Cave.'

Woman said, 'Then why did you not come with First Friend on the first night?'

Cat grew very angry and said, 'Has Wild Dog told tales of me?'

Then the Woman laughed and said, 'You are the Cat who walks by himself, and all places are alike to you. You are neither a friend nor a servant. You have said it yourself. Go away and walk by yourself in all places alike.'

Then Cat pretended to be sorry and said, 'Must I never come into the Cave? Must I never sit by the warm fire? Must I never drink the warm white milk? You are very wise and very beautiful. You should not be cruel even to a Cat.'

Woman said, 'I knew I was wise, but I did not know I was beautiful. So I will make a bargain with you. If ever I say one word in your praise, you may come into the Cave.'

'And if you say two words in my praise?' said the Cat.

'I never shall,' said the Woman, 'but if I say two words in your praise, you may sit by the fire in the Cave.'

'And if you say three words?' said the Cat.

'I never shall,' said the Woman, 'but if I say three words in your praise, you may drink the warm white milk three times a day for always and always and always.'

Then the Cat arched his back and said, 'Now let the Curtain at the mouth of the Cave, and the Fire at the back of the Cave, and the Milk-pots that stand beside the Fire, remember what my Enemy and the Wife of my Enemy has said.' And he went away through the Wet Wild Woods waving his wild tail and walking by his wild lone.

That night when the Man and the Horse and the Dog came home from hunting, the Woman did not tell them of the bargain that she had made with the Cat, because she was afraid that they might not like it.

Cat went far and far away and hid himself in the Wet Wild Woods by his wild lone for a long time till the Woman forgot all about him. Only the Bat – the little upside-down Bat – that hung inside the Cave

[23]

knew where Cat hid; and every evening Bat would fly to Cat with news of what was happening.

One evening Bat said, 'There is a Baby in the Cave. He is new and pink and fat and small, and the Woman is very fond of him.'

'Ah,' said the Cat, listening. 'But what is the Baby fond of?'

'He is fond of things that are soft and tickle,' said the Bat. 'He is fond of warm things to hold in his arms when he goes to sleep. He is fond of being played with. He is fond of all those things.'

'Ah,' said the Cat, listening. 'Then my time has come.'

Next night Cat walked through the Wet Wild Woods and hid very near the Cave till morning-time, and Man and Dog and Horse went hunting. The Woman was busy cooking that morning, and the Baby cried and interrupted. So she carried him outside the Cave and gave him a handful of pebbles to play with. But still the Baby cried.

Then the Cat put out his paddy paw and patted the Baby on the cheek, and it cooed; and the Cat rubbed against its fat knees and tickled it under its fat chin with his tail. And the Baby laughed; and the Woman heard him and smiled.

Then the Bat – the little upside-down Bat – that hung in the mouth of the Cave said, 'O my Hostess and Wife of my Host and Mother of my Host's Son, a Wild Thing from the Wild Woods is most beautifully playing with your Baby.'

'A blessing on that Wild Thing whoever he may be,' said the Woman, straightening her back, 'for I was a busy woman this morning and he has done me a service.'

That very minute and second, Best Beloved, the dried horse-skin Curtain that was stretched tail-down at the mouth of the Cave fell down – *woosh!* – because it remembered the bargain she had made with the Cat; and when the Woman went to pick it up – lo and behold! – the Cat was sitting quite comfy inside the Cave.

'O my Enemy and Wife of my Enemy and Mother of my Enemy,' said the Cat, 'it is I: for you have spoken a word in my praise, and now I can sit within the Cave for always and always and always. But still I am the Cat who walks by himself, and all places are alike to me.'

The Woman was very angry, and shut her lips tight and took up her spinning-wheel and began to spin.

But the Baby cried because the Cat had gone away, and the Woman could not hush it, for it struggled and kicked and grew black in the face.

'O my Enemy and Wife of my Enemy and Mother of my Enemy,' said the Cat, 'take a strand of the thread that you are spinning and tie

Cat, Gwen John (*Tate Gallery, London*)

it to your spindle-whorl and drag it along the floor, and I will show you a Magic that shall make your Baby laugh as loudly as he is now crying.'

'I will do so,' said the Woman, 'because I am at my wits' end; but I will not thank you for it.'

She tied the thread to the little clay spindle-whorl and drew it across the floor, and the Cat ran after it and patted it with his paws and rolled head over heels, and tossed it backward over his shoulder and chased it between his hind legs and pretended to lose it, and pounced down upon it again, till the Baby laughed as loudly as it had been crying, and scrambled after the Cat and frolicked all over the Cave till it grew tired and settled down to sleep with the Cat in its arms.

'Now,' said Cat, 'I will sing the Baby a song that shall keep him asleep for an hour.' And he began to purr, loud and low, low and loud, till the Baby fell fast asleep. The Woman smiled as she looked down upon the two of them, and said, 'That was wonderfully done. No question but you are very clever, O Cat.'

That very minute and second, Best Beloved, the smoke of the Fire at the back of the Cave came down in clouds from the roof – *puff!* – because it remembered the bargain she had made with the Cat; and when it had cleared away – lo and behold! – the Cat was sitting quite comfy close to the fire.

'O my Enemy and Wife of my Enemy and Mother of my Enemy,' said the Cat, 'it is I: for you have spoken a second word in my praise, and now I can sit by the warm fire at the back of the Cave for always and always and always. But still I am the Cat who walks by himself, and all places are alike to me.'

Then the Woman was very very angry, and let down her hair and put more wood on the fire and brought out the broad blade-bone of the shoulder of mutton and began to make a Magic that should prevent her from saying a third word in praise of the Cat. It was not a Singing Magic, Best Beloved, it was a Still Magic; and by and by the Cave grew so still that a little wee-wee mouse crept out of a corner and ran across the floor.

'O my Enemy and Wife of my Enemy and Mother of my Enemy,' said the Cat, 'is that little mouse part of your Magic?'

'Ouh! Chee! No indeed!' said the Woman, and she dropped the blade-bone and jumped upon the footstool in front of the fire and braided up her hair very quick for fear that the mouse should run up it.

'Ah,' said the Cat, watching. 'Then the mouse will do me no harm if I eat it?'

[26]

'No,' said the Woman, braiding up her hair, 'eat it quickly and I will ever be grateful to you.'

Cat made one jump and caught the little mouse, and the Woman said, 'A hundred thanks. Even the First Friend is not quick enough to catch little mice as you have done. You must be very wise.'

That very minute and second, O Best Beloved, the Milk-pot that stood by the fire cracked in two pieces – *ffft!* – because it remembered the bargain she had made with the Cat; and when the Woman jumped down from the footstool – lo and behold! – the Cat was lapping up the warm white milk that lay in one of the broken pieces.

'O my Enemy and Wife of my Enemy and Mother of my Enemy,' said the Cat, 'it is I: for you have spoken three words in my praise, and now I can drink the warm white milk three times a day for always and always and always. But *still* I am the Cat who walks by himself, and all places are alike to me.'

Then the Woman laughed and set the Cat a bowl of the warm white milk and said, 'O Cat, you are as clever as a man, but remember that your bargain was not made with the Man or the Dog, and I do not know what they will do when they come home.'

'What is that to me?' said the Cat. 'If I have my place in the Cave by the fire and my warm white milk three times a day I do not care what the Man or the Dog can do.'

That evening when the Man and the Dog came into the Cave, the Woman told them all the story of the bargain, while the Cat sat by the fire and smiled. Then the Man said, 'Yes, but he has not made a bargain with *me* or with all proper Men after me.' Then he took off his two leather boots and he took up his little stone axe (that makes three) and he fetched a piece of wood and a hatchet (that is five altogether), and he set them out in a row and he said, 'Now we will make *our* bargain. If you do not catch mice when you are in the Cave for always and always and always, I will throw these five things at you whenever I see you, and so shall all proper Men do after me.'

'Ah!' said the Woman, listening. 'This is a very clever Cat, but he is not so clever as my Man.'

The Cat counted the five things (and they looked very knobby) and he said, 'I will catch mice when I am in the Cave for always and always and always; but *still* I am the Cat who walks by himself, and all places are alike to me.'

'Not when I am near,' said the Man. 'If you had not said that last I would have put all these things away for always and always and always;

[27]

but now I am going to throw my two boots and my little stone axe (that makes three) at you whenever I meet you. And so shall all proper Men do after me!'

Then the Dog said, 'Wait a minute. He has not made a bargain with *me* or with all proper Dogs after me.' And he showed his teeth and said, 'If you are not kind to the Baby while I am in the Cave for always and always and always, I will hunt you till I catch you, and when I catch you I will bite you. And so shall all proper Dogs do after me.'

'Ah!' said the Woman, listening. 'This is a very clever Cat, but he is not so clever as the Dog.'

Cat counted the Dog's teeth (and they looked very pointed) and he said, 'I will be kind to the Baby while I am in the Cave, as long as he does not pull my tail too hard, for always and always and always. But *still* I am the Cat who walks by himself, and all places are alike to me.'

'Not when I am near,' said the Dog. 'If you had not said that last I would have shut my mouth for always and always and always; but *now* I am going to hunt you up a tree whenever I meet you. And so shall all proper Dogs do after me.'

Then the Man threw his two boots and his little stone axe (that makes three) at the Cat, and the Cat ran out of the Cave and the Dog chased him up a tree; and from that day to this, Best Beloved, three proper Men out of five will always throw things at a Cat whenever they meet him, and all proper Dogs will chase him up a tree. But the Cat keeps his side of the bargain too. He will kill mice, and he will be kind to Babies when he is in the house, just as long as they do not pull his tail too hard. But when he has done that, and between times, and when the moon gets up and night comes, he is the Cat that walks by himself, and all places are alike to him. Then he goes out to the Wet Wild Woods or up the Wet Wild Trees or on the Wet Wild Roofs, waving his wild tail and walking by his wild lone.

Midwife Cat

MARK VAN DOREN

Beyond the fence she hesitates,
  And drops a paw, and tries the dust.
It is a clearing, but she waits
  No longer minute than she must.

Though a dozen foes may dart
  From out the grass, she crouches by,
Then runs to where the silos start
  To heave their shadows far and high.

Here she folds herself and sleeps;
  But in a moment she has put
The dreams aside; and now she creeps
  Across the open, foot by foot,

Till at the threshold of a shed
  She smells the water and the corn
Where a sow is on her bed
  And little pigs are being born.

Silently she leaps, and walks
  All night upon a narrow rafter,
Whence at intervals she talks
  Wise to them she watches after.

PART II

Cat's Meat

Milk for the Cat

HAROLD MONRO

When the tea is brought at five o'clock,
And all the neat curtains are drawn with care,
The little black cat with bright green eyes
Is suddenly purring there.

At first she pretends, having nothing to do,
She has come in merely to blink by the grate,
But though tea may be late or the milk may be sour,
She is never late.

And presently her agate eyes
Take a soft large milky haze,
And her independent casual glance
Becomes a stiff, hard gaze.

Then she stamps her claws or lifts her ears
Or twists her tail and begins to stir,
Till suddenly all her lithe body becomes
One breathing, trembling purr.

The children eat and wriggle and laugh;
The two old ladies stroke their silk;
But the cat is grown small and thin with desire,
Transformed to a creeping lust for milk.

The white saucer like some full moon descends
At last from the cloud of the table above;
She sighs and dreams and thrills and glows,
Transfigured with love.

She nestles over the shining rim,
Buries her chin in the creamy sea;
Her tail hangs loose; each drowsy paw
Is doubled under each bending knee.

A long dim ecstasy holds her life;
Her world is an infinite shapeless white,
Till her tongue has curled the last holy drop
Then she sinks back into the night,

Draws and dips her body to heap
Her sleepy nerves in the great arm-chair,
Lies defeated and buried deep
Three or four hours unconscious there.

The Cat's Dinner, Marguerite Gérard (*Musée Fragonard, Grasse*)

[34]

War Cat

DOROTHY L. SAYERS

I am sorry, my little cat, I am sorry –
if I had it, you should have it;
but there is a war on.

No, there are no table-scraps;
there was only an omelette
made from dehydrated eggs,
and baked apples to follow, and we finished it all.
The butcher has no lights,
the fishmonger has no cod's heads –
there is nothing for you
but cat-biscuit
and those remnants of yesterday's ham;
you must do your best with it.

Round and pathetic eyes,
baby mouth opened in a reproachful cry,
how can I explain to you?
I know, I know:
'Mistress, it is not nice;
the ham is very salt
and the cat-biscuit very dull,
I sniffed at it, and the smell was not enticing.
Do you not love me any more?
Mistress, I do my best for the war-effort;
I killed four mice last week,
yesterday I caught a young stoat.
You stroked and praised me,
you called me a clever cat.
What have I done to offend you?
I am industrious, I earn my keep;
I am not like the parrot, who sits there
using bad language and devouring
parrot-seed at eight-and-sixpence a pound
without working for it.

If you will not pay me my wages
there is no justice;
if you have ceased to love me
there is no charity.

'See, now, I rub myself against your legs
to express my devotion,
which is not altered by any unkindness.
My little heart is contracted
because your goodwill is withdrawn from me;
my ribs are rubbing together
for lack of food,
but indeed I cannot eat this –
my soul revolts at the sight of it.
I have tried, believe me,
but it was like ashes in my mouth.
If your favour is departed
and your bowels of compassion are shut up,
then all that is left me
is to sit in a draught on the stone floor and look miserable
till I die of starvation
and a broken heart.'

Cat with the innocent face,
what can I say?
Everything is very hard on everybody.
If you were a little Greek cat,
or a little Polish cat,
there would be nothing for you at all,
not even cat-food:
indeed, you would be lucky
if you were not eaten yourself.
Think if you were a little Russian cat
prowling among the cinders of a deserted city!
Consider that pains and labour
and the valour of merchant-seamen and fishermen
have gone even to the making of this biscuit
which smells so unappetizing.
Alas! there is no language
in which I can tell you these things.

Harriet Martineau with her Cat, Alfred Croquis

Well, well!
If you will not be comforted
we will put the contents of your saucer
into the chicken-bowl – there!
all gone! nasty old cat-food –
The hens, I dare say,
will be grateful for it.

Wait only a little
and I will go to the butcher
and see if by any chance
he can produce some fragments of the insides of something.

[37]

Only stop crying
and staring in that unbearable manner –
as soon as I have put on my hat
we will try to do something about it.
My hat is on,
I have put on my shoes,
I have taken my shopping basket –
What are you doing on the table?

The chicken-bowl is licked clean;
there is nothing left in it at all.
Cat,
hell-cat, Hitler-cat, human,
all-too-human cat,
cat corrupt, infected,
instinct with original sin,

The Cat's Meat Man, W. J. Webb

cat of a fallen and perverse creation,
hypocrite with the innocent and limpid eyes –
is nothing desirable
till somebody else desires it?

Is anything and everything attractive
so long as it is got by stealing?
Furtive and squalid cat,
green glance, squinted over a cringing shoulder,
streaking hurriedly out of the back door
in expectation of judgment,
your manners and morals are perfectly abhorrent to me,
you dirty little thief and liar.

Nevertheless,
although you have made a fool of me,
yet, bearing in mind your pretty wheedling ways
(not to mention the four mice and the immature stoat),
and having put on my hat to go to the butcher's,
I may as well go.

Five Eyes

WALTER DE LA MARE

In Hans' old mill his three black cats
Watch the bins for the thieving rats.
Whisker and claw, they crouch in the night,
Their five eyes smouldering green and bright:
Squeaks from the flour-sacks, squeaks from where
The cold wind stirs on the empty stair,
Squeaking and scampering everywhere.
Then down they pounce, now in, now out,
At whisking tail, and sniffing snout;
While lean old Hans he snores away
Till peep of light at break of day;
Then up he climbs to his creaking mill,
Out come his cats all grey with meal –
Jekkel, and Jessup, and one-eyed Jill.

[39]

The Story of Webster

P. G. WODEHOUSE

'CATS are not dogs!'

There is only one place where you can hear good things like that thrown off quite casually in the general run of conversation, and that is the bar parlour of the *Angler's Rest*. It was there, as we sat grouped about the fire, that a thoughtful Pint of Bitter had made the statement just recorded.

Although the talk up to this point had been dealing with Einstein's Theory of Relativity, we readily adjusted our minds to cope with the new topic. Regular attendance at the nightly sessions over which Mr Mulliner presides with such unfailing dignity and geniality tends to produce mental nimbleness. In our little circle I have known an argument on the Final Destination of the Soul to change inside forty seconds into one concerning the best method of preserving the juiciness of bacon fat.

'Cats,' proceeded the Pint of Bitter, 'are selfish. A man waits on a cat hand and foot for weeks, humouring its lightest whim, and then it goes and leaves him flat because it has found a place down the road where the fish is more frequent.'

'What I've got against cats,' said a Lemon Sour, speaking feelingly, as one brooding on a private grievance, 'is their unreliability. They lack candour and are not square shooters. You get your cat and you call him Thomas or George, as the case may be. So far, so good. Then one morning you wake up and find six kittens in the hat-box and you have to re-open the whole matter, approaching it from an entirely different angle.'

'If you want to know what's the trouble with cats,' said a red-faced man with glassy eyes, who had been rapping on the table for his fourth whisky, 'they've got no tact. That's what's the trouble with them. I remember a friend of mine had a cat. Made quite a pet of that cat, he did. And what occurred? What was the outcome? One night he came home rather late and was feeling for the keyhole with his corkscrew; and, believe me or not, his cat selected that precise moment to jump on the back of his neck out of a tree. No tact.'

Mr Mulliner shook his head.

'I grant you all this,' he said, 'but still, in my opinion, you have not got to the root of the matter. The real objection to the great majority of cats is their insufferable air of superiority. Cats, as a class, have never completely got over the snootiness caused by the fact that in Ancient Egypt they were worshipped as gods. This makes them too prone to set themselves up as critics and censors of the frail and erring human beings whose lot they share. They stare rebukingly. They view with concern. And on a sensitive man this often has the worst effects, inducing an inferiority complex of the gravest kind. It is odd that the conversation should have taken this turn,' said Mr Mulliner, sipping his hot Scotch and lemon, 'for I was thinking only this afternoon of the rather strange case of my cousin Edward's son, Lancelot.'

'I knew a cat – ' began a Small Bass.

My cousin Edward's son, Lancelot (said Mr Mulliner), was, at the time of which I speak, a comely youth of some twenty-five summers. Orphaned at an early age, he had been brought up in the home of his Uncle Theodore, the saintly Dean of Bolsover; and it was a great shock to that good man when Lancelot, on attaining his majority, wrote from London to inform him that he had taken a studio in Bott Street, Chelsea, and proposed to remain in the metropolis and become an artist.

The Dean's opinion of artists was low. As a prominent member of the Bolsover Watch Committee, it had recently been his distasteful duty to be present at a private showing of the super-super-film, *Palettes of Passion*; and he replied to his nephew's communication with a vibrant letter in which he emphasized the grievous pain it gave him to think that one of his flesh and blood should deliberately be embarking on a career which must inevitably lead sooner or later to the painting of Russian princesses lying on divans in the semi-nude with their arms round tame jaguars. He urged Lancelot to return and become a curate while there was yet time.

But Lancelot was firm. He deplored the rift between himself and a relative whom he had always respected; but he was dashed if he meant to go back to an environment where his individuality had been stifled and his soul confined in chains. And for four years there was silence between uncle and nephew.

During these years Lancelot had made progress in his chosen profession. At the time at which this story opens, his prospects seemed bright. He was painting the portrait of Brenda, only daughter of Mr and Mrs B. B. Carberry-Pirbright, of 11 Maxton Square, South Kensington, which meant thirty pounds in his sock on delivery. He had learned to cook eggs and bacon. He had practically mastered the ukulele. And, in addition, he was engaged to be married to a fearless young vers libre poetess of the name of Gladys Bingley, better known as The Sweet Singer of Garbidge Mews, Fulham – a charming girl who looked like a pen-wiper.

It seemed to Lancelot that life was very full and beautiful. He lived joyously in the present, giving no thought to the past.

But how true it is that the past is inextricably mixed up with the present and that we can never tell when it may spring some delayed bomb beneath our feet. One afternoon, as he sat making a few small alterations in the portrait of Brenda Carberry-Pirbright, his fiancée entered.

He had been expecting her to call, for today she was going off for a three weeks' holiday to the South of France, and she had promised to look in on her way to the station. He laid down his brush and gazed at her with a yearning affection, thinking for the thousandth time how he worshipped every spot of ink on her nose. Standing there in the doorway with her bobbed hair sticking out in every direction like a golliwog's, she made a picture that seemed to speak to his very depths.

'Hullo, Reptile!' he said lovingly.

The Cat, unknown American artist (*National Gallery of Art, Washington, D.C., Collection of Edgar William and Bernice Chrysler Garbisch*)

[42]

'What ho, Worm!' said Gladys, maidenly devotion shining through the monocle which she wore in her left eye. 'I can stay just half an hour.'

'Oh, well, half an hour soon passes,' said Lancelot. 'What's that you've got there?'

'A letter, ass. What did you think it was?'

'Where did you get it?'

'I found the postman outside.'

Lancelot took the envelope from her and examined it.

'Gosh!' he said.

'What's the matter?'

'It's from my Uncle Theodore.'

'I didn't know you had an Uncle Theodore.'

'Of course I have. I've had him for years.'

'What's he writing to you about?'

'If you'll kindly keep quiet for two seconds, if you know how,' said Lancelot, 'I'll tell you.'

And in a clear voice which, like that of all the Mulliners, however distant from the main branch, was beautifully modulated, he read as follows:

The Deanery,
Bolsover, Wilts.

My dear Lancelot,

As you have, no doubt, already learned from your *Church Times*, I have been offered and have accepted the vacant Bishopric of Bongo-Bongo, in West Africa. I sail immediately to take up my new duties, which I trust will be blessed.

In these circumstances it becomes necessary for me to find a good home for my cat Webster. It is, alas, out of the question that he should accompany me, as the rigours of the climate and the lack of essential comforts might well sap a constitution which has never been robust.

I am dispatching him, therefore, to your address, my dear boy, in a straw-lined hamper, in the full confidence that you will prove a kindly and conscientious host.

With cordial good wishes,

Your affectionate uncle,
Theodore Bongo-Bongo

For some moments after he had finished reading this communication, a thoughtful silence prevailed in the studio.

'Of all the nerve!' she said. 'I wouldn't do it.'

'Why not?'

'What do you want with a cat?'

Lancelot reflected.

'It is true,' he said, 'that, given a free hand, I would prefer not to have my studio turned into a cattery or cat-bin. But consider the special circumstances. Relations between Uncle Theodore and self have for the last few years been a bit strained. In fact, you might say we have definitely parted brass-rags. It looks to me as if he were coming round. I should describe this letter as more or less what you might call an olive-branch. If I lush this cat up satisfactorily, shall I not be in a position later on to make a swift touch?'

'He is rich, this bean?' said Gladys, interested.

'Extremely.'

'Then,' said Gladys, 'consider my objections withdrawn. A good stout cheque from a grateful cat-fancier would undoubtedly come in very handy. We might be able to get married this year.'

'Exactly,' said Lancelot. 'A pretty loathsome prospect, of course; but still, as we've arranged to do it, the sooner we get it over, the better, what?'

'Absolutely.'

'Then that's settled. I accept custody of cat.'

'It's the only thing to do,' said Gladys. 'Meanwhile, can you lend me a comb? Have you such a thing in your bedroom?'

'What do you want with a comb?'

'I got some soup in my hair at lunch. I won't be a minute.'

She hurried out, and Lancelot, taking up the letter again, found that he had omitted to read a continuation of it on the back page.

It was to the following effect:

ps. In establishing Webster in your home, I am actuated by another motive than the simple desire to see to it that my faithful friend and companion is adequately provided for.

From both a moral and an educative standpoint, I am convinced that Webster's society will prove of inestimable value to you. His advent, indeed, I venture to hope, will be a turning-point in your life. Thrown, as you must be, incessantly among loose and immoral Bohemians, you will find in this cat an example of upright conduct which cannot but act as an antidote to the poison cup of temptation which is, no doubt, hourly pressed to your lips.

pps. Cream only at midday, and fish not more than three times a week.

He was reading these words for the second time, when the front-door bell rang and he found a man on the steps with a hamper. A discreet mew from within revealed its contents, and Lancelot, carrying it into the studio, cut the strings.

'Hi!' he bellowed, going to the door.

'What's up?' shrieked his betrothed from above.

'The cat's come.'

'All right. I'll be down in a jiffy.'

Lancelot returned to the studio.

'What ho, Webster!' he said cheerily. 'How's the boy?'

The cat did not reply. It was sitting with bent head, performing that wash and brush up which a journey by rail renders so necessary.

In order to facilitate these toilet operations, it had raised its left leg and was holding it rigidly in the air. And there flashed into Lancelot's mind an old superstition handed on to him, for what it was worth, by one of the nurses of his infancy. If, this woman had said, you creep up to a cat when its leg is in the air, and give it a pull, then you make a wish and your wish comes true in thirty days.

It was a pretty fancy, and it seemed to Lancelot that the theory might as well be put to the test. He advanced warily, therefore, and was in the act of extending his fingers for the pull, when Webster, lowering the leg, turned and raised his eyes.

He looked at Lancelot. And suddenly with sickening force there came to Lancelot the realization of the unpardonable liberty he had been about to take.

Until this moment, though the postscript to his uncle's letter should have warned him, Lancelot Mulliner had had no suspicion of what manner of cat this was that he had taken into his home. Now, for the first time, he saw him steadily and saw him whole.

Webster was very large and very black and very composed. He conveyed the impression of being a cat of deep reserves. Descendant of a long line of ecclesiastical ancestors who had conducted their decorous courtships beneath the shadow of cathedrals and on the back walls of bishops' palaces, he had that exquisite poise which one sees in high dignitaries of the Church. His eyes were clear and steady, and seemed to pierce to the very roots of the young man's soul, filling him with a sense of guilt.

Once, long ago, in his hot childhood, Lancelot, spending his summer holidays at the Deanery, had been so far carried away by ginger-beer and original sin as to plug a senior canon in the leg with his air-gun – only to discover, on turning, that a visiting archdeacon had been a spectator of the entire incident from his immediate rear. As he felt then, when meeting the archdeacon's eye, so did he feel now as Webster's gaze played silently upon him.

Webster, it is true, had not actually raised his eyebrows. But this, Lancelot felt, was simply because he hadn't any.

[45]

He backed, blushing.

'Sorry!' he muttered.

There was a pause. Webster continued his steady scrutiny. Lancelot edged towards the door.

'Er – excuse me – just a moment ...' he mumbled. And, sidling from the room, he ran distractedly upstairs.

'I say,' said Lancelot.

'Now what?' asked Gladys.

'Have you finished with the mirror?'

'Why?'

'Well, I – er – I thought,' said Lancelot, 'that I might as well have a shave.'

The girl looked at him, astonished.

'Shave? Why, you shaved only the day before yesterday.'

'I know. But, all the same ... I mean to say, it seems only respectful. That cat, I mean.'

Large Cat, who weighed 25¾ lb.

'What about him?'

'Well, he seems to expect it, somehow. Nothing actually said, don't you know, but you could tell by his manner. I thought a quick shave and perhaps change into my blue serge suit –'

'He's probably thirsty. Why don't you give him some milk?'

'Could one, do you think?' said Lancelot doubtful. 'I mean I hardly seem to know him well enough.' He paused. 'I say, old girl,' he went on, with a touch of hesitation.

'Hullo?'

'I know you won't mind my mentioning it, but you've got a few spots of ink on your nose.'

'Of course I have. I always have spots of ink on my nose.'

'Well ... you don't think ... a quick scrub with a bit of pumice-stone ... I mean to say, you know how important first impressions are ...'

The girl stared.

'Lancelot Mulliner,' she said, 'if you think I'm going to skin my nose to the bone just to please a mangy cat –'

'Sh!' cried Lancelot, in agony.

'Here, let me go down and look at him,' said Gladys petulantly.

As they re-entered the studio, Webster was gazing with an air of quiet distaste at an illustration from *La Vie Parisienne* which adorned one of the walls. Lancelot tore it down hastily.

Gladys looked at Webster in an unfriendly way.

'So that's the blighter!'

'Sh!'

'If you want to know what I think,' said Gladys, 'that cat's been living too high. Doing himself a dashed sight too well. You'd better cut his rations down a bit.'

In substance, her criticism was not unjustified. Certainly, there was about Webster more than a suspicion of embonpoint. He had that air of portly well-being which we associate with those who dwell in cathedral closes. But Lancelot winced uncomfortably. He had so hoped that Gladys would make a good impression, and here she was, starting right off by saying the tactless thing.

He longed to explain to Webster that it was only her way; that in the Bohemian circles of which she was such an ornament genial chaff of a personal order was accepted and, indeed, relished. But it was too late. The mischief had been done. Webster turned in a pointed manner and withdrew silently behind the chesterfield.

Gladys, all unconscious, was making preparations for departure.

[47]

'Well, bung-ho,' she said lightly. 'See you in three weeks. I suppose you and that cat'll both be out on the tiles the moment my back's turned.'

'Please! Please!' moaned Lancelot. 'Please!'

He had caught sight of the tip of a black tail protruding from behind the chesterfield. It was twitching slightly, and Lancelot could read it like a book. With a sickening sense of dismay, he knew that Webster had formed a snap judgement of his fiancée and condemned her as frivolous and unworthy.

It was some ten days later that Bernard Worple, the neo-Vorticist sculptor, lunching at the Puce Ptarmigan, ran into Rodney Scollop, the powerful young surrealist. And after talking for a while of their art:

'What's all this I hear about Lancelot Mulliner?' asked Worple. 'There's a wild story going about that he was seen shaved in the middle of the week. Nothing in it, I suppose?'

Scollop looked grave. He had been on the point of mentioning Lancelot himself, for he loved the lad and was deeply exercised about him.

'It is perfectly true,' he said.

'It sounds incredible.'

Scollop leaned forward. His fine face was troubled.

'Shall I tell you something, Worple?'

'What?'

'I know for an absolute fact,' said Scollop, 'that Lancelot Mulliner now shaves every morning.'

Worple pushed aside the spaghetti which he was wreathing about him and through the gap stared at his companion.

'Every morning?'

'Every single morning. I looked in on him myself the other day, and there he was, neatly dressed in blue serge and shaved to the core. And, what is more, I got the distinct impression that he had used talcum powder afterwards.'

'You don't mean that!'

'I do. And shall I tell you something else? There was a book lying open on the table. He tried to hide it, but he wasn't quick enough. It was one of those etiquette books!'

'An etiquette book!'

'*Polite Behaviour*, by Constance, Lady Bodbank.'

Worple unwound a stray tendril of spaghetti from about his left ear. He was deeply agitated. Like Scollop, he loved Lancelot.

'He'll be dressing for dinner next!' he exclaimed.

'I have every reason to believe,' said Scollop gravely, 'that he does dress for dinner. At any rate, a man closely resembling him was seen furtively buying three stiff collars and a black tie at Hope Brothers in the King's Road last Tuesday.'

Worple pushed his chair back, and rose. His manner was determined.

'Scollop,' he said, 'we are friends of Mulliner's, you and I. It is evident from what you tell me that subversive influences are at work and that never has he needed our friendship more. Shall we not go round and see him immediately?'

'It was what I was about to suggest myself,' said Rodney Scollop.

Twenty minutes later they were in Lancelot's studio, and with a significant glance Scollop drew his companion's notice to their host's appearance. Lancelot Mulliner was neatly, even foppishly, dressed in blue serge with creases down the trouser-legs, and his chin, Worple saw with a pang, gleamed smoothly in the afternoon light.

At the sight of his friends' cigars, Lancelot exhibited unmistakable concern.

'You don't mind throwing those away, I'm sure,' he said pleadingly.

Rodney Scollop drew himself up a little haughtily.

'And since when,' he asked, 'have the best fourpenny cigars in Chelsea not been good enough for you?'

Lancelot hastened to soothe him.

'It isn't me,' he exclaimed. 'It's Webster. My cat. I happen to know he objects to tobacco smoke. I had to give up my pipe in deference to his views.'

Bernard Worple snorted.

'Are you trying to tell us,' he sneered, 'that Lancelot Mulliner allows himself to be dictated to by a blasted cat?'

'Hush!' cried Lancelot, trembling. 'If you knew how he disapproves of strong language!'

'Where is this cat?' asked Rodney Scollop. 'Is that the animal?' he said, pointing out of the window to where, in the yard, a tough-looking Tom with tattered ears stood mewing in a hardboiled way out of the corner of its mouth.

'Good heavens, no!' said Lancelot. 'That is an alley cat which comes round here from time to time to lunch at the dustbin. Webster is quite different. Webster has a natural dignity and repose of manner. Webster is a cat who prides himself on always being well turned out and whose high principles and lofty ideals shine from his eyes like beacon fires ...' And then suddenly, with an abrupt change of manner, Lancelot broke down and in a low voice added, 'Curse him! Curse him! Curse him! Curse him!'

[49]

Worple looked at Scollop. Scollop looked at Worple.

'Come, old man,' said Scollop, laying a gentle hand on Lancelot's bowed shoulder. 'We are your friends. Confide in us.'

'Tell us all,' said Worple. 'What's the matter?'

Lancelot uttered a bitter, mirthless laugh.

'You want to know what's the matter? Listen, then. I'm cat-pecked!'

'Cat-pecked?'

'You've heard of men being hen-pecked, haven't you?' said Lancelot with a touch of irritation. 'Well, I'm cat-pecked.'

And in broken accents he told his story. He sketched the history of his association with Webster from the latter's first entry into the studio. Confident now that the animal was not within earshot, he unbosomed himself without reserve.

'It's something in the beast's eye,' he said in a shaking voice. 'Something hypnotic. He casts a spell upon me. He gazes at me and disapproves. Little by little, bit by bit, I am degenerating under his influence from a wholesome, self-respecting artist into ... well, I don't know what you call it. Suffice it to say that I have given up smoking, that I have ceased to wear carpet slippers and go about without a collar, that I never dream of sitting down to my frugal evening meal without dressing, and' – he choked – 'I have sold my ukulele.'

'Not that!' said Worple, paling.

'Yes,' said Lancelot. 'I felt he considered it frivolous.'

There was a long silence.

'Mulliner,' said Scollop, 'this is more serious than I had supposed. We must brood upon your case.'

'It may be possible,' said Worple, 'to find a way out.'

Lancelot shook his head hopelessly.

'There is no way out. I have explored every avenue. The only thing that could possibly free me from this intolerable bondage would be if once – just once – I could catch that cat unbending. If once – merely once – it would lapse in my presence from its austere dignity for but a single instant, I feel that the spell would be broken. But what hope is there of that?' cried Lancelot passionately. 'You were pointing just now to that alley cat in the yard. There stands one who has strained every nerve and spared no effort to break down Webster's inhuman self-control. I have heard that animal say things to him which you would think no cat with red blood in its veins would suffer for an instant. And Webster merely looks at him like a Suffragan Bishop eyeing an erring choirboy and turns his head and falls into a refreshing sleep.'

The Painter with a Lovable Cat, I. Kay

He broke off with a dry sob. Worple, always an optimist, attempted in his kindly way to minimize the tragedy.

'Ah, well,' he said. 'It's bad, of course, but still, I suppose there is no actual harm in shaving and dressing for dinner and so on. Many great artists ... Whistler, for example –'

'Wait!' cried Lancelot. 'You have not heard the worst.'

He rose feverishly, and, going to the easel, disclosed the portrait of Brenda Carberry-Pirbright.

'Take a look at that,' he said, 'and tell me what you think of her.'

His two friends surveyed the face before them in silence. Miss Carberry-Pirbright was a young woman of prim and glacial aspect. One sought in vain for her reasons for wanting to have her portrait painted. It would be a most unpleasant thing to have about any house.

Scollop broke the silence.

'Friend of yours?'

'I can't stand the sight of her,' said Lancelot vehemently.

'Then,' said Scollop, 'I may speak frankly. I think she's a pill.'

'A blister,' said Worple.

[51]

'A boil and a disease,' said Scollop, summing up.

Lancelot laughed hackingly.

'You have described her to a nicety. She stands for everything most alien to my artist soul. She gives me a pain in the neck. I'm going to marry her.'

'What!' cried Scollop.

'But you're going to marry Gladys Bingley,' said Worple.

'Webster thinks not,' said Lancelot bitterly. 'At their first meeting he weighed Gladys in the balance and found her wanting. And the moment he saw Brenda Carberry-Pirbright he stuck his tail up at right angles, uttered a cordial gargle, and rubbed his head against her leg. Then turning, he looked at me. I could read that glance. I knew what was in his mind. From that moment he has been doing everything in his power to arrange the match.'

'But, Mulliner,' said Worple, always eager to point out the bright side, 'why should this girl want to marry a wretched, scrubby, hard-up footler like you? Have courage, Mulliner. It is simply a question of time before you repel and sicken her.'

Lancelot shook his head.

'No,' he said. 'You speak like a true friend, Worple, but you do not understand. Old Ma Carberry-Pirbright, this exhibit's mother, who chaperons her at the sittings, discovered at an early date my relationship to my Uncle Theodore, who, as you know, has got it in gobs. She knows well enough that some day I shall be a rich man. She used to know my Uncle Theodore when he was Vicar of St Botolph's in Knightsbridge, and from the very first she assumed towards me the repellent chumminess of an old family friend. She was always trying to lure me to her At Homes, her Sunday luncheons, her little dinners. Once she actually suggested that I should escort her and her beastly daughter to the Royal Academy.'

He laughed bitterly. The mordant witticisms of Lancelot Mulliner at the expense of the Royal Academy were quoted from Tite Street in the south to Holland Park in the north and eastward as far as Bloomsbury.

'To all these overtures,' resumed Lancelot, 'I remained firmly unresponsive. My attitude was from the start one of frigid aloofness. I did not actually say in so many words that I would rather be dead in a ditch than at one of her At Homes, but my manner indicated it. And I was just beginning to think I had choked her off when in crashed Webster and upset everything. Do you know how many times I have been to that infernal house in the last week? Five. Webster seemed to wish it. I tell you, I am a lost man.'

He buried his face in his hands. Scollop touched Worple on the arm, and together the two men stole silently out.

'Bad!' said Worple.

'Very bad,' said Scollop.

'It seems incredible.'

'Oh, no. Cases of this kind are, alas, by no means uncommon among those who, like Mulliner, possess to a marked degree the highly-strung, ultra-sensitive artistic temperament. A friend of mine, a rhythmical interior decorator, once rashly consented to put his aunt's parrot up at his studio while she was away visiting friends in the north of England. She was a woman of strong evangelical views, which the bird had imbibed from her. It had a way of putting its head on one side, making a noise like someone drawing a cork from a bottle, and asking my friend if he was saved. To cut a long story short, I happened to call on him a month later and he had installed a harmonium in his studio and was singing hymns, ancient and modern, in a rich tenor, while the parrot, standing on one leg on its perch, took the bass. A very sad affair. We were all much upset about it.'

Worple shuddered.

'You appal me, Scollop! Is there nothing we can do?'

Rodney Scollop considered for a moment.

'We might wire Gladys Bingley to come home at once. She might possibly reason with the unhappy man. A woman's gentle influence ... Yes, we could do that. Look in at the post office on your way home and send Gladys a telegram. I'll owe you for my half of it.'

In the studio they had left, Lancelot Mulliner was staring dumbly at a black shape which had just entered the room. He had the appearance of a man with his back to the wall.

'No!' he was crying. 'No! I'm dashed if I do!'

Webster continued to look at him.

'Why should I?' demanded Lancelot weakly.

Webster's gaze did not flicker.

'Oh, all right,' said Lancelot sullenly.

He passed from the room with leaden feet, and, proceeding upstairs, changed into morning clothes and a top hat. Then, with a gardenia in his buttonhole, he made his way to 11 Maxton Square, where Mrs Carberry-Pirbright was giving one of her intimate little teas ('just a few friends') to meet Clara Throckmorton Stooge, authoress of *A Strong Man's Kiss*.

*   *   *

[53]

Gladys Bingley was lunching at her hotel in Antibes when Worple's telegram arrived. It occasioned her the gravest concern.

Exactly what it was all about she was unable to gather, for emotion had made Bernard Worple rather incoherent. There were moments, reading it, when she fancied that Lancelot had met with a serious accident; others when the solution seemed to be that he had sprained his brain to such an extent that rival lunatic asylums were competing eagerly for his custom; others, again, when Worple appeared to be suggesting that he had gone into partnership with his cat to start a harem. But one fact emerged clearly. Her loved one was in serious trouble of some kind, and his best friends were agreed that only her immediate return could save him.

Gladys did not hesitate. Within half an hour of the receipt of the telegram she had packed her trunk, removed a piece of asparagus from her right eyebrow, and was negotiating for accommodation on the first train going north.

Arriving in London, her first impulse was to go straight to Lancelot. But a natural feminine curiosity urged her, before doing so, to call upon Bernard Worple and have light thrown on some of the more abstruse passages in the telegram.

Worple, in his capacity of author, may have tended towards obscurity, but, when confining himself to the spoken word, he told a plain story well and clearly. Five minutes of his society enabled Gladys to obtain a firm grasp on the salient facts, and there appeared on her face that grim, tight-lipped expression which is seen only on the faces of fiancées who have come back from a short holiday to discover that their dear one has been straying in their absence from the straight and narrow path.

'Brenda Carberry-Pirbright, eh?' said Gladys, with ominous calm. 'I'll give him Brenda Carberry-Pirbright! My gosh, if one can't go off to Antibes for the merest breather without having one's betrothed getting it up his nose and starting to act like a Mormon Elder, it begins to look a pretty tough world for a girl.'

Kind-hearted Bernard Worple did his best.

'I blame the cat,' he said. 'Lancelot, to my mind, is more sinned against than sinning. I consider him to be acting under undue influence or duress.'

'How like a man!' said Gladys. 'Shoving it all off on to an innocent cat!'

'Lancelot says it has a sort of something in its eye.'

[54]

'Well, when I meet Lancelot,' said Gladys, 'he'll find that I have a sort of something in my eye.'

She went out, breathing flame quietly through her nostrils. Worple, saddened, heaved a sigh and resumed his neo-Vorticist sculpting.

It was some five minutes later that Gladys, passing through Maxton Square on her way to Bott Street, stopped suddenly in her tracks. The sight she had seen was enough to make any fiancée do so.

Along the pavement leading to No. 11 two figures were advancing. Or three, if you counted a morose-looking dog of a semi-dachshund nature which preceded them, attached to a leash. One of the figures was that of Lancelot Mulliner, natty in grey herring-bone tweed and a new Homburg hat. It was he who held the leash. The other Gladys recognized from the portrait which she had seen on Lancelot's easel as that modern Du Barry, that notorious wrecker of homes and breaker-up of love-nests, Brenda Carberry-Pirbright.

The next moment they had mounted the steps of No. 11, and had gone in to tea, possibly with a little music.

It was perhaps an hour and a half later that Lancelot, having wrenched himself with difficulty from the lair of the Philistines, sped homeward in a swift taxi. As always after an extended tête-à-tête with Miss Carberry-Pirbright, he felt dazed and bewildered, as if he had been swimming in a sea of glue and had swallowed a good deal of it. All he could think of clearly was that he wanted a drink and that the materials for that drink were in the cupboard behind the chesterfield in his studio.

He paid the cab and charged in with his tongue rattling dryly against his front teeth. And there before him was Gladys Bingley, whom he had supposed far, far away.

'You!' exclaimed Lancelot.

'Yes, me!' said Gladys.

Her long vigil had not helped to restore the girl's equanimity. Since arriving at the studio she had had leisure to tap her foot three thousand, one hundred and forty-two times on the carpet, and the number of bitter smiles which had flitted across her face was nine hundred and eleven. She was about ready for the battle of the century.

She rose and faced him, all the woman in her flashing from her eyes.

'Well, you Casanova!' she said.

'You who?' said Lancelot.

'Don't say "Yoo-hoo!" to me!' cried Gladys. 'Keep that for your Brenda Carberry-Pirbright. Yes, I know all about it, Lancelot Don Juan

[55]

Cat as Painter, 1890

Henry the Eighth Mulliner! I saw you with her just now. I hear that you and she are inseparable. Bernard Worple says you said you were going to marry her.'

'You mustn't believe everything a neo-Vorticist sculptor tells you,' quavered Lancelot.

'I'll bet you're going back to dinner there tonight,' said Gladys.

She had spoken at a venture, basing the charge purely on a possessive cock of the head which she had noticed in Brenda Carberry-Pirbright at their recent encounter. There, she had said to herself at the time, had gone a girl who was about to invite – or had just invited – Lancelot Mulliner to dine quietly and take her to the pictures afterwards. But the shot went home. Lancelot hung his head.

'There was some talk of it,' he admitted.

'Ah!' exclaimed Gladys.

Lancelot's eyes were haggard.

'I don't want to go,' he pleaded. 'Honestly, I don't. But Webster insists.'

'Webster!'

'Yes, Webster. If I attempt to evade the appointment, he will sit in front of me and look at me.'

'Tchah!'

'Well, he will. Ask him for yourself.'

Gladys tapped her foot six times in rapid succession on the carpet, bringing the total to three thousand, one hundred and forty-eight. Her manner had changed and was now dangerously calm.

'Lancelot Mulliner,' she said, 'you have your choice. Me, on the one hand, Brenda Carberry-Pirbright on the other. I offer you a home where you will be able to smoke in bed, spill the ashes on the floor, wear pyjamas and carpet slippers all day and shave only on Sunday mornings. From her, what have you to hope? A house in South Kensington – possibly the Brompton Road – probably with her mother living with you. A life that will be one long round of stiff collars and tight shoes, of morning coats and top hats.'

Lancelot quivered, but she went on remorselessly.

'You will be at home on alternate Thursdays, and will be expected to hand the cucumber sandwiches. Every day you will air the dog, till you become a confirmed dog-airer. You will dine out in Bayswater and go for the summer to Bournemouth or Dinard. Choose well, Lancelot Mulliner! I will leave you to think it over. But one last word. If by seven-thirty on the dot you have not presented yourself at 6a Garbidge Mews ready to take me out to dinner at the Ham and Beef, I shall know what to think and shall act accordingly.'

And brushing the cigarette ashes from her chin, the girl strode haughtily from the room.

'Gladys!' cried Lancelot.

But she had gone.

For some minutes Lancelot Mulliner remained where he was, stunned. Then, insistently, there came to him the recollection that he had not had that drink. He rushed to the cupboard and produced the bottle. He uncorked it, and was pouring out a lavish stream, when a movement on the floor below him attracted his attention.

Webster was standing there, looking up at him. And in his eyes was that familiar expression of quiet rebuke.

'Scarcely what I have been accustomed to at the Deanery,' he seemed to be saying.

Lancelot stood paralysed. The feeling of being bound hand and foot, of being caught in a snare from which there was no escape, had become more poignant than ever. The bottle fell from his nerveless fingers and rolled across the floor, spilling its contents in an amber river, but he was too heavy in spirit to notice it. With a gesture such as Job might have made on discovering a new boil, he crossed to the window and stood looking moodily out.

Then, turning with a sigh, he looked at Webster again – and, looking, stood spell-bound.

The spectacle which he beheld was of a kind to stun a stronger man than Lancelot Mulliner. At first, he shrank from believing his eyes. Then, slowly, came the realization that what he saw was no mere figment of a disordered imagination. This unbelievable thing was actually happening.

Webster sat crouched upon the floor beside the widening pool of whisky. But it was not horror and disgust that had caused him to crouch. He was crouched because, crouching, he could get nearer to the stuff and obtain crisper action. His tongue was moving in and out like a piston.

And then abruptly, for one fleeting instant, he stopped lapping and glanced up at Lancelot, and across his face there flitted a quick smile – so genial, so intimate, so full of jovial camaraderie, that the young man found himself automatically smiling back, and not only smiling but winking. And in answer to that wink Webster winked too – a

The Artist's Studio (detail), Gustave Courbet (*Musée du Louvre, Paris*)

whole-hearted, roguish wink that said as plainly as if he had spoken the words:

'How long has this been going on?'

Then with a slight hiccough he turned back to the task of getting his drink before it soaked into the floor.

Into the murky soul of Lancelot Mulliner there poured a sudden flood of sunshine. It was as if a great burden had been lifted from his shoulders. The intolerable obsession of the last two weeks had ceased to oppress him, and he felt a free man. At the eleventh hour the reprieve had come. Webster, that seeming pillar of austere virtue, was one of the boys, after all. Never again would Lancelot quail beneath his eye. He had the goods on him.

Webster, like the stag at eve, had now drunk his fill. He had left the pool of alcohol and was walking round in slow, meditative circles. From time to time he mewed tentatively, as if he were trying to say 'British Constitution'. His failure to articulate the syllables appeared to tickle him, for at the end of each attempt he would utter a slow, amused chuckle. It was about this moment that he suddenly broke into a rhythmic dance, not unlike the old Saraband.

It was an interesting spectacle, and at any other time Lancelot would have watched it raptly. But now he was busy at his desk, writing a brief note to Mrs Carberry-Pirbright, the burden of which was that if she thought he was coming within a mile of her foul house that night or any other night she had vastly underrated the dodging powers of Lancelot Mulliner.

And what of Webster? The Demon Rum now had him in an iron grip. A lifetime of abstinence had rendered him a ready victim to the fatal fluid. He had now reached the stage when geniality gives way to belligerence. The rather foolish smile had gone from his face, and in its stead there lowered a fighting frown. For a few moments he stood on his hind legs, looking about him for a suitable adversary: then, losing all vestiges of self-control, he ran five times round the room at a high rate of speed and, falling foul of a small footstool, attacked it with the utmost ferocity, sparing neither tooth nor claw.

But Lancelot did not see him. Lancelot was not there. Lancelot was out in Bott Street, hailing a cab.

'6a Garbidge Mews, Fulham,' said Lancelot to the driver.

On Lutestrings Catt-Eaten

THOMAS MASTER

Are these the strings that poets feigne
Have clear'd the Ayre, and calm'd the mayne?
Charm'd wolves, and from the mountaine creasts
Made forests dance with all their beasts?
Could these neglected shreads you see
Inspire a Lute of Ivorie
And make it speake? Oh! think then what
Hath beene committed by my catt,
Who, in the silence of this night
Hath gnawne these cords, and marr'd them quite;
Leaving such reliques as may be
For fretts, not for my lute, but me.
Pusse, I will curse thee; may'st thou dwell
With some dry Hermit in a cell
Where Ratt neere peep'd, where mouse neere fedd,
And flyes goes supperlesse to bedd;
Or with some close-par'd Brother, where
Thou'lt fast each Saboath in the yeare;
Or else, prophane, be hang'd on Munday,
For butchering a mouse on Sunday;
Or May'st thou tumble from some tower,
And misse to light upon all fower,
Taking a fall that may untie
Eight of nine lives, and let them flye;
Or may the midnight embers sindge
Thy daintie coate, or Jane beswinge
Thy hide, when she shall take thee biting
Her cheese clouts, or her house beshiting.
What, was there neere a ratt nor mouse,
Nor Buttery ope? nought in the house
But harmlesse Lutestrings could suffice
Thy paunch, and draw thy glaring eyes?
Did not thy conscious stomach finde
Nature prophan'd, that kind with kind

[61]

The Cats' Concert (British Library, London)

Should stanch his hunger? thinke on that,
Thou caniball, and Cyclops catt.
For know, thou wretch, that every string
Is a catt-gutt, which art doth spinne
Into a thread; and how suppose
Dunstan, that snuff'd the divell's nose,
Should bid these strings revive, as once
He did the calfe, from naked bones;
Or I, to plague thee for thy sinne,
Should draw a circle, and beginne
To conjure, for I am, look to't,
An Oxford scholler, and can doo't.
Then with three setts of mapps and mowes,
Seaven of odd words, and motley showes,
A thousand tricks, that may be taken
From Faustus, Lambe, or Fryar Bacon:
I should beginne to call my strings
My catlings, and my mynikins;

[62]

A Cat Piano, 1883

And they recalled, straight should fall
To mew, to purr, to catterwaule
From puss's belly. Sure as death,
Pusse should be an Engastranith;
Pusse should be sent for to the king
For a strange bird, or some rare thing.
Pusse should be sought to farre and neere,
As she some cunning woman were.
Pusse should be carried up and downe,
From shire to shire, from Towne to Towne,
Like to the camell, Leane as Hagg,
The Elephant, or Apish negg,
For a strange sight; pusse should be sung
In Lousy Ballads, midst the Throng
At markets, with as good a grace
As Agincourt, or Chevy-chase.
The Troy-sprung Brittan would forgoe
His pedigree he chaunteth soe,

[63]

And singe that Merlin – long deceast –
Returned is in a nyne-liv'd beast.
   Thus, pusse, thou seest what might betyde thee;
But I forbeare to hurt or chide thee;
For may be pusse was melancholy
And so to make her blythe and jolly,
Finding these strings, shee'ld have a fitt
Of mirth; nay, pusse, if that were it,
Thus I revenge mee, that as thou
Hast played on them, I've plaid on you;
And as thy touch was nothing fine,
Soe I've but scratch'd these notes of mine.

The Diminutive Lyon or Catus, *the Cat*

WILLIAM SALMON

I. It is called in Hebrew, בטול,מחנר, *Catul, Schanar*; in Chaldean, חתול,
pl. חתוליז, *Chatul, pl. Chatulin*; in Greek, Κάτλης, αἴλουρος; in Latin,
Catus, felis; in English, *the Cat*, but the wild Cat is supposed to be called
in Hebrew, אייס, *Jim. Isa.* 13, 22, and 34, 14, for so *Arius Montanus* trans-
lates it; as for *Kat* or *Cat*, it is the most usual name that almost all Nations
call it by.

II. It is bred and is an Inhabitant of almost all Countries in the World,
all *Cats* were at first wild, but were at length tamed by the industry of
Mankind; it is a Beast of prey, even the tame one, more especially the
wild, it being in the opinion of many nothing but a diminutive Lyon.

III. It is now said to be of three kinds, 1. *The tame Cat*. 2. *The wild
wood Cat*. 3. *The Cat of Mountain*, all which are of one nature, and agree
much in one Shape, save as to their magnitude, the *wild Cat* being larger
much than the Tame, and the *Cat of Mountain* much larger than the
wild Cat.

IV. It has a broad Face almost like a Lyon, short Ears, large Whiskers,
shining Eyes, short smooth Hair, long Tail, rough Tongue, and armed
on its Feet with Claws, being a crafty, subtle watchful Creature, very
loving and familiar with Man-kind, the mortal enemy to the Rat, Mouse,

Cat from *The Historie of Foure-Footed Beastes*, 1607, by Edward Topsell

and all sorts of Birds, which it seizes on as its prey. As to its Eyes, Authors say that they shine in the Night, and see better at the full, and more dimly at the change of the Moon; as also that the Cat doth vary his Eyes with the Sun, the Apple of its Eye being long at Sun rise, round towards Noon, and not to be seen at all at night, but the whole Eye shining in the night. These appearances of the Cats Eyes I am sure are true, but whether they answer to the times of the day, I never observed.

V. It is a neat and cleanly creature, often licking it self, to keep it fair and clean, and washing its Face with its fore-feet; the best are such as are of a fair and large kind, and of an exquisite Tabby color, called *Cyprus* Cats. They usually generate in the winter Season, making a great noise, go 56 Days or 8 weeks with young, and bring forth 2, 3, 4, 5, 6, or more at a time, they cover their excrements, and love to keep their old habitations.

VI. *Its Flesh* is not usually eaten, yet in some Countries it is accounted an excellent Dish, but the Brain is said to be poisonous, causing madness, stupidity, and loss of memory, which is cured only by vomiting, and taking musk in Wine. The Flesh applied easeth the pain of Hæmorrhoids and the back, and salted, beaten, and applied, draws Thorns, *&c.* out of the Flesh, and is said particularly to help the Gout, especially that of the wild Cat.

VII. *The Fat* is hot, dry, emollient, discussive, and Anodyne: R *Cat's Grease*, ℨij. *Palm Oyl*, ℨβ. *Oil of Anniseed*, ℨj. *mix them*; it dissolves tumors, eases pain, and prevails against nodes in the Shin, and the cold Gout.

VIII. *The Head*: R *the Ashes of a Cat's Head* ℨj. *white vitriol in fine Pouder*, Saccharum Saturni *ana* ℈j. *mix them for a Pouder*; or mix them with Honey for a Balsam, blown into the Eyes, or annointed thrice aday; it cures Blindness, and most Diseases of the Eyes, as the Pin and Web, Pearls, Clouds, Films, *&c.*

IX. *The Liver*: R *the Ashes, or rather pouder of it*, ℨj. *Borax, Nitre, Volatile Sal Armoniack, Pouder of Elecampane, Roots of Bay-berries*, ana ℨij. *mix them*. Dose ℨij. in any convenient Vehicle, against Gravel and stoppage of Urine.

X. *The Gall*: ℞ *of Cat's Gall*, ℥β. *of our* Aqua Regulata ʒij. *Honey*, ʒj. *mix them for a* Collyrium to wash the Eyes often with against Pearls, Films, Blindness, and Dimness of the sight: ℞ *Cat's Gall* ℥β. Colo quintida, *Fine Aloes*, *Ana* q.s. *Musk gr*. xvi. *mix and make a pessary*. It brings away the birth and after birth, and extracts a Mola.

XI. *The Blood*, some affirms it kills Worms in the Nose, and other places of the Skin: ℞ *the Bloud of the Tail of a Bore-Cat* gut. x. *Salt of Man's Skull*, *gr*. vj. *pouder of Ox horns*, gr. 10. *mix them for a Dose*. It is said to cure the Falling-Sickness.

XII. *The Dung and Urine*: ℞ *Pouder of Cats Dung*, ℥j. *Mustard-seed in Pouder*, ʒiij. *Juice of Onions*, ʒii. *Bears Grease enough to make an Oyntment*. It cures Baldness and the Alopecia.

PART III

Cat's Games

Poem

WILLIAM CARLOS WILLIAMS

As the cat
climbed over
the top of

the jamcloset
first the right
forefoot

carefully
then the hind
stepped down

into the pit of
the empty
flowerpot

The White Cat

W. W. JACOBS

THE traveller stood looking from the taproom window of the *Cauliflower* at the falling rain. The village street below was empty, and everything was quiet with the exception of the garrulous old man smoking with much enjoyment on the settle behind him.

'It'll do a power o' good,' said the ancient, craning his neck round the edge of the settle and turning a bleared eye on the window. 'I ain't like some folk; I never did mind a drop o' rain.'

The traveller grunted and, returning to the settle opposite the old man, fell to lazily stroking a cat which had strolled in attracted by the warmth of the small fire which smouldered in the grate.

'He's a good mouser,' said the old man, 'but I expect that Smith the landlord would sell 'im to anybody for arf a crown, but we 'ad a cat in

[71]

Claybury once that you couldn't ha' bought for a hundred golden sovereigns.'

The traveller continued to caress the cat.

'A white cat, with one yaller eye and one blue one,' continued the old man. 'It sounds queer, but it's as true as I sit 'ere wishing that I 'ad another mug o' ale as good as the last you gave me.'

The traveller, with a start that upset the cat's nerves, finished his own mug, and then ordered both to be refilled. He stirred the fire into a blaze, and, lighting his pipe and putting one foot on to the hob, prepared to listen.

It used to belong to old man Clark, young Joe Clark's uncle, said the ancient, smacking his lips delicately over the ale and extending a tremulous claw to the tobacco-pouch pushed towards him; and he was never tired of showing it off to people. He used to call it 'is blue-eyed darling, and the fuss 'e made o' that cat was sinful.

Young Joe Clark couldn't bear it, but being down in 'is uncle's will for five cottages and a bit o' land bringing in about forty pounds a year, he 'ad to 'ide his feelings and pretend as he loved it. He used to take it little drops o' cream and tid-bits o' meat, and old Clark was so pleased

White Cat, photo Sean C. Coombs (*Barnaby's Picture Library*)

[72]

that 'e promised 'im that he should 'ave the cat along with all the other property when 'e was dead.

Young Joe said he couldn't thank 'im enough, and the old man, who 'ad been ailing a long time, made 'im come up every day to teach 'im 'ow to take care of it arter he was gone. He taught Joe 'ow to cook its meat and then chop it up fine: 'ow it liked a clean saucer every time for its milk; and 'ow he wasn't to make a noise when it was asleep.

'Take care your children don't worry it, Joe,' he ses one day, very sharp. 'One o' your boys was pulling its tail this morning, and I want you to clump his 'ead for 'im.'

'Which one was it?' ses Joe.

'The slobbery-nosed one,' ses old Clark.

'I'll give 'im a clout as soon as I get 'ome,' ses Joe, who was very fond of 'is children.

'Go and fetch 'im and do it 'ere,' ses the old man; 'that'll teach 'im to love animals.'

Joe went off 'ome to fetch the boy, and arter his mother 'ad washed his face, and wiped his nose, an' put a clean pinneyfore on 'im, he took 'im to 'is uncle's and clouted his 'ead for 'im. Arter that Joe and 'is wife 'ad words all night long, and next morning old Clark, coming in from the garden, was just in time to see 'im kick the cat right acrost the kitchen.

He could 'ardly speak for a minute, and when 'e could Joe see plain wot a fool he'd been. Fust of all 'e called Joe every name he could think of – which took 'im a long time – and then he ordered 'im out of 'is house.

'You shall 'ave my money when your betters have done with it,' he ses, 'and not afore. That's all you've done for yourself.'

Joe Clark didn't know wot he meant at the time, but when old Clark died three months afterwards 'e found out. His uncle 'ad made a new will and left everything to old George Barstow for as long as the cat lived, providing that he took care of it. When the cat was dead the property was to go to Joe.

The cat was only two years old at the time, and George Barstow, who was arf crazy with joy, said it shouldn't be 'is fault if it didn't live another twenty years.

The funny thing was the quiet way Joe Clark took it. He didn't seem to be at all cut up about it, and when Henery Walker said it was a shame, 'e said he didn't mind, and that George Barstow was a old man, and he was quite welcome to 'ave the property as long as the cat lived.

'It must come to me by the time I'm an old man,' he ses, 'and that's all I care about.'

[73]

A Blockade Runner, Briton Rivière (*Tate Gallery, London*)

Henery Walker went off, and as 'e passed the cottage where old Clark used to live, and which George Barstow 'ad moved into, 'e spoke to the old man over the palings and told 'im wot Joe Clark 'ad said. George Barstow only grunted and went on stooping and prying over 'is front garden.

'Bin and lost something?' ses Henery Walker, watching 'im.

'No; I'm finding,' ses George Barstow, very fierce, and picking up something. 'That's the fifth bit o' powdered liver I've found in my garden this morning.'

Henery Walker went off whistling, and the opinion he'd 'ad o' Joe Clark began to improve. He spoke to Joe about it that arternoon, and Joe said that if 'e ever accused 'im o' such a thing again he'd knock 'is 'ead off. He said that he 'oped the cat 'ud live to be a hundred, and that 'e'd no more think of giving it poisoned meat than Henery Walker would of paying for 'is drink so long as 'e could get anybody else to do it for 'im.

They 'ad bets up at this 'ere *Cauliflower* public-'ouse that evening as to 'ow long that cat 'ud live. Nobody gave it more than a month, and Bill Chambers sat and thought o' so many ways o' killing it on the sly that it was wunnerful to hear 'im.

George Barstow took fright when he 'eard of them, and the care 'e took o' that cat was wunnerful to behold. Arf its time it was shut up in the back bedroom, and the other arf George Barstow was fussing arter it till that cat got to hate 'im like pison. Instead o' giving up work as he'd thought to do, 'e told Henery Walker that 'e'd never worked so 'ard in his life.

'Wot about Joe Clark?' ses George Barstow. 'I'm tied 'and and foot. I dursent leave the house for a moment. I ain't been to the *Cauliflower* since I've 'ad it, and three times I got out o' bed last night to see if it was safe.'

'Mark my words,' ses Henery Walker, 'if that cat don't 'ave exercise, you'll lose it.'

'I shall lose it if it does 'ave exercise,' ses George Barstow, 'that I know.'

He sat down thinking arter Henery Walker 'ad gone, and then he 'ad a little collar and chain made for it, and took it out for a walk. Pretty nearly every dog in Claybury went with 'em, and the cat was in such a state o' mind afore they got 'ome he couldn't do anything with it. It 'ad a fit as soon as they got indoors, and George Barstow, who 'ad read about children's fits in the almanac, gave it a warm bath. It brought it round immediate, and then it began to tear round the room and up and down stairs till George Barstow was afraid to go near it.

It was so bad that evening, sneezing, that George Barstow sent for Bill Chambers, who'd got a good name for doctoring animals, and asked 'im to give it something. Bill said he'd got some powders at 'ome that would cure it at once, and he went and fetched 'em and mixed one up with a bit o' butter.

'That's the way to give a cat medicine,' he ses; 'smear it with butter and then it'll lick it off, powder and all.'

He was just going to rub it on the cat when George Barstow caught 'old of 'is arm and stopped 'im.

'How do I know it ain't pison?' he ses. 'You're a friend o' Joe Clark's, and for all I know he may ha' paid you to pison it.'

'I wouldn't do such a thing,' ses Bill. 'You ought to know me better than that.'

'All right,' ses George Barstow; 'you eat it then, and I'll give you two shillings instead o' one. You can easy mix some more.'

'Not me,' ses Bill Chambers, making a face.

'Well, three shillings, then,' ses George Barstow, getting more and more suspicious like; 'four shillings – five shillings.'

Bill Chambers shook his 'ead, and George Barstow, more and more certain he 'ad caught 'im trying to kill 'is cat and that 'e wouldn't eat the stuff, rose 'im up to ten shillings.

Bill looked at the butter and then 'e looked at the ten shillings on the table, and at last he shut 'is eyes and gulped it down and put the money in 'is pocket.

'You see, I 'ave to be careful, Bill,' ses George Barstow, rather upset.

Bill Chambers didn't answer 'im. He sat there as white as a sheet, and making such extraordinary faces that George was arf afraid of 'im.

'Anything wrong, Bill?' he ses at last.

Bill sat staring at 'im, and then all of a sudden he clapped 'is 'andker-chief to 'is mouth and, getting up from his chair, opened the door and rushed out. George Barstow thought at fust that he 'ad eaten pison for the sake o' ten shillings, but when 'e remembered that Bill Chambers 'ad got the most delikit stummick in Claybury he altered 'is mind.

The cat was better the next morning, but George Barstow had 'ad such a fright about it 'e wouldn't let it go out of 'is sight, and Joe Clark began to think that 'e would 'ave to wait longer for that property than 'e had thought, arter all. To 'ear 'im talk anybody'd ha' thought that 'e loved the cat. We didn't pay much attention to it up at the *Cauliflower* 'ere, except maybe to wink at 'im – a thing he couldn't a bear – but at 'ome, o' course, his young 'uns thought as everything he said was Gospel; and one day, coming 'ome from work, as he was passing George Barstow's he was paid out for his deceitfulness.

'I've wronged you, Joe Clark,' ses George Barstow, coming to the door, 'and I'm sorry for it.'

'Oh!' ses Joe staring.

'Give that to your little Jimmy,' ses George Barstow, giving 'im a shilling. 'I've give 'im one, but I thought arterwards it wasn't enough.'

'What for?' ses Joe, staring at 'im agin.

'For bringing my cat 'ome,' ses George Barstow. ' 'Ow it got out I can't think, but I lost it for three hours, and I'd about given it up when your little Jimmy brought it to me in 'is arms. He's a fine little chap and 'e does you credit.'

Joe Clark tried to speak, but he couldn't get a word out, and Henery Walker, wot 'ad just come up and 'eard wot passed, took hold of 'is arm and helped 'im home. He walked like a man in a dream, but arf-way he stopped and cut a stick from the hedge to take 'ome to little Jimmy. He said the boy 'ad been asking him for a stick for some time, but up till then 'e'd always forgotten it.

At the end o' the fust year that cat was still alive, to everybody's surprise; but George Barstow took such care of it 'e never let it out of 'is sight. Every time 'e went out he took it with 'im in a hamper, and, to prevent its being pisoned, he paid Isaac Sawyer, who 'ad the biggest family in Claybury, sixpence a week to let one of 'is boys taste its milk before it had it.

The second year it was ill twice, but the horse-doctor that George Barstow got for it said that it was as 'ard as nails, and with care it might live to be twenty. He said that it wanted more fresh air and exercise; but when he 'eard 'ow George Barstow come by it he said that p'rhaps it would live longer indoors arter all.

At last one day, when George Barstow 'ad been living on the fat o' the land for nearly three years, that cat got out agin. George 'ad raised the front-room winder two or three inches to throw something outside, and, afore he knew wot was 'appening, the cat was outside and going up the road about twenty miles an hour.

George Barstow went arter it, but he might as well ha' tried to catch the wind. The cat was arf wild with joy at getting out agin, and he couldn't get within arf a mile of it.

He stayed out all day without food or drink, follering it about until it came on dark, and then, o' course, he lost sight of it, and, hoping against 'ope that it would come home for its food, he went 'ome and waited for it. He sat up all night dozing in a chair in the front room with the door left open, but it was all no use; and arter thinking for a long time wot was best to do, he went out and told some o' the folks it was lost and offered a reward of five pounds for it.

You never saw such a hunt then in all your life. Nearly every man, woman, and child in Claybury left their work or school and went to try and earn that five pounds. By the arternoon George Barstow made it ten pounds provided the cat was brought 'ome safe and sound, and people as was too old to walk stood at their cottage doors to snap it up as it came by.

Joe Clark was hunting for it 'igh and low, and so was 'is wife and the boys. In fact, I b'lieve that everybody in Claybury excepting the parson and Bob Pretty was trying to get that ten pounds.

O' course, we could understand the parson – 'is pride wouldn't let 'im; but a low, poaching, thieving rascal like Bob Pretty turning up 'is nose at ten pounds was more than we could make out. Even on the second day, when George Barstow made it ten pounds down and a shilling a week for a year besides, he didn't offer to stir; all he did was to try and make fun o' them as *was* looking for it.

'Have you looked everywhere you can think of for it, Bill?' he ses to Bill Chambers.

'Yes, I 'ave,' ses Bill.

'Well, then, you want to look everywhere else,' ses Bob Pretty. 'I know where I should look if I wanted to find it.'

'Why don't you find it, then?' ses Bill.

''Cos I don't want to make mischief,' ses Bob Pretty. 'I don't want to be unneighbourly to Joe Clark by interfering at all.'

'Not for all that money?' ses Bill.

'Not for fifty pounds,' ses Bob Pretty; 'you ought to know me better than that, Bill Chambers.'

'It's my belief that you know more about where that cat is than you ought to,' ses Joe Gubbins.

'You go on looking for it, Joe,' ses Bob Pretty, grinning; 'it's good exercise for you, and you've only lost two days' work.'

'I'll give you arf a crown if you let me search your 'ouse, Bob,' ses Bill Chambers, looking at 'im very 'ard.

'I couldn't do it at the price, Bill,' ses Bob Pretty, shaking his 'ead. 'I'm a pore man, but I'm very partikler who I 'ave come into my 'ouse.'

O' course, everybody left off looking at once when they heard about Bob – not that they believed that he'd be such a fool as to keep the cat in his 'ouse; and that evening, as soon as it was dark, Joe Clark went round to see 'im.

'Don't tell me as that cat's found, Joe,' ses Bob Pretty, as Joe opened the door.

'Not as I've 'eard of,' said Joe, stepping inside. 'I wanted to speak to you about it; the sooner it's found the better I shall be pleased.'

'It does you credit, Joe Clark,' ses Bob Pretty.

'It's my belief that it's dead,' ses Joe, looking at 'im very 'ard; 'but I want to make sure afore taking over the property.'

Bob Pretty looked at 'im and then he gave a little cough. 'Oh, you want it to be found dead,' he ses. 'Now, I wonder whether that cat's worth most dead or alive?'

Joe Clark coughed then. 'Dead, I should think,' he ses at last.

'George Barstow's just 'ad bills printed offering fifteen pounds for it,' ses Bob Pretty.

'I'll give that or more when I come into the property,' ses Joe Clark.

'There's nothing like ready-money, though, is there?' ses Bob.

'I'll promise it to you in writing, Bob,' ses Joe, trembling.

'There's some things that don't look well in writing, Joe,' ses Bob Pretty, considering; 'besides, why should you promise it to *me*?'

'O' course, I meant if you found it,' ses Joe.

'Well, I'll do my best, Joe,' ses Bob Pretty; 'and none of us can do no more than that, can they?'

They sat talking and argufying over it for over an hour, and twice Bob Pretty got up and said 'e was going to see whether George Barstow wouldn't offer more. By the time they parted they was as thick as thieves, and next morning Bob Pretty was wearing Joe Clark's watch and chain, and Mrs Pretty was up at Joe's 'ouse to see whether there was any of 'is furniture as she 'ad a fancy for.

She didn't seem to be able to make up 'er mind at fust between a chest o' drawers that 'ad belonged to Joe's mother and a grandfather clock. She walked from one to the other for about ten minutes, and then Bob, who'd come to 'elp her, told 'er to 'ave both.

'You're quite welcome,' he ses; 'ain't she, Joe?'

Joe Clark said 'Yes,' and arter he 'ad helped them carry 'em 'ome the Prettys went back and took the best bedstead to pieces, cos Bob said as it was easier to carry that way. Mrs Clark 'ad to go and sit down at the bottom o' the garden with the neck of 'er dress undone to give herself air, but when she saw the little Prettys each walking 'ome with one of 'er best chairs on their 'eads she got up and walked up and down like a mad thing.

[79]

'I'm sure I don't know where we are to put it all,' ses Bob Pretty to Joe Gubbins, wot was looking on with other folks, 'but Joe Clark is that generous he won't 'ear of our leaving anything.'

'Has 'e gorn mad?' ses Bill Chambers, staring at 'im.

'Not as I knows on,' ses Bob Pretty. 'It's 'is good-'artedness, that's all. He feels sure that that cat's dead, and he'll 'ave George Barstow's cottage and furniture. I told 'im he'd better wait till he'd made sure, but 'e wouldn't.'

Before they'd finished the Prettys 'ad picked that 'ouse as clean as a bone, and Joe Clark 'ad to go and get clean straw for his wife and children to sleep on; not that Mrs Clark 'ad any sleep that night, nor Joe neither.

Henery Walker was the fust to see what it really meant, and he went rushing off as fast as 'e could run to tell George Barstow. George couldn't believe 'im at fust, but when 'e did he swore that if a 'air of that cat's 'ead was harmed 'e'd 'ave the law o' Bob Pretty, and arter Henery Walker 'ad gone 'e walked round to tell 'im so.

'You're not yourself, George Barstow, else you wouldn't try and take away my character like that,' ses Bob Pretty.

'Wot did Joe Clark give you all them things for?' ses George, pointing to the furniture.

'Took a fancy to me, I s'pose,' ses Bob. 'People do sometimes. There's something about me at times that makes 'em like me.'

'He gave 'em to you to kill my cat,' ses George Barstow. 'It's plain enough for anybody to see.'

Bob Pretty smiled. 'I expect it'll turn up safe and sound one o' these days,' he ses, 'and then you'll come round and beg my pardon. P'r'aps –'

'P'r'aps wot?' ses George Barstow, arter waiting a bit.

'P'r'aps somebody 'as got it and is keeping it till you've drawed the fifteen pounds out o' the bank,' ses Bob, looking at 'im very hard.

'I've taken it out o' the bank,' ses George, starting; 'if that cat's alive, Bob, and you've got it, there's the fifteen pounds the moment you 'and it over.'

'Wot d'ye mean – me got it?' ses Bob Pretty. 'You be careful o' my character.'

'I mean if you know where it is,' ses George Barstow trembling all over.

'I don't say I couldn't find it, if that's wot you mean,' ses Bob. 'I can gin'rally find things when I want to.'

'You find me that cat, alive and well, and the money's yours, Bob,' ses George, 'ardly able to speak, now that 'e fancied the cat was still alive.

[80]

Bob Pretty shook his 'ead. 'No, that won't do,' he ses. 'S'pose I did 'ave the luck to find that pore animal, you'd say I'd had it all the time and refuse to pay.'

'I swear I wouldn't, Bob,' ses George Barstow, jumping up.

'Best thing you can do if you want me to try and find that cat,' ses Bob Pretty, 'is to give me the fifteen pounds now, and I'll go and look for it at once. I can't trust you, George Barstow.'

'And I can't trust you,' ses George Barstow.

'Very good,' ses Bob, getting up; 'there's no 'arm done. P'r'aps Joe Clark'll find the cat is dead and p'r'aps you'll find it's alive. It's all one to me.'

George Barstow walked off 'ome, but he was in such a state o' mind 'e didn't know wot to do. Bob Pretty turning up 'is nose at fifteen pounds like that made 'im think that Joe Clark 'ad promised to pay 'im more if the cat was dead; and at last, arter worrying about it for a couple o' hours, 'e came up to this 'ere *Cauliflower* and offered Bob the fifteen pounds.

'Wot's this for?' ses Bob.

'For finding my cat,' ses George.

'Look here,' ses Bob, handing it back, 'I've 'ad enough o' your insults; I don't know where your cat is.'

'I mean for trying to find it, Bob,' ses George Barstow.

'Oh, well, I don't mind that,' ses Bob, taking it. 'I'm a 'ard-working man, and I've got to be paid for my time; it's on'y fair to my wife and children. I'll start now.'

He finished up 'is beer, and while the other chaps was telling George Barstow wot a fool he was Joe Clark slipped out arter Bob Pretty and began to call 'im all the names he could think of.

'Don't you worry,' ses Bob; 'the cat ain't found yet.'

'Is it dead?' ses Joe Clark, 'ardly able to speak.

''Ow should I know?' ses Bob; 'that's wot I've got to try and find out. That's wot you gave me your furniture for, and wot George Barstow gave me the fifteen pounds for, ain't it? Now, don't you stop me now, 'cos I'm goin' to begin looking.'

He started looking there and then, and for the next two or three days George Barstow and Joe Clark see 'im walking up and down with his 'ands in 'is pockets looking over garden fences and calling 'Puss'. He asked everybody 'e see whether they 'ad seen a white cat with one blue eye and one yaller one, and every time 'e came into the *Cauliflower* he put 'is 'ead over the bar and called 'Puss,' 'cos, as 'e said, it was as likely to be there as anywhere else.

[81]

Jack Russell and Persian, Frederick Rutherford (*Michael Parkin Fine Arts Ltd*)

It was about a week after the cat 'ad disappeared that George Barstow was standing at 'is door talking to Joe Clark, who was saying the cat must be dead and 'e wanted 'is property, when he sees a man coming up the road carrying a basket stop and speak to Bill Chambers. Just as 'e got near them an awful 'miaow' come from the basket and George Barstow and Joe Clark started as if they'd been shot.

'He's found it!' shouts Bill Chambers, pointing to the man.

'It's been living with me over at Ling for a week pretty nearly,' ses the man. 'I tried to drive it away several times, not knowing that there was fifteen pounds offered for it.'

George Barstow tried to take 'old of the basket.

'I want that fifteen pounds fust,' ses the man.

'That's on'y right and fair, George,' ses Bob Pretty, who 'ad just come up. 'You've got all the luck, mate. We've been hunting 'igh and low for that cat for a week.'

Then George Barstow tried to explain to the man and call Bob Pretty names at the same time; but it was all no good. The man said it 'ad nothing to do with 'im wot he 'ad paid to Bob Pretty; and at last they fetched Policeman White over from Cudford, and George Barstow signed a paper to pay five shillings a week till the reward was paid.

George Barstow 'ad the cat for five years arter that, but he never let it get away agin. They got to like each other in time and died within a fortnight of each other, so Joe Clark got 'is property arter all.

Peter

MARIANNE MOORE

Strong and slippery, built for the midnight grass-party confronted
                                            by four cats,
   he sleeps his time away – the detached first claw on the foreleg,
                                            which corresponds
      to the thumb, retracted to its tip; the small tuft of fronds
         or katydid-legs above each eye, still numbering the units in each
                                            group;
         the shadbones regularly set about the mouth, to droop or rise

in unison like the porcupine's quills – motionless. He lets himself be flattened out by gravity, as it were a piece of seaweed tamed and weakened by
      exposure to the sun; compelled when extended, to lie
         stationary. Sleep is the result of his delusion that one must do as
            well as one can for oneself; sleep – epitome of what is to

him as to the average person, the end of life. Demonstrate on him how
   the lady caught the dangerous southern snake, placing a forked stick
      side of its innocuous neck; one need not try to stir on either
         him up; his prune-shaped head and alligator eyes are not a party
                                            to the
            joke. Lifted and handled, he may be dangled like an eel or set

up on the forearm like a mouse; his eyes bisected by pupils of a pin's
   width, are flickeringly exhibited, then covered up. May be? I should say
      might have been; when he has been got the better of in a
         dream – as in a fight with nature or with cats – we all know it.
                                            Profound sleep is
               not with him a fixed illusion. Springing about with froglike ac-

[83]

Contemplation, Henry Rogers (*Jellinek & Sampson*)

curacy, emitting jerky cries when taken in the hand, he is himself
  again; to sit caged by the rungs of a domestic chair would be unprofit-
  able – human. What is the good of hypocrisy? It
      is permissible to choose one's employment, to abandon the wire nail,
                                                                        the
        roly-poly, when it shows signs of being no longer a pleas-

ure, to score the adjacent magazine with a double line of strokes. He can
  talk, but insolently says nothing. What of it? When one is frank, one's
                                                                      very
      presence is a compliment. It is clear that he can see
        the virtue of naturalness, that he is one of those who do not regard
        the published fact as a surrender. As for the disposition

invariably to affront, an animal with claws wants to have to use
  them; that eel-like extension of trunk into tail is not an accident. To
  leap, to lengthen out, divide the air – to purloin, to pursue.
      To tell the hen: fly over the fence, go in the wrong way in your
                                                                perturba-
        tion – this is life; to do less would be nothing but dishonesty.

[84]

The White and Black Dynasties

THÉOPHILE GAUTIER

(*translated by Lady Chance*)

A CAT brought from Havana by Mademoiselle Aïta de la Penuela, a young Spanish artist whose studies of white angoras may still be seen gracing the printsellers' windows, produced the daintiest little kitten imaginable. It was just like a swan's-down powder-puff, and on account of its immaculate whiteness it received the name of Pierrot. When it grew big this was lengthened to Don Pierrot de Navarre as being more grandiose and majestic.

Don Pierrot, like all animals which are spoiled and made much of, developed a charming amiability of character. He shared the life of the household with all the pleasure which cats find in the intimacy of the domestic hearth. Seated in his usual place near the fire, he really appeared to understand what was being said, and to take an interest in it.

His eyes followed the speakers, and from time to time he would utter little sounds, as though he too wanted to make remarks and give his

Cats on the Tiles, 1878

[85]

opinion on literature, which was our usual topic of conversation. He was very fond of books, and when he found one open on a table he would lie on it, look at the page attentively, and turn over the leaves with his paw; then he would end by going to sleep, for all the world as if he were reading a fashionable novel.

Directly I took up a pen he would jump on my writing-desk and with deep attention watch the steel nib tracing black spider-legs on the expanse of white paper, and his head would turn each time I began a new line. Sometimes he tried to take part in the work, and would attempt to pull the pen out of my hand, no doubt in order to write himself, for he was an aesthetic cat, like Hoffman's Murr, and I strongly suspect him of having scribbled his memoirs at night on some house-top by the light of his phosphorescent eyes. Unfortunately these lucubrations have been lost.

Don Pierrot never went to bed until I came in. He waited for me inside the door, and as I entered the hall he would rub himself against my legs and arch his back, purring joyfully all the time. Then he proceeded to walk in front of me like a page, and if I had asked him, he would certainly have carried the candle for me. In this fashion he escorted me to my room and waited while I undressed; then he would jump on the bed, put his paws round my neck, rub noses with me, and lick me with his rasping little pink tongue, while giving vent to soft inarticulate cries, which clearly expressed how pleased he was to see me again. Then when his transports of affection had subsided, and the hour for repose had come, he would balance himself on the rail of the bedstead and sleep there like a bird perched on a bough. When I woke in the morning he would come and lie near me until it was time to get up. Twelve o'clock was the hour at which I was supposed to come in. On this subject Pierrot had all the notions of a concierge.

At that time we had instituted little evening gatherings among a few friends, and had formed a small society, which we called the Four Candles Club, the room in which we met being, as it happened, lit by four candles in silver candlesticks, which were placed at the corners of the table.

Sometimes the conversation became so lively that I forgot the time, at the risk of finding, like Cinderella, my carriage turned into a pumpkin and my coachman into a rat.

Pierrot waited for me several times until two o'clock in the morning, but in the end my conduct displeased him, and he went to bed without me. This mute protest against my innocent dissipation touched me so much that ever after I came home regularly at midnight. But it was a long time before Pierrot forgave me. He wanted to be sure that it was not a sham repentance; but when he was convinced of the sincerity of my conversion, he deigned to take me into favour again, and he resumed his nightly post in the entrance-hall.

To gain the friendship of a cat is not an easy thing. It is a philosophic, well-regulated, tranquil animal, a creature of habit and a lover of order and cleanliness. It does not give its affections indiscriminately. It will consent to be your friend if you are worthy of the honour, but it will not be your slave. With all its affection, it preserves its freedom of judgement, and it will not do anything for you which it considers unreasonable; but once it has given its love, what absolute confidence, what fidelity of affection! It will make itself the companion of your hours of work, of loneliness, or of sadness. It will lie the whole evening on your knee, purring and happy in your society, and leaving the company of creatures of its own kind to be with you. In vain the sound of caterwauling reverberates from the house-tops, inviting it to one of those cats' evening parties where essence of red-herring takes the place of tea. It will not be tempted, but continues to keep its vigil with you. If you put it down it climbs up again quickly, with a sort of crooning noise, which is like a gentle reproach. Sometimes, when seated in front of you, it gazes at you with such soft, melting eyes, such a human and caressing look, that you are almost awed, for it seems impossible that reason can be absent from it.

Don Pierrot had a companion of the same race as himself, and no less white. All the imaginable snowy comparisons it were possible to pile up would not suffice to give an idea of that immaculate fur, which would have made ermine look yellow.

I called her Seraphita, in memory of Balzac's Swedenborgian romance. The heroine of that wonderful story, when she climbed the snow peaks of the Falberg with Minna, never shone with a more pure white radiance. Seraphita had a dreamy and pensive character. She would lie motionless on a cushion for hours, not asleep, but with eyes fixed in rapt attention on scenes invisible to ordinary mortals.

Caresses were agreeable to her, but she responded to them with great reserve, and only to those of people whom she favoured with her esteem, which it was not easy to gain. She liked luxury, and it was always in the newest armchair or on the piece of furniture best calculated to show off her swan-like beauty, that she was to be found. Her toilette took an immense time. She would carefully smooth her entire coat every morning, and wash her face with her paw, and every hair on her body shone like new silver when brushed by her pink tongue. If anyone touched her she would immediately efface all traces of the contact, for she could not endure being ruffled. Her elegance and distinction gave one an idea of aristocratic birth, and among her own kind she must have been at least a duchess. She had a passion for scents. She would plunge her nose into bouquets, and nibble a perfumed handkerchief with little paroxysms of delight. She would walk about on the dressing-table sniffing the stoppers of the scent-bottles, and she would have loved to use the violet powder if she had been allowed.

Such was Seraphita, and never was a cat more worthy of a poetic name.

Don Pierrot de Navarre, being a native of Havana, needed a hot-house temperature. This he found indoors, but the house was surrounded by large gardens, divided up by palings through which a cat could easily slip, and planted with big trees in which hosts of birds twittered and sang; and sometimes Pierrot, taking advantage of an open door, would go out hunting of an evening and run over the dewy grass and flowers. He would then have to wait till morning to be let in again, for although he might come mewing under the windows, his appeal did not always wake the sleepers inside.

He had a delicate chest, and one colder night than usual he took a chill which soon developed into consumption. Poor Pierrot, after a year of coughing, became wasted and thin, and his coat, which formerly boasted such a snowy gloss, now put one in mind of the lustreless white of a shroud. His great limpid eyes looked enormous in his attenuated face. His pink nose had grown pale, and he would walk sadly along the sunny wall with slow steps, and watch the yellow autumn leaves whirling up in spirals. He looked as though he were reciting Millevoye's elegy.

There is nothing more touching than a sick animal; it submits to suffering with such gentle, pathetic resignation.

Everything possible was done to try and save Pierrot. He had a very clever doctor who sounded him and felt his pulse. He ordered him asses' milk, which the poor creature drank willingly enough out of his little china saucer. He lay for hours on my knee like the ghost of a sphinx, and I could feel the bones of his spine like the beads of a rosary under my fingers. He tried to respond to my caresses with a feeble purr which was like a death rattle.

When he was dying he lay panting on his side, but with a supreme effort he raised himself and came to me with dilated eyes in which there

[88]

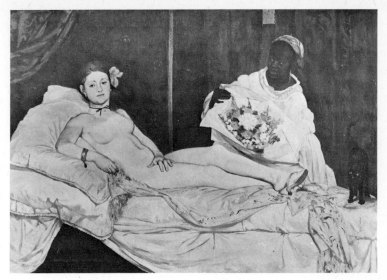

Olympia, Edouard Manet (*Musée du Louvre, Paris*)

was a look of intense supplication. This look seemed to say: 'Cannot you save me, you who are a man?' Then he staggered a short way with eyes already glazing, and fell down with such a lamentable cry, so full of despair and anguish, that I was pierced with silent horror.

He was buried at the bottom of the garden under a white rosebush which still marks his grave.

Seraphita died two or three years later of diphtheria, again which no science could prevail.

She rests not far from Pierrot. With her the white dynasty became extinct, but not the family. To this snow-white pair were born three kittens as black as ink.

Let him explain this mystery who can.

Just at that time Victor Hugo's *Misérables* was in great vogue, and the names of the characters in the novel were on everyone's lips. I called the two male kittens Enjolras and Gavroche, while the little female received the name of Eponine.

They were perfectly charming in their youth. I trained them like dogs to fetch and carry a bit of paper crumpled into a ball, which I threw for them. In time they learnt to fetch it from the tops of cupboards, from

[89]

behind chests or from the bottom of tall vases, out of which they would pull it very cleverly with their paws. When they grew up they disdained such frivolous games, and acquired that calm philosophic temperament which is the true nature of cats.

To people landing in America in a slave colony all negroes are negroes, and indistinguishable from one another. In the same way, to careless eyes, three black cats are three black cats; but attentive observers make no such mistake. Animal physiognomy varies as much as that of men, and I could distinguish perfectly between those faces, all three as black as Harlequin's mask, and illuminated by emerald disks shot with gold.

Enjolras was by far the handsomest of the three. He was remarkable for his great leonine head and big ruff, his powerful shoulders, long back and splendid feathery tail. There was something theatrical about him, and he seemed to be always posing like a popular actor who knows he is being admired. His movements were slow, undulating and majestic. He put each foot down with as much circumspection as if he were walking on a table covered with Chinese bric-à-brac or Venetian glass. As to his character, he was by no means a stoic, and he showed a love of eating which that virtuous and sober young man, his namesake, would certainly have disapproved. Enjolras would undoubtedly have said to him, like the angel to Swedenborg: 'You eat too much.'

I humoured this gluttony, which was as amusing as a gastronomic monkey's, and Enjolras attained a size and weight seldom reached by the domestic cat. It occurred to me to have him shaved poodle-fashion, so as to give the finishing touch to his resemblance to a lion.

We left him his mane and a big tuft at the end of his tail, and I would not swear that we did not give him mutton-chop whiskers on his haunches like those Munito wore. Thus tricked out, it must be confessed he was much more like a Japanese monster than an African lion. Never was a more fantastic whim carved out of a living animal. His shaven skin took odd blue tints, which contrasted strangely with his black mane.

Gavroche, as though desirous of calling to mind his namesake in the novel, was a cat with an arch and crafty expression of countenance. He was smaller than Enjolras, and his movements were comically quick and brusque. In him absurd capers and ludicrous postures took the place of the banter and slang of the Parisian *gamin*. It must be confessed that Gavroche had vulgar tastes. He seized every possible occasion to leave the drawing-room in order to go and make up parties in the back-yard, or even in the street, with stray cats, '*De naissance quelconque et de sang peu prouvé*', in which doubtful company he completely forgot his dignity as cat of Havana, son of Don Pierrot de Navarre, grandee of Spain of the first order, and of the aristocratic and haughty Doña Seraphita.

Sometimes in his truant wanderings he picked up emaciated comrades, lean with hunger, and brought them to his plate of food to give them a treat in his good-natured, lordly way. The poor creatures, with ears laid back and watchful side-glances, in fear of being interrupted in their free meal by the broom of the housemaid, swallowed double, triple, and quadruple mouthfuls, and, like the famous dog Siete-Aguas (seven waters) of Spanish *posadas* (inns), they licked the plate as clean as if it had been washed and polished by one of Gerard Dow's or Mieris's Dutch housewives.

Seeing Gavroche's friends reminded me of a phrase which illustrates one of Gavarni's drawings, '*Ils sont jolis les amis dont vous êtes susceptible d'aller avec!*' ('Pretty kind of friends you like to associate with!')

But that only proved what a good heart Gavroche had, for he could easily have eaten all the food himself.

The cat named after the interesting Eponine was more delicate and slender than her brothers. Her nose was rather long, and her eyes slightly oblique, and green as those of Pallas Athene, to whom Homer always applied the epithet of $\gamma\lambda\alpha\nu\kappa\varpi\pi\iota\varsigma$. Her nose was of velvety black, with the grain of a fine Périgord truffle; her whiskers were in a perpetual state of agitation, all of which gave her a peculiarly expressive countenance. Her superb black coat was always in motion, and was watered and shot with shadowy markings. Never was there a more sensitive, nervous, electric animal. If one stroked her two or three times in the dark, blue sparks would fly crackling out of her fur.

Eponine attached herself particularly to me, like the Eponine of the novel to Marius, but I, being less taken up with Cosette than that handsome young man, could accept the affection of this gentle and devoted cat, who still shares the pleasures of my suburban retreat, and is the inseparable companion of my hours of work.

She comes running up when she hears the front-door bell, receives the visitors, conducts them to the drawing-room, talks to them – yes, talks to them – with little chirruping sounds, that do not in the least resemble the language cats use in talking to their own kind, but which simulate the articulate speech of man. What does she say? She says in the clearest way, 'Will you be good enough to wait till monsieur comes down? Please look at the pictures, or chat with me in the meantime, if that will amuse you.' Then when I come in she discreetly retires to an armchair or a corner of the piano, like a well-bred animal who knows what is correct in good society. Pretty little Eponine gave so many proofs of intelligence, good disposition and sociability, that by common consent she was raised to the dignity of a *person*, for it was quite evident that she was possessed of higher reasoning power than mere instinct. This dignity conferred on her the privilege of eating at table like a person instead of out of a saucer in a corner of the room like an animal.

So Eponine had a chair next to me at breakfast and dinner, but on account of her small size she was allowed to rest her two front paws on the edge of the table. Her place was laid, without spoon or fork, but she had her glass. She went right through dinner dish by dish, from soup to dessert, waiting for her turn to be helped, and behaving with such propriety and nice manners as one would like to see in many children. She made her appearance at the first sound of the bell, and on going into the dining-room one found her already in her place, sitting up in her chair with her paws resting on the edge of the table-cloth, and seeming to offer you her little face to kiss, like a well-brought-up little girl who is affectionately polite towards her parents and elders.

As one finds flaws in diamonds, spots on the sun, and shadows on perfection itself, so Eponine, it must be confessed, had a passion for fish. She shared this in common with all other cats. Contrary to the Latin proverb, '*Catus amat pisces, sed non vult tingere plantas*,' she would willingly have dipped her paw into the water if by so doing she could have pulled out a trout or a young carp. She became nearly frantic over fish, and, like a child who is filled with the expectation of dessert, she sometimes rebelled at her soup when she knew (from previous investigations in the kitchen) that fish was coming. When this happened she was not helped, and I would say to her coldly: 'Mademoiselle, a person who is not hungry for soup cannot be hungry for fish,' and the dish would be pitilessly carried away from under her nose. Convinced that matters were serious, greedy Eponine would swallow her soup in all haste, down to the last drop, polishing off the last crumb of bread or bit of macaroni, and would then turn round and look at me with pride, like someone who has conscientiously done his duty. She was then given her portion, which she consumed with great satisfaction, and after tasting of every dish in turn, she would finish up by drinking a third of a glass of water.

When I am expecting friends to dinner Eponine knows there is going to be a party before she sees the guests. She looks at her place, and if she sees a knife and fork by her plate she decamps at once and seats herself on a music-stool, which is her refuge on these occasions.

Let those who deny reasoning powers to animals explain if they can

[92]

this little fact, apparently so simple, but which contains a whole series of inductions. From the presence near her plate of those implements which man alone can use, this observant and reflective cat concludes that she will have to give up her place for that day to a guest, and promptly proceeds to do so. She never makes a mistake; but when she knows the visitor well she climbs on his knee and tries to coax a tit-bit out of him by her pretty caressing ways.

Cat

ALAN BROWNJOHN

Sometimes I am an unseen
marmalade cat, the friendliest colour,
making off through a window without permission,
pacing along a broken-glass wall to the greenhouse,
jumping down with a soft, four-pawed thump,
finding two inches open of the creaking door
with the loose brass handle,
slipping impossibly in,

[93]

Cat at Foxes' Bait, photo D. N. Dalton (*Natural History Photographic Agency*)

flattening my fur at the hush and touch of the sudden warm air,
avoiding the tiled gutter of slow green water,
skirting the potted nests of tetchy cactuses,
and sitting with my tail flicked
skilfully underneath me, to sniff
the azaleas   the azaleas   the azaleas.

Rhymes for the Nursery (*1839*)

Pussy-cat Mew

Pussy-cat Mew jumped over a coal,
And in her best petticoat burnt a great hole.
Pussy-cat Mew shall have no more milk
Till she has mended her gown of silk.

[94]

Kitty: How to Treat Her

I like little Pussy, her coat is so warm,
And if I don't hurt her she'll do me no harm;
So I'll not pull her tail, nor drive her away,
But Pussy and I very gently will play.

Ten Little Mice

Ten little mice sat down to spin;
Pussy passed by, and just looked in,
'What are you doing, my jolly ten?'
'We're making coats for gentlemen.'
'Shall I come in and cut your threads?'
'No! No! Mistress Pussy – you'd bite off our heads.'

The Graham Children, William Hogarth (*Tate Gallery, London*)

[95]

From *The Cat by the Fire*

LEIGH HUNT

POOR Pussy! she looks up at us again, as if she thanked us for those vindications of dinner; and symbolically gives a twist of a yawn and a lick of her whiskers. Now she proceeds to clean herself all over, having a just sense of the demands of her elegant person – beginning judiciously with her paws, and fetching amazing tongues at her hind-hips. Anon, she scratches her neck with a foot of rapid delight, leaning her head towards it, and shutting her eyes, half to accommodate the action of the skin, and half to enjoy the luxury. She then rewards her paws with a few more touches; look at the action of her head and neck, how pleasing it is, the ears pointed forward, and the neck gently arching to and fro. Finally, she gives a sneeze, and another twist of mouth and whiskers, and then, curling her tail towards her front claws, settles herself on her hind quarters, in an attitude of bland meditation ...

She is a sprightly cat, hardly past her youth; so, happening to move the fringe of the rug a little with our foot, she darts out a paw, and begins plucking it and inquiring into the matter, as if it were a challenge to play, or something lively enough to be eaten. What a graceful action of that foot of hers, between delicacy and petulance! – combining something of a thrust out, a beat and a scratch. There seems even something of a little bit of fear in it, as if just enough to provoke her courage, and give her the excitement of a sense of hazard. We remember being much amused with seeing a kitten manifestly making a series of experiments upon the patience of its mother – trying how far the latter would put up with positive bites and thumps. The kitten ran at her every moment, gave her a knock or a bite of the tail; then ran back again, to recommence the assault. The mother sat looking at her, as if betwixt tolerance and admiration, to see how far the spirit of the family was inherited by her sprightly offspring. At length, however, the 'little Pickle' presumed too far, and the mother, lifting up her paw, and meeting her at the very nick of the moment, gave her one of the most unsophisticated boxes on the ear we ever beheld. It sent her rolling half over the room, and made her come to the most ludicrous pause, with the oddest little look of premature and wincing meditation ...

At the Zoo

MARK TWAIN

In the great Zoological Gardens [of Marseilles] we found specimens of all the animals the world produces, I think … The boon companion of the colossal elephant was a common cat! This cat had a fashion of climbing up the elephant's hind legs, and roosting on his back. She would sit up there, with her paws curved under her breast, and sleep in the sun half the afternoon. It used to annoy the elephant at first and he would reach up and take her down, but she would go aft and climb up again. She persisted until she finally conquered the elephant's prejudices, and now they are inseparable friends. The cat plays about her comrade's forefeet or his trunk often, until dogs approach, and then she goes aloft out of danger. The elephant has annihilated several dogs lately, that pressed his companion too closely.

The Family Cat

ROY FULLER

This cat was bought upon the day
That marked the Japanese defeat;
He was anonymous and gay,
But timorous and not discreet.

Although three years have gone, he shows
Fresh sides of his uneven mind:
To us – fond, lenient – he grows
Still more eccentric and defined.

He is a grey, white-chested cat,
And barred with black along the grey;
Not large, and the reverse of fat,
His profile good from either way.

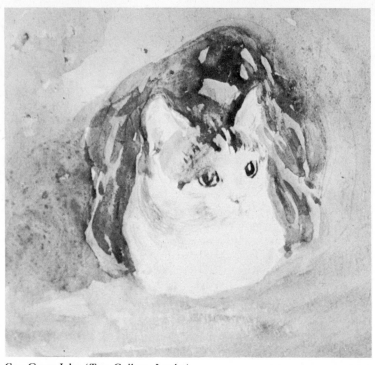

Cat, Gwen John (*Tate Gallery, London*)

The poet buys especial fish,
Which is made ready by his wife;
The poet's son holds out the dish:
They thus maintain the creature's life.

It's not his anniversary
Alone that's his significance:
In any case mortality
May not be thought of in his presence.

For brief as are our lives, more brief
Exist. Our stroking hides the bones,
Which none the less cry out in grief
Beneath the mocking, loving tones.

[98]

The Ballad of Tough Tom

PAUL GALLICO

That's right!
Those are tufts of my fur you're looking at.
What about it?
You don't see the other cat, do you?
What are a few hairs
Compared to an ear?
I didn't get the whole of his off
Because by then he was already heading south,
Having had enough.
But it was eminently satisfactory.
My name is Tough Tom,
And I am King of the Car Park.
When the sun shines
It warms the hoods of the cars for us.
We like that.
We lie on them.
Sometimes we get chased because
We leave footmarks on the cars,
But most of the time nobody bothers,
We have our own crowd that comes here
To sun.
But I say who does and who doesn't.
See?
Because I'm King of the Car Park.
So one day this stranger walks up and says,
'What's your name?'
So I says, 'Tough Tom
And I'm King of the Car Park. What's yours?'
And he says, 'Tough Charlie, and I guess
You ain't King of the Car Park anymore.'
'Oh, I get it,' I says, 'You're looking for a little action.'
'How did you guess?' says Tough Charlie.
I'm measuring him up in the meantime
And he's a lot of cat.

Tough Tom, photo Osamu Nishikawa

Yellow and white.
Yellow is a colour I ain't partial to.
And although I wasn't looking for trouble that morning,
Like now by being King of the Car Park,
It was up to me to oblige. So I says,
'Shall we dispense with the preliminaries?
See now, like the growling
And the fluffing
And the humping up
And the exchange of insults?'
Waste of time
When you know you're going to mix.
'Okay by me,' says Tough Charlie, 'Let's go!'
And he's up and onto me, leading with his right.

Oh boy, a sucker punch.
But I guess I'm a little dopey,
Lying out in that hot sun,
On that warm hood
And maybe he's got a half a pound on me as well.
So I'm on my back before I know it,
And he just misses getting my eye out.
Tough Charlie he was all right.
I give my left on the end of his nose
And try a roll-over
But he's too smart for that
And goes for my eye again, only this time
I'm waiting for it.
He don't get the eye,
But I get his ear.
Brother!
We're all over the car,
Down on the ground,
And underneath,
And back up on top again,
With the gang sitting around
Waiting to see
Who is the King of the Car Park.
He gives me the raking kick
With the back legs.
That's when I lost all that fur
You see about.
But I've still got that ear,
And it's starting to come away.
Tough Tom and Tough Charlie
And the battle of the Car Park!
They'll sing about that one on the tiles
For many a night.
So I guess maybe Tough Charlie thinks it over,
That with only one ear
He ain't gonna do so good anymore
With the broads, and he says,
'Okay, so I was wrong. Leggo!
You're still King of the Car Park.'
So I had to laugh, and he's off

Fighting Cats (Museo del Prado, Madrid)

With what's left of his ear.
That's the story.
So now for a little clean-up.
I'm still Tough Tom,
King of the Car Park.

From *Jubilate Agno*

CHRISTOPHER SMART

For I will consider my Cat Jeoffrey.

For he is the servant of the Living God, duly and daily serving him.

For at the first glance of the glory of God in the East he worships in his way.

For this is done by wreathing his body seven times round with elegant quickness.

For then he leaps up to catch the musk, which is the blessing of God upon his prayer.

For he rolls upon prank to work it in.

For having done duty and received blessing he begins to consider himself.

For this he performs in ten degrees.

For first he looks upon his fore-paws to see if they are clean.

For secondly he kicks up behind to clear away there.

For thirdly he works it upon stretch with the fore-paws extended.

For fourthly he sharpens his paws by wood.

For fifthly he washes himself.

For sixthly he rolls upon wash.

For Seventhly he fleas himself, that he may not be interrupted upon the beat.

For Eighthly he rubs himself against a post.

For Ninthly he looks up for his instructions.

For Tenthly he goes in quest of food.

For having consider'd God and himself he will consider his neighbour.

For if he meets another cat he will kiss her in kindness.

For when he takes his prey he plays with it to give it a chance.

For one mouse in seven escapes by his dallying.

For when his day's work is done his business more properly begins.

For he keeps the Lord's watch in the night against the adversary.

For he counteracts the powers of darkness by his electrical skin & glaring eyes.

For he counteracts the Devil, who is death, by brisking about the life.

For in his morning orisons he loves the sun and the sun loves him.

For he is of the tribe of Tiger.

For the Cherub Cat is a term of the Angel Tiger.

For he has the subtlety and hissing of a serpent, which in goodness he suppresses.

For he will not do destruction, if he is well fed, neither will he spit without provocation.

For he purrs in thankfulness, when God tells him he's a good Cat.

For he is an instrument for the children to learn benevolence upon.

For every house is incomplete without him and a blessing is lacking in the spirit.

For the Lord commanded Moses concerning the cats at the departure of the Children of Israel from Egypt.

For every family had one cat at least in the bag.

For the English Cats are the best in Europe.

For he is the cleanest in the use of his fore-paws of any quadrupede.

For the dexterity of his defence is an instance of the love of God to him exceedingly.

[103]

For he is the quickest to his mark of any creature.

For he is tenacious of his point.

For he is a mixture of gravity and waggery.

For he knows that God is his Saviour.

For there is nothing sweeter than his peace when at rest.

For there is nothing brisker than his life when in motion.

For he is of the Lord's poor and so indeed is he called by benevolence perpetually – Poor Jeoffry! poor Jeoffry! the rat has bit thy throat.

For I bless the name of the Lord Jesus that Jeoffry is better.

For the divine spirit comes about his body to sustain it in complete cat.

For his tongue is exceedingly pure so that it has in purity what it wants in music.

For he is docile and can learn certain things.

For he can set up with gravity which is patience upon approbation.

For he can fetch and carry, which is patience in employment.

For he can jump over a stick which is patience upon proof positive.

Two Boys with Pets, unknown American artist (*Philadelphia Museum of Art, The Edgar William and Bernice Chrysler Garbisch Collection*)

[104]

For he can spraggle upon waggle at the word of command.

For he can jump from an eminence into his master's bosom.

For he can catch the cork and toss it again.

For he is hated by the hypocrite and miser.

For the former is afraid of detection.

For the latter refuses the charge.

For he camels his back to bear the first notion of business.

For he is good to think on, if a man would express himself neatly.

For he made a great figure in Egypt for his signal services.

For he killed the Ichneumon-rat very pernicious by land.

For his ears are so acute that they sting again.

For from this proceeds the passing quickness of his attention.

For by stroking of him I have found out electricity.

For I perceived God's light upon him both wax and fire.

For the Electrical fire is the spiritual substance, which God sends from
heaven to sustain the bodies both of man and beast.

For God has blessed him in the variety of his movements.

For, tho he cannot fly, he is an excellent clamberer.

For his motions upon the face of the earth are more than any other
quadrupede.

For he can tread to all the measures upon the music.

For he can swim for life.

For he can creep.

From *A Letter to his Daughter*

THEODORE ROOSEVELT

White House, 6th January 1903

Dear Kermit,

We felt very melancholy after you and Ted left and the house seemed
empty and lonely. But it was the greatest possible comfort to feel that
you both really have enjoyed school and are both doing well there.

Tom Quartz is certainly the cunningest kitten I have ever seen. He
is always playing pranks on Jack and I get very nervous lest Jack should
grow too irritated. The other evening they were both in the library –
Jack sleeping before the fire – Tom Quartz scampering about, an exceedingly playful little creature – which is about what he is. He would race

The Girl with Cat, Alfred Dehodencq (*Private Collection*)

across the floor, then jump upon the curtain or play with the tassel. Suddenly he spied Jack and galloped up to him. Jack, looking exceedingly sullen and shame-faced, jumped out of the way and got upon the sofa and around the table, and Tom Quartz instantly jumped upon him again. Jack suddenly shifted to the other sofa, where Tom Quartz again went after him. Then Jack started for the door, while Tom made a rapid turn under the sofa and around the table and just as Jack reached the door leaped on his hind-quarters. Jack bounded forward and away and the two went tandem out of the room – Jack not co-operating at all; and about five minutes afterwards Tom Quartz stalked solemnly back.

Another evening, the next Speaker of the House, Mr Cannon, an exceedingly solemn, elderly gentleman with chin whiskers, who certainly does not look to be of playful nature, came to call upon me. He is a great friend of mine, and we sat talking over what our policies for the session should be until about eleven o'clock and when he went away I accompanied him to the head of the stairs. He had gone about half-way down when Tom Quartz strolled by, his tail erect and very fluffy. He spied Mr Cannon going down the stairs, jumped to the conclusion that he was a playmate escaping, and raced after him, suddenly grasping him by the leg the way he does Archie and Quentin when they play hide and seek with him; then loosening his hold he tore downstairs ahead of Mr Cannon, who eyed him with an iron calm and not one particle of surprise ...

Striped Cat, Walter Bell Currie (*Crane Kalman Gallery*)

PART IV

Cat's Love

Esther's Tomcat

TED HUGHES

Daylong this tomcat lies stretched flat
As an old rough mat, no mouth and no eyes.
Continual wars and wives are what
Have tattered his ears and battered his head.

Like a bundle of old rope and iron
Sleeps till blue dusk. Then reappear
His eyes, green as ringstones: he yawns wide red,
Fangs fine as a lady's needle and bright.

A tomcat sprang at a mounted knight,
Locked round his neck like a trap of hooks
While the knight rode fighting its clawing and bite.
After hundreds of years the stain's there

On the stone where he fell, dead of the tom:
That was at Barnborough. The tomcat still
Grallochs odd dogs on the quiet,
Will take the head clean off your simple pullet,

Is unkillable. From the dog's fury,
From gunshot fired point-blank he brings
His skin whole, and whole
From owlish moons of bekittenings

Among ashcans. He leaps and lightly
Walks upon sleep, his mind on the moon.
Nightly over the round world of men,
Over the roofs go his eyes and outcry.

Cat and Lady

PAUL VERLAINE

(translated by Arthur Symons)

They were at play, she and her cat,
And it was marvellous to mark
The white paw and the white hand pat
Each other in the deepening dark.

The stealthy little lady hid
Under her mittens' silken sheath
Her deadly agate nails that thrid
The silk-like dagger points of death.

The cat purred primly and drew in
Her claws that were of steel filed thin:
The devil was in it all the same.

And in the boudoir, while a shout
Of laughter in the air rang out,
Four sparks of phosphor shone like flame.

Nature Notes: Cats

LOUIS MACNEICE

Incorrigible, uncommitted,
They leavened the long flat hours of my childhood,
Subtle, the opposite of dogs,
And, unlike dogs, capable
Of flirting, falling, and yawning anywhere,
Like women who want no contract
But going their own way
Make the way of their lovers lighter.

[112]

Woman with a Cat, Edouard Manet (*Tate Gallery, London*)

The Jealous One

GILES GORDON

THEY stood at the threshold, the lintel above their heads, like the blade of a guillotine. Hand in hand, they would have been stunned as they waited there, had the blade fallen, as they felt each other, as they looked at the faces that looked at them. But their end was not thus ordained at this moment in time. Their new life had just begun.

They entered the room in which the reception was being held (the room that was to become the bedroom, if not the bridal chamber), she in white, he in – mainly – black.

Ninety-seven faces were turned towards the door, not expectantly, confidently. Some of them forgot to hold their smiles. All were bored, most without knowing it.

Her lips were smeared red, cherry wet. Not a hair on his usually unruly scalp was out of place. They smiled – at those who smiled at them, at the room itself, at the pictures on the wall, at the mirror (if they could see themselves in it!), at the memory and anticipation of the bed. Now they were inside the room, they smiled at each other. Edward. Angela.

From a place known to him but not to them, the cat smiled.

'Please ... Kiss each other. Yes, like that. Just like that. Thank you. Hold it.'

Flash. A premonition of lightning. Someone looked up at the ceiling, that had become sky, that had become blue. An aircraft glittered past the bright sun. They rubbed their eyes. Inside the room again.

'Thank you, Mr and Mrs ... em ... yes, Mr and Mrs. Ha!'

'A family group. We must have a family group.'

The individuals were assembled, pushed together, smiled (again) without being persuaded to do so.

Flash. A premonition of blinding. Staggering about in the darkness, unable to see the sun that beat down so sweatily.

The sixteen people in the portrait tumbled apart, moved away from each other, avoiding the honey pot. Laughter reverberated as the two pairs of lips touched again. Peck, peck. Snap. Already they had memories to treasure, to store up and misinterpret. Their mouths glued together. Gobble, gobble. Held. After the shot.

Woman with Cat, Alexander Archipenko (*Kunstmuseum, Düsseldorf*)

Champagne glasses were raised in the direction of the heavens; hard, dry, curranty wedding cake was washed down.

The cat was almost sick, would have been had Edward not forgotten to feed him that morning, before he left the house in such a rush amidst so much clatter and turmoil. The beginning of the end, the first time in four years he'd forgotten to feed him.

There were eighty – two hundred – people in the room. Parents, in-laws, aunts, cousins, nephews, a step-brother, bridesmaids, sisters, colleagues from work, a grand-parent, a school-friend not encountered for six years, a best man (a brother), vague distant relatives not seen or even spoken of previously, Angela's ballet mistress (her legs were muscular but no varicose veins apparent to the naked eye), Edward's sometime stamp collector friend. The I-thee-wed man, imagining himself a bishop, was present in the flesh but not in the spirit.

'Hold it.'

Another caught-in-the-act job.

[115]

Puss in Boots, Gustave Doré

The laughter ceased. Sssh ... Flash. The laughter built up again. The cat nipped an ankle, but when he-who-was-nipped looked down there was no cat to be seen.

Shaking hands, eating, smiling, kissing, crying, drinking, oh the happy (unconsummated) scene, knew him (her) when he (she) was so high, so low. Always been pretty (ugly), has Angela. I know someone who'll be very jealous of him. Very jealous. Maternal tears into a scented, embroidered handkerchief. The cut of the cake, cutting the cake. Flash. Again. And again. His hand up her dress, no one (else) noticing, all eyes upon her face, the veil thrown back, abused. Her lips open, thrust apart, her face at the moment of orgasm (the camera doesn't lie), the cake popped in. A contraceptive pill, a wafer. Wired corks ricocheting across the room, hitting walls and ceiling, raining down on the guests like bullets. The happy couple.

The remark was not recorded, then or now, but someone said: Funny, a cat at a wedding.

Others noticed Edward's cat, those who knew him, knew his cat. The cat, surprisingly, believed that no one – least of all Edward, which was true – had noticed him.

And they cried, those who wore their emotions near to their eyes, after he was dead.

Rat-tat-tat-tat.

One bullet. In the forehead, in the temple. Goliath felled by David. Or some such comparison.

And he fell over in slow fast slow motion.

'A priest!'

The vicar had departed. He'd drunk the couple's health, stuffed his mouth with crumbling, flaky white icing, and left after ten minutes, the bishopric no nearer. Others to administer to, services to officiate at. You know? I do apologize. Beautiful wedding, thank you vicar.

His words were a little odd, as was his presence, as they'd been married at a registry office. He'd come along for history's sake.

Not a Catholic. Neither, obviously, were they. A bun in the ovary (orifice).

Edward checked the cake, the champagne, the guests, his wife. And they cried after he was dead. Fell over slow, slow, faster. Stop. No more movement. A pin didn't drop.

Then they began to crowd around, Angela alone not near him, having fled the scene of carnage and tragedy for what reason we can but speculate. A heartless girl, you think? Or an over-sensitive child?

[117]

Rat-tat-tat-tat.

They turned round, the guests, their heads moving as if they belonged to an immaculately drilled opera chorus. A generation ago, most of them might have crossed themselves. He fell, fell, fell. Who could have. Loved by everyone. Such a promising career. No enemies. Knew his father. Mafia? IRA? On his wedding day!

The cat stood by the door, a revolver in his left hand.

(Impossible. Cats have four legs, four paws; no hands. They do not stand on two legs, except occasionally when leaning against an upright surface, when they desire to reach a height a few feet or more above them. If a cat is said to stand on two legs, there must be an error. The animal seen thus cannot have been a cat.)

The revolver smoked, smouldered. Was hot. The cat tilted the barrel towards his green, oriental eyes; looked up the barrel. There was no bullet to be seen, only smoke coiling out of the muzzle.

The cat looked up from the revolver, at the wedding guests. His ego was wounded: no one was looking at him. They all looked at Edward, at the body.

'Do not panic,' said the cat, in a loud, toneless voice.

(Impossible. Cats do not speak. Their vocal chords are different in kind from those of humans. I never thought, never imagined, that the day would come when we would be able to understand each other, so-called cats and so-called humans.)

'Do not panic,' said the cat, and the figures caught in the act of bending over the recumbent (now dead) body of the groom turned – as if caught with their trousers round their ankles – to look at him from whom emanated the voice, the words. They could see nobody, nobody again in the act of making a public utterance.

There were three people bending over the corpse. His bride of less than an hour (presumably having had second thoughts about where her duty lay); Dr Cole, a physician friend on the groom's side of the family; and Angela's mother.

'There's nobody there,' said Mrs Ankarah (Angela's mama; her present husband – not at the wedding – not being Angela's father).

'There's nobody there,' repeated Mrs Ankarah, having risen to her feet, and peered short-sightedly towards the entrance of the room where stood (only) the cat. Everyone in the room looked towards the door, as that was where the voice undoubtedly spoke from, except for the dead Edward.

Such fools, thought the cat. They don't even notice a pussy when he's holding a smoking revolver.

[118]

The cat waved the revolver, determined to attract attention. Would he have to kill them all before they saw him? And then who would notice?

Dr Cole was bending over the recent Edward, undoing buttons. He had undone so many, yet there still seemed more to undo than there had been at the beginning. Why was he trying to expose what he was trying to expose? Had he not felt the heart, known it was not beating?

Angela was weeping, shaking her head, willing the mascara to run. The tragic heroine, the wronged bride, the lustful widow – of all this she still knew nothing. She would have the photographs.

'There's nobody there,' repeated Mrs Ankarah.

As unintelligent as she looks, thought the cat. He slunk forward, towards the family pietà attended by family doctor. A path was cleared for him, the funeral guests moved aside to let him through without giving the impression that they were moving, for him or for anyone. He was grateful for this, as it added to his dignity. He *could* have gone through their legs, but he'd had to have crawled.

He stood next to the body. And spoke:

'I knew Edward more ... intimately than any of you did. He had no right to marry Sonia.'

A few murmurs. Now they saw who was speaking, who was holding a revolver. It had ceased to smoke.

'Angela,' said her mother. 'We thought of Sonia but decided against.'

'Mother!' screamed and sobbed the wronged bride, if screaming and sobbing can be accomplished simultaneously.

'What's in a name?' said the cat, shrugging his shoulders. 'I'm called just pussy, and I get by.'

There was an indrawing of breath throughout the room. Outrageous. Appalling. Wicked. Scandalous. Should be put down. This moment. Dangerous animal.

The mourners moved away from the body, perhaps (but unlikely, as Edward was dead; though nobody as yet had said so) to allow it to breathe, perhaps afraid of the cat. The cat stood, one eye on the hundred, two hundred people in what had been, would be again, the centre of the house, the room of the bed; the other on his Edward.

Lazarus-like, if Edward desired sufficiently to return to life, thought the cat, to prove that his heart hadn't ceased to breathe, this was his moment. The cat willed him to live. But there was one provision; and Edward knew it; and knew that the cat knew that he knew. He would have to choose – Angela, or pussy.

Until this moment (he was thinking in death), Edward hadn't realized what the choice was; that there *was* a choice. Now he understood everything, certainly why his beloved pussy had shot him. How thoughtless he'd been, how insensitive. But why not both? He could make Angela understand, he was sure of that. She was a pliable girl, and she could hardly feel challenged by a cat. But pussy wouldn't accept her – under any circumstances? Under none – that was clear.

Edward thought on the past, on the four ... idyllic years he and pussy had had. But what had happened had happened, pussy was behind him, Angela was in front. Couldn't the three of them live together, love together? He had no desire to hurt the cat, to cause him pain. No, Edward finally decided, he couldn't make the choice. It was too much for him. It was unfair of pussy to expect him to be able to make it. He would have to remain dead.

Rat-tat-tat-tat.

And he wheeled over in slow fast slow motion, grasping at what he'd never clutched. The icing of the wedding cake disintegrated in a cascade of powder, lifted into the air. The guests began coughing and choking. His body brushed the floor lightly, as if trying to protect the carpet. There was no blood to be seen.

The guests began talking to each other again, exchanging news of relatives some of them had thought long since dead. They resumed gorging themselves on the fare provided, downing glass after glass of champagne, to drown the memory of anything unpleasant or distasteful that might have happened.

Edward – still on the ground; on the ground not to rise again – crawled towards the door of the room on all fours, uncertain whether it was entrance or exit, the beginning or end. No one in the room appeared to notice his progress, except for the cat. Of course, except for the cat.

'I've phoned for an ambulance,' Dr Cole whispered to Mrs Ankarah; and she would have communicated the news to Edward's parents had they been alive. 'Told the ambulance people there was nothing for them to do, except take the body away.'

Mrs Ankarah nodded gratefully, and gulped. As long as Angela didn't think of a nunnery, or something extreme like that.

The cat watched the man crawling, looked down at him. Towards the door, towards the exit, about to leave his own wedding.

And they cried after he was dead.

As he died.

Rat-tat-tat-tat.

[120]

On the Prowl, Henry Rogers (*Jellinek & Sampson*)

I, Edward Anigram, dearly beloved husband of Angela Ankarah Anigram, leave all my worldly possessions to my wife, and the recesses of my mind to pussy (my cat), who has been my sensual adviser and consort for so many seasons. As I draw up this will, I sincerely wish it were I who were dying, not he ...

But it is, Edward, it is, thought pussy; and I have killed you.

No human being would have done it, only an insensitive, jealous animal.

The cat donned dark glasses, so that no one could see his eyes. All those people might be mourning Edward's end; what did they imagine that he, Edward's lover, felt? No one could see if he had an expression of remorse, or of sorrow, on his visage. Angela wondered, and he sensed her thought and was grateful, whether he regretted what he had done; did he care; could he feel; did he realize that ... she had loved, that she still loved Edward? Why didn't he stick to catching mice or rats, or if he must sparrows? Though certainly not budgies, which Edward had told her he'd once done when some child's pet bird had been released temporarily from its gilded prison, then forgotten until too late.

The cat decided to instil in what passed for Angela's mind the idea that he, pussy, had loved Edward, and allow her mind to play on that concept.

Someone, not Dr Cole, dialled 999. Ambulance – *and* police. Then you have to make two separate calls, Mrs. Yes, to the same number.

Someone else dialled 999.

The cat purred, but no one listened. He'd triumphed in adversity. They were all tense, neurotic, bewildered, the guests. They'd come to a wedding, found themselves witnesses to a murder of a peculiar kind. Witnesses, yet none of them had seen it happen. There'd been a cat, some thought with a gun, but the idea was ... ridiculous.

'Murder?' said a would-be husband's of Angela's. 'Don't you think murder's rather a strong word?'

Rat-tat-tat-tat.

The angle from immediately inside the door to where Edward and Angela stood, tickling each other's clammy palms.

'Look, there's my beloved pussy,' said Edward to his bride.

But he didn't say that, he hadn't referred to the cat at all. He might not have existed. What would my life be without Edward, thought the cat, and though the intention presumably was – Edward hadn't confided – that he and Mrs Edward would live in the house together, the three of them, well, it wouldn't be the same. He knew they'd do things together, the two of them, have a relationship, maybe even a child, who would tweak him, pull his tail, worse still his whiskers. Such a ghastly domestic scene must be pre-empted, thought pussy as bride and groom arrived at their reception. Better to do it now than when the heart (his, hers) grows fond.

The cat understood certain things about man, not others. Had Edward even alluded to him once, given him a credit, he wouldn't then have asked to be centre of the stage. A backroom boy, he'd have been satisfied. If Edward was fit to wed Angela today, the relationship that had existed between him and pussy had to be important. If no one else knew this, he and Edward did; and now Angela knew.

Rat-tat-tat-tat.

Edward lay down and died. Angela ran from the room, her mouth open in a soundless scream that encompassed her whole life up to that moment. Out of the room, across the hall, into the bedroom ... But the bedroom was the room in which the guests were, where Edward was. The cat rose up in front of her. Larger, larger, larger. As he stretched out two paws towards her, to hold her body, she ... fainted.

Edward and he knew things, between each other, intuitively. It wasn't

[122]

as if they had talked together, had understood each other's minds. Nothing so advanced as that. Empathy, maybe; logic, no. Therefore.

His eyes were closed at the moment the bullet hit him. Of course he had known it was coming. He'd known his affair with the cat could only be ended by his marrying somebody; and he loved Angela.

And they cried after he was dead.

The ambulance men removed the body, on a stretcher, and covered it with a red blanket as if to compensate for the lack of blood shed.

The police officers took a few notes, asked a few questions, removed the revolver, holding it on a cloth so as not to smudge the paw-prints.

Thank you all for your cooperation. Desperately sorry. The worst case of its kind I've come across. Thank you. Try to forget it.

Hands shaken, heads bowed. The caterers cleared up the dead bottles, the cardboard plates, the crumbs, the remaining sandwiches, biscuits, melted ice-cream, jelly, the accoutrements of a wedding.

Angela couldn't leave.

'Come along, my poor love,' said her mother, when everyone else had gone.

She shook her head, her face damp and dirty, her mind confused, her world in turmoil.

'I'm staying.'

Her mother tried to pull her by the elbow, Angela drew herself away.

'I want to stay.'

'Not here. On your own. In this house.'

'In our house. In my house.'

She smiled at her mother, stood close beside her.

'Mother, please leave me here for a little while. On my own. I want to be alone. To think. Just to be here.'

'Very well. But don't be long; not too long.'

Mrs Ankarah smiled at her daughter, Angela smiled back. She watched her mother walk through the house, stood for a few seconds following her progress out of the front door, down the garden path. Her mother didn't look back, and Angela closed the front door.

She stood, leaning against the inside of the door for half a minute, her eyes closed. Then she began to walk towards the bedroom.

The cat was standing there, waiting for her. She knew he would be. It was what she wanted, what she had learned to want.

She smiled at pussy. He was purring.

'Angela,' he said.

'Edward,' she said.

[123]

To My Lord Buckhurst, Very Young, Playing with a Cat

MATTHEW PRIOR

The am'rous Youth, whose tender Breast
Was by his darling Cat possest,
Obtain'd of VENUS his Desire,
Howe'er irregular his Fire:
Nature the Pow'r of Love obey'd:
The Cat became a blushing Maid;
And, on the happy Change, the Boy
Imploy'd his Wonder and his Joy.

   Take care, O beauteous Child, take care,
Lest Thou prefer so rash a Pray'r:
Nor vainly hope, the Queen of Love
Will e'er thy Fav'rite's Charms improve.
O quickly from her Shrine retreat;
Or tremble for thy Darling's Fate.

   The Queen of Love, who soon will see
Her own ADONIS live in Thee,
Will lightly her first Loss deplore;
Will easily forgive the Boar:
Her Eyes with Tears no more will flow;
With jealous Rage her Breast will glow:
And on her tabby Rival's Face
She deep will mark her new Disgrace.

Chalk sketch, Léopold Louis Boilly (*Achenbach Foundation, California Palace of the Legion of Honor, San Francisco*)

the song of mehitabel

DON MARQUIS

– the song is written by archy who is a cockroach who writes free verse
on an office typewriter; mehitabel is an alley cat –

this is the song of mehitabel
of mehitabel the alley cat
as i wrote you before boss
mehitabel is a believer
in the pythagorean
theory of the transmigration
of the souls and she claims
that formerly her spirit
was incarnated in the body
of cleopatra
that was a long time ago
and one must not be
surprised if mehitabel
has forgotten some of her
more regal habits

i have had my ups and downs
but wotthehell wotthehell
yesterday sceptres and crowns
fried oysters and velvet gowns
and today i herd with bums
but wotthehell wotthehell

i wake the world from sleep
as i caper and sing and leap
when i sing my wild free tune
wotthehell wotthehell
under the blear eyed moon
i am pelted with cast off shoon
but wotthehell wotthehell

do you think that i would change
my present freedom to range
for a castle or moated grange
wotthehell wotthehell
cage me and i d go frantic
my life is so romantic
capricious and corybantic
and i m toujours gai toujours gai

Feline, Alan Durst (*Tate Gallery, London*)

[127]

Blue Eyes, Martin Leman (*Private Collection*)

i know that i am bound
for a journey down the sound
in the midst of a refuse mound
but wotthehell wotthehell
oh i should worry and fret
death and i will coquette
there s a dance in the old dame yet
toujours gai toujours gai

[128]

i once was an innocent kit
wotthehell wotthehell
with a ribbon my neck to fit
and bells tied onto it
o wotthehell wotthehell
but a maltese cat came by
with a come hither look in his eye
and a song that soared to the sky
and wotthehell wotthehell
and i followed adown the street
the pad of his rhythmical feet
o permit me again to repeat
wotthehell wotthehell

my youth i shall never forget
but there s nothing i really regret
wotthehell wotthehell
there s a dance in the old dame yet
toujours gai toujours gai

the things that i had not ought to
i do because i ve gotto
wotthehell wotthehell
and i end with my favourite motto
toujours gai toujours gai

boss sometimes i think
that our friend mehitabel
is a trifle too gay

> archy

mehitabel s extensive past

DON MARQUIS

mehitabel the cat claims that
she has a human soul
also and has transmigrated
from body to body and it

[129]

may be so boss you
remember i told you she accused
herself of being cleopatra once i
asked her about antony

anthony who she asked me are
you thinking of that
song about rowley and gammon and
spinach heigho for anthony rowley

no i said mark antony the
great roman the friend of
caesar surely cleopatra you
remember j caesar

listen archy she said i
have been so many different
people in my time and met
so many prominent gentlemen i
wont lie to you or stall i
do get my dates mixed sometimes
think of how much i have had a
chance to forget and i have
always made a point of not
carrying grudges over
from one life to the next archy

i have been
used something fierce in my time but
i am no bum sport archy
i am a free spirit archy i
look on myself as being
quite a romantic character oh the
queens i have been and the
swell feeds i have ate
a cockroach which you are
and a poet which you used to be
archy couldn t understand
my feelings at having come
down to this i have
had bids to elegant feeds where poets

and cockroaches would
neither one be mentioned without a
laugh archy i have had
adventures but i
have never been an adventuress
one life up and the next life
down archy but always a lady
through it all and a
good mixer too always the
life of the party archy but never
anything vulgar always free footed
archy never tied down to
a job or housework yes looking
back on it all i can say is
i had some romantic
lives and some elegant times i
have seen better days archy but

Cat Eating a Bird, Pablo Picasso (*Photographie Giraudon*)

[131]

what is the use of kicking kid its
all in the game like a gentleman
friend of mine used to say
toujours gai kid toujours gai he
was an elegant cat he used
to be a poet himself and he made up
some elegant poetry about me and him

lets hear it i said and
mehitabel recited

persian pussy from over the sea
demure and lazy and smug and fat
none of your ribbons and bells for me
ours is the zest of the alley cat
over the roofs from flat to flat
we prance with capers corybantic
what though a boot should break a slat
mehitabel us for the life romantic
we would rather be rowdy and gaunt and free
and dine on a diet of roach and rat

roach i said what do you
mean roach interrupting mehitabel
yes roach she said that s the
way my boy friend made it up
i climbed in amongst the typewriter
keys for she had an excited
look in her eyes go on mehitabel i
said feeling safer and she
resumed her elocution

we would rather be rowdy and gaunt and free
and dine on a diet of roach and rat
than slaves to a tame society
ours is the zest of the alley cat
fish heads freedom a frozen sprat
dug from the gutter with digits frantic
is better than bores and a fireside mat
mehitabel us for the life romantic
when the pendant moon in the leafless tree
clings and sways like a golden bat

i sing its light and my love for thee
ours is the zest of the alley cat
missiles around us fall rat a tat tat
but our shadows leap in a ribald antic
as over the fences the world cries scat
mehitabel us for the life romantic

persian princess i don t care that
for your pedigree traced by scribes pedantic
our is the zest of the alley cat
mehitabel us for the life romantic

aint that high brow stuff
archy i always remembered it
but he was an elegant gent
even if he was a highbrow and a
regular bohemian archy him and
me went aboard a canal boat
one day and he got his head into
a pitcher of cream and couldn t get
it out and fell overboard
he come up once before he
drowned toujours gai kid he
gurgled and then sank for ever that
was always his words archy toujours
gai kid toujours gai i
have known some swell gents
in my time dearie

                                    archy

My cat and i

ROGER MCGOUGH

Girls are simply the prettiest things
My cat and i believe
And we're always saddened
When it's time for them to leave

[133]

Portrait of Pierre Loti, Henri Rousseau (*Kunsthaus, Zürich*)

We watch them titivating
(that often takes a while)
And though they keep us waiting
My cat & i just smile

We like to see them to the door
Say how sad it couldn't last
Then my cat and i go back inside
And talk about the past.

[134]

What Did You Do There?

HARVEY JACOBS

MARVIN Carton's affair with Eileen Vincent-Norman was complicated by a cat named Humphrey, a white cat that grew to enormous size after he was fixed.

When Eileen Vincent-Norman told Marvin Carton that Humphrey was 'altered' Marvin Carton was not only surprised, he was angry. The whole idea was outrageous. On the other hand, after the surgery, Humphrey stopped leaping onto Marvin Carton's back at embarrassing moments. And Marvin Carton no longer thought the great fluffy cat a threat to his privates. So, the action that first seemed to reveal a strange and dark part of Eileen Vincent-Norman's personality (fixer of cats), ultimately proved to be good common sense.

With Humphrey's new behaviour, a contented withdrawal, an occasional desire for a scratch on the belly, in contrast with a former male-volence and terrible energy, Marvin Carton found it easier and less complicated to lie naked with Eileen Vincent-Norman. He lost the need to keep alert for frenzied furry attack and to repress more rage when Eileen Vincent-Norman interpreted those feline assaults as 'cute' or 'darling'. Also he was less worried about having to carry paw marks on his sensitive back, or God knows where else, and explain those to his wife.

Even the cat syndrome that seemed so important to Eileen Vincent-Norman annoyed Marvin Carton less. The box of litter and cat-do in the bathroom, the bowls of fish, the rubber toys shaped like mice – all were easier to take after the traumatic operation. Marvin Carton was, in fact, freer to appreciate Eileen Vincent-Norman's delicious young beauty and sensual response. For a girl so young – she was hardly twenty – she knew so much, knew it with a flesh knowledge that was really splen-did and amazing. Marvin Carton, just past forty, felt her move against him and was renewed, sparks of human nourishment leapt between them, it was all very good from the first and better still since Humphrey's visit to the veterinarian.

One problem remained, it had been there all along, but since the undo-ing of Humphrey's equipment seemed to grow worse. The cat shed snow-falls of hair. Everything in Eileen Vincent-Norman's apartment was prey to cat-hair, white, long cat-hair. In the winter of their affair steam heat

[135]

and dry air filled her apartment with static electricity that made the hairs stand up and fly toward Marvin Carton's clothes. He was a magnet.

'You're getting prematurely grey,' was a joke of Eileen Vincent-Norman's as she ran over his business suit with a fuzz remover, or a band-aid, or a damp turkish towel.

Yes, winter was the worst time since Marvin Carton's suits were mostly blue. The hairs clung and covered his pants and jacket like graffiti. And because he always visited Eileen Vincent-Norman after work, he was always dressed in conservative clothes. He longed for summer and a new pale wardrobe – wash and wear garments of white or seersucker that would camouflage the cat hairs like soldiers in the bush.

The prevalence of Humphrey's shed hairs disturbed three aspects of Marvin Carton's affair. First, he could no longer simply rip off his clothes in abandon and leave them on the carpet while he carried Eileen Vincent-Norman to the bedroom or sofa. She liked it when he did that because of the spontaneity and because of Marvin Carton's easy disregard for the crease in his $200 Cardin pants. Now if he did anything but pause to hang his clothes they came up saturated with white. Even the hangers had cat-hair on them, impossible though that seemed. Second, because of the sheddings, Eileen Vincent-Norman had to de-fuzz Marvin Carton as he was about to leave for home. His pleasure in leaving her naked, sleepy, drowsing while he departed like a phantom after filling her with warmth and honey, was ruined by the necessary ritual act of having a roller of sticky tape run over him collar to cuffs. The abrupt return to reality not only broke the mood but led to practical conversation as to the ultimate dimensions of their sparkling relationship, how long it would last, whether it was right or wrong. Once Eileen Vincent-Norman asked Marvin Carton to stay a moment and help balance her cheque-book. He did, sitting at a bridge-table, and had to be rolled again because the table was full of cat. The third and most annoying problem was Marvin Carton's wife and daughter. They both had terrific eyes, better than 20–20, a joy to the optometrist. If there was a crumb in the house they could see it in darkness. Cat-hairs, white long cat-hairs on a blue suit, made them blink as if they were staring into sun. And despite Eileen Vincent-Norman's care, and Marvin Carton's pickings on the way home, a few of Humphrey's hairs always remained. It was impossible to get them all.

'Where have you been sitting?'

'Nowhere.'

'Look, Daddy. Another one. Whee!'

'Marvin, where *have* you been sitting?'

[136]

The Family, Gustaaf De Smet (*Musées royaux des Beaux-Arts, Brussels*)

'Now how the hell do I answer a question like that?'
'Daddy said hell. God will bite you.'
'Where does she learn things like that?'
'Look, Marvin. Under your arm.'
'This city is filthy.'
Because of all this, Marvin Carton had to change the rhythm of his visits to Eileen Vincent-Norman. He came later to her apartment and he left later. By leaving later he could get home after his child was sleeping and his wife was weary. He could slide through the darkened apartment,

into the bathroom, and de-fuzz himself of leftovers. The leftovers, two or three white strands each visit, he dropped cleverly into an unused laundry cabinet. If he threw them into the sink or the john they could form a clogging knot. Some plumber would come when the water rose and say something like, 'Did you drown a horse down here, lady?' to his wife. But the laundry cabinet, a metal built-in thing, was never used except to store old work-clothes. Some day, alone, Marvin Carton could clean out the multitudes of cat hairs and dispose of them quietly and efficiently.

Meanwhile, because of his later visits, he could see less of Eileen Vincent-Norman. To find an excuse for working until midnight was much more complicated than finding an excuse for coming home at ten. Visitors from out-of-town would not come in more than a few times a month. Eileen Vincent-Norman was very understanding. She never made trouble. She liked the affair with married Marvin Carton and was not possessive beyond the normal moments of clutch and hold. She did not want a permanent alliance, why should she, he was old enough to be her father. Marvin Carton adored the girl as well he might. She was worth the guilt feelings, the deceptions, the lies, even the cat-hairs. When he began to see less of her it was, curiously, at a time when he wanted to see more of her. And Marvin Carton did not want Eileen Vincent-Norman to think for a minute that he was growing tired of her. She was beautiful, nubile, intelligent, and superb in bed. Their sex woke him to new energy.

'I feel like a kid,' he would say to the immortal young girl. 'I feel like I came over a ridge and discovered the Pacific.'

'Thank you,' Eileen Vincent-Norman would say.

She even reminded him when it was time to go home. If he told her they had guests coming she set her alarm radio so he would be unpressured. And setting the alarm she always turned the radio to semi-classical music, not hard rock. And left ten minutes for rolling the tape over Marvin Carton's blue knit. She only asked about his wife occasionally, and then, her questions were never personal. That was a girl to be cherished, God knows, to be defended and treasured.

'At home one night, near four in the morning, Marvin Carton's wife woke him.

'I heard something,' she said.

'From upstairs,' Marvin Carton said, yawning.

'A meow.'

'From outside.'

[138]

'From the bathroom.'

'From the what?'

'I must have been dreaming.'

They went back to sleep.

It happened again the next night. Marvin Carton had been with Eileen Vincent-Norman earlier, and had made love with her three times. That was a lot after a full business day and he was depleted beyond his vitamin E. He hit the pillow and slept hard, dreaming of an elevator that went up and down a thousand times. His wife shook him awake and said, 'There is a meowing in the bathroom.'

Marvin Carton got up, went to investigate. Only a few hours before he had added a few strands of Humphrey's errant hair to the collection in the laundry cabinet. Now here he was checking out a mystical 'meow', fighting to keep conscious.

'There's nothing meowing. Lord, it must be plumbing. Or a neighbour's pussycat.'

'I suppose.'

Marvin Carton got back into bed, dreamed again, and was blasted awake by a cat shriek.

'From the yard. They must be mating.'

'It came from the bathroom.'

Their daughter was wakened too and already in the bathroom 'doing her business'.

'It's making me nervous,' said Marvin Carton's wife.

'Ah.'

Then their daughter came out, hiking up her pyjamas, holding a kitten.

'Mommy, Daddy, a pussy.'

The parents looked.

'The pussy came out of the laundry house,' their daughter said. 'Can I keep him?'

In the morning, Marvin Carton took two Librium. His wife decided the cat had somehow crawled in through a window and gotten into the cabinet, though she marvelled at its resourcefulness. Their daughter was assured she could keep the cat, it was time she had a pet other than a mangy turtle that said Welcome to Miami Beach on its back.

Marvin Carton continued the normal routine of his life. He continued to use the laundry cabinet to store Humphrey's hairs, which may have been a mistake since a month later another white pussycat wandered into the bedroom and climbed into the bed where he and his wife slept bottom to bottom.

Cat and Mirror, photo Lynwood M. Chace (*Frank W. Lane*)

'It's really some kind of miracle,' his wife said. 'What a darling.'

It was decided to keep the second cat as a companion to the first. This meant more litter, more fish, more water in the cup on the kitchen floor. And as the cats grew, it meant more fixing, a stiff bill from the veterinarian (he used the same veterinarian as Eileen Vincent-Norman who recommended him highly), subsequent larger cats and shedding of their own.

He never told Eileen Vincent-Norman that the operation was for his cats. He told her he had a friend whose cats needed the full treatment. He never mentioned the cats to Eileen Vincent-Norman in any shape, size or form. There was surely a spooky force at work, and he didn't want to upset the girl. Besides he was ashamed of himself. It had occurred to him that the cats, spinoffs of Humphrey, were somehow sent to do harm to his wife and daughter. Messengers from Eileen Vincent-Norman to dispose of competition so that she could have Marvin Carton for her own. That was ridiculous. The cats were nothing but loving. Besides, Eileen Vincent-Norman told Marvin Carton she was dating an accountant and that it might turn serious. There was never any doubt that if that happened their affair would turn to warm friendship and nothing more.

The upshot of two cats at home and one cat at Eileen Vincent-Norman's was that Marvin Carton's business suits were gardens of fuzz. He was forever having tape run over him or pulling at himself. Even his ivory summer suit and subsequent seersucker held the hairs. And the warm months passed too quickly. Before he knew it his wife told him,

'Marvin, you can't wear those light things any more. It's practically October.'

Now, back to darker fabrics, the cat-hair explosion was definitely a plague to be contended with. His boss had mentioned 'good grooming' more than once. The hairs became harder to remove. And one night, in the shower, washing Eileen Vincent-Norman's delicious love with Ivory soap, he noticed cat-hairs on his very body. And they were hard to get rid of. They hurt when he went at them. And left welts. So he stopped trying.

Six months later, Marvin Carton stopped wearing clothes. He was totally covered with a lush, Siamese growth, so clothes were redundant.

'You'd better comb yourself more carefully,' his wife said. And he did. He spent inordinate amounts of time combing and brushing and licking his pelt.

At work, his boss was forced to level with him.

'Marvin, I don't give a damn about a man's dress. But upstairs they do. And you're an executive. They don't want an abominable snowman walking around. You'll get a fine severance check. And you're vested in the pension plan. Of course, upon termination, you'll have to furnish your own Blue Cross.'

[141]

So Marvin Carton was unemployed. It never rains, it pours. Eileen Vincent-Norman fell in love with her accountant and told Marvin Carton that they could no longer sleep together. They had slept together little enough since his hair grew. He tickled and Eileen Vincent-Norman was turned off by her own giggles. Humphrey, on the other hand, was very friendly. Marvin Carton played with him on the floor, chasing a pimpled rubber ball and crunching cellophane from cigarette packages.

After a session with Humphrey he had to go home and play with his own cats, East and West they were named. It was quite exhausting. And Marvin Carton was concerned because he had heard his wife on the telephone with the veterinarian recommended by Eileen Vincent-Norman. They talked in whispers.

'I'm taking you downtown for some shots and a trim,' his wife said to Marvin Carton.

'Where?'

'To the vet. To the nice vet. He's promised to give you a collar and a bell if you behave yourself.'

'Shots and a trim? Is that all?'

'Certainly, dear.'

'A collar and a bell?'

'If you behave yourself.'

'Nothing more? Right?'

'Right. Would I kid you?'

'No.'

'The same vet we used before?'

'The same one. You'll feel at home with him, won't you?'

'Sure. Sure. No problem.'

'I've got some nice chicken parts for you.'

'Expensive chicken parts?'

'Yes. And champagne.'

'How come? Why the celebration?'

'No special reason,' his wife said.

'No special reason?'

'What reason would there be?'

'No reason.'

'That's what I said, dear,'

Marvin Carton jumped at a fly. There was something going on. He couldn't put his paw on it.

Woman Holding a White Pussy Cat, Sylvia Emmons (*Crane Kalman Gallery*)

PART V

Cat's Magic

Cat-Goddesses

ROBERT GRAVES

A perverse habit of cat-goddesses –
Even the blackest of them, black as coals
Save for a new moon blazing on each breast,
With coral tongues and beryl eyes like lamps,
Long-leggèd, pacing three by three in nines –
This obstinate habit is to yield themselves
In verisimilar love-ecstasies,
To tatter-eared and slinking alley-toms
No less below the common run of cats
Than they above it; which they do for spite,
To provoke jealousy – not the least abashed
By such gross-headed, rabbit-coloured litters
As soon they shall be happy to desert.

Black Cat, photo Kevin MacDonnell
(*Natural History Photographic Agency*)

[147]

Broomsticks

WALTER DE LA MARE

MISS Chauncey's cat, Sam, had been with her many years before she noticed anything unusual, anything *disturbing*, in his conduct. Like most cats who live under the same roof with but one or two humans, he had always been more sagacious than cats of a common household. He had learned Miss Chauncey's ways. He acted, that is, as nearly like a small mortal dressed up in a hairy coat as one could expect a cat to act. He was what is called an 'intelligent' cat.

But though Sam had learned much from Miss Chauncey, I am bound to say that Miss Chauncey had learned very little from Sam. She was a kind indulgent mistress; she could sew, and cook, and crochet, and make a bed, and read and write and cipher a little. And when she was a girl she used to sing 'Kathleen Mavourneen' to the piano. Sam, of course, could do nothing of this kind.

But then, Miss Chauncey could no more have caught and killed a mouse or a blackbird with her five naked fingers than she could have been Pope of Rome. Nor could she run up a six-foot brick wall, or leap clean from the hearth-mat in her parlour on to the shelf of her chimney-piece without disturbing a single ornament, or even tinkle one crystal glass-drop against another. Unlike Sam, she could not find her way in the dark, or by her sense of smell; or keep in good health by merely nibbling grass in the garden. If, moreover, as a little girl she had been held up by her feet and hands two or three feet above the ground and then dropped, she would have at once fallen plump on her back, whereas when Sam was only a three-month-old, he could have managed to twist clean about in the air in twelve inches and come down on his four feet as firm as a table.

While Sam, then, had learned a good deal from Miss Chauncey, she had learned nothing from him. And even if she had been willing to be taught, it is doubtful if she would ever have proved even a promising pupil. What is more, she knew much less about Sam than he knew about his mistress – until, at least, that afternoon when she was doing her hair in the glass. And then she could hardly believe her own eyes. It was a moment that completely changed her views about Sam – and nothing after that experience was ever quite the same again.

[148]

Young Woman Holding a Black Cat, Gwen John (*Tate Gallery, London*)

Sam had always been a fine upstanding creature, his fur jet-black and silky, his eyes a lambent green, even in sunshine, and at night a-glow like green topazes. He was now full seven years of age, and had an unusually powerful miaou. Living as he did quite alone with Miss Chauncey at Post Houses, it was natural that he should become her constant companion. For Post Houses was a singularly solitary house, standing almost in the middle of Haggurdsdon Moor, just where two wandering byways cross each other like the half-closed blades of a pair of shears or scissors.

It was a mile and a half from its nearest neighbour, Mr Cullings, the carrier; and yet another quarter of a mile from the village of Haggurdsdon. Its roads were extremely ancient. They had been sheep-tracks long before the Romans came to England and had cut *their* roads from shore to shore. But for many years past few travellers or carts or even sheep with their shepherd came Miss Chauncey's way. You could have gazed from her windows for hours together, even on a summer's day, without seeing so much as a tinker's barrow or a gipsy's van.

Post Houses, too, was perhaps the ugliest house there ever was. Its four corners stood straight up on the moor like a house of nursery bricks. From its flat roof on a clear day the eye could see for miles across the moor, Mr Cullings' cottage being out of sight in a shallow hollow. It had belonged to Miss Chauncey's ancestors for numbers of generations. Many people in Haggurdsdon indeed called it Chauncey's. And though in a great wind it was almost as full of noises as an organ, though it was a cold barn in winter and though another branch of the family had as far back as the seventies gone to live in the Isle of Wight, Miss Chauncey still remained faithful to its four walls. In fact she loved the ugly old place, for she had lived in it ever since she was a little girl with knicker-bockers showing under her skirts and pale-blue ribbon shoulder knots.

This fact alone made Sam's conduct the more reprehensible, for never cat had kinder mistress. Miss Chauncey herself was now about sixty years of age – fifty-three years older than Sam. She was five foot ten-and-a-half inches in height. On weekdays she wore black alpaca, and on Sundays a watered silk. Her large round steel spectacles straddling across her high nose gave her a look of being keen as well as cold. But truly she was neither. For even so stupid a man as Mr Cullings could take her in over the cartage charge of a parcel – just by looking tired or sighing as he glanced at his rough-haired, knock-kneed mare. And there was the warmest of hearts under her stiff bodice.

Being so far from the village, milk and cream were a little difficult, of course. But Miss Chauncey could deny Sam nothing – in reason. She paid a whole sixpence a week to a little girl called Susan Ard who brought these dainties from the nearest farm. They were dainties indeed, for though the grasses on Haggurdsdon Moor were of dark sour green, the cows that grazed on it gave an uncommonly rich milk, and Sam flourished on it. Mr Cullings called once a week on his round, and had a standing order to bring with him a few sprats or fresh herrings, or any other toothsome fish that was in season. Miss Chauncey would not even withhold her purse from expensive whitebait, if no other cheaper fish were procurable. And Mr Cullings would eye Sam fawning about his cartwheel, or gloating up at his dish, and say, ' 'Ee be a queer animal, shure enough; 'ee be a wunnerful queer animal, 'ee be.'

As for Miss Chauncey herself, she was a niggardly eater, though much attached to her tea. She made her own bread and biscuits. On Saturday a butcher-boy drove up in a striped apron. Besides which she was a wonderful manager. Her cupboards were full of homemade jams and bottled fruits and dried herbs – everything of that kind, for Post Houses had a nice long strip of garden behind it, surrounded by a high old yellow brick wall.

Quite early in life Sam, of course, had learned to know his mealtime – though how he 'told' it was known only to himself, for he never appeared even to glance at the face of the grandfather's clock on the staircase. He was punctual, particularly in his toilet, and a prodigious sleeper. He had learned to pull down the latch of the back door, if, in the months when an open window was not to be found, he wished to go out. Indeed at last he preferred the latch. He never slept on Miss Chauncey's patchwork quilt, unless his own had been placed over it. He was particular almost to a foppish degree in his habits, and he was no thief. He had a mew on one note to show when he wanted something to eat; a mew a semitone or two higher if he wanted drink (that is, cold water, for which he had a great taste); and yet another mew – gentle and sustained – when he wished, so to speak, to converse with his mistress.

Not, of course, that the creature talked *English*, but he liked to sit up on one chair by the fireside, especially in the kitchen – for he was no born parlour-cat – and to look up at the glinting glasses of Miss Chauncey's spectacles, and then down awhile at the fire-flames (drawing his claws in and out as he did so, and purring the while), almost as if he might be preaching a sermon, or reciting a poem.

But this was in the happy days when all seemed well. This was in the days when Miss Chauncey's mind was innocent of all doubts and suspicions. Like others of his kind, too, Sam delighted to lie in the window

[151]

and idly watch the birds in the apple-trees – tits and bullfinches and dun-nocks – or to crouch over a mouse-hole for hours together. Such were his amusements (for he never ate his mice) while Miss Chauncey with cap and broom, duster and dishclout, went about her housework. But he also had a way of examining things in which cats are not generally interested. He as good as told Miss Chauncey one afternoon that a hole was coming in her parlour carpet. For he walked to and fro and back and forth with his tail up, until she attended to him. And he certainly warned her, with a yelp like an Amazonian monkey, when a red-hot coal had set her kitchen mat on fire.

He would lie or sit with his whiskers to the North before noonday, and due South afterwards. In general his manners were perfection. But occasionally when she called him, his face would appear to knot itself into a frown – at any rate to assume a low sullen look, as if he expostulated 'Why must you be interrupting me, Madam, when I am thinking of some-thing else?' And now and then, Miss Chauncey fancied he would deliber-ately secrete himself or steal out and in of Post Houses unbeknown.

Miss Chauncey, too, would sometimes find him trotting from room to room as if on a visit of inspection. On his fifth birthday he had brought an immense mouse and laid it beside the patent toe-cap of her boot, as she sat knitting by the fire. She smiled and nodded merrily at him, as usual, but on this occasion he had looked at her intently, and then deliber-ately shook his head. After that, he never paid the smallest attention to mouse or mouse-hole or mousery, and Miss Chauncey was obliged to purchase a cheese-bait trap, else she would have been overrun.

Almost any domestic cat may do things of this nature, and of course all this was solely on Sam's domestic side. For he shared a house with Miss Chauncey and, like any two beings that live together, he was bound to keep up certain appearances. He met her half-way, as the saying goes. When, however, he was 'on his own', he was no longer Miss Chauncey's Sam, he was no longer merely the cat at Post Houses, but just *himself*. He went back, that is, to his own free independent life; to his own private habits.

Then the moor on which he roved was his own country, and the humans and their houses on it were no more to him in his wild, privy existence than molehills or badgers' earths, or rabbits' mounds, are to us. Of this side of his life his mistress knew practically nothing. She did not consider it. She supposed that Sam behaved like other cats, though it was evident that at times he went far abroad, for he now and then brought home a Cochin China chick, and the nearest Cochin China fowls

[152]

were at the vicarage, a good four miles off. Sometimes of an evening, too, when Miss Chauncey was taking a little walk herself, she would see him – a swiftly-moving black speck – far along the road, hastening home. And there was more purpose expressed in his gait and appearance than ever Mr Cullings showed!

It was pleasant to observe, too, when he came within miaouing distance how his manner changed. He turned at once from being a Cat into being a Domestic Cat. He was instantaneously no longer the Feline Adventurer, the Nocturnal Marauder and Haunter of Haggurdsdon Moor (though Miss Chauncey would not have so expressed it), but simply his mistress' spoiled pet, Sam. She loved him dearly. But, as again with human beings who are accustomed to live together, she did not *think* very much about him. It could not but be a shock then that latish afternoon, when without the slightest warning Miss Chauncey discovered that Sam was deliberately deceiving her!

She was brushing her thin brown front hair before her looking-glass. And this moment it hung down over her face like a fine loose veil. And as she always mused of other things when she was brushing her hair, she was somewhat absentminded the while. Then suddenly on raising her eyes behind this mesh of hair, she perceived not only that Sam's reflection was in sight of the looking-glass, but that something a little mysterious was happening. Sam was sitting up as if to beg. There was nothing in that. It had been a customary feat of his since he was six months old. Still, for what might he be begging, no one by?

Now the window to the right of the chintz-valanced dressing-table was open at the top. Without, it was beginning to grow dark. All Haggurdsdon Moor lay hushed and still in the evening's coming gloom. And apart from begging when there was nothing to beg for, Sam seemed, so to speak, to be gesticulating with his paws. He appeared, that is, to be making signs, just as if there were someone or something looking in at the window at him from out of the air – which was quite impossible. And there was a look upon his face that certainly Miss Chauncey had never seen before.

She stayed a moment with her hair-brush uplifted, her long lean arm at an angle with her head. On seeing this, Sam had instantly desisted from these motions. He had dropped to his fours again, and was now apparently composing himself for another nap. No; this too was a pretence, for presently as she watched, he turned restlessly about so that his whiskers were once again due South. His backward part toward the window, he was now gazing straight in front of him out of a far from

[153]

friendly face. Far indeed from friendly for a creature that has lived with you ever since he opened the eyes of his first kittenhood.

As if he had read her thoughts, Sam at that moment lifted his head to look at his mistress; she withdrew her eyes to the glass only in the nick of time and when she turned from her toilet there sat he – so serene in appearance, so puss-like, so ordinary once more that Miss Chauncey could scarcely believe anything whatever had been amiss. Had her eyes deluded her – her glass? Was that peculiar motion of Sam's fore-paws (almost as if he were knitting), was that wide excited stare only due to the fact that he was catching what was, to her, an invisible fly?

Miss Chauncey having now neatly arranged her 'window-curtains' – the sleek loops of hair she wore on either side her high forehead – glanced yet again at the window. Nothing there but the silence of the moor; nothing there but the faint pricking of a star as the evening darkened.

Sam's cream was waiting on the hearthrug in the parlour as usual at five o'clock. The lamp was lit. The red blinds were drawn. The fire crackled in the grate. There they sat, these two; the walls of the four-cornered house beside the crossroads rising up above them like a huge oblong box under the immense starry sky that saucered in the wide darkness of the moor.

And while she so sat – with Sam there, seemingly fast asleep – Miss Chauncey was thinking. What had occurred in the bedroom that early evening had reminded her of other odd little bygone happenings. Trifles she had scarcely noticed but which now returned clearly to memory. How often in the past, for example, Sam at this hour would be sitting as if fast asleep (as now), his paws tucked neatly in, looking much like a stout alderman after a high dinner. And then suddenly, without warning, as if a distant voice had called him, he would leap to his feet and run straight out of the room. And somewhere in the house – door ajar or window agape – he would find his egress and be up and away into the night. This had been a common thing to happen.

Once, too, Miss Chauncey had found him squatting on his hind-quarters on the window-ledge of a little room that had been entirely disused since her fair little Cousin Milly had stayed at Post Houses when Miss Chauncey was a child of eight. She had cried out at sight of him, 'You foolish Sam, you! Come in, sir. You will be tumbling out of the window next!' And she remembered as if it were yesterday that though at this he had stepped gingerly in at once from his dizzy perch, he had not looked at her. He had passed her without a sign.

On moonlight evenings, too – why, you could never be sure where

Paris Through the Window, Marc Chagall (*The Solomon R. Guggenheim Museum, New York*)

he was. You could never be sure from what errand he had *returned*. Was she sure indeed where he was on *any* night? The longer she reflected, the deeper grew her doubts and misgivings. This night, at any rate, Miss Chauncey determined to keep watch. But she was not happy in doing so. She hated all manner of spying. They were old companions, Sam and she; and she without him, in bleak Post Houses, would be sadly desolate. She loved Sam dearly. None the less, the spectacle of that afternoon haunted her, and it would be wiser to know all that there was to be known, even if for Sam's sake only.

Now Miss Chauncey always slept with her bedroom door ajar. She had slept so ever since her nursery days. Being a rather timid little girl, she liked in those far-away times to hear the grown-up voices downstairs

[155]

Animals in a Fantasy Landscape, Otto Dix (*Kunstmuseum, Düsseldorf*)

and the spoons and forks clinking. As for Sam, he always slept in his basket beside her fireplace. Every morning there he would be, though on some mornings Miss Chauncey's eyes would open gently to find herself gazing steadily into his pale-green ones as he stood on his hind-paws, resting his front ones on her bed-side, and looking up into her face. 'Time for your milk, Sam?' his mistress would murmur. And Sam would mew, as distantly almost as a seagull in the height of the sky.

Tonight, however, Miss Chauncey only pretended to fall asleep. It was difficult, however, to keep wholly awake, and she was all but drowsing off when there came a faint squeak from the hinge of her door, and she realized that Sam was gone out. After waiting a moment or two, she struck a match. Yes, there was his empty basket in the dark silent room, and presently from far away – from the steeple at Haggurdsdon Village – came the knolling of midnight.

Miss Chauncey placed the dead end of the match in the saucer of her candlestick, and at that moment fancied she heard a faint *whssh* at her window, as of a sudden gust or scurry of wind, or the wings of a fast-flying bird – of a wild goose. It even reminded Miss Chauncey of half-forgotten Guy Fawkes Days and of the sound the stick of a rocket makes as it sweeps down through the air while its green and ruby lights die out in the immense heavens above. Miss Chauncey gathered up her long legs in the bed, drew on the flannel dressing-gown that always hung on her bed-rail, and lifting back the blind an inch or two, looked out of the window.

It was a high starry night, and a brightening in the sky above the roof seemed to betoken there must be a moon over the backward parts of the house. Even as she watched, a streak of pale silver descended swiftly out of the far spaces of the heavens where a few large stars were gathered as if in the shape of a sickle. It was a meteorite; and at that very instant Miss Chauncey fancied she heard a faint remote dwindling *whssh* in the air. Was *that* a meteor too? Could she have been deceived? Was she being deceived in everything? She drew back.

And then, as if in deliberate and defiant answer, out of the distance, from what appeared to be the extreme end of her long garden, where grew a tangle of sloe bushes, there followed a prolonged and as if half-secret caterwaul; very low – contralto, one might say – *Meearou-rou-rou-rou-rou*.

Heaven forbid! Was *that* Sam's tongue? The caterwauling ceased. Yet still Miss Chauncey could not suppress a shudder. She knew Sam's voice of old. But surely not that! Surely not that!

[157]

Strange and immodest, too, though it was to hear herself in that solitary place calling out in the dead of night, she none the less at once opened the window and summoned Sam by name. There was no response. The trees and bushes of the garden stood motionless; their faint shadows on the ground revealing how small a moon was actually in the sky, and how low it hung towards its setting. The vague undulations of the moor stretched into the distance. Not a light to be seen except those of the firmament. Again, and yet again, Miss Chauncey cried, 'Sam, Sam! Come away in! Come away in, sir, you bad creature!' Not a sound. Not the least stir of leaf or blade of grass.

When, after so broken a night, Miss Chauncey awoke a little late the next morning, the first thing her eyes beheld when she sat up in bed was Sam – couched as usual in his basket. It was a mystery, an uneasy one. After supping up his morning bowl, he slept steadily on until noonday. This happened to be the day of the week when Miss Chauncey made bread. On and on she steadily kneaded the dough with her knuckled hands, glancing ever and again towards the motionless creature. With fingers clotted from the great earthenware bowl, she stood over him at last for a few moments, and looked at him closely.

He was lying curled round with his whiskered face to one side towards the fire. And it seemed to Miss Chauncey that she had never noticed before that faint peculiar grin on his face. 'Sam!' she cried sharply. An eye instantly opened, fiercely green as if a mouse had squeaked. He stared at her for an instant; then the lid narrowed. The gaze slunk away a little, but Sam began to purr.

The truth of it is, all this was making Miss Chauncey exceedingly unhappy. Mr Cullings called that afternoon with a basket of some fine comely young sprats. 'Them'll wake his Royal Highness up,' he said. 'They'm fresh as daisies. Lor, m'm, what a Nero that beast be!'

'Cats *are* strange creatures, Mr Cullings,' replied Miss Chauncey reflectively, complacently, supposing that Mr Cullings had misplaced an *h* and had meant to say *an hero*. And Sam himself, with uplifted tail, and as if of the same opinion, was rubbing his head gently against her boot.

Mr Cullings eyed her closely. 'Why, yes, they be,' he said. 'What I says is, is that as soon as they're out of sight, you are out of their mind. There's no more gratitood nor affection in a cat than in a pump. Though so far as the pump is concerned, the gratitood should be on our side. I knew a Family of Cats once what fairly druv their mistress out of house and home.'

[158]

'But you wouldn't have a cat *only* a pet?' said Miss Chauncey faintly; afraid to ask for further particulars of the peculiar occurrence.

'Why no, m'm,' said the carrier. 'As the Lord made 'em, so they be. But I'll be bound they could tell some knotty stories if they had a human tongue in their heads!'

Sam had ceased caressing his mistress's foot, and was looking steadily at Mr Cullings, his hair roughed a little about the neck and shoulders. And the carrier looked back.

'No, m'm. We wouldn't keep 'em,' he said at last, 'if they was *four* times that size. Or, not for long!'

Having watched Mr Cullings' little cart bowl away into the distance, Miss Chauncey returned into the house, more disturbed than ever. Nor did her uneasiness abate when Sam refused even to sniff at his sprats. Instead, he crawled under a low table in the kitchen, behind the old sea-man's chest in which Miss Chauncey kept her kindling-wood. She fancied she heard his claws working in the wood now and again; once he seemed to be expressing his natural feelings in what vulgar people with little sympathy for animals describe as 'swearing'.

Her caressing 'Sams', at any rate, were all in vain. His only reply was a kind of sneeze which uncomfortably resembled 'spitting'. Miss Chauncey's feelings had already been hurt. It was now her mind that suffered.

Witches from *The Book of Days*

Something the carrier had said, or the way he had said it, or the peculiar look she had noticed on his face when he was returning Sam's stare in the porch, haunted her thoughts. She was no longer young; was she becoming fanciful? Or must she indeed conclude that for weeks past Sam had been steadily deceiving her, or at any rate concealing his wanderings and his interests? What nonsense! Worse still: – Was she now so credulous as to believe that Sam had in actual fact been making signals – and secretly, behind her back – to some confederate that must either have been up in the sky, or in the moon!

Whether or not, Miss Chauncey determined to keep a sharper eye on him, if for his own sake only. She would at least make sure that he did not leave the house that night. But then: why not? she asked herself. Why shouldn't the creature choose his own hour and season? Cats, like owls, *see* best in the dark. They go best a-mousing in the dark, and may prefer the dark for their private, social, and even public affairs. Post Houses, after all, was only rather more than two miles from Haggurdsdon Village, and there were cats there in plenty. Poor fellow, her own dumb human company must sometimes be dull enough!

Such were Miss Chauncey's reflections; and as if to reassure her, Sam himself at that moment serenely entered the room and leaped up on to

Villagers Attacking a Witch

1. Advancing Cat, Louis Wain (© *Guttman Maclay Collection, Institute of Psychiatry, London*)

2. *Don Manuel Osorio de Zuñiga*, Francisco de Goya (*The Metropolitan Museum of Art, The Jules S. Bache Collection, 1949*)

3. *Charles Waterton, Naturalist*, C. W. Peale (*National Portrait Gallery, London*)

4. Kitty Fisher, Nathaniel Hone (*National Portrait Gallery, London*)

5. Lady Chasing Cat with Parrot, Kangra, *c.* 1810 (*Victoria and Albert Museum. Crown Copyright*)

6. *Miss Brummell*, Thomas Gainsborough (*Iveagh Bequest, Kenwood*)

7. *Mr and Mrs Clark and Percy*, David Hockney (*Tate Gallery, London*)

8. *Girl with a Kitten*, Lucian Freud (*Private Collection*)

9. Cat and Mouse, James Lloyd (*Tate Gallery, London*)

11. Red Tabby, Sheila Robinson (*Artist's Collection*)

10. Inlaid choir stall (detail), Fra Raffaele de Brescia (*Monte Oliveto Maggiore, Siena*)

13. Cat with Spider, Jillian Peccinotti (*Michael Parkin Fine Art Ltd*)

12. Flowercat, Johan Hermsen (© *Verkerke Reprodukties BV*)

14. Trixie, Martin Leman (*Private Collection*)

15. Ginger Persian Cat, photo Hans Reinhard (*Bruce Coleman Ltd*)

16. Cat with a Fish in its Mouth, Kalighat, *c.* 1890 (*Victoria and Albert Museum. Crown Copyright*)

the empty chair beside her tea-table. As if, too, to prove that he had thought better of his evil temper, or to insinuate that there had been nothing amiss between himself and Mr Cullings, he was licking his chops, and there was no mistaking the odour of fish which he brought in with him from his saucer.

'So you have thought better of it, my boy?' thought Miss Chauncey, though she did not utter the words aloud. And yet as she returned his steady feline gaze, she realized how difficult it was to read the intelligence behind those eyes. You might say that, Sam being only a cat, there was no meaning in them at all. But Miss Chauncey knew she couldn't have said it if such eyes had looked out of a *human* shape at her! She would have been acutely alarmed.

Unfortunately, and almost as if Sam had overheard his mistress' speculations regarding possible cat friends in the Village, there came at that moment a faint wambling mew beneath the open window. In a flash Sam was out of his chair and over the window ledge, and Miss Chauncey rose only just in time to see him in infuriated pursuit of a slim sleek tortoise-shell creature that had evidently come to Post Houses in hope of a friendlier reception, and was now fleeing in positive fear of its life.

Sam returned from his chase as fresh as paint, and Miss Chauncey

Witches, Francisco de Goya
(*Museo del Prado, Madrid*)

was horrified to detect – caught up between the claws of his right foot – a tuft or two of tortoiseshell fur, which, having composed himself by the fire, he promptly removed by licking.

Still pondering on these disquieting events, Miss Chauncey took her usual evening walk in the garden. Candytuft and Virginia stock were blossoming along the shell-lined path, and roses were already beginning to blow on the high brick wall which shut off her narrow strip of land from the vast lap of the moor. Having come to the end of the path, Miss Chauncey pushed on a little farther than usual, to where the grasses grew more rampant, and where wild headlong weeds raised their heads beneath her few lichenous apple trees. Still farther down – for hers was a long, though narrow, garden – there grew straggling bushes of sloe, spiny white-thorn. These had blossomed there indeed in the moor's bleak springs long before Post Houses had raised its chimney-pots into the sky. Here, too, flourished a dense drift of dead-nettles – their sour odour haunting the air.

And it was in this forlorn spot that – like Robinson Crusoe before her – Miss Chauncey was suddenly brought to a standstill by the sight of what appeared to be nothing else than a strange footprint in the mould. Nearby the footprint, moreover, showed what might be the impression of a walking-cane or possibly of something stouter and heavier – a crutch. Could she again be deceived? The footprint, it was true, was unlike most human footprints, the heel sunk low, the toe square. Might it be accidental? *Was* it a footprint?

Miss Chauncey glanced up across the bushes toward the house. It loomed gaunt and forbidding in the moorland dusk. And she fancied she could see, though the evening light might be deceiving her, the cowering shape of Sam looking out at her from the kitchen-window. To be watched! To be herself spied upon – and watched.

But then of course, Sam was always watching her. What oddity was there in that? Where else would his sprats come from, his cream, his saucer of milk, his bowl of fresh well-water? Nevertheless Miss Chauncey returned to her parlour gravely discomposed.

It was an uncommonly still evening, and as she went from room to room locking the windows, she noticed there was already a moon in the sky. She eyed it with misgiving. And at last bedtime came, and when Sam, as usual, after a lick or two had composed himself in his basket, Miss Chauncey, holding the key almost challengingly within view, deliberately locked her bedroom door.

When she awoke next morning Sam was sleeping in his basket as usual, and during the daytime he kept pretty closely to the house. So, too, on the Wednesday and the Thursday. It was not until the following Friday that having occasion to go into an upper bedroom that had no fireplace, and being followed as usual by Sam, Miss Chauncey detected the faint rank smell of soot in the room. No chimney, and a smell of soot! She turned rapidly on her companion; he had already left the room.

And when that afternoon she discovered a black sooty smear upon her own patchwork quilt, she realized not only that her suspicions had been justified, but that for the first time in his life Sam had deliberately laid himself down there in her absence. At this act of sheer defiance, she was no longer so much hurt as exceedingly angry. There was no doubt now. Sam was deliberately defying her. No two companions could share a house on such terms as these. He must be taught a lesson.

That evening in full sight of the creature, having locked her bedroom door, she stuffed a large piece of mattress ticking into the mouth of her chimney and pulled down the register. Having watched these proceedings, Sam rose from his basket, and with an easy spring, leapt up on to the dressing-table. Beyond the window, the moor lay almost as bright as day. Ignoring Miss Chauncey, the creature squatted there steadily and openly staring into the empty skies, for a whole stretch of them was visible from where he sat.

Miss Chauncey proceeded to make her toilet for the night, trying in vain to pretend that she was entirely uninterested in what the animal was at. Faint sounds – not exactly mewings or growlings – but a kind of low inward caterwauling, hardly audible, were proceeding from his throat. But whatever these sounds might mean, Sam himself can have been the only listener. There was not a sign or movement at the window or in the world without. And then Miss Chauncey promptly drew down the blind. At this Sam at once raised his paw for all the world as if he were about to protest, and then, apparently thinking better of it, he pretended instead that the action had been only for the purpose of commencing his nightly wash.

Long after her candle had been extinguished, Miss Chauncey lay listening. Every stir and movement in the quiet darkness could be clearly followed. First there came a furtive footing and tapping at the register of the fireplace, so closely showing what was happening that Miss Chauncey could positively see in her imagination Sam on the hearth-stone, erecting himself there upon his hind-legs, vainly attempting to push the obstacle back.

This being in vain, he appeared to have dropped back on to his fours.

Then came a pause. Had he given up his intention? No; now he was at the door, pawing, gently scratching. Then a leap, even towards the handle; but one only – the door was locked. Retiring from the door, he now sprang lightly again on to the dressing-table. What now was he at? By covertly raising her head from her pillow, Miss Chauncey could see him with paw thrust out, gently drawing back the blind from the moon-flooded window-pane. And even while she listened and watched, she heard yet again – and yet again – the faint *whssh* as of a wild swan cleaving the air; and then what might have been the cry of a bird, but which to Miss Chauncey's ears resembled a shrill cackle of laughter. At this Sam hastily turned from the window and without the least attempt at concealment pounced clean from the dressing-table on to the lower rail of her bed.

This unmannerly conduct could be ignored no longer. Poor Miss Chauncey raised herself in her sheets, pulled her night-cap a little closer down over her ears, and thrusting out her hand towards the chair beside the bed, struck a match and relit her candle. It was with a real effort that she then slowly turned her head and faced her night-companion. His hair was bristling about his body as if he had had an electric shock. His whiskers stood out at stiff angles with his jaws. He looked at least twice his usual size, and his eyes blazed in his head, as averting his face from her regard he gave vent to a low sustained *Miariou-rou-rou!*

'I say you shall *not*,' cried Miss Chauncey at the creature. At the sound of her words, he turned slowly and confronted her. And it seemed that until that moment Miss Chauncey had never actually seen Sam's countenance as in actual fact it really was. It was not so much the grinning tigerish look it wore, but the sullen assurance upon it of what he wanted and that he meant to get it.

All thought of sleep was out of the question. Miss Chauncey could be obstinate too. The creature seemed to shed an influence on the very air which she could hardly resist. She rose from her bed and thrusting on her slippers made her way to the window. Once more a peculiar inward cry broke out from the bed-rail. She raised the blind and the light of the moon from over the moor swept in upon her little apartment. And when she turned to remonstrate with her pet at his ingratitude, and at all this unseemliness and the deceit of his ways, there was something so menacing and pitiless in his aspect that Miss Chauncey hesitated no more.

'Well, mark me!' she cried in a trembling voice. 'Go out of the *door* you shan't. But if you enjoy soot, soot it shall be.'

With that she thrust back the register with the poker, and drew down the bundle of ticking with the tongs. And before the fit of coughing caused by the consequent smotheration that followed had ceased, the lithe black shape had sprung from the bed-rail, and with a scramble was into the hearth, over the firebars, up the chimney, and away.

Trembling from head to foot, Miss Chauncey sat down on a cane rocking-chair that stood nearby to reflect what next she must be doing. *Wh-ssh! Wh-ssh!* Again at the window came that mysterious rushing sound, but now the flurrying murmur as of a rocket shooting up with its fiery train of sparks thinning into space, rather than the sound of its descending stick. And then in the hush that followed, there sounded yet again, like a voice from the foot of the garden – a caterwauling piercing and sonorous enough to arouse the sleeping cocks in the Haggurdsdon hen-roosts and for miles around. Out of the distance their chanticleering broke shrill on the night air; to be followed a moment afterwards by the tardy clang of midnight from the church steeple. Then once more silence; utter quiet. Miss Chauncey returned to her bed, but that night she slept no more.

Her mind overflowed with unhappy thoughts. Her faith in Sam was gone. Far worse she had lost faith even in her affection for him. To have wasted that! – all the sprats, all the whitebait in the wide seas were as nothing by comparison. That Sam had wearied of her company was at least beyond question. It shamed her to think how much this meant to her – a mere animal! But she knew what was gone; knew how dull and spiritless in future the day's round would seem – the rising, the housework, the meals, a clean linen collar – the long, slow afternoon, forsaken and companionless! The solitary tea, her candle, prayers, bed – on and on. In what wild company was her cat Sam now? At her own refusal to face that horrid question it was as if she had heard the hollow clanging slam of an immense iron door.

Next morning – still ruminating on these strange events, grieved to the heart at this dreadful rift between herself and one who had been her honest companion of so many years; ashamed, too, that Sam should have had his way with her when she had determined not to allow him to go out during the night – the next morning Miss Chauncey, as if merely to take a little exercise, once again ventured down to the foot of her garden. A faint, blurred mark (such as she had seen on the previous evening) in the black mould of what *might* be a footprint is nothing very much.

But now – in the neglected patch beyond the bushes of white-thorn and bramble – there was no doubt in the world appeared the marks of many. And surely no cats' paw-prints these! Of what use, too, to a cat could a crutch or a staff be? A staff or crutch which – to judge from the impression it had left in the mould – must have been at least as thick as a broomstick.

More disquieted and alarmed than ever over this fresh mystery, Miss Chauncey glanced up and back towards the chimney-pots of the house, clearly and sharply fretted against the morning light of the eastern skies. And she realized what perils even so sure-footed a creature as Sam had faced when he skirred up out of the chimney in his wild effort to emerge into the night. Having thus astonishingly reached the rim of the chimney-pot – the burning stars above and the wilderness of the moor spread out far beneath and around him – he must have leaped from the top of the pot to a narrow brick ledge not three inches wide. Thence on to the peak of the roof and thence down a steep slippery slope of slates to a leaden gutter.

And how then? The thick tod of ivy matting the walls of the house reached hardly more than half-way up. Could Sam actually have plunged from gutter to tod? The very thought of such peril drew Miss Chauncey's steps towards the house again, in the sharpest anxiety to assure herself that he was still in the land of the living.

And lo and behold, when she was but half-way on her journey, she heard a succession of frenzied cries and catcalls in the air from over the moor. Hastily placing a flower-pot by the wall, she stood on tiptoe and peered over. And even now, at this very moment, in full sight across the nearer slope of the moor she descried her Sam, not now in chase of a foolishly trustful visitor, but hotly pursued by what appeared to be the complete rabblement of Haggurdsdon's cats. Sore spent though he showed himself to be, Sam was keeping his distance. Only a few lank tabby gibs, and what appeared to be a grey-ginger Manx (unless he was an ordinary cat with his tail chopped off) were close behind.

'Sam! Sam!' Miss Chauncey cried, and yet again, 'Sam!' but in her excitement and anxiety her foot slipped on the flower-pot and in an instant the feline chase had fallen out of sight. Gathering herself together again, she clutched a long besom or garden broom that was leaning against the wall, and rushed down to the point at which she judged Sam would make his entrance into the garden. She was not mistaken, nor an instant too soon. With a bound he was up and over, and in three seconds the rabble had followed in frenzied pursuit.

What came after Miss Chauncey could never very clearly recall. She could but remember plying her besom with might and main amid the rabble and mêlée of animals, while Sam, no longer a fugitive, turned on his enemies and fought them cat for cat. None the less, it was by no means

[166]

an easy victory. And had not the over-fatted cur from the butcher's in Haggurdsdon – which had long since started in pursuit of this congregation of his enemies – had he not at last managed to overtake them, the contest might very well have had a tragic ending. But at the sound of his baying and at sight of the cur's teeth snapping at them as he vainly attempted to surmount the wall, Sam's enemies turned and fled in all directions. And faint and panting, Miss Chauncey was able to fling down her besom and to lean for a brief respite against the trunk of a tree.

At last she opened her eyes again. 'Well, Sam,' she managed to mutter at last, 'we got the best of them, then?'

But to her amazement she found herself uttering these friendly words into a complete vacancy. The creature was nowhere to be seen. His cream disappeared during the day, however, and by an occasional rasping sound Miss Chauncey knew that he once more lay hidden in his dingy resort behind the kindling-wood box. And there she did not disturb him.

Not until tea-time of the following day did Sam reappear. And then – after attending to his hurts – it was merely to sit with face towards the fire, sluggish and sullen and dumb as a dog. It was not Miss Chauncey's 'place' to make advances, she thought. She took no notice of the beast except to rub in a little hog's fat on the raw places of his wounds. She was rejoiced to find, however, that he kept steadily to Post Houses for the next few days, though her dismay was reawakened at hearing on the third night a more dismal wailing and wauling than ever from the sloe-bushes, even while Sam himself sat motionless beside the fire. His ears twitched, his fur seemed to bristle; he sneezed or spat, but remained otherwise motionless.

When Mr Cullings called again, Sam at once hid himself in the coal-cellar, but gradually his manners towards Miss Chauncey began to recover their usual suavity. And within a fortnight after the full-moon, the two of them had almost returned to their old friendly companionship. He was healed, sleek, confident and punctual. No intruder of his species had appeared from Haggurdsdon. The night noises had ceased; Post Houses to all appearances – apart from its strange ugliness – was as peaceful and calm as any other solitary domicile in the United Kingdom.

But alas and alas. With the very first peeping of the crescent moon, Sam's mood and habits began to change again. He mouched about with a sly and furtive eye. And when he fawned on her, purring and clawing, the whole look of him was full of deceit. If Miss Chauncey chanced softly to enter the room wherein he sat, he would at once leap down from the window at which he had been perched as if in the attempt to prove that

Sacred Cat (*British Museum*)

he had *not* been looking out of it. And once, towards evening, though she was no spy, she could not but pause at the parlour door. She had peeped through its crack as it stood ajar. And there on the hard sharp back of an old prie-dieu chair that had belonged to her pious great-aunt Jemima, there sat Sam on his hind-quarters. And without the least doubt in the world he was vigorously signalling to some observer outside with his forepaws. Miss Chauncey turned away sick at heart.

From that hour on Sam more and more steadily ignored and flouted his mistress, was openly insolent, shockingly audacious. Mr Cullings gave her small help indeed. 'If I had a cat, m'm, what had manners like that, after all your kindness, fresh fish and all every week, and cream, as I understand, not skim, I'd – I'd give him away.'

'To whom?' said Miss Chauncey shortly.

'Well,' said the carrier, 'I don't know as how I'd much mind to who. Just a home, m'm.'

'He seems to have no friends in the Village,' said Miss Chauncey in as light a tone as she could manage.

'When they're as black as that, with them saucer eyes, you can never tell,' said Mr Cullings. 'There's that old trollimog what lives in Hogges Bottom. She's got a cat that might be your Sam's twin.'

'Indeed no, he has the mange,' said Miss Chauncey, loyal to the end. The carrier shrugged his shoulders, climbed into his cart, and bowled away off over the moor. And Miss Chauncey returning into the house, laid the platter of silvery sprats on the table, sat down and burst into tears.

It was, then, in most ways a fortunate thing that the very next morning – three complete days, that is, before the next full-moontide – she received a letter from her sister-in-law in Shanklin, in the Isle of Wight, entreating her to pay them a long visit.

My dear Emma, you must sometimes be feeling very lonely (it ran), shut up in that great house so far from any neighbours. We often think of you, and particularly these last few days. It's nice to have that Sam of yours for company, but after all, as George says, a pet is only a pet. And we do all think it's high time you took a little holiday with us. I am looking out of my window at this moment. The sea is as calm as a mill-pond, a solemn beautiful blue. The fishing boats are coming in with their brown sails. This is the best time of the year with us, because as it's not yet holy-day-time there are few of those horrid visitors to be seen, and no crowds. George says you *must* come. He joins with me in his love as would Maria if she weren't out shopping, and will meet you at the station in the trap. Emmie is now free of her cough, only whooping when the memory takes her and never sick. And we shall all be looking forward to seeing you in a few days.

At this kindness, and with all her anxieties, Miss Chauncey all but broke down. When the butcher drove up in his cart an hour or two afterwards, he took a telegram for her back to the Village, and on the Monday her box was packed and all that remained was to put Sam in his basket in preparation for the journey. But I am bound to say it took more than the persuasion of his old protectress to accomplish this. Indeed Mr Cullings had actually to hold the creature with his gloved hands and none too gently, while Miss Chauncey pressed down the lid and pushed the skewer in to hold it close.

'What's done's dumned done!' said the carrier, as he rubbed a pinch of earth into his scratches. 'But what I say is, better done forever. Mark my words, m'm!'

Miss Chauncey took a shilling out of her large leather purse; but made no reply.

Indeed all this trouble proved at last in vain. Thirty miles distant from Haggurdsdon, at Blackmoor Junction, Miss Chauncey had to change trains. Her box and Sam's basket were placed together on the station platform beside half-a-dozen empty milk-cans and some fowls in a crate, and Miss Chauncey went to inquire of the station-master to make sure of her platform.

It was the furious panic-stricken cackling of these fowls that brought her hastily back to her belongings, only to find that by hook or by crook Sam had managed to push the skewer of the basket out of its cane loops. The wicker lid yawned open – the basket was empty. Indeed one poor gaping hen, its life fluttering away from its helpless body, was proof not only of Sam's prowess but of his cowardly ferocity.

A few days afterwards, as Miss Chauncey sat in the very room to which her sister-in-law had referred in her invitation, looking over the placid surface of the English Channel, the sun gently shining in the sky, there came a letter from Mr Cullings. It was in pencil and written upon the back of a baker's bag:

Dear Madam, i take the libberty of riteing you in referense to the Animall as how i helped put in is bawskit which has cum back returned empty agenn by rail me having okashun to cart sum hop powles from Haggurdsdon late at nite ov Sunday. I seez him squattin at the parlor windy grimasin out at me fit to curdle your blood in your vanes and lights at the upper windies and a yowling and screetching such as i never hopes to hear agen in a Christian lokalety. And that ole wumman from Hogges Botom sitting in the porch mi own vew being that there is no good in the place and the Animall be bewitched. Mr Flint the fysh-munger agrees with me as how now only last mesures is of any use and as i have said afore i am wiling to take over the house the rent if so be being low and mod-drate considering of the bad name it as in these parts around Haggurdsdon. I remain dear madam waitin your orders and oblidge yours truely William Cullings.

To look at Miss Chauncey you might have supposed she was a strong-minded woman. You might have supposed that this uncivil reference to the bad name her family house had won for itself would have mortified her beyond words. Whether or not, she neither showed this letter to her sister-in-law nor for many days together did she even answer it. Sitting on the Esplanade, and looking out to sea, she brooded on and on in the warm, salt, yet balmy air. It was a distressing problem. But, 'No, he must go his own way,' she sighed to herself at last; 'I have done my best for him.'

What is more, Miss Chauncey never returned to Post Houses. She sold it at last, house and garden and for a pitiful sum, to the carrier, Mr Cullings. By that time Sam had vanished, had been never seen again.

Not that Miss Chauncey was faithless of memory. Whenever the faint swish of a seagull's wing sounded in the air above her head; or the crackling of an ascending rocket for the amusement of the visitors broke the silence of the nearer heavens over the sea; whenever even she became conscious of the rustling frou-frou of her Sunday watered-silk gown as she sallied out to church from the neat little villa she now rented on the Shanklin Esplanade – she never noticed such things without being instantly transported back in imagination to her bedroom at Post Houses, to see again that strange deluded animal, once her Sam, squatting there on her patchwork counterpane, and as it were knitting with his fore-paws the while he stood erect upon his hind.

The Cat and the Moon

W. B. YEATS

The cat went here and there
And the moon spun round like a top,
And the nearest kin of the moon,
The creeping cat, looked up.
Black Minnaloushe stared at the moon,
For, wander and wail as he would,
The pure cold light in the sky
Troubled his animal blood.
Minnaloushe runs in the grass
Lifting his delicate feet.
Do you dance, Minnaloushe, do you dance?
When two close kindred meet,
What better than call a dance?
Maybe the moon may learn,
Tired of that courtly fashion,
A new dance turn.

[171]

The Mount of the Sacred Cat, Paul Klee (*Private Collection*)

Minnaloushe creeps through the grass
From moonlit place to place,
The sacred moon overhead
Has taken a new phase.
Does Minnaloushe know that his pupils
Will pass from change to change,
And that from round to crescent,
From crescent to round they range?
Minnaloushe creeps through the grass
Alone, important and wise,
And lifts to the changing moon
His changing eyes.

Diamond Cut Diamond

EWART MILNE

Two cats
One up a tree
One under the tree
The cat up a tree is he
The cat under the tree is she
The tree is witch elm, just incidentally.
He takes no notice of she, she takes no notice of he.
He stares at the woolly clouds passing, she stares at the tree.
There's been a lot written about cats, by Old Possum, Yeats and Company
But not Alfred de Musset or Lord Tennyson or Poe or anybody
Wrote about one cat under, and one cat up, a tree.
God knows why this should be left for me
Except I like cats as cats be
Especially one cat up
And one under
A witch elm
Tree

The Cat

GILES LYTTON STRACHEY

Dear creature by the fire a-purr,
 Strange idol, eminently bland,
Miraculous puss! As o'er your fur
 I trail a negligible hand

And gaze into your gazing eyes,
 And wonder in a demi-dream
What mystery it is that lies
 Behind those slits that glare and gleam,

[173]

Two Cats (Mansell Collection)

An exquisite enchantment falls
    About the portals of my sense;
Meandering through enormous halls
    I breathe luxurious frankincense.

An ampler air, a warmer June
    Enfold me, and my wondering eye
Salutes a more imperial moon
    Throned in a more resplendent sky

Than ever knew this northern shore.
    Oh, strange! For you are with me too,
And I, who am a cat once more,
    Follow the woman that was you.

With tail erect and pompous march,
    The proudest puss that ever trod,
Through many a grove, 'neath many an arch,
    Impenetrable as a god,

Down many an alabaster flight
    Of broad and cedar-shaded stairs,
While over us the elaborate night
    Mysteriously gleams and glares!

The Cat Horoscope

ANN CURRAH

ARIES (March 21–April 20): The original cat on a hot tin roof, most active and ambitious of them all. From clean laundry to flower beds, he makes a (hollow) impression everywhere. Fond of wandering, and when at home liable to create his own obstacle course with no inhibitions about broken ornaments. Fond of fighting, impetuous at loving.
Best Owners (only owners able to survive him): Sagittarius, Leo.

TAURUS (April 21–May 20): So placid and imperturbable that humans can understand him. So far from flighty that even danger will not stir

Cat on the Floor, Théophile Steinlen (*Achenbach Foundation, California Palace of the Legion of Honor, San Francisco*)

his lazy bones. Taurus is dependable – you can depend on him to be forever in your way.
Best Owners: Capricorn, Virgo, Cancer.

GEMINI (May 21–June 20): Essentially the kitten-cat, that exaggeratedly playful pussy with the gift of eternal youth. So far as felines fret, Gemini frets. He desires change of scene, balls of wool; is much in demand for TV commercials. Incorrigibly bossy.
Best Owners: Libra, Aquarius, but never Taurus.

CANCER (June 21–July 20): Inconstant as the moon, deceitful as women, emotional as a Foreign Secretary, he swings from the chandelier and meows piteously in the corner; nobody can understand this cat. Regards humans as furniture.
Best Owners: Pisces, Scorpio.

LEO (July 21–August 21): Pretentious – like his sign – authoritative, domineering, and ostentatious. From kittenhood, goes through life with the look of one who has his nose immediately above the smell of a rotting mouse. No tabby can resist him.
Best Owners: Aries, Sagittarius, but never Capricorn.

VIRGO (August 22–September 22): Conscientious, dedicated, down-to-earth. So domesticated that if you leave the beds until teatime, he glowers in disapproval. Careful never to harm a growing petunia, fussy enough to demand fresh food. Choosy about friends.
Best Owners: Capricorn, Taurus.

LIBRA (September 23–October 22): Remember copy cats? That's Libra – which is why he studies his owner to an extent, learning his mannerisms, adopting his habits. He prefers to look at life from your lap, to breakfast off eggs and bacon.
Best Owners: Leo, but never Aries.

SCORPIO (October 23–November 22): Hidden beneath his prettily patterned fur lurks enough power for a fleet of bulldozers. Nobody ever got the better of this cat. He sums you up from the start. A hospitable cat, usually at your expense; likely to expect you to maintain his mate.
Best Owners: Cancer, Pisces.

SAGITTARIUS (November 23–December 20): A dreamy cat with the speed of a horse but the brain of a bird. This unsettling combination usually makes him as uncomfortable as he makes you. Not good in town – a dilapidated castle or old manor keeps him happiest.
Best Owners: Sagittarius, Leo, but never Cancer.

CAPRICORN (December 21–January 19): A serious cat, most aptly named Prudence; cool, deliberate, a calculating cat indeed. If he cannot improve his owners, then he seeks a new family. Quickly house-trained, but too flirty for a happy love life.
Best Owners: Virgo, Libra, Taurus.

AQUARIUS (January 20–February 18): Meddlesome moggie, keen to have a paw in everybody's business. Appears to be kleptomaniac, but only steals a neighbour's petticoat or next-door's strawberry plants because he heard you admire them. Fond of humans.
Best Owners: Libra, Gemini, Aquarius.

PISCES (February 19–March 20): A difficult cat, often gay and moody, friendly but uncommunicative at the same time. Easily placated with promises of 'fish tomorrow'. The ideal ship's cat or theatre cat, for he loves the sea as much as play-acting.
Best Owners: Cancer, Scorpio, but never Capricorn.

Chinese Cats from *Jeux des nuages et de la pluie*

From *The Hsien-i*

LIU YUAN-CH'ING

(*translated by Martin Booth*)

THE Chi-Yen family kept a cat which the master of the house held very highly indeed, calling it *Tiger*. One day, a passer-by said to him, 'A tiger is a ferocious creature, but not as strange and mystical as a dragon. Cats are so. I suggest you change the cat's name to *Dragon*.'

Not long afterwards, a stranger saw the cat and said, 'A dragon is definitely more mysterious than a tiger. When it flies high in the firmament, it rests on the clouds. This means the clouds are greater than the dragon. So call the cat *Cloud*.'

[178]

Others came by with their own ideas, furthering the idea and the development of the cat's name.

'When the clouds are heavy and grey, the wind dispels them: now that's great! The wind is the greatest thing in the world. Re-name your cat *Wind*.'

'The wind is powerful: when a typhoon rises and screams about we shelter from it behind the walls of the house. They withstand the blast of the wind. The wall is the thing that holds back all power from us. The cat should be called *Wall*.'

'So walls are strong. But when they are riddled with rat-holes, they are weakened, the wood splinters and the wall falls. Now cats hit out at rats: always have – they kill them. *Rat* would be a fitting name for your cat!'

Through all this, an old man from Tung-lii butted in. He laughed wryly and said, 'No! No! Look, my friends, a cat's a cat. It lives to kill rats. Why try to change its way of being?'

Chinese Cat Merchants at the Port of Peking, T. Allom

From *A Voyage to Lisbon*

HENRY FIELDING

Thursday, July 11th 1754. A most tragical incident fell out this day at sea. While the ship was under sail, but making as will appear no great way, a kitten, one of four of the feline inhabitants of the cabin, fell from the window into the water: an alarm was immediately given to the captain, who was then upon deck, and received it with the utmost concern and many bitter oaths. He immediately gave orders to the steersman in favour of the poor thing, as he called it; the sails were instantly slackened, and all hands, as the phrase is, employed to recover the poor animal. I was, I own, extremely surprised at all this; less indeed at the captain's extreme tenderness than at his conceiving any possibility of success; for if puss had had nine thousand instead of nine lives, I concluded they had been all lost. The boatswain, however, had more sanguine hopes, for having stripped himself of his jacket, breeches and shirt, he leaped boldly into the water, and to my great astonishment, in a few minutes returned to the ship, bearing the motionless animal in his mouth. Nor was this, I observed, a matter of such great difficulty as it appeared to my ignorance, and possibly may seem to that of my fresh-water reader. The kitten was now exposed to air and sun on the deck, where its life, of which it retained no symptoms, was despaired of by all.

The captain's humanity, if I may so call it, did not so totally destroy his philosophy as to make him yield himself up to affliction on this melancholy occasion. Having felt his loss like a man, he resolved to shew he could bear it like one; and, having declared he had rather have lost a cask of rum or brandy, betook himself to threshing at backgammon with the Portuguese friar, in which innocent amusement they passed about two-thirds of their time.

But as I have, perhaps, a little too wantonly endeavoured to raise the tender passions of my readers in this narrative, I should think myself unpardonable if I concluded it without giving them the satisfaction of hearing that the kitten at last recovered, to the great joy of the good captain, but to the great disappointment of some of the sailors, who asserted that the drowning cat was the very surest way of raising a favourable wind; a supposition of which, though we have heard several plausible accounts, we will not presume to assign the true original reason.

Wednesday. He even extended his humanity, if I may so call it, to animals, and even his cats and kittens had large shares in his affection. An instance of which we saw this evening, when the cat, which had shewn it could not be drowned, was found suffocated under a feather-bed in the cabin. I will not endeavour to describe his lamentations with more prolixity than barely by saying they were grievous, and seemed to have some mixture of the Irish howl in them.

Cats

CHARLES BAUDELAIRE

(translated by Roy Fuller)

Lovers and austere dons are equally
(In their maturity) attached to cats –
Cats soft but cruel, emperors of flats,
Touchy like these and like those sedentary.

Friends of the sensual, the cerebral,
They seek the quiet and horror of the dark;
If they had ever bent their pride to work
They might have pulled the funeral cars of hell.

Asleep they take the noble attitude
Of the great sphinxes that appear to brood,
Stretched in the wastes, in dreams that have no end;
Their loins are electric with fecundity,
And particles of gold, like finest sand,
Star vaguely their unfathomable eye.

The Seventh Knight and the Green Cat: A Variation on the Gawain Poet

ALAN BROWNJOHN

Curious about her seven daughters, in turn came
The seven fortitudinous knights. And the first
To sit by the swarming fire, sipping mead with

The Return of Odysseus, Pintoricchio (*National Gallery, London*)

Mother and eldest daughter, saw with much delight
The white cat pace to him, as he loved them,
Cats.
   The creature was unbleached to a queer
Shifting shade of green by the colours of the room
– Green hangings, green velvet on the couches,
Green branches at the window, green eyes in matron and girl,
Green even in the flames of the fire because
They cast salt in the crevices of the coals to
Make matching colours.
       So the white cat
Mewed at him, nudged his ankle, mounted his lap,

[182]

And the mother murmured, 'You are much honoured.
She has never before walked in such a way up to a man.'
This flattery went deep, the proposals were made, and the pair
Duly wed.
           And since daughters must dutifully marry,
And mothers must needs be mothers, and marry off,
A second knight came seeking the second daughter
And chose a green chair by the great fire while
The mother poured wine.
           Again, willingly, the white
Cat rose on her green cushion, stood stretching,
And pattered the flagstones to the handsome second knight
To form fond figures-of-eight round the man's thin legs.
'There's a something about you that attracts her, she
Has never lingered with any man,' the lady said.
In this style was her second daughter secured
To a cat-adoring knight.
           This way it went too
With the third, the fourth, the fifth, and the sixth, on
A succession of green days with the cat casually
Trusting its truly said-to-be-so-untypical
Affection to the different knights, whether of
Aragon, Transylvania, Tartary or Tibet, being
Similar only in their peculiar pride at pre-empting,
Uniquely, an unsociable animal unsure of men:
Cat-lovers but gullible with it, which is rare.

On the last and greenest day, green curtains gathered
Across the storm which sent the green branches seething
Over the sky in a frenzied trellis-work of green,
The seventh knight finally knocked; one who knew
And loved cats more than any of these lovers, and
He yearned for the youngest daughter's hand.
                 Her mother
Decanted liquor as usual, and the lovely daughter sat,
And green flames flashed in the hearth as the cat
Began again, greenly, its meaningful trek of the floor.
'She will not go to you, she has never gone to greet a man,'
The matron predicted; but the cat pounced all at once,
From no definable angle, on the very codpiece of the doting

Knight, and neatly nestled.
                              So the mother and girl
Cried equally with eagerness and ecstasy as before

– At which the knight bounded up from his bench of green,
Shouting, 'I am getting out, out of here at once!'
And 'I know what sort of situation this is,'
Dropping the cat, flat-eared and snarling, with dire dismay,
To the stones, decapitating the thing with a dirk;
With screams from all, except himself and the evil cat's
Head which jeered, and rejoined itself to the body
And said, 'What was that intended to imply?'
'The true friend of cat,' said the knight, 'knows
That cat in ninety-nine which walks for women
And not for itself alone, the animal which is
The familiar of witches.
                              But it seems as if
I have not exorcised this particular one enough.'

'You are remarkably right,' said the reconstructured cat
Sapiently, 'and for this wisdom you will wend,
By a promise you will here and now provide,
One year through numerous travails of the world and come
To the terrible temple of the great cat-goddess,
The mere pictures of whom inflict fevers and death
On the temerarious beholder who braves them,
Leading lady of many a lousy psychotropic
Trance. There we shall truly meet again,
And I shall take my turn.'
                              So the seventh knight
Ground on grimly over the bogs and crags of the world
Lodging roughly, going rudely his slow way
On his bewildered horse through innumerable bleak,
Colourless, sleazy, subtopiate regions,
Demoralizing tracts of megalosuburbia,
And came, just after eleven heavy months, to a splendid
Castle where he was welcomed very festively.
                              There,
In the course of after-dinner prattle of the price of property,
He thought he might try to elicit where the temple

[184]

European with Servants, c. 1605–10, Mughal (*India Office Library*)

Of the great cat-goddess stood, half-hoping it had not
Survived redevelopment.
                              'My fine fellow, I can
Tell you the lie of the land,' said the lord his host,
'But linger a day or two here, love, enjoy some relaxation'
– And his lady smiled in sly sympathy and accord –
'While I do some terribly tedious hunting. And, by the way,
Be good!'
            With an inward feeling of distant déjà vu,
The seventh knight agreed; and for three successive days,
Was allowed to lie lazily in bed while his host
Hunted and left his lady behind (just as he had read somewhere:
Because, to truncate a tangled tale,
Coming in sleek, scarlet, delightful garments,
She insisted on sleeping with him thoroughly each of the three
Days her husband was out happily hunting the evening meal,
Which the knight acquiesced in with an uneasy
Sense of compromise, and suspicion).
                                       Each night, the master,
Hot and bothered, and scenting himself, brought back
The special spoils of a strenuous day in the field;
For this supper asking nothing in return and reward
But the knight's company in anecdotes and carousing;
And on the last day, as promised, he provided
Instructions for getting to the great cat-goddess' place.

It proved a daunting plod over muddy areas,
An extremely unclean excursion, so that when the knight
Arrived there, both he and his horse exhausted,
Spattered in the saddle from travel, he thought it was his tiredness
That stopped him from seeing where it was. But suddenly,
He saw it, a low brick thing nearly hidden in the grasses
Of a thistly field, with peculiar peep-holes from which
Any occupant, sitting in a safe nook, could
Scan out.
            Dismounting the knight called, clearly, and
Loudly as he was able, on whoever lurked inside to
Emerge, and there expeditiously appeared a
Truly tremendous cat, the size of a full-grown woman.
'As I promised and pledged I would do, in all duty,'

[186]

Stated the knight, 'I have travelled to the temple
Of the great cat-goddess to pay the penalty for
Following up certain suspicions too rashly,
And acting in anger.'
                              The vast cat mysteriously smiled,
Saying, 'Listen. As an artful knight, you showed
Some shrewdness in discerning a witch's cat;
As a truly brave one you moved boldly
Against a defenceless, domestic animal; as

Superbia, Hieronymus Bosch (*Museo del Prado, Madrid*)

[187]

A plodder you showed some powerful persistence
In going your way through the world for a whole year
To find out this frightful place; as a seizer of chances
You lay three times with the lady of the castle,
Obviously not having offered any oath you would
Thereby break; thus, a clean code of knightly
Tactics you have most tightly kept, and
Will be rightly rewarded.'
                                    At which the vast beast
Cast off its outer cat-costume to step calmly
Forth as the seventh daughter, dressed in the delightful,
Scarlet, sleek garments of the mistress of the castle.
'I was,' she said, 'all the time secretly concealed
In the little anatomy of the cat, and in the body
Of the lady of the castle you came to know a bit,
And the knight of the castle, my master and lord,
Was all the time my own dear mother in drag.
So on the basis of all that you may bow, and beg now
The hand of the seventh daughter you came to collect.
There is no way out.'
                                    So, haltingly heeding
These dreadful words, the dumbstruck fellow put
His proposals, too perplexed to do other, and the pair
Were rapidly wed. And they went on to work through
Many years of irrefrangible, retributive wedlock
(For she turned out termagant as well as witch)

– Yet concerning these travails I cannot, truthfully, say
I am sad or sorry, and I cannot make this knight an
Object of pity, because as a grown-up I genuinely regard
Knights and knighthood and weapons and the mores
Of a warrior society as both juvenile and degrading.

Tobermory

SAKI

IT was a chill, rain-washed afternoon of a late August day, that indefinite season when partridges are still in the security of cold storage, and there is nothing to hunt – unless one is bounded on the north by the Bristol Channel, in which case one may lawfully gallop after fat red stags. Lady Blemley's house-party was not bounded on the north by the Bristol Channel, hence there was a full gathering of her guests round the tea-table on this particular afternoon. And, in spite of the blankness of the season and the triteness of the occasion, there was no trace in the company of that fatigued restlessness which means a dread of the pianola and a subdued hankering for auction bridge. The undisguised, open-mouthed attention of the entire party was fixed on the homely, negative personality of Mr Cornelius Appin. Of all her guests, he was the one who had come to Lady Blemley with the vaguest reputation. Someone had said he was 'clever', and he had got his invitation in the moderate expectation, on the part of his hostess, that some portion at least of his cleverness would be contributed to the general entertainment. Until tea-time that day she had been unable to discover in what direction, if any, his cleverness lay. He was neither a wit nor a croquet champion, a hypnotic force nor a begetter of amateur theatricals. Neither did his exterior suggest the sort of man in whom women are willing to pardon a generous measure of mental deficiency. He had subsided into mere Mr Appin, and the Cornelius seemed a piece of transparent baptismal bluff. And now he was claiming to have launched on the world a discovery beside which the invention of gun powder, of the printing-press, and of steam locomotion were inconsiderable trifles. Science had made bewildering strides in many directions during recent decades, but this thing seemed to belong to the domain of miracle rather than to scientific achievement.

'And do you really ask us to believe,' Sir Wilfrid was saying, 'that you have discovered a means for instructing animals in the art of human speech, and that dear old Tobermory has proved your first successful pupil?'

'It is a problem at which I have worked for the last seventeen years,' said Mr Appin, 'but only during the last eight or nine months have I been rewarded with glimmerings of success. Of course I have experi-

[189]

The Cat, Bart A. van der Leck (*Rijksmuseum Kröller-Müller, Otterlo*)

mented with thousands of animals, but latterly only with cats, those wonderful creatures which have assimilated themselves so marvellously with our civilization while retaining all their highly developed feral instincts. Here and there among cats one comes across an outstanding superior intellect, just as one does among the ruck of human beings, and when I made the acquaintance of Tobermory a week ago I saw at once that I was in contact with a "Beyond-cat" of extraordinary intelligence. I had gone far along the road to success in recent experiments; with Tobermory, as you call him, I have reached the goal.'

[190]

Mr Appin concluded his remarkable statement in a voice which he strove to divest of a triumphant inflexion. No one said 'Rats', though Clovis's lips moved in a monosyllabic contortion which probably invoked those rodents of disbelief.

'And do you mean to say,' asked Miss Resker, after a slight pause, 'that you have taught Tobermory to say and understand easy sentences of one syllable?'

'My dear Miss Resker,' said the wonder-worker patiently, 'one teaches little children and savages and backward adults in that piecemeal fashion; when one has once solved the problem of making a beginning with an animal of highly developed intelligence one has no need for those halting methods. Tobermory can speak our language with perfect correctness.'

This time Clovis very distinctly said, 'Beyond-rats!' Sir Wilfrid was more polite, but equally sceptical.

'Hadn't we better have the cat in and judge for ourselves?' suggested Lady Blemley.

Sir Wilfrid went in search of the animal, and the company settled themselves down to the languid expectation of witnessing some more or less adroit drawing-room ventriloquism.

In a minute Sir Wilfrid was back in the room, his face white beneath its tan and his eyes dilated with excitement.

'By Gad, it's true!'

His agitation was unmistakably genuine, and his hearers started forward in a thrill of awakened interest.

Collapsing into an armchair he continued breathlessly; 'I found him dozing in the smoking-room, and called after him to come for his tea. He blinked at me in his usual way, and I said, "Come on, Toby; don't keep us waiting;" and, by Gad! he drawled out in a most horribly natural voice, that he'd come when he dashed well pleased! I nearly jumped out of my skin!'

Appin had preached to absolutely incredulous hearers; Sir Wilfrid's statement carried instant conviction. A Babel-like chorus of startled exclamation arose, amid which the scientist sat mutely enjoying the first fruit of his stupendous discovery.

In the midst of the clamour Tobermory entered the room and made his way with velvet tread and studied unconcern across to the group seated round the tea-table.

A sudden hush of awkwardness and constraint fell on the company. Somehow there seemed an element of embarrassment in addressing on equal terms a domestic cat of acknowledged mental ability.

'Will you have some milk, Tobermory?' asked Lady Blemley in a rather strained voice.

'I don't mind if I do,' was the response, couched in a tone of even indifference. A shiver of suppressed excitement went through the listeners, and Lady Blemley might be excused for pouring out the saucerful of milk rather unsteadily.

'I am afraid I have spilled a good deal of it,' she said apologetically.

'After all, it's not my Axminster,' was Tobermory's rejoinder.

Another silence fell on the group, and then Miss Resker, in her best district-visitor manner, asked if the human language had been difficult to learn. Tobermory looked squarely at her for a moment and then fixed his gaze serenely on the middle distance. It was obvious that boring questions lay outside his scheme of life.

'What do you think of human intelligence?' asked Mavis Pellington lamely.

'Of whose intelligence in particular?' asked Tobermory coldly.

'Oh, well, mine for instance,' said Mavis, with a feeble laugh.

'You put me in an embarrassing position,' said Tobermory, whose tone and attitude certainly did not suggest a shred of embarrassment. 'When your inclusion in this house party was suggested, Sir Wilfrid protested that you were the most brainless woman of his acquaintance, and that there was a wide distinction between hospitality and the care of the feeble-minded. Lady Blemley replied that your lack of brain-power was the precise quality which had earned you your invitation, as you were the only person she could think of who might be idiotic enough to buy their old car. You know, the one they call "The Envy of Sisyphus", because it goes quite nicely uphill if you push it.'

Lady Blemley's protestations would have had greater effect if she had not casually suggested to Mavis only that morning that the car in question would be just the thing for her down at her Devonshire home.

Major Barfield plunged in heavily to effect a diversion.

'How about your carryings-on with the tortoiseshell puss up at the stables, eh?'

The moment he had said it everyone realized the blunder.

'One does not usually discuss these matters in public,' said Tobermory frigidly. 'From a slight observation of your ways since you've been in this house I should imagine you'd find it inconvenient if I were to shift the conversation on to your own little affairs.'

The panic which ensued was not confined to the Major.

'Would you like to go and see if cook has got your dinner ready?' sug-

Proverb, XVIIth century, Flemish (*Musée du Berry, Bourges*)

gested Lady Blemley hurriedly, affecting to ignore the fact that it wanted
at least two hours to Tobermory's dinner-time.

'Thanks,' said Tobermory, 'not quite so soon after my tea. I don't want
to die of indigestion.'

'Cats have nine lives, you know,' said Sir Wilfrid heartily.

'Possibly,' answered Tobermory; 'but only one liver.'

'Adelaide!' said Mrs Cornett, 'do you mean to encourage that cat to
go out and gossip about us in the servants' hall?'

The panic had indeed become general. A narrow ornamental balu-
strade ran in front of most of the bedroom windows at the Towers, and
it was recalled with dismay that this had formed a favourite promenade
for Tobermory at all hours, whence he could watch the pigeons – and
heaven knew what else besides. If he intended to become reminiscent
in his present outspoken strain the effect would be something more than
disconcerting. Mrs Cornett, who spent much time at her toilet table, and
whose complexion was reputed to be of a nomadic though punctual disposition, looked as ill at ease as the Major. Miss Scrawen, who wrote

fiercely sensuous poetry and led a blameless life, merely displayed irritation; if you are methodical and virtuous in private you don't necessarily want everyone to know it. Bertie van Tahn, who was so depraved at seventeen that he had long ago given up trying to be any worse, turned a dull shade of gardenia white, but he did not commit the error of dashing out of the room like Odo Finsberry, a young gentleman who was understood to be reading for the Church and who was possibly disturbed at the thought of scandals he might hear concerning other people. Clovis had the presence of mind to maintain a composed exterior; privately he was calculating how long it would take to procure a box of fancy mice through the agency of the *Exchange and Mart* as a species of hush-money.

Even in a delicate situation like the present, Agnes Resker could not endure to remain too long in the background.

'Why did I ever come down here?' she asked dramatically. Tobermory immediately accepted the opening.

'Judging by what you said to Mrs Cornett on the croquet lawn yesterday, you were out for food. You described the Blemleys as the dullest people to stay with that you knew, but said they were clever enough to employ a first-rate cook; otherwise they'd find it difficult to get anyone to come down a second time.'

'There's not a word of truth in it! I appeal to Mrs Cornett –' exclaimed the discomfitted Agnes.

'Mrs Cornett repeated your remark afterwards to Bertie van Tahn,' continued Tobermory, 'and said, "That woman is a regular Hunger Marcher; she'd go anywhere for four square meals a day," and Bertie van Tahn said–'

At this point the chronicle mercifully ceased. Tobermory had caught a glimpse of the big yellow Tom from the Rectory working his way through the shrubbery towards the stable wing. In a flash he had vanished through the open French window.

With the disappearance of his too brilliant pupil Cornelius Appin found himself beset by a hurricane of bitter upbraiding, anxious inquiry, and frightened entreaty. The responsibility for the situation lay with him, and he must prevent matters from becoming worse. Could Tobermory impart his dangerous gift to other cats? was the first question he had to answer. It was possible, he replied, that he might have initiated his intimate friend the stable puss into his new accomplishment, but it was unlikely that his teaching could have taken a wider range as yet.

'Then,' said Mrs Cornett, 'Tobermory may be a valuable cat and a great pet; but I'm sure you'll agree, Adelaide, that both he and the stable cat must be done away with without delay.'

'You don't suppose I've enjoyed the last quarter of an hour, do you?' said Lady Blemley bitterly. 'My husband and I are very fond of Tobermory – at least, we were before this horrible accomplishment was infused into him; but now, of course, the only thing is to have him destroyed as soon as possible.'

'We can put some strychnine in the scraps he always gets at dinnertime,' said Sir Wilfrid, 'and I will go and drown the stable cat myself. The coachman will be very sore at losing his pet, but I'll say a very catching form of mange has broken out in both cats and we're afraid of it spreading to the kennels.'

'But my great discovery!' expostulated Mr Appin; 'after all my years of research and experiment—'

Apollo Killing the Cyclops (detail), Domenichino (*National Gallery, London*)

'You can go and experiment on the short-horns at the farm, who are under proper control,' said Mrs Cornett, 'or the elephants at the Zoological Gardens. They're said to be highly intelligent, and they have this recommendation, that they don't come creeping about our bedrooms and under chairs, and so forth.'

An archangel ecstatically proclaiming the Millennium, and then finding that it clashed with Henley and would have to be indefinitely postponed, could hardly have felt more crestfallen than Cornelius Appin at the reception of his wonderful achievements. Public opinion, however, was against him – in fact, had the general voice been consulted on the subject it is probable that a strong minority vote would have been in favour of including him in the strychnine diet.

Defective train arrangements and a nervous desire to see matters brought to a finish prevented an immediate dispersal of the party, but dinner that evening was not a social success. Sir Wilfrid had had rather a trying time with the stable cat and subsequently with the coachman. Agnes Resker ostentatiously limited her repast to a morsel of dry toast, which she bit as though it were a personal enemy, while Mavis Pellington maintained a vindictive silence throughout the meal. Lady Blemley kept up a flow of what she hoped was conversation, but her attention was fixed on the doorway. A plateful of carefully dosed fish scraps was in readiness on the sideboard, but sweets and savoury and dessert went their way, and no Tobermory appeared either in the dining-room or kitchen.

The sepulchral dinner was cheerful compared with the subsequent vigil in the smoking-room. Eating and drinking had at least supplied a distraction and cloak to the prevailing embarrassment. Bridge was out of the question in the general tension of nerves and tempers, and after Odo Finsberry had given a lugubrious rendering of 'Melisande in the Wood' to a frigid audience, music was tacitly avoided. At eleven the servants went to bed, announcing that the small window in the pantry had been left open as usual for Tobermory's private use. The guests read steadily through the current batch of magazines, and fell back gradually on the 'Badminton Library' and bound volumes of *Punch*. Lady Blemley made periodic visits to the pantry, returning each time with an expression of listless depression which forestalled questioning.

At two o'clock Clovis broke the dominating silence.

'He won't turn up to-night. He's probably in the local newspaper office at the present moment, dictating the first instalment of his reminiscences. Lady What's-her-name's book won't be in it. It will be the event of the day.'

Having made this contribution to the general cheerfulness, Clovis went to bed. At long intervals the various members of the house party followed his example.

The servants taking round the early tea made a uniform announcement in reply to a uniform question. Tobermory had not returned.

Breakfast was, if anything, a more unpleasant function than dinner had been, but before its conclusion the situation was relieved. Tobermory's corpse was brought in from the shrubbery, where a gardener had just discovered it. From the bites on his throat and the yellow fur which coated his claws it was evident that he had fallen in unequal combat with the big Tom from the Rectory.

By midday most of the guests had quitted the Towers, and after lunch Lady Blemley had sufficiently recovered her spirits to write an extremely nasty letter to the Rectory about the loss of her valuable pet.

Tobermory had been Appin's one successful pupil, and he was destined to have no successor. A few weeks later an elephant in the Dresden Zoological Garden, which had shown no previous signs of irritability, broke loose and killed an Englishman who had apparently been teasing it. The victim's name was variously reported in the papers as Oppin and Eppelin, but his front name was faithfully rendered Cornelius.

'If he was trying German irregular verbs on the poor beast,' said Clovis, 'he deserved all he got.'

The Singing Cat

STEVIE SMITH

It was a little captive cat
　　Upon a crowded train
His mistress takes him from his box
　　To ease his fretful pain.

She holds him tight upon her knee
　　The graceful animal
And all the people look at him
　　He is so beautiful.

[197]

A Girl with a Kitten, Jean-Baptiste Perronneau (*National Gallery, London*)

But oh he pricks and oh he prods
 And turns upon her knee
Then lifteth up his innocent voice
 In plaintive melody.

He lifteth up his innocent voice
 He lifteth up, he singeth
And to each human countenance
 A smile of grace he bringeth.

[198]

He lifteth up his innocent paw
   Upon her breast he clingeth
And everybody cries, Behold
   The cat, the cat that singeth.

He lifteth up his innocent voice
   He lifteth up, he singeth
And all the people warm themselves
   In the love his beauty bringeth.

'When In Doubt – Wash'

PAUL GALLICO

These extracts are taken, with the author's permission, from Jennie, *by Paul Gallico. At the beginning of the adventure Peter, the boy turned into a white cat, is thrown out to shift for himself in London. Hounded and pursued from the West End to the Docks, he is half-killed by a tough tom cat, and his life is only saved when Jennie, a stray London tabby, who lives in a dockside warehouse, finds him unconscious in the street and drags him into her hideout.*

' "WHEN in doubt – any kind of doubt – *Wash!*" That is Rule No. 1,' said Jennie. She sat now primly and a little stiffly, with her tail wrapped around her feet, near the head of the big bed beneath the Napoleon Initial and Crown, rather like a schoolmistress. But it was obvious that the role of teacher and the respectful attention Peter bestowed upon her were not unendurable, because she had a pleased expression and her eyes were again gleaming brightly.

The sun had reached its noon zenith in the sky in the world that lay outside the dark and grimy warehouse, and coming in slantwise through the small window sent a dusty shaft that fell like a theatrical spotlight about Jennie's head and shoulders as she lectured.

'If you have committed any kind of an error and anyone scolds you – wash,' she was saying. 'If you slip and fall off something and somebody laughs at you – wash. If you are getting the worst of an argument and want to break off hostilities until you have composed yourself, start washing. Remember, *every* cat respects another cat at her toilet. That's our first rule of social deportment, and you must also observe it.

[199]

'Whatever the situation, whatever difficulty you may be in, you can't go wrong if you wash. If you come into a room full of people you do not know, and who are confusing to you, sit right down in the midst of them and start washing. They'll end up by quieting down and watching you. Some noise frightens *you* into a jump, and somebody you know saw you were frightened – begin washing immediately.

'If somebody calls you and you don't care to come and still you don't wish to make it a direct insult – wash. If you've started off to go somewhere and suddenly can't remember where it was you wanted to go, sit right down and begin brushing up a little. It will come back to you. Something hurt you? Wash it. Tired of playing with someone who has been kind enough to take time and trouble and you want to break off without hurting his or her feelings – start washing.

'Oh, there are dozens of things! Door closed and you're burning up because no one will open it for you – have yourself a little wash and forget it. Somebody petting another cat or dog in the same room, and you are annoyed over *that* – be nonchalant; wash. Feel sad – wash away your blues. Been picked up by somebody you don't particularly fancy and who didn't smell good – wash him off immediately and pointedly where he can see you do it. Overcome by emotion – a wash will help you to get a grip on yourself again. Any time, anyhow, in any manner, for whatever

A Farmyard Cat (Pictorial Press Ltd)

purpose, wherever you are, whenever and why ever that you want to clear the air, or get a moment's respite or think things over – WASH!

'And,' concluded Jennie, drawing a long breath, 'of course you also wash to get clean and to keep clean.'

'Goodness!' said Peter, quite worried. 'I don't see how I could possibly remember them all.'

'You don't have to remember any of it, actually,' Jennie explained. 'All that you have to remember is Rule 1: "When in doubt – WASH!"'

Peter, who, like all boys, had no objection to being reasonably clean, but not *too* clean, saw the problem of washing looming up large and threatening to occupy all of his time. 'It's true, I remember, you always do seem to be washing,' he protested to Jennie. 'I mean, all cats I've seen, but I don't see why. Why do cats spend so much of their time at it?'

Jennie considered his question for a moment, and then replied, 'Because it feels so good to be clean.'

'Well, at any rate I shall never be capable of doing it,' Peter remarked, 'because I won't be able to reach places now that I am a cat and cannot use my hands. And even when I was a boy, Nanny used to have to wash my back for me ...'

'Nothing of the kind,' said Jennie. 'The first thing you will learn that there isn't an inch of herself or himself that a cat cannot reach to wash. If you had ever owned one of us, you would know. Now watch me. We'll begin with the back. I'll do it first, and then you come over here alongside of me and do as I do.'

And thereupon sitting upright, she turned her head around over her shoulder with a wonderful ease and grace, using little short strokes of her tongue and keeping her chin down close to her body, she began to wash over and around her left shoulder-blade, gradually increasing the amount of turn and the length of the stroking movement of her head until her rough, pink tongue was travelling smoothly and firmly along the region of her upper spine.

'Oh, I never could!' cried Peter, 'because I cannot twist my head around as far as you can. I never know what is going on behind me unless I turn right around.'

'Try,' was all Jennie replied.

Peter did, and to his astonishment found that whereas when he had been a boy he had been unable to turn his head more left and right than barely to be able to look over his shoulders, now he could swivel it quite around on his neck so that he was actually gazing out behind him. And when he stuck out his tongue and moved his head in small circles as he had seen Jennie do, there he was washing around his left shoulder.

'Oh, bravo! Splendid!' applauded Jennie. 'There, you see! Well done, Peter. Now turn a little more – you're bound to be a bit stiff at first – and down the spine you go!'

And indeed, down the spine, about half-way from below his neck to the middle of his back, Peter went. He was so delighted that he tried to purr and wash at the same time, and actually achieved it.

'Now,' Jennie coached, 'for the rest of the way down, you can help yourself and make it easier – like this. Curve your body around and go a little lower so that you are half-sitting, half-lying. That's it! Brace yourself against your right paw and pull your left paw in a little closer to you so that it is out of the way. There ... Now, you see, that brings the rest of you nicely around in a curve where you can get at it. Finish off the left side of your back and hind-quarters and then shift around and do the other side.'

Peter did so, and was amazed to find with what little effort the whole of his spine and hindquarters was brought within ample reach of his busy tongue. He even essayed to have a go at his tail from this position, but found this a more elusive customer. It would keep squirming away.

Jennie smiled. 'Try putting a paw on it to hold it down. The right one. You can still brace yourself with it. That's it. We'll get at the underside of it later on.'

Peter was so enchanted with what he had learned that he would have gone on washing and washing the two sides of his back and his flanks and quarters if Jennie hadn't said, 'There, that's enough of that. There's still plenty left, you know. Now you must do your front and the stomach and the inside of your paws and quarters.'

The front limbs and paws, of course, proved easy for Peter, for they were quite close, but when he attempted to tackle his chest, it was something else.

'Try lying down first,' Jennie suggested. 'After a while you'll get so supple you will be able to wash your chest sitting up just by sticking your tongue out a little more and bobbing your head. But it's easier lying down on your side. Here, like this,' and she suited the action to the word, and soon Peter found that he actually was succeeding in washing his chest-fur just beneath his chin.

'But I can't get at my middle,' he complained, for indeed the underside of his belly defied his clumsy attempts to reach it, bend and twist as he would.

[202]

Simpkin Housekeeping, Beatrix Potter (*Tate Gallery, London*)

Jennie smiled. ' "*Can't* catches no mice," ' she quoted. 'That is more difficult. Watch me now. You won't do it lying on your side. Sit up a bit and rock on your tail. That's it, get your tail right under you. You can brace with either of your forepaws, or both. Now, you see, that bends you right around again and brings your stomach within reach. You'll get it with practice. It's all curves. That's why we were made that way.'

Peter found it more awkward to balance than in the other position and fell over several times, but soon found that he was getting better at it and that each portion of his person that was thus made accessible to him through Jennie's knowledge, experience and teaching brought him a new enjoyment and pleasure of accomplishment. And, of course, Jennie's approval made him very proud.

He was forging ahead so rapidly with his lesson that he decided to see whether he could go and learn by himself. 'Now how would you go about doing the inside of the hind-quarter?' she asked.

'Oh, that's easy,' Peter cried. But it wasn't at all. In fact, the more he tried and strained and reached and curved, the further away did his hind leg seem to go. He tried first the right and then the left, and finally got himself tangled in such a heap of legs, paws and tail that he fell right over in a manner that Jennie had to take a few quick dabs at herself to keep from laughing.

'I can't – I mean, I don't see how ...' wailed Peter, 'there isn't any way ...'

Jennie was contrite at once and hoped Peter had not seen she had been amused. 'Oh, I'm sorry,' she declared. 'That wasn't fair of me. There is, but it's most difficult, and you have to know how. It took me the longest time when my mother tried to show me. Here, does this suggest anything to you – Leg of Mutton? I'm sure you've seen it dozens of times,' and she assumed an odd position with her right leg sticking straight up in the air and somehow close to her head, almost like the contortionist that Peter had seen at the circus at Olympia who had twisted himself right around so that his head came down between his legs. He was sure that he could never do it.

Peter tried to imitate Jennie, but only succeeded in winding himself into a worse knot. Jennie came to his rescue once more. 'See here,' she said, 'let's try it by counts, one stage at a time. Once you've done it, you know, you'll never forget it. Now–

'One – rock on your tail.' Peter rocked.

'Two – brace yourself with your left forepaw.' Peter braced.

'Three – half-sit, and bend your back.' Peter managed that, and made himself into the letter C.

'Four – stretch out the left leg all the way. That will keep you from falling over the other side and provide a balance for the paw to push against.' This, too, worked out exactly as Jennie described it when Peter tried it.

'Five – swing your right leg from the hip – you'll find it will go – with the foot pointing straight up into the air. Yes, like that, but *outside*, not inside the right forepaw.' It went better this time. Peter got it almost up.

'Six – NOW you've got it. Hold yourself steady by bracing the right front forepaw. SO!'

Peter felt like shouting with joy. For there he was, actually sitting, leg of mutton, his hind-quarter shooting up right past his cheek and the whole inside of his leg exposed. He felt that he was really doubled back on himself like the contortionist, and he wished that Nanny were there so that he could show her.

[204]

By twisting and turning a little, there was no part of him underneath that he could not reach, and he washed first one side and then, without any further instruction from Jennie managed to reverse the position and get the left leg up, which drew forth an admiring 'Oh, you are clever!' from Jennie – 'it took me just ages to learn to work the left side. It all depends whether you are left or right pawed, but you caught on to it immediately. Now there's only one thing more. The back of the neck, the ears and the face.'

In a rush to earn more praise Peter went nearly cross-eyed trying to get his tongue out and around to reach behind him and on top of him, and of course it wouldn't work. He cried, 'Oh, dear, THAT must be the most complicated of all.'

'On the contrary,' smiled Jennie, 'it's quite the simplest. Wet the side of your front paw.' Peter did so. 'Now rub it around over your ears and the back of your neck.'

Now it was Peter's turn to laugh at himself. 'How stupid I am,' he said. 'That part is just the way I do it at home. Except I use a flannel, and Nanny stands there watching to make certain I go behind the ears.'

'Well,' said Jennie, '*I'm* watching you now ...'

So Peter completed his bath by wetting one paw and then the other, on the side and in the middle on the pads, and washing first his ears, then both sides of his face, the back of his neck, his whiskers, and even a little under his chin, and over his nose and eyes.

And now he found that having washed himself all over, from head to foot, the most wonderful feeling of comfort and relaxation had come over him. It was quite a different sensation from the time that Jennie had washed him and which had somehow taken him back to the days when he was very little and his mother was looking after him.

This time he felt a kind of glow in his skin and a sense of well-being in his muscles as though every one of them had been properly used and stretched. In the light from the last of the shaft of the sun that was just passing from the window of the store-house he could see how his white fur glistened from the treatment he had given it, as smooth as silk and as soft.

Peter felt a delicious drowsiness. His eyes began to close, and as from a distance he heard Jennie say 'It's good to take a nap after washing. I always do. You've earned it.'

Just before he dropped off to sleep, Peter felt her curl up against him, her back touching his, warm and secure, and the next moment he was off in sweet and dreamless slumber.

*　　*　　*

'I'm awfully thirsty, Jennie,' Peter whispered.

They had been crouching there around the bend of the warehouse corridor for the better part of an hour waiting for the men to finish the work of carrying out the furniture from the storage bin.

Jennie flattened herself and peered around the corner. 'Soon,' she said. 'There are only a few pieces left.'

'How I wish I had a tall, cool glass of milk,' Peter said.

Jennie turned her head and looked at him. 'Dish of milk, you mean. You wouldn't be able to drink it out of a glass. And as for milk – do you know how long it is since I have seen or tasted milk? In our kind of life, I mean, cut off from humans, there isn't any milk. If you're thirsty you find some rain-water or some slops in the gutter or in a pail left out, or you can go down the stone steps to the river landings when they are deserted at night, if you don't mind your water a little oily and brackish.'

Peter was not at all pleased with the prospect and he had not yet got used to the fact that he was no longer a boy, with a home and family, but a white cat with no home at all and no one to befriend him but another scrawny stray.

He was so desperately thirsty and the picture drawn by Jennie so gloomy and unpleasant that he could not help bursting into tears and crying. 'But I'm *used* to milk! I like it, and Nanny gives me some every day ...'

'Sshhh!' cautioned Jennie, 'they'll hear you.' Then she added: 'There's nobody goes about setting out dishes of milk for strays. You'll get used to not having it eventually.'

But Peter didn't think so, and continued to cry softly to himself while Jennie Baldrin watched him with growing concern and bewilderment. She seemed to be trying to make up her mind about something which apparently she did not very much wish to do. But finally, when it appeared that she could bear his unhappiness no longer, she whispered to him 'Come, now ... don't take on so! I know a place where I think I can get you a dish of milk. We'll go there.'

The thought caused Peter to stop crying and brighten up immediately. 'Yes?' he said. 'Where?'

'There's an old watchman lives in a shack down by the tea docks,' Jennie told him. 'He's lonely, likes cats, and is always good for a titbit, especially for me. He's been after me to come and live with him for months. Of course, I wouldn't dream of it.'

'But,' said Peter, not wishing to argue himself out of milk but only

Two Men and Four Cats, Jean-Antoine Watteau (*Musée Bonnat, Bayonne*)

desiring to understand clearly the terms under which they were to have it, 'that *is* taking it from people, isn't it?'

'It's taking, but not *giving* anything,' Jennie said, with that strange, unhappy intenseness that came over her whenever she discussed anything to do with human beings. 'We'll *have it* and then walk out on him.'

'Would that be right?' Peter asked. It slipped out almost before he was aware of it, for he very much wanted the milk and he equally did not wish to offend Jennie. But it was just that he had been taught certain ways of behaviour, or felt them to be so by instinct, and this seemed a poor way of repaying a kindness. Clearly he had somewhat put Jennie out, for she stiffened slightly and with the nearest thing to a cold look she had bestowed upon him since they had met, said 'You can't have it both ways, Peter. If you want to live my kind of life, and I can't see where you have very much choice at the moment –'

'But of course I do!' Peter hastened to explain, 'it's just that I'm not yet quite familiar with the different way cats feel than the way people feel. And I will do as you say, and I do want to learn ...'

From her expression, Jennie did not appear to be too pleased with this speech either, but before she could remark upon it there came a loud call from the movers, 'That's the lot, then,' and another voice replied, 'Righty-ho!' Jennie peered around the corner and said, 'They've finished. We'll wait a few minutes to make sure they don't come back, and then we'll start.'

When they were certain that the aisle was quite deserted again, they set off, Jennie leading, past the empty bin and down the corridor in the direction the men had taken, but before they had gone very far Jennie branched off to the right on a new track until she came to a bin close to the outside wall of the warehouse, filled with horrible, new, modern kind of furniture, chrome-bound leather and overstuffed plush. She led Peter to the back where there was a good-sized hole in the baseboard. It looked dark and forbidding inside.

'Don't be afraid,' Jennie said. 'Just follow me. We go to the right and then to the left, but it gets light very quickly.'

She slipped in with Peter after her, and it soon grew pitch black. Peter now discovered that he was feeling through the ends of his whiskers, rather than seeing where Jennie was, and he had no difficulty in following

Cat, photo Will Green

her, particularly inasmuch as it soon became bright enough to see that they were in a tunnel through which a large iron pipe more than a foot in diameter was running. Then Peter saw where the light was coming from. There was a hole in the pipe where it had rusted through a few feet from where it gave exit to the street.

Apparently the pipe was used as some kind of air intake, or had something to do with the ventilation of the warehouse, for it had once had a grating over the end of it, but the fastenings of that had long since rusted and it had fallen away, and there was nothing to bar their way out.

Peter was so pleased and excited at the prospect of seeing the sun and being out of doors again that he hurried past Jennie and would have rushed out into the street had not the alarm in her warning cry checked him just before he emerged from the opening.

'Peter! Wait!' she cried. 'Not like that! Cats never, *never* rush out from places. Don't you know about Pausing on the Threshold, or Lingering on the Sill? But then, of course, you wouldn't. Oh, dear, I don't mean always to be telling you what to do and what not to do, but this is really Important. It's almost Lesson No. 2. You never hurry out of any place, and particularly not outdoors.'

Peter saw that Jennie had quite recovered her good nature and apparently had forgotten that she had been upset with him. He was curious to find out the reasons for her warning. He said 'I don't quite understand, Jennie. You mean, I'm not to stop before coming in, but I am whenever I go out?'

'Of course. What else?' replied Jennie, sitting down quite calmly in the mouth of the exit and showing not the slightest disposition to go through it and into the street. 'You know what's inside because you come from there. You don't know what's outside because you haven't been there. That's common ordinary sense for anyone, I should think.'

'Yes, but what is there outside to be afraid of, really?' inquired Peter. 'I mean, after all, if you know where you live and the street and houses and all which don't change –'

'Oh, my goodness,' said Jennie. 'I couldn't try to tell you them all. To begin with – dogs, people, moving vehicles, the weather and changes in temperature, the condition of the street, is it wet or dry, clean or dirty, what has been left lying about, what is parked at the kerb, and whether anybody is coming along, on which side of the street and in how much of a hurry.

'And it isn't that you're actually afraid. It's just that you want to *know*.

And you ought to know, if you have your wits about you, everything your eyes, your ears, your nose and the ends of your whiskers can tell you. And so you stop, look, listen, and *feel*. We have a saying: "Heaven is over-crowded with kittens who rushed out of doors without first stopping and *receiving* a little."

'There might be another cat in the vicinity, bent on mischief, or looking for a fight. You'd certainly want to know about that before you stepped out into something you weren't prepared for. Then you'd want to know all about the weather, not only what it's like at the moment, but what it's going to be doing later, say an hour from then. If it's going to come on to rain or thunder, you wouldn't want to be too far from home. Your whiskers and your skin tell you that.

'And then, anyway,' Jennie concluded, 'it's a good idea on general principles not to rush into things. When you go out there are very few places to go to that won't be there just the same five minutes later, and the chances of your getting there will be ever so much better. Come here and squat down beside me and we'll just have a look.'

Peter did as she suggested and lay down directly in the opening with his paws tucked under him, and felt quite natural doing it, and suddenly he was glad that Jennie had stopped him and that he hadn't gone charging out into goodness knows what.

Feet went by at intervals. By observation he got to know something about the size of the shoes, which were mostly the heavy boots belonging to workmen, their speed, and how near they came to the wall of the warehouse. The wheeled traffic was of the heavy type – huge horse-drawn drays, and motor lorries that rumbled past ominously loud, and the horses' feet, huge things with big, shaggy fetlocks, were another danger. Far in the distance, Peter heard Big Ben strike four. The sound would not have reached him as a human being, perhaps, but it travelled all the distance from the Houses of Parliament to his cat's ears and informed him of the time.

Now he used his nostrils and sniffed the scents that came to his nose and tried to understand what they told him. There was a strong smell of tea and a queer odour that he could not identify, he just knew he didn't like it. He recognized dry goods, machinery, musk and spices, and horses and burned petrol, exhaust gases, tar and soft coal smoke, the kind that comes from railway engines.

Jennie had got up now and was standing on the edge of the opening with only her head out, whiskers extended forward, quivering a little, and making small wrinkly movements with her nose. After a moment

[210]

or so of this she turned to Peter quite relaxed and said 'All clear. We can go now. No cats around. There's a dog been by, but only a mangy cur probably scared of his own shadow. There's a tea-boat just docked. That's good. The Watchman won't really have any responsibilities until she's unloaded. Rain's all cleared away. Probably won't rain for at least another forty-eight hours. Goods train just gone down into the docks area. That's fine. Means the gates'll be open, and besides, we can use the wagons for cover.'

'Goodness!' Peter marvelled. 'I don't see how you can tell all that from just one tiny sniff around. Do you suppose I'll ever –?'

'Of course you will,' Jennie laughed, and with a bit of a purr added, 'It's only a matter of getting used to it and looking at things the way a cat would. It's really nothing.' And here she gave herself two or three self-conscious licks, for, truth to tell, she was just a trifle vain and nothing delighted her so much as to appear clever in Peter's eyes, which was only feline.

Cat and Dog Merchant, Paris 1774

'Well, I don't understand –' Peter began, saying just the right thing and giving her the lead which she was quick to take up.

'It's really quite simple,' she explained. 'For instance, you can smell the tea. Well, that wasn't around last time I was outside. Means a tea-boat has come in and they've opened the hatches. No cats about – I don't get any signals on my receiver, at least not hostile ones. The dog that went by, well, goodness knows, you can smell *him*. If he had any class or self-respect that might lead him to chase cats, he'd be clean, and a clean dog smells different. This one was filthy, and that's why I say he's nothing to worry about. He'll be slinking along down back alleys and glad to be left alone. And as for the goods train that went by, after you get to know the neighbourhood it'll be easy for you too. You see, the smoke smell comes from the left, down where the docks are, so of course it went that way. And you know it was a goods train, because you can smell everything that was in the wagons. There, you see how easy it is?'

Peter again said the right thing, for he was learning how to please Jennie. 'I think you're *enormously* clever,' he told her. Her purr almost drowned out the sound of a passing horse-drawn dray. Then she cried to him gaily, 'Come along, Peter! We're off!' and the two friends went out into the cobbled street.

Macavity: The Mystery Cat

T. S. ELIOT

Macavity's a Mystery Cat: he's called the Hidden Paw –
For he's the master criminal who can defy the Law.
He's the bafflement of Scotland Yard, the Flying Squad's despair:
For when they reach the scene of crime – *Macavity's not there*!

Macavity, Macavity, there's no one like Macavity,
He's broken every human law, he breaks the law of gravity.
His powers of levitation would make a fakir stare,
And when you reach the scene of crime – *Macavity's not there*!
You may seek him in the basement, you may look up in the air –
But I tell you once and once again, *Macavity's not there*!

[212]

Pole Cat, photo S. C. Reynolds (*Pictorial Press Ltd*)

Macavity's a ginger cat, he's very tall and thin;
You would know him if you saw him, for his eyes are sunken in.
His brow is deeply lined with thought, his head is highly domed;
His coat is dusty from neglect, his whiskers are uncombed.
He sways his head from side to side, with movements like a snake;
And when you think he's half asleep, he's always wide awake.

Macavity, Macavity, there's no one like Macavity,
For he's a fiend in feline shape, a monster of depravity.
You may meet him in a by-street, you may see him in the square –
But when a crime's discovered, then *Macavity's not there!*

He's outwardly respectable. (They say he cheats at cards.)
And his footprints are not found in any file of Scotland Yard's.
And when the larder's looted, or the jewel-case is rifled,
Or when the milk is missing, or another Peke's been stifled,
Or the greenhouse glass is broken, and the trellis past repair –
Ay, there's the wonder of the thing! *Macavity's not there!*

And when the Foreign Office find a Treaty's gone astray,
Or the Admiralty lose some plans and drawings by the way,
There may be a scrap of paper in the hall or on the stair –
But it's useless to investigate – *Macavity's not there!*
And when the loss has been disclosed, the Secret Service say:
'It *must* have been Macavity!' – but he's a mile away.
You'll be sure to find him resting, or a-licking of his thumbs,
Or engaged in doing complicated long division sums.

Macavity, Macavity, there's no one like Macavity,
There never was a Cat of such deceitfulness and suavity.
He always has an alibi, and one or two to spare:
At whatever time the deed took place – MACAVITY WASN'T THERE!
And they say that all the Cats whose wicked deeds are widely known
(I might mention Mungojerrie, I might mention Griddlebone)
Are nothing more than agents for the Cat who all the time
Just controls their operations: the Napoleon of Crime!

The Latecomer, Louis Wain (*Michael Parkin Fine Art Ltd*)

PART VI

Cat's Killings

Growltiger's Last Stand

T. S. ELIOT

Growltiger was a Bravo Cat, who travelled on a barge:
In fact he was the roughest cat that ever roamed at large.
From Gravesend up to Oxford he pursued his evil aims,
Rejoicing in his title of 'The Terror of the Thames'.

His manners and appearance did not calculate to please;
His coat was torn and seedy, he was baggy at the knees;
One ear was somewhat missing, no need to tell you why,
And he scowled upon a hostile world from one forbidding eye.

The cottages of Rotherhithe knew something of his fame;
At Hammersmith and Putney people shuddered at his name.
They would fortify the hen-house, lock up the silly goose,
When the rumour ran along the shore: GROWLTIGER'S
ON THE LOOSE!

Woe to the weak canary, that fluttered from its cage;
Woe to the pampered Pekinese, that faced Growltiger's rage;
Woe to the bristly Bandicoot, that lurks on foreign ships,
And woe to any Cat with whom Growltiger came to grips!

But most to Cats of foreign race his hatred had been vowed;
To Cats of foreign name and race no quarter was allowed.
The Persian and the Siamese regarded him with fear –
Because it was a Siamese had mauled his missing ear.

Now on a peaceful summer night, all nature seemed at play,
The tender moon was shining bright, the barge at Molesey lay.
All in the balmy moonlight it lay rocking on the tide –
And Growltiger was disposed to show his sentimental side.

His bucko mate, GRUMBUSKIN, long since had disappeared,
For to the Bell at Hampton he had gone to wet his beard,
And his bosun, TUMBLEBRUTUS, he too had stol'n away –
In the yard behind the Lion he was prowling for his prey.

The Cat and the Old Rat, Gustave Doré

In the forepeak of the vessel Growltiger sate alone,
Concentrating his attention on the Lady GRIDDLEBONE,
And his raffish crew were sleeping in their barrels and their bunks –
As the Siamese came creeping in their sampans and their junks.

Growltiger had no eye or ear for aught but Griddlebone,
And the Lady seemed enraptured by his manly baritone,
Disposed to relaxation, and awaiting no surprise –
But the moonlight shone reflected from a thousand bright blue eyes.

And closer still and closer the sampans circled round,
And yet from all the enemy there was not heard a sound.
The lovers sang their last duet, in danger of their lives –
For the foe was armed with toasting forks and cruel carving knives.

Then GILBERT gave the signal to his fierce Mongolian horde;
With a frightful burst of fireworks the Chinks they swarmed aboard.
Abandoning their sampans, and their pullaways and junks,
They battened down the hatches on the crew within their bunks.

Then Griddlebone she gave a screech, for she was badly skeered;
I am sorry to admit it, but she quickly disappeared.
She probably escaped with ease, I'm sure she was not drowned –
But a serried ring of flashing steel Growltiger did surround.

The ruthless foe pressed forward, in stubborn rank on rank;
Growltiger to his vast surprise was forced to walk the plank.
He who a hundred victims had driven to that drop,
At the end of all his crimes was forced to go ker-flip, ker-flop.

Oh there was joy in Wapping when the news flew through the land;
At Maidenhead and Henley there was dancing on the strand.
Rats were roasted whole at Brentford, and at Victoria Dock,
And a day of celebration was commanded in Bangkok.

A Cat

EDWARD THOMAS

She had a name among the children;
But no one loved though some one owned
Her, locked her out of doors at bedtime,
And had her kittens duly drowned.

Cat Accompanying Game, Jan Fyt (*Musée des Beaux-Arts, Nantes*)

In spring, nevertheless, this cat
Ate blackbirds, thrushes, nightingales,
And birds of bright voice, and plume, and flight,
As well as scraps from neighbours' pails.

I loathed and hated her for this;
One speckle on a thrush's breast
Was worth a million such; and yet
She lived long till God gave her rest.

Ming's Biggest Prey

PATRICIA HIGHSMITH

MING was resting comfortably on the foot of his mistress' bunk, when the man picked him up by the back of the neck, stuck him out on the deck and closed the cabin door. Ming's blue eyes widened in shock and brief anger, then nearly closed again because of the brilliant sunlight. It was not the first time Ming had been thrust out of the cabin rudely, and Ming realized that the man did it when his mistress, Elaine, was not looking.

The sailboat now offered no shelter from the sun, but Ming was not yet too warm. He leapt easily to the cabin roof and stepped onto the coil of rope just behind the mast. Ming liked the rope coil as a couch, because he could see everything from the height, the cup shape of the rope protected him from strong breezes, and also minimized the swaying and sudden changes of angle of the *White Lark*, since it was more or less the centre point. But just now the sail had been taken down, because Elaine and the man had eaten lunch, and often they had a siesta afterward, during which time, Ming knew, the man didn't like him in the cabin. Lunchtime was all right. In fact, Ming had just lunched on delicious grilled fish and a bit of lobster. Now, lying in a relaxed curve on the coil of rope, Ming opened his mouth in a great yawn, then with his slant eyes almost closed against the strong sunlight, gazed at the beige hills and the white and pink houses and hotels that circled the bay of Acapulco. Between the *White Lark* and the shore where people plashed inaudibly, the sun twinkled on the water's surface like thousands of tiny electric lights going on and off. A water-skier went by, skimming up white spray behind him. Such activity! Ming half dozed, feeling the heat of the sun sink into his fur. Ming was from New York, and he considered Acapulco a great improvement over his environment in the first weeks of his life. He remembered a sunless box with straw on the bottom, three or four other kittens in with him, and a window behind which giant forms paused for a few moments, tried to catch his attention by tapping, then passed on. He did not remember his mother at all. One day a young woman who smelled of something pleasant came into the place and took him away – away from the ugly, frightening smell of dogs, of medicine and parrot dung. Then they went on what Ming now knew was an aeroplane.

[223]

He was quite used to aeroplanes now and rather liked them. On aeroplanes he sat on Elaine's lap, or slept on her lap, and there were always
titbits to eat if he was hungry.

Elaine spent much of the day in a shop in Acapulco, where dresses
and slacks and bathing suits hung on all the walls. This place smelled
clean and fresh, there were flowers in pots and in boxes out front, and
the floor was of cool blue and white tile. Ming had perfect freedom to
wander out into the patio behind the shop, or to sleep in his basket in
a corner. There was more sunlight in front of the shop, but mischievous
boys often tried to grab him if he sat in front, and Ming could never
relax there.

Ming liked best lying in the sun with his mistress on one of the long
canvas chairs on their terrace at home. What Ming did not like were the
people she sometimes invited to their house, people who spent the night,
people by the score who stayed up very late eating and drinking, playing
the gramophone or the piano – people who separated him from Elaine.
People who stepped on his toes, people who sometimes picked him up
from behind before he could do anything about it, so that he had to
squirm and fight to get free, people who stroked him roughly, people
who closed a door somewhere, locking him in. *People!* Ming detested
people. In all the world, he liked only Elaine. Elaine loved him and understood him.

Especially this man called Teddie Ming detested now. Teddie was
around all the time lately. Ming did not like the way Teddie looked at
him, when Elaine was not watching. And sometimes Teddie, when Elaine
was not near, muttered something which Ming knew was a threat. Or
a command to leave the room. Ming took it calmly. Dignity was to be
preserved. Besides, wasn't his mistress on his side? The man was the
intruder. When Elaine was watching, the man sometimes pretended a
fondness for him, but Ming always moved gracefully but unmistakably
in another direction.

Ming's nap was interrupted by the sound of the cabin door opening.
He heard Elaine and the man laughing and talking. The big red-orange
sun was near the horizon.

'Ming!' Elaine came over to him. 'Aren't you getting *cooked*, darling?
I thought you were *in*!'

'So did I!' said Teddie.

Ming purred as he always did when he awakened. She picked him up
gently, cradled him in her arms, and took him below into the suddenly
cool shade of the cabin. She was talking to the man, and not in a gentle

[224]

The Music Lesson, Jean-Honoré Fragonard (*Musée du Louvre, Paris*)

tone. She set Ming down in front of his dish of water, and though he was not thirsty, he drank a little to please her. Ming did feel addled by the heat, and he staggered a little.

Elaine took a wet towel and wiped Ming's face, his ears and his four paws. Then she laid him gently on the bunk that smelled of Elaine's perfume but also of the man whom Ming detested.

Now his mistress and the man were quarrelling. Ming could tell from the tone. Elaine was staying with Ming, sitting on the edge of the bunk. Ming at last heard the splash that meant Teddie had dived into the water. Ming hoped he stayed there, hoped he drowned, hoped he never came back. Elaine wet a bathtowel in the aluminium sink, wrung it out, spread it on the bunk, and lifted Ming onto it. She brought water, and now Ming was thirsty, and drank. She left him to sleep again while she washed and put away the dishes. These were comfortable sounds that Ming liked to hear.

[225]

But soon there was another *plash* and *plop*, Teddie's wet feet on the deck, and Ming was awake again.

The tone of quarrelling recommenced. Elaine went up the few steps onto the deck. Ming, tense but with his chin still resting on the moist bathtowel, kept his eyes on the cabin door. It was Teddie's feet that he heard descending. Ming lifted his head slightly, aware that there was no exit behind him, that he was trapped in the cabin. The man paused with a towel in his hands, staring at Ming.

Ming relaxed completely, as he might do preparatory to a yawn, and this caused his eyes to cross. Ming then let his tongue slide a little way out of his mouth. The man started to say something, looked as if he wanted to hurl the wadded towel at Ming, but he wavered, whatever he had been going to say never got out of his mouth, and he threw the towel in the sink, then bent to wash his face. It was not the first time Ming had let his tongue slide out at Teddie. Lots of people laughed when Ming did this, if they were people at a party, for instance, and Ming rather enjoyed that. But Ming sensed that Teddie took it as a hostile gesture of some kind, which was why Ming did it deliberately to Teddie, whereas among other people, it was often an accident when Ming's tongue slid out.

The quarrelling continued. Elaine made coffee. Ming began to feel better, and went on deck again, because the sun had now set. Elaine had started the motor, and they were gliding slowly toward the shore. Ming caught the song of birds, the odd screams like shrill phrases of certain birds that cried only at sunset. Ming looked forward to the adobe house on the cliff that was his and his mistress' home. He knew that the reason she did not leave him at home (where he would have been more comfortable) when she went on the boat, was because she was afraid that people might trap him, even kill him. Ming understood. People had tried to grab him from almost under Elaine's eyes. Once he had been all the way in a cloth bag suddenly, and though fighting as hard as he could, he was not sure he would have been able to get out, if Elaine had not hit the boy herself and grabbed the bag from him.

Ming had intended to jump up on the cabin roof again, but after glancing at it, he decided to save his strength, so he crouched on the warm, gently sloping deck with his feet tucked in, and gazed at the approaching shore. Now he could hear guitar music from the beach. The voices of his mistress and the man had come to a halt. For a few moments, the loudest sound was the chug-chug-chug of the boat's motor. Then Ming heard the man's bare feet climbing the cabin steps. Ming did not turn his head

The Woman with Cat, Pierre Bonnard (*Kunsthalle, Bremen*)

to look at him, but his ears twitched back a little, involuntarily. Ming looked at the water just the distance of a short leap in front of him and below him. Strangely, there was no sound from the man behind him. The hair on Ming's neck prickled, and Ming glanced over his right shoulder.

At that instant, the man bent forward and rushed at Ming with his arms outspread.

Ming was on his feet at once, darting straight toward the man which was the only direction of safety on the railless deck, and the man swung his left arm and cuffed Ming in the chest. Ming went flying backward, claws scraping the deck, but his hind legs went over the edge. Ming clung with his front feet to the sleek wood which gave him little hold, while his hind legs worked to heave him up, worked at the side of the boat which sloped to Ming's disadvantage.

The man advanced to shove a foot against Ming's paws, but Elaine came up the cabin steps just then.

'What's happening? *Ming!*'

Ming's strong hind legs were getting him onto the deck little by little. The man had knelt as if to lend a hand. Elaine had fallen onto her knees, also, and had Ming by the back of the neck now.

Ming relaxed, hunched on the deck. His tail was wet.

'He fell overboard!' Teddie said. 'It's true he's groggy. Just lurched over and fell when the boat gave a dip.'

'It's the sun. Poor *Ming!*' Elaine held the cat.

The man came down into the cabin. Elaine had Ming on the bunk and was talking softly to him. Ming's heart was still beating fast. He was alert against the man at the wheel, even though Elaine was with him. Ming was aware that they had entered the little cove where they always went before getting off the boat.

Here were the friends and allies of Teddie, whom Ming detested by association, although these were merely Mexican boys. Two or three boys in shorts called 'Señor Teddie!' and offered a hand to Elaine to climb onto the dock, took the rope attached to the front of the boat, offered to carry 'Ming! – Ming!' Ming leapt onto the dock himself and crouched, waiting for Elaine, ready to dart away from any other hand that might reach for him. And there were several brown hands making a rush for him, so that Ming had to keep jumping aside. There were laughs, yelps, stomps of bare feet on wooden boards. But there was also the reassuring voice of Elaine, warning them off. Ming knew she was busy carrying off the plastic satchels, locking the cabin door. Teddie with the aid of one

[228]

of the Mexican boys was stretching the canvas over the cabin now. And Elaine's sandalled feet were beside Ming. Ming followed her as she walked away. A boy took the things Elaine was carrying, then she picked Ming up.

They got into the big car without a roof that belonged to Teddie, and drove up the winding road toward Elaine's and Ming's house. One of the boys was driving. Now the tone in which Elaine and Teddie were speaking was calmer, softer. The man laughed. Ming sat tensely on his mistress' lap. He could feel her concern for him in the way she stroked him and touched the back of his neck. The man reached out to put his fingers on Ming's back, and Ming gave a low growl that rose and fell and rumbled deep in his throat.

'Well, well,' said the man, pretending to be amused and took his hand away.

Elaine's voice had stopped in the middle of something she was saying. Ming was tired, and wanted nothing more than to take a nap on the big bed at home. The bed was covered with a red and white striped blanket of thin wool.

Hardly had Ming thought of this, when he found himself in the cool, fragrant atmosphere of his own home, being lowered gently onto the bed with the soft woollen cover. His mistress kissed his cheek, and said something with the word hungry in it. Ming understood, at any rate. He was to tell her when he was hungry.

Ming dozed, and awakened at the sound of voices on the terrace a couple of yards away, past the open glass doors. Now it was dark. Ming could see one end of the table, and could tell from the quality of the light that there were candles on the table. Concha, the servant who slept in the house, was clearing the table. Ming heard her voice, then the voices of Elaine and the man. Ming smelled cigar smoke. Ming jumped to the floor and sat for a moment looking out the door toward the terrace. He yawned, then arched his back and stretched, and limbered up his muscles by digging his claws into the thick straw carpet. Then he slipped out to the right on the terrace and glided silently down the long stairway of broad stones to the garden below. The garden was like a jungle or a forest. Avocado trees and mango trees grew as high as the terrace itself, there were bougainvilleas against the wall, orchids in the trees, and magnolias and several camellias which Elaine had planted. Ming could hear birds twittering and stirring in their nests. Sometimes he climbed trees to get at their nests, but tonight he was not in the mood, though he was no longer tired. The voices of his mistress and the man disturbed him.

His mistress was not a friend of the man's tonight, that was plain.

Concha was probably still in the kitchen, and Ming decided to go in and ask her for something to eat. Concha liked him. One maid who had not liked him had been dismissed by Elaine. Ming thought he fancied barbecued pork. That was what his mistress and the man had eaten tonight. The breeze blew fresh from the ocean, ruffling Ming's fur slightly. Ming felt completely recovered from the awful experience of nearly falling into the sea.

Now the terrace was empty of people. Ming went left, back into the bedroom, and was at once aware of the man's presence, though there was no light on and Ming could not see him. The man was standing by the dressing-table, opening a box. Again involuntarily Ming gave a low growl which rose and fell, and Ming remained frozen in the position he had been in when he first became aware of the man, his right front paw extended for the next step. Now his ears were back, he was prepared to spring in any direction, although the man had not seen him.

'*Ssss-st!* Damn you!' the man said in a whisper. He stamped his foot, not very hard, to make the cat go away.

Ming did not move at all. Ming heard the soft rattle of the white necklace which belonged to his mistress. The man put it into his pocket, then moved to Ming's right, out the door that went into the big living-room. Ming now heard the clink of a bottle against glass, heard liquid being poured. Ming went through the same door and turned left toward the kitchen.

Here he miaowed, and was greeted by Elaine and Concha. Concha had her radio turned on to music.

'Fish? – Pork. He likes pork,' Elaine said, speaking the odd form of words which she used with Concha.

Ming, without much difficulty, conveyed his preference for pork, and got it. He fell to with a good appetite. Concha was exclaiming 'Ah-eee-ee!' as his mistress spoke with her, spoke at length. Then Concha bent to stroke him, and Ming put up with it, still looking down at his plate, until she left off and he could finish his meal. Then Elaine left the kitchen. Concha gave him some of the tinned milk, which he loved, in his now empty saucer, and Ming lapped this up. Then he rubbed himself against her bare leg by way of thanks, and went out of the kitchen, made his way cautiously into the living-room en route to the bedroom. But now his mistress and the man were out on the terrace. Ming had just entered the bedroom, when he heard Elaine call:

'Ming? Where are you?'

There is always Another, Marcus Stone (*Tate Gallery, London*)

Ming went to the terrace door and stopped, and sat on the threshold.

Elaine was sitting sideways at the end of the table, and the candlelight was bright on her long fair hair, on the white of her trousers. She slapped her thigh, and Ming jumped onto her lap.

The man said something in a low tone, something not nice.

Elaine replied something in the same tone. But she laughed a little.

Then the telephone rang.

Elaine put Ming down, and went into the living-room toward the telephone.

The man finished what was in his glass, muttered something at Ming, then set the glass on the table. He got up and tried to circle Ming, or to get him toward the edge of the terrace, Ming realized, and Ming also realized that the man was drunk – therefore moving slowly and a little clumsily. The terrace had a parapet about as high as the man's hips, but it was broken by grilles in three places, grilles with bars wide enough for Ming to pass through, though Ming never did, merely looked through the grilles sometimes. It was plain to Ming that the man wanted to drive him through one of the grilles, or grab him and toss him over the terrace parapet. There was nothing easier for Ming than to elude him. Then the man picked up a chair and swung it suddenly, catching Ming on the hip. That had been quick, and it hurt. Ming took the nearest exit, which was down the outside steps that led to the garden.

The man started down the steps after him. Without reflecting, Ming dashed back up the few steps he had come, keeping close to the wall which was in shadow. The man hadn't seen him, Ming knew. Ming leapt to the terrace parapet, sat down and licked a paw once to recover and collect himself. His heart beat fast as if he were in the middle of a fight. And hatred ran in his veins. Hatred burned his eyes as he crouched and listened to the man uncertainly climbing the steps below him. The man came into view.

Ming tensed himself for a jump, then jumped as hard as he could, landing with all four feet on the man's right arm near the shoulder. Ming clung to the cloth of the man's white jacket, but they were both falling. The man groaned. Ming hung on. Branches crackled. Ming could not tell up from down. Ming jumped off the man, became aware of direction and of the earth too late and landed on his side. Almost at the same time, he heard the thud of the man hitting the ground, then of his body rolling a little way, then there was silence. Ming had to breathe fast with his mouth open until his chest stopped hurting. From the direction of the man, he could smell drink, cigar, and the sharp odour that meant fear. But the man was not moving.

Ming could now see quite well. There was even a bit of moonlight. Ming headed for the steps again, had to go a long way through the bush, over stones and sand, to where the steps began. Then he glided up and arrived once more upon the terrace.

Elaine was just coming onto the terrace.

'Teddie?' she called. Then she went back into the bedroom where she turned on a lamp. She went into the kitchen. Ming followed her. Concha had left the light on, but Concha was now in her own room, where the radio played.

Elaine opened the front door.

The man's car was still in the driveway, Ming saw. Now Ming's hip had begun to hurt, or now he had begun to notice it. It caused him to limp a little. Elaine noticed this, touched his back, and asked him what was the matter. Ming only purred.

'Teddie? – Where are you?' Elaine called.

She took a torch and shone it down into the garden, down among the great trunks of the avocado trees, among the orchids and the lavender and pink blossoms of the bougainvilleas. Ming, safe beside her on the terrace parapet, followed the beam of the torch with his eyes and purred with content. The man was not below here, but below and to the right. Elaine went to the terrace steps and carefully, because there was no rail here, only broad steps, pointed the beam of the light downward. Ming did not bother looking. He sat on the terrace where the steps began.

'Teddie!' she said. '*Teddie!*' Then she ran down the steps.

Ming still did not follow her. He heard her draw in her breath. Then she cried:

'*Concha!*'

Elaine ran back up the steps.

Concha had come out of her room. Elaine spoke to Concha. Then Concha became excited. Elaine went to the telephone, and spoke for a short while, then she and Concha went down the steps together. Ming settled himself with his paws tucked under him on the terrace, which was still faintly warm from the day's sun. A car arrived. Elaine came up the steps, and went and opened the front door. Ming kept out of the way on the terrace, in a shadowy corner, as three or four strange men came out on the terrace and tramped down the steps. There was a great deal of talk below, noises of feet, breaking of bushes, and then the smell of all of them mounted the steps, the smell of tobacco, sweat, and the familiar smell of blood. The man's blood. Ming was pleased, as he was pleased when he killed a bird and created this smell of blood under his own teeth. This was big prey. Ming, unnoticed by any of the others, stood up to his full height as the group passed with the corpse, and inhaled the aroma of his victory with a lifted nose.

Then suddenly the house was empty. Everyone had gone, even Concha. Ming drank a little water from his bowl in the kitchen, then went to his mistress' bed, curled against the slope of the pillows, and fell fast asleep. He was awakened by the rr-rr-r of an unfamiliar car. Then the

[233]

Woman with Leaping Cat, Robert Colquhoun (*Tate Gallery, London*)

front door opened, and he recognized the step of Elaine and then Concha. Ming stayed where he was. Elaine and Concha talked softly for a few minutes. Then Elaine came into the bedroom. The lamp was still on. Ming watched her slowly open the box on her dressing table, and into it she let fall the white necklace that made a little clatter. Then she closed the box. She began to unbutton her shirt, but before she had finished, she flung herself on the bed and stroked Ming's head, lifted his left paw and pressed it gently so that the claws came forth.

'Oh Ming – Ming,' she said.

Ming recognized the tones of love.

The Colubriad

WILLIAM COWPER

Close by the threshold of a door nail'd fast
Three kittens sat: each kitten look'd aghast.
I, passing swift and inattentive by,
At the three kittens cast a careless eye;
Not much concern'd to know what they did there,
Not deeming kittens worth a poet's care.
But presently a loud and furious hiss
Caused me to stop, and to exclaim – what's this?
When, lo! upon the threshold met my view,
With head erect, and eyes of fiery hue,
A viper, long as Count de Grasse's queue.
Forth from his head his forkèd tongue he throws,
Darting it full against a kitten's nose;
Who having never seen in field or house
The like, sat still and silent, as a mouse:
Only, projecting with attention due
Her whisker'd face, she ask'd him – who are you?
On to the hall went I, with pace not slow,
But swift as lightning, for a long Dutch hoe;
With which well arm'd I hasten'd to the spot,
To find the viper. But I found him not,
And, turning up the leaves and shrubs around,
Found only, that he was not to be found.
But still the kittens, sitting as before,
Sat watching close the bottom of the door.
I hope – said I – the villain I would kill
Has slipt between the door and the door's sill;
And if I make dispatch, and follow hard,
No doubt but I shall find him in the yard –

For long ere now it should have been rehears'd,
'Twas in the garden that I found him first.
E'en there I found him; there the full-grown cat
His head with velvet paw did gently pat,
As curious as the kittens erst had been
To learn what this phenomenon might mean.
Fill'd with heroic ardour at the sight,
And fearing every moment he might bite,
And rob our household of our only cat
That was of age to combat with a rat,
With outstretch'd hoe I slew him at the door,
And taught him NEVER TO COME THERE NO MORE.

Aunty and Her Cats

PAUL ABLEMAN

SOMETIMES my great-aunt would be sitting at her dressing-table, in the curve of the big bow window, brushing her white, fine, still abundant hair with a matched set of engraved silver hair-brushes, the gift of a Viennese count perhaps – or a German baron. More probably, at that time of day, she would be seated on the low sofa in front of the blazing gas-fire, legs apart to reveal the ends of long, silk bloomers, spectacles perched on her dainty nose, round, astonishingly-smooth face wrinkled into a frown of dismay as she studied the *Evening Standard*.

'Ach! Terrible it is – terrible!'

'What is?'

'Have you not heard? This earthquake in – Brazil, is it?'

She would peer forwards at the elusive print and then amend, 'Ah – Mehico – Mehico! Twelve people killed and three buried alive! This is – such a tragedy! These poor people! Terrible!'

In my callow intolerance, I felt merely irritated by her distress. In the midst of a desperate war that had, amongst greater enormities, deprived her of everything she owned, Aunty would fuss endlessly about some trivial natural disaster. But the thing that, shamefully, annoyed me most about her was her devotion to Nicki and Simon, her two sluggish, overfed cats. These were regularly the recipient of tidbits which in wartime should clearly have been reserved for human beings. It infuriated me to see Aunty slip morsels of precious meat into the cats' mouths or even pour them a saucer of priceless cream. I sensed that Aunty loved those cats more than any other living things and this seemed to me monstrous when my aunt Olga had, with incredible pains, snatched her from Nazi Germany and installed her in the greatest luxury our guest-house could offer. There was no prospect of any material return since all Aunty's possessions in Bavaria had been seized. The old lady, who had been the mistress of many aristocrats, was now a pauper.

I was angered then by Aunty's pampering of her cats but perhaps even more so by her intermittent bursts of fury with them. Through the thin ceiling, if I happened to be in Olga's basement room, I might suddenly hear a hubbub from Aunty's room above:

'Pfa! Pfooi! Villain! Verdamt! Aus! Aus! Geh – Schwein!'

We would also hear dismal thudding and scratching sounds. Olga would leap to her feet, exclaiming, 'Oh my God – not again!'

And hasten out of the room and up the stairs. I would listen sardonically to Aunty's voice, shrill with denunciation, and Olga's soothing one. I knew, from abundant precedent, exactly what had happened. Nicki or Simon, shaking off its overfed torpor and responding to atavistic impulse, would once again have caught a bird and, blissfully and idiotically forgetful of its reception after the last such escapade, would have carried the bedraggled corpse up the garden steps, along the balcony ledge, through the noble French windows and finally deposited it proudly at Aunty's feet. The old lady would then have risen like one of the Furies, stamped her foot at the disconcerted animal and abused it in ringing terms. She could never bring herself actually to assault her darlings but sometimes she went so far as to pursue fat, tortoiseshell Simon or black, bulging Nicki with a broom and many a menacing feint. And, sometimes for days on end, she would be inconsolable. When Olga attempted to defend the obese predator, extolling some imaginary feline virtue, Aunty would angrily contradict her:

'No, Nicki is a swine! I have told him before – he must not kill the birds! Ach, the pig! I never will see him again!'

Sadly, tenderly, she would take up the little huddle of feathers and stump off with it across the room, down the steps to the garden and there, right at the end under the plane tree, bury it with a trowel, pausing repeatedly to make a fierce gesture towards a black nose and a pair of glowing, carnivore's eyes that peered apprehensively out at her from the jungle of a peony bush.

[237]

I found these episodes baffling and excessively irritating. Once or twice, I tried to remonstrate with Aunty, 'After all, it's part of their nature.'

'Ja, ja.' She would nod sadly.

Cat with Cock

'I mean it's instinct. Cats are hunting animals.'

'He is a swine, that Nicki!'

'But, Aunty, it's utterly illogical. It's like – like setting something on fire and then being upset because it burns.'

'He will not get any cream on Sunday. I will punish him.'

'But that's crazy.'

'Ach, the poor little bird! The little bird!'

And I would note, with uncomfortable surprise, that Aunty's large, grey-blue eyes, a little discoloured with age, were full of tears. She had no imagination, no philosophical or scientific view of the universe, but – rivalling feats attributed to deity – she noted and mourned the fall of a sparrow.

The Rat-Catcher and Cats

JOHN GAY

The rats by night such mischief did,
Betty was every morning chid.
They undermined whole sides of bacon,
Her cheese was sapp'd, her tarts were taken.
Her pasties, fenced with thickest paste,
Were all demolish'd, and laid waste.
She cursed the Cat for want of duty,
Who left her foes a constant booty.

An engineer, of noted skill,
Engaged to stop the growing ill.

From room to room he now surveys
Their haunts, their works, their secret ways;
Finds where they 'scape and ambuscade,
And whence the nightly sally's made,

And envious Cat, from place to place,
Unseen attends his silent pace.
She saw that if his trade went on,
The purring race must be undone;
So, secretly removes his baits,
And ev'ry stratagem defeats.

Again he sets the poison'd toils,
And Puss again the labour foils.

[239]

The Ratcatcher, Thomas Woodward (*Tate Gallery, London*)

What foe (to frustrate my designs)
My schemes thus nightly countermines?
Incensed, he cries, this very hour
The wretch shall bleed beneath my power.
    So said, a pond'rous trap he brought,
And in the fact poor Puss was caught.
    Smuggler, says he, thou shalt be made
A victim to our loss of trade.
    The captive Cat, with piteous mews,
For pardon, life, and freedom sues.
A sister of the science spare;
One int'rest is our common care.
    What insolence! the man replied;
Shall cats with us the game divide?
Were all your interloping band
Extinguish'd or expell'd the land,

We Rat-catchers might raise our fees,
Sole guardians of a nation's cheese!
  A Cat, who saw the lifted knife,
Thus spoke, and saved her sister's life:
  In ev'ry age and clime we see,
Two of a trade can ne'er agree.
Each hates his neighbour for encroaching;
'Squire stigmatizes 'squire for poaching;
Beauties with beauties are in arms,
And scandal pelts each other's charms;
Kings, too, their neighbour kings dethrone,
In hope to make the world their own,
But let us limit our desires,
Not war like beauties, kings, and 'squires!
For though we both one prey pursue,
There's game enough for us and you.

Cat and Fiddle

ROY FULLER

DINNER at the Club: always a blend of boredom and, à la Henry James,
stimulation at hearing of the lives of others. When Bobby Freeman sat
next to me at the round table the mix seemed likely to have gone wrong
for the evening. He talked, as he often does, about crime, fictional and
real, even recounting a few plots. He is one of those who talk so much
that food accompanies their words, sometimes flecking one's clothes. He
made the ancient point that we can never know about the 'perfect' crime
precisely because of its perfection. Still, there were a few murders which
might be classed as perfect simply by reason of the meagre number of
people who suspected them of being murders. Who, for example, except
himself, was aware of the Guild case?

'Sir Hugh's?' I asked jokingly, really envisaging something involving
a political or craft organization of the slightly eccentric kind, which Bobby
might well have special information about. We both knew Hugh Guild,
Bobby better than I.

'Yes.'

Even as I laughed an uneasy memory came of the deaths in Hugh's life. 'Oh, really, Bobby.'

'This is what I had from Hugh himself,' said Bobby. 'As a novelist you'll be interested.'

When Hugh retired from the Museum, he and his wife went to live in some village on the far side of Newbury. (I put down what Bobby told me, embellished with my own knowledge.) The house was called 'The Cottages': someone had converted three cottages into the one dwelling. Hugh bought an adjoining paddock with an eye to enlarging the garden. He had enough money to do so and to titivate the place further, having sold the Chelsea house he'd owned all the time he'd directed the Museum.

Odd to contemplate Hugh Guild in the country. He had been a dogged world traveller on Museum business: when at home, an equally dogged party-goer and diner-out. I remember the first time I saw him at an evening-dress function being amazed at the splendour of his decorations – which included a fair selection of foreign orders – and thinking that perhaps a strong motive for such appearances was the opportunity to display the evidence of his honours. At cocktail parties his shiny black hair (which never changed colour, even in his sixties) could be seen surrounded by the more desiccated and abundant hair of the young – his books, and exhibitions at the Museum, which always seemed just to anticipate new enthusiasms and shifts in taste, ensured him an audience of that constitution.

Not that he appeared to do more than accept their homage. In England at any rate he was always accompanied by Lady Guild, growing more and more to seem mother rather than wife. Though she, too, had kept thin, a somewhat battered mask was quite early presented: one eyelid was inclined to droop; the chin sported a sprouting mole. The figure, by no means straight-backed, was surmounted by white hair in a very old-fashioned 'bob'. The total effect was inclined to the witchlike.

Helen Guild's transmogrification into a countrywoman was also surprising, since she too had been active in urban affairs, mainly of an obscure 'good works' kind. The fact was that at sixty-five they were both rather weary and possessed ailments not less lowering for being scarcely definable. Hugh found himself relieved to give up the responsibilities of administration. Their notion of regular London 'days' was not fulfilled. They dropped almost completely out of their former worlds.

Yet Hugh didn't feel that his life was on a finally downward slope. Rather he saw himself as re-charging his batteries for a 'final period' of somewhat changed scope – the authorship of different kinds of books

[242]

and articles, possibly some new appointment in the public service sphere. The decorations had not been permanently mothballed, as it were: they would eventually re-emerge, perhaps with a couple of distinguished additions.

Nevertheless, the Guilds at first were quiet and shaky. Hugh's insomnia wasn't mathematically more severe than in London but since he hadn't to be on parade the following day he positively indulged his nocturnal wakefulness – going downstairs to read for long periods, making himself drinks and snacks, even strolling in the enlarging garden.

'We've got mice,' he told his wife at breakfast one day.

'Have we?'

'I saw one when I came down to make my Ovaltine last night.'

'We had mice at Bramerton Street,' said Lady Guild.

'I never saw any.'

'Well, in those days you didn't make a habit of visiting the kitchen in the middle of the night.'

Quite soon, Hugh raised the question again.

'Those bloody mice come out and sit up and watch me.'

'I expect they're only field mice,' said Lady Guild.

'I don't care what they are, I don't like them. I find I've an unreasoning fear of them. I'm quite uneasy when I have to go into the kitchen and switch on the light.'

'You should try harder to get to sleep again upstairs.'

'I think we ought to buy a cat.'

'We've never had pets,' said Lady Guild. 'We don't know how to deal with them.'

'A cat wouldn't need "dealing with".'

'Um.'

The pub on the village green had been raised in status by the brewers – with a licensee to match, possessing a military title. The Guilds had begun by patronizing the bar luncheon and then Hugh took to dropping in at the end of an evening stroll. To the landlord he told his mice story. Also behind the bar was a Mrs Farrer, a pale young woman, usually with a cigarette sticking out of her mouth. She said that the pub's charwoman's cat, nondescript itself, had had kittens, the father reputed to be a Persian of prize breed. They were going gratis.

'Which kind do you want?' Mrs Farrer asked Hugh. 'Boy or girl?'

Had he been entirely serious about acquiring a cat? Under Mrs Farrer's laconic but penetrating interrogation he felt suddenly carried along by events.

'Girl,' he said, matching her off-handedness, but with a sense of some unusual step taken, not wholly displeasing.

Lady Guild disclaimed any responsibility for the slight new complication in their lives. Though not actively hostile, she was uncharmed by the mainly black, diminutive animal that after a few hours of cowering and peeing under furniture scuttled across the floors, climbed curtains and attacked feet.

'That kitten is very bold,' Hugh observed with satisfaction. 'The mice had better look out.'

He began to refer to the creature as 'Boldero'. When Lady Guild asked him if that was to be its name and he affirmed it, she remarked it was an odd one.

' "Boldero" was a *nom de plume* assumed by the poet Grigson in the Thirties,' he said.

'Grigson?'

'You remember him. Friend of Bill Coldstream.'

In a few days' time Lady Guild heard her husband shouting 'Martin, Martin' in the garden. When challenged, he said he'd been calling the kitten.

'I thought it was called Boldero,' said Lady Guild.

'The *nom de plume* was "Martin Boldero". I've shortened it to Martin.'

'But the animal is female.'

'That's true,' Hugh had to admit.

'Besides, it has fleas.'

Though Hugh would have been on safer ground in attacking this final statement merely as a *non sequitur*, he disputed the actual infestation. 'The *Cat and Fiddle* cleaner is a very well turned out person and I'm sure her house is the same.'

It was an indication of Hugh's ignorance of 'pets' that he seemed to confuse human and feline parasites. Stroking Boldero (or Martin) the very day of this conversation, he saw an insect on the back of his thumb which, instead of flying or crawling away in an ordinary manner, disappeared with a disreputable leap. Far more for Boldero's comfort than in the interests of domestic hygiene, Hugh took action without delay, plunging the animal in a wash-basinful of tepid water, tinctured with shampoo and Dettol. Its struggles were fairly effectively mastered but the immediate result was appalling. In his hands shivered a skeletal kitten, all the more horrifying for the thin layer of fur plastered to the bone. The apparition jerked out of the towel Hugh had ready, and disappeared downstairs under a chiffonier which Hugh laboriously moved,

Temptation, Gabriel Gresly (*Musée du Dijon*)

fearing that Boldero would catch a chill, even pneumonia. The kitten, cornered, flew out of the window, breaking a nice little saucer in the process.

In the evening, when the parties were reconciled, Hugh saw a flea slither from a patch of Boldero's preternaturally-shining white to the ampler cover of the black. He removed the kitten from his knee to the floor, but without haste, since Lady Guild was in the room and she had already commented adversely on the breakage and other depredations of the afternoon bathe. 'I'm afraid that flea-ridden beast will have to go,' she had concluded unemotionally.

Hugh was agreeably surprised to see that Boots in Newbury devoted considerable shelf space to feline remedies and cosmetics: it was like finding a cache of books of one's special interest in an unpromising second-hand shop. He came away with several items, including anti-flea powder, which as soon as Lady Guild was out of the way for half an hour he used according to the directions.

[245]

The parasites went on being apparent. The mice have been extirpated only to be replaced by fleas, he thought, emitting a wry snigger. He would have passed on the jest to his wife had he not feared her irony: moreover, he was still carrying on his fleaing in secrecy. This eventually had to be done in his dressing-room, for the final and most effective mode involved a comb and a bowl of water, the latter hard to conceal at short notice. The fleas emerged dazed on the comb or, with even greater chance of capture, trapped in its teeth. They were drowned in the bowl of water; in later sessions more humanely cracked between Hugh's thumb-nails, the betraying water dispensed with.

The resultant blood or guts – or, indeed, any part of the operation – did not disgust him. The small black specks, discernible against the white parts of the fur, which he had thought to be flea eggs, left a trail of red in the water: obviously they were flea excrement, composed of Boldero's gore. The discovery held the impersonality and pleasure of scientific knowledge. Nevertheless, the whole process undoubtedly brought on a rapid intimacy and sympathy, as between patient and nurse.

'How are you getting on with that kitten?' Mrs Farrer asked Hugh when he had dropped into the *Cat and Fiddle* soon after these pulicine sessions. She had proved to be the landlady's daughter by a former marriage, now living, presumably more or less permanently, at the pub.

'Had great flea trouble,' said Hugh, only too pleased to find a neutral ear in which to spill a prolix account of his therapy.

When he got home he saw that his wife had a long sticking plaster on the back of her hand. 'What have you been doing to yourself?'

'Boldero scratched me.'

'What were you doing to her?'

'Absolutely nothing.'

'Are you sure?'

'Of course I'm sure,' said Lady Guild.

'I mean are you sure you didn't do it pruning that rambler?'

'You must allow me to know whether or not I've been scratched by a cat.'

'It's utterly out of character. Even when I tease her she knows exactly how far to go with her teeth and claws.' He visualized raising his fist, Boldero clinging to it like the fur trimming of a sleeve. His mind was full of the touching flea saga, just related to Mrs Farrer. Also, the few drinks he'd had on an empty stomach encouraged his challenge of events which really it seemed unlikely his wife would be misconceived or mendacious about. Lady Guild, indeed, gave him a pitying look and went out of the room.

'I'm sick of that cat,' she was heard to say before she died, though the words were not distinct and Hugh's view was that she was still delirious and actually referring to a hat – the only one she possessed and which in their more public days she had to put on her bobbed locks when attending a garden party at Buck House and the like. It was an object of which she had made previous criticism. Rose-thorn or Boldero – medical opinion was neutral. The only certainty was that the septicaemia spreading from the scratched hand seemed unusually resistant. In a way, Hugh was thus supported in his persistence in his darling's defence.

Besides, to have admitted the cat's guilt would surely have lessened the comfort she afforded him in the early days of his widowerhood. It would have been tantamount to forgiving the crime in the most heinous possible manner – cohabiting happily with the criminal. The weeks following the funeral marked Boldero's transition from foolish kittendom to vigorous young queenliness. Perhaps in the end the charm and condescending companionship were slightly overdone: Hugh began to feel himself the inferior partner in an alliance of the human and animal worlds.

'I'm glad we're seeing you here once more,' said Mrs Farrer to Hugh in the saloon bar of the *Cat and Fiddle*. 'If you don't mind my saying so, we thought you'd cut yourself off completely from the village. That would have been a pity.'

Attaching himself to humanity again (if that was how the process was to be described), Hugh solved the faint mystery of Mrs Farrer's presence – or, rather, Mr Farrer's absence. During Lady Guild's illness Mrs Farrer's divorce had been finalized. For the time being she intended to stay on at the *Cat and Fiddle*, helping out her mother and the Captain. The status of her presence had changed from a lucky accident to a more or less permanent bonus the place might have superficially seemed ill-equipped to confer.

Returning home from his evening drink at what more and more inclined to be a latish hour, Hugh was always struck with Boldero's beauty. The face was blunt (stemming from her Persian ancestry) but the mongrel strain had prevented any exaggeration of the quality. The white on the face avoided eyes and nose so that – coral nostrils, peeled yellow-grape eyes supported by the glossiest black – she seemed permanently masked and enigmatic. The legs were short (feline mark of beauty, in contrast

Simpkin at the Tailor's Bedside, Beatrix Potter (*Tate Gallery, London*)

to the human), the feet substantial. It was a critical evening when this aesthetic sight prompted Hugh to think: Mrs Farrer is pretty, too.

His anticipation of ancient but not forgotten sensual enjoyment was fulfilled in the early days of his marriage with Mrs Farrer. It was months, perhaps a year or so, before he could think that *her* motive might have been to get away from the *Cat and Fiddle* and to be called Lady Guild. He disliked the appearance of male figures from her past life, even though she returned to sleep under his roof. And what came home to one in the second half of one's sixties was the rapidity and irreversibleness of emotional change. After all, he thought, sitting at his desk surrounded by the notebooks and card indices of his unfinished life's work, art is both the only sensible and the only enduring thing. Boldero's tail (she also was on the desk) waved slowly across the photograph of an Armenian stele. He seized the cursive object: the head came round, the little double keyhole of the nose astonishingly cold and wet – almost equally as astonishing as the phenomena his new marriage had reintroduced him to.

Very early one morning he found the second Lady Guild at the foot of the staircase, in a bad way. The conversion of the original three cottages involved, in the conception of the then owner, two staircases, one at either end of the resultant house. It was the minor staircase down which Lady Guild had tumbled. This was merely the original staircase of one of the constituent cottages, with its excessive proportion of riser to tread, and undeviating precipitousness from one floor to the other. Possibly the converter had envisaged a servant's end, a servant young and agile enough to move freely up and down what was scarcely more than a ladder.

'I fell over a cat,' moaned Lady Guild, as Hugh held her hand, waiting for the ambulance.

'How could that be?'

'A strange cat must have got in.'

'Strange', naturally, since Boldero could hardly be conceived as lurking in that uncomfortable area. Or was the *ci-devant* Mrs Farrer seeking to excuse Boldero, so beloved of Hugh, because she herself was guilty? It occurred too late to Hugh to ask her what she was doing at that hour using the staircase so remote from their bedrooms, because she lost consciousness in the ambulance and never recovered it. The haemorrhage spread rapidly through the brain.

I noticed (said Bobby) that Hugh didn't attempt in this case to interpret the crucial remark made as 'Fell over a hat'. Too outré to think Helen's envious shade had planted there the famous royal headgear. Nor would Bobby hear anything of my own suggestion that there *had* been an intruding cat – a tom after Boldero. He explained that Boldero had been spayed, adding that it was a pity the second Lady Guild hadn't been too – all things considered.

The swift double loss might have put Hugh off The Cottages. But in fact he went on living there. Yet the image wasn't quite that of a bereaved old man consoled only by his cat. He began to be seen in London again, even (particularly when 'decorations' were specified) at night. Somehow his batteries had been re-charged; or perhaps he had learned better how to draw on their remaining resources.

'Are you suggesting,' I asked Bobby, 'that that animal – Martin or whatever its name was – was the perfect murderer? Fiction has long ceased to deal with such whimsicalities.' However, one has to admit that mysteries are often inclined to arise where cats are concerned, though more usually in such realms as unexplained absences or missing delicacies.

'You wouldn't acknowledge that a jealous cat – or a zealous cat – might direct a campaign against those it conceived to be damaging its master?'

'No.'

'Nor would I.'

'You wouldn't?'

'No,' said Bobby.

'What on earth have we been talking about then?'

'I put it delicately to Hugh that in the eyes of some imaginative policeman *he* could have been the culprit. I called on him with the point in mind.'

'Good Lord!'

'You see some possible lines of investigation,' Bobby said. 'Hugh collects Helen's penicillin prescription, or whatever it was, from the doctor and substitutes aspirin. Knowing the former Mrs Farrer has been using the far stairs for her illicit purposes, he stretches a wire across the top of them.'

'What did he say?'

'What could he say? Only emphasize the accidental nature of the events.'

'Did you see the less likely suspect?'

'Not on view. Not even a lingering grin. Though probably she was aware of my visit. When I drove away there was a bird in the car.'

'What?' One momentarily conceived a female hitchhiker trading on her youth by actually seating herself in the parked vehicle.

'My Peugeot has a sun-roof. It had been open. A young starling had dropped – or been deposited – in the aperture. Awkward blind turn at the end of Hugh's lane. What with the squawking and fluttering I nearly failed to see a Post Office van. Eventually I stopped and let down the windows and managed to shoo the bird out. It didn't seem injured. Whether it was old enough to fly was doubtful. I didn't spend too much time worrying about it because when I got on the A4 I found the mice.'

Drawing, Chas. Adams (© *1975 The New Yorker Magazine Inc.*)

'In the car you mean?' One positively drained one's cognac. 'You're having me on.'

'Put in – or making their own way – through the sun-roof, as with the starling. Doubtless relatives of the mice that started the whole affair off. I don't share Hugh's unreasoning fear of mice but I must say it was awkward dèaling with the beasts among the traffic. However, I survived, as is obvious.'

'You knew too much. They wanted to get rid of you.' Unusually with Bobby, one was carried away by his narrative.

'You mean Hugh and Boldero were actually working in concert?'

'Well, then, *she* wanted to get rid of you.'

'I think the pronoun required is masculine,' said Bobby.

The Black Cat

EDGAR ALLAN POE

FOR the most wild, yet most homely, narrative which I am about to pen, I neither expect nor solicit belief. Mad indeed would I be to expect it, in a case where my very senses reject their own evidence. Yet, mad am I not – and very surely do I not dream. But tomorrow I die, and today I would unburthen my soul. My immediate purpose is to place before the world, plainly, succinctly, and without comment, a series of mere household events. In their consequences, these events have terrified – have tortured – have destroyed me. Yet I will not attempt to expound them. To me they have presented little but horror – to many they still seem less terrible than *baroques*. Hereafter, perhaps, some intellect may be found which will reduce my phantasm to the commonplace – some intellect more calm, more logical, and far less excitable than my own, which will perceive, in the circumstances I detail with awe, nothing more than an ordinary succession of very natural causes and effects.

From my infancy I was noted for the docility and humanity of my disposition. My tenderness of heart was even so conspicuous as to make me the jest of my companions. I was especially fond of animals, and was indulged by my parents with a great variety of pets. With these I spent most of my time, and never was so happy as when feeding and caressing them. This peculiarity of character grew with my growth, and, in my manhood, I derived from it one of my principal sources of pleasure. To those who have cherished an affection for a faithful and sagacious dog, I need hardly be at the trouble of explaining the nature or the intensity of the gratification thus derivable. There is something in the unselfish and self-sacrificing love of a brute which goes directly to the heart of him who has had frequent occasion to test the paltry friendship and gossamer fidelity of mere *Man*.

I married early, and was happy to find in my wife a disposition not uncongenial with my own. Observing my partiality for domestic pets, she lost no opportunity of procuring those of the most agreeable kind. We had birds, gold-fish, a fine dog, rabbits, a small monkey, and *a cat*.

This latter was a remarkably large and beautiful animal, entirely black, and sagacious to an astonishing degree. In speaking of his intelligence, my wife, who at heart was not a little tinctured with superstition, made

[252]

Children Playing with a Cat, Jan Mienz Molenaer (*Musée du Dunkerque*)

frequent allusion to the ancient popular notion, which regarded all black cats as witches in disguise. Not that she was ever *serious* upon this point – and I mention the matter at all for no better reason than that it happens, just now, to be remembered.

Pluto – this was the cat's name – was my favourite pet and playmate. I alone fed him, and he attended me wherever I went about the house. It was even with difficulty that I could prevent him from following me through the streets.

Our friendship lasted, in this manner, for several years, during which my general temperament and character – through the instrumentality of the Fiend Intemperance – had (I blush to confess it) experienced a radical alteration for the worse. I grew, day by day, more moody, more irritable, more regardless of the feelings of others. I suffered myself to use intemperate language to my wife. At length, I even offered her personal violence. My pets, of course, were made to feel the change in my disposition. I not only neglected, but ill-used them. For Pluto, however, I still retained sufficient regard to restrain me from maltreating him, as I made no scruple of maltreating the rabbits, the monkey, or even the dog, when by accident, or through affection, they came in my way. But my disease grew upon me – for what disease is like Alcohol! – and at length even Pluto, who was now becoming old, and consequently somewhat peevish – even Pluto began to experience the effects of my ill-temper.

One night, returning home, much intoxicated, from one of my haunts about town, I fancied that the cat avoided my presence. I seized him: when, in his fright at my violence, he inflicted a slight wound upon my hand with his teeth. The fury of a demon instantly possessed me. I knew myself no longer. My original soul seemed, at once, to take its flight from my body; and a more than fiendish malevolence, gin-nurtured, thrilled every fibre of my frame. I took from my waistcoat pocket a pen-knife, opened it, grasped the poor beast by the throat, and deliberately cut one of its eyes from the socket! I blush, I burn, I shudder, while I pen the damnable atrocity.

When reason returned with the morning – when I had slept off the fumes of the night's debauch – I experienced a sentiment half of horror, half of remorse, for the crime of which I had been guilty: but it was, at best, a feeble and equivocal feeling, and the soul remained untouched. I again plunged into excess, and soon drowned in wine all memory of the deed.

In the meantime the cat slowly recovered. The socket of the lost eye presented, it is true, a frightful appearance, but he no longer appeared to suffer any pain. He went about the house as usual, but, as might be expected, fled in extreme terror at my approach. I had so much of my old heart left as to be at first grieved by this evident dislike on the part of a creature which had once so loved me. But this feeling soon gave place to irritation. And then came, as if to my final and irrevocable overthrow, the spirit of PERVERSENESS. Of this spirit philosophy takes no account. Yet I am not more sure that my soul lives, than I am that perverseness is one of the primitive impulses of the human heart – one of

[254]

the indivisible primary faculties, or sentiments, which give direction to the character of Man. Who has not, a hundred times, found himself committing a vile or a silly action for no other reason than because he knows he should *not*? Have we not a perpetual inclination, in the teeth of our last judgement, to violate that which is *Law*, merely because we understand it to be such? This spirit of perverseness, I say, came to my final overthrow. It was this unfathomable longing of the soul to *vex itself* – to offer violence to its own nature – to do wrong for the wrong's sake only – that urged me to continue and finally to consummate the injury I had inflicted upon the unoffending brute. One morning, in cold blood, I slipped a noose about its neck and hung it to the limb of a tree – hung it with the tears streaming from my eyes, and with the bitterest remorse at my heart; hung it *because* I knew that it had loved me, and *because* I felt it had given me no reason of offence; hung it *because* I knew that in so doing I was committing a sin – a deadly sin that would so jeopardize my immortal soul as to place it – if such a thing were possible – even beyond the reach of the infinite mercy of the Most Merciful and Most Terrible God.

On the night of the day on which this cruel deed was done, I was aroused from sleep by the cry of fire. The curtains of my bed were in flames. The whole house was blazing. It was with great difficulty that my wife, a servant, and myself made our escape from the conflagration. The destruction was complete. My entire worldly wealth was swallowed up, and I resigned myself thenceforward to despair.

I am above the weakness of seeking to establish a sequence of cause and effect, between the disaster and the atrocity. But I am detailing a chain of facts – and wish not to leave even a possible link imperfect. On the day succeeding the fire, I visited the ruins. The walls, with one exception, had fallen in. This exception was found in a compartment wall, not very thick, which stood about the middle of the house, and against which had rested the head of my bed. The plastering had here, in great measure, resisted the action of the fire – a fact which I attributed to its having been recently spread. About this wall a dense crowd were collected, and many persons seemed to be examining a particular portion of it with very minute and eager attention. The words 'strange!' 'singular!' and other similar expressions excited my curiosity. I approached and saw, as if graven in bas-relief upon the white surface, the figure of a gigantic *cat*. The impression was given with an accuracy truly marvellous. There was a rope about the animal's neck.

When I first beheld this apparition – for I could scarcely regard it as

Portrait of Girl with Cat, Charles Chaplin (*Château de Compiègne*)

less – my wonder and my terror were extreme. But at length reflection came to my aid. The cat, I remember, had been hung in a garden adjacent to the house. Upon the alarm of fire, this garden had been immediately filled by the crowd – by some one of whom the animal must have been cut from the tree and thrown, through an open window, into my chamber. This had probably been done with the view of arousing me from sleep. The falling of other walls had compressed the victim of my cruelty into the substance of the freshly spread plaster: the lime of which with the flames, and the *ammonia* from the carcase, had then accomplished the portraiture as I saw it.

Although I thus readily accounted to my reason, if not altogether to my conscience, for the startling fact just detailed, it did not the less fail to make a deep impression upon my fancy. For months I could not rid myself of the phantasm of the cat; and, during this period, there came back into my spirit a half-sentiment that seemed, but was not, remorse. I went so far as to regret the loss of the animal, and to look about me, among the vile haunts which I now habitually frequented, for another pet of the same species, and of somewhat similar appearance, with which to supply its place.

One night as I sat, half stupefied, in a den of more than infamy, my attention was suddenly drawn to some black object, reposing upon the head of one of the immense hogsheads of gin, or of rum, which constituted the chief furniture of the apartment. I had been looking steadily at the top of this hogshead for some minutes, and what now caused me surprise was the fact that I had not sooner perceived the object thereupon. I approached it, and touched it with my hands. It was a black cat – a very large one – fully as large as Pluto, and closely resembling him in every respect but one. Pluto had not a white hair upon any portion of his body; but this cat had a large, although indefinite splotch of white, covering nearly the whole region of the breast.

Upon my touching him, he immediately arose, purred loudly, rubbed against my hand, and appeared delighted with my notice. This, then, was the very creature of which I was in search. I at once offered to purchase it of the landlord; but this person made no claim to it – knew nothing of it – had never seen it before.

I continued my caresses, and when I prepared to go home, the animal evinced a disposition to accompany me. I permitted it to do so; occasionally stopping and patting it as I proceeded. When it reached the house it domesticated itself at once, and became immediately a great favourite with my wife.

[257]

For my own part, I soon found a dislike to it arising within me. This was just the reverse of what I had anticipated; but – I know not how or why it was – its evident fondness for myself rather disgusted and annoyed. By slow degrees, these feelings of disgust and annoyance rose into the bitterness of hatred. I avoided the creature; a certain sense of shame, and the remembrance of my former deed of cruelty, preventing me from physically abusing it. I did not, for some weeks, strike or otherwise violently ill-use it; but gradually – very gradually – I came to look upon it with unutterable loathing, and to flee silently from its odious presence, as from the breath of a pestilence.

What added, no doubt, to my hatred of the beast was the discovery, on the morning after I brought it home, that, like Pluto, it also had been deprived of one of its eyes. This circumstance, however, only endeared it to my wife, who, as I have already said, possessed, in a high degree, that humanity of feeling which had once been my distinguishing trait, and the source of many of my simplest and purest pleasures.

With my aversion to this cat, however, its partiality for myself seemed to increase. It followed my footsteps with a pertinacity which it would be difficult to make the reader comprehend. Whenever I sat, it would crouch beneath my chair, or spring upon my knees, covering me with its loathsome caresses. If I arose to walk, it would get between my feet, and thus nearly throw me down, or, fastening its long and sharp claws in my dress, clamber, in this manner, to my breast. At such times, although I longed to destroy it with a blow, I was yet withheld from so doing, partly by a memory of my former crime, but chiefly – let me confess it at once – by absolute *dread* of the beast.

This dread was not exactly a dread of physical evil – and yet I should be at a loss how otherwise to define it. I am almost ashamed to own – yes, even in this felon's cell, I am almost ashamed to own – that the terror and horror with which the animal inspired me had been heightened by one of the merest chimeras it would be possible to conceive. My wife had called my attention, more than once, to the character of the mark of white hair, of which I have spoken, and which constituted the sole visible difference between the strange beast and the one I had destroyed. The reader will remember that this mark, although large, had been originally very indefinite; but, by slow degrees – degrees almost imperceptible, and which for a long time my reason struggled to reject as fanciful – it had, at length, assumed the rigorous distinctness of outline. It was now the representation of an object that I shudder to name – and for this, above all, I loathed and dreaded, and would have rid myself

[258]

of the monster *had I dared* – it was now, I say, the image of a hideous – of a ghastly thing – of the GALLOWS! – oh, mournful and terrible engine of Horror and of Crime – of Agony and of Death!

And now was I indeed wretched beyond the wretchedness of mere Humanity. And *a brute beast* – whose fellow I had contemptuously destroyed – *a brute beast* to work out for *me* – for me, a man, fashioned in the image of the High God – so much of insufferable woe! Alas! neither by day nor by night knew I the blessing of Rest any more! During the former the creature left me no moment alone; and, in the latter, I started, hourly, from dreams of unutterable fear, to find the hot breath of *the thing* upon my face, and its vast weight – an incarnate Nightmare that I had no power to shake off – incumbent eternally upon my *heart!*

Beneath the pressure of torments such as these, the feeble remnant of the good within me succumbed. Evil thoughts became my sole intimates – the darkest and most evil of thoughts. The moodiness of my usual temper increased to hatred of all things and of all mankind; while, for the sudden, frequent, and ungovernable outbursts of a fury to which I now blindly abandoned myself, my uncomplaining wife, alas! was the most usual and the most patient of sufferers.

One day she accompanied me, upon some household errand, into the cellar of the old building which our poverty compelled us to inhabit. The

The Distressed Poet, William Hogarth

cat followed me down the steep stairs, and, nearly throwing me headlong, exasperated me to madness. Uplifting an axe, and forgetting, in my wrath, the childish dread which had hitherto stayed my hand, I aimed a blow at the animal which, of course, would have proved instantly fatal had it descended as I wished. But this blow was arrested by the hand of my wife. Goaded by the interference into a rage more than demoniacal, I withdrew my arm from her grasp and buried the axe in her brain. She fell dead upon the spot, without a groan.

This hideous murder accomplished, I set myself forthwith, and with entire deliberation, to the task of concealing the body. I knew that I could not remove it from the house, either by day or by night, without the risk of being observed by the neighbours. Many projects entered my mind. At one period I thought of cutting the corpse into minute fragments, and destroying them by fire. At another, I resolved to dig a grave for it in the floor of the cellar. Again, I deliberated about casting it in the well in the yard – about packing it in a box, as if merchandise, with the usual arrangements, and so getting a porter to take it from the house. Finally I hit upon what I considered a far better expedient than either of these. I determined to wall it up in the cellar – as the monks of the Middle Ages are recorded to have walled up their victims.

For a purpose such as this the cellar was well adapted. Its walls were loosely constructed, and had lately been plastered throughout with a rough plaster, which the dampness of the atmosphere had prevented from hardening. Moreover, in one of the walls was a projection caused by a false chimney or fireplace, that had been filled up, and made to resemble the rest of the cellar. I made no doubt that I could readily displace the bricks at this point, insert the corpse, and wall the whole up as before, so that no eye could detect anything suspicious.

And in this calculation I was not deceived. By means of a crow-bar I easily dislodged the bricks, and, having carefully deposited the body against the inner wall, I propped it in that position, while, with little trouble, I re-laid the whole structure as it originally stood. Having procured mortar, sand, and hair, with every possible precaution, I prepared a plaster which could not be distinguished from the old, and with this I very carefully went over the new brickwork. When I had finished I felt satisfied that all was right. The wall did not present the slightest appearance of having been disturbed. The rubbish on the floor was picked up with the minutest care. I looked around triumphantly, and said to myself: 'Here, at least, then, my labour has not been in vain.'

My next step was to look for the beast which had been the cause of so much wretchedness, for I had, at length, firmly resolved to put it to death. Had I been able to meet with it, at the moment, there could have been no doubt of its fate; but it appeared that the crafty animal had been alarmed at the violence of my previous anger, and forbore to present itself in my present mood. It is impossible to describe, or to imagine, the deep, the blissful sense of relief which the absence of the detested creature occasioned in my bosom. It did not make its appearance during the night – and thus for one night at least, since its introduction into the house, I soundly and tranquilly slept; aye, *slept*, even with the burden of murder upon my soul!

The second and third day passed, and still my tormenter came not. Once again I breathed as a free man. The monster, in terror, had fled the premises for ever! I should behold it no more! My happiness was supreme! The guilt of my dark deed disturbed me but little. Some few inquiries had been made, but these had been readily answered. Even a search had been instituted – but, of course, nothing was to be discovered. I looked upon my future felicity as secured.

Upon the fourth day of the assassination, a party of the police came, very unexpectedly, into the house, and proceeded again to make rigorous investigation of the premises. Secure, however, in the inscrutability of my place of concealment, I felt no embarrassment whatever. The officers bade me accompany them in their search. They left no nook or corner unexplored. At length, for the third or fourth time, they descended into the cellar. I quivered not in a muscle. My heart beat calmly as that of one who slumbers in innocence. I walked the cellar from end to end. I folded my arms upon my bosom, and roamed easily to and fro. The police were thoroughly satisfied, and prepared to depart. The glee at my heart was too strong to be restrained. I burned to say if but one word, by way of triumph, and to render doubly sure their assurance of my guilt-lessness.

'Gentlemen,' I said at last, as the party ascended the steps, 'I delight to have allayed your suspicions. I wish you all health and a little more courtesy. By the by, gentlemen, this – this is a very well-constructed house.' – (In the rabid desire to say something easily, I scarcely knew what I uttered at all.) – 'I may say an *excellently* well-constructed house. These walls – are you going, gentlemen? – these walls are solidly put together'; and here, through the mere frenzy of bravado, I rapped heavily with a cane, which I held in my hand, upon that very portion of the brick-work behind which stood the corpse of the wife of my bosom.

But may God shield and deliver me from the fangs of the Arch-Fiend!

The Black Cat, Harry Clarke

No sooner had the reverberation of my blows sunk into silence, than I was answered by a voice from within the tomb! – by a cry, at first muffled and broken, like the sobbing of a child, and then quickly swelling into one long, loud, and continuous scream, utterly anomalous and inhuman – a howl – a wailing shriek, half of horror and half of triumph, such as might have arisen only out of hell, conjointly from the throats of the damned in their agony and of the demons that exult in their damnation.

Of my own thoughts it is folly to speak. Swooning, I staggered to the opposite wall. For one instant the party upon the stairs remained motionless, through extremity of terror and of awe. In the next, a dozen stout arms were toiling at the wall. It fell bodily. The corpse, already greatly decayed and clotted with gore, stood erect before the eyes of the spectators. Upon its head, with red extended mouth and solitary eye of fire, sat the hideous beast whose craft had seduced me into murder, and whose informing voice had consigned me to the hangman! I had walled the monster up within the tomb!

PART VII

Cat's Age

The Kitten

OGDEN NASH

The trouble with a kitten is
THAT
Eventually it becomes a
CAT.

Prince Edward, Martin Leman (*Private Collection*)

[267]

The Woman and the Mouse, Martin Drolling (*Musée des Beaux-Arts, Orléans*)

Memoir of the Cats of Greta Hall

ROBERT SOUTHEY

FOR as much, most excellent Edith May, as you must always feel a natural and becoming concern in whatever relates to the house wherein you were born, and in which the first part of your life has thus far so happily been spent, I have for your instruction and delight composed these Memoirs of the Cats of Greta Hall: to the end that the memory of such worthy animals may not perish, but be held in deserved honour by my children, and those who shall come after them. And let me not be supposed unmindful of Beelzebub of Bath, and Senhor Thomaz de Lisboa, that I have not gone back to an earlier period, and included them in my design. Far be it from me to intend any injury or disrespect to their shades! Opportunity of doing justice to their virtues will not be wanting at some future time, but for the present I must confine myself within the limits of these precincts.

In the autumn of the year 1803, when I entered upon this place of abode, I found the hearth in possession of two cats, whom my nephew Hartley Coleridge (then in the 7th year of his age) had named Lord Nelson, and Bona Marietta. The former, as the name implies, was of the

[268]

worthier gender: it is as decidedly so in Cats, as in Grammar and in law. He was an ugly specimen of the streaked-carrotty, or Judas-coloured kind; which is one of the ugliest varieties. But *nimium ne crede colori*. In spite of his complexion, there was nothing treacherous about him. He was altogether a good Cat, affectionate, vigilant and brave; and for services performed against the Rats was deservedly raised in succession to the rank of Baron, Viscount and Earl. He lived to a good old age; and then, being quite helpless and miserable, was in mercy thrown into the river. I had more than once interfered to save him from this fate; but it became at length plainly an act of compassion to consent to it. And here let me observe that in a world wherein death is necessary, the law of nature by which one creature preys upon another is a law of mercy, not only because death is thus made instrumental to life, and more life exists in consequence, but also because it is better for the creatures themselves to be cut off suddenly, than to perish by disease or hunger – for these are the only alternatives.

There are still some of Lord Nelson's descendants in the town of Keswick. Two of the family were handsomer than I should have supposed any Cats of this complexion could have been; but their fur was fine, the colour a rich carrot, and the striping like that of the finest tyger or tabby kind. I named one of them William Rufus; the other Danayr le Roux, after a personage in the Romance of Gyron le Courtoys.

Bona Marietta was the mother of Bona Fidelia, so named by my nephew aforesaid. Bona Fidelia was a tortoiseshell cat. She was filiated upon Lord Nelson, others of the same litter having borne the unequivocal stamp of his likeness. It was in her good qualities that she resembled him, for in truth her name rightly bespoke her nature. She approached as nearly as possible in disposition, to the ideal of a perfect cat: he who supposes that animals have not their difference of disposition as well as men, knows very little of animal nature. Having survived her daughter Madame Catalani, she died of extreme old age, universally esteemed and regretted by all who had the pleasure of her acquaintance.

Bona Fidelia left a daughter and a granddaughter; the former I called Madame Bianchi – the latter Pulcheria. It was impossible ever to familiarize Madame Bianchi, though she had been bred in all respects like her gentle mother, in the same place, and with the same persons. The nonsense of that arch-philosophist Helvétius would be sufficiently confuted by this single example, if such rank folly, contradicted as it is by the experience of every family, needed confutation. She was a beautiful and singular creature, white, with a fine tabby tail, and two or three spots of tabby, always delicately clean; and her wild eyes were bright and green as the Duchess de Cadaval's emerald necklace. Pulcheria did not correspond as she grew up to the promise of her kittenhood and her name; but she was as fond as her mother was shy and intractable. Their fate was extraordinary as well as mournful. When good old Mrs Wilson died, who used to feed and indulge them, they immediately forsook the house, nor could they be allured to enter it again, though they continued to wander and moan round it, and came for food. After some weeks Madame Bianchi disappeared, and Pulcheria soon afterwards died of a disease endemic at that time among cats.

For a considerable time afterwards, an evil fortune attended all our attempts at re-establishing a Cattery. Ovid disappeared and Virgil died of some miserable distemper. You and your cousin are answerable for these names: the reasons which I could find for them were, in the former case the satisfactory one that the same Ovid might be presumed to be a master in the Art of Love; and in the latter, the probable one that something like Ma-ro might be detected in the said Virgil's notes of courtship.

There was poor Othello: most properly named, for black he was, and jealous undoubtedly he would have been, but he in his kittenship followed Miss Wilbraham into the street, and there in all likelihood came to an untimely end. There was the Zombi – (I leave the Commentators to explain that title, and refer them to my History of Brazil to do it) – his marvellous story was recorded in a letter to Bedford – and after that adventure he vanished. There was Prester John, who turned out not to be of John's gender, and therefore had the name altered to Pope Joan. The Pope I am afraid came to a death of which other Popes have died. I suspect that some poison which the rats had turned out of their holes, proved fatal to their enemy. For some time I feared we were at the end of our Cat-a-logue: but at last Fortune as if to make amends for her late severity sent us two at once – the never-to-be-enough-praised Rumpelstilzchen, and the equally-to-be-admired Hurlyburlybuss.

And 'first for the first of these' as my huge favourite and almost namesake, Robert South, says in his Sermons.

When the Midgeleys went away from the next house, they left this creature to our hospitality, cats being the least movable of all animals because of their strong local predilections; they are indeed in a domesticated state the serfs of the animal creation, and properly attached to the soil. The change was gradually and therefore easily brought about, for he was already acquainted with the children and with me; and having the same precincts to prowl in was hardly sensible of any other difference in his condition than that of obtaining a name; for when he was consigned to us he was an anonymous cat; and I having just related at breakfast with universal applause the story of Rumpelstilzchen from a German tale in Grimm's Collection, gave him that strange and magnisonant appellation; to which upon its being ascertained that he came when a kitten from a bailiff's house, I added the patronymic of Macbum. Such is his history, his character may with most propriety be introduced after the manner of Plutarch's parallels when I shall have given some previous account of his great compeer and rival Hurlyburlybuss – that name also is of Germanic and Grimmish extraction.

Strange Contents, Sal Meijer (*Stedelijk Museum, Amsterdam*)

[271]

Whence Hurlyburlybuss came was a mystery when you departed from the Land of Lakes, and a mystery it long remained. He appeared here, as Mango Gapac did in Peru, and Quetzalcohuatl among the Aztecas, no one knew from whence. He made himself acquainted with all the philofelists of the family – attaching himself more particularly to Mrs Lovell, but he never attempted to enter the house, frequently disappeared for days, and once since my return for so long a time that he was actually believed to be dead and veritably lamented as such. The wonder was whither did he retire at such times – and to whom did he belong; for neither I in my daily walks, nor the children, nor any of the servants ever by any chance saw him anywhere except in our own domain. There was something so mysterious in this, that in old times it might have excited strong suspicion, and he would have been in danger of passing for a Witch in disguise, or a familiar. The mystery however was solved about four weeks ago, when as we were returning from a walk up the Greta, Isabel saw him on his transit across the road and the wall from Shulicrow in a direction towards the Hill. But to this day we are ignorant who has the honour to be his owner in the eye of the law; and the owner is equally ignorant of the high honour in which Hurlyburlybuss is held, of the heroic name which he has obtained, and that his fame has extended far and wide – even unto Norwich in the East, and Escott and Crediton and Kellerton in the West, yea – that with Rumpelstilzchen he has been celebrated in song, by some hitherto undiscovered poet, and that his glory will go down to future generations.

The strong enmity which unhappily subsists between these otherwise gentle and most amiable cats, is not unknown to you. Let it be imputed, as in justice it ought, not to their individual characters (for Cats have characters – and for the benefit of philosophy, as well as felisophy, this truth ought generally to be known) but to the constitution of Cat nature – an original sin, or an original necessity, which may be only another mode of expressing the same thing:

> Two stars keep not their motion in one sphere,
> Nor can one purlieu brook a double reign
> Of Hurlyburlybuss and Rumpelstilzchen.

When you left us, the result of many a fierce conflict was that Hurly remained master of the green and garden, and the whole of the out of door premises, Rumpel always upon the appearance of his victorious enemy retiring into the house as a citadel or sanctuary. The conqueror was perhaps in part indebted for this superiority to his hardier habits

Night Meeting, photo A. Eidenbenz (*Frank W. Lane*)

of life, living always in the open air, and providing for himself; while Rumpel (who though born under a bum-bailiff's roof was nevertheless kittened with a silver spoon in his mouth) past his hours in luxurious repose beside the fire, and looked for his meals as punctually as any two-legged member of the family. Yet I believe that the advantage on Hurley's side is in a great degree constitutional also, and that his superior courage arises from a confidence in his superior strength, which as you well know is visible in his make. What Benito and Maria Rosa used to say of my poor Thomaz, that he was *muito hidalgo*, is true of Rumpelstilzchen, his countenance, deportment and behaviour being such that he is truly a gentleman-like Tom-cat. Far be it from me to praise him beyond his deserts – he is not beautiful, the mixture, tabby and white, is not good (except under very favourable combinations) and the tabby is not good of its kind. Nevertheless he is a fine cat, handsome enough for his sex, large, well-made, with good features, and an intelligent countenance, and carrying a splendid tail, which in Cats and Dogs is undoubtedly the seat of honour. His eyes which are soft and expressive are of a hue between chrysolite and emerald. Hurlyburlybuss's are between chrysolite and topaz. Which may be the more esteemed shade for the *olho de gato* I am not lapidary enough to decide. You should ask my Uncle. But both are of the finest water. In all his other features Hurly must yield the palm, and in form also; he has no pretensions to elegance, his size is ordinary

[273]

and his figure bad: but the character of his face and neck is so masculine, that the Chinese, who use the word bull as synonymous with male, and call a boy a bull-child, might with great propriety denominate him a bull-cat. His make evinces such decided marks of strength and courage that if cat-fighting were as fashionable as cock-fighting, no cat would stand a fairer chance of winning a Welsh main. He would become as famous as the Dog Billy himself, whom I look upon as the most distinguished character that has appeared since Buonaparte.

Some weeks ago Hurlyburlybuss was manifestly emaciated and enfeebled by ill health, and Rumpelstilzchen with great magnanimity made overtures of peace. The whole progress of the treaty was seen from the parlour window. The caution with which Rumpel made his advances, the sullen dignity with which they were received, their mutual uneasiness when Rumpel, after a slow and wary approach, seated himself whisker-to-whisker with his rival, the mutual fear which restrained not only teeth and claws, but even all tones of defiance, the mutual agitation of their tails which, though they did not expand with anger, could not be kept still for suspense, and lastly the manner in which Hurly retreated, like Ajax still keeping his face towards his old antagonist, were worthy to have been represented by that painter who was called the Rafaelle of Cats. The overture I fear was not accepted as generously as it was made; for no sooner had Hurlyburlybuss recovered strength than hostilities were recommenced with greater violence than ever. Rumpel, who had not abused his superiority while he possessed it, had acquired meantime a confidence which made him keep the field. Dreadful were the combats which ensued, as their ears, faces and legs bore witness. Rumpel had a wound which went through one of his feet. The result had been so far in his favour that he no longer seeks to avoid his enemy, and we are often compelled to interfere and separate them. Oh it is awful to hear the 'dreadful note of preparation' with which they prelude their encounters! – the long low growl slowly rises and swells till it becomes a high sharp yowl – and then it is snapt short by a sound which seems as if they were spitting fire and venom at each other. I could half persuade myself that the word felonious is derived from the feline temper as displayed at such times. All means of reconciling them and making them understand how goodly a thing it is for cats to dwell together in peace, and what fools they are to quarrel and tear each other, are in vain. The proceedings of the Society for the Abolition of War are not more utterly ineffectual and hopeless.

All we can do is to act more impartially than the Gods did between Achilles and Hector, and continue to treat both with equal regard.

And thus having brought down these Memoirs of the Cats of Greta Hall to the present day, I commit the precious memorial to your keeping, and I remain

> Most dissipated and light-heeled daughter,
> Your most diligent and light-hearted father,
> Robert Southey

Keswick, 18th June 1824

Sermons in Cats

ALDOUS HUXLEY

I MET, not long ago, a young man who aspired to become a novelist. Knowing that I was in the profession, he asked me to tell him how he should set to work to realize his ambition. I did my best to explain. 'The first thing,' I said, 'is to buy quite a lot of paper, a bottle of ink, and a pen. After that you merely have to write.' But this was not enough for my young friend. He seemed to have a notion that there was some sort of esoteric cookery book, full of literary recipes, which you had only to follow attentively to become a Dickens, a Henry James, a Flaubert – 'according to taste', as the authors of recipes say, when they come to the question of seasoning and sweetening. Wouldn't I let him have a glimpse of this cookery book? I said that I was sorry, but that (unhappily – for what an endless amount of time and trouble it would save!) I had never even seen such a work. He seemed sadly disappointed; so, to console the poor lad, I advised him to apply to the professors of dramaturgy and short-story writing at some reputable university; if any one possessed a trustworthy cookery book of literature, it should surely be they. But even this was not enough to satisfy the young man. Disappointed in his hope that I would give him the fictional equivalent of 'One Hundred Ways of Cooking Eggs' or the 'Carnet de la Ménagère', he began to cross-examine me about my methods of 'collecting material'. Did I keep a notebook or a daily journal? Did I systematically frequent the drawing-rooms of the rich and fashionable? Or did I, on the contrary, inhabit the Sussex downs? Or spend my evenings looking for 'copy' in East End gin-palaces?

[275]

Cats

Did I think it was wise to frequent the company of intellectuals? Was it a good thing for a writer of novels to try to be well educated, or should he confine his reading exclusively to other novels? And so on. I did my best to reply to these questions – as non-committally, of course, as I could. And as the young man still looked rather disappointed, I volunteered a final piece of advice, gratuitously. 'My young friend,' I said, 'if you want to be a psychological novelist and write about human beings, the best thing you can do is to keep a pair of cats.' And with that I left him.

I hope, for his own sake, that he took my advice. For it was good advice – the fruit of much experience and many meditations. But I am afraid that, being a rather foolish young man, he merely laughed at what he must have supposed was only a silly joke: laughed, as I myself foolishly laughed when, years ago, that charming and talented and extraordinary man, Ronald Firbank, once told me that he wanted to write a novel about life in Mayfair and so was just off to the West Indies to look for copy among the Negroes. I laughed at the time; but I see now that he was quite right. Primitive people, like children and animals, are simply civilized people with the lid off, so to speak – the heavy elaborate lid of manners, conventions, traditions of thought and feeling beneath which each one of us passes his or her existence. This lid can be very conveniently studied in Mayfair, shall we say, or Passy, or Park Avenue. But what goes on underneath the lid in these polished and elegant districts? Direct observation (unless we happen to be endowed with a very penetrating intuition) tells us but little; and, if we cannot infer what is going on under the other lids from what we see, introspectively, by peeping under our own, then the best thing we can do is to take the next boat for the West Indies, or else, less expensively, pass a few mornings in the nursery, or alternatively, as I suggested to my literary young friend, buy a pair of cats.

Yes, a pair of cats. Siamese by preference; for they are certainly the most 'human' of all the race of cats. Also the strangest, and, if not the most beautiful, certainly the most striking and fantastic. For what disquieting pale blue eyes stare out from the black velvet masks of their faces! Snow-white at birth, their bodies gradually darken to a rich mulatto colour. Their fore-paws are gloved almost to the shoulder like the long black kid arms of Yvette Guilbert; over their hind legs are tightly drawn the black silk stockings with which Félicien Rops so perversely and indecently clothed his pearly nudes. Their tails, when they have tails – and I would always recommend the budding novelist buy the tailed variety; for the tail, in cats, is the principal organ of emotional expression and a Manx cat is the equivalent of a dumb man – their tails are tapering black serpents endowed, even when the body lies in Sphinx-like repose, with a spasmodic and uneasy life of their own. And what strange voices they have! Sometimes like the complaining of small children; sometimes like the noise of lambs; sometimes like the agonized and furious howling of lost souls. Compared with these fantastic creatures, other cats, however beautiful and engaging, are apt to seem a little insipid.

Well, having bought his cats, nothing remains for the would-be novelist but to watch them living from day to day; to mark, learn, and inwardly digest the lessons about human nature which they teach; and finally – for, alas, this arduous and unpleasant necessity always arises – finally write his book about Mayfair, Passy, or Park Avenue, whichever the case may be.

Let us consider some of these instructive sermons in cats, from which the student of human psychology can learn so much. We will begin – as every good novel should begin, instead of absurdly ending – with marriage. The marriage of Siamese cats, at any rate as I have observed it, is an extraordinarily dramatic event. To begin with, the introduction of the bridegroom to his bride (I am assuming that, as usually happens in the world of cats, they have not met before their wedding day) is the signal for a battle of unparalleled ferocity. The young wife's first reaction to the advances of her would-be husband is to fly at his throat. One is thankful, as one watches the fur flying and listens to the piercing yells of rage and hatred, that a kindly providence has not allowed these devils to grow any larger. Waged between creatures as big as men, such battles would bring death and destruction to everything within a radius of hundreds of yards. As things are, one is able, at the risk of a few scratches, to grab them, still writhing and spitting, apart. What would happen if the newly-wedded pair were allowed to go on fighting to the bitter end I do not know, and have never had the scientific curiosity or the strength of mind to try to find out. I suspect that, contrary to what happened in Hamlet's family, the wedding baked meats would soon be serving for a funeral. I have always prevented this tragical consummation by simply shutting up the bride in a room by herself and leaving the bridegroom for a few hours to languish outside the door. He does not languish dumbly; but for a long time there is no answer, save an occasional hiss or growl, to his melancholy cries of love. When, finally, the bride begins replying in tones as soft and yearning as his own, the door may be opened. The bridegroom darts in and is received, not with tooth and claw as on the former occasion, but with every demonstration of affection.

At first there would seem, in this specimen of feline behaviour, no special 'message' for humanity. But appearances are deceptive; the lids under which civilized people live are so thick and so profusely sculptured with mythological ornaments, that it is difficult to recognize the fact, so much insisted upon by D. H. Lawrence in his novels and stories, that there is almost always a mingling of hate with the passion of love and that young girls very often feel (in spite of their sentiments and even their desires) a real abhorrence of the fact of physical love. Unlidded, the cats make manifest this ordinary obscure mystery of human behaviour. After witnessing a cats' wedding no young novelist can rest content with the falsehood and banalities which pass, in current fiction, for descriptions of love.

Time passes and, their honeymoon over, the cats begin to tell us things about humanity which even the lid of civilization cannot conceal in the world of men. They tell us – what, alas, we already know – that husbands soon tire of their wives, particularly when they are expecting or nursing families; that the essence of maleness is the love of adventure and infidelity; that guilty consciences and good resolutions are the psychological symptoms of that disease which spasmodically affects practically every male between the ages of eighteen and sixty – the disease called 'the morning after'; and that with the disappearance of the disease the psychological symptoms also disappear, so that when temptation comes again, conscience is dumb and good resolutions count for nothing. All these unhappily too familiar truths are illustrated by the cats with a most comical absence of disguise. No man has ever dared to manifest his boredom so insolently as does a Siamese tom-cat, when he yawns in the face of his amorously importunate wife. No man has ever dared to proclaim his illicit amours so frankly as this same tom caterwauling on the tiles. And how

JOHN KAY

Drawn & Engraved by Himself 1786.

John Kay and His Cat

slinkingly – no man was ever so abject – he returns next day to the con-
jugal basket by the fire! You can measure the guiltiness of his conscience
by the angle of his back-pressed ears, the droop of his tail. And when,
having sniffed him and so discovered his infidelity, his wife, as she always
does on these occasions, begins to scratch his face (already scarred, like
a German student's, with the traces of a hundred duels), he makes no
attempt to resist; for, self-convicted of sin, he knows that he deserves
all he is getting.

It is impossible for me in the space at my disposal to enumerate all

[279]

the human truths which a pair of cats can reveal or confirm. I will cite only one more of the innumerable sermons in cats which my memory holds – an acted sermon which, by its ludicrous pantomime, vividly brought home to me the most saddening peculiarity of our human nature, its irreducible solitariness. The circumstances were these. My she-cat, by now a wife of long standing and several times a mother, was passing through one of her occasional phases of amorousness. Her husband, now in the prime of life and parading that sleepy arrogance which is the characteristic of the mature and conquering male (he was now the feline equivalent of some herculean young Alcibiades, of the Guards), refused to have anything to do with her. It was in vain that she uttered her love-sick mewing, in vain that she walked up and down in front of him rubbing herself voluptuously against doors and chair legs as she passed, it was in vain that she came and licked his face. He shut his eyes, he yawned, he averted his head, or, if she became too importunate, got up and slowly, with an air of insulting dignity and detachment, stalked away. When the opportunity presented itself, he escaped and spent the next twenty-four hours upon the tiles. Left to herself, the wife went wandering disconsolately about the house, as though in search of a vanished happiness, faintly and plaintively mewing to herself in a voice and with a manner that reminded one irresistibly of Mélisande in Debussy's opera, '*Je ne suis pas heureuse ici*,' she seemed to be saying. And, poor little beast, she wasn't. But, like her big sisters and brothers of the human world, she had to bear her unhappiness in solitude, uncomprehended, unconsoled. For in spite of language, in spite of intelligence and intuition and sympathy, one can never really communicate anything to anybody. The essential substance of every thought and feeling remains incommunicable, locked up in the impenetrable strong-room of the individual soul and body. Our life is a sentence of perpetual solitary confinement. This mournful truth was overwhelmingly borne in on me as I watched the abandoned and love-sick cat as she walked unhappily round my room. '*Je ne suis pas heureuse ici*,' she kept mewing, '*je ne suis pas heureuse ici*.' And her expressive black tail would lash the air in a tragical gesture of despair. But each time it twitched, hop-la! from under the armchair, from behind the book-case, wherever he happened to be hiding at the moment, out jumped her only son (the only one, that is, we had not given away), jumped like a ludicrous toy tiger, all claws out, on to the moving tail. Sometimes he would miss, sometimes he caught it, and getting the tip between his teeth would pretend to worry it, absurdly ferocious. His mother would have to jerk it violently to get it out of his mouth. Then,

[280]

he would go back under his armchair again and, crouching down, his hindquarters trembling, would prepare once more to spring. The tail, the tragical, despairingly gesticulating tail, was for him the most irresistible of playthings. The patience of the mother was angelical. There was never a rebuke or a punitive reprisal; when the child became too intolerable, she just moved away; that was all. And meanwhile, all the time, she went on mewing, plaintively, despairingly. '*Je ne suis pas heureuse ici, je ne suis pas heureuse ici.*' It was heartbreaking. The more so as the antics of the kitten were so extraordinarily ludicrous. It was as though a slap-stick comedian had broken in on the lamentations of Mélisande – not mischievously, not wittingly, for there was not the smallest intention to hurt the little cat's performance, but simply from lack of comprehension. Each was alone serving his life-sentence of solitary confinement. There was no communication from cell to cell. Absolutely no communication. These sermons in cats can be exceedingly depressing.

Fourteen Ways Of Touching The Peter

GEORGE MACBETH

I

You can push
your thumb
in the
ridge
between his
shoulder-blades
to please him.

II

Starting
at its root,
you can let
his whole
tail
flow
through your hand.

[281]

The Two Beggars (detail), Giacomo Ceruti (*Pinacoteca Tosio Martinengo, Brescia*)

III
Forming
a fist
you can let
him rub
his bone
skull
against it, hard.

IV
When he makes
bread,
you can lift
him
by his under-
sides on your
knuckles.

[282]

V

In hot
weather
you can itch
the fur
under
his chin. He
likes that.

VI

At night
you can hoist
him
out of his bean-stalk,
sleepily
clutching
paper bags.

VII

Pressing
his head against
your cheek,
you can carry
him
in the dark,
safely.

VIII

In late Autumn
you can find
seeds
adhering
to his fur.
There are
plenty.

IX

You can prise
his jaws
open,
helping
any medicine
he won't
abide, go down.

X

You can touch
his
feet, only
if
he is relaxed.
He
doesn't like it.

XI

You can comb
spare thin
fur
from his coat,
so he won't
get
fur-ball.

XII

You can shake
his rigid
chicken-leg leg,
scouring his
hind-quarters
with his Vim
tongue.

[284]

Rosie stalking, photo Simon Playle

XIII
Dumping
hot fish
on his plate, you can
fend
him off,
pushing
and purring.

XIV
You can have
him shrimp
along you,
breathing,
whenever
you want
to compose poems.

[285]

Cat Writing Poem (*British Library, London*)

Cat

MICHAEL HAMBURGER

Unfussy lodger, she knows what she wants and gets it:
Food, cushions, fires, the run of the garden.
I, her night porter in the small hours,
Don't bother to grumble, grimly let her in.
To that coldness she purrs assent,
Eats her fill and outwits me,
Plays hide and seek in the dark house.

Only at times, by chance meeting the gaze
Of her amber eyes that can rest on me
As on a beech-bole, on bracken or meadow grass
I'm moved to celebrate the years between us,
The farness and the nearness:
My fingers graze her head.
To that fondness she purrs assent.

[286]

Jeremy Bentham's Cat

DR BOWRING

BENTHAM was very fond of animals, particularly 'pussies', as he called them, when they had domestic virtues, but he had no particular affection for the common race of cats. He had one, however, of which he used to boast that he had 'made a man of him', and whom he was wont to invite to eat macaroni at his own table. This puss got knighted, and rejoiced in the name of Sir John Langbourne. In his early days he was a frisky, inconsiderate, and, to say the truth, somewhat profligate gentleman; and had, according to the report of his patron, the habit of seducing light and giddy young ladies, of his own race, into the garden of Queen's Square Place: but tired at last, like Solomon, of pleasures and vanities, he became sedate and thoughtful – took to the church, laid down his knightly title, and was installed as the Reverend John Langbourne. He gradually obtained a great reputation for sanctity and learning, and a Doctor's degree was conferred upon him. When I knew him, in his declining days, he bore no other name than the Reverend Doctor John Langbourne: and he was alike conspicuous for his gravity and philosophy. Great respect was invariably shown his reverence: and it was supposed that he was not far off from a mitre, when old age interfered with his hopes and honours. He departed amidst the regrets of his many friends, and was gathered to his fathers, and to eternal rest, in a cemetery in Milton's garden.

From *Wild Wales*

GEORGE BORROW

AS I and my family sat at tea in our parlour, an hour or two after we had taken possession of our lodgings, the door of the room and that of the entrance of the house being open, on account of the fineness of the weather, a poor black cat entered hastily, sat down on the carpet by the table, looked up towards us, and mewed piteously. I never had seen so wretched a looking creature. It was dreadfully attenuated, being little

[287]

more than skin and bone, and was sorely afflicted with an eruptive malady. And here I may as well relate the history of this cat previous to our arrival which I subsequently learned by bits and snatches. It had belonged to a previous vicar of Llangollen, and had been left behind at his departure. His successor brought with him dogs and cats, who, conceiving that the late vicar's cat had no business at the vicarage, drove it forth to seek another home, which, however, it could not find. Almost all the people of the suburb were dissenters, as indeed were the generality of the people at Llangollen, and knowing the cat to be a church cat, not only would not harbour it, but did all they could to make it miserable; whilst the few who were not dissenters, would not receive it into their houses, either because they had cats of their own, or dogs, or did not want a cat, so that the cat had no home and was dreadfully persecuted by nine-tenths of the suburb. Oh, there never was a cat so persecuted as that poor Church of England animal, and solely on account of the opinions which it was supposed to have imbibed in the house of its late master, for I never could learn that the dissenters of the suburb, nor indeed of Llangollen in general, were in the habit of persecuting other cats;

Slumbering Cat, photo Will Green

the cat was a Church of England cat, and that was enough: stone it, hang it, drown it! were the cries of almost everybody. If the workmen of the flannel factory, all of whom were Calvinistic Methodists, chanced to get a glimpse of it in the road from the windows of the building, they would sally forth in a body, and with sticks, stones, or for want of other weapons, with clots of horse-dung, of which there was always plenty on the road, would chase it up the high bank or perhaps over the Camlas – the inhabitants of a small street between our house and the factory leading from the road to the river, all of whom were dissenters, if they saw it moving about the perllan, into which their back windows looked, would shriek and hoot at it, and fling anything of no value, which came easily to hand, at the head or body of the ecclesiastical cat. The good woman of the house, who though a very excellent person, was a bitter dissenter, whenever she saw it upon her ground or heard it was there, would make after it, frequently attended by her maid Margaret, and her young son, a boy about nine years of age, both of whom hated the cat, and were always ready to attack it, either alone or in company, and no wonder, the maid being not only a dissenter, but a class teacher, and the boy not only a dissenter, but intended for the dissenting ministry. Where it got its food, and food it sometimes must have got, for even a cat, an animal known to have nine lives, cannot live without food, was only known to itself, as was the place where it lay, for even a cat must lie down sometimes; though a labouring man who occasionally dug in the garden told me he believed that in the springtime it ate freshets, and the woman of the house once said that she believed it sometimes slept in the hedge, which hedge, by the bye, divided our perllan from the vicarage grounds, which were very extensive. Well might the cat having led this kind of life for better than two years look mere skin and bone when it made its appearance in our apartment, and have an eruptive malady, and also a bronchitic cough, for I remember it had both. How it came to make its appearance there is a mystery, for it had never entered the house before, even when there were lodgers; that it should not visit the woman, who was its declared enemy, was natural enough, but why, if it did not visit her other lodgers, did it visit us? Did instinct keep it aloof from them? Did instinct draw it towards us? We gave it some bread-and-butter, and a little tea with milk and sugar. It ate and drank and soon began to purr. The good woman of the house was horrified when on coming in to remove the things she saw the church cat on her carpet. 'What impudence!' she exclaimed, and made towards it, but on our telling her that we did not expect that it should be disturbed, she let it alone. A very remarkable circumstance was, that though the cat had hitherto been in the habit of flying not only from her face, but the very echo of her voice, it now looked her in the face with perfect composure, as much as to say, 'I don't fear you, for I know that I am now safe and with my own people.' It stayed with us two hours and then went away. The next morning it returned. To be short, though it went away every night, it became our own cat, and one of our family. I gave it something which cured it of its eruption, and through good treatment it soon lost its other ailments and began to look sleek and bonny.

We were at first in some perplexity with respect to the disposal of the ecclesiastical cat; it would of course not do to leave it in the garden to the tender mercies of the Calvinistic Methodists of the neighbourhood, more especially those of the flannel manufactory, and my wife and daughter could hardly carry it with them. At length we thought of applying to a young woman of sound church principles who was lately married and lived over the water on the way to the railway station, with whom we were slightly acquainted, to take charge of the animal, and she on the first intimation of our wish willingly acceded to it. So with her poor puss was left along with a trifle for its milk-money, and with her, as we subsequently learned, it continued in peace and comfort till one morning it sprang suddenly from the hearth into the air, gave a mew and died. So much for the ecclesiastical cat.

The Cat

ROBIN SKELTON

– for Sam –

The cat stood under the lilac.
It was black.
The sky was blue, the grass green,
and it stood
black under the lilac
that was lilac
under the sky that was all over blue.

[290]

Dog and Cat, Frantz Snyders (*Musée des Beaux-Arts, Grenoble*)

No matter that the way we say is how
the thing is in the mind, a proof of sorts
that where we stand and look is what we are,
sometimes a black cat stands black under lilac
and the grass is green, the sky unknown.

To Mrs Reynolds' Cat

JOHN KEATS

Cat! who hast pass'd thy grand climacteric,
  How many mice and rats hast in thy days
  Destroy'd? How many tit bits stolen? Gaze
With those bright languid segments green, and prick
Those velvet ears – but pr'ythee do not stick
  Thy latent talons in me – and upraise
  Thy gentle mew – and tell me all thy frays,
Of fish and mice, and rats and tender chick.

[291]

Nay, look not down, nor lick thy dainty wrists –
  For all thy wheezy asthma – and for all
Thy tail's tip is nick'd off – and though the fists
  Of many a maid have given thee many a maul,
Still is that fur as soft, as when the lists
  In youth thou enter'dest on glass bottled wall.

A Sleeping Maid, Nicolaes Maes (*National Gallery, London*)

[292]

On a Cat Ageing

ALEXANDER GRAY

He blinks upon the hearth-rug
And yawns in deep content,
Accepting all the comforts
That Providence has sent.

Louder he purrs, and louder,
In one glad hymn of praise,
For all the night's adventures,
For quiet, restful days.

Life will go on for ever,
With all that cat can wish;
Warmth, and the glad procession
Of fish, and milk and fish.

Only – the thought disturbs him –
He's noticed once or twice,
The times are somehow breeding
A nimbler race of mice.

Old Tom

RICHARD EBERHART

An old, black, rutting tomcat,
The brother of his female,
Expressed nature in his sister
Begetting again in his future.

I eye this old, mangy fellow
With a certain sympathy.
His progeny already
Have suffered fortune and misfortune

Cat, 1804

Teaching us, as larger animals,
Something of ourselves.
As poets will to survive,
Cats survive by force.

A kitten could not be expected
To understand a moving car.
One, atop my front wheel,
Was rolled down to mutilation.

I had to kill her with a club
And buried her in the bushes,
Shaking with the dread of this
But doing it nevertheless.

Her little brother very soon
Had caught a bird so beautiful
I hated to see it mutilated,
And left only feathers and the spleen.

They are the most civilized creatures,
Sleep all day and hunt by night,
Elegance in the drawing room,
Merciless in dusk or in moonlight.

But most it is their indifference
To death of their own fellows
I applaud; they go about their business,
Unquestioning the fates of those fellows.

Old Tom, here is a handout,
Some meal and some milk for you.
Go rough it under the stars,
You teach us what we are

When our policies are riven
And our pretensions are bare,
And we are subservient to nature
Very much as you are.

PART VIII

Cat's Death

My Old Cat

HAL SUMMERS

My old cat is dead,
Who would butt me with his head.
He had the sleekest fur.
He had the blackest purr.
Always gentle with us
Was this black puss,
But when I found him today
Stiff and cold where he lay
His look was a lion's,
Full of rage, defiance:
Oh, he would not pretend
That what came was a friend
But met it in pure hate.
Well died, my old cat.

On Clem: A Cat

GEOFFREY HOLLOWAY

A thing of piebald moods, true to his born colours –
querulous if shook from noonday beds
yet mornings given to nudging one awake
breathy, tickling, with stubborn tenderness ...
not much at bouncing intruder toms
but liked to prowl for dogs, the bigger the tastier ...
could saunter with a mannequin's rubato
but was never that feline about birds
save once: dozing on a sill
he snapped a breakneck bluetit rebounding off the pane ...

The Cat Loves Fish ..., Joseph Low (*Museum of Fine Arts, Boston, William A. Sargent Fund*)

We had him thirteen years.
Then something grew between:
he'd drool, subside in road-middles,
mess anywhere.
So, the vets. The last time
– oddly enough –
he purred like a sun-tuned grasshopper.
After, we couldn't open
that cardboard box – all the way back
colder, heavier –
but buried him with it.

[300]

He's there, by the garden-fence,
two sticks looped over with washing-line.
A rough job ... like death generally ...
but fitting somehow (he was farm stock)
and lasts, has meaning; if not perhaps
for the robin that sometimes lingers
wind-flaked, on its cross.

Dostoievsky

ROBERT LEACH

Our cat had gone
When we returned from holiday.
A week forgetting him,
Browning our pallor miles away,

And he was gone. Walked out on us.
His alert, delicate contempt had suggested Dostoievsky,
And so I'd called him:
The name satisfied my intellectual vanity.

The kids called him Dusty
And profligated the love of youth
On him. He ignored them, preferring
To snap wasps with his red mouth,

Eating them, stings and all. He was like that –
A baroque destroyer, researching
A library of garbage with taloned eloquence,
Minutely secret as a professor.

When we came back from the seaside
He was gone. No goodbye,
Merely an absent wish
And something to remember him by –

Self-portrait 1928, Tsugouharu Foujita (*Musée Nationale d'Art Moderne, Paris*)

A pillow's worth of feathers
And two dead birds on the living-room floor,
Guts spilling from the half-open corpses like
Underclothing from a dowager's boudoir drawer.

[302]

Among the intestine clots
A million maggots wagged,
Bulbous whitey things, wriggling, squirming, gorging
In half-gore carcasses stiff like crags.

The children missed him,
Dusty, they searched and called.
He didn't come. This indifference
Was once for all.

I'd only called him Dostoievsky
Out of intellectual pride;
When Dusty went,
The children cried.

Cat, Warwick Hutton (*The Keepsake Press*)

Last Words to a Dumb Friend

THOMAS HARDY

Pet was never mourned as you
Purrer of the spotless hue,
Plumy tail, and wistful gaze
While you humoured our queer ways,
Or outshrilled your morning call
Up the stairs and through the hall –
Foot suspended in its fall –
While expectant, you would stand
Arched to meet the stroking hand;
Till your way you chose to wend
Yonder, to your tragic end.

Never another pet for me!
Let your place all vacant be;
Better blankness day by day
Than companion torn away.
Better bid his memory fade,
Better blot each mark he made,
Selfishly escape distress
By contrived forgetfulness,
Than preserve his prints to make
Every morn and eve an ache.

From the chair whereon he sat
Sweep his fur, nor wince thereat;
Rake his little pathways out
Mid the bushes roundabout;
Smooth away his talons' mark
From the claw-worn pine-tree bark,
Where he climbed as dusk embrowned,
Waiting us who loitered round.

Girl and Cat, John Russell (*Tate Gallery, London*)

Strange it is this speechless thing,
Subject to our mastering,
Subject for his life and food
To our gift, and time, and mood;
Timid pensioner of us Powers,
His existence ruled by ours,
Should – by crossing at a breath
Into safe and shielded death,

[305]

By the merely taking hence
Of his insignificance –
Loom as largened to the sense,
Shape as part, above man's will,
Of the Imperturbable.

As a prisoner, flight debarred,
Exercising in a yard,
Still retain I, troubled, shaken,
Mean estate, by him forsaken;
And this home, which scarcely took
Impress from his little look,
By his faring to the Dim
Grows all eloquent of him.

Housemate, I can think you still
Bounding to the window-sill,
Over which I vaguely see
Your small mound beneath the tree,
Showing in the autumn shade
That you moulder where you played.

In Memory of My Cat, Domino: 1951–66

ROY FULLER

Rising at dawn to pee, I thought I saw you
Curved in a chair, with head raised to look at me,
As you did at such hours. But the next moment,
More used to the gloom, there was only a jar
And a face-cloth. Time enough, nonetheless,
For love's responsibilities to return
To me.
          The unique character of the dead
Is the source of our sense of mourning and loss;
So, back in bed, I avoided calling up
What I know is intact in my mind, your life,
Entirely possessed as it was by my care.

I could conceive you not as dead but merely
Gone before me to a world that sends to us
Decreasing intimations of its beings –
No doubt because they find us in the end
Pathetic, worthy, but of small importance.

So long had we been together it never
Occurred to me I might fall somewhat behind.
Even when, familiar fur in my hands,
The sickly wave of barbiturate rose up,
I thought it was I who was journeying on –
But looking back there is only emptiness,
Your dusty medicaments and my portrait
Taken with you: sad mode of life you've outpaced.

On the Death of a Favourite Cat, Drowned in a Tub of Gold Fishes

THOMAS GRAY

'Twas on a lofty vase's side,
Where China's gayest art had dy'd
   The azure flowers that blow;
Demurest of the tabby kind,
The pensive Selima, reclin'd,
   Gaz'd on the lake below.

Her conscious tail her joy declar'd;
The fair round face, the snowy beard,
   The velvet of her paws,
Her coat, that with the tortoise vies,
Her ears of jet, and emerald eyes,
   She saw; and purr'd applause.

[307]

Horace Walpole's Cat, Selima

Still had she gaz'd; but 'midst the tide
Two angel forms were seen to glide,
　　The Genii of the stream:
Their scaly armour's Tyrian hue
Thro' richest purple to the view
　　Betray'd a golden gleam.

The hapless Nymph with wonder saw:
A whisker first, and then a claw,
　　With many an ardent wish,
She stretch'd in vain to reach the prize.
What female heart can gold despise?
　　What Cat's averse to fish?

Presumptuous Maid! with looks intent
Again she stretch'd, again she bent,
　　Nor knew the gulf between.
(Malignant Fate sat by, and smil'd.)
The slipp'ry verge her feet beguil'd,
　　She tumbled headlong in.

[308]

Eight times emerging from the flood
She mew'd to ev'ry wat'ry God,
     Some speedy aid to send.
No Dolphin came, no Nereid stirr'd:
Nor cruel *Tom*, nor *Susan* heard.
     A Fav'rite has no friend!

From hence, ye Beauties, undeceiv'd,
Know, one false step is ne'er retriev'd,
     And be with caution bold.
Not all that tempts your wand'ring eyes
And heedless hearts, is lawful prize;
     Nor all that glisters, gold.

Death of the Cat

IAN SERRAILLIER

Alas! Mowler, the children's pride,
Has slipped on a water-butt, tumbled inside
And died.

The seamstress on her sewing machine
Stitched a shroud of satin sheen.

The carpenter hammered and planed a coffin
Of seasoned oak without a knot in.

The sexton – he loved dear Mowler well –
Mournfully, mournfully tolled the bell.

Few were the prayers the parson spoke.
All he could do, poor fellow, was choke.

But saddest of all in the funeral train
Were the children. Deep were their sorrow and pain,

For they knew, as they followed the churchyard through,
They'd never set eyes on Mowler again.

[309]

In silence behind the coffin they stepped,
Solemnly, slowly. Everyone wept

Except
The little mice hid in the hedge – not they!

'Twas not *their* hearts that bled.
'Let's out and play,'
They cried. 'Oh, spread
The butter thick on the bread!
Dance in cream cheese right up to our knees,
For the cat is dead!
Hooray!
The cat
        is
           dead!'

Mike

SIR ERNEST A. WALLIS BUDGE

(The cat who assisted in keeping the main gate of the British Museum
from February 1909 to January 1929)

IN the days when that famous and learned man, Sir Richard Garnett,
ruled over the Department of Printed Books in the British Museum, he
was frequently visited by a cat who was generally known among the staff
as 'Black Jack'.

He was a very handsome black creature, with a white shirt front and
white paws, and whiskers of great length. He was fond of sitting on the
desks in the Reading Room, and he never hesitated to ask a reader to
hold open both folding doors when he wanted to go out into the corridor.
Being shut in one of the newspaper rooms one Sunday, and being bored,
he amused himself by sharpening his claws on the bindings of the volumes
of newspapers, and it must be confessed did much damage. This brought
down upon him the wrath of the officials, and he was banished from the
library; the Clerk of the Works was ordered to get rid of him, and tried
to do so, but failed, for Black Jack had disappeared mysteriously. The
truth was that two of the members of the staff arranged for him to be

Dressing the Kitten, Joseph Wright of Derby (*The Iveagh Bequest, Kenwood*)

kept in safety in a certain place, and provided him with food and milk. An official report was written to the effect that Black Jack had disappeared, and he was 'presumed dead'; the bindings of the volumes of newspapers were repaired, and the official mind was once more at peace. A few weeks later Black Jack reappeared, and everyone was delighted to see him again; and the chief officials asked no questions!

[311]

Early in the spring of 1908 the Keeper of the Egyptian Cat Mummies in the British Museum was going down the steps of his official residence, when he saw Black Jack coming towards the steps and carrying something rather large in his mouth. He came to the steps and deposited his burden on the steps at the Keeper's feet and then turned and walked solemnly away. The something which he deposited on the steps was a kitten, and that kitten was later known to fame as 'Mike'. The kitten was taken in and cared for and grew and flourished, and by great good luck was adopted as a pal by the two cats already in the house. So all was well.

When Mike was a little older he went and made friends with the kind-hearted gatekeeper at the main gate, and he began to frequent the lodge. By day and night he was always sure of a welcome, and thus he was the happy possessor of two homes. On Sunday mornings the house cat taught him to stalk pigeons in the colonnade. Mike was set to 'point' like a dog, and the house cat little by little drove the pigeons up into a corner. The pigeons became dazed, and fell down, and then each cat seized a bird and carried it into the house uninjured. The Housekeeper took the pigeons from the cats, and in return for them gave a slice of beef or mutton and milk to each cat. The pigeons were taken into a little side room, and after they had eaten some maize and drunk water, they flew out of the window none the worse for their handling by the cats. The fact was that neither cat liked to eat game with dirty, sooty, feathers on it; they preferred clean, cooked meat.

Cat, Louis Wain (*Michael Parkin Fine Art Ltd*)

[312]

As time went on, Mike, wishing to keep his proceedings during the hours of night uncriticized by the household, preferred the lodge to the house, and finally he took up his abode there; the corner shelf out of the draughts was prepared for him to sleep on, and he could go out and come in at any time he pleased both by day and by night. The Keeper of the Mummied Cats took care to feed him during the lean years of the war, and whoever went short, Mike did not. During the last two years he was difficult to feed because of his decaying teeth, but a diet of tender meat and fish on alternate days kept him going. He preferred sole to whiting, and whiting to haddock, and sardines to herrings; for cod he had no use whatever. He owed much to the three kind-hearted gatekeepers who cooked his food for him, and treated him as a man and a brother.

A Case of Murder

VERNON SCANNELL

They should not have left him there alone,
Alone that is except for the cat.
He was only nine, not old enough
To be left alone in a basement flat,
Alone, that is, except for the cat.
A dog would have been a different thing,
A big gruff dog with slashing jaws,
But a cat with round eyes mad as gold,
Plump as a cushion with tucked-in paws –
Better have left him with a fair-sized rat!
But what they did was leave him with a cat.
He hated that cat; he watched it sit,
A buzzing machine of soft black stuff,
He sat and watched and he hated it,
Snug in its fur, hot blood in a muff,
And its mad gold stare and the way it sat
Crooning dark warmth: he loathed all that.
So he took Daddy's stick and he hit the cat.
Then quick as a sudden crack in glass
It hissed, black flash, to a hiding place
In the dust and dark beneath the couch,

[313]

And he followed the grin on his new-made face,
A wide-eyed, frightened snarl of a grin,
And he took the stick and he thrust it in,
Hard and quick in the furry dark.
The black fur squealed and he felt his skin
Prickle with sparks of dry delight.
Then the cat again came into sight,
Shot for the door that wasn't quite shut,
But the boy, quick too, slammed fast the door:
The cat, half-through, was cracked like a nut
And the soft black thud was dumped on the floor.
Then the boy was suddenly terrified
And he bit his knuckles and cried and cried;
But he had to do something with the dead thing there.
His eyes squeezed beads of salty prayer
But the wound of fear gaped wide and raw;
He dared not touch the thing with his hands
So he fetched a spade and shovelled it
And dumped the load of heavy fur
In the spidery cupboard under the stair
Where it's been for years, and though it died
It's grown in that cupboard and its hot low purr
Grows slowly louder year by year:
There'll not be a corner for the boy to hide
When the cupboard swells and all sides split
And the huge black cat pads out of it.

The King of the Cats is Dead

JENI COUZYN

The king of the cats is dead
Tom the all time conqueror
Tom the invincible bushytailed
Tom the monarch of eternity.
Hazel-eyed
he could see around the world

[314]

Cat with Bird (Museo Nazionale, Naples)

knew the hiding places of birds
terror of rats and squirrels he
played games on the wild heath
with credible pretty witches
Tom the slant-eyed
Tom the cunning deceitful trickster of men
Tom the hero among cats
Tom the wise of many generations.

Alas Tom is dead.
I sing his praises who would not have noticed
contemptible me. Alas Tom the hero
I see you everywhere, in black cats
everywhere I am looking for you
who betrayed you.
Your yellow eyes plague my vision.

The king of the cats is dead.
They are building the Royal Free
where he ruled generations of cats who were
knights among cats, the round table of
noble cats, the merry men among cats

[315]

scorning the dandy domestics.
Wildcat of dustbin and midnight
they were sovereign
where whitecoated men lurk now in the
old places, scum of the earth with your nets and
poised syringes, a pox on your endeavours.

The king of the cats is dead, dead.
Old ladies leave scraps for the scattered
hundred in alleyways.
They are building the Royal Free where he
was tyrant.
Tom is dead. I am glad he is not alive
to see what they are doing.

The King of the Cats is Dead

PETER PORTER

The light on his thigh was like
a waterfall in Iceland, and his hair
was the tidal rip between two rocks,
his claws retracted sat in softness
deeper than the ancient moss of Blarney,
his claws extended were the coulter
of the gods and a raw March wind
was in his merely agricultural yawn.
Between his back legs was a catapult
of fecundity and he was riggish
as a red-haired man. The girls
of our nation felt him brush their legs
when they were bored with telling rosaries –
at night he clawed their brains in their
coffined beds and his walnut mind
wrinkled on their scalps. His holidays
were upside down in water and then
his face was like the sun: his smell

was in the peat smoke and even his midden
was a harmony of honey. When he stalked
his momentary mice the land shook
as though Atlantic waves were bowling
at the western walls. But his eyes
were the greatest thing about him.
They burned low and red so that drunks
saw them like two stars above a hedge,
they held the look of last eyes
in a drowning man, they were the sight
the rebel angels saw the first morning
of expulsion. And he is dead – a voice
from the centre of the earth told of his death
by treachery, that he lies in a hole
of infamy, his kidneys and his liver
torn from his body.

The late Fosdyke, photo Roy Deverell

Therefore tell
the men and horses of the marketplace,
the swallows laying twigs, the salmon
on the ladder that nothing is
as it has been
time is explored
and all is known, the portents
are of brief and brutal things, since
all must hear the words of desolation,
The King of the Cats is Dead
and it
is only Monday in the world.

From *The Age of Reason*

JEAN-PAUL SARTRE

(*translated by Eric Sutton*)

'POPPAEA!' cried Daniel. 'Poppaea, Poppaea!' Poppaea hardly ever came
when called: Daniel had to go and fetch her from the kitchen. When
she saw him, she jumped on to the gas stove with a sharp peevish growl.
She was a stray cat, heavily scarred across her right side. Daniel had found
her in the Luxembourg one winter evening, just before the garden closed,
and had taken her home. She was imperious and bad-tempered, and she
often bit Malvina: Daniel was fond of her. He took her in his arms, and
she drew her head back, flattening her ears and arching her neck: she
looked quite scandalized. He stroked her nose, and she nibbled the tip
of one finger with angry playfulness: then he pinched her in the loose
flesh of the neck, and she lifted a defiant little head. She did not purr –
Poppaea never purred – but she looked at him, straight in the face, and
Daniel thought, as indeed he often did: 'A cat that looks you in the eyes
is very rare.' At the same time, he felt an intolerable anguish take possession of him, and had to turn his eyes away: 'There, there,' he said, 'there,
there, my beauty,' and smiled at her with eyes averted. The two others
had remained side by side; purring idiotically, like a grasshopper chorus.
Daniel eyed them with a sort of malignant relief: 'Rabbit-stew,' he
thought. He remembered Malvina's pink teats. It was no end of a business
to get Poppaea into the basket: he had to push her in headfirst, but she

Bagging the Cat, A. V. Venne

turned and spat and tried to claw him. 'Oh, would you now?' said Daniel. He picked her up by the neck and hindquarters, and crammed her forcibly into the basket, which creaked as Poppaea clawed it from within. Daniel took advantage of the cat's momentary stupor to slam down the lid and snap the two clasps.

'Ouf!' he ejaculated. His hand smarted slightly – with a dry little pain that was almost a tickle. He got up and eyed the basket with ironical satisfaction: safe and secure. On the back of his hand were two scratches, and in his innermost self an odd tickling sensation that promised to become unpleasant. He picked up the ball of string off the table and put it in his trouser pocket.

Then he hesitated: 'It's a goodish way, I shall get pretty hot.' He would have liked to wear his flannel jacket, but it was not a habit of his to yield easily to his inclinations, and besides it would be rather comical to march along in the bright sunshine, flushed and perspiring, with that burden in his arms. Comical and a trifle ridiculous: the vision made him smile and he chose his brown tweed jacket, which he had not been able to wear since the end of May. He lifted the basket by the handle, and thought; 'Curse the little brutes, how heavy they are.' He pictured their attitudes, humiliated and grotesque, their fury and their terror. 'And that is what I was so fond of!' No sooner had he shut the three idols into a wicker basket than they became cats once more, just simply cats, small, vain, stupid mammals, stricken with panic – very far from being sacred. 'Cats: merely cats.' He began to laugh: he had the feeling that he was going to play an excellent trick on somebody. As he passed the flat door, his heart turned over, but the sensation soon passed: once on the staircase he felt hard and resolute, with an underside of strange sickliness, reminiscent of raw meat. The concierge was in her doorway, and she smiled at him. She liked Daniel because he was so ceremonious and polite.

'You are out early this morning, Monsieur Sereno.'

'I was afraid you were ill, dear lady,' replied Daniel with an air of concern. 'I got back late last night, and I saw a light under the lodge door.'

'Just imagine,' said the concierge. 'I was so done up that I fell asleep without turning the light off. Suddenly I heard the sound of your bell. Ah, I said to myself, there's Monsieur Sereno coming in. (You were the only tenant out.) I turned the light out immediately afterwards. I think it was about three o'clock.'

'Just about . . .'

'Well,' she said, 'that's a large basket you've got.'

'They're my cats.'

'Are they ill – poor little things?'

'No, but I'm taking them to my sister's at Meudon. The vet told me they needed air.' And he added gravely, 'Cats tend to become tuberculous, you know.'

'Tuberculous!' said the concierge, in a voice of consternation. 'You must look after them carefully. All the same,' she added, 'they'll be missed in your flat. I had got used to seeing the little dears when I was cleaning up. You will be sorry to lose them.'

'I shall indeed, Madame Dupuy,' said Daniel.

He smiled at her gravely and walked on. The old mole, she gave herself away. She must have played about with them when I wasn't there; she'd much better have been attending to her daughter. Emerging from the archway he was dazzled by the light, an unpleasant, scorching, stabbing light. It hurt his eyes, which was only to be expected: when a man has been drinking the night before, a misty morning suits him best. He could no longer see anything, he was afloat in the encompassing light, with a ring of iron round his skull. Suddenly, he saw his shadow, a grotesque and stocky figure, with the shadow of the wicker basket dangling from the end of his arm. Daniel smiled: he was very tall. He drew himself to his full height, but the shadow remained squat and misshapen, like that of a chimpanzee. 'Doctor Jekyll and Mr Hyde. No; I won't take a taxi,' he said to himself: 'I have plenty of time. I shall take Mr Hyde for an airing as far as the 72 stop.' The 72 would take him to Charenton. Half a mile from there, Daniel knew a little solitary corner on the bank of the Seine. 'At any rate,' he said to himself, 'I shan't be sick, that would be the last straw.' The water of the Seine was particularly dark and dirty at that spot, being covered with greenish patches of oil from the Vitry factories. Daniel envisaged himself with disgust: he felt, within himself, so benevolent, so truly benevolent that it wasn't natural. 'That,' he thought, 'is the real man,' with a sort of satisfaction. His was a hard, forbidding character, but underneath it all was a shrinking victim pleading for mercy. It was odd, he thought, that a man could hate himself as though he were someone else. Not that that was really true: whatever he might do there was only one Daniel. When he despised himself he had the feeling of detachment from his own being, as though he were poised like an impartial judge above a noisome turmoil, then suddenly he found himself plunging downwards caught again in his own toils. 'Damnation,' thought he to himself. 'I must ge a drink.' He had to make a little detour for this purpose, he would stop at Championnet's in the rue Tailledouce. When he pushed open the door, the bar was deserted. The waiter was dusting the red, wooden cask-like tables. The darkness was grateful to Daniel's eyes. 'I've got a cursed headache,' he thought, as he put down the basket and clambered on to one of the stools by the bar.

'A nice double whisky, I suppose,' said the barman.

'No,' said Daniel curtly.

'Confound these fellows' mania for classifying human beings as though they were umbrellas or sewing-machines. I am *not* so-and-so; one isn't ever anything. But they pin you down as quick as look at you. One chap gives good tips, another is always ready with a joke, and I am fond of double whiskies.'

'A gin-fizz,' said Daniel.

The barman served him without comment: he was no doubt offended. 'So much the better,' thought Daniel. He would not enter the place again, the people were too familiar. Anyway, gin-fizz tasted like a lemon-flavoured purgative. It scattered a sort of acidulated dust upon the tongue, and left a steely savour behind it. 'It no longer has any effect on me,' thought Daniel.

'Give me a peppered Vodka in a balloon glass.'

He swallowed the Vodka and remained for a moment plunged in meditation, with a firework in his mouth. 'Won't it ever end?' he thought to himself. But these were surface thoughts, as usual, cheques without funds to meet them. 'What won't ever end? What won't ever end?' Whereupon a shrill miaow was heard, and the sound of scratching. The barman gave a start.

'They are cats,' said Daniel curtly.

He got off the stool, flung twenty francs on to the counter and picked up the basket. As he lifted it, he noticed a tiny red drop on the floor: blood. 'What can they be up to inside there,' thought Daniel distressfully. But he could not bring himself to lift the lid. For the moment the little cage contained nothing but a solid, undifferentiated fear: if he opened the basket, that fear would dissolve once more into *his cats*, which Daniel could not have endured. 'You couldn't endure it, eh? And supposing I did lift that lid?' But Daniel was already outside, and again the blindness fell, a clear and dewy blindness: your eyes itched, fire seemed to fill the vision, then came the sudden realization that for moments past you have been looking at houses, houses a hundred yards ahead, airy and insubstantial, edifices of smoke. At the end of the road stood a high blue wall. 'It's uncanny to see too clearly,' thought Daniel. It was thus that he imagined Hell: a vision that penetrated everything, and saw to the very end of the world – the depths of a man's self. The basket shook at the extremity of his arm: the creatures inside it were clawing each other. The terror that he felt so near to his hand – Daniel wasn't sure whether it disgusted or delighted him: anyway, it came to the same thing. 'There is always something to reassure them, they can smell me.' And Daniel thought, 'I am, indeed, for them, a smell.' Patience, though: Daniel would soon be divested of that familiar smell, he would walk about without a smell, alone amid his fellow-men, who haven't fine enough senses to spot a man by his smell. Without a smell or a shadow, without a past, nothing more than an invisible uprootment from the self towards the future. Daniel noticed that he was a few steps in advance of his body – yonder, at the level of the gas-jet, and that he was watching his own progress, hobbling a little under his burden, stiff-jointed and already soaked in sweat: he saw himself come, he was no more than a disembodied

Penitent Cat at the Birth of the Ganges River, photo Paolo Koch

vision. But the shop-window of a dyeing establishment presented his reflection, and the illusion was dispelled. Daniel filled himself with viscous, vapid water: himself: the water of the Seine, vapid and viscous, would fill the basket, and they would claw each other to pieces. A vast revulsion came upon him – this was surely a wanton act. He had stopped and set the basket on the ground. One could only damage oneself through the harm one did to others. One could never get directly at oneself. Once more he thought of Constantinople where faithless spouses were put in a sack with hydrophobic cats, and the sack thrown into the Bosphorus. Barrels, leather sacks, wicker baskets: prisons. 'There are worse things.' Daniel shrugged his shoulders: another thought without funds to meet it. He didn't want to adopt a tragic attitude, he had done that too often in the past. Besides, that meant taking oneself seriously. Never, never again would Daniel take himself seriously. The motor-bus suddenly appeared, Daniel waved to the driver and got into the first-class compartment.

'As far as you go.'

'Six tickets,' said the conductor.

Seine water would drive them crazy. Coffee-coloured water with violet gleams in it. A woman came in and sat opposite him, a prim, respectable female, with a little girl. The little girl observed the basket with interest: 'Nasty little insect,' thought Daniel. The basket miaowed, and Daniel started, as though he had been caught in the act of murder.

'What is it?' asked the little girl in a shrill voice.

'Hush,' said her mother. 'Don't annoy the gentleman.'

'It's cats,' said Daniel.

'Are they yours?' asked the little girl.

'Yes.'

'Why are you taking them about in a basket?'

'Because they're ill,' said Daniel mildly.

'May I see them?'

'Jeannine,' said her mother, 'mind what you're saying.'

'I can't show them to you, they're ill, and rather savage.'

'Oh,' said the little girl in a calm, insinuating tone; 'they'll be quite all right with me, the little darlings.'

'Do you think so? Look here, my dear,' said Daniel in a low, hurried voice, 'I'm going to drown my cats, that's what I'm going to do, and do you know why? Because, no longer ago than this morning, they clawed the face of a pretty little girl like you, who came to bring me some flowers, and now she'll have to have a glass eye.'

[324]

'Oh!' cried the little girl in consternation. She threw a terror-stricken glance at the basket, and clung to her mother's skirts.

'There, there,' said the mother, turning indignant eyes upon Daniel. 'You must keep quiet, you see, and not chatter to everyone you meet. Don't be frightened, darling, the gentleman was only joking.'

Daniel returned her look placidly. 'She detests me,' he thought, with satisfaction. Behind the windows he could see the grey houses gliding by, and he knew that the good woman was looking at him. 'An angry mother: she's looking for something to dislike in me. And it won't be my face.' No one ever disliked Daniel's face. 'Nor my suit, which is new and handsome. My hands perhaps.' His hands were short and strong, a little fleshy, with black hairs at the joints. He spread them out on his knees ('Look at them – just look at them'). But the woman had abandoned the encounter; she was staring straight ahead of her with a crass expression on her face: she was at rest. Daniel eyed her with a kind of eagerness; these people who rested – how did they manage it? She had let her whole person sag into herself and sat dissolved in it. There was nothing in that head of hers that resembled a frantic flight from self, neither curiosity, nor hatred, nor any motion, not the faintest undulation: nothing but the thick integument of sleep. Abruptly she awoke, and an air of animation took possession of her face.

'Why, we're there,' said she. 'Come along! You bad little girl, you never notice anything.'

She took her daughter by the hand, and dragged her off. The bus re-started and then pulled up. People passed in front of Daniel laughing.

'All change,' shouted the conductor.

Daniel started: the vehicle was empty. He got up and climbed out. It was a populous square containing a number of taverns: a group of workmen and women had gathered round a hand-cart. Women eyed him with surprise. Daniel quickened his step and turned down a dirty alley that led towards the Seine. On both sides of the road there were barrels and warehouses. The basket was now miaowing incessantly, and Daniel almost ran: he was carrying a leaky bucket from which water oozed out drop by drop. Every miaow was a drop of water. The bucket was heavy, Daniel transferred it to his left hand, and wiped his forehead with his right. He must not think about the cats. Oh? So you don't want to think about the cats? Well, that's just why you *must* think of them. You can't get away with it so easily. Daniel recalled Poppaea's golden eyes, and quickly thought of whatever came first into his head – of the Bourse, where he had made ten thousand francs the day before, of Marcelle –

he was going to see her that evening, it was his day: 'Archangel!' Daniel grinned: he despised Marcelle profoundly. 'They haven't the courage to admit that they're no longer in love. If Mathieu saw things as they were, he would have to make a decision. But he didn't want to: he didn't want to lose his bearings. He is a normal fellow,' thought Daniel ironically. The cats were miaowing as though they had been scalded, and Daniel felt he would soon lose his self-control. He put the basket on the ground, and gave it a couple of violent kicks. This produced a tremendous commotion in the interior, after which the cats were silent. Daniel stood for a moment motionless, conscious of an odd shiver like a tuft behind his ears. Some workmen came out of a warehouse and Daniel resumed his journey. Here was the place. He made his way down a stone stair to the bank of the Seine and sat down on the ground, beside an iron ring and between a barrel of tar and a heap of paving-stones. The Seine was yellow under a blue sky. Black barges loaded with casks lay moored against the opposite quay. Daniel was sitting in the sun and his temples ached. He eyed the rippling stream, swollen with patches of opal iridescence. He took the ball of string out of his pocket, and cut off a long strand with his clasp-knife: then, without getting up, and with his left hand, he picked out a paving stone. He fastened one of the ends of the string to the handle of the basket, rolled the rest of it round the stone, made several knots and replaced the stone on the ground. It looked a singular contrivance. Daniel's idea was to carry the basket in his right hand and the stone in his left hand: he would drop them into the water at the same moment. The basket would perhaps float for the tenth of a second after which it would be forcibly dragged beneath the surface and abruptly disappear. Daniel felt hot, and cursed his thick jacket, but did not want to take it off. Within him something throbbed, something pleaded for mercy, and Daniel, the hard and resolute Daniel, heard himself say in mournful tones: 'When a man hasn't the courage to kill himself wholesale, he must do so retail.' He would walk down to the water and say: 'Farewell to what I love most in the world ...' He raised himself slightly on his hands and looked about him: on his right the bank was deserted, on his left – some distance away, he could see a fisherman, a black figure in the sunshine. The ripples would spread *under water* to the cork on the man's line. 'He'll think he's had a bite.' Daniel laughed and pulled out his handkerchief to wipe away the sweat that beaded his forehead. The hands of his wrist-watch stood at eleven twenty-five. 'At half-past eleven!' He must prolong that strange moment: Daniel had split into two entities; he felt himself *lost* in a scarlet cloud, under a leaden sky.

He thought of Mathieu with a sort of pride. 'It is *I* who am free,' he said to himself. But it was an impersonal pride, for Daniel was no longer a person. At eleven twenty-nine he got up and felt so weak that he had to lean against the barrel. He got a smear of tar on to his tweed jacket, and looked at it.

He saw the black smear on the brown material, and suddenly he felt that he was one person and no more. One only. A coward. A man who liked his cats and could not chuck them in the river. He picked up his pocket-knife, bent down, and cut the string. In silence. Even within himself there was silence now, he was too ashamed to talk in his own presence. He picked up the basket again, and climbed the stair: it was as though he were walking with averted head past someone who regarded him with contempt. Within himself desolation and silence still reigned. When he reached the top of the steps he ventured to speak his first words to himself: 'What was that drop of blood?' But he didn't dare open the basket: he walked on, limping as he went. It is I: it is I: it is I. The evil thing. But in the depths of him there was an odd little smile because he had saved Poppaea.

'Taxi!' he shouted.

PART IX

Cat's Resurrection

Extract from the Will of Miss Topping, who died in Vendôme, May 1841

I DESIRE that there shall be raised from the most easily convertible part of my property a capital sum sufficient to produce 800 f. a year, which shall be paid quarterly to such person as I may name ... on condition of taking the care and nourishment of my three favourite cats, Nina, Fanfan and Mini ... The person [so] appointed shall live on a groundfloor, to which shall adjoin a terrace easy of access and a garden enclosed within walls, of which they shall have full and free enjoyment ... They are to sleep in the house, and therefore are to be shut up after their supper.

The Times, March 1843

Three Cats, Benjamin Cam Norton (*Michael Parkin Fine Art Ltd*)

[331]

Car Fights Cat

ALAN SILLITOE

In a London crescent curving vast
A cat sat –
Between two rows of molar houses
With birdsky in each grinning gap.

Cat small – coal and snow
Road wide – a zone of tar set hard and fast
With four-wheeled speedboats cutting
A dash
    for it from
        time to time.

King Cat walked warily midstream
As if silence were no warning on this silent road
Where even a man would certainly have crossed
With hands in pockets and been whistling.

The cat heard it, but royalty and indolence
Weighed its paws to hobnailed boots
Held it from the dragons-teeth of safety first and last,
Until some Daimler hurrying from work
Caused cat to stop and wonder where it came from –
Instead of zig-zag scattering to hide itself.

Maybe a deaf malevolence descended
And cat thought car would pass in front –
So spun and walked all fur and confidence
Into the dreadful tyre-treads ...
A wheel caught hold of it and
FEARSOME THUDS
Sounded from the night-time of black axles in
UNEQUAL FIGHT
That stopped the heart to hear it.

But cat shot out with limbs still solid,
Bolted – spitting fire and gravel
At unjust God who built such massive
Catproof motorcars in his graven image,
Its mind made up to lose and therefore win
By winging towards
The wisdom toothgaps of the canyon houses
LEGS AND BRAIN INTACT.

Let No Man Put Asunder

GRAHAM FAWCETT

THE road ran straight for the first mile, as far as the signpost. The white arms pointed black letters to the Church and the Mouth. The Church road coiled its way under the shadow of high hedges and then out into sunlight, stretching beyond the graveyard and the Saxon tower to pitch forward easing to a slope down several hundred yards to the bridge.

Here the two rivers became one: Torridge from the Northern moor, Bere from the valley to the West. Priestlike the old bridge received their union, an altargate to the ordination of water by water seconds before its unmaking. Higher than the bridge and astride the narrowing land between the currents stood the Mill, where the man and the woman lived and nearly a century had passed since the last turning of the wheels.

For this Mill had two wheels: quite independent, they waited only on the mood or season of water from moor or valley. And yet it was said that when one had turned, the other had stood still – no sound from its shackchamber but the simple sameness of shallow water trickling beneath the silent wheel and on towards the bridge.

When the man and the woman had come to the house, they had found a cat which already belonged there. She'd been called Mouthwatch because she would sit every day on the parapet of the bridge below the Mill and watch the two rivers joining together and stumbling down to the Mouth and the open sea. Mouthwatch had led them everywhere from that first day: through the high wooden gates, along the short drive which forked to avoid trees and stopped before the orchard. Then into the kitchen garden and over the fence to the meadow surrounded by steep wooded banks. At the far end of the meadow the trees closed in and the only path – the cat went slowly here – crossed the shallower Torridge on large smooth stones before drifting along cart tracks and disappearing suddenly through a gap in the low rock wall which marked the boundary between Mill land and the lost world on the other side of the trees. That wall – and Mouthwatch would never cross it – ran cleanly along a line of massive elms into a wild climb of struggling branches and no eventual light.

The night that Mouthwatch was due to give birth there was a gale and rain. Mouthwatch left the house in search of shelter. Towards midnight, they took lanterns and went outside to listen in the dark and the steady rain for sound of her. They looked in all the usual places, stood and held their breath in the night and heard nothing. Then as they turned to go inside, they stopped. Below the house from the direction of the bridge there was a single cry. Then silence. They headed towards the noise, its echo already deadened by the rain. The sound of running water increased as they came out on to the road that led to the bridge. The rain fell harder, and, in the light of the lantern, straighter. There was no more noise. They saw nothing.

The next morning the rain had stopped and the sky was light with cloud. After breakfast they went out and took the same path as the night before. When they reached the bridge, they stopped to rest and leaned on the parapet looking towards the Mouth and the falling, single river. If they had not then looked directly down, they might never have noticed Mouthwatch half-hidden from sight and lying on the narrow bank beneath the bridge. They climbed down to look closer. She was alive, clearly, and so were her clinging young. It was not until the man took a small twig and stirred them gently that he realized: the kittens were clinging not only to her but to each other. They were joined together at the side.

Mouthwatch would not let them touch her or the litter. The man and the woman could only turn away and walk back along the road towards the high wooden gates of the house. At the end of the drive they continued across the orchard and into the meadow, past the disused caravan and the corn elevator haunched on its large iron wheels in the tall grass. Through the gap in the trees they could see as they drew nearer that the wind had brought down branches which had dammed Torridge's flat-stone crossing. The man reflected: if that had not happened, the river would have been higher, much higher at the bridge and the cats could not have survived the height and power of the double rush of water. He walked down into the water and made to begin to clear the fallen branches. Then he stopped. They were still there, under the bridge. The water was lower now but the stream must stay blocked until they could be moved.

The rain came back the next night, harder than before. The woman pleaded that they should go to the cats and try to bring them home, however difficult it might be and at whatever risk of injury to them. It was already dark when the man went out to get them. At the top of the steps leading down from the door he stumbled and fell. The lantern smashed on the stone and the smell of warm paraffin mixed with that of wet grass. Picking himself up, he turned back inside the house for the keys to the caravan in the meadow. There was an old lantern in there – he had to get it – which had not been used for a long time. He hurried through the kitchen garden, climbed the rough wood fence and ran on into the meadow. He had just reached the caravan and felt the lock take the key when he heard a creaking and then a rushing of water. The dam had given way and the river, swollen by new rain, was already racing down the course towards the bridge. It would be too late. He was stepping out of the caravan with the lit lantern in his hand before he heard another, quite different sound. As he hurried back towards the house and passed the shackchamber of the Torridge wheel, he knew. With the onrush of the flood the wheel had begun to turn. He ran back across the orchard, out into the road and down to the bridge. He leaned straining over the parapet and held the lantern down as far as he could reach in the direction of Mouthwatch's hiding place. There was nothing; and as he watched he saw the water rising as it washed the bank.

Newborn Kitten, photo Will Green

[335]

When day came, the urgency of the darkness had gone. Neither of them wanted to go outside. But as the sun came out and the air grew warmer, the woman opened the window and looked out across the orchard. She was looking at the chamber of the Torridge wheel and the man saw her. Together they went out to see for themselves what signs there might be that it had turned in the storm. It lay, still again, in the breathing sunlight, with no trace of sudden life. But there was something else. In the deep well of the wheel was a small black separate kitten. Across the stone pathway, in the well of the Bere stream wheel, lay the other. Each bore a patch of white skin on one side. And as the man and the woman watched, so did a third cat – sitting on the parapet of the bridge below the Mill watching the two rivers become one on their way to the Mouth and the open sea.

To A Slow Drum

GEORGE MACBETH

I

Solitary thoughts,
and burial mounds,
begin this dirge,
and mournful sounds.

II

Now to the dead march
troop in twos,
the granite owls
with their *Who Was Who's,*
the bat, and the grave, yew
bear on his wheels,
Tuborg the pig
with his hard wood heels.

[336]

Creation of the Animals, Paul Brill (*Galleria Doria, Rome*)

III

Gemmed with a dew
of morning tears,
    the weeping armadillo
has brought his shears:
    the droop-ear dog
and the lion come,
    dipping their long waists
to meet the drum.

IV

On the bare chafing-dish
as each one hears,
    the grey lead pigs
reverse their spears:
    grooved in line,
they show no grief,
    grouped above a sere
and yellow leaf,
    a tree's life blown
through a crack in the door.

[337]

V

Over the red-black
kitchen floor,
Jeremy the spider
stalks to his place,
all eight legs
wet from the waste:
he climbed up the drain
to be here on time.

VI

Now, to the slow
egg-timer's chime,
shiny in state
come things from the grime:
tiny slaters
with wings and hoods,
beetles from the closet
under the stairs:
gashed with sorrow
each fixed eye stares.

VII

Fairbanks crawls
from his winter leaves:
he rubs his eyes
on his prickling sleeves:
rattling his plate
for a sad sound,
his black legs cover
the chill ground
at a fair speed:
he creeps to our need.

VIII

Now the hall resounds
to the tread of toes
as each one gathers,
and the crowd grows:

[338]

broken-spirited,
the bears upstairs
troop to the banisters
and droop their ears:
the brown one squats,
glum cheeks in his paws,
the blue one strums
a melancholy string.

IX

From all feasts of fish
he wove good fur:
alas, no fish
stale death can deter.

X

As the drum beats,
the long cortège
winds to the attic
as towards the stage:
some hop and skip,
some crawl or run,
the sad music
holds every one:
crouched by the window
all weep to view
Peter, poor Peter,
drift up the flue.

The Garden of Delights (detail), Hieronymus Bosch (*Museo del Prado, Madrid*)

XI

Now, all together
they chant his dirge,
grouped by the ledge
where the chimneys merge.

XII

Peter, salt Peter
fish-eating cat,
feared by the blackbird,
stung by the gnat,
wooden-spider collector,
lean as a rat,
soon you shall fall
to a fine grey fat.

XIII

Peter, salt Peter,
drift into the wind,
enter the water
where all have sinned:
forgive us our trespasses
as we forgive yours:
remember us in heaven
as clean scales and furs,
as we you on earth here
when any cat purrs.

XIV

Peter, salt Peter,
farewell and live,
as we do remembering
and so forgive.

XV

Over the world
a sad pall falls,
            fur into fine air,
bone into ash:
            a chill water
wets every lash.

XVI

Peter, salt Peter,
by pleurisy slain,
            the pale glass weeps
in its wooden pane,
            come to the cat-flap
and slap in again.

XVII

Peter, salt Peter,
the bird of death,
            a boding raven
chokes off my breath.

XVIII

Wrung warm tears,
and doleful words
            end this dirge,
and the screams of birds.

Pets

TED HUGHES

A dark November night. Late. The back door wide.
Beyond the doorway, the step off into space.
On the threshold, looking out,
With foxy furry tail lifted, a kitten.

Somewhere out there a badger, our lodger,
A stripe-faced rusher at cats, a grim savager,
Is crunching the bones and meat of a hare
That I left out for her twilight emergence
From under the outhouses.
The kitten flirts its tail, arches its back,
All its hairs are inquisitive.
Dare I go for a pee?
Something is moving there – just in dark.
A prowling lump. A tabby Tom. Grows.
And the battered master of the house
After a month at sea, comes through the doorway,
Recovered from his nearly fatal mauling,
Two probably three pounds heavier
Since that last appearance
When he brought in his remains to die or be doctored.
He deigns to recognize me,
With his criminal eyes, his deformed voice.
Then poises, head lowered, muscle-bound,
Like a bull for the judges,
A thick Devon bull,
Sniffing the celebration of sardines.

Gunner

MARTIN BOOTH

Dropped in a cannon's maw
upon the 'Victory'
grandfather named him *Gunner*
out of fact and quandary
disliking *Drake* or *Nelson*

through Essex and life's countryside
he bore himself with dignity
in glory or defeat
or astride a seasoning queen
under the gooseberry bushes
when I was five

Gunner, photo Martin Booth

now just a fading sepia plate
in childhood's album
he haunts my dreams
re-lives his scars and killings
while I sleep
and has his paw pressed firmly to my pulse

[343]

over the twenty years
since his death
(guardian of my grandmother's fire-tongs)
he has kept re-occurring
as king cat
feles universalis
the harbinger of good tidings in early hours
– warned me of my marriage
and scorns my adult love of dogs

today
for the first time
I've bought a home he'd like:
cornfields
an old church
oblivious thrushes tugging at the lawn

even my dog *Chester*
ageing
would bow and let dead *Gunner* by

under the ripe apples
he suns and squints at distance:
under the gooseberries
his echo is shrieking for a mate

The Cat as Cat

DENISE LEVERTOV

The cat on my bosom
sleeping and purring
– fur-petalled chrysanthemum,
squirrel-killer –

is a metaphor only if I
force him to be one,
looking too long in his pale, fond,
dilating, contracting eyes

[344]

Child with Cat, François Drouais (*Musée Cognacq-Jay, Paris*)

that reject mirrors, refuse
to observe what bides
stockstill.
        Likewise

flex and reflex of claws
gently pricking through sweater to skin
gently sustains their own tune,
not mine. I-Thou, cat, I-Thou.

[345]

Epitaph on the Duchess of Maine's Cat

LA MOTHE LE VAYER

(*translated by Sir Edmund Gosse*)

Puss passer-by, within this simple tomb
Lies one whose life fell Atropos hath shred;
The happiest cat on earth hath heard her doom,
And sleeps for ever in a marble bed.
Alas! what long delicious days I've seen!
O cats of Egypt, my illustrious sires,
You who on altars, bound with garlands green,
Have melted hearts, and kindled fond desires,
Hymns in your praise were paid, and offerings too,
But I'm not jealous of those rights divine,
Since Ludovisa loved me, close and true,
Your ancient glory was less proud than mine.
To live a simple pussy by her side
Was nobler far than to be deified.

INDEX OF AUTHORS

Index of Artists

Numbers in bold type refer to the pages of the colour inset.

TEXT ACKNOWLEDGEMENTS

The publishers gratefully acknowledge the permission of the following to reprint the copyright material in this book:

Paul Ableman: *Aunty and Her Cats*, the author.

Alan Brownjohn: *Cat* from *Brownjohn's Beasts*, Macmillan of London and Basingstoke; *The Seventh Knight and the Green Cat*, the author.

Jeni Couzyn: *The King of the Cats is Dead* from *Monkeys' Wedding*, Jonathan Cape Ltd.

Walter de la Mare: *Broomsticks* and *Five Eyes*, The Literary Trustees of Walter de la Mare, and the Society of Authors as their representative.

Richard Eberhart: *Old Tom* from *Collected Poems 1930–1976*, Copyright © by Richard Eberhart 1960, 1976. Chatto & Windus and Oxford University Press, Inc.

T. S. Eliot: *Growltiger's Last Stand* and *Macavity* from *Old Possum's Book of Practical Cats*, Copyright, 1939, by T. S. Eliot; copyright, 1967, by Esme Valerie Eliot. Faber and Faber Ltd, and Harcourt Brace Jovanovich, Inc.

Graham Fawcett: *Let No Man Put Asunder*, the author.

Roy Fuller: *Cat and Fiddle*, the author; *The Family Cat* and *In Memory of My Cat Domino*, André Deutsch Ltd.

Paul Gallico: *The Ballad of Tough Tom* from *Honourable Cat* published by William Heinemann Ltd and Crown Publishers, Inc.; '*When in Doubt – Wash*' from *The Abandoned*, Copyright 1950, published by William Heinemann Ltd and Alfred A. Knopf, Inc.; by permission of Hughes Massie Ltd and Harold Ober Associates Inc.

Giles Gordon: *The Jealous One*, the author.

Robert Graves: *Cat-Goddesses* from *Collected Poems 1965*, the author.

Michael Hamburger: *Cat* from *Travelling* published by Fulcrum Press, the author.

Thomas Hardy: *Last Words to a Dumb Friend* from *Collected Poems of Thomas Hardy*, Copyright 1925 by Macmillan Publishing Co, Inc. The Trustees of the Hardy Estate, Macmillan of London and Basingstoke, Macmillan Company of Canada Limited, Macmillan Publishing Co., Inc.

Patricia Highsmith: *Ming's Biggest Prey*, the author.

Geoffrey Holloway: *On Clem*, the author and London Magazine Editions.

Ted Hughes: *Esther's Tomcat* from *Lupercal*, Faber and Faber Ltd and Harper & Row, Publishers; *How the Cat Became* from *How the Whale Became*, Faber and Faber Ltd and Atheneum Publishers; *Pets*, the author.

Aldous Huxley: *Sermons in Cats* from *Collected Essays*, Bantam Books, Inc.

Harvey Jacobs: *What Did You Do There?*, the author.

W. W. Jacobs: *The White Cat*, the Society of Authors as the literary representatives of the Estate of W. W. Jacobs.

Rudyard Kipling: *The Cat that Walked by Himself* from *The Just So Stories*, the late Mrs George Bambridge, the Macmillan Company of London and Basingstoke, Doubleday & Co., Inc.

Robert Leach: *Dostoievsky* from *Cats Free & Familiar* published by The Keepsake Press, the author.

[351]

ILLUSTRATION ACKNOWLEDGEMENTS

In addition to the owners named under the illustrations, the following sources must be acknowledged most gratefully by the publishers: John Bignell, 108, 143; John Blackwell, 317; Mary Evans Picture Library, 22, 37, 38, 46, 51, 56, 63, 85, 116, 211, 279; Photographie Giraudon, 34, 59, 89, 106, 131, 172, 193, 207, 222, 225, 227, 253, 256, 268, 291, 302; Mansell Collection, 159, 160, 161, 168, 174, 221, 238, 245, 276, 294, 315, 319, 337, 345; Eileen Tweedy, colour plates 1, 5, 11, 13, 16; John Webb, colour plate 7.

The following copyright owners must also be thanked for their permission to reproduce: ADAGP, 155, 227; William Heinemann Ltd, 100 (from *Honourable Cat*); Office du Livre, Fribourg, 178; Portal Gallery, colour plate 9; SPADEM, 131, 172; Frederick Warne & Co. Ltd, 203, 248 (from *The Tailor of Gloucester*).

MORE ABOUT PENGUINS
AND PELICANS

Penguinews, which appears every month, contains details of all the new books issued by Penguins as they are published. From time to time it is supplemented by our stocklist, which includes around 5,000 titles.

A specimen copy of *Penguinews* will be sent to you free on request. Please write to Dept EP, Penguin Books Ltd, Harmondsworth, Middlesex, for your copy.

In the U.S.A.: For a complete list of books available from Penguins in the United States write to Dept CS, Penguin Books, 625 Madison Avenue, New York, New York 10022.

In Canada: For a complete list of books available from Penguins in Canada write to Penguin Books Canada Ltd, 2801 John Street, Markham, Ontario L3R 1B4.

In Australia: For a complete list of books available from Penguins in Australia write to the Marketing Department, Penguin Books Australia Ltd, P.O. Box 257, Ringwood, Victoria 3134.

DEAR ME

PETER USTINOV

'Mr Ustinov's own memory is both abundant and imaginative: hence *Dear Me*, a controversial autobiography, bursting at the seams with uproarious stories, wise saws and modern instances, and ablaze with images' – J. W. Lambert in the *Sunday Times*

'There are actually six Peter Ustinovs, and I admire them all: actor, author, designer, director, film star, playwright ... Their latest contribution, *Dear Me*, is the minaret gracing their careers, which appear – thank Fortune – to have no end in sight' – Garson Kanin

THE COUNTRY RAILWAY

DAVID ST JOHN THOMAS

For those who regret the passing of Britain's country railways, this loving portrayal will bring back the charm and nostalgic delight of that halcyon time when rural branch lines were a necessary and much appreciated lifeline for people living in country outposts. Trim station platforms, colourful gardens, tank engines' shining brasswork, daringly built viaducts, decorative bridges and embankments carpeted with flowers – all these features are celebrated in words and pictures in this unique labour of love.

THE PENGUIN BOOK OF THE BICYCLE

RODERICK WATSON AND MARTIN GRAY

Richly illustrated, entertaining and packed with fascinating detail, this is a sparkling celebration of the bicycle in all its forms and fashions. The authors examine the evolution of cycling, the drama of cycle sport, the modern cycle revival, and many practical aspects of buying, assembling, maintaining and riding a bicycle with enthusiasm and experience. Above all, this is a book about the aesthetic and technical beauty of the simplest – and most harmless – mechanical contraptions ever devised by man.

INDIA: A WOUNDED CIVILIZATION

V. S. NAIPAUL

'This is a stern attempt to break through the understandable yet entirely disabling sentimentality with which India is invariably viewed. Much less diverting than the earlier memoir *An Area of Darkness*, and intentionally so; but much more worrying' – Martin Amis in the *Observer*

India: A Wounded Civilization challenges so many clichés that it is bound to raise protest, but it is a book written out of love and with the creative sympathy of a great novelist.

WORDPOWER

An Illustrated Dictionary of Vital Words

EDWARD DE BONO

'Wordpower is to the mind what horsepower is to the car.' The 265 specialized words that Dr de Bono defines here are most of them familiar, at least in part; some, because of their usefulness, are borrowed from scientific, technical and business fields. All are powerful tools of expression if used precisely. Here they are defined in terms of usage and with the help of cartoons and illustrations to enable the reader to adopt them into his everyday vocabulary. The wordpower they offer makes a dynamic addition to anyone's education.

BIKO

DONALD WOODS

This book is at once a powerful biographical sketch of the young South African leader Steve Biko, and a flaming indictment of the South African Government. Donald Woods, the outspoken editor of the *East London Daily Despatch*, escaped from South Africa in 1977 and is already established as an eloquent and informed commentator on South African affairs. His *Biko* recounts the arrest and the violent death in custody of this remarkable young politician. It makes harrowing reading.